Models
for
Writers

Short Essays for Composition

Models
for
Writers

Short Essays for Composition

EIGHTH EDITION

Alfred Rosa
Paul Eschholz

University of Vermont

BEDFORD/ST. MARTIN'S
Boston ◆ *New York*

For Bedford/St. Martin's

Developmental Editor: Bennett Morrison
Editorial Assistant: Kristy Bredin
Assistant Editor, Publishing Services: Maria Burwell
Senior Production Supervisor: Dennis J. Conroy
Production Associate: Christie Gross
Project Management: Books By Design, Inc.
Cover Design: Lucy Krikorian
Cover Art: Alexander Calder, *Poisson Rouge, Queue Jaune,* 1968. Painted
metal mobile. Overall size: 27 × 55 inches (67.3 × 139.7 cm.) © 2003
Estate of Alexander Calder/Artists Rights Society (ARS), New York.
Photo copyright of Sotheby's.
Composition: Pine Tree Composition, Inc.
Printing and Binding: R. R. Donnelley & Sons Company

President: Joan E. Feinberg
Editorial Director: Denise B. Wydra
Editor in Chief: Nancy Perry
Director of Marketing: Karen Melton Soeltz
Director of Editing, Design, and Production: Marcia Cohen
Manager, Publishing Services: Emily Berleth

Library of Congress Control Number: 2003113554

Manufactured in the United States of America.

9 8 7 6 5 4
f e d c b

For information, write: Bedford/St. Martin's, 75 Arlington Street, Boston,
MA 02116 (617–399–4000)

ISBN: 0–312–40686–X

Acknowledgments

Acknowledgments and copyrights are continued at the back of the book
on pages 613–17, which constitute an extension of the copyright page.

PREFACE

Models for Writers provides students and instructors with readable, high-interest essays that model rhetorical elements, principles, and patterns. As important as it is for students to read while they are learning to write college-level essays, *Models for Writers* offers more than a collection of essays. The questions and activities that accompany each selection allow students to see how rhetorical strategies and techniques enhance what the authors are saying. In addition, writing activities and assignments help students stitch the various rhetorical elements together into coherent, forceful essays of their own. This approach, which has helped students for over a quarter century to become better writers, remains at the heart of the book.

In this eighth edition, the classic features of *Models for Writers* that have won praise from teachers and students alike continue to be emphasized. In addition, we have not only introduced new selections and new voices but also developed new features that will help students become better readers and writers.

Favorite Features of *Models for Writers*

- **Lively Readings.** Most of the selections in *Models for Writers* are comparable in length (two to three pages) to the essays students will write themselves, and each clearly illustrates a basic rhetorical element, principle, or pattern. Just as important, the essays deal with subjects that we know from our own teaching experience will spark the interest of most college students. Drawn from a wide range of sources, the essays represent a variety of popular contemporary prose styles.

- **Expanded Rhetorical Organization.** Each of the eighteen rhetorically-based chapters in *Models for Writers* is devoted to a particular element or pattern important to college writing. Chapters 3 through 9 focus on the concepts of thesis, unity, organization, beginnings and endings, paragraphs, transitions, and effective sentences. Chapter 10 illustrates the importance of controlling diction and tone, and Chapter 11, the uses of figurative language. Chapters 12 through 20 explore the types of writing most often required of college students: illustration, narration, description, process analysis, definition, division and classification, comparison and contrast, cause and effect, and argument.

• **Abundant Study Materials** To help students use the readings to improve their writing, every essay is accompanied by ample study materials.

For Your Journal activities precede each reading and prompt students to explore their own ideas and experiences regarding the issues presented in the reading.

Questions for Study and Discussion focus on the content and the author's purpose, and the particular strategy used to achieve that purpose, with at least one question in each series focusing on a writing concern other than the one highlighted in the chapter to remind students that good writing is never one-dimensional.

Vocabulary sections identify several words from the reading that students will find worth adding to their vocabularies and ask students to define each word as it is used in the context of the selection and then to use the word in a new sentence of their own.

Classroom Activities provide brief exercises enabling students to work in the classroom (often in groups) on rhetorical elements, techniques, or patterns. These activities range from developing thesis statements to using strong action verbs and building argumentative evidence. Classroom activities help students apply concepts modeled in the readings to their own writing.

Suggested Writing Assignments provide two writing assignments for each essay, one encouraging students to use the reading selection as a direct model and the other asking them to respond to the content of the reading.

• **Flexible Arrangement.** Each chapter is self-contained so that instructors can easily follow their own teaching sequences, omitting or emphasizing certain chapters according to the needs of their students. Whatever sequence is followed, thematic connections among the selections can be made by referring to the alternate Thematic Contents at the beginning of the book.

• **Concise and Helpful Chapter Introductions.** Writing instructors who use *Models for Writers* have continued to be generous in their praise for the brief chapter introductions, which explain the various rhetorical elements and patterns. In each one, students will find numerous illuminating examples—many written by students—of the feature or principle being discussed.

• **Glossary of Useful Terms.** Cross-referenced in many of the questions and writing assignments throughout the book, this helpful list covers rhetorical and literary terms that student writers need to know. Terms that are defined in the Glossary are shown in boldface the first time they appear in text.

- **Appendix on Writing a Research Paper.** A brief, helpful appendix, which includes a sample documented student essay, offers guidance on conducting research using print and online sources; evaluating, quoting, and integrating sources; and using MLA citation style.

- **Instructor's Resource Manual.** In the manual that accompanies *Models for Writers,* we offer insights into the rhetorical features of each essay as well as advice on how best to use the materials in class. Suggested answers for study questions, vocabulary, and classroom activities are included.

Highlights of the Eighth Edition of *Models for Writers*

New Readings on Topics of Current Interest. The eighth edition of *Models for Writers* has twenty-eight new essays, many on topics of current interest such as the terrorist attacks of September 11, growing up in a bilingual household, the influence of the Internet on studying, and allowing women to register for selective service. We chose these essays for their brevity, clarity, and potential for developing critical thinking and writing skills in student writers. Among the new readings included in this edition are essays by popular writers such as Judith Ortiz Cofer, Thomas Friedman, Pico Iyer, Barbara Kingsolver, Rita Dove, Sarah Vowell, and Pete Hamill.

Longer readings in each part. To provide a greater variety of essays for students and to help them progress to more demanding reading, each part of *Models for Writers* now includes at least one longer essay. These essays, by William Lutz, Judith Ortiz Cofer, Bruce Catton, and Barbara Dafoe Whitehead, introduce students to more complex forms of the genre.

New Part on Reading and Writing Well. The new Part One includes two chapters to help students understand the writing process and use the essays they read to improve their own writing. The first chapter, "The Writing Process," details the steps in the writing process and illustrates them with a student essay in progress. The second chapter, "From Reading to Writing," shows students how to use the apparatus in the text, provides them with guidelines for critical reading, and demonstrates with three student papers how they can generate their own writing from reading.

New and Updated Footnotes Providing Contextual Information. Explanatory footnotes that accompany the readings help students understand important cultural and historical references that might otherwise be unfamiliar to them.

New Arguments on Contemporary Issues. The argument chapter features two new sets of essays on important issues being debated today: Affirmative Action in Higher Education and The Influence of the Media. The Influence of the Media set includes three essays to show students that an argument can have many sides, not just pro and con.

Acknowledgments

In response to the many helpful reviews from instructors who use this book, we have maintained the solid foundation of the previous edition of *Models for Writers* while adding fresh readings and writing topics to stimulate today's student writers.

We are indebted to many people for their advice as we prepared this eighth edition. We are especially grateful to Kathy Cantley Ackerman, Isothermal Community College; Michael Bertsch, Butte College; Luis A. Contreros, Fresno City College; Roy Flannagan, Francis Marion University; Tammy Frankland, Casper College; Richard Johnson, Kirkwood Community College; Rita Kahn, California State University; Jesse Kavadlo, Winona State University; Alisa Klinger, Cuesta College; Karen Kreeger, California Polytechnic State University; Mary Ann Linden, Black Hawk College; Vernice McCullough, Glendale Community College; Jacqueline Goffe McNish, Dutchess Community College; Silvia Milosevich, Butte College; Kitty M. Nard, California State University, Northridge; Amy Olsen, Cuesta College; Claudia P. Pineo, Fullerton College; Marian Rooney, Glendale Community College; June Roque, Milwaukee Area Technical College; Stephanie Satie, California State University, Northridge; Sharon Schakel, Mesa State College; Janet M. Selitto, University of Central Florida; Neal Snidow, Butte College; Anna Tripp, California State University, Northridge; Tondalaya W. Van Lear, Dabney S. Lancaster Community College; Kathryn Leslie Zipperian, Cuesta College.

It has been our good fortune to have the editorial guidance of Ben Morrison, our developmental editor on this book, our longtime colleague and mentor Nancy Perry, and the rest of the excellent team at Bedford/St. Martin's as we worked on this new edition.

Thanks also to our colleague Brian Kent, who authored the new material for the *Instructor's Resource Manual,* and to Cara Simone Bader, Susan Wanner, Dick Sweterlitsch, and Betsy Eschholz, who have shared their experiences using *Models for Writers* in the classroom. Our greatest debt is, as always, to our students — especially to Lisa Drive, Susan Francis, Jake Jamieson, Zoe Ockenga, and Jeffrey Olesky, whose papers appear in this text—for all they have taught us over the years.

Alfred Rosa
Paul Eschholz

Contents

part two **The Elements of the Essay**

3 Thesis 67

4 Unity 86

18 Comparison and Contrast 431

19 Cause and Effect 457

20 Argument 487

Thematic Contents

Education

The Urban Experience

Health and Medicine

Writers and Writing

Introduction for Students

Models for Writers is designed to help you learn to write by providing you with a collection of model essays — that is, essays that are examples of good writing. Good writing is direct and purposeful and communicates its message without confusing the reader. It doesn't wander from the topic, and it answers the reader's questions. While good writing is well developed and detailed, it also accomplishes its task with the fewest possible words and with the simplest language appropriate to the writer's topic and thesis.

We know that one of the best ways to learn to write and to improve our writing is to read. By reading we can begin to see how other writers have communicated their experiences, ideas, thoughts, and feelings. We can study how they have used the various elements of the essay — words, sentences, paragraphs, organizational patterns, transitions, examples, evidence, and so forth — and thus learn how we might effectively do the same. When we see, for example, how a writer like James Lincoln Collier develops an essay from a strong thesis statement, we can better appreciate the importance of having a clear thesis statement in our own writing. When we see the way Russell Baker uses transitions to link key phrases and important ideas so that readers can recognize clearly how the parts of his essay are meant to fit together, we have a better idea of how to achieve such clarity in our own writing.

But we do not learn only by observing, by reading. We also learn by doing — that is, by writing, and in the best of all situations, we engage in these two activities in conjunction with one another. *Models for Writers* encourages you, therefore, to practice what you are learning, to move from reading to writing.

Part One of *Models for Writers* provides you with strategies to do just that. Chapter 1 introduces you to the writing process, gives you guidelines for writing, and illustrates the writing process with a student essay. Chapter 2 shows you how to use what you learn from the essays that you will read to generate your own essays. You will soon see that an effective essay has a clear purpose, often provides useful information, has an effect on the reader's thoughts and feelings, and is usually a pleasure to read.

Those essays that you will read in *Models for Writers* were chosen because they are effective essays.

All well-written essays also share a number of structural and stylistic features that are illustrated by the various essays in *Models for Writers*. One good way to learn what these features are and how you can incorporate them into your own writing is to look at each of them in isolation. For this reason, we have divided the readings in *Models for Writers* into three major sections and, within these sections, into eighteen chapters, each with its own particular focus and emphasis.

Part Two, "The Elements of the Essay," includes chapters on the following subjects: thesis, unity, organization, beginnings and endings, paragraphs, transitions, and effective sentences. All of these elements are essential to a well-written essay, but the concepts of thesis, unity, and organization underlie all the others and so come first in our sequence. "Thesis" shows how authors put forth or state the main ideas of their essays and how they use such statements to develop and control content. "Unity" shows how authors achieve a sense of wholeness in their essays, and "Organization" illustrates some important patterns that authors use to organize their thinking and writing. The next chapter, "Beginnings and Endings," offers advice and models of ways to begin and conclude essays, while "Paragraphs" concentrates on the importance of well-developed paragraphs and what is necessary to achieve them. "Transitions" concerns the various devices that writers use to move from one idea or section of an essay to the next. Finally, "Effective Sentences" focuses on techniques to make sentences powerful and to create stylistic variety.

Part Three, "The Language of the Essay," includes a chapter on diction and tone and one on figurative language. "Diction and Tone" shows how carefully writers choose words either to convey exact meanings or to be purposely suggestive. In addition, this chapter shows how the words a writer uses can create a particular tone or relationship between the writer and reader—one of irony, for example, or humor or great seriousness. "Figurative Language" concentrates on the usefulness of the special devices of language—such as simile, metaphor, and personification—that add richness and depth to writing.

Part Four of *Models for Writers,* "Types of Essays," includes chapters on the various types of writing most often required of college writing students: illustration (how to use examples to illustrate a point or idea); narration (how to tell a story or give an account of an event); description (how to present a verbal picture); process analysis (how to explain how something is done or happens); definition (how to explain what something is); division and classification (how to divide a subject into its parts and place items into appropriate categories); comparison and contrast (how to explain the similarities and/or differences between two or more items); cause and effect (how to explain the causes of an event or the effects of an action); and argument (how to use reason and logic to persuade someone to your way of thinking). These types of writing are referred to as *organizational patterns* or *rhetorical modes.*

Studying the organizational patterns and practicing them are very important in any effort to broaden one's writing skills. In *Models for Writers,* we look at each pattern separately; we believe this is the simplest and most effective way to introduce them. However, this does not mean that a well-written essay is necessarily one that chooses a single pattern and sticks to it exclusively and rigidly. Confining oneself to comparison and contrast throughout an entire essay, for instance, might prove impractical and may yield a strained, unnatural piece of writing. In fact, it is often best to use a single pattern to organize your essay and then to use other patterns as your material dictates. As you read the model essays in this text, you will find that in the service of the dominant pattern, a good many of them utilize a combination of other patterns.

Combining organizational patterns is probably not something you want to plan or even think about when you first tackle a writing assignment. Rather, such combinations of patterns will develop naturally as you organize, draft, and revise your materials. Such combinations of patterns will also enhance the interest and impact of your writing. See Chapter 1 for a discussion on combining patterns.

Chapters 3 to 20 are organized in the same way. Each opens with an explanation of the element or principle under discussion. These introductions are intended to be brief, clear, and practical. Here you will also usually find one or more short examples of the feature or principle being studied, including examples from students such as yourself. Following the introduction, we present three or four model essays (Chapter 20, with 11 essays is an exception), each with a brief introduction of its own, providing information about the author and

On Reading
and Writing Well

chapter 1

The Writing Process

The essays in this book will help you understand the elements of good writing and provide ample opportunity to practice writing in response to the model essays. As you write your own essays, pay attention to your writing process. This chapter focuses on the stages of the writing process—prewriting, writing the first draft, revising, and editing and proofreading. It concludes with a sample student process that you can model your own writing after, from start to finish. The strategies suggested in this chapter for each stage of the writing process will help you overcome many of the problems you may face while writing your own essays.

■ Prewriting

Writers rarely rely on inspiration alone to produce an effective piece of writing. Good writers prewrite or plan, write the first draft, revise and edit, and proofread. It is worth remembering, however, that the writing process is rarely as simple and as straightforward as this. Often the process is recursive, moving back and forth among the four stages. Moreover, writing is personal; no two people go about it exactly the same way. Still, it is possible to learn the steps in the process and thereby have a reassuring and reliable method for undertaking a writing task and producing a good composition.

Your reading can give you ideas and information, of course. But reading also helps expand your knowledge of the organizational patterns available to you, and, consequently, it can help direct all your prewriting activities. In *prewriting*, you select your subject and topic, gather ideas and information, and determine the thesis and organizational pattern or patterns you will use. Once you have worked through the prewriting process, you will be ready to start on your first draft. Let's explore how this works.

UNDERSTAND YOUR ASSIGNMENT

When you first receive an assignment, read it over several times. Focus on each word and each phrase to make sure you understand what you are being asked to do. Try restating the assignment in your own words to make sure you understand it. For example, consider the following assignments:

1. Narrate an experience that taught you that every situation has at least two sides.
2. Explain what is meant by *theoretical modeling* in the social sciences.
3. Write a persuasive essay in which you support or refute the following proposition: "Violence in the media is in large part responsible for an increase in violence in American society today."

Each of these assignments asks you to write in different ways. The first assignment asks you to tell the story of an event that showed you that every situation has more than one perspective. To complete the assignment, you might choose simply to narrate the event, or you might choose to analyze it in depth. In either case, you have to explain to your reader how you came to this new understanding of multiple perspectives and why it was important to you. The second assignment asks you to explain what theoretical modeling is and why it is used. To accomplish this assignment, you first need to read about the concept to gain a thorough understanding of it, and then you'll need to define it in your own words and explain its purpose and usefulness to your readers. You will also want to demonstrate the abstract concept with concrete examples to help your readers understand it. Finally, the third assignment asks you to take a position on a controversial issue for which there are many studies on both sides of the question. You will need to research the studies, consider the evidence they present, and then take a stand of your own. Your argument will necessarily have to draw on the sources and evidence you have researched, and you will need to refute the arguments and evidence presented by those experts who take an opposing position.

If, after reading the assignment several times, you are still unsure about what is being asked of you or about any additional requirements of the assignment, such as length or format, be sure to consult with your instructor. He or she should be willing to clear up any confusion before you start writing.

CHOOSE A SUBJECT AREA, AND FOCUS ON A TOPIC

Although you will usually be given specific assignments in your writing course, you may sometimes have the freedom to write on any subject that interests you. In such a case, you may already have a specific idea in mind. For example, if you are interested in sports, you might argue against the use of performance-enhancing drugs by athletes. What happens, however, when you are free to choose your own subject and cannot think of anything to write about? If you find yourself in this situation, begin by determining a broad subject that you like to think about and might enjoy writing about—a general subject like virtual reality, medical ethics, amateur sports, or foreign travel. Also consider what you've recently read—essays in *Models for Writers,* for example—or your career ambitions when choosing a subject. Select several likely subjects, and let your mind explore their potential for interesting topics. Your goal is to arrive at an appropriately limited topic.

A topic is the specific part of a subject on which a writer focuses. Subjects such as the environment, literature, and sports are too broad to be dealt with adequately in a single essay. Entire books are written about these and other subjects. Start with your broad subject, and make it more specific. Thus if your subject is sports, you might choose as your topic rule violations in college recruiting, violence in ice hockey, types of fan behavior, the psychology of marathon runners, or the growth of sports medicine.

Suppose, for example, you select farming and advertising as possible subject areas. The following examples illustrate how to focus these broad subjects into manageable topics:

General ⎯⎯⎯⎯⎯⎯⎯⎯⎯⎯⎯⎯⎯⎯⎯⎯⎯⎯⎯⎯⎯⎯⎯⎯➤Specific

farming ► livestock ► cows ► dairy cow disease ► parasite control in dairy cows

advertising ► TV advertising ► TV advertising of food ► TV advertising of cereals ► TV advertising of high-fiber cereals

Notice how each successive topic is more limited than the one before it. Moving from the general to the specific, the topics become appropriate for essay-length writing.

In moving from a broad subject to a particular topic, you should take into account any assigned constraints on length or format. You will also want to consider the amount of time you have to write. These practical considerations will affect the scope of your topic.

GET IDEAS AND COLLECT INFORMATION

Once you have found your topic, you will need to determine what you want to say about it. The best way to do this is to gather information. Your ideas about a topic must be supported by information, such as facts, and examples. The information you gather about a topic will influence your ideas about the topic and what you want to say. Here are some of the ways you can gather information:

1. *Ask questions about your topic.* If you were assigned the topic of theoretical modeling, for example, you could ask, what is *theoretical modeling?* Why, where, and by whom is theoretical modeling used? What are the benefits of using it? Is it taught in school? Is it difficult to learn to use? Once the questioning starts, one question will lead to another, and the answers to these questions will be the stuff of your writing. Like a newspaper reporter going after a story, asking questions and getting answers is an essential way to understand a topic before trying to explain it to others.

2. *Brainstorm.* List the things you know about a topic, freely associating ideas and information as a way to explore the topic and its possibilities. Don't censor or edit your list making, and don't worry about spelling or punctuation. The objective is to free up your thinking before you start to write. You may want to set aside your list and return to it over several days. Once you have a substantial brainstorming list, you might want to sort your entries by highlighting them with colored markers.

3. *Cluster.* Another strategy for stimulating your thinking about a topic is *clustering.* Place your topic in a circle, and draw lines from that circle to other circles in which you write related key words or phrases. Around each of these key words, generate more circles representing the various aspects of the key word that come to mind. (See p. 23 for an example.) The value of clustering over brainstorming is that you are generating ideas and organizing them at the same time. Both techniques work very well, but you may prefer one over the other or may find that one works better with one topic than another.

4. *Research.* You may want to add to what you already know about your topic with research. Research can take many forms beyond

formal research carried out in your library. For example, first-hand observations and interviews with people knowledgeable about your topic can provide up-to-date information. Whatever your form of research, take careful notes so you can accurately paraphrase an author or quote an interviewee. The appendix to this book will help you research a topic.

5. *Think creatively.* To push an idea one step further, to make a connection not easily recognized by others, to step to one side of your topic and see it in a new light, to ask a question no one else would, to arrive at a fresh insight is to be creative. Don't be afraid to step outside conventional wisdom and ask a basic or unorthodox question. Such bravery adds creativity to your writing.

ESTABLISH YOUR THESIS

Once you have generated ideas and information, you are ready to begin the important task of establishing a controlling idea, or *thesis.* The thesis of a paper is its main idea, the point the writer is trying to make. The thesis is often expressed in one or two sentences called a *thesis statement.* Here's an example:

> The so-called serious news programs are becoming too much like tabloid news shows in both their content and their presentation.

The thesis statement should not be confused with your purpose for writing. While a thesis statement makes an assertion about your topic and actually appears in your essay as such, your purpose is what you are trying to do in the essay — to express, to explain, or to argue. For example, the purpose behind the preceding thesis statement might be expressed as follows:

> By comparing the transcripts of news shows like the *CBS Evening News* and tabloid shows like *Entertainment Tonight*, I will show troubling parallels in what the two genres of programs find "newsworthy."

This type of purpose statement should not appear in your essay.

A thesis statement should be

- the most important point you make about a topic;
- more general than the ideas and facts used to support it; and
- focused enough to be covered in the space allotted for the essay.

A thesis statement should not be a question, but rather an assertion. If you find yourself writing a question for a thesis statement, answer the question first, and then write your statement.

An effective method for developing a thesis statement is to begin by writing, *"What I want to say is that . . . ."*

> What I want to say is that unless language barriers between patients and health care providers are bridged, the lives of many patients in our more culturally diverse cities will be endangered.

Later you can delete the formulaic opening, and you will be left with a thesis statement:

> Unless language barriers between patients and health care providers are bridged, many patients' lives in our more culturally diverse cities will be endangered.

A good way to determine whether your thesis is too general or too specific is to consider how easy it will be to present information and examples to support it. If you stray too far in either direction, your task will become much more difficult. A thesis statement that is too general will leave you overwhelmed by the number of issues you must address. For example, the statement, "Malls have ruined the fabric of American life" would lead to the question "How?" To answer it, you would probably have to include information about traffic patterns, urban decay, environmental damage, economic studies, and so on. You would obviously have to take shortcuts, and your paper would be ineffective. On the other hand, too specific a thesis statement will leave you with too little information to present. "The Big City Mall should not have been built because it reduced retail sales at the existing Big City stores by 21.4%" does not leave you with any opportunities to develop an argument.

The thesis statement is usually set forth near the beginning of the essay, although writers sometimes begin with a few sentences that establish a context for the piece. One common strategy is to position the thesis as the final sentence of the first paragraph. In the opening paragraph of an essay on the harmful effects of quick weight-loss diets, student Marcie Turple builds a context for her thesis statement, which she presents in her last sentence:

> Americans are obsessed with thinness—even at the risk of dying. In the 1930s, people took dinitrophenol, an industrial poison, to lose weight. It boosted metabolism but caused blindness and some deaths. Since then dieters have used hormone injections, amphetamines, liquid protein diets, and, more recently, the controversial fen-phen. What most dieters need to realize is that there is no magic way to lose weight—no pill, no crash diet plan. *The only way to permanent weight loss is through sensible eating and exercise.*
>
> –Marcie Turple, student

Will Your Thesis Hold Water?

Once you have selected a possible thesis for an essay, ask yourself the following questions:

1. Does my thesis statement take a clear stance on an issue? And if so, what is that stance?
2. Is my thesis too general?
3. Is my thesis too specific?
4. Does my thesis apply to a larger audience than myself? If so, who is that audience?

For more on the various ways to build an effective thesis, see Chapter 3, "Thesis."

KNOW YOUR AUDIENCE

While it is not always possible to know who your readers are, you nevertheless need to consider your intended audience. Your attitude toward your topic, your tone, your sentence structure, and your choice of words are just some of the important considerations that rely on your awareness of audience. For a list of questions to help you determine your audience, see page 14.

DETERMINE YOUR METHOD OF DEVELOPMENT

Part Four of *Models for Writers* includes chapters on the various types of writing most often required of college students. These types of writing are referred to as *methods of development* or *rhetorical patterns.*

Audience Questions

1. Who are my readers?
2. Is my audience specialized (for example, all those in my geology lab) or more general (college students)?
3. What do I know about my audience's age, gender, education, religious affiliation, socioeconomic status, and political attitudes?
4. What does my audience need to know that I can tell them?
5. Will my audience be interested, open-minded, resistant, objective, or hostile to what I am saying?
6. Is there any specialized language that my audience must have to understand my subject or that I should avoid?
7. What do I want my audience to do as a result of reading my essay?

Studying the organizational patterns and practicing the use of them are very important in any effort to broaden one's writing skills. In *Models for Writers,* we look at each pattern separately because we believe this is the most effective way to introduce them. However, this does not necessarily mean that a well-written essay adheres ex-

---

Methods of Development

Illustration	Using examples to illustrate a point or idea
Narration	Telling a story or giving an account of an event
Description	Presenting a picture with words
Process Analysis	Explaining how something is done or happens
Definition	Explaining what something is
Division and Classification	Dividing a subject into its parts and placing them in appropriate categories
Comparison and Contrast	Demonstrating likenesses and differences
Cause and Effect	Explaining the causes of an event or the effects of an action
Argument	Using reason and logic to persuade someone to your way of thinking

clusively and rigidly to a single pattern of development. Confining oneself exclusively to comparison and contrast throughout an entire essay, for instance, might prove impractical and might yield a strained, unnatural piece of writing. In fact, it is often best to use a single pattern to organize and develop your essay and then use the other patterns as your material dictates. For a description of what each method of development involves, see page 14. As you read the model essays in this text, you will find that many of them utilize a combination of patterns to support the dominant pattern.

Combining organization patterns is probably not something you want to plan or even think about when you first tackle a writing assignment. Instead, let organizational patterns develop naturally as you organize, draft, and revise your materials. The combination of patterns will enhance the interest and impact of your writing.

If you're still undecided or concerned about combining patterns, try the following steps:

1. Summarize the point you want to make in a single phrase or sentence.
2. Restate the point as a question—in effect, the question your essay will answer.
3. Look closely at both the summary and the question for key words or concepts that suggest a particular pattern.
4. Consider other strategies that could support your primary pattern.

Here are some examples:

SUMMARY: Venus and Serena Williams are among the best women tennis players in the history of the game.

QUESTION: How do Venus and Serena Williams compare with other tennis players?

PATTERN: Comparison and contrast. The writer must compare the Williams sisters with other women players and provide evidence to support the claim that they are "among the best."

SUPPORTING PATTERNS: Illustration and description. Good evidence includes examples of their superior ability and accomplishments and descriptions of their athletic feats.

SUMMARY: How to build a personal Web site.

QUESTION: How do you build a personal Web site?

PATTERN: Process analysis. The word *how,* especially in the phrase *how to,* implies a procedure that can be explained in steps or stages.

SUPPORTING PATTERNS: Description. It will be necessary to describe the Web site at various points in the process, especially the look and design of the site.

SUMMARY: Petroleum and natural gas prices should be federally controlled.

QUESTION: What should be done about petroleum and natural gas prices?

PATTERN: Argument. The word *should* signals an argument, calling for evidence and reasoning in support of the conclusion.

SUPPORTING PATTERNS: Comparison and contrast and cause-and-effect analysis. The writer should present evidence from a comparison of federally controlled pricing with deregulated pricing as well as from a discussion of the effects of deregulation.

These are just a few examples showing how to decide on a pattern of development and supporting patterns that are suitable for your topic and what you want to say about it. In every case, your reading can guide you in recognizing the best plan to follow.

MAP YOUR ORGANIZATION

Once you decide what you want to write about and you come up with some ideas about what you might like to say, your next task is to jot down the main ideas for your essay in an order that seems both natural and logical to you. In other words, make a scratch outline. In constructing this outline, if you discover that one of the organizational patterns will help you in generating ideas, you might consider using that as your overall organizing principle.

Whether you write a formal outline, simply set down a rough sequence of the major points of your thesis, or take a middle ground between those two strategies, you need to think about the overall organization of your paper. Some writers make a detailed outline and fill it out point by point, while others follow a general plan and let the writing take them where it will, making any necessary adjustments to the plan when they revise.

Some major patterns of organization that you may use for your outline are:

- chronological (oldest to newest, or the reverse)
- spatial (top to bottom, left to right, inside to outside, and so forth)

- least familiar to most familiar
- easiest to most difficult to comprehend
- easiest to most difficult to accept
- according to similarities or differences

You will notice that some of these organizational patterns correspond to the rhetorical patterns in Part Four of this book. For example, a narrative essay generally follows a chronological organization. If you are having trouble developing or mapping an effective organization, refer to the introduction and readings in Chapter 5, "Organization." Once you have settled on an organizational pattern you are ready to write a first draft.

■ Writing the First Draft

Your goal in writing a first draft is to get your ideas down on paper. Write quickly, and let the writing follow your thinking. Do not be overly concerned about spelling, word choice, or grammar because such concerns will break the flow of your ideas. After you have completed your first draft, you will go over your paper to revise and edit it.

As you write your draft, pay attention to your outline, but do not be a slave to it. It is there to help you, not restrict you. Often, when writing, you discover something new about your subject; follow that idea freely. Wherever you deviate from your plan, place an X in the margin to remind yourself of the change. When you revise, you can return to that part of your writing and reconsider the change you made.

It may happen that while writing your first draft, you run into difficulty that prevents you from moving forward. For example, suppose you want to tell the story of something that happened to you, but you aren't certain whether you should be using the pronoun *I* so often. Turn to the essays in Chapters 10 and 13 to see how the authors use diction and tone and how other narrative essays handle this problem. You will find that the frequent use of *I* isn't necessarily a problem at all. For an account of a personal experience, it's perfectly acceptable to use *I* as often as you need to. Or suppose that after writing several pages describing someone you think is quite a character, you find that your draft seems flat and doesn't express how lively and funny the subject really is. If you read the introduction to Chapter 12, you will learn that descriptions need lots of factual, concrete detail; the selections in that chapter give further proof of this. You can use those guidelines to add details that are missing from your draft.

If you do run into difficulties writing your first draft, don't worry or get upset. Even experienced writers run into problems at the beginning. Just try to keep going and take the pressure off yourself. Think about your topic, and consider your details and what you want to say. You might even want to go back and look over the ideas and information you've gathered.

CREATE A TITLE

What makes a good title? There are no hard-and-fast rules, but most writers would agree that an effective title attracts attention and hooks the reader into reading the essay, either because the title is unusual or colorful and intrigues the reader or because it asks a question and the reader is curious to know the answer. A good title announces your subject and prepares your reader for the approach you take. You can create a title while writing your first draft or after you have seen how your ideas develop. Either way, the important thing is to brainstorm a list of titles and not simply use the first one that comes to mind. With at least a half dozen to choose from, you will have a much better sense of how to pick an effective one, one that does important work explaining your subject to the reader. Spend several minutes reviewing the titles of the essays in *Models for Writers* (see the table of contents, pp. xi–xx). You'll like some better than others, but reflecting on the effectiveness of each one will help you strengthen your own titles.

FOCUS ON BEGINNINGS AND ENDINGS

The beginning of your essay is vitally important to its success. Indeed, if your opening doesn't attract and hold your reader's attention, your reader may be less than enthusiastic about proceeding.

Your ending is almost always equally important as your beginning. An effective conclusion does more than end your essay. It wraps up your thoughts and leaves the reader satisfied with the presentation of your ideas and information. Your ending should be a natural outgrowth of the development of your ideas. Avoid trick endings, mechanical summaries, and cutesy comments, and never introduce new concepts or information in the ending. Review the notes on page 19 and Chapter 6 for more help developing your beginnings and endings.

Notes on Beginnings and Endings

Beginnings and endings are very important to the effectiveness of an essay, but they can be daunting to write. Inexperienced writers often feel that they must write their essays sequentially when, in fact, it is better to write both the beginning and the ending after you have completed most of the rest of your paper. Pay particular attention to both parts during revision. Ask yourself the following questions:

1. Does my introduction grab the reader's attention?
2. Is my introduction confusing in any way? How well does it relate to the rest of the essay?
3. If I state my thesis in the introduction, how effectively is it presented?
4. Does my essay come to a logical conclusion, or does it seem to just stop?
5. How well does the conclusion relate to the rest of the essay? Am I careful not to introduce new topics or issues that I did not address in the essay?
6. Does the conclusion help to underscore or illuminate important aspects of the body of the essay, or is it redundant, a reproduction of what I wrote earlier?

■ Revising

Once you have completed a first draft, set it aside for a few hours or even until the next day. Removed from the process of drafting, you can approach the revision of your draft with a clear mind. When you revise, consider the most important elements of your draft first. You should focus on your thesis, purpose, content, organization, and paragraph structure. You will have a chance to look at grammar, punctuation, and mechanics after you revise. This way you will make sure that your essay is fundamentally solid and says what you want it to say before dealing with the task of editing.

It is very helpful to have someone—your roommate or another member of your writing class—listen to your essay as you read it aloud. The process of reading aloud allows you to determine if your writing sounds clear and natural. If you have to strain your voice to

---

Questions for Revising

1. Have I focused on my topic?
2. Does my thesis make a clear statement about my topic?
3. Is the organizational pattern I have used the best one, given my purpose?
4. Does the topic sentence of each paragraph relate to my thesis? Does each paragraph support its topic sentence?
5. Do I have enough supporting details, and are my examples the best ones that I can develop?
6. How effective are my beginning and my ending? Can I improve them?
7. Do I have a good title? Does it indicate what my subject is and hint at my thesis?

---

provide emphasis, try rephrasing the idea to make it clearer. Whether you revise your work on your own or have someone assist you, the questions above will help you focus on the largest, most important elements of your essay early in the revision process.

■ Editing and Proofreading

Once you are sure that the large elements in your essay are in place and that you have said what you intended, you are ready to begin editing your essay. At this stage, you will correct any mistakes in grammar, punctuation, mechanics, and spelling. Use a dictionary and a grammar handbook as you edit. The questions on page 21 should help you in editing your paper.

Edit and proofread your work carefully. You don't want to use *your* when you intended *you're* or *to* when you wanted *too*. If you know that you are prone to certain mistakes, you might want to go once through your essay looking for those particular problems. If, for example, you often misspell or mistype certain words, or are often confused about where the punctuation should go with quotation marks, read your paper for that specific problem. Above all, do not assume that because you made proofreading corrections on your word processor that your paper will print out correctly. Give the hard copy of your paper one final check before submitting it to your instructor.

Questions for Editing Sentences

1. Are my sentences clear, and do they convey my thoughts accurately?
2. Are my sentences complete thoughts? Did I use any unintentional sentence fragments?
3. Do my verbs agree in number with their subjects?
4. Do my pronouns have clear antecedents—that is, do they clearly refer to specific nouns earlier in my sentences?
5. Have I made any unnecessary shifts in person, tense, or number?
6. Have I used the comma properly in all instances?
7. Is my word choice appropriate? Does each word convey exactly what I meant?
8. Have I avoided slang or other inappropriate words and expressions?
9. Have I punctuated accurately in every instance? Have I consulted my handbook or instructor to get answers to punctuation questions?
10. Have I misspelled or incorrectly typed any words? Has my spellchecker inadvertently approved commonly confused words like *it's* and *its,* or *their, there,* and *they're?*
11. Have I formatted my paper according to my instructor's directions?

It's surprising how quickly a number of small errors can add up and distract your reader. More importantly, such errors can cause the reader to doubt the important points you are trying to make.

■ Writing an Expository Essay: A Student Essay in Progress

While he was a student in a writing class at the University of Vermont, Jeffrey Olesky was asked to write an essay on any topic using a suitable method of development. After making a brief list of the subjects that interested him, he chose to write about golf. Golf has been a part of Olesky's life since he was a youngster, so he figured he would have enough material for an essay.

First, he needed to focus on a specific topic within the broad subject area of golf. Having considered a number of aspects of the game—how it's played, its recent popularity because of Tiger Woods, the controversies of private clubs excluding women and minorities—he kept coming back to how much golf meant to him. Focusing on his love of golf, he then established his tentative thesis: Golf has taught me a lot.

Olesky needed to develop a number of examples to support his thesis, so he brainstormed for ideas, examples, and anecdotes—anything that came to mind that would help him develop his essay. This is his list:

Brainstorming List

Golf is my life—I can't imagine being who I am without it.

I love to be out on the course early in the morning.

It's been embarrassing and stressful sometimes.

There's so much to know and remember about the game, even before you try to hit the ball.

The story about what my father taught me—felt badly and needed to apologize.

"You know better than that, Jeffrey."

I have pictures of me on the greens with a cut-down golf putter.

All kinds of character building goes on.

It's all about rules and playing fairly.

Wanted to be like my father.

The frustration is awesome, but you can learn to deal with it.

Golf is methodical.

I use golf to clear my head.

Golf teaches life's lessons.

Golf teaches you manners, to be respectful of others.

Golf teaches you to abide by the rules.

Golf is an internal tool.

When he thought that he had amassed enough information, he began to sort it out. He needed an organizational plan, some way to present his information that was not random but rather showed a logical progression. He realized that the character-building benefits of golf that he included in his brainstorming list clustered around some key subtopics. He decided to do some clustering and drew circles that included his ideas about golf: the physical and mental demands of the game, the social values and morals it teaches, and the reflective benefits of golf. He then sorted out his related ideas and examples and added them, mapping their relationship in the diagram. Here is his clustering diagram:

Clustering Diagram

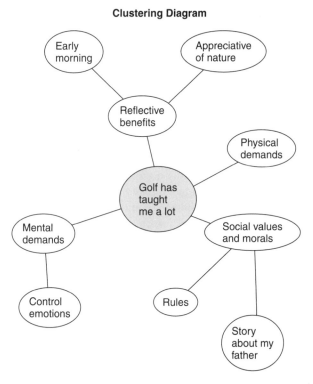

Before beginning to write the first draft of his paper, Olesky thought it would be a good idea to list in an informal outline the major points he wanted to make.

Outline of First Draft

1. Brief introductory paragraph announcing the topic
2. An expansion of the introductory paragraph and the *thesis statement:* Golf has taught me a lot
3. A discussion of how, above all, golf teaches one to control one's emotions
4. A discussion of how much one needs to know and remember to play golf well
5. The values that golf teaches
6. A multiparagraph example illustrating a valuable lesson taught through golf

7. Golf provides an opportunity to reflect
8. Reflection, in turn, leads to a deeper appreciation of nature

With his outline before him, Olesky felt ready to try a rough draft of his paper. He wrote quickly, keeping his organizational plan in mind but striving to keep the writing going and get his thoughts down on paper. He knew that once he had a draft, he could determine how to improve it. Olesky wrote some fairly solid paragraphs, but he sensed that they were on different aspects of his topic and that the logical order of the points he was making was not quite right. He needed an organizational plan, some way to present his information that was not random but rather showed a logical progression.

Reviewing his outline, Olesky could see that there was a natural progression from the physical lessons of the sport to the social and moral lessons to the psychological, emotional, and even spiritual benefits that one could derive. He decided therefore to move item 3 ("A discussion of how, above all, golf teaches one to control one's emotions") in his original organization and make it item 6 in the revision. Here is his reordered outline:

Revised Outline

1. Brief introductory paragraph announcing the topic
2. An expansion of the introductory paragraph and the *thesis statement:* Golf has taught me a lot
3. A discussion of how much one needs to know and remember to play golf well
4. The social values that golf teaches
5. A multiparagraph example illustrating a valuable lesson taught through golf
6. A discussion of how, above all, golf teaches one to control one's emotions
7. Golf provides an opportunity to reflect
8. Reflection, in turn, leads to a deeper appreciation of nature

Olesky was satisfied that his essay now had a natural and logical organization. In short, it moved from matters of lesser to greater importance to him personally. However, he now needed to revise his thesis to better suit the argument he had established. He needed his revised thesis to be more focused and specific and to include the idea that the lessons and values golf taught him could not be as easily learned in other ways.

> *Revised thesis statement:* In its simplicity, golf has taught me many lessons and values other people have trouble learning elsewhere.

After revising the organization, he was now ready to edit his essay and to correct those smaller but equally important errors in word choice, wordiness, punctuation, and mechanics. He had put aside these errors to make sure his essay had the appropriate content. Now he needed to make sure it was grammatically correct. Here are several sample paragraphs showing the editing that Olesky did on his essay:

EDITED PARAGRAPHS FROM OLESKY'S ESSAY

Ever since I was a little boy, no older than two or three, I have had a golf club in my hand.

Addition for clarity

My mother has pictures of me ∧*as a toddler* with my father on

Elimination of unessential information

the putting green of the golf course, ~~that my father belonged to~~. With a cut-down putter, the shaft ~~had been~~ reduced in length so that it would fit me, I would spend hours trying to place the small white ball into the little round hole. I'm sure at first that I took to the game to be like

Change of period to colon to eliminate sentence fragment and introduce appositive phrase

my father. ⊙ ⊤o act like him, play like him, and hit the ball as far as he did. However, it is not what I have learned about the mechanics of the golf swing, or ~~all~~ ∧*about* the facts ~~and figures~~ of the game that have caused golf to mean so much to me, but rather ∧*it is* the things golf has taught

Correction of it's *to* its

me about everyday life ∧*in general*. In it's simplicity, golf has taught me many lessons and values other people have trouble learning elsewhere.

*Elimina-
tion of
wordiness*

Golf is a good teacher because there
~~Along the same lines, t~~There are many variables and aspects to the game~~ of golf~~. You ~~are~~

your position and strategy
constantly hav̂ing to think, analyze, and evaluate∧

~~That is the difficulty of the game of golf.~~
that rely on   *ing*
Unlike many sports,∧ ~~once you~~ committ~~ing~~~~ed the~~
golf requires
action*s* to muscle memory,∧~~there is no guarantee~~
~~you will still perform well. There is~~ a phenomenal amount of information to think about
and keys to remember. Legs shoulder-width apart,
knees flexed, fingers interlocked, body loose . . .
and you haven't even tried to hit the ball yet.
in golf
But having to go about things so methodically∧
the skills of patience and analysis

*Addition
of specific
informa-
tion for
clarity*

has enabled me to apply∧ ~~the methods of golf~~ to
many other parts of my life. I don't believe I
would have nearly the same personality if golf

*Improved
dicton*

integral
had not played such an ~~intricate~~ role in my development.

In addition to editing his revised paper, Olesky reexamined his title, "Character Builder." Olesky considered a half-dozen alternatives. He finally settled on the use of "Golf" as a main title because it was such a key word for his topic and thesis; he used "Character Builder" as his subtitle. He also thought about his conclusion, wondering whether it was forceful enough. After considerable thought, and having sought the advice of his classmates, Olesky decided to end with the rather low-key but significantly meaningful final paragraphs he generated in his original draft. Here is the final version of his essay:

Golf: A Character Builder

Jeffrey Olesky

*Title: sug-
gests what
the essay
will be
about*

Golf is what I love. It is what I do, and it
is who I am. In many respects it has defined and
shaped my character and personality. I couldn't

Beginning:
*effective
opening
paragraph
sets the
context
for the
paper*
possibly imagine my life without golf and what it has meant for me.

Ever since I was a little boy, no older than two or three, I have had a golf club in my hand. My mother has pictures of me as a toddler with my father on the putting green of the golf course. With a cut-down putter, the shaft reduced in length so that it would fit me, I would spend hours trying to place the small white ball in the little round hole. I'm sure at first that I took to the game to be like my father: to act like him, play like him, and hit the ball as far as he did. However, it is not what I have learned about the mechanics of the golf swing or about the facts of the game that have caused golf to mean so much to me, but rather it is the things golf has taught me about everyday life in general. In

Thesis
statement:
*sets clear
expecta-
tion in the
reader's
mind*
its simplicity, golf has taught me many lessons and values other people have trouble learning elsewhere.

Golf is a good teacher because there are many variables and aspects to the game. You constantly have to think, analyze, and evaluate your

*Golf re-
quires lots
of infor-
mation,
both phys-
ical and
mental.*
position and strategy. Unlike many sports that rely on committing actions to muscle memory, golf requires a phenomenal amount of information to think about and keys to remember. Legs shoulder-width apart, knees flexed, fingers interlocked,

Transition:
*discussion
moves to
how the
game in-
fluences
personality*
body loose . . . and you haven't even tried to hit the ball yet. But having to go about things so methodically in golf has enabled me to apply the skills of patience and analysis to many other

parts of my life. I don't believe I would have nearly the same personality if golf had not played such an integral role in my development.

Golf teaches life lessons, too.

Golf has also changed and shaped my personality by repeatedly reinforcing many of the lessons of life. You know the ones I'm referring to, the rules you learn in kindergarten: Treat others as you would like to be treated; respect other people and their property . . . the list goes on. Golf may not blare them out as obviously as my kindergarten teacher, but in its own subtle, respectful tone, golf has imbued me with many of the values and morals I have today. Simply by learning the rules of such a prestigious, honest, and respected game, you gradually learn the reasoning behind them and how they relate to life.

Illustration: extended example in narrative form of some of the lessons golf teaches

A good example of such a life lesson comes from the first time my father ever took me out on an actual golf course. I had been waiting for this day for quite some time and was so excited when he finally gave me the chance. He had gone out to play with a few of his friends early one Saturday morning in one of the larger tournaments. I was caddying for my father. Although I was too young to actually carry his bag, I would clean his golf ball, rake the bunkers for him, and do the other minor tasks that caddies do. But the fact that I was actually out "with the big boys," watching them play golf, was enough to make me happy. Besides, none of the other gentlemen my father was playing with seemed to mind that I was along for the ride.

Narrative example continues

The lesson I learned that day appears rather simple now. It came on the putting green of the second hole. My father had finished putting out, and I was holding the flagstick off to the side of the green while the other players finished. Generally my father would come stand next to me and give me a hand, but due to circumstances we ended up on opposite sides of the green. During the next player's putt my father lowered his eyebrows at me and nodded his head to one side a few times. Curious as to what he wanted me to do, I almost let the question slip out of my mouth. But I knew better. I had already learned the rules of not talking or moving while other golfers were hitting. I quietly stood my ground until everyone was finished, then placed the flagstick back in the hole. While walking towards the next tee box, I neared my father. Regardless of what he had wanted me to do I thought he would commend me for not talking or moving during the ordeal.

Dialogue: "shows rather than tells" and puts the reader in the scene

"You know better than that, Jeffrey," he said.

"What?" I asked curiously, disappointed that he had not praised me on a job well done.

"You never stand so that your shadow is in someone's line."

How could I be so stupid? He had reminded me a thousand times before. You never allow your shadow to fall in the line of someone's putt because it is distracting to the person putting. I rationalized to my father that maybe the man hadn't noticed or that it didn't bother him.

Unfortunately my father wasn't going to take that as an excuse. After explaining to me what I had done wrong, he suggested that I go over and apologize to the gentleman. I was still a young boy, and the figure of the older man was somewhat intimidating. This task was no easy chore because I was obviously very scared, and this is perhaps what made the lesson sink in a little deeper. I remember gradually approaching my father's friend and periodically looking back to my father for help. Once I realized I was on my own, I bashfully gave him my apologies and assured him that it wouldn't happen again. As you can probably guess, the repercussions were not as dramatic as I had envisioned them to be. Once my father had pointed out my mistake, I begged him to reconcile with the gentleman for me. However, in apologizing for myself, I learned a valuable lesson. Golf is important because it has taught me many social values such as this, but it can also be a personal, internal tool.

Golf has taught me how to deal with frustration and to control myself mentally in difficult and strenuous situations. Golf is about mastering your emotions in stressful times and prevailing with a methodical, calm mind. I have dealt with the disappointment of missing a two-foot putt on the last hole to break eighty and the embarrassment of shanking my drive off the first hole in front of dozens of people. In dealing with these circumstances and continuing with my game, I have

Transition: Golf can also be a personal, internal tool.

Organization: continues to move from concrete practical concerns to those that are more abstract

learned how to control my emotions. Granted, golf is not the most physically strenuous sport, but it is the mental challenge of complete and utter concentration that makes it difficult. People who are not able to control their temper or to take command of their emotions generally do not end up playing this game for very long.

Organization: Olesky moves to more philosophic influences.

Golf gives me the opportunity to be reflective—time to myself when I can debate and organize the thoughts in my head. There are few places where you can find the peace and tranquility like that of a golf course in the early morning or late afternoon. When I am playing by myself, which I make an effort to do when I need to "get away," I am able to reflect and work out some of the difficulties I am facing. I can think in complete quietness, but at the same time I have something to do while I am thinking. There are few places in the world offering this type of sanctuary that are easily accessible.

Organization: Olesky discusses finally golf's ability to bring him close to nature.

It is in these morning reflections that I also gain an appreciation of my surroundings. I often like to get up early on a Saturday or Sunday and be the first one on the course. There are many things I love about the scenery of a golf course during the morning hours. I love the smell of the freshly cut grass as the groundskeepers crisscross their patterns onto the fairways and greens. I love looking back on my progress toward the tee box on the first hole to witness my solitary foot tracks in the morning dew. I love the chirp of the yellow finches as they signal the break of dawn. All these conditions help to create the feeling I perceive as I walk down the *Ending: a quiet but appropriate conclusion* first fairway. Thinking back to those days on the putting green with my father, I realize how dear golf is to me. Golf has created my values, taught me my lessons, and been my outlet. I love the game for all these reasons.

chapter 2

From Reading to Writing

To move from reading to writing, you need to read actively, in a thoughtful spirit, and with an alert, inquiring mind. Reading actively means learning how to analyze what you read. You must be able to discover what is going on in an essay, to figure out the writer's reasons for shaping the essay in a particular way, to decide whether the result works well or poorly — and why. At first, such digging may seem odd, and for good reason. After all, we all know how to read. But do we know how to read actively?

Active reading is a skill that takes time to acquire. By becoming more familiar with different types of writing, you will sharpen your critical thinking skills and learn how good writers make decisions in their writing. After reading an essay, most people feel more confident talking about the content of the piece than about the writer's style. Content is more tangible than style, which always seems so elusive. In large part, this discrepancy results from our schooling. Most of us have been taught to read for ideas. Not many of us, however, have been trained to read actively, to engage a writer and his or her writing, to ask why we like one piece of writing and not another. Similarly, most of us do not ask ourselves why one piece of writing is more convincing than another. When you learn to read actively, you begin to answer these important questions and come to appreciate the craftsmanship involved in writing. Active reading, then, is a skill you need if you are truly to engage and understand the content of a piece of writing as well as the craft that shapes the writer's ideas into a presentable form. Active reading will repay your efforts by helping you read more effectively and write more persuasively.

■ Getting the Most Out of Your Reading

Active reading requires, first of all, that you commit time and effort. Second, try to take a positive interest in what you are reading, even if the subject matter is not immediately appealing. Remember, you are not reading for content alone but also to understand a writer's methods—to see firsthand the kinds of choices writers make while they write.

To help you get the most out of your reading, here are some guidelines for (1) preparing yourself to read a selection, (2) reading the selection the first time, (3) rereading the selection, (4) annotating the text with marginal notes, and (5) analyzing the text with questions.

PREREADING: PREPARING YOURSELF

Instead of diving right into any given selection in *Models for Writers* or any other book, there are a few things that you can do first that will prepare you to get the most out of what you will be reading. It's helpful, for example, to get a context for what it is you'll be reading. What's the essay about? What do you know about the writer's background and reputation? Where was the essay first published? Who was the intended audience for the essay? And, finally, how much do you already know about the subject of the reading selection? We encourage you to consider carefully the materials that precede each selection in this book.

Each selection begins with a title, a headnote, and a journal prompt. From the title, you often discover the writer's position on an issue or attitude toward the topic. On occasion, the title provides clues about the intended audience and the writer's purpose in writing the piece. The headnote contains a biographical note about the author, publication information, and rhetorical highlights of the selection. In addition to information on the person's life and work, you'll find out something about his or her reputation and authority to write on the subject of the piece. The publication information tells you when the essay was published and in what book or magazine it appeared. This information, in turn, gives you insight about the intended audience. The rhetorical highlights direct your attention to one or more aspects of how the selection was written. Finally, the journal prompt encourages you to collect your own thoughts and opinions about the topic or related subjects before you commence reading. The journal prompt makes it easy for you to keep a record of your own knowledge or thinking about a topic before you see what the writer has to offer in the essay.

To demonstrate how these context-building materials can work for you, carefully review the following materials that accompany H. Allen Smith's essay "Claude Fetridge's Infuriating Law." The essay itself appears later in this chapter.

Claude Fetridge's Infuriating Law

■ H. Allen Smith

During his lifetime, H. Allen Smith (1907–1976) **Headnote**
*had a reputation as an authority on humor of all
kinds. He wrote many articles, for example, about
the famous Hugh Troy, a man he dubbed "the
world's greatest practical joker." He authored* **Biographical note**
many humorous books, among them Low Man on
the Totem Pole *(1941),* Life in a Putty Knife Factory *(1943), and* Larks in the Popcorn *(1948). As
can be seen in the following selection, first published in* Reader's Digest *in June 1963, Smith ap-* **Publication**
preciated the humor in everyday life and sought to **information**
*share this humor with his readers. As you read this
selection, notice how Smith's topic sentences con-* **Rhetorical**
trol and focus the material in each of the essay's **highlights**
*five paragraphs and how well his examples illus-
trate the range of activities covered by Fetridge's
Law.*

FOR YOUR JOURNAL

Have you ever observed what seems like a remark- **Journal prompt**
ably consistent pattern of behavior in the people
around you or in the events of everyday life? For example, do your friends ask you to go out on the
nights when you have an important exam the next
day? Do you always do well on exams—or some
other activity—when you wear your favorite old
sweatshirt? Do your favorite sports teams lose when
you attend their games?

From reading these preliminary materials, what expectations do
you have for the selection itself? And how does this knowledge equip
you to engage the selection before you read it? From the title, you
probably inferred that Smith will tell you who Claude Fetridge is,

what the law that carries his name is all about, and why people find it "infuriating." His purpose clearly is to inform readers about his subject. The short biographical note reveals that Smith is no longer living, that he enjoyed a reputation as an authority on humor and wrote a number of books, including three which have "funny" titles, and that this essay, written in 1963, appeared after he had established himself as a humor expert. This background material suggests that the subject of the essay is likely to be light and humorous, perhaps intended to entertain. This assumption is strengthened when you learn that the essay first appeared in *Reader's Digest*, a popular magazine intended for a general readership. The rhetorical highlight advises you to look at Smith's use of topic sentences to control or direct the content of each paragraph as well as at the examples that Smith has selected to illustrate the range of application for Fetridge's Law. Finally, the journal prompt asks you to look for and consider patterns—with both good or bad results—in your everyday life. After reading the essay, you will discover whether the patterns you wrote about in your journal qualify as examples of Fetridge's Law in action.

READING: GETTING AN OVERVIEW OF THE SELECTION

Always read the selection at least twice, no matter how long it is. The first reading gives you a chance to get acquainted with the essay and to form your first impressions of it. With the first reading, you want to get an overall sense of what the writer is saying, keeping in mind the essay's title and what you know about the writer. The essay will offer you information, ideas, and arguments—some you may have expected, some you may not have expected. As you read, you may find yourself modifying your sense of the writer's message and purpose. If there are any words that you do not recognize, circle them so that you can look them up later in a dictionary. Put a "?" alongside any passages that are not immediately clear. You may, in fact, want to delay most of your annotating until a second reading so that your first reading can be fast and free, enabling you to concentrate on the larger issues.

REREADING: COMING TO AN UNDERSTANDING
OF THE SELECTION

Your second reading should be quite different from the first. You will know what the essay is about, where it is going, and how it gets there; now you can relate the parts of the essay more accurately to the whole. Use your second reading to test your first impressions against the words on the page, developing and deepening your sense of how the essay is written, and how well. Because you now have a general understanding of the essay, you can pay special attention to the author's purpose and means of achieving that purpose. You can look for features of organization and style that you can learn from and adapt to your own work.

RESPONDING TO YOUR READING: MAKING MARGINAL NOTES

When you annotate a text, you should do more than simply underline or highlight important points to remember. It is easy to underline so much that the notations become almost meaningless because you forget why you underlined the passages in the first place. Instead, as you read, write down your thoughts in the margins or on a separate piece of paper. Mark the selection's main point when you find it stated directly. Look for the pattern or patterns of development the author uses to explore and support that point, and jot the information down. If you disagree with a statement or conclusion, object in the margin: "No!" If you feel skeptical, indicate that response: "Why?" or "Explain." If you are impressed by an argument or turn of phrase, compliment the writer: "Good point!" Place vertical lines or a star in the margin to indicate important points.

Jot down whatever marginal notes come naturally to you. Most readers combine brief responses written in the margins with underlining, circling, highlighting, stars, or question marks.

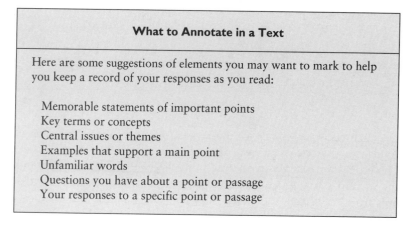

What to Annotate in a Text

Here are some suggestions of elements you may want to mark to help you keep a record of your responses as you read:

Memorable statements of important points
Key terms or concepts
Central issues or themes
Examples that support a main point
Unfamiliar words
Questions you have about a point or passage
Your responses to a specific point or passage

Remember that there are no hard-and-fast rules for which elements you annotate. Choose a method of annotation that works best for you and that will make sense to you when you go back to recollect your thoughts and responses to the essay. When annotating a text, don't be timid. Mark up your book as much as you like, or jot down as many responses in your notebook as you think will be helpful. Don't let annotating become burdensome. A word or phrase is usually as good as a sentence. One helpful way to focus your annotations is to ask yourself questions as you read the selection a second time.

ANALYZING: ASKING YOURSELF QUESTIONS AS YOU READ

As you read the essay a second time, probing for a deeper understanding of and appreciation for what the writer has done, focus your attention by asking yourself some basic questions about its content and its form. Here are some questions you may find useful:

Questions to Ask Yourself as You Read

1. What does the writer want to say? What is the writer's main point or thesis?
2. Why does the writer want to make this point? What is the writer's purpose?
3. What pattern or patterns of development does the writer use?
4. How does the writer's pattern of development suit his or her subject and purpose?
5. What, if anything, is noteworthy about the writer's use of this pattern?
6. How effective is the essay? Does the writer make his or her points clearly?

Each essay in *Models for Writers* is followed by study questions similar to the ones suggested here, but more specific to the essay. These questions help you analyze both the content of the essay and the writer's craft. As you read the essay a second time, look for details from the selection that will support your answers to these questions, and then answer the questions as fully as you can.

An Example: Annotating H. Allen Smith's
"Claude Fetridge's Infuriating Law"

Notice how one of our students, guided by the six questions above, recorded her responses to Smith's text with marginal annotations.

Definition of Fetridge's Law

Fetridge's Law, in simple language, states that important things that are supposed to happen do not happen, especially when people are looking; or, conversely, things that are supposed not to happen do happen, especially when people are looking. Thus a dog that will jump through a hoop a thousand times a day for his owner will not jump through a hoop when a neighbor is called in to watch; and a baby that will say "Dada" in the presence of its proud parents will, when friends are summoned, either clam up or screech like a jaybird.

Two examples illustrate definition

Background information on Fetridge and the incident on which Fetridge's Law is based

Fetridge's Law takes its name from a onetime radio engineer named Claude Fetridge. Back in 1936, Mr. Fetridge thought up the idea of broadcasting the flight of the famous swallows from San Juan de Capistrano mission in Southern California. As is well known, the swallows depart from the mission each year on St. John's Day, October 23, and return on March 19, St. Joseph's Day. Claude Fetridge conceived the idea of broadcasting the flutter of wings of the departing swallows on October 23. His company went to considerable expense to set up its equipment at the mission; then, with the whole nation waiting anxiously for the soul-stirring event, it was discovered that this year the swallows, out of sheer orneriness, had departed a day ahead of schedule. Thus did a flock of birds lend immortality to Claude Fetridge.

Series of three examples of Fetridge's Law at work

Example 1: television

Television sets, of course, are often subject to the workings of Fetridge's Law. If a friend tells me he is going to appear on a television show and asks me to watch it, I groan inwardly, knowing this is going to cost me money. The moment his show comes on the air, my screen will snow up or acquire the look of an old-school-tie pattern. I turn it off and call the repairman. He travels three miles to my house and turns the set on. The picture emerges bright and clear, the contrast exactly right, a better picture than I've ever had before. It's that way always and forever, days without end.

Example 2:
human
behavior

An attractive woman neighbor of mine drives her husband to the railroad station every morning. On rare occasions she has been late getting her backfield in motion, and hasn't had time to get dressed. These times she has thrown a coat over her nightgown and, wearing bedroom slippers, headed for the depot. Fetridge's Law always seems to give her trouble. Once she clashed fenders with another car on the highway and had to go to the police station in her night shift. Twice she has had motor trouble in the depot plaza, requiring that she get out of her car in robe and slippers and pincurlers. The last I heard, she was considering sleeping in her street clothes.

Example 3:
toothache

Fetridge's Law operates fiercely in the realm of dentistry. In my own case, I have often noted that whenever I develop a raging toothache it is a Sunday and the dentists are all on the golf course. Not long ago, my toothache hung on through the weekend, and Monday morning it was still throbbing and pulsating like a diesel locomotive, I called my dentist, proclaimed an emergency, and drove to his office. As I was going up the stairway, the ache suddenly vanished. By the time I got into his chair, I was confused and embarrassed and unable to tell him with certainty which tooth it was that had been killing me. The X-ray showed no shady spots, though it would have shown several if he had pointed the thing at my brain. Claude Fetridge's Law clearly has its good points; it can exasperate, but it can also cure toothaches.

Now that you have learned about the essentials of the reading process—what you can do to prepare yourself to read a selection, what you should look for during a first reading, what you should annotate, and what questions you might ask yourself as you reread a selection—you are ready to read an entire selection to practice what you have learned.

Practice Reading and Annotating Rachel Carson's "A Fable for Tomorrow"

Before you read the following essay, think about its title, the biographical and rhetorical information in the headnote, and the journal prompt. Make some marginal notes of your expectations for the essay, and write out a response to the journal prompt. Then, as you read the essay itself for the first time, try not to stop; take it all in as if in one breath. The second time, however, pause to annotate key points in the text, using the marginal rules we have provided alongside each paragraph. As you read, remember the six basic questions we mentioned earlier:

1. What does Carson want to say? What is her main point or thesis?
2. Why does she want to make this point? What is her purpose?
3. What pattern or patterns of development does Carson use?
4. How does Carson's pattern of development suit her subject and purpose?
5. What, if anything, is noteworthy about Carson's use of this pattern?
6. How effective is Carson's essay? Does Carson make her points clearly?

Fable for Tomorrow

Title:

■ Rachel Carson

Naturalist Rachel Carson (1907–1964) majored in biology at the Pennsylvania College for Women (which later became Chatham College) in the mid-1920s and earned a master's degree in marine zoology from Johns Hopkins University. Later she worked as an aquatic biologist for the U.S. Bureau of Fisheries in Washington, D.C. She wrote Under the Sea Wind *(1941),* The Sea around Us *(1951), and* The Edge of the Sea *(1955)—all sensitive investigations of marine life. But it was* Silent Spring *(1962), her study of herbicides and insecticides, that made Carson a controversial figure. Once denounced as an alarmist, she is now regarded as an early prophet of the ecology movement. In the following fable (a short tale teaching a moral) taken from* Silent Spring, *Carson uses contrast to show her readers the devastating effects of the indiscriminate use of pesticides.*

Biographical note:

Publication
information:

Rhetorical
highlight:

FOR YOUR JOURNAL

Hardly a week goes by that we don't hear a news story about the poisoning of the environment. Popular magazines have run cover stories about Americans' growing interest in organic foods. Where do you stand on the issue of using chemical fertilizers, herbicides, and pesticides to grow our nation's food? Do you seek out organic products when you shop? Why, or why not?

Journal prompt:

There was once a town in the heart of America where all life seemed to live in harmony with its surroundings. The town lay in the midst of a checkerboard of prosperous farms, with fields of grain and hillsides of orchards where, in spring, white clouds of bloom drifted above the green fields. In autumn, oak and maple and birch set up a blaze of color that flamed and flickered across a backdrop of pines. Then foxes barked in the hills and deer silently crossed the fields, half hidden in the mists of the fall mornings.

Along the roads, laurels, viburnum and alder, great ferns and wildflowers delighted the traveler's eye through much of the year. Even in winter the roadsides were places of beauty, where countless birds came to feed on the berries and on the seed heads of the dried weeds rising above the snow. The countryside was, in fact, famous for the abundance and variety of its bird life, and when the flood of migrants was pouring through in spring and fall people traveled from great distances to observe them. Others came to fish the streams, which flowed clear and cold out of the hills and contained shady pools where trout lay. So it had been from the days many years ago when the first settlers raised their houses, sank their wells, and built their barns.

Then a strange blight crept over the area and everything began to change. Some evil spell had settled on the community: mysterious maladies swept the flocks of chickens; the cattle and sheep sickened and died. Everywhere was a shadow of death. The farmers spoke of much illness among their families. In the town the doctors had become more and more puzzled by new kinds of sickness appearing among their patients. There had been several sudden and unexplained deaths, not only among adults but even among children, who would be stricken suddenly while at play and die within a few hours.

There was a strange stillness. The birds, for example — where had they gone? Many people spoke of them, puzzled and disturbed. The feeding stations in the backyards were deserted. The few birds seen anywhere were moribund; they trembled violently and could not fly. It was a spring without voices. On the mornings that had once throbbed with the dawn chorus of robins, catbirds, doves, jays, wrens, and scores of other bird voices there was now no sound; only silence lay over the fields and woods and marsh.

On the farms the hens brooded, but no chicks 5 hatched. The farmers complained that they were unable to raise any pigs—the litters were small and the young survived only a few days. The apple trees were coming into bloom but no bees droned among the blossoms, so there was no pollination and there would be no fruit.

The roadsides, once so attractive, were now 6 lined with browned and withered vegetation as though swept by fire. These, too, were silent, deserted by all living things. Even the streams were now lifeless. Anglers no longer visited them, for all the fish had died.

In the gutters under the eaves and between the 7 shingles of the roofs, a white granular powder still showed a few patches; some weeks before it had fallen like snow upon the roofs and the lawns, the fields and streams.

No witchcraft, no enemy action had silenced 8 the rebirth of new life in this stricken world. The people had done it themselves.

This town does not actually exist, but it might 9 easily have a thousand counterparts in America or elsewhere in the world. I know of no community that has experienced all the misfortunes I describe. Yet every one of these disasters has actually happened somewhere, and many real communities have already suffered a substantial number of them. A grim specter has crept upon us almost unnoticed, and this imagined tragedy may easily become a stark reality we all shall know.

Once you have read and reread Carson's essay and annotated the text, write your own answers to the six basic questions listed on page 41. Then compare your answers with the set of answers that follows.

1. *What does Carson want to say? What is her main point or thesis?* Carson wants to tell her readers a fable, a short narrative that makes an edifying or cautionary point. Carson draws the "moral" of her fable in the final paragraph. She believes that we have in our power the ability to upset the balance of nature, to turn what is an idyllic countryside into a wasteland. As she states in paragraph 8, "The people had done it [silenced the landscape] themselves." Human beings need to take heed and understand their role in environmental stewardship.

2. *Why does she want to make this point? What is her purpose?* Carson's purpose is to alert us to the clear danger of pesticides (the "white granular powder," paragraph 7) to the environment. Even though the composite environmental disaster she describes has not occurred yet, she feels compelled to inform her readers that each of the individual disasters has happened somewhere in a real community. Although Carson does not make specific recommendations for what each of us can do, her message is clear: To do nothing about pesticides is to invite environmental destruction.

3. *What pattern or patterns of development does Carson use?* Carson's dominant pattern of development is comparison and contrast. In paragraphs 1 and 2, she describes the mythical town before the blight ("all life seemed to live in harmony with its surroundings"); in paragraphs 3 through 7, the same town after the blight ("some evil spell had settled on the community"). Carson seems less interested in making specific contrasts than in drawing a total picture of the town before and after the blight. In this way, she makes the change dramatic and powerful. Carson enhances her contrast by using vivid descriptive details that appeal to our senses to paint her pictures of the town before and after the "strange blight." The countryside before the blight is full of life; the countryside after, barren and silent.

4. *How does Carson's pattern of development suit her subject and purpose?* Carson selects comparison and contrast as her method of development because she wants to shock her readers into seeing what happens when humans use pesticides indiscriminately. By contrasting a mythical American town before the blight with the same town after the blight, Carson is able to *show* us the differences, not merely tell us about them. The descriptive details enhance this contrast: for example, "checkerboard of prosperous farms," "white clouds of bloom," "foxes barked," "seed heads

of the dried weeds," "cattle and sheep sickened," "they trembled violently," "no bees droned," and "browned and withered vegetation." Perhaps the most striking detail is the "white granular powder" that had "fallen like snow upon the roofs and the lawns, the fields and streams." The powder is the residue of the all-pervasive use of insecticides and herbicides in farming. Carson waits to introduce the powder for dramatic impact. Readers absorb the horror of the changing scene, wonder at its cause, and then suddenly realize it is not an unseen, uncontrollable force, but human beings who have caused the devastation.

5. *What, if anything, is noteworthy about Carson's use of this pattern?* In her final paragraph, Carson says, "A grim specter has crept upon us almost unnoticed." And this is exactly what happens in her essay. By starting with a two-paragraph description of "a town in the heart of America where all life seemed to live in harmony with its surroundings," Carson lulls her readers into thinking that all is well. But then at the beginning of paragraph 3, she introduces change: "a strange blight crept over the area." By opting to describe the preblight town in its entirety first and then to contrast it with the blighted town, she makes the change more dramatic and thus enhances its impact on readers.

6. *How effective is Carson's essay? Does Carson make her points clearly?* Instead of writing a strident argument against the indiscriminate use of pesticides, Carson chooses to engage her readers with a fable with an educational message. In reading her story of this American town, we witness what happens when farmers blanket the landscape with pesticides. When we learn in the last paragraph that "this town does not actually exist," we are given cause for hope. In spite of the fact that "every one of these disasters has actually happened somewhere," we are led to believe that there is still time to act before "this imagined tragedy" becomes "a stark reality we all shall know." Interestingly, Carson was considered an alarmist when she wrote *Silent Spring* in 1962, and now almost daily we read reports of water pollution, oil spills, hazardous waste removal, toxic waste dumps, or the greenhouse effect. Her warning is as appropriate today as it was when she first wrote it more than four decades ago.

▓ Using Your Reading in the Writing Process

Reading and writing are the two sides of the same coin. Many people view writing as the making of reading. But the connection does not end there. Active reading is a means to help you become a better writer. We know that one of the best ways to learn to write and to improve our writing is to read. By reading we can begin to see how other writers have communicated their experiences, ideas, thoughts, and feelings in their writing. We can study how they have effectively used the various elements of the essay—thesis, unity, organization, beginnings and endings, paragraphs, transitions, effective sentences, diction and tone, and figurative language—to say what they wanted to say. By studying the style, technique, and rhetorical strategies of other writers, we learn how we might effectively do the same. The more we read and write, the more we begin to read as writers and, in turn, to write knowing what readers expect.

READING AS A WRITER

What does it mean to read as a writer? As mentioned earlier, most of us have not been taught to read with a writer's eye, to ask why we like one piece of writing and not another. Similarly, most of us do not ask ourselves why one piece of writing is more convincing than another. When you learn to read with a writer's eye, you begin to answer these important questions and, in the process, you come to appreciate what is involved in selecting and focusing a subject as well as the craftsmanship involved in writing—how a writer selects descriptive details, uses an unobtrusive organizational pattern, opts for fresh and lively language, chooses representative and persuasive examples, and emphasizes important points with sentence variety.

On one level, reading stimulates your thinking by providing you with subjects to write about. For example, after reading Annie Dillard's essay "Hitting Pay Dirt" or Helen Keller's "Three Days to See," you might take up your pen to write about a turning point in your life or about what you would choose to do if you had only three days with vision. Or, by reading Mike Rose's "I Just Wanna Be Average," Carl T. Rowan's "Unforgettable Miss Bessie," and Thomas L. Friedman's "My Favorite Teacher," you might see how each writer creates a dominant impression of an influential person in his or her life and write about an influential person in your own life.

On a second level, reading provides you with information, ideas, and perspectives for developing your own paper. In this way, you respond to what you read, using material from what you've read in your essay. For example, after reading Rene Sanchez's essay "Surfing's Up and Grades Are Down," you might want to elaborate on what he has written and either agree with his examples or generate better ones of your own. You could also qualify his argument or take issue against it. Similarly, if you wanted to write about the effects of television on America's youth, you will find the essays by Joanmarie Kalter, Barbara Kingsolver, and Pete Hamill in Chapter 20 an invaluable resource.

On a third level, active reading can increase your awareness of how others' writing affects you, thus making you more sensitive to how your own writing will affect your readers. For example, if you have ever been impressed by an author who uses convincing evidence to support each of her claims, you might be more likely to back up your own claims carefully. If you have been impressed by an apt turn of phrase or absorbed by a writer's new idea, you may be less inclined to feed your readers dull, worn-out, and trite phrases. More to the point, however, the active reading that you are encouraged to do in *Models for Writers* will help you recognize and analyze the essential elements of the essay. When you see, for example, how a writer like Witold Rybczynski uses a strong thesis statement to control the parts of his essay on machine-made screws, you can better appreciate the importance of having a clear thesis statement in your writing. When you see the way Steve Brody uses transitions to link key phrases and important ideas so that readers can recognize clearly how the parts of his essay are meant to flow together, you have a better idea of how to achieve such coherence in your own writing. And when you see how Rita Dove uses a point-by-point organizational pattern to show the differences between reality and television, you see a powerful way in which you too can organize an essay using comparison and contrast.

Another important reason, then, to master the skills of active reading is that, for everything you write, you will be your own first reader and critic. How well you are able to scrutinize your own drafts will powerfully affect how well you revise them, and revising well is crucial to writing well. So reading others' writing with a critical eye is useful and important practice; the more you read, the more practice you will have in sharpening your skills.

Remember, writing is the making of reading. The more sensitive you become to the content and style decisions made by the writers in *Models for Writers*, the more skilled you will be at making similar decisions in your own writing.

WRITING FROM READING: THREE SAMPLE STUDENT ESSAYS

A Narrative Essay

Reading often triggers memories of experiences that we have had. After reading several personal narratives about growing up—Steve Brody's "How I Got Smart," Dick Gregory's "Shame," and Roger Hoffmann's "The Dare," in particular—student Lisa Driver found herself thinking about what it was like growing up in rural Vermont. When her classmates asked her to share with them a childhood experience that they wouldn't be able to forget, Driver told them of an experience that she'd had in the sixth grade. She confided that as a sixth grader the experience felt very traumatic. In retrospect, however, she was able to appreciate the humor in the uncomfortable situation. Encouraged by her classmates, Driver wrote the following narrative in which she captures her memorable encounter with Mrs. Armstrong, her teacher.

Title: introduces subject and provides focus

The Strong Arm of a Sixth-Grade Teacher

Lisa V. Driver

Point of view: first-person narration

Sometimes experiences that we have had in a classroom leave an indelible imprint on our lives. For me, it was one experience that I had with Mrs. Armstrong, a powerful, overbearing

Context: description of self, classroom setting, and other student

teacher. I was a scrawny, sixth-grade girl. I sat in the back of the classroom in the third row behind Todd, the class troublemaker. There was a little bit of safety in sitting behind Todd. Usually Mrs. Armstrong targeted him and not anyone close by. Todd was the type of kid who loved to get into trouble. He had a heart of gold but had absolutely no use for school. He was not at all intimidated by Mrs. Armstrong and her academic credentials, her perfect children, her world travel, and, most of all, her condescending manner to her rural farm students.

Context: description of teacher foreshadows later action

Mrs. Armstrong was a very large, domineering, and commanding figure. She loved jelly donuts, and it showed. Her hands, desk, and papers always had globs of sticky jam on them. She's the only person I've ever known who could make almost a whole donut disappear in one bite. The bright, red jam would ooze out the sides of the donut and get all over her face. My classmates and I all drooled at the thought of having such a treat ourselves. Most days she managed to devour a half-dozen Koffee Kup jelly donuts.

Narrative begins: antonym/ synonym drill

On one particular dull and dreary day, Mrs. Armstrong was droning on about antonyms and synonyms. She loved to use her knowledge to evoke fear and terror in her sixth-grade students, and none of us was immune to her reign of terror. She was the type of teacher who expected the right answer right away. The drill sergeant strutted around the room that day, snapping her pudgy, sticky fingers in our faces and expecting answers on the spot. If a student did not deliver immediately, then she would yell at and humiliate that student in front of his or her classmates. Many of my classmates had suffered her snapping

Description: dominant impression of teacher as "drill sergeant"

fingers and been left embarrassed and defeated. But I was safe—I was behind Todd.

The class dragged on as Mrs. Armstrong de-

Organiza-tion: chrono-logical sequence of events

lighted in her antonym game. She'd march down each aisle and point to two different things, ex-pecting us to quickly state the correct antonyms. For example, if she pointed to the ceiling and the floor, we were supposed to respond "up and down." Or, if she pointed to the classroom and the window, the answer would be "inside and out-side." As she neared my desk, I was feeling pretty safe, hidden as I was behind Todd. But

Details

then Todd cleverly knocked his pencil to the floor and leaned over to retrieve it. Well, there I was totally exposed to Mrs. Armstrong. I froze. Suddenly, she pointed to herself and then pointed at me and snapped those fingers, demanding an an-

Climactic moment

swer. Before I realized what I was saying, I blurted out, "fat and skinny"!

Mrs. Armstrong exploded. She started yelling and then grabbed hold of my shirt, dragged me to the door, and marched me down the hallway, screaming at me all the way. She stormed into the principal's office and deposited me in a hard wooden chair. In a loud voice she told Mr. Alder-man, the principal, that I was not to come back to her class for an entire week. She slammed the door on her way out, leaving me with the princi-pal. By now I was shaking and crying because I'd never ever been sent to the principal's office.

Details

Mr. Alderman sat in his old swivel chair and behind him on the wall hung a wooden paddle with the words "Board of Education" etched in large letters. Todd often bragged that he had firsthand knowledge of the purpose of that paddle. All that kept going through my head was that my parents were going to kill me after I'd been spanked by this man.

Mr. Alderman was a huge man with a short crew cut. Everyone except Todd was afraid of him. With steely eyes peering out over his glasses straight at me, the principal raised his eyebrows and demanded an explanation for my visit. I choked out the story to him between crying spells. When I told him that I had said, "fat and skinny," in response to Mrs. Armstrong's antonym problem, he leaned back in his chair and started laughing as hard as I'd ever seen a person laugh. When he finished laughing and drying his eyes, he told me that the correct response should have been "teacher and student." Slowly it dawned on me that I had mistakenly given the wrong antonym to Mrs. Armstrong, and I started to giggle with the principal. I spent the entire week in Mr. Alderman's office, answering the phone and being his secretary. I think he was afraid of that teacher also.

*Conclu-
sion: re-
flection
on the
incident*

A Response Essay

For an assignment following the James Lincoln Collier reading in Chapter 3, Zoe Ockenga tackled the topic of anxiety. In her first draft, she explored the anxiety she felt the night before her first speech in a public speaking class and how in confronting that anxiety she benefited from the course. Ockenga read her paper aloud in class, and other students had an opportunity to ask her questions and to offer constructive criticism. Several students suggested that she might want to relate her experiences to those that Collier recounts in his essay. Another asked if she had other examples that she could include to bolster the point she wanted to make. At this point in the discussion, Ockenga recalled a phone conversation she had had with her mother regarding her mother's indecision about accepting a new job. The thought of working outside the home for the first time in more than twenty years brought out her mother's worst fears and threatened to keep her from accepting the challenge. Armed with these valuable suggestions and ideas, Ockenga went back to work. In subsequent drafts, she worked on the Collier connection, actually citing his essay on several occasions, and developed the example of the anxiety surrounding her mother's decision. What follows is the final draft of her essay, which incorporates the changes she made based on the peer evaluation of her first draft.

Title: indicates main idea of the essay

The Excuse "Not To"

Zoe Ockenga

Beginning: captures reader's attention

I cannot imagine anything worse than the nervous, anxious feeling I got the night before my first speech in public speaking class last spring semester. The knots in my stomach were so fierce that I racked my brain for an excuse to give the teacher so that I would not have to go through with the dreaded assignment. Once in bed, I lay awake thinking of all the mistakes that I might make while standing alone in front of my classmates. I spent the rest of the night tossing and turning, frustrated that now, on top of my panic, I would have to give my speech with huge bags under my eyes.

Anxiety is an intense emotion that can strike at any time or place, before a simple daily activity or a life-changing decision. For some people, anxiety is only a minor interference in the process of achieving a goal. For others, it can be a force that is impossible to overcome. In these instances, anxiety can prevent the accomplishment of lifelong hopes and dreams. Avoiding the causes of stress or fear can make us feel secure and safe. Avoiding anxiety, however, may mean forfeiting a once-in-a-lifetime opportu-

Thesis   nity. Confronting anxiety can make for a richer, more fulfilling existence.

First exam-   The next day I trudged to class and sat on
ple: contin-
ues story   the edge of my seat until I could not stand the
introduced
in opening   tension any longer. At this point, I forced my-
paragraph
to support   self to raise my hand to volunteer to go next
thesis   simply to end my suffering. As I walked to the front of the room and assumed my position at the podium, the faces of the twenty-five classmates I had been sitting beside a minute ago suddenly seemed like fifty. I probably fumbled over a word or two as I discussed the harmful aspects of animal testing, but my mistakes were not nearly as severe as I had imagined the night before. Less than five minutes later the whole nightmare was over, and it had been much less painful than I had anticipated. As I sat down with a huge sigh of relief to listen to the next victim stumble repeatedly over how to milk dairy cows, I real-ized that I had not been half bad.

Although I still dreaded giving the next series of speeches, I eventually became more accustomed to speaking in front of my peers. I would still have to force myself to volunteer, secretly hoping the teacher would forget about me, but the audience that once seemed large and forbidding eventually became much more human. A speech class is something that I would never have taken if it had not been a requirement, but I can honestly say that I am better off because of it. I was forced to grapple with my anxiety and in the process become a stronger, more self-confident individual. Before this class I had been able to hide out in large lectures, never offering any comments or insights. For the first time at college I was forced to participate, and I realized that I could speak effectively in front of strangers and, more importantly, that I had something to say.

Second example: cites essay from Models for Writers *to support thesis*

The insomnia-inducing anticipation of giving a speech was a type of anxiety that I had to overcome to meet my distribution requirements for graduation. In the essay "Anxiety: Challenge by Another Name" by James Lincoln Collier, the author tells of his own struggles with anxiety. He tells of one particular event that happened between his sophomore and junior years in college when he was asked to spend a summer in Argentina with a good friend. He writes about how he felt after he made his decision not to go:

I had turned down something I wanted to do because I was scared, and had ended up feeling depressed. I stayed that way for a long time. And it didn't help when I went back to college in the fall to discover that Ted and his friend had had a terrific time. (38)

The proposition of going to Argentina was an extremely difficult choice for Collier as it meant abandoning the comfortable routine of the past and venturing completely out of his element. Although the idea of the trip was exciting, the author could not bring himself to choose the summer in Argentina because of his uncertainties.

The summer abroad that Collier denied himself in his early twenties left him with such a feeling of regret that he vowed to change his approach to life. From then on, he faced challenges that made him uncomfortable and was able to accomplish feats he would never have dreamed possible: interviewing celebrities, traveling extensively throughout Europe, parachuting, and even learning to ski at age forty. Collier emphasizes that he was able to make his life fulfilling and exciting by adhering to his belief that anxiety cannot be stifled by avoidance; it can only be stifled by confrontation (39).

Third example: introduces mother's dilemma

Anxiety prevents many individuals from accepting life's challenges and changes. My own mother is currently struggling with such a dilemma. At age fifty-three, having never had a

career outside the home, my mother has been recommended to manage a new art gallery. The River
Gallery, as it will be called, will be opening in
our town of Ipswich, Massachusetts, this spring.
An avid collector and art lover as well as a
budding potter, my mother would, I believe, be
exceptional at this job.

Anticipating this new opportunity and responsibility has caused my mother great anxiety.
Re-entering the workforce after over twenty years
is as frightening for my mother as the trip to
Argentina was for Collier. When I recently discussed the job prospect with my mother, she was
negative and full of doubt. "There's no way I
could ever handle such a responsibility," she commented. "I have no business experience. I would
look like a fool if I actually tried to pull something like this off. Besides, I'm sure the artists
would never take me seriously." Just as my mother
focused on all the possible negative aspects of
the opportunity in front of her, Collier questioned the value of his opportunity to spend a
summer abroad. He describes having second thoughts
about just how exciting the trip would be:

*Quotation:
quotes Col-
lier to help
explain
mother's
indecision*

I had never been very far from New England, and I had been homesick my first few
weeks at college. What would it be like in
a strange country? What about the language? And besides, I had promised to
teach my younger brother to sail that summer. (37-38)

Focusing on all the possible problems accompanying a new opportunity can arouse such a sense of fear that it can overpower the ability to take a risk. Both my mother and Collier found out that dwelling on possible negative outcomes allowed them to ignore the benefits of a new experience and thus maintain their safe current situations.

Currently my mother is using anxiety as an excuse "not to" act. To confront her anxiety and take an opportunity in which there is a possibility of failure as well as success is a true risk. Regardless of the outcome, to even contemplate a new challenge has changed her life. The summer forgone by Collier roused him to never again pass up an exciting opportunity and thus to live his life to the fullest. Just the thought of taking the gallery position has prompted my mother to contemplate taking evening classes so that if she refuses the offer she may be better prepared for a similar challenge in the future. Although her decision is unresolved, her anxiety has made her realize the possibilities that may be opening for her, whether or not she chooses to take them. If in the end her answer is no, I believe that the lingering feeling of "what if" will cause her to re-evaluate her expectations and goals for the future.

Conclusion　　Anxiety can create confidence and optimism or depression, low self-esteem, and regret. The outcome of anxiety is entirely dependent on whether the individual runs from it or embraces it. Some forms of anxiety can be conquered merely by repeating the activity that causes them, such as giving speeches in a public speaking class. Anxiety brought on by unique opportunities or life-changing decisions, such as a summer in a foreign country or a new career, must be harnessed. Opportunities forgone due to anxiety and fear could be the chances of a lifetime. Although the unpleasant feelings that may accompany anxiety may make it initially easier to do nothing, the road not taken will never be forgotten. Anxiety is essentially a blessing in disguise. It is a physical and emotional trigger that tells us when and where there is an opportunity for us to grow and become stronger human beings.

WORKS CITED

Collier, James Lincoln. "Anxiety: Challenge by Another Name." Models for Writers. Eds. Alfred Rosa and Paul Eschholz. 7th ed. New York: Bedford/St. Martin's, 2001. 37-40.

An Analytical Essay

When student Susan Francis wrote an analysis of George Orwell's "A Hanging," her purpose was to show that she had understood the essay and to help her readers increase their understanding of it, too. She started by thinking about aspects of the work's meaning, structure, and style that are important but not obvious. Her analysis grew directly out of her reading and, more specifically, out of the notes she made during her first and subsequent readings of the text.

From the start, Francis knew that she had to decide what point she most wanted to make — what her thesis would be. With a little thought, she developed a list of four theses that she could use in her analytical paper:

1. In "A Hanging," George Orwell carefully selects details to persuade readers that capital punishment is wrong.
2. "A Hanging" reveals how thoroughly the British had imposed their laws, customs, and values on colonial Burma.
3. Though "A Hanging" appeals powerfully to the emotions, it does not make a reasoned argument against capital punishment.
4. In "A Hanging," George Orwell employs simile and metaphor, personification, and dialogue to express people's inhumanity to other people.

After considering the merits of each of her four choices, Francis chose the last thesis to use in her paper. She thought she could support this one most strongly and effectively using evidence from Orwell's essay. The following is the final draft of her analytical paper. Her discussion is clear and coherent, and it is firmly based on Orwell's text. She cites many details that capture Orwell's attitude toward the hanging and toward his imperial colleagues, and she has interpreted them so that her readers can plainly see how those details contribute to the total effect of "A Hanging."

The Disgrace of Man

Susan Francis

Thesis: statement of central idea and order in which evidence is to be presented

George Orwell's "A Hanging" graphically depicts the execution of a prisoner in a way that expresses a universal tragedy. He artfully employs simile and metaphor, personification, and dialogue to indicate people's inhumanity toward other people regardless of nationality and to prompt readers' sympathy and self-examination.

*Point 1:
examples
of simile
and
metaphor*

Orwell uses simile and metaphor to show that the prisoner is treated more like an animal than like a human being. The cells of the condemned men, "a row of sheds [. . .] quite bare within," are "like small animal cages"(220). The warders grip the prisoner "like men handling a fish" (221). Though they refer to the prisoner as "this

*Parenthetical in-text
citations in
MLA style*

man"(222) or "our friend"(224), the other characters view him as less than human. Even his cry resounds like the "tolling of a bell" rather than a human "prayer or cry for help"(223), and after he is dead, the superintendent pokes at the body with a stick. These details direct readers' attention to the lack of human concern for the condemned prisoner.

*Point 2:
examples
of personification—
prisoner's
body parts*

In contrast, Orwell emphasizes the "wrongness of cutting life short"(222) by representing the parts of the prisoner's body as taking on human behavior. He describes how the lock of hair "danced" on the man's scalp, how his feet "printed themselves" on the gravel, and how all his organs were "toiling away"(222) like a team of laborers at some collective project. In personifying these bodily features, Orwell forces readers to confront the prisoner's vitality, his humanity. Readers, in turn, associate each bodily part with themselves; they become highly aware of the fragility of life. As the author focuses on

how easily these actions can be stopped in any
human being "with a sudden snap"(222), readers
feel the "wrongness" of the hanging as if their
own lives were threatened.

Personifi-
cation:
example of
dog

In addition to creating this sense of unmistakable life, Orwell uses the dog as a standard
for evaluating the characters' appreciation of
human life. The dog loves people--he is "wild
with glee to find so many human beings together"
(221)--and the person he loves the most is the
prisoner, who has been treated as less than human
by the jail attendants. When the prisoner starts
to pray, the other people are silent, but the dog
answers "with a whine"(223). Even after the
hanging, the dog runs directly to the gallows to
see the prisoner again. Readers are forced to reflect on their own reactions: Which is more
shocking, the dog's actions or the observers'
cold response?

Point 3: in-
sensitive
dialogue
regardless
of nation-
ality

Finally, Orwell refers to the characters'
nationalities to stress that this insensitivity
extends to all nationalities and races. The hanging takes place in Burma, in a jail run by a
European army doctor and a native of southern
India. The warders are also Indians, and the
hangman is actually a fellow prisoner. The author
calls attention to each of these participants and
implies that each one of them might have halted
the brutal proceeding. He was there, too, and
could have intervened when he suddenly realized

that killing the prisoner would be wrong. Yet the formality of the hanging goes on.

As he reflects on the meaning of suddenly destroying human life, Orwell emphasizes the similarities among all men, regardless of nationality. Before the hanging, they are "seeing, hearing, feeling, understanding the same world," and afterward there would be "one mind less, one world less"(222). Such insights do not affect the other characters, who think of the hanging not as a killing but as a job to be done, a job made unpleasant by those reminders (the incident of the dog, the prisoner's praying) that they are dealing with a human being. Orwell uses dialogue to show how selfish and callous the observers are. Though they have different accents—the superintendent's "for God's sake hurry up"(221), the Dravidian's "All has passed off with the utmost satisfactoriness"(224)--they think and feel the same. Their words, such as "He's all right" (223), show that they are more concerned about their own lives than the one they are destroying.

Conclusion: value of human life

Although George Orwell sets his story in Burma, his point is universal; although he deals with capital punishment, he implies other questions about life and death. We are all faced with issues such as capital punishment, abortion, and euthanasia, and sometimes we find ourselves directly involved, as Orwell was in Burma. "A Hanging" confronts us with a situation that won't go

away and urges us to take very seriously the
value of human life.

WORKS CITED

Orwell, George. "A Hanging." <u>Models for Writers.</u>
    Eds. Alfred Rosa and Paul Eschholz. 7th ed.
    Boston: Bedford/St. Martin's, 2001. 220-224.

The Elements
of the Essay

Thesis

The *thesis* of an essay is its main idea, the point it is trying to make. The thesis is often expressed in a one- or two-sentence statement, although sometimes it is implied or suggested rather than stated directly. The thesis statement determines the content of the essay: Everything that the writer says must be logically related to the thesis statement.

Because everything you say in your composition must be logically related to your thesis statement, the thesis statement controls and directs the choices you make about the content of your essay. This does not mean that your thesis statement is a straitjacket. As your essay develops, you may want to modify your thesis statement to accommodate your new thinking. This urge is not only acceptable, it is normal. One way to develop a working thesis is to determine a question that you are trying to answer in your paper. A one- or two-sentence answer to this question often produces a tentative thesis statement. For example, a student wanted to answer the following question in her essay:

Do men and women have different conversational speaking styles?

Her preliminary answer to this question was this:

Men and women appear to have different objectives when they converse.

After writing two drafts, she modified her thesis to better fit the examples she had gathered:

Very often, conversations between men and women become situations in which the man gives a mini-lecture and the woman unwittingly turns into a captive audience.

A thesis statement should be

1. More general than the ideas and facts used to support it
2. Appropriately focused for the length of your paper
3. The most important point you make about your topic

A thesis statement should not be a question, but an assertion—a claim made about a debatable issue that can be supported with evidence.

Another effective strategy for developing a thesis statement is to begin by writing *What I want to say is that* . . .

> *What I want to say is that* unless the university administration enforces its strong anti-hazing policy, the well-being of many of its student-athletes will be endangered.

Later you can delete the formulaic opening, and you will be left with a thesis statement:

> Unless the university administration enforces its strong anti-hazing policy, the well-being of many of its student-athletes will be endangered.

Usually the thesis is presented early in an essay, sometimes in the first sentence. Here are some thesis statements that begin essays:

> One of the most potent elements in body language is eye behavior.
> —Flora Davis

> Americans can be divided into three groups—smokers, nonsmokers, and that expanding pack of us who have quit.
> —Franklin E. Zimring

> Over the past ten to fifteen years it has become apparent that eating disorders have reached epidemic proportions among adolescents.
> —Helen A. Guthrie

> Clutter is the disease of American writing. We are a society strangling in unnecessary words, circular construction, pompous frills, and meaningless jargon.
> —William Zinsser

Each of these sentences does what a good thesis statement should do: It identifies the topic and makes an assertion about it.

Often writers prepare readers for a thesis statement with one or several sentences that establish a context. Notice in the following example how the author eases the reader into his thesis about television instead of presenting it abruptly in the first sentence:

> With the advent of television, for the first time in history, all aspects of animal and human life and death, of societal and individual behavior have been condensed on the average to a 19-inch diagonal screen and a 30-minute time slot. Television, a unique medium, claiming to be neither a reality nor art, has become reality for many of us, particularly for our children who are growing up in front of it.
>
> –Jerzy Kosinski

On occasion a writer may even purposely delay the presentation of a thesis until the middle or the end of an essay. If the thesis is controversial or needs extended discussion and illustration, the writer might present it later to make it easier for the reader to understand and accept it. Appearing near or at the end of an essay, a thesis also gains prominence. For example, after an involved discussion about why various groups put pressure on school libraries to ban books, a student ended an essay with her thesis:

> The effort to censor what our children are reading can turn into a potentially explosive situation and cause misunderstanding and hurt feelings within our schools and communities. If we can gain an understanding of why people have sought to censor children's books, we will be better prepared to respond in a sensitive and reasonable manner. More importantly, we will be able to provide the best educational opportunity for our children through a sensible approach, one that neither overly restricts the range of their reading nor allows them to read all books, no matter how inappropriate.   *thesis*
>
> –Tara Ketch, student

Some kinds of writing do not need thesis statements. These include descriptions, narratives, and personal writing such as letters and diaries. But any essay that seeks to explain or prove a point has a thesis that is usually set forth in a thesis statement.

The Most Important Day

■ **Helen Keller**

Helen Keller (1880–1968) was afflicted by a disease that left her blind and deaf at the age of eighteen months. With the aid of her teacher, Anne Sullivan, she was able to overcome her severe handicaps, to graduate from Radcliffe College, and to lead a productive and challenging adult life. In the following selection from her autobiography, The Story of My Life *(1902), Keller tells of the day she first met Anne Sullivan, a day she regarded as the most important in her life. As you read, note that Keller states her thesis in the first paragraph and that the remaining paragraphs maintain unity by emphasizing the importance of the day her teacher arrived, even though they deal with the days and weeks following.*

FOR YOUR JOURNAL

Imagine what your life would be like without the use of your eyes and your ears. What would your other senses be able to tell you? Try to imagine how you would communicate with others.

The most important day I remember in all my life is the one on which my teacher, Anne Mansfield Sullivan, came to me. I am filled with wonder when I consider the immeasurable contrast between the two lives which it connects. It was the third of March, 1887, three months before I was seven years old. 1

On the afternoon of that eventful day, I stood on the porch, dumb, expectant. I guessed vaguely from my mother's signs and from the hurrying to and fro in the house that something unusual was about to happen, so I went to the door and waited on the steps. The afternoon sun penetrated the mass of honeysuckle that covered the porch and fell on my upturned face. My fingers lingered almost unconsciously on the familiar leaves and blossoms which had just come forth to greet the sweet southern spring. I did not know what the future held of marvel or surprise for me. Anger and bitterness had preyed upon me continually for weeks and a deep languor had succeeded this passionate struggle. 2

Have you ever been at sea in a dense fog, when it seemed as if a 3
tangible white darkness shut you in, and the great ship, tense and
anxious, groped her way toward the shore with plummet and sounding-
line, and you waited with beating heart for something to happen? I
was like that ship before my education began, only I was without
compass or sounding-line, and had no way of knowing how near the
harbor was. "Light! give me light!" was the wordless cry of my soul,
and the light of love shone on me in that very hour.

I felt approaching footsteps. I stretched out my hand as I sup- 4
posed to my mother. Someone took it, and I was caught up and held
close in the arms of her who had come to reveal all things to me, and,
more than all things else, to love me.

The morning after my teacher came she led me into her room and 5
gave me a doll. The little blind children at the Perkins Institution had
sent it and Laura Bridgman had dressed it; but I did not know this
until afterward. When I had played with it a little while, Miss
Sullivan slowly spelled into my hand the word "d-o-l-l." I was at
once interested in this finger play and tried to imitate it. When I
finally succeeded in making the letters correctly I was flushed with
childish pleasure and pride. Running downstairs to my mother I held
up my hand and made the letters for doll. I did not know that I was
spelling a word or even that words existed; I was simply making my
fingers go in monkeylike imitation. In the days that followed I
learned to spell in this uncomprehending way a great many words,
among them *pin, hat, cup* and a few verbs like *sit, stand,* and *walk.*
But my teacher had been with me several weeks before I understood
that everything has a name.

One day, while I was playing with my new doll, Miss Sullivan 6
put my big rag doll into my lap also, spelled "d-o-l-l" and tried to
make me understand that "d-o-l-l" applied to both. Earlier in the day
we had had a tussle over the words "m-u-g" and "w-a-t-e-r." Miss
Sullivan had tried to impress it upon me that "m-u-g" is *mug* and
that "w-a-t-e-r" is *water,* but I persisted in confounding the two. In
despair she had dropped the subject for the time, only to renew it at
the first opportunity. I became impatient at her repeated attempts
and, seizing the new doll, I dashed it upon the floor. I was keenly
delighted when I felt the fragments of the broken doll at my feet.
Neither sorrow nor regret followed my passionate outburst. I had not
loved the doll. In the still, dark world in which I lived there was no
strong sentiment or tenderness. I felt my teacher sweep the fragments
to one side of the hearth, and I had a sense of satisfaction that the

cause of my discomfort was removed. She brought me my hat, and I knew I was going out into the warm sunshine. This thought, if a wordless sensation may be called a thought, made me hop and skip with pleasure.

We walked down the path to the well-house, attracted by the fra- 7
grance of the honeysuckle with which it was covered. Someone was drawing water and my teacher placed my hand under the spout. As the cool stream gushed over one hand she spelled into the other the word *water*, first slowly, then rapidly. I stood still, my whole attention fixed upon the motions of her fingers. Suddenly I felt a misty consciousness as of something forgotten—a thrill of returning thought; and somehow the mystery of language was revealed to me. I knew then that "w-a-t-e-r" meant the wonderful cool something that was flowing over my hand. The living word awakened my soul, gave it light, hope, joy, set it free! There were barriers still, it is true, but barriers that could in time be swept away.

I left the well-house eager to learn. Everything had a name, and 8
each name gave birth to a new thought. As we returned to the house every object which I touched seemed to quiver with life. That was because I saw everything with the strange, new sight that had come to me. On entering the door I remembered the doll I had broken. I felt my way to the hearth and picked up the pieces. I tried vainly to put them together. Then my eyes filled with tears; for I realized what I had done, and for the first time I felt repentance and sorrow.

I learned a great many new words that day. I do not remember 9
what they all were; but I do know that *mother, father, sister, teacher* were among them—words that were to make the world blossom for me, "like Aaron's rod, with flowers."[1] It would have been difficult to find a happier child than I was as I lay in my crib at the close of that eventful day and lived over the joys it had brought me, and for the first time longed for a new day to come.

QUESTIONS FOR STUDY AND DISCUSSION

1. What is Keller's thesis in this essay? What question do you think Keller is trying to answer? How does this question help focus her subject? Does her thesis answer her question?

---

[1]*Aaron's rod:* in Jewish and Christian traditions, a rod similar to Moses' staff that, in the high priest Aaron's hands, had miraculous power. [Eds.]

2. What is Keller's purpose in this essay? (Glossary: *Purpose*)

3. What was Keller's state of mind before Anne Sullivan arrived to help her? To what does she compare herself? (Glossary: *Analogy*) How effective is this comparison? Explain.

4. Why was the realization that everything has a name important to Keller?

5. How was the "mystery of language" (7) revealed to Keller? What were the consequences for her of this new understanding of the nature of language?

6. Keller narrates the events of the day Sullivan arrived (2–4), the morning after she arrived (5), and one day several weeks after her arrival (6–9). Describe what happens on each day, and explain how these separate incidents support Keller's thesis.

VOCABULARY

Refer to your dictionary to define the following words as they are used in this selection. Then use each word in a sentence of your own.

dumb (2)	plummet (3)
preyed (2)	tussle (6)
languor (2)	vainly (8)
passionate (2)	

CLASSROOM ACTIVITY USING THESIS

One effective way of focusing on your subject is to brainstorm a list of specific questions about it at the start. This strategy has a number of advantages. Each question narrows the general subject area, suggesting a more manageable essay. Also, simply phrasing your topic as a question gives you a starting point; your work has focus and direction from the outset. Finally, a one- or two-sentence answer to your question often provides you with a preliminary thesis statement.

To test this strategy, develop a list of five questions about the subject of "recycling paper waste on campus." To get you started, here is one possible question: Should students be required to recycle paper waste?

1. _____

2. _____

3. _____

4. _____

5. _____

SUGGESTED WRITING ASSIGNMENTS

1. Think about an important day in your own life. Using the thesis statement "The most important day of my life was _____," write an essay in which you show the significance of that day by recounting and explaining the events that took place as Keller does in her essay.

2. For many people around the world, the life of Helen Keller is a symbol of what an individual can achieve despite seemingly insurmountable disabilities. Her achievements have also inspired many who have no disabilities, leading them to believe that they can accomplish more than they ever thought possible. Consider the role of disabled people in our society, develop an appropriate thesis, and write an essay on the topic.

Anxiety: Challenge by Another Name

■ James Lincoln Collier

James Lincoln Collier is a freelance writer with more than six hundred articles to his credit. He was born in New York in 1928 and graduated from Hamilton College in 1950. Among his published books are many works of fiction, including novels for young adults. His nonfiction writing has often focused on American music, particularly jazz. Collier *has produced biographies of Louis Armstrong, Duke Ellington, and Benny Goodman, but his best-known book is* The Making of Jazz: A Comprehensive History *(1978). With his son Christopher he has written a number of history books, including* A Century of Immigration: 1820–1924 *(2000),* The Civil War *(2000),* The Changing Face of American Society: 1945–2000 *(2001), and a series of biographies for young readers covering major figures in American history. As you read the following essay, which first appeared in* Reader's Digest *in 1986, pay particular attention to where Collier places his thesis. Note also how his thesis statement identifies the topic (anxiety) and makes an assertion about it (that it can have a positive impact on our lives).*

FOR YOUR JOURNAL

Many people tend to associate anxiety with stress and to think of it as a negative thing. Are there good kinds of anxiety, too? Provide an example of anxiety that has been beneficial to you or to someone you know.

Between my sophomore and junior years at college, a chance came   1
up for me to spend the summer vacation working on a ranch in Argentina. My roommate's father was in the cattle business, and he wanted Ted to see something of it. Ted said he would go if he could take a friend, and he chose me.

2

---

[1]*Pampas:* a vast plain in central Argentina. [Eds.]

The idea of spending two months on the fabled Argentine Pampas[1] was exciting. Then I began having second thoughts. I had never been very far from New England, and I had been homesick my first few weeks at college. What would it be like in a strange country? What about the language? And besides, I had promised to teach my younger brother to sail that summer. The more I thought about it, the more the prospect daunted me. I began waking up nights in a sweat.

In the end I turned down the proposition. As soon as Ted asked   3
somebody else to go, I began kicking myself. A couple of weeks later I went home to my old summer job, unpacking cartons at the local supermarket, feeling very low. I had turned down something I wanted to do because I was scared, and had ended up feeling depressed. I stayed that way for a long time. And it didn't help when I went back to college in the fall to discover that Ted and his friend had had a terrific time.

In the long run that unhappy summer taught me a valuable les-   4
son out of which I developed a rule for myself: *do what makes you anxious; don't do what makes you depressed.*

I am not, of course, talking about severe states of anxiety or de-   5
pression, which require medical attention. What I mean is that kind of anxiety we call stage fright, butterflies in the stomach, a case of nerves—the feelings we have at a job interview, when we're giving a big party, when we have to make an important presentation at the office. And the kind of depression I am referring to is that downhearted feeling of the blues, when we don't seem to be interested in anything, when we can't get going and seem to have no energy.

I was confronted by this sort of situation toward the end of my   6
senior year. As graduation approached, I began to think about taking a crack at making my living as a writer. But one of my professors was urging me to apply to graduate school and aim at a teaching career.

I wavered. The idea of trying to live by writing was scary—a lot   7
more scary than spending a summer on the Pampas, I thought. Back and forth I went, making my decision, unmaking it. Suddenly, I realized that every time I gave up the idea of writing, that sinking feeling went through me; it gave me the blues.

The thought of graduate school wasn't what depressed me. It was   8
giving up on what deep in my gut I really wanted to do. Right then I learned another lesson. To avoid that kind of depression meant, inevitably, having to endure a certain amount of worry and concern.

The great Danish philosopher Søren Kierkegaard believed that   9
anxiety always arises when we confront the possibility of our own

development. It seems to be a rule of life that you can't advance
without getting that old, familiar, jittery feeling.

Even as children we discover this when we try to expand our-   10
selves by, say, learning to ride a bike or going out for the school play.
Later in life we get butterflies when we think about having that first
child, or uprooting the family from the old hometown to find a better
opportunity halfway across the country. Any time, it seems, that we
set out aggressively to get something we want, we meet up with anxiety. And it's going to be our traveling companion, at least part of the
way, into any new venture.

When I first began writing magazine articles, I was frequently re-   11
quired to interview big names — people like Richard Burton,[2] Joan
Rivers,[3] sex authority William Masters, baseball-great Dizzy Dean.
Before each interview I would get butterflies and my hands would
shake.

At the time, I was doing some writing about music. And one per-   12
son I particularly admired was the great composer Duke Ellington.
Onstage and on television, he seemed the very model of the confident, sophisticated man of the world. Then I learned that Ellington
still got stage fright. If the highly honored Duke Ellington, who had
appeared on the bandstand some 10,000 times over 30 years, had
anxiety attacks, who was I to think I could avoid them?

I went on doing those frightening interviews, and one day, as I   13
was getting onto a plane for Washington to interview columnist
Joseph Alsop, I suddenly realized to my astonishment that I was
looking forward to the meeting. What had happened to those butterflies?

Well, in truth, they were still there, but there were fewer of them.   14
I had benefited, I discovered, from a process psychologists call "extinction." If you put an individual in an anxiety-provoking situation
often enough, he will eventually learn that there isn't anything to be
worried about.

Which brings us to a corollary to my basic rule: *you'll never elimi-*   15
nate anxiety by avoiding the things that caused it. I remember how
my son Jeff was when I first began to teach him to swim at the lake
cottage where we spent our summer vacations. He resisted, and when

---

[2]*Richard Burton* (1925–1984): a well-known British stage and Hollywood movie actor.
[Eds.]
[3]*Joan Rivers* (b 1933): a stand-up comedienne and talk-show host. [Eds.]

I got him into the water he sank and sputtered and wanted to quit. But I was insistent. And by summer's end he was splashing around like a puppy. He had "extinguished" his anxiety the only way he could—by confronting it.

The problem, of course, is that it is one thing to urge somebody else to take on those anxiety-producing challenges; it is quite another to get ourselves to do it.   16

Some years ago I was offered a writing assignment that would re-quire three months of travel through Europe. I had been abroad a couple of times on the usual "If it's Tuesday this must be Belgium" trips, but I hardly could claim to know my way around the continent. Moreover, my knowledge of foreign languages was limited to a little college French.   17

I hesitated. How would I, unable to speak the language, totally unfamiliar with local geography or transportation systems, set up in-terviews and do research? It seemed impossible, and with consider-able regret I sat down to write a letter begging off. Halfway through, a thought—which I subsequently made into another corollary to my basic rule—ran through my mind: *you can't learn if you don't try.* So I accepted the assignment.   18

There were some bad moments. But by the time I had finished the trip I was an experienced traveler. And ever since, I have never hesitated to head for even the most exotic of places, without guides or even advanced bookings, confident that somehow I will manage.   19

The point is that the new, the different, is almost by definition scary. But each time you try something, you learn, and as the learning piles up, the world opens to you.   20

I've made parachute jumps, learned to ski at 40, flown up the Rhine[4] in a balloon. And I know I'm going to go on doing such things. It's not because I'm braver or more daring than others. I'm not. But I don't let the butterflies stop me from doing what I want. Accept anxi-ety as another name for challenge and you can accomplish wonders.   21

QUESTIONS FOR STUDY AND DISCUSSION

1. What is Collier's thesis in this essay? Based on your own experiences, do you think that Collier's thesis is valid? Explain.
2. What is the process known to psychologists as "extinction"?
3. What caused Collier to come up with his basic rule for himself:

---

[4]*Rhine:* a major river and waterway of western Europe. [Eds.]

"Do what makes you anxious; don't do what makes you depressed" (4)? (Glossary: *Cause and Effect*) How did he develop the two corollaries to his basic rule? How do the basic rule and the two corollaries prepare you for his thesis?

4. What do you think Collier's purpose was in writing this essay? (Glossary: *Purpose*) Explain.

5. Identify the figure of speech that Collier uses toward the end of paragraph 10. (Glossary: *Figure of Speech*)

6. Explain how paragraphs 17–19 function within the context of Collier's essay. (Glossary: *Illustration*)

VOCABULARY

Refer to your dictionary to define the following words as they are used in this selection. Then use each word in a sentence of your own.

daunted (2)

proposition (3)

anxiety (5)

depression (5)

butterflies (5)

crack (6)

venture (10)

corollary (15)

CLASSROOM ACTIVITY USING THESIS

A good thesis statement identifies the topic and makes an assertion about it. Evaluate each of the following sentences as a thesis statement, and explain why each one either works or doesn't work as one.

1. Americans are suffering from overwork.

2. Life is indeed precious, and I believe the death penalty helps to affirm this fact.

3. Birthday parties are loads of fun.

4. New York is a city of sounds: muted sounds and shrill sounds; shattering sounds and soothing sounds; urgent sounds and aimless sounds.

5. Everyone is talking about the level of violence in American society.

6. Neighborhoods are often assigned human characteristics, one of which is a life cycle: They have a birth, a youth, a middle age, and an old age.

SUGGESTED WRITING ASSIGNMENTS

1. Building on your own experiences and the reading you have done, write an essay in which you use as your thesis either Collier's basic rule or one of his corollaries to that basic rule.

2. Write an essay in which you use any one of the following as your thesis:

   Good manners are a thing of the past.

   We need rituals in our lives.

   To tell a joke well is an art.

   We are a drug-dependent society.

   A regular low-dosage regimen of aspirin can be therapeutic.

   Regular exercise offers many benefits.

One Good Turn: The Importance of Machine-Made Screws

■ **Witold Rybczynski**

An architectural historian and professor of urban studies at the University of Pennsylvania, Witold Rybczynski graduated from McGill University with a degree in architecture in 1966. He received his masters in architecture from McGill in 1973. Rybczynski has written widely on design, building, and architecture, contributing regularly to the New Yorker *and* Time *magazine. His books include* Home: A Short History of an Idea *(1987),* Looking Around: A Journey through Architecture *(1993),* City Life: Urban Expectations in a New World *(1996) and* A Clearing in the Distance: Frederick Law Olmsted and America in the Nineteenth Century *(1999). In 2002, he published two books:* The Perfect House: A Journey with the Renaissance Master Andrea Palladio *and* The Look of Architecture. *In the following essay, which first appeared in the* New York Times Magazine *in 1999, Rybczynski draws on his personal experience building his own house as well as his knowledge of architectural history to tell the story of the ordinary machine-made screw and its impact on humankind. As you read, pay particular attention to the way Rybczynski presents his thesis.*

FOR YOUR JOURNAL

What's been your experience using the equipment associated with an activity you do — gardening and lawn tools for yard work, kitchen tools and utensils for cooking, carpentry tools for building, or even the "tools" or functional capabilities provided with a software program? What kinds of tools do you use? Do you have a preference for hand tools or power tools? Why?

Some years ago my wife and I built a house. I mean really built it—ourselves, from the ground up. Electricity being unavailable, we used hand tools. I did not have a large toolbox. It contained different-size saws, a mallet and chisels, a plane, several hammers (for friends conscripted into our work force), and, for correcting major mistakes, a heavy sledge. In addition I had a number of tools for measuring: a tape, a square, a spirit level, and a plumb line. That was all we needed.

One of the rewards of building something yourself is the pleasure of using tools. Hand tools are really extensions of the human body, for they have evolved over centuries—millenniums—of trial and error. Power tools are more convenient, of course, but they lack precisely this sense of refinement. Using a clumsy nailing gun is work, but swinging a claw hammer is satisfying work.

Had a medieval[1] carpenter come along—untutored neophytes, we could have used his help—he would have found most of my tools familiar. Indeed, even an ancient Roman carpenter would have found few surprises in my toolbox. He would recognize my plane, a version of his *plana;* he might admire my retractable tape measure, an improvement on his bronze folding *regula.* He would be puzzled by my brace and bit, a medieval invention, but being familiar with the Egyptian bow drill, he would readily infer its purpose. No doubt he would be impressed by my hard steel nails, so much superior to his hand-forged spikes.

Saws, hammers (and nails), chisels, drills, and squares all date from the Bronze[2] and early Iron Ages.[3] Many types of modern tools originated even earlier, in the Neolithic period, about 8,000 years ago. In fact, there is only one tool in my toolbox that would puzzle a Roman and a medieval carpenter: my screwdriver. They would understand the principle of screws; after all, Archimedes invented the screw in the third century B.C. Ancient screws were large wood contraptions, used for raising water. One of the earliest devices that used a screw to apply pressure was a Roman clothes press; presses were also used to make olive oil and wine. The Middle Ages[4] applied the

---

[1]*Medieval:* of or relating to the Middle Ages. [Eds.]

[2]*Bronze Age:* the period during which humans first used metal (bronze) instead of stone to make technological and cultural implements. [Eds.]

[3]*Iron Age:* the subsequent period during which iron essentially replaced bronze in the making of implements. [Eds.]

[4]*Middle Ages:* the period in European history between the collapse of Roman civilization in the fifth century C.E. and the Italian Renaissance of the fourteenth century. [Eds.]

same principle to the printing press and to that fiendish torturing device, the thumbscrew. Yet the ordinary screw as a small fixing device was unknown.

Wood screws originated sometime in the sixteenth century. The 5 first screwdrivers were called turn-screws, flat-bladed bits that could be attached to a carpenter's brace. The inventor of the handheld screwdriver remains unknown, but the familiar tool does not appear in carpenters' toolboxes until after 1800. There was not a great call for screwdrivers, because screws were expensive. They had to be painstakingly made by hand and were used in luxury articles like clocks. It was only after 1850 that wood screws were available in large quantities.

Inexpensive screws are quintessentially modern. Their mass pro- 6 duction requires a high degree of precision and standardization. The wood screw also represents an entirely new method of attachment, more durable than nails—which can pop out if the wood dries out or expands. (This makes screws particularly useful in shipbuilding.) The tapered, gimlet-pointed wood screw—like its cousin the bolt—squeezes the two joined pieces together. The more you tighten the screw—or the nut—the greater the squeeze. In modern steel buildings, for example, high-tension bolts are tightened so hard that it is the friction between the two pieces of steel—not the bolt itself—that gives strength to the joint. On a more mundane level, screws enable a vast array of convenient attachments in the home: door hinges, drawer pulls, shelf hangers, towel bars. Perhaps that is why if you rummage around most people's kitchen drawers you will most likely find at least one screwdriver.

Wood screws are stronger and more durable than nails, pegs or 7 staples. But the aristocrat of screws is the precision screw. This was first made roughly—by hand—and later on screw-cutting lathes, which is a chicken-and-egg story, since it was the screw that made machine lathes possible. The machined screw represented a technological breakthrough of epic proportions. Screws enabled the minute adjustment of a variety of precision instruments like clocks, microscopes, telescopes, sextants, theodolites,[5] and marine chronometers.

It is not an exaggeration to say that accurately threaded screws 8 changed the world. Without screws, entire fields of science would have languished, navigation would have remained primitive, and

---

[5]*Theodolites:* a surveying instrument used to measure horizontal and vertical angles. [Eds.]

naval warfare as well as routine maritime commerce in the eighteenth and nineteenth centuries would not have been possible. Without screws there would have been no machine tools, hence no industrial products and no Industrial Revolution. Think of that the next time you pick up a screwdriver to pry open a can of paint.

QUESTIONS FOR STUDY AND DISCUSSION

1. After talking about the house that he and his wife built and giving a brief history of hand tools, Rybczynski introduces his topic in the middle of paragraph 4 when he mentions the screwdriver. At what point does Rybczynski reveal his thesis, and does he state it directly or imply it? How effective is its placement and the way Rybczynski reveals it? Explain.

2. What, for Rybczynski, is the pleasure of using hand tools? How do they differ from other tools?

3. Rybczynski claims, "It is not an exaggeration to say that accurately threaded screws changed the world" (8). How does he support this claim?

4. How does Rybczynski make the transition between paragraphs 4 and 5, between paragraphs 5 and 6, and between paragraphs 7 and 8? (Glossary: *Transition*)

5. Explain how Rybczynski uses examples to develop his thesis. (Glossary: *Example*) Which examples do you find most effective? Why?

6. How does Rybczynski's diction help to establish him as an authority on the subject of hand tools in general and wood screws and machine-made screws in particular? (Glossary: *Diction*)

VOCABULARY

Refer to your dictionary to define the following words as they are used in this selection. Then use each word in a sentence of your own.

conscripted (1)	infer (3)
untutored (3)	quintessentially (6)
neophytes (3)	mundane (6)
retractable (3)	epic (7)

CLASSROOM ACTIVITY USING THESIS

Based on your reading of Rybczynski's essay, write at least one thesis statement for each of the following questions:

1. How are hand tools different from power tools?
2. Why is an accurately threaded, machine-made screw so useful?
3. Which recent technological advancements have changed, or will change, our lives as dramatically as the screw did?

SUGGESTED WRITING ASSIGNMENTS

1. In an age of automation, when everything is faster, easier, and more convenient, Rybczynski celebrates the pleasure of doing things by hand. Do you enjoy baking bread from scratch, shoveling snow with a shovel, or paddling a canoe, or do you prefer a bread machine, a snowblower, or a power boat? Write an essay in which you defend your preference for using old-fashioned tools or techniques to accomplish a task or for using modern, high-powered tools. You might start by reading what you wrote in response to the journal prompt for this selection. Be sure to illustrate your essay with well-chosen examples.

2. Using Rybczynski's essay as a model, write about a tool, an appliance, a device, or a service that you frequently use, such as a toothbrush, a computer mouse, a pencil, an electric saw, a coffeemaker, a personal digital assistant (PDA), or a Web site. You may find it helpful to consider the following questions before you start writing: Under what circumstances do you use this item? What do you know of its history? What impact has it had on your life or on the lives of others?

Unity

Unity is an essential quality in a well-written essay. The principle of
unity requires that every element in a piece of writing—whether a
paragraph or an essay—be related to the main idea. Sentences that
stray from the subject, even though they might be related to it or provide additional information, can weaken an otherwise strong piece of
writing. Note how the italicized segments in the following paragraph
undermine its unity and divert our attention from its main idea:

> When I was growing up, one of the places I enjoyed most was
> the cherry tree in the backyard. *Behind the yard was an alley and
> then more houses.* Every summer when the cherries began to ripen,
> I used to spend hours high up in the tree, picking and eating the
> sweet, sun-warmed cherries. *My mother always worried about my
> falling out of the tree, but I never did.* But I had some competition
> for the cherries—flocks of birds that enjoyed them as much as I did
> and would perch all over the tree, devouring the fruit whenever I
> wasn't there. I used to wonder why the grown-ups never ate any of
> the cherries—*my father loved all kinds of fruit*—but actually,
> when the birds and I had finished, there weren't many left.
>
> – Betty Burns, student

When the italicized sentences are eliminated, the paragraph is unified
and reads smoothly.

Now consider another paragraph, this one from an essay about
family photographs and how they allowed the author to learn about
her past and to stay connected with her family in the present.

> Photographs have taken me to places I have never been and have
> shown me people alive before I was born. I can visit my grand-
> mother's childhood home in Vienna, Austria, and walk down the high-
> ceilinged, iron staircase by looking through the small, white album my
> grandma treasures. I also know of the tomboy she once was, wear-
> ing lederhosen instead of the dirndls worn by her friends. And I have

seen her as a beautiful young woman who traveled with the Red
Cross during the war, uncertain of her future. The photograph that
rests in a red leather frame on my grandma's nightstand has allowed me to meet the man she would later marry. He died before I was born. I have been told that I would have loved his calm
manner, and I can see for myself his gentle smile and tranquil expression.

—Carrie White, student

Did you notice that the first sentence gives focus and direction to the
paragraph and that all of the subsequent sentences are directly related
to it?

A well-written essay should be unified both within and between
paragraphs; that is, everything in it should be related to its **thesis,** the
main idea of the essay. The first requirement for unity is that the thesis
itself be clear, either through a direct statement, called the *thesis statement,* or by implication. The second requirement is that there be no digressions, no discussion or information that is not shown to be logically
related to the thesis. A unified essay stays within the limits of its thesis.

Here, for example, is a short essay called "Over-Generalizing"
about the dangers of making generalizations. As you read, notice
how carefully author Stuart Chase sticks to his point.

One swallow does not make a summer, nor can two or three   1
cases often support a dependable generalization. Yet all of us, including the most polished eggheads, are constantly falling into
this mental peopletrap. It is the most common, probably the most
seductive, and potentially the most dangerous, of all the fallacies.

You drive through a town and see a drunken man on the   2
sidewalk. A few blocks further on you see another. You turn to
your companion: "Nothing but drunks in this town!" Soon you
are out in the country, bowling along at fifty. A car passes you as
if you were parked. On a curve a second whizzes by. Your companion turns to you: "All the drivers in this state are crazy!" Two
thumping generalizations, each built on two cases. If we stop to
think, we usually recognize the exaggeration and the unfairness
of such generalizations. Trouble comes when we do not stop to
think—or when we build them on a prejudice.

This kind of reasoning has been around for a long time.   3
Aristotle was aware of its dangers and called it "reasoning by
example," meaning too few examples. What it boils down to is

failing to count your swallows before announcing that summer is here. Driving from my home to New Haven the other day, a distance of about forty miles, I caught myself saying: "Every time I look around I see a new ranch-type house going up." So on the return trip I counted them; there were exactly five under construction. And how many times had I "looked around"? I suppose I had glanced to right and left—as one must at side roads and so forth in driving—several hundred times.

In this fallacy we do not make the error of neglecting facts altogether and rushing immediately to the level of opinion. We start at the fact level properly enough, but *we do not stay there*. A case of two and up we go to a rousing over-simplification about drunks, speeders, ranch-style houses—or, more seriously, about foreigners, African Americans, labor leaders, teen-agers.   4

Why do we over-generalize so often and sometimes so disastrously? One reason is that the human mind is a generalizing machine. We would not be people without this power. The old academic crack: "All generalizations are false, including this one," is only a play on words. We *must* generalize to communicate and to live. But we should beware of beating the gun; of not waiting until enough facts are in to say something useful. Meanwhile it is a plain waste of time to listen to arguments based on a few handpicked examples.   5

– Stuart Chase

Everything in the essay relates to Chase's thesis statement, which is included in the essay's first sentence: ". . . nor can two or three cases often support a dependable generalization." Paragraphs 2 and 3 document the thesis with examples; paragraph 4 explains how over-generalizing occurs; paragraph 5 analyzes why people over-generalize; and, for a conclusion, Chase restates his thesis in different words. An essay may be longer, more complex, and more wide-ranging than this one, but to be effective it must also avoid digressions and remain close to the author's main idea.

A good way to check that your essay is indeed unified is to underline your thesis and then to explain to yourself how each paragraph in your essay is related to the thesis. If you find a paragraph that does not appear to be logically connected, you can revise it so that the relationship is clear. Similarly, it is useful to make sure that each sentence in a paragraph is related to the topic sentence.

My Name

■ Sandra Cisneros

Sandra Cisneros was born in Chicago in 1954. After graduating from Loyola University in Chicago and attending the Iowa Writers' Workshop in the late 1970s, she moved to the Southwest and now lives in San Antonio, Texas. Cisneros has had numerous occupations within the fields of education and the arts and has been a visiting writer at various universities. Although she has written two well-received books of poetry, My Wicked, Wicked Ways *(1987) and* Loose Woman *(1994), she is better known for the autobiographical fiction of* The House on Mango Street *(1984)—from which the following selection was taken—and for* Woman Hollering Creek and Other Stories *(1991). In 1995 she was awarded a grant from the prestigious MacArthur Foundation. In 2002 she published a novel,* Caramelo. *As you read "My Name," pay particular attention to how tightly Cisneros unifies her paragraphs by intertwining the meanings of her name (originally Esperanza) and her feelings about the great-grandmother with whom she shares that name.*

FOR YOUR JOURNAL

Who chose your name, and why was it given to you? Does your name have a special meaning for the person who gave it to you? What does the sound of your name suggest to you? Are you happy with your name?

In English my name means hope. In Spanish it means too many letters. It means sadness, it means waiting. It is like the number nine. A muddy color. It is the Mexican records my father plays on Sunday mornings when he is shaving, songs like sobbing.

It was my great-grandmother's name and now it is mine. She was a horse woman too, born like me in the Chinese year of the horse—which is supposed to be bad luck if you're born female—but I think this is a Chinese lie because the Chinese, like the Mexicans, don't like their women strong.

My great-grandmother. I would've liked to have known her, a wild horse of a woman, so wild she wouldn't marry until my great-grandfather threw a sack over her head and carried her off. Just like that, as if she were a fancy chandelier. That's the way he did it.

And the story goes she never forgave him. She looked out the window all her life, the way so many women sit their sadness on an elbow. I wonder if she made the best with what she got or was she sorry because she couldn't be all the things she wanted to be. Esperanza. I have inherited her name, but I don't want to inherit her place by the window. 4

At school they say my name funny as if the syllables were made out of tin and hurt the roof of your mouth. But in Spanish my name is made out of a softer something like silver, not quite as thick as my sister's name Magdalena which is uglier than mine. Magdalena who at least can come home and become Nenny. But I am always Esperanza. 5

I would like to baptize myself under a new name, a name more like the real me, the one nobody sees. Esperanza as Lisandra or Maritza or Zeze the X. Yes. Something like Zeze the X will do. 6

QUESTIONS FOR STUDY AND DISCUSSION

1. What is Cisneros's thesis? (Glossary: *Thesis*) Where does she state her thesis?

2. Are there any digressions, discussions, or information in this essay that do not logically connect to Cisneros's thesis? Explain how each paragraph in the essay relates to her thesis.

3. What is Cisneros's purpose in writing the essay? (Glossary: *Purpose*) Explain your answer.

4. In what way do you think a name can be like the number nine? Like a muddy color? What is your impression of the author's name, based on these similes? (Glossary: *Figure of Speech*)

5. What is Cisneros's tone in the essay? (Glossary: *Tone*) How does she establish the tone? What does it tell the reader about how she feels about her name?

6. Why do you think Cisneros waits until the end of paragraph 4 to reveal her given name?

7. Why do you think Cisneros chose "Zeze the X" as a name that better represents her inner self?

VOCABULARY

Refer to your dictionary to define the following words as they are used in this selection. Then use each word in a sentence of your own.

sobbing (1)   chandelier (3)   baptize (6)

CLASSROOM ACTIVITY USING UNITY

Take a paragraph from a draft of a paper you have been working on, and test it for unity. Be prepared to read the paragraph in class and explain why it is unified, or why it is not, and what you need to do to make it unified.

SUGGESTED WRITING ASSIGNMENTS

1. If you, like Cisneros, wished to choose a different name for yourself, what would it be? Write an essay that reveals your choice of a new name and explains why you like it or why it might be particularly appropriate for you. Make sure the essay is unified and that every paragraph directly supports your name choice.

2. Choose a grandparent or other relative at least two generations older than you about whom you know an interesting story. What impact has the relative, or the stories about him or her, had on your life? Write a unified narrative essay about the relative and what is interesting about him or her.

The Meanings of a Word

■ Gloria Naylor

American novelist, essayist, and screenwriter Gloria Naylor was born in 1950 in New York City, where she lives today. She worked first as a missionary for the Jehovah's Witnesses from 1967 to 1975, then as a telephone operator until 1981. That year she graduated from Brooklyn College of the City University of New York. She also holds a graduate degree in African American studies from Yale University. Naylor has taught writing and literature at George Washington University, New York University, and Cornell University, in addition to publishing several novels: The Women of Brewster Place *(1982),* Linden Hills *(1985),* Mama Day *(1988),* Bailey's Cafe *(1992), and* The Men of Brewster Place *(1998). The following essay first appeared in the* New York Times *in 1986. In it Naylor examines the ways in which words can take on meaning, depending on who uses them and for what purpose. Notice how the paragraphs describing her experiences with the word* nigger *relate back to a clearly stated thesis at the end of paragraph 2.*

FOR YOUR JOURNAL

Have you ever been called a derogatory name? What was the name, and how did you feel about it?

Language is the subject. It is the written form with which I've managed to keep the wolf away from the door and, in diaries, to keep my sanity. In spite of this, I consider the written word inferior to the spoken, and much of the frustration experienced by novelists is the awareness that whatever we manage to capture in even the most transcendent passages falls far short of the richness of life. Dialogue achieves its power in the dynamics of a fleeting moment of sight, sound, smell, and touch. 1

I'm not going to enter the debate here about whether it is language that shapes reality or vice versa. That battle is doomed to be waged whenever we seek intermittent reprieve from the chicken and egg dispute. I will simply take the position that the spoken word, like 2 the written word, amounts to a nonsensical arrangement of sounds or letters without a consensus that assigns "meaning." And building from the meanings of what we hear, we order reality. Words themselves are innocuous; it is the consensus that gives them true power.

I remember the first time I heard the word *nigger*. In my third-   3
grade class, our math tests were being passed down the rows, and as I handed the papers to a little boy in back of me, I remarked that once again he had received a much lower mark than I did. He snatched his test from me and spit out that word. Had he called me a nymphomaniac or a necrophiliac, I couldn't have been more puzzled. I didn't know what a nigger was, but I knew that whatever it meant, it was something he shouldn't have called me. This was verified when I raised my hand, and in a loud voice repeated what he had said and watched the teacher scold him for using a "bad" word. I was later to go home and ask the inevitable question that every black parent must face — "Mommy, what does *nigger* mean?"

And what exactly did it mean? Thinking back, I realize that this   4
could not have been the first time the word was used in my presence. I was part of a large extended family that had migrated from the rural South after World War II and formed a close-knit network that gravitated around my maternal grandparents. Their ground-floor apartment in one of the buildings they owned in Harlem was a weekend mecca for my immediate family, along with countless aunts, uncles, and cousins who brought along assorted friends. It was a bustling and open house with assorted neighbors and tenants popping in and out to exchange bits of gossip, pick up an old quarrel, or referee the ongoing checkers game in which my grandmother cheated shamelessly. They were all there to let down their hair and put up their feet after a week of labor in the factories, laundries, and shipyards of New York.

Amid the clamor, which could reach deafening proportions —   5
two or three conversations going on simultaneously, punctuated by the sound of a baby's crying somewhere in the back rooms or out on the street — there was still a rigid set of rules about what was said and how. Older children were sent out of the living room when it was time to get into the juicy details about "you-know-who" up on the third floor who had gone and gotten herself "p-r-e-g-n-a-n-t!" But my parents, knowing that I could spell well beyond my years, always demanded that I follow the others out to play. Beyond sexual misconduct and death, everything else was considered harmless for our young ears. And so among the anecdotes of the triumphs and

disappointments in the various workings of their lives, the word *nigger* was used in my presence, but it was set within contexts and inflections that caused it to register in my mind as something else.

In the singular, the word was always applied to a man who had   6
distinguished himself in some situation that brought their approval for his strength, intelligence, or drive:

"Did Johnny *really* do that?"   7

"I'm telling you, that nigger pulled in $6,000 of overtime last   8
year. Said he got enough for a down payment on a house."

When used with a possessive adjective by a woman—"my nig-   9
ger"—it became a term of endearment for her husband or boyfriend. But it could be more than just a term applied to a man. In their mouths it became the pure essence of manhood—a disembodied force that channeled their past history of struggle and present survival against the odds into a victorious statement of being: "Yeah, that old foreman found out quick enough—you don't mess with a nigger."

In the plural, it became a description of some group within the   10
community that had overstepped the bounds of decency as my family defined it. Parents who neglected their children, a drunken couple who fought in public, people who simply refused to look for work, those with excessively dirty mouths or unkempt households were all "trifling niggers." This particular circle could forgive hard times, unemployment, the occasional bout of depression—they had gone through all of that themselves—but the unforgivable sin was a lack of self-respect.

A woman could never be a "nigger" in the singular, with its con-   11
notation of confirming worth. The noun *girl* was its closest equivalent in that sense, but only when used in direct address and regardless of the gender doing the addressing. *Girl* was a token of respect for a woman. The one-syllable word was drawn out to sound like three in recognition of the extra ounce of wit, nerve, or daring that the woman had shown in the situation under discussion.

"G-i-r-l, stop. You mean you said that to his face?"   12

But if the word was used in a third-person reference or shortened   13
so that it almost snapped out of the mouth, it always involved some element of communal disapproval. And age became an important factor in these exchanges. It was only between individuals of the same generation, or from any older person to a younger (but never the other way around), that *girl* would be considered a compliment.

I don't agree with the argument that use of the word *nigger* at this   14
social stratum of the black community was an internalization of
racism. The dynamics were the exact opposite: the people in my grandmother's living room took a word that whites used to signify worth-
lessness or degradation and rendered it impotent. Gathering there
together, they transformed *nigger* to signify the varied and complex
human beings they knew themselves to be. If the word was to disappear
totally from the mouths of even the most liberal of white society, no one
in that room was naive enough to believe it would disappear from white
minds. Meeting the word head-on, they proved it had absolutely
nothing to do with the way they were determined to live their lives.

So there must have been dozens of times that *nigger* was spoken   15
in front of me before I reached the third grade. But I didn't "hear" it
until it was said by a small pair of lips that had already learned it
could be a way to humiliate me. That was the word I went home and
asked my mother about. And since she knew that I had to grow up in
America, she took me in her lap and explained.

QUESTIONS FOR STUDY AND DISCUSSION

1. Naylor states her thesis in the last sentence of paragraph 2. How
   does what she says in the first two paragraphs build unity by
   connecting to her thesis statement? (Glossary: *Thesis*)
2. What are the two meanings of the word *nigger* as Naylor uses it
   in her essay? Where in the essay is the clearest definition of each
   use of the word presented? (Glossary: *Definition*)
3. Naylor says she must have heard the word *nigger* many times
   while she was growing up; yet she "heard" it for the first time
   when she was in the third grade. How does she explain this
   seeming contradiction?
4. Naylor gives a detailed narration of her family and its lifestyle in
   paragraphs 4 and 5. What kinds of details does she include in her
   brief story? (Glossary: *Narration; Details*) How does this narration contribute to your understanding of the word *nigger* as used
   by her family? Why do you suppose she offers so little in the way
   of a definition of the other use of the word *nigger*? Explain.
5. Would you characterize Naylor's tone as angry, objective, cynical, or something else? (Glossary: *Tone*) Cite examples of her
   diction to support your answer. (Glossary: *Diction*)

6. What is the meaning of Naylor's last sentence? How well does it work as an ending for her essay? (Glossary: *Beginnings and Endings*)

VOCABULARY

Refer to your dictionary to define the following words as they are used in this selection. Then use each word in a sentence of your own.

transcendent (1)	anecdotes (5)
innocuous (2)	inflections (5)
consensus (2)	unkempt (10)
nymphomaniac (3)	trifling (10)
necrophiliac (3)	internalization (14)
mecca (4)	impotent (14)
clamor (5)	

CLASSROOM ACTIVITY USING UNITY

Carefully read the following five-paragraph sequence, paying special attention to how each paragraph relates to the writer's thesis. Identify the paragraph that disrupts the unity of the sequence, and explain why it doesn't belong.

Though "experts" differ as to the best technique to follow 1
when building a fire, one generally accepted method consists of
first laying a generous amount of crumpled newspaper on the
hearth between the andirons. Kindling wood is then spread gener-
ously over this layer of newspaper and one of the thickest logs is
placed across the back of the andirons. This should be as close to
the back of the fireplace as possible, but not quite touching it. A
second log is then placed an inch or so in front of this, and a few additional sticks of kindling are laid across these two. A third log is
then placed on top to form a sort of pyramid with air space
between all logs so that flames can lick freely up between them.

Roaring fireplace fires are particularly welcome during the 2
winter months, especially after hearty outdoor activities. To
avoid any mid-winter tragedies, care should be taken to have a
professional inspect and clean the chimney before starting to use

the fireplace in the fall. Also, be sure to clean out the fireplace after each use.

A mistake frequently made is building the fire too far forward so that the rear wall of the fireplace does not get properly heated. A heated back wall helps increase the draft and tends to suck smoke and flames rearward with less chance of sparks or smoke spurting out into the room.

Another common mistake often made by the inexperienced fire-tender is to try to build a fire with only one or two logs, instead of using at least three. A single log is difficult to ignite properly, and even two logs do not provide an efficient bed with adequate fuel-burning capacity.

Use of too many logs, on the other hand, is also a common fault and can prove hazardous. Building too big a fire can create more smoke and draft than the chimney can safely handle, increasing the possibility of sparks or smoke being thrown out into the room. For best results, the homeowner should start with three medium-size logs as described above, then add additional logs as needed if the fire is to be kept burning.

The five paragraphs on "How to Build a Fire in a Fireplace" are taken from Bernard Gladstone's book *The New York Times Complete Manual of Home Repair.*

SUGGESTED WRITING ASSIGNMENTS

1. Naylor disagrees with the notion that use of the word *nigger* in the African American community can be taken as an "internalization of racism." Reexamine her essay and discuss in what ways her definition of the word *nigger* affirms or denies her position. Draw on your own experiences, observations, and reading to support your answer.

2. Write a short essay in which you define a word, for example, *wife, macho, liberal, success,* or *marriage,* that has more than one meaning, depending on one's point of view.

Learning to See

■ Samuel H. Scudder

Samuel H. Scudder (1837–1911) was a graduate of Williams College and Harvard University and was a university professor and a leading scientist of his day. His special field of study was butterflies, grasshoppers, and crickets, and in 1888 and 1889 he published the results of his thirty years of research on butterflies in The Butterflies of the Eastern United States and Canada with Special Reference to New England.

The following essay about the famous zoologist and geologist Louis Agassiz was first published in 1874. However, the approach Agassiz took with Scudder, his student, and the lesson he imparted to him are as valid for us today as when Scudder first met his great teacher. As you read Scudder's story of his initial encounter with Louis Agassiz, notice how each narrative detail supports the idea that the lesson he learned—though exasperating at times—was the best he had ever had.

FOR YOUR JOURNAL

How observant do you consider yourself to be? Have teachers ever told you that you have a keen eye for detail? Do you think you see most everything there is to see in an object or a person you're looking at, or have you noticed that others see more than you do?

It was more than fifteen years ago that I entered the laboratory of Professor Agassiz, and told him I had enrolled my name in the Scientific School as a student of natural history. He asked me a few questions about my object in coming, my antecedents generally, the mode in which I afterwards proposed to use the knowledge I might acquire, and, finally, whether I wished to study any special branch. To the latter I replied that, while I wished to be well grounded in all departments of zoology, I purposed to devote myself specially to insects.

"When do you wish to begin?" he asked.

"Now," I replied.

This seemed to please him, and with an energetic "Very well!" he 4
reached from the shelf a huge jar of specimens in yellow alcohol.

"Take this fish," he said, "and look at it; we call it a haemulon;[1] 5
by and by I will ask what you have seen."

With that he left me, but in a moment returned with explicit in- 6
structions as to the care of the object entrusted to me.

"No man is fit to be a naturalist," said he, "who does not know 7
how to take care of specimens."

I was to keep the fish before me in a tin tray, and occasionally 8
moisten the surface with alcohol from the jar, always taking care to
replace the stopper tightly. Those were not the days of ground-glass
stoppers and elegantly shaped exhibition jars; all the old students will
recall the huge neckless glass bottles with their leaky, wax-besmeared
corks, half eaten by insects, and begrimed with cellar dust. Entomology[2] was a cleaner science than ichthyology,[3] but the example of the
Professor, who had unhesitatingly plunged to the bottom of the jar to
produce the fish, was infectious; and though this alcohol had a "very
ancient and fishlike smell," I really dared not to show any aversion
within these sacred precincts, and treated the alcohol as though it
were pure water. Still I was concious of a passing feeling of disappointment, for gazing at a fish did not commend itself to an ardent
entomologist. My friends at home, too, were annoyed when they discovered that no amount of eau-de-Cologne[4] would drown the perfume which haunted me like a shadow.

In ten minutes I had seen all that could be seen in that fish, and 9
started in search of the Professor—who had, however, left the Museum; and when I returned, after lingering over some of the odd animals stored in the upper apartment, my specimen was dry all over. I
dashed the fluid over the fish as if to resuscitate the beast from a
fainting-fit, and looked with anxiety for a return of the normal
sloppy appearance. This little excitement over, nothing was to be
done but to return to a steadfast gaze at my mute companion. Half
an hour passed—an hour—another hour; the fish began to look
loathsome. I turned it over and around; looked it in the face—
ghastly, from behind, beneath, above, sideways, at a three-quarters'
view—just as ghastly. I was in despair; at an early hour I concluded

---

[1]*Haemulon:* a major subdivision in the classification of fishes. [Eds.]
[2]*Entomology:* a branch of zoology dealing with insects. [Eds.]
[3]*Ichthyology:* a branch of zoology dealing with fishes. [Eds.]
[4]*Eau-de-Cologne:* perfumed water. [Eds.]

that lunch was necessary; so, with infinite relief, the fish was carefully placed in the jar, and for an hour I was free.

On my return, I learned that Professor Agassiz had been at the Mu- 10 seum, but had gone, and would not return for several hours. My fellow-students were too busy to be disturbed by continued conversation. Slowly I drew forth that hideous fish, and with a feeling of desperation again looked at it. I might not use a magnifying glass; instruments of all kinds were interdicted. My two hands, my two eyes, and the fish; it seemed a most limited field. I pushed my finger down its throat to feel how sharp the teeth were. I began to count the scales in the different rows, until I was convinced that that was nonsense. At last a happy thought struck me—I would draw the fish; and now with surprise I began to discover new features in the creature. Just then the Professor returned.

"That is right," said he, "a pencil is one of the best eyes. I am 11 glad to notice, too, that you keep your specimen wet, and your bottle corked."

With these encouraging words, he added: 12

"Well, what is it like?" 13

He listened attentively to my brief rehearsal of the structure of 14 parts whose names were still unknown to me: the fringed gill-arches and movable operculum;[5] the pores of the head, fleshy lips and lidless eyes; the lateral line, the spinous fins and forked tail; the compressed and arched body. When I had finished, he waited as if expecting more, and then with an air of disappointment:

"You have not looked very carefully; why," he continued more 15 earnestly, "you haven't even seen one of the most conspicuous features of the animal, which is as plainly before your eyes as the fish itself; look again, look again!" and he left me to my misery.

I was piqued; I was mortified. Still more of that wretched fish! 16 But now I set myself to my task with a will, and discovered one new thing after another, until I saw how just the Professor's criticism had been. The afternoon passed quickly; and when, toward its close, the Professor inquired:

"Do you see it yet?" 17

"No," I replied, "I am certain I do not, but I see how little I saw 18 before."

"That is the next best," said he, earnestly, "but I won't hear you 19 now; put away your fish and go home; perhaps you will be ready

---

[5]*operculum:* a lid or flap covering an opening, the gill cover in fish. [Eds.]

with a better answer in the morning. I will examine you before you look at the fish."

This was disconcerting. Not only must I think of my fish all night, studying, without the object before me, what this unknown but most visible feature might be; but also, without my discoveries, I must give an exact account of them the next day. I had a bad memory; so I walked home by Charles River[6] in a distracted state, with my two perplexities. 20

The cordial greeting from the Professor the next morning was reassuring; here was a man who seemed to be quite as anxious as I that I should see for myself what he saw. 21

"Do you perhaps mean," I asked, "that the fish has symmetrical sides with paired organs?" 22

His thoroughly pleased "Of course! Of course!" repaid the wakeful hours of the previous night. After he had discoursed most happily and enthusiastically — as he always did — upon the importance of this point, I ventured to ask what I should do next. 23

"Oh, look at your fish!" he said, and left me again to my own devices. In a little more than an hour he returned, and heard my new catalogue. 24

"That is good, that is good!" he repeated; "but that is not all; go on"; and so for three long days he placed that fish before my eyes, forbidding me to look at anything else, or to use any artificial aid. "Look, look, look," was his repeated injunction. 25

The fourth day, a second fish of the same group was placed beside the first, and I was bidden to point out the resemblances and differences between the two; another and another followed, until the entire family lay before me, and a whole legion of jars covered the table and surrounding shelves; the odor had become a pleasant perfume; and even now, the sight of an old, six-inch, worm-eaten cork brings fragrant memories. 26

The whole group of haemulons was thus brought in review; and, whether engaged upon the dissection of the internal organs, the preparation and examination of the body framework, or the description of the various parts, Agassiz's training in the method of observing facts and their orderly arrangement was ever accompanied by the urgent exhortation not to be content with them. 27

---

[6]*Charles River:* a river in eastern Massachusetts. Boston and Cambridge are on opposite banks of the Charles. [Eds.]

"Facts are stupid things," he would say, "until brought into con- 28
nection with some general law."

At the end of eight months, it was almost with reluctance that I 29
left these friends and turned to insects; but what I had gained by this
outside experience has been of greater value than years of later inves-
tigation in my favorite groups.

This was the best entomological lesson I ever had—a lesson 30
whose influence has extended to the details of every subsequent
study; a legacy the Professor has left me, as he has left it to many
others, of inestimable value, which we could not buy, with which we
cannot part.

A year afterward, some of us were amusing ourselves with chalk- 31
ing outlandish beasts on the Museum blackboard. We drew prancing
starfishes; frogs in mortal combat; hydra-headed worms; stately
crawfishes, standing on their tails, bearing aloft umbrellas; and
grotesque fishes with gaping mouths and staring eyes. The Professor
came in shortly after, and was as amused as any at our experiments.
He looked at the fishes.

"Haemulons, every one of them," he said; "Mr.——— drew 32
them."

True; and to this day, if I attempt a fish, I can draw nothing but 33
haemulons.

QUESTIONS FOR STUDY AND DISCUSSION

1. What important lesson did Scudder learn from his experience
   with Professor Agassiz? Where is the lesson referred to in the
   essay?
2. Explain the meaning of Scudder's title. (Glossary: *Title*) How
   effectively does the title focus attention on the point of Scudder's
   essay? Explain.
3. Briefly describe Professor Agassiz's teaching technique or method.
   What aspect of his style made his teaching effective with
   Scudder? How would you respond to Agassiz's teaching methods? Explain.
4. How did Scudder happen to draw the fish? How did his drawing the fish help him better understand or know the fish? What
   does Agassiz mean when he says "a pencil is one of the best
   eyes" (11)?

5. Identify some of the transitional expressions or devices Scudder uses to maintain continuity in his narrative. (Glossary: *Transition*) Explain how each works to ensure unity in the context of this essay.

6. What in Scudder's style and diction shows that this essay was written in the nineteenth century and not the twenty-first? (Glossary: *Diction*)

VOCABULARY

Refer to your dictionary to define the following words as they are used in this selection. Then use each word in a sentence of your own.

antecedents (1)	interdicted (10)
specimens (4)	conspicuous (15)
begrimed (8)	piqued (16)
infectious (8)	discoursed (23)
resuscitate (9)	injunction (25)
loathsome (9)	legacy (30)

CLASSROOM ACTIVITY USING UNITY

Mark Wanner, a student, wrote the following paragraphs for an essay using this thesis statement:

> In order to provide a good learning environment in school, the teachers and administrators need to be strong leaders.

Unfortunately, some of the sentences disrupt the unity of the essay. Find these sentences, eliminate them, and reread the essay.

STRONG SCHOOL LEADERS

School administrators and teachers must do more than 1 simply supply students with information and a school building. They must also provide students with an atmosphere that allows them to focus on learning within the walls of the school. Whether the walls are brick, steel, or cement, they are only walls, and they do not help to create an appropriate atmosphere. Strong leadership both inside and outside the classroom yields a school in which students are able to excel in their studies, because they know how to conduct themselves in their relationships with their teachers and fellow students.

A recent change in the administration of Eastside High   2
School demonstrated how important strong leadership is to learning. Under the previous administration, parents and students complained that not enough emphasis was placed on studies. Most of the students lived in an impoverished neighborhood that had only one park for several thousand residents. Students were allowed to leave school at any time of the day, and little was done to curb the growing substance abuse problem. "What's the point of trying to teach algebra to students who are just going to get jobs as part-time sales clerks, anyway?" Vice Principal Iggy Norant said when questioned about his school's poor academic standards. Mr. Norant was known to students as Twiggy Iggy because of his tall, thin frame. Standardized test scores at the school lagged well behind the state average, and only 16% of the graduates attended college within two years.

Five years ago, the school board hired Mary Peña, former   3
chair of the state educational standards committee, as principal. A cheerleader in college, Ms. Peña got her B.A. in recreation science before getting her masters in education. She immediately emphasized the importance of learning, replacing any faculty members who did not share her high expectations of the students. Among those she fired was Mr. Norant; she also replaced two social studies teachers, one math teacher, four English teachers, and a lab instructor who let students play Gameboy in lab. She also established a code of conduct, which clearly stated the rules all students had to follow. Students were allowed second chances, but those who continued to conduct themselves in a way that interfered with the other students' ability to learn were dealt with quickly and severely. "The attitude at Eastside has changed so much since Mary Peña arrived," said math teacher Jeremy Rifkin after Peña's second year. "Students come to class much more relaxed and ready to learn. I feel like I can teach again." Test scores at Eastside are now well above state averages, and 68% of the most recent graduating class went straight to college.

– Mark Wanner, student

SUGGESTED WRITING ASSIGNMENTS

1. Using Scudder's essay as a model, write about a teacher, coach, or other adult figure who had a significant impact or powerful influence on you and your education. Describe the learning experience you had in as much detail as you can. What was it about the way that your teacher approached learning that has stayed with you?

2. What do you think Professor Agassiz meant when he said, "Facts are stupid things until brought into connection with some general law" (28)? Living in the so-called information age, we have facts at our fingertips. Some people complain that we are bombarded with factual information, that we have too much information and too few ideas to balance it. In a unified essay, explore the relevance of Agassiz's comment for our world.

chapter 5

Organization

In an essay, ideas and information cannot be presented all at once; they have to be arranged in some order. That order is the essay's **organization.**

The pattern of organization in an essay should be suited to the writer's subject and **purpose.** For example, if you are writing about your experience working in a fast-food restaurant and your purpose is to tell about the activities of a typical day, you might present those activities in chronological order. If, on the other hand, you wish to argue that working in a bank is an ideal summer job, you might proceed from the least rewarding to the most rewarding aspect of this job; this is called *climactic order.*

Some often-used patterns of organization are time order, space order, and logical order. Time order, or chronological order, is used to present a sequence of events as they occurred. A personal narrative, a report of a campus incident, or an account of a historical event can be most naturally and easily related in chronological order. In the following paragraph, the author uses chronological order to recount a disturbing childhood memory:

> I clearly remember my sixth birthday because Dad was in the hospital with pneumonia. He was working so hard he paid very little attention to his health. As a result, he spent almost the entire summer before I entered the first grade in the hospital. Mom visited him nightly. On my birthday I was allowed to see him. I have memories of sitting happily in the lobby of the hospital talking to the nurses, telling them with a big smile that I was going to see my dad because it was my birthday. I couldn't wait to see him because children under 12 were not allowed to visit patients, so I had not seen him in a long time. When I entered the hospital room, I saw tubes inserted into his nose and needles stuck in his arm. He was very, very thin. I was frightened and wanted to cry, but I was determined to have a good visit. So I stayed for a while, and he wished me a

happy birthday. When it was time to go, I kissed him good-bye and waited until I left his room to cry.

–Grace Ming-Yee Wai

Of course, the order of events can sometimes be rearranged for special effect. For, example, an account of an auto accident may begin with the collision itself and then flash back in time to the events leading up to it. The description of a process—such as framing a poster, constructing a bookcase with cinder blocks and boards, or serving a tennis ball—almost always calls for a chronological organization.

When analyzing a causally related series of events, writers often use a chronological organization to clarify for readers the exact sequence of events. In the following selection, the writer examines sequentially the series of malfunctions that led to the near disaster at the Three Mile Island nuclear facility in Harrisburg, Pennsylvania, showing clearly how each one led to the next:

> On March 28, 1979, at 3:53 A.M., a pump at the Harrisburg plant failed. Because the pump failed, the reactor's heat was not drawn off in the heat exchanger and the very hot water in the primary loop overheated. The pressure in the loop increased, opening a release valve that was supposed to counteract such an event. But the valve stuck open and the primary loop system lost so much water (which ended up as a highly radioactive pool, six feet deep, on the floor of the reactor building) that it was unable to carry off all the heat generated within the reactor core. Under these circumstances, the intense heat held within the reactor could, in theory, melt its fuel rods, and the resulting "meltdown" could then carry a hugely radioactive mass through the floor of the reactor. The reactor's emergency cooling system, which is designed to prevent this disaster, was then automatically activated, but when it was, apparently, turned off too soon, some of the fuel rods overheated. This produced a bubble of hydrogen gas at the top of the reactor. (The hydrogen is dissolved in the water in order to react with oxygen that is produced when the intense reactor radiation splits water molecules into their atomic constituents. When heated, the dissolved hydrogen bubbles out of the solution.) This bubble blocked the flow of cooling water so that despite the action of the emergency cooling system the reactor core was again in danger of melting down. Another danger was that the gas might contain enough oxygen to cause an explosion that could rupture the huge containers that surround the reactor and release a deadly cloud of radioactive material into the surrounding countryside. Working desperately, technicians were able to

gradually reduce the size of the gas bubble using a special apparatus brought in from the atomic laboratory at Oak Ridge, Tennessee, and the danger of a catastrophic release of radioactive materials subsided. But the sealed-off plant was now so radioactive that no one could enter it for many months—or, according to some observers, for years—without being exposed to a lethal dose of radiation.

–Barry Commoner

Space order is used when describing a person, place, or thing. This organizational pattern begins at a particular point and moves in some direction, such as left to right, top to bottom, east to west, outside to inside, front to back, near to far, around, or over. In describing a house, for example, a writer could move from top to bottom, from outside to inside, or in a circle around the outside.

In the following paragraph, the subject is a baseball, and the writer describes it from the inside out, moving from its composition-cork nucleus to the print on its stitched cowhide cover.

It weighs just over five ounces and measures between 2.86 and 2.94 inches in diameter. It is made of a composition-cork nucleus encased in two thin layers of rubber, one black and one red, surrounded by 121 yards of tightly wrapped blue-gray wool yarn, 45 yards of white wool yarn, 54 more yards of blue-gray wool yarn, 150 yards of fine cotton yarn, a coat of rubber cement, and a cowhide (formerly horsehide) exterior, which is held together with 216 slightly raised red cotton stitches. Printed certifications, endorsements, and outdoor advertising spherically attest to its authenticity.

–Roger Angell

Logical order can take many forms, depending on the writer's purpose. Often used patterns include general to specific, most familiar to least familiar, and smallest to biggest. Perhaps the most common type of logical order is order of importance. Notice how the writer uses this order in the following paragraph:

The Egyptians have taught us many things. They were excellent farmers. They knew all about irrigation. They built temples which were afterwards copied by the Greeks and which served as the earliest models for the churches in which we worship nowadays. They invented a calendar which proved such a useful instrument for the purpose of measuring time that it has survived with few changes until today. But most important of all, the Egyptians learned how to preserve speech for the benefit of future generations. They invented the art of writing.

By organizing the material according to the order of increasing importance, the writer places special emphasis on the final sentence.

A student essay on outdoor education provides another example of logical order. In the paragraph below, the writer describes some of the special problems students have during the traditionally difficult high school years. She then goes on to explain the benefits of involving such students in an outdoor education curriculum as a possible remedy, offers a quotation from a noteworthy text on outdoor education to support her views, and then offers her thesis statement in the final sentence of the paragraph — all logical steps in her writing.

For many students, the normally difficult time of high school is especially troublesome. These students may have learning disabilities, emotional-behavioral disorder, low self-esteem, or be labeled "at-risk" because of socioeconomic background, delinquency, or drug and alcohol abuse. Any of these factors contributes negatively to students' success in school. Often the traditional public or private high school may not be the ideal environment in which these students can thrive and live up to their highest potential. Outdoor Education can benefit these high schoolers and provide them with the means necessary to overcome their personal issues and develop skills, knowledge, and self-esteem that will enable them to become successful, self-aware, emotionally stable, and functional adults. In their book *Outdoor Education,* authors Smith, Carlson, Donaldson, and Masters state poignantly that Outdoor Education "can be one of the most effective forces in the community to prevent human erosion as well as land erosion; it can be one of the means of saving youngsters from the education scrap heap" (49). Outdoor Education builds a relationship between students and the natural environment that might not be formed otherwise and gives students a respect for the world in which they live. Aspects of Outdoor Education should be implemented in the

Statement of problem

Possible remedy is offered and explained.

Authorities are quoted to support suggested solution.

Thesis is given after preliminary discussion to increase its acceptability.

curriculums of high schools in order to achieve these
results in all students.

–Jinsie Ward, student

As explained above, logical order can take many different forms,
but the exact rationale is always dependent upon the topic of the
writing. For example, in writing a descriptive essay about a place you
visited, you can move from the least striking to the most striking detail, so as to keep your readers interested and involved in the description. In an essay explaining how to pick individual stocks for
investment, you can start with the point that readers will find least
difficult to understand and move on to the most difficult. (That's
how teachers organize many courses.) Or, in writing an essay arguing
for more internships and service learning courses, you can move from
your least controversial point to the most controversial, preparing
your reader gradually to accept your argument.

A simple way to check the organization of an essay is to outline it
once you have a draft. Does the outline represent the organizational
pattern—chronological, spatial, or logical—that you set out to use?
Problems in outlining will naturally indicate sections that you need to
revise.

A View from the Bridge

■ Cherokee Paul McDonald

A fiction writer, memoirist, and journalist, Cherokee Paul McDonald was raised and schooled in Fort Lauderdale, Florida. In 1970 he returned home from a tour of duty in Vietnam and joined the Fort Lauderdale Police Department, where he rose to the rank of sergeant. In 1980, after receiving a degree in criminal science from Broward Community College, McDonald left the police department to become a writer. He worked a number of odd jobs before publishing his first book, The Patch, *in 1986. McDonald has said that almost all of his writing comes from his police work, and his common themes of justice, balance, and fairness reflect his life as part of the "thin blue line" (the police department). In 1991, he published* Blue Truth, *a memoir. His novel,* Summer's Reason, *was released in 1994, and his most recent book, a memoir of the Vietnam War titled* Into the Green: A Reconnaissance by Fire, *was published in 2001. "A View from the Bridge" was originally published in* Sunshine *magazine in 1990. Notice how McDonald uses dialogue to narrate his experience of a chance encounter with a young fisherman.*

FOR YOUR JOURNAL

Make a list of your interests, focusing on those to which you devote a significant amount of time. Do you share any of these interests with people you know? What does a shared interest do for a relationship between two people?

I was coming up on the little bridge in the Rio Vista neighborhood   1
of Fort Lauderdale, deepening my stride and my breathing to negotiate the slight incline without altering my pace. And then, as I neared the crest, I saw the kid.

He was a lumpy little guy with baggy shorts, a faded T-shirt and   2
heavy sweat socks falling down over old sneakers.

Partially covering his shaggy blond hair was one of those blue   3
baseball caps with gold braid on the bill and a sailfish patch sewn

onto the peak. Covering his eyes and part of his face was a pair of those stupid-looking '50s-style wrap-around sunglasses.

He was fumbling with a beat-up rod and reel, and he had a little bait bucket by his feet. I puffed on by, glancing down into the empty bucket as I passed. 4

"Hey mister! Would you help me, please?" 5

The shrill voice penetrated my jogger's concentration, and I was determined to ignore it. But for some reason, I stopped. 6

With my hands on my hips and the sweat dripping from my nose I asked, "What do you want, kid?" 7

"Would you please help me find my shrimp? It's my last one and I've been getting bites and I know I can catch a fish if I can just find that shrimp. He jumped outta my hand as I was getting him from the bucket." 8

Exasperated, I walked slowly back to the kid, and pointed. 9

"There's the damn shrimp by your left foot. You stopped me for *that?*" 10

As I said it, the kid reached down and trapped the shrimp. 11

"Thanks a lot, mister," he said. 12

I watched as the kid dropped the baited hook down into the canal. Then I turned to start back down the bridge. 13

That's when the kid let out a "Hey! Hey!" and the prettiest tarpon I'd ever seen came almost six feet out of the water, twisting and turning as he fell through the air. 14

"I got one!" the kid yelled as the fish hit the water with a loud splash and took off down the canal. 15

I watched the line being burned off the reel at an alarming rate. The kid's left hand held the crank while the extended fingers felt for the drag setting. 16

"No, kid!" I shouted. "Leave the drag alone . . . just keep that damn rod tip up!" 17

Then I glanced at the reel and saw there were just a few loops of line left on the spool. 18

"Why don't you get yourself some decent equipment?" I said, but before the kid could answer I saw the line go slack. 19

"Ohhh, I lost him," the kid said. I saw the flash of silver as the fish turned. 20

"Crank, kid, crank! You didn't lose him. He's coming back toward you. Bring in the slack!" 21

The kid cranked like mad, and a beautiful grin spread across his face. 22

"He's heading in for the pilings," I said. "Keep him out of those 23 pilings!"

The kid played it perfectly. When the fish made its play for the 24 pilings, he kept just enough pressure on to force the fish out. When the water exploded and the silver missile hurled into the air, the kid kept the rod tip up and the line tight.

As the fish came to the surface and began a slow circle in the 25 middle of the canal, I said, "Whooee, is that a nice fish or what?"

The kid didn't say anything, so I said, "Okay, move to the 26 edge of the bridge and I'll climb down to the seawall and pull him out."

When I reached the seawall I pulled in the leader, leaving the fish 27 lying on its side in the water.

"How's that?" I said. 28

"Hey, mister, tell me what it looks like." 29

"Look down here and check him out," I said. "He's beautiful." 30

But then I looked up into those stupid-looking sunglasses and it 31 hit me. The kid was blind.

"Could you tell me what he looks like, mister?" he said again. 32

"Well, he's just under three, uh, he's about as long as one of your 33 arms," I said. "I'd guess he goes about 15, 20 pounds. He's mostly silver, but the silver is somehow made up of *all* the colors, if you know what I mean." I stopped. "Do you know what I mean by colors?"

The kid nodded. 34

"Okay. He has all these big scales, like armor all over his body. 35 They're silver too, and when he moves they sparkle. He has a strong body and a large powerful tail. He has big round eyes, bigger than a quarter, and a lower jaw that sticks out past the upper one and is very tough. His belly is almost white and his back is a gunmetal gray. When he jumped he came out of the water about six feet, and his scales caught the sun and flashed it all over the place."

By now the fish had righted itself, and I could see the bright-red 36 gills as the gill plates opened and closed. I explained this to the kid, and then said, more to myself, "He's a beauty."

"Can you get him off the hook?" the kid asked. "I don't want to 37 kill him."

I watched as the tarpon began to slowly swim away, tired but 38 still alive.

By the time I got back up to the top of the bridge the kid had his 39 line secured and his bait bucket in one hand.

He grinned and said, "Just in time. My mom drops me off here, 40
and she'll be back to pick me up any minute."

He used the back of one hand to wipe his nose. 41

"Thanks for helping me catch that tarpon," he said, "and for 42
helping me to see it."

I looked at him, shook my head, and said, "No, my friend, thank 43
you for letting *me* see that fish."

I took off, but before I got far the kid yelled again. 44

"Hey, mister!" 45

I stopped. 46

"Someday I'm gonna catch a sailfish and a blue marlin and a 47
giant tuna and *all* those big sportfish!"

As I looked into those sunglasses I knew he probably would. I 48
wished I could be there when it happened.

QUESTIONS FOR STUDY AND DISCUSSION

1. How has McDonald organized his essay? What period of time would you estimate is covered in this essay?

2. What clues lead up to the revelation that the kid is blind? Why does it take McDonald so long to realize it?

3. Notice the way McDonald chooses and adjusts some of the words he uses to describe the fish to the kid in paragraphs 33–36. Why does he do this? How does he organize his description of the fish so that the boy can visualize it better?

4. By the end of the essay, we know much more about the kid than the fact that he is blind, but after the initial description, McDonald characterizes him only indirectly. As the essay unfolds, what do we learn about the kid, and how does the author convey this knowledge?

5. McDonald tells much of his experience through dialogue. (Glossary: *Dialogue*) What does this dialogue add to the narration? What would have been lost had McDonald not used it? (Glossary: *Narration*)

6. Near the end of the story, why does the narrator say to the kid, "No, my friend, thank you for letting *me* see that fish"(43)?

7. What is the connotation of the word *view* in the title? Of the word *bridge*? (Glossary: *Connotation/Denotation*)

VOCABULARY

Refer to your dictionary to define the following words as they are used in this selection. Then use each word in a sentence of your own.

negotiate (1)   tarpon (14)
exasperated (9)   pilings (23)

CLASSROOM ACTIVITY USING ORGANIZATION

Consider the ways in which you might organize a discusssion of the seven states listed below. For each state, we have provided you with some basic information: the date it entered the Union, population, land area, and number of electoral votes in a presidential election.

MAINE
March 15, 1820
1,274,923 people
30,865 square miles
4 electoral votes

MONTANA
November 8, 1889
902,165 people
145,556 square miles
3 electoral votes

ALASKA
January 3, 1959
626,932 people
570,374 square miles
3 electoral votes

ARIZONA
February 14, 1912
5,130,632 people
113,642 square miles
10 electoral votes

FLORIDA
March 3, 1845
16,396,515 people
53,937 square miles
27 electoral votes

OREGON
February 14, 1859
3,472,867 people
98,386 square miles
7 electoral votes

MISSOURI
August 10, 1821
5,595,211 people
69,709 square miles
11 electoral votes

SUGGESTED WRITING ASSIGNMENTS

1. In groups of two or three, take turns describing a specific beautiful or remarkable thing to the others as if they were blind. You may want to actually bring an object to observe while your classmates cover their eyes. Help each other find the best words to create a vivid verbal picture. Using McDonald's paragraphs 33–36 as a model, write a brief description of your object, retaining the informal style of your speaking voice.

2. Recall a time when you and one other person held a conversation that helped you see something more clearly—visually, in terms of understanding, or both. Using McDonald's narrative as an organizational model, tell the story of that moment, re-creating the dialogue exactly as you remember it.

The Corner Store

■ **Eudora Welty**

One of the most honored and respected writers of the twentieth century, Eudora Welty was born in 1909 in Jackson, Mississippi, where she lived most of her life and where she died in 2001. Her first book, A Curtain of Green *(1941), was a collection of short stories. Although she went on to become a successful writer of novels, essays, and book reviews, among other genres (as well as a published photographer), she is most often remembered as a master of the short story.* The Collected Stories of Eudora Welty *was published in 1980. Her other best-known works include a collection of essays,* The Eye of the Story *(1975); her autobiography,* One Writer's Beginnings *(1984); and a collection of book reviews and essays,* The Writer's Eye *(1994). Peggy Prenshaw also published two collections of interviews with Eudora Welty: the first in 1984 and the second in 1995. Welty's novel* The Optimist's Daughter *won the Pulitzer Prize for fiction in 1973, and in 1999 the Library of Congress published two collections of her work:* Welty: Collected Novels *and* Welty: Collected Essays and Memoirs. *Welty's description of the corner store, taken from an essay about growing up in Jackson, recalls for many readers the neighborhood store in the town or city where they grew up. As you read, pay particular attention to the effect Welty's spatial arrangement of descriptive details has on the dominant impression of the store.*

FOR YOUR JOURNAL

Write about a store you frequented as a child. Maybe it was the local supermarket, the hardware store, or the corner convenience store. Using your five senses (sight, smell, taste, touch, and hearing), describe what you remember about the place.

O ur Little Store rose right up from the sidewalk; standing in a   1
street of family houses, it alone hadn't any yard in front, any tree or flower bed. It was a plain frame building covered over with brick. Above the door, a little railed porch ran across on an upstairs

level and four windows with shades were looking out. But I didn't catch on to those.

Running in out of the sun, you met what seemed total obscurity inside. There were almost tangible smells—licorice recently sucked in a child's cheek, dill pickle brine that had leaked through a paper sack in a fresh trail across the wooden floor, ammonia-loaded ice that had been hoisted from wet croker sacks[1] and slammed into the icebox[2] with its sweet butter at the door, and perhaps the smell of still un-trapped mice. 2

Then through the motes of cracker dust, cornmeal dust, the Gold Dust of the Gold Dust Twins that the floor had been swept out with, the realities emerged. Shelves climbed to high reach all the way around, set out with not too much of any one thing but a lot of things—lard, molasses, vinegar, starch, matches, kerosene, Octagon soap (about a year's worth of octagon-shaped coupons cut out and saved brought a signet ring addressed to you in the mail). It was up to you to remember what you came for, while your eye traveled from cans of sardines to tin whistles to ice-cream salt to harmonicas to fly-paper (over your head, batting around on a thread beneath the blades of the ceiling fan, stuck with its testimonial catch). 3

Its confusion may have been in the eye of its beholder. Enchant-ment is cast upon you by all those things you weren't supposed to have need for, to lure you close to wooden tops you'd outgrown, boys' marbles and agates in little net pouches, small rubber balls that wouldn't bounce straight, frail, frazzly kite string, clay bubble pipes that would snap off in your teeth, the stiffest scissors. You could con-template those long narrow boxes of sparklers gathering dust while you waited for it to be the Fourth of July or Christmas, and noisemak-ers in the shape of tin frogs for somebody's birthday party you hadn't been invited to yet, and see that they were all marvelous. 4

You might not have even looked for Mr. Sessions when he came around his store cheese (as big as a doll's house) and in front of the counter looking for you. When you'd finally asked him for, and re-ceived from him in its paper bag, whatever single thing it was that you had been sent for, the nickel that was left over was yours to spend. 5

---

[1]*Croker sacks:* sacks or bags made of burlap, a coarse woven fabric. [Eds.]
[2]*Icebox:* a wooden box or cupboard that held ice in a lower compartment to cool a second compartment above it, which was used for storing perishable food. [Eds.]

Down at a child's eye level, inside those glass jars with mouths in 6
their sides through which the grocer could run his scoop or a child's
hand might be invited to reach for a choice, were wineballs, all-day
suckers, gumdrops, peppermints. Making a row under the glass of a
counter were the Tootsie Rolls, Hershey bars, Goo Goo Clusters,
Baby Ruths. And whatever was the name of those pastilles that came
stacked in a cardboard cylinder with a cardboard lid? They were thin
and dry, about the size of tiddledy-winks,[3] and in the shape of
twisted rosettes. A kind of chocolate dust came out with them when
you shook them out in your hand. Were they chocolate? I'd say,
rather, they were brown. They didn't taste of anything at all, unless it
was wood. Their attraction was the number you got for a nickel.

Making up your mind, you circled the store around and around, 7
around the pickle barrel, around the tower of Crackerjack boxes; Mr.
Sessions had built it for us himself on top of a packing case like a
house of cards.

If it seemed too hot for Crackerjacks, I might get a cold drink. Mr. 8
Sessions might have already stationed himself by the cold-drinks barrel,
like a mind reader. Deep in ice water that looked black as ink, murky
shapes—that would come up as Coca-Colas, Orange Crushes, and various flavors of pop—were all swimming around together. When you
gave the word, Mr. Sessions plunged his bare arm in to the elbow and
fished out your choice, first try. I favored a locally bottled concoction
called Lake's Celery. (What else could it be called? It was made by a Mr.
Lake out of celery. It was a popular drink here for years but was not
known universally, as I found out when I arrived in New York and ordered one in the Astor bar.) You drank on the premises, with feet set
wide apart to miss the drip, and gave him back his bottle and your nickel.

But he didn't hurry you off. A standing scale was by the door, 9
with a stack of iron weights and a brass slide on the balance arm,
that would weigh you up to three hundred pounds. Mr. Sessions,
whose hands were gentle and smelled of carbolic, would lift you up
and set your feet on the platform, hold your loaf of bread for you,
and taking his time while you stood still for him, he would make certain of what you weighed today. He could even remember what you
weighed the last time, so you could subtract and announce how much
you'd gained. That was goodbye.

---

[3]*Tiddledy-winks:* playing pieces from the game Tiddledy-Winks, flat and round in
shape, the size of quarters (tiddledies) and dimes (winks). [Eds.]

QUESTIONS FOR STUDY AND DISCUSSION

1. Which of the three patterns of organization has Welty used in this essay: chronological, spatial, or logical? If she has used more than one, where precisely has she used each type?

2. In paragraph 2, Welty describes the smells that a person encountered when entering the corner store. Why do you think she presents these smells before giving any visual details of the inside of the store?

3. What is the dominant impression that Welty creates in her description of the corner store? (Glossary: *Dominant Impression*) How does Welty create this dominant impression?

4. What impression of Mr. Sessions does Welty create? What details contribute to this impression? (Glossary: *Details*)

5. Welty places certain pieces of information in parentheses in this essay. Why are they in parentheses? What, if anything, does this information add to our understanding of the corner store? Might this information be left out? Explain.

6. Comment on Welty's ending. (Glossary: *Beginnings and Endings*) Is it too abrupt? Why or why not?

VOCABULARY

Refer to your dictionary to define the following words as they are used in this selection. Then use each word in a sentence of your own.

frame (1)	signet (3)
tangible (2)	agates (4)
brine (2)	concoction (8)
motes (3)	scales (9)

CLASSROOM ACTIVITY USING ORGANIZATION

Yesterday, while cleaning out the center drawer of his desk, a student found the following items:

2 no. 2 pencils	2 pairs of scissors
3 rubber bands	1 book mailing bag
1 roll of adhesive tape	1 mechanical pencil
1 plastic comb	3 first-class postage stamps

25 3 × 5 cards	5 postcards
3 ballpoint pens	2 clasps
1 eraser	2 8 × 10 manila envelopes
6 paper clips	7 thumbtacks
1 nail clipper	1 bottle of correction fluid
1 highlighting marker	1 nail file
1 bottle of glue	1 toothbrush
3 business envelopes	1 felt-tip pen
6 postcard stamps	2 airmail stamps

To organize the student's drawer, into what categories would you divide these items? Explain which items you would place in each category, and suggest an order you might use to discuss the categories in a paper. (Glossary: *Division and Classification*)

SUGGESTED WRITING ASSIGNMENTS

1. Using Welty's essay as a model, describe your neighborhood store or supermarket. Gather a large quantity of detailed information from memory and from an actual visit to the store if that is still possible. You may find it helpful to reread what you wrote in response to the journal prompt for this essay. Once you have gathered your information, try to select those details that will help you create a dominant impression of the store. Finally, organize your examples and illustrations according to some clear organizational pattern.

2. Write an essay on one of the following topics:

   local restaurants
   reading materials
   television shows
   ways of financing a college education
   types of summer employment

   Be sure to use an organizational pattern that is well thought out and suited to both your material and your purpose.

Doubts about Doublespeak

William Lutz

William Lutz is a professor of English at Rutgers University and was the editor of the Quarterly Review of Doublespeak *for fourteen years. Born in Racine, Wisconsin, in 1940, Lutz is best known for his important works* Doublespeak: From Revenue Enhancement to Terminal Living *(1990) and* The New Doublespeak: Why No One Knows What Anyone's Saying Anymore *(1996).* His most recent book, Doublespeak Defined: Cut through the Bull**** and Get to the Point, *was published in 1999. (The term* doublespeak *comes from the Newspeak vocabulary of George Orwell's novel* Nineteen Eighty-Four. *It refers to speech or writing that presents two or more contradictory ideas in such a way that an unsuspecting audience is not consciously aware of the contradiction and is likely to be deceived.) As chair of the National Council of Teachers of English's Committee on Public Doublespeak, Lutz has been a watchdog of public officials who use language to "mislead, distort, deceive, inflate, circumvent, and obfuscate." Each year the committee presents the Orwell Awards, recognizing the most outrageous uses of doublespeak in government and business. In the following essay, which first appeared in the July 1993 issue of* State Government News, *Lutz argues that, far from harmless, "doublespeak alters our perception of reality. It deprives us of the tools we need to develop, advance and preserve our society, our culture, our civilization."*

FOR YOUR JOURNAL

Imagine that you work for a manufacturing plant in your town and that your boss has just told you that you are on the list of people who will be "dehired" or that you are part of a program of "negative employee retention." What would you think was happening to you? Would you be happy about it? What would you think of the language your boss used to describe your situation?

During the past year, we learned that we can shop at a "unique retail biosphere" instead of a farmers' market, where we can buy items made of "synthetic glass" instead of plastic, or purchase a "high velocity, multipurpose air circulator," or electric fan. A "waste-water conveyance facility" may "exceed the odor threshold" from time to time due to the presence of "regulated human nutrients," but that is not to be confused with a sewage plant that stinks up the neighborhood with sewage sludge. Nor should we confuse a "resource development park" with a dump. Thus does doublespeak continue to spread.

Doublespeak is language which pretends to communicate but doesn't. It is language which makes the bad seem good, the negative seem positive, the unpleasant seem attractive, or at least tolerable. It is language which avoids, shifts, or denies responsibility; language which is at variance with its real or purported meaning. It is language which conceals or prevents thought.

Doublespeak is all around us. We are asked to check our packages at the desk "for our convenience" when it's not for our convenience at all but for someone else's convenience. We see advertisements for "preowned," "experienced," or "previously distinguished" cars, not used cars and for "genuine imitation leather," "virgin vinyl," or "real counterfeit diamonds." Television offers not reruns but "encore telecasts." There are no slums or ghettos, just the "inner city" or "substandard housing" where the "disadvantaged" or "economically nonaffluent" live and where there might be a problem with "substance abuse." Nonprofit organizations don't make a profit, they have "negative deficits" or experience "revenue excesses." With doublespeak it's not dying but "terminal living" or "negative patient care outcome."

There are four kinds of doublespeak. The first kind is the euphemism, a word or phrase designed to avoid a harsh or distasteful reality. Used to mislead or deceive, the euphemism becomes doublespeak. In 1984 the U.S. State Department's annual reports on the status of human rights around the world ceased using the word "killing." Instead the State Department used the phrase "unlawful or arbitrary deprivation of life," thus avoiding the embarrassing situation of government-sanctioned killing in countries supported by the United States.

A second kind of doublespeak is jargon, the specialized language of a trade, profession, or similar group, such as doctors, lawyers, plumbers, or car mechanics. Legitimately used, jargon allows members of a group to communicate with each other clearly, efficiently, and quickly. Lawyers and tax accountants speak to each other of an "involuntary conversion" of property, a legal term that means the loss or destruction of property through theft, accident, or condemnation. But when lawyers or tax accountants use unfamiliar terms to speak to others, then the jargon becomes doublespeak.

In 1978 a commercial 727 crashed on takeoff, killing three passengers, injuring 21 others and destroying the airplane. The insured value of the airplane was greater than its book value, so the airline made a profit of $1.7 million, creating two problems: the airline didn't want to talk about one of its airplanes crashing, yet it had to account for that $1.7 million profit in its annual report to its stockholders. The airline solved both problems by inserting a footnote in its annual report which explained that the $1.7 million was due to "the involuntary conversion of a 727." 6

A third kind of doublespeak is gobbledygook or bureaucratese. Such doublespeak is simply a matter of overwhelming the audience with words—the more the better. Alan Greenspan, a polished practitioner of bureaucratese, once testified before a Senate committee that "it is a tricky problem to find the particular calibration in timing that would be appropriate to stem the acceleration in risk premiums created by falling incomes without prematurely aborting the decline in the inflation-generated risk premiums." 7

The fourth kind of doublespeak is inflated language, which is designed to make the ordinary seem extraordinary, to make everyday things seem impressive, to give an air of importance to people or situations, to make the simple seem complex. Thus do car mechanics become "automotive internists," elevator operators become "members of the vertical transportation corps," grocery store checkout clerks become "career associate scanning professionals," and smelling something becomes "organoleptic analysis." 8

Doublespeak is not the product of careless language or sloppy thinking. Quite the opposite. Doublespeak is language carefully designed and constructed to appear to communicate when in fact it doesn't. It is language designed not to lead but mislead. Thus, it's not a tax increase but "revenue enhancement" or "tax-base broadening." So how can you complain about higher taxes? Those aren't useless, billion dollar pork barrel projects; they're really "congressional projects of national significance," so don't complain about wasteful government spending. That isn't the Mafia in Atlantic City; those are just 9 "members of a career-offender cartel," so don't worry about the influence of organized crime in the city.

New doublespeak is created every day. The Environmental Protection Agency once called acid rain "poorly-buffered precipitation" then dropped that term in favor of "atmospheric deposition of anthropogenically-derived acidic substances," but recently decided that acid rain should be called "wet deposition." The Pentagon, which has in the past given us such classic doublespeak as "hexiform rotatable surface compression unit" for steel nut, just published a pamphlet warning soldiers that exposure to nerve gas will lead to "immediate permanent incapacitation." That's almost as good as the Pentagon's official term "servicing the target," meaning to kill the enemy. Meanwhile, the Department of Energy wants to establish a "monitored retrievable storage site," a place once known as a dump for spent nuclear fuel.

Bad economic times give rise to lots of new doublespeak designed to avoid some very unpleasant economic realities. As the "contained depression" continues so does the corporate policy of making up even more new terms to avoid the simple, and easily understandable, term "layoff." So it is that corporations "reposition," "restructure," "reshape," or "realign" the company and "reduce duplication" through "release of resources" that involves a "permanent downsizing" or a "payroll adjustment" that results in a number of employees being "involuntarily terminated."

Other countries regularly contribute to doublespeak. In Japan, where baldness is called "hair disadvantaged," the economy is undergoing a "severe adjustment process," while in Canada there is an "involuntary downward development" of the work force. For some government agencies in Canada, wastepaper baskets have become "user friendly, space effective, flexible, deskside sortation units." Politicians in Canada may engage in "reality augmentation," but they never lie. As part of their new freedom, the people of Moscow can visit "intimacy salons," or sex shops as they're known in other countries. When dealing with the bureaucracy in Russia, people know that they should show officials "normal gratitude," or give them a bribe.

The worst doublespeak is the doublespeak of death. It is the language, wrote George Orwell in 1946, that is "largely the defense of the indefensible . . . designed to make lies sound truthful and murder respectable, and to give an appearance of solidity to pure wind." In the doublespeak of death, Orwell continued, "defenseless villages are bombarded from the air, the inhabitants driven out into the country-side, the cattle machine-gunned, the huts set on fire with incendiary bullets. This is called pacification. Millions of peasants are robbed of their farms and sent trudging along the roads with no more than they can carry. This is called transfer of population or rectification of frontiers." Today, in a country once called Yugoslavia, this is called "ethnic cleansing."[1]

It's easy to laugh off doublespeak. After all, we all know what's   14 going on, so what's the harm? But we don't always know what's going on, and when that happens, doublespeak accomplishes its ends. It alters our perception of reality. It deprives us of the tools we need to develop, advance, and preserve our society, our culture, our civilization. It breeds suspicion, cynicism, distrust, and, ultimately, hostility. It delivers us into the hands of those who do not have our interests at heart. As Samuel Johnson[2] noted in 18th century England, even the devils in hell do not lie to one another, since the society of hell could not subsist without the truth, any more than any other society.

QUESTIONS FOR STUDY AND DISCUSSION

1. What is Lutz's thesis in this essay? (Glossary: *Thesis*) Where is it stated?

2. Lutz treats four kinds of doublespeak in his essay. What are they? Is there an organizational pattern to his presentation? What is that pattern, and why do you suppose he arranges his discussion of each type of doublespeak in the manner that he does?

3. After reading Lutz's discussion of the second type of double-speak, that which is akin to jargon, what advice would you give someone about when to use jargon? (Glossary: *Jargon*)

4. Lutz's use of illustrative examples is all but mandatory. (Glossary: *Examples*) Are his examples good ones? Why or why not?

---

[1]Lutz is referring to the breakup of the Federal Republic of Yugoslavia in the Balkan region of southeastern Europe in the early 1990s and the 1992–95 genocide centered in the cites of Sarajevo and Srebrenica. [Eds.]
[2]*Samuel Johnson* (1709–1784): an important English literary figure. [Eds.]

Should he have used fewer examples? Does the essay need more examples?

5. Could the order of Lutz's first two paragraphs be reversed? What would be gained or lost if they were? (Glossary: *Beginnings and Endings*)

6. Reread Lutz's last paragraph, where he makes some serious claims about the importance of doublespeak. Is such seriousness on his part justified by what he has written about doublespeak in the body of his essay? Why or why not?

VOCABULARY

Refer to your dictionary to define the following words as they are used in this selection. Then use each word in a sentence of your own.

conveyance (1)   bureaucratese (7)
purported (2)   pacification (13)
jargon (5)   trudging (13)
gobbledygook (7)

CLASSROOM ACTIVITY USING ORGANIZATION

Carefully read the following paragraph from *Blue Highways* by William Least Heat Moon, and identify the organizational pattern he uses to structure his description.

The old store, lighted only by three fifty-watt bulbs, smelled of coal and baking bread. In the middle of the rectangular room, where the oak floor sagged a little, stood an iron stove. To the right was a wooden table with an unfinished game of checkers and a stool made from an apple tree stump. On the shelves around the walls sat earthen jugs with corncob stoppers . . . , a few canned goods, and some of the two-thousand old clocks and clockworks Thurmond Watts owned. Only one was ticking; the others he just looked at. I asked how long he had been in the store.

Based on Least Heat Moon's description, sketch the inside of Thurmond Watts's store. Compare your sketch with those of your classmates, and discuss how the paragraph's organization influenced the relative prominence of various objects in your sketch.

SUGGESTED WRITING ASSIGNMENTS

1. Write an essay in which you consider the effects of doublespeak. Is it always a form of lying? Is it harmful to our society, and if so, how? How can we measure its effects? Be sure to cite some instances of doublespeak that are not included in Lutz's essay, examples that you uncover yourself through your reading, Web browsing, or library research.

2. Think of a commonplace subject that people might take for granted but that you find interesting. Write an essay on that subject, using one of the following types of logical order:

Least important to most important
Most familiar to least familiar
Smallest to biggest
Oldest to newest
Easiest to understand to most difficult to understand
Good news to bad news
General to specific

chapter 6

Beginnings and Endings

"Begin at the beginning and go on till you come to the end: then stop," advised the King of Hearts in *Alice in Wonderland*. "Good advice, but more easily said than done," you might be tempted to reply. Certainly, no part of writing essays can be more daunting than coming up with effective **beginnings and endings**. In fact, many writers feel these are the most important parts of any piece of writing regardless of its length. Even before coming to your introduction, your readers will usually know something about your intentions from your title. Titles like "The Case against Euthanasia," "How to Buy a Used Car," or "What Is a Migraine Headache?" indicate both your subject and approach and prepare your readers for what is to follow.

■ Beginnings

What makes for an effective beginning? Not unlike a personal greeting, a good beginning should catch a reader's interest and then hold it. The experienced writer realizes that many readers would rather do almost anything than make a commitment to read, so the opening or "lead," as journalists refer to it, requires a lot of thought and much revising to make it right and to keep the reader's attention from straying. The inexperienced writer, on the other hand, knows that the beginning is important but tries to write it first and to perfect it before moving on to the rest of the essay. Although there are no "rules" for writing introductions, we can offer one bit of general advice: Wait until the writing process is well under way or almost completed before focusing on your lead. Following this advice will keep you from spending too much time on an introduction that you will undoubtedly revise. More important, once you actually see how your essay develops, you will know better how to introduce it to your reader.

In addition to capturing your reader's attention, a good beginning usually introduces your thesis and either suggests or actually reveals the structure of the composition. Keep in mind that the best beginning is not necessarily the most catchy or the most shocking but the one most appropriate for the job you are trying to do.

There are many effective ways of beginning an essay. Consider using one of the following.

ANECDOTE

Introducing your essay with an anecdote, a brief narrative drawn from current news events, history, or your personal experience, can be an effective way to capture your reader's interest. In the following example, the writer introduces an essay on the topic of integrity by recounting a surprising experience he had as a public speaker.

> A couple of years ago I began a university commencement address by telling the audience that I was going to talk about integrity. The crowd broke into applause. Applause! Just because they had heard the word "integrity": that's how starved for it they were. They had no idea how I was using the word, or what I was going to say about integrity, or, indeed, whether I was for it or against it. But they knew they liked the idea of talking about it.
>
> –Stephen L. Carter

ANALOGY/COMPARISON

An analogy or comparison can be useful in getting readers to contemplate a topic they might otherwise reject as unfamiliar or uninteresting. In the following multiparagraph example, Roger Garrison introduces a subject few would consider engrossing—writing—with an analogy to stone wall building. By pairing these two seemingly unrelated concepts, he both introduces and vividly illustrates the idea he will develop in his essay: that writing is a difficult, demanding craft with specific skills to be learned.

> In northern New England, where I live, stone walls mark boundaries, border meadows, and march through the woods that grew up around them long ago. Flank-high, the walls are made of granite rocks stripped from fields when pastures were cleared and are used to fence in cattle. These are dry walls, made without mortar, and the stones in them, all shapes and sizes, are fitted to one another with such care that a wall, built a hundred years ago, still runs as straight and solid as it did when people cleared the land.
>
> Writing is much like wall building. The writer fits together separate chunks of meaning to make an understandable statement.

Like the old Yankee wall builders, anyone who wants to write well must learn some basic skills, one at a time, to build soundly. This [essay] describes these skills and shows you how to develop them and put them together. You can learn them.

Building a stone wall is not easy: It is gut-wrenching labor. Writing is not easy either. It is a complex skill, mainly because it demands a commitment of our own complicated selves. But it is worth learning how to do well—something true of any skill. Solid walls do get built, and good writing does get done. We will clear alway some underbrush and get at the job.

–Roger Garrison

DIALOGUE/QUOTATION

Although relying heavily on the ideas of others can weaken an effective introduction, opening your essay with a quotation or a brief dialogue can attract a reader's attention and can succinctly illustrate a particular attitude or point that you want to discuss. In the following example, the writer introduces an essay about the three main types of stress in our lives by recounting a brief dialogue with one of her roommates.

My roommate, Megan, pushes open the front door, throws her keys on the counter, and flops down on the couch.

"Hey, Megan, how are you?" I yell from the kitchen.

"I don't know what's wrong with me. I sleep all the time, but I'm still tired. No matter what I do, I just don't feel well."

"What did the doctor say?"

"She said it sounds like chronic fatigue syndrome."

"Do you think it might be caused by stress?" I ask.

"Nah, stress doesn't affect me very much. I like keeping busy and running around. This must be something else."

Like most Americans, Megan doesn't recognize the numerous factors in her life that cause her stress.

–Sarah Federman

FACTS AND STATISTICS

For the most part, you should support your argument with facts and statistics rather than letting them speak for you, but a brief and startling fact or statistic can be an effective way to engage readers in your essay.

Charles Darwin and Abraham Lincoln were born on the same day —February 12, 1809. They are also linked in another curious way —for both must simultaneously play, and for similar reasons, the role of man and legend.

–Stephen Jay Gould

IRONY OR HUMOR

It is often effective to introduce an essay with irony or humor. Humor, especially, signals to the reader that your essay will be entertaining to read, and irony can indicate an unexpected approach to a topic. In his essay "Shooting an Elephant," George Orwell begins by simultaneously establishing a wry tone and indicating to the reader that he, the narrator, occupies the position of outsider in the events he is about to relate.

> In Moulmein, in lower Burma, I was hated by large numbers of people—the only time in my life that I have been important enough for this to happen to me.
>
> > –George Orwell

There are several other good ways to begin an essay; the following opening sentences illustrate each approach.

SHORT GENERALIZATION

> It is a miracle that New York works at all.
>
> > –E. B. White

STARTLING CLAIM

> It is possible to stop most drug addiction in the United States within a very short time.
>
> > –Gore Vidal

RHETORICAL QUESTIONS

> Just how interconnected *is* the animal world? Is it true that if we change any part of that world we risk unduly damaging life in other, larger parts of it?
>
> > –Matthew Douglas

There are also ways of beginning an essay that should be avoided. Some of these follow.

APOLOGY

I am a college student and do not consider myself an expert on the computer industry, but I think that many computer companies make false claims about just how easy it is to learn to use a computer.

COMPLAINT

I'd rather write about a topic of my own choice than the one that is assigned, but here goes.

WEBSTER'S DICTIONARY

Webster's New Collegiate Dictionary defines the verb *to snore* as follows: "to breathe during sleep with a rough hoarse noise due to vibration of the soft palate."

PLATITUDE

America is the land of opportunity, and no one knows it better than Madonna.

REFERENCE TO TITLE

As you can see from my title, this essay is about why we should continue to experiment with human heart transplants.

▓ Endings

An effective ending does more than simply indicate where the writer stopped writing. A conclusion may summarize; may inspire the reader to further thought or even action; may return to the beginning by repeating key words, phrases, or ideas; or may surprise the reader by providing a particularly convincing example to support a thesis. Indeed, there are many ways to write a conclusion, but the effectiveness of any choice must be measured by how appropriately it fits what has gone before it. You might consider concluding with a restatement of your thesis, with a prediction, or with a recommendation.

In an essay contrasting the traditional Hispanic understanding of the word *macho* with the meaning it has developed in mainstream

American culture, Rose Del Castillo Guilbault begins her essay with a succinct, two-sentence paragraph offering her thesis:

> What is *macho?* That depends which side of the border you come from.

She concludes her essay by restating her thesis, but in a manner that reflects the detailed examination she has given the concept of *macho* in her essay:

> The impact of language in our society is undeniable. And the misuse of *macho* hints at a deeper cultural misunderstanding that extends beyond mere word definitions.
>
> –Rose Del Castillo Guilbault

In the following conclusion to a long chapter on weasel words, a form of deceptive advertising language, the writer summarizes the points that he has made, ending with a recommendation to the reader:

> A weasel word is a word that's used to imply a meaning that cannot be truthfully stated. Some weasels imply meanings that are not the same as their actual definition, such as "help," "like," or "fortified." They can act as qualifiers and/or comparatives. Other weasels, such as "taste" and "flavor," have no definite meanings, and are simply subjective opinions offered by the manufacturer. A weasel of omission is one that implies a claim so strongly that it forces you to supply the bogus fact. Adjectives are weasels used to convey feelings and emotions to a greater extent than the product itself can.
>
> In dealing with weasels, you must strip away the innuendos and try to ascertain the facts, if any. To do this, you need to ask questions such as: How? Why? How many? How much? Stick to basic definitions of words. Look them up if you have to. Then, apply the strict definition to the text of the advertisement or commercial. "Like" means similar to, but not the same as. "Virtually" means the same in essence, but not in fact.
>
> Above all, never underestimate the devious qualities of a weasel. Weasels twist and turn and hide in dark shadows. You must come to grips with them, or advertising will rule you forever.
>
> My advice to you is: Beware of weasels. They are nasty and untrainable, and they attack pocketbooks.
>
> –Paul Stevens

In the following conclusion to a composition entitled "Title IX Just Makes Sense," the writer offers an overview of her argument and concludes by predicting the outcome of the solution she advocates:

> There have undeniably been major improvements in the treatment of female college athletes since the enactment of Title IX. But most colleges and universities still don't measure up to the actual regulation standards, and many have quite a ways to go. The Title IX fight for equality is not a radical feminist movement, nor is it intended to take away the privileges of male athletes. It is, rather, a demand for fairness, for women to receive the same opportunities that men have always had. When colleges and universities stop viewing Title IX budget requirements as an inconvenience and start complying with the spirit and not merely the letter of the law, collegiate female athletes will finally reach the parity they deserve.
>
> –Jen Jarjosa, student

If you are having trouble with your conclusion—and this is not an uncommon occurrence—it may be because of problems with your essay itself. Frequently, writers do not know when to end because they are not sure about their overall purpose. For example, if you are taking a trip and your purpose is to go to Chicago, you'll know when you get there and will stop. But if you don't really know where you are going, it's very difficult to know when to stop.

It's usually a good idea in your conclusion to avoid such overworked expressions as "In conclusion," "In summary," "I hope I have shown," or "Finally." Your conclusion should also do more than simply repeat what you've said in your opening paragraph. The most satisfying essays are those in which the conclusion provides an interesting way of wrapping up ideas introduced in the beginning and developed throughout.

You might find it revealing as your course progresses to read with special attention the beginnings and endings of the essays throughout *Models for Writers*. Take special note of the varieties of beginnings and endings, the possible relationship between a beginning and an ending, and the general appropriateness of these elements to the writer's subject and purpose.

Of My Friend Hector and My Achilles Heel

■ **Michael T. Kaufman**

The former writer of the "About New York" column for the New York Times, Michael T. Kaufman was born in 1938 in Paris and grew up in the United States. He studied at the Bronx High School of Science, City College of New York, and Columbia University. He began his career at the New York Times *as a reporter and feature writer, and before assuming his position as columnist, he served as bureau chief in Ottawa and Warsaw. The experience in Warsaw is evident in his book about Poland,* Mad Dreams, Saving Graces, *published in 1989. Kaufman is also a past winner of the George Polk Award for International Reporting. His most recent book is* Soros: The Life and Times of a Messianic Billionaire *(2002). In the following selection, which appeared in the* New York Times *in 1992, Kaufman uses the story of his childhood friend Hector Elizondo to reflect on his own "prejudice and stupidity." Take note of how the two very brief sentences at the beginning establish the chronological and narrative structure of what follows.*

FOR YOUR JOURNAL

Many schools "track" students by intellectual ability into such categories as "honors," "college bound," "vocational," "remedial," or "terminal." Did you go to a high school that tracked its students? How did the tracking system work? How did you feel about your placement? What did you think about classmates who were on tracks higher or lower than yours?

This story is about prejudice and stupidity. My own.   1

It begins in 1945 when I was a 7-year-old living on the fifth floor   2
of a tenement walkup on 107th Street between Columbus and Manhattan Avenues in New York City. The block was almost entirely

Irish and Italian, and I believe my family was the only Jewish one around.

One day a Spanish-speaking family moved into one of the four 3 apartments on our landing. They were the first Puerto Ricans I had met. They had a son who was about my age named Hector, and the two of us became friends. We played with toy soldiers and I particularly remember how, using rubber bands and wood from orange crates, we made toy pistols that shot off little squares we cut from old linoleum.

We visited each other's homes and I know that at the time I liked 4 Hector and I think he liked me. I may even have eaten my first avocado at his house.

About a year after we met, my family moved to another part of 5 Manhattan's West Side and I did not see Hector again until I entered Booker T. Washington Junior High School as an 11-year-old.

THE SPECIAL CLASS

The class I was in was called 7SP-1; the SP was for special. Earlier, I 6 recall, I had been in the IGC class, for "intellectually gifted children." The SP class was to complete the seventh, eighth and ninth grades in two years and almost all of us would then go to schools like Bronx Science, Stuyvesant or Music and Art, where admission was based on competitive exams. I knew I was in the SP class and the IGC class. I guess I also knew that other people were not.

Hector was not. He was in some other class, maybe even 7-2, the 7 class that was held to be the next-brightest, or maybe 7-8. I remember I was happy to see him whenever we would meet, and sometimes we played punchball during lunch period. Mostly, of course, I stayed with my own classmates, with other Intellectually Gifted Children.

Sometimes children from other classes, those presumably not so 8 intellectually gifted, would tease and taunt us. At such times I was particularly proud to have Hector as a friend. I assumed that he was tougher than I and my classmates and I guess I thought that if necessary he would come to my defense.

DIFFERENT HIGH SCHOOLS

For high school, I went uptown to Bronx Science. Hector, I think, 9 went downtown to Commerce. Sometimes I would see him in Riverside Park, where I played basketball and he worked out on the parallel bars. We would acknowledge each other, but by this time the conversations we held were perfunctory — sports, families, weather.

After I finished college, I would see him around the neighbor- 10 hood pushing a baby carriage. He was the first of my contemporaries to marry and to have a child.

A few years later, in the 60's, married and with children of my own, 11 I was once more living on the West Side, working until late at night as a reporter. Some nights as I took the train home I would see Hector in the car. A few times we exchanged nods, but more often I would pretend that I didn't see him, and maybe he also pretended he didn't see me. Usually he would be wearing a knitted watch cap, and from that I deduced that he was probably working on the docks as a longshoreman.

I remember quite distinctly how I would sit on the train and think 12 about how strange and unfair fate had been with regard to the two of us who had once been playmates. Just because I had become an intellectually gifted adult or whatever and he had become a longshoreman or whatever, was that any reason for us to have been left with nothing to say to each other? I thought it was wrong and unfair, but I also thought that conversation would be a chore or a burden. That is pretty much what I thought about Hector, if I thought about him at all, until one Sunday in the mid-70's, when I read in the drama section of this newspaper that my childhood friend, Hector Elizondo, was replacing Peter Falk[1] in the leading role in "The Prisoner of Second Avenue."[2]

Since then, every time I have seen this versatile and acclaimed 13 actor in movies or on television I have blushed for my assumptions. I have replayed the subway rides in my head and tried to fathom why my thoughts had led me where they did.

In retrospect it seems far more logical that the man I saw on the 14 train, the man who had been my friend as a boy, was coming home from an Off Broadway theater or perhaps from a job as a waiter while taking acting classes. So why did I think he was a longshoreman? Was it just the cap? Could it be that his being Puerto Rican had something to do with it? Maybe that reinforced the stereotype I concocted, but it wasn't the root of it.

---

[1]*Peter Falk* (b. 1927): a well-known stage, television, and movie actor who starred as the rumpled television detective Columbo. [Eds.]

[2]*"The Prisoner of Second Avenue"*: a play by Neil Simon, which premiered at the Eugene O'Neill Theatre in New York City in 1971. The Broadway hit was made into a movie released in 1975. [Eds.]

WHEN IT GOT STARTED

No, the foundation was laid when I was 11, when I was in 7SP-1 and he 15
was not, when I was in the IGC class and he was not.

I have not seen him since I recognized how I had idiotically kept 16
tracking him for years and decades after the school system had
tracked both of us. I wonder now if my experience was that unusual,
whether social categories conveyed and absorbed before puberty do
not generally tend to linger beyond middle age. And I wonder, too,
that if they affected the behavior of someone like myself who had
been placed on the upper track, how much more damaging it must
have been for someone consigned to the lower.

I have at times thought of calling him, but kept from doing it be- 17
cause how exactly does one apologize for thoughts that were never expressed? And there was still the problem of what to say. "What have you
been up to for the last 40 years?" Or "Wow, was I wrong about you!"
Or maybe just, "Want to come over and help me make a linoleum gun?"

QUESTIONS FOR STUDY AND DISCUSSION

1. How do Kaufman's first two sentences affect how the reader views
   the rest of the essay? Did they catch your attention? Why or why not?
2. If you are unfamiliar with the Greek myth of Hector and Achilles, look it up in a book on mythology. Why does Kaufman allude to Hector and Achilles in his title? (Glossary: *Allusion*)
3. How does Kaufman organize his essay? (Glossary: *Organization*)
4. What is Kaufman's purpose in the essay? (Glossary: *Purpose*) How
   does his organization of the essay help him express his purpose?
5. Why did Kaufman ignore Hector after graduating from college?
   What does this tell him about society in general?
6. Why is Kaufman's ending effective? What point does he want to
   emphasize with the ending he uses?

VOCABULARY

Refer to your dictionary to define the following words as they are
used in this selection. Then use each word in a sentence of your own.

intellectually (6)	acclaimed (13)
perfunctory (9)	concocted (14)
contemporaries (10)	

CLASSROOM ACTIVITY USING BEGINNINGS AND ENDINGS

Carefully read the following three beginnings for an essay on the world's most famous practical joker, Hugh Troy. What are the advantages and disadvantages of each? Which one would you select as an opening paragraph? Why?

> Whether questioning the values of American society or simply relieving the monotony of daily life, Hugh Troy always managed to put a little of himself into each of his stunts. One day he attached a plaster hand to his shirt sleeve and took a trip through the Holland Tunnel. As he approached the tollbooth, with his toll ticket between the fingers of the artificial hand, Troy left both ticket and hand in the grasp of the stunned tollbooth attendant and sped away.

> Nothing seemed unusual. In fact, it was a rather common occurrence in New York City. Five men dressed in overalls roped off a section of busy Fifth Avenue in front of the old Rockefeller residence, hung out MEN WORKING signs, and began ripping up the pavement. By the time they stopped for lunch, they had dug quite a hole in the street. This crew was different, however, from all the others that had descended upon the streets of the city. It was led by Hugh Troy — the world's greatest practical joker.

> Hugh Troy was born in Ithaca, New York, where his father was a professor at Cornell University. After graduating from Cornell, Troy left for New York City, where he became a successful illustrator of children's books. When World War II broke out, he went into the army and eventually became a captain in the 21st Bomber Command, 20th Air Force, under General Curtis LeMay. After the war he made his home in Garrison, New York, for a short while before finally settling in Washington, D.C., where he lived until his death.

SUGGESTED WRITING ASSIGNMENTS

1. Kaufman's essay is a deeply personal one. Use it as a model to write an essay about a time or an action in your life that you are not proud of. What happened? Why did it happen? What would you do differently if you could? Be sure to catch the reader's attention in the beginning and to end your essay with a thought-provoking conclusion.

2. Everyone has childhood friends that we either have lost track of or don't communicate with as often as we would like. Choose an old friend whom you have lost track of and would like to see again. Write an essay about your relationship. What made your friend special to you as a child? Why did you lose touch? What does the future hold? Organize your essay chronologically.

Shame

■ **Dick Gregory**

Dick Gregory, a well-known comedian and nutrition expert, was born in St. Louis, Missouri, in 1932 and has long been active in the civil rights movement. During the 1960s, Gregory was also an outspoken critic of America's involvement in Vietnam. His most recent book is the autobiography, Callus on My Soul *(2000). In the following episode from his first autobiography,* Nigger *(1964), he narrates the story of a childhood experience that taught him the meaning of shame. Through his use of realistic dialogue and vivid details, he dramatically re-creates the experience for readers. Notice also how he uses the first three paragraphs to establish a context for the events that follow.*

FOR YOUR JOURNAL

We all learn many things in school beyond the lessons we study formally. Some of the extracurricular truths we learn stay with us for the rest of our lives. Write about something you learned in school that you still find very useful—something that has made life easier or more understandable for you.

I never learned hate at home, or shame. I had to go to school for 1
that. I was about seven years old when I got my first big lesson. I was in love with a little girl named Helene Tucker, a light-complexioned little girl with pigtails and nice manners. She was always clean and she was smart in school. I think I went to school then mostly to look at her. I brushed my hair and even got me a little old handkerchief. It was a lady's handkerchief, but I didn't want Helene to see me wipe my nose on my hand. The pipes were frozen again, there was no water in the house, but I washed my socks and shirt every night. I'd get a pot, and go over to Mister Ben's grocery store, and stick my pot down into his soda machine. Scoop out some chopped ice. By evening the ice melted to water for washing. I got sick a lot that winter because the fire would go out at night before the

clothes were dry. In the morning I'd put them on, wet or dry, because they were the only clothes I had.

Everybody's got a Helene Tucker, a symbol of everything you want. I loved her for her goodness, her cleanness, her popularity. She'd walk down my street and my brothers and sisters would yell, "Here comes Helene," and I'd rub my tennis sneakers on the back of my pants and wish my hair wasn't so nappy and the white folks' shirt fit me better. I'd run out on the street. If I knew my place and didn't come too close, she'd wink at me and say hello. That was a good feeling. Sometimes I'd follow her all the way home, and shovel the snow off her walk and try to make friends with her Momma and her aunts. I'd drop money on her stoop late at night on my way back from shining shoes in the taverns. And she had a Daddy, and he had a good job. He was a paper hanger.

I guess I would have gotten over Helene by summertime, but something happened in that classroom that made her face hang in front of me for the next twenty-two years. When I played the drums in high school it was for Helene and when I broke track records in college it was for Helene and when I started standing behind microphones and heard applause I wished Helene could hear it, too. It wasn't until I was twenty-nine years old and married and making money that I finally got her out of my system. Helene was sitting in that classroom when I learned to be ashamed of myself.

It was on a Thursday. I was sitting in the back of the room, in a seat with a chalk circle drawn around it. The idiot's seat, the troublemaker's seat.

The teacher thought I was stupid. Couldn't spell, couldn't read, couldn't do arithmetic. Just stupid. Teachers were never interested in finding out that you couldn't concentrate because you were so hungry, because you hadn't had any breakfast. All you could think about was noontime, would it ever come? Maybe you could sneak into the cloakroom and steal a bite of some kid's lunch out of a coat pocket. A bite of something. Paste. You can't really make a meal of paste, or put it on bread for a sandwich, but sometimes I'd scoop a few spoonfuls out of the paste jar in the back of the room. Pregnant people get strange tastes. I was pregnant with poverty. Pregnant with dirt and pregnant with smells that made people turn away, pregnant with cold and pregnant with shoes that were never bought for me, pregnant with five other people in my bed and no Daddy in the next room, and pregnant with hunger. Paste doesn't taste too bad when you're hungry.

The teacher thought I was a troublemaker. All she saw from the 6
front of the room was a little black boy who squirmed in his idiot's
seat and made noises and poked the kids around him. I guess she
couldn't see a kid who made noises because he wanted someone to
know he was there.

It was on a Thursday, the day before the Negro payday. The 7
eagle always flew on Friday. The teacher was asking each student
how much his father would give to the Community Chest. On Friday
night, each kid would get the money from his father, and on Monday
he would bring it to the school. I decided I was going to buy me a
Daddy right then. I had money in my pocket from shining shoes and
selling papers, and whatever Helene Tucker pledged for her Daddy I
was going to top it. And I'd hand the money right in. I wasn't going
to wait until Monday to buy me a Daddy.

I was shaking, scared to death. The teacher opened her book and 8
started calling out names alphabetically.

"Helene Tucker?" 9

"My daddy said he'd give two dollars and fifty cents." 10

"That's very nice, Helene. Very, very nice indeed." 11

That made me feel pretty good. It wouldn't take too much to top 12
that. I had almost three dollars in dimes and quarters in my pocket. I
stuck my hand in my pocket and held onto the money, waiting for
her to call my name. But the teacher closed her book after she called
everybody else in the class.

I stood up and raised my hand. 13

"What is it now?" 14

"You forgot me." 15

She turned toward the blackboard. "I don't have time to be play- 16
ing with you, Richard."

"My Daddy said he'd . . ." 17

"Sit down, Richard, you're disturbing the class." 18

"My Daddy said he'd give . . . fifteen dollars." 19

She turned around and looked mad. "We are collecting this 20
money for you and your kind, Richard Gregory. If your Daddy can
give fifteen dollars you have no business being on relief."

"I got it right now, I got it right now, my Daddy gave it to me to 21
turn in today, my Daddy said . . ."

"And furthermore," she said, looking right at me, her nostrils 22
getting big and her lips getting thin and her eyes opening wide, "we
know you don't have a Daddy."

Helene Tucker turned around, her eyes full of tears. She felt sorry 23
for me. Then I couldn't see her too well because I was crying, too.

"Sit down, Richard." 24

And I always thought the teacher kind of liked me. She always 25
picked me to wash the blackboard on Friday, after school. That was
a big thrill, it made me feel important. If I didn't wash it, come
Monday the school might not function right.

"Where are you going, Richard?" 26

I walked out of school that day, and for a long time I didn't go 27
back very often. There was shame there.

Now there was shame everywhere. It seemed like the whole 28
world had been inside that classroom, everyone had heard what the
teacher had said, everyone had turned around and felt sorry for me.
There was shame in going to the Worthy Boys Annual Christmas
Dinner for you and your kind, because everybody knew what a worthy boy was. Why couldn't they just call it the Boys Annual Dinner;
why'd they have to give it a name? There was shame in wearing the
brown and orange and white plaid mackinaw the welfare gave to
three thousand boys. Why'd it have to be the same for everybody so
when you walked down the street the people could see you were on
relief? It was a nice warm mackinaw and it had a hood, and my
Momma beat me and called me a little rat when she found out I
stuffed it in the bottom of a pail full of garbage way over on Cottage
Street. There was shame in running over to Mister Ben's at the end of
the day and asking for his rotten peaches, there was shame in asking
Mrs. Simmons for a spoonful of sugar, there was shame in running
out to meet the relief truck. I hated that truck, full of food for you
and your kind. I ran into the house and hid when it came. And then I
started to sneak through alleys, to take the long way home so the
people going into White's Eat Shop wouldn't see me. Yeah, the whole
world heard the teacher that day, we all know you don't have a
Daddy.

QUESTIONS FOR STUDY AND DISCUSSION

1. How do the first three paragraphs of the essay help to establish a
   context for the narrative that follows?

2. What does Gregory mean by "shame"? What precisely was he
   ashamed of, and what in particular did he learn from the incident? (Glossary: *Definition*)

3. Why do you think Gregory narrates this episode from the first-person point of view? (Glossary: *Point of View*) What would be gained or lost if he instead wrote it from the third-person point of view?

4. What is the teacher's attitude toward Gregory? Consider her own words and actions as well as Gregory's opinion in arriving at your answer.

5. What role does money play in Gregory's experience? How does money relate to his sense of shame?

6. Specific details can enhance the reader's understanding and appreciation of a subject. (Glossary: *Details*) Gregory's description of Helene Tucker's manners or the plaid of his mackinaw, for example, makes his account vivid and interesting. Cite several other specific details he gives, and consider how the essay would be different without them.

7. Reread this essay's first and last paragraphs, and compare how much each one emphasizes shame. Which emotion other than shame does Gregory reveal in the first paragraph, and does it play a role in the last one? Is the last paragraph an effective ending? Explain.

VOCABULARY

Refer to your dictionary to define the following words as they are used in this selection. Then use each word in a sentence of your own.

nappy (2)   mackinaw (28)

CLASSROOM ACTIVITY USING BEGINNINGS AND ENDINGS

Gregory uses two startling sentences to grab his reader's attention at the beginning of his essay: "I never learned hate at home, or shame. I had to go to school for that." He then goes on to establish the context for the events that follow. Sometimes it is possible to find an alternate beginning within the essay itself. For example, Gregory could have started his essay with paragraph 4 or with the dialogue starting in paragraph 8. Think about how Gregory's essay would have changed had he used one of these alternate beginnings. What kinds of changes do you think would have had to be made?

SUGGESTED WRITING ASSIGNMENTS

1. Using Gregory's essay as a model, write an essay narrating an experience that made you especially afraid, angry, surprised, embarrassed, or proud. Include sufficient detail so that your readers will know exactly what happened and pay particular attention to how you use your first and last paragraphs to present the emotion your essay focuses on.

2. Most of us grow up with some sense of the socioeconomic class that our family belongs to, and often we are aware of how we are, or believe we are, different from people of other classes. Write an essay in which you describe a possession or activity that you thought revealed your socioeconomic standing and made you self-conscious about how you were different from others. Be sure to recount an experience that seemed to confirm your belief, and discuss why it did. Pay particular attention to your essay's first and last paragraphs so that they serve your purpose.

The Wounds That Can't Be Stitched Up

■ **Ruth Russell**

Ruth Russell was born in Greenfield, Massachusetts, and graduated from Greenfield Community College. When we selected Russell's essay for inclusion in Models for Writers, *we had no idea that she had used the sixth edition as the textbook in her college composition course. Russell said of her experience with* Models, *"The book was tremendously helpful to me in learning to write. I would do a lot of the exercises at the end of the essays, even when they were not assigned, as a way of deconstructing them, of finding out how they were written, what their essential parts were. I was really interested in improving my writing." After writing the following essay for her course, she submitted it to the "My Turn" column in* Newsweek, *where it appeared in December 1999, without much editing by the column's editor, Pam Hammer. "Her suggestions helped to make it a little shorter and stronger," recalls Russell, who feels very proud to have made so much progress with her writing. "At one point I had entitled the piece 'Full Circle,' but I much prefer the present title. I often think how amazing it is that the incident that caused me to write the essay occurred on about the twentieth anniversary of my mother's accident."*

FOR YOUR JOURNAL

Everyone has childhood fears that are often associated with a particular event or experience, fears that can last for years. What particular fear or fears did you have as a child? Were they caused by a specific incident that you can recall? How have they affected your life as a teenager and young adult?

It was a mild December night. Christmas was only two weeks away. 1
The evening sky was overcast, but the roads were dry. All was quiet in our small town as I drove to my grandmother's house.

I heard the sirens first. Red lights and blue lights strobed in tandem. Ambulances with their interiors lit like television screens in a dark room flew by, escorted by police cruisers on the way to the hospital.

When I arrived at my gram's, she was on the porch steps struggling to put on her coat. "Come on," she said breathlessly, "your mother has been in an accident." I was 17 then, and it would take a long time before sirens lost their power to reduce me to tears.

Twenty-three years have passed, but only recently have I realized how deeply affected I was by events caused by a drunk driver so long ago.

When the accident occurred, my youngest brother was 8. He was sitting in the back seat of our family's large, sturdy sedan. The force of the crash sent him flying headlong into the back of the front seat, leaving him with a grossly swollen black eye. He was admitted to the hospital for observation. He didn't talk much when I visited him that night. He just sat in the bed, a lonely little figure in a darkened hospital room.

My sister, who was 12, was sitting in the front seat. She confided to me later how much she missed the beautiful blue coat she'd been wearing at the time. It was an early Christmas present, and it was destroyed beyond repair by the medical personnel who cut it off her body as they worked to save her life. She had a severely fractured skull that required immediate surgery. The resulting facial scar became for our family a permanent reminder of how close she came to dying that night.

My mother was admitted to the intensive-care unit to be stabilized before her multiple facial cuts could be stitched up. Dad tried to prepare me before we went in to see her by telling me that she looked and sounded worse than she was. One eye was temporarily held in place by a bandage wrapped around her head. Her lower lip hideously gaped, exposing a mouthful of broken teeth. Delirious, she cried out for her children and apologized for an accident she neither caused nor could have avoided. An accident that happened when her car was hit head-on by a drunk driver speeding down the wrong side of the road in a half-ton truck with no headlights.

My dad, my brothers, my sister and I spent Christmas at the hospital visiting my mother. Sometimes she was so out of it from medication that she barely recognized us. We celebrated two of my brothers' birthdays—one only days after Christmas and the other in early January—there too.

I remember watching the police escort the drunk driver out of the 9
hospital the night of the accident. He looked about 35 years old, but
his face was so distorted by rage and alcohol that I could only guess.
A bandaged wrist was his only visible injury. He kept repeating that
he'd done nothing wrong as several officers tried to get him into the
cruiser waiting outside the emergency-room exit.

The man was jailed over the weekend and lost his license for 30 10
days for driving while intoxicated. I don't know if that was his first
alcohol-related traffic violation, but I know it wasn't the last. Now
and then I'd see his name in the court log of our local paper for another DWI, and wonder how he could still be behind the wheel.

Sometimes when I tell this story, I'd be asked in an accusatory 11
tone if my mom and siblings were wearing seat belts. I think that's a
lot like asking a rape victim how she was dressed. The answer is no.
This all happened before seat-belt-awareness campaigns began. In
fact, if they had been in a smaller car, seat belts or not, I believe my
mother and sister would have died.

Many local people who know the driver are surprised when they 12
hear about the accident, and they are quick to defend him. They tell
me he was a war hero. His parents aren't well. He's an alcoholic. Or
my favorite: "He's a good guy when he doesn't drink."

Two years ago I discovered this man had moved into my apart- 13
ment building. I felt vaguely apprehensive, but I believed the accident
was ancient history. Nothing could have prepared me for what
happened next.

It was a mild afternoon, just a few days before Christmas. I had 14
started down the back staircase of the building, on my way to visit
my son, when I recognized my neighbor's new pickup truck as it
roared down the street. The driver missed the entrance to our shared
parking lot. He reversed crookedly in the road, slammed the transmission into forward, then quickly pulled into his parking space.
Gravel and sand flew as he stomped on the brakes to halt his truck
just inches from where I stood frozen on the staircase. As he staggered from his vehicle, he looked at me and asked drunkenly, "Did I
scare you?"

QUESTIONS FOR STUDY AND DISCUSSION

1. Russell begins her essay with a somewhat generic description —
   season, weather, road conditions — of the day of her mother's

accident. Why are such details important in her memory? How does her first paragraph work with her title to draw the reader in?

2. Russell provides the reader with an image of her little brother—the least injured of the three in the car—before discussing her sister and mother. What is the image? Why is it an effective introduction to the scene at the hospital?

3. What is Russell's tone in her essay? (Glossary: *Tone*) How does she establish it? Cite specific examples from the text.

4. Russell ironically describes the platitude, "He's a good guy when he doesn't drink," as her "favorite" (12). Why is the statement ironic? (Glossary: *Irony*) Why do you think Russell emphasizes it as her favorite excuse for the man?

5. Russell's ending does not offer a neat conclusion to her situation and makes no concrete statement about her own feelings. Why does she leave the interaction between the drunk driver and herself so open-ended? How does her ending tie in with her purpose for writing the essay? (Glossary: *Purpose*)

VOCABULARY

Refer to your dictionary to define the following words as they are used in the selection. Then use each word in a sentence of your own.

confided (6)   accusatory (11)
gaped (7)   apprehensive (13)
distorted (9)

CLASSROOM ACTIVITY USING BEGINNINGS AND ENDINGS

Choose one of the essays you have been writing for your course, and write at least two different beginnings for it. If you are having trouble coming up with two, check to see whether one of the paragraphs in the body of your essay would be appropriate, or consult the list of effective beginnings in the introduction to this chapter. After you have finished, have several classmates read your beginnings and select their favorite. Do any of your new beginnings suggest ways that you can improve the focus, the organization, or the ending of your essay? Explain these revision possibilities to your partners.

SUGGESTED WRITING ASSIGNMENTS

1. Russell's essay says a lot about how our society reacts to drunk drivers, but she never directly argues a point. Her experiences alone speak to the problem very clearly. Using her essay as a model, write an essay in which you present an indirect argument about a topic that is important to you, using your experiences and observations to lead the reader to the desired conclusion. Construct your beginning and ending with care so that the reader immediately understands how your experiences are relevant to the issue and is left with a strong image or statement that supports your point of view. (Glossary: *Argumentation*)

2. Write a short essay about an ongoing conflict or situation that you are either working to resolve or hoping will be resolved in the near future. For example, you can use a test you are studying for, an up-and-down relationship, or a search for employment. Have a clear purpose in mind regarding how you want the reader to react—with anger, sympathy, amusement, and so on—and craft your essay to accomplish your goal. Pay particular attention to the conclusion, which will be open-ended but should clearly communicate your purpose to the reader.

Unforgettable Miss Bessie

■ **Carl T. Rowan**

In addition to being a popular syndicated newspaper columnist, Carl T. Rowan (1925–2000) was a former ambassador to Finland and director of the U.S. Information Agency. Born in Ravenscroft, Tennessee, he received degrees from Oberlin College and the University of Minnesota. He worked as a columnist for the Minneapolis Tribune *and the* Chicago Sun-Times *before moving to Washington, D.C. In 1996, Washington College awarded Rowan an honorary Doctor of Letters degree in recognition not only of his achievements as a writer, but also for his many contributions to minority youth, most notably through the organization he founded in 1987, Project Excellence. In 1991, Rowan published* Breaking Barriers: A Memoir. *He is also the author of two biographies, one of baseball great Jackie Robinson, the other of former Supreme Court Justice Thurgood Marshall. His last book,* The Coming Race War in America, *appeared in 1996. In the following essay, he describes a high school teacher whose lessons went far beyond the subjects she taught. After reading the details Rowan presents about Miss Bessie's background, behavior, and appearance, determine what kind of dominant impression of Miss Bessie he leaves you with.*

FOR YOUR JOURNAL

Perhaps you have at some time taught a friend or younger brother or sister how to do something—tie a shoe, hit a ball, read, solve a puzzle, drive a car—but you never thought of yourself as a teacher. Did you enjoy the experience of sharing what you know with someone else? Would you consider becoming a teacher someday?

She was only about five feet tall and probably never weighed more 1
than 110 pounds, but Miss Bessie was a towering presence in the classroom. She was the only woman tough enough to make me read *Beowulf* and think for a few foolish days that I liked it. From 1938 to 1942, when I attended Bernard High School in McMinnville, Tenn., she taught me English, history, civics—and a lot more than I realized.

I shall never forget the day she scolded me into reading *Beowulf*.   2

"But Miss Bessie," I complained, "I ain't much interested in it."   3

Her large brown eyes became daggerish slits. "Boy," she said,   4
"how dare you say 'ain't' to me! I've taught you better than that."

"Miss Bessie," I pleaded, "I'm trying to make first-string end on   5
the football team, and if I go around saying 'it isn't' and 'they aren't,'
the guys are gonna laugh me off the squad."

"Boy," she responded, "you'll play football because you have   6
guts. But do you know what *really* takes guts? Refusing to lower
your standards to those of the crowd. It takes guts to say you've got
to live and be somebody fifty years after all the football games are
over."

I started saying "it isn't" and "they aren't," and I still made first-   7
string end—and class valedictorian—without losing my buddies' respect.

During her remarkable 44-year career, Mrs. Bessie Taylor   8
Gwynn taught hundreds of economically deprived black youngsters—including my mother, my brother, my sisters, and me. I remember her now with gratitude and affection—especially in this era
when Americans are so wrought-up about a "rising tide of medioc-
rity" in public education and the problems of finding competent, caring teachers. Miss Bessie was an example of an informed, dedicated
teacher, a blessing to children, and an asset to the nation.

Born in 1895, in poverty, she grew up in Athens, Ala., where   9
there was no public school for blacks. She attended Trinity School, a
private institution for blacks run by the American Missionary Association, and in 1911 graduated from the Normal School (a "super"
high school) at Fisk University in Nashville. Mrs. Gwynn, the essence
of pride and privacy, never talked about her years in Athens; only in
the months before her death did she reveal that she had never attended Fisk University itself because she could not afford the four-
year course.

At Normal School she learned a lot about Shakespeare, but most   10
of all about the profound importance of education—especially, for a
people trying to move up from slavery. "What you put in your head,
boy," she once said, "can never be pulled out by the Ku Klux Klan,[1]
the Congress, or anybody."

---

[1]*Ku Klux Klan:* a secret organization in the United States hostile toward African Americans (eventually other groups as well), founded in 1915 and continuing to the present.
[Eds.]

Miss Bessie's bearing of dignity told anyone who met her that she   11
was "educated" in the best sense of the word. There was never a discipline problem in her classes. We didn't dare mess with a woman
who knew about the Battle of Hastings, the Magna Carta, and the
Bill of Rights—and who could also play the piano.

This frail-looking woman could make sense of Shakespeare,   12
Milton, Voltaire, and bring to life Booker T. Washington and
W. E. B. Du Bois.[2] Believing that it was important to know who the
officials were that spent taxpayers' money and made public policy,
she made us memorize the names of everyone on the Supreme Court
and in the President's Cabinet. It could be embarrassing to be unpre-
pared when Miss Bessie said, "Get up and tell the class who Frances
Perkins[3] is and what you think about her."

Miss Bessie knew that my family, like so many others during the   13
Depression,[4] couldn't afford to subscribe to a newspaper. She knew
we didn't even own a radio. Still, she prodded me to "look out for
your future and find some way to keep up with what's going on in
the world." So I became a delivery boy for the Chattanooga *Times*. I
rarely made a dollar a week, but I got to read a newspaper every day.

Miss Bessie noticed things that had nothing to do with school-   14
work, but were vital to a youngster's development. Once a few classmates made fun of my frayed, hand-me-down overcoat, calling me
"Strings." As I was leaving school, Miss Bessie patted me on the back
of that old overcoat and said, "Carl, never fret about what you *don't*
have. Just make the most of what you *do* have—a brain."

Among the things that I did not have was electricity in the little   15
frame house that my father had built for $400 with his World War I
bonus. But because of her inspiration, I spent many hours squinting
beside a kerosene lamp reading Shakespeare and Thoreau, Samuel
Pepys and William Cullen Bryant.

No one in my family had ever graduated from high school, so   16
there was no tradition of commitment to learning for me to lean on.

---

[2]*W. E. B. Du Bois* (1868–1963): American sociologist, the most important black
protest leader in the United States during the first half of the twentieth century, cofounder of the National Association for the Advancement of Colored People (NAACP)
in 1909. [Eds.]

[3]*Frances Perkins:* the U.S. secretary of labor during the presidency of Franklin D.
Roosevelt and the first woman appointed to a cabinet post. [Eds.]

[4]*Depression:* the longest and most severe economic slump in North America, Europe,
and other industrialized areas of the world, which began in 1929 and ended around
1939. Also called the *Great Depression*. [Eds.]

Like millions of youngsters in today's ghettos and barrios, I needed the push and stimulation of a teacher who truly cared. Miss Bessie gave plenty of both, as she immersed me in a wonderful world of similes, metaphors and even onomatopoeia. She led me to believe that I could write sonnets as well as Shakespeare, or iambic-pentameter verse to put Alexander Pope to shame.

In those days the McMinnville school system was rigidly "Jim Crow,"[5] and poor black children had to struggle to put anything in their heads. Our high school was only slightly larger than the once-typical little red schoolhouse, and its library was outrageously inadequate—so small, I like to say, that if two students were in it and one wanted to turn a page, the other one had to step outside.

Negroes, as we were called then, were not allowed in the town library, except to mop floors or dust tables. But through one of those secret Old South arrangements between whites of conscience and blacks of stature, Miss Bessie kept getting books smuggled out of the white library. That is how she introduced me to the Brontës, Byron, Coleridge, Keats and Tennyson. "If you don't read, you can't write, and if you can't write, you might as well stop dreaming," Miss Bessie once told me.

So I read whatever Miss Bessie told me to, and tried to remember the things she insisted that I store away. Forty-five years later, I can still recite her "truths to live by," such as Henry Wadsworth Longfellow's lines from "The Ladder of St. Augustine":[6]

> The heights by great men reached and kept
> Were not attained by sudden flight.
> But they, while their companions slept,
> Were toiling upward in the night.

Years later, her inspiration, prodding, anger, cajoling, and almost osmotic infusion of learning finally led to that lovely day when Miss Bessie dropped me a note saying, "I'm so proud to read your column in the Nashville *Tennessean*."

Miss Bessie was a spry 80 when I went back to McMinnville and visited her in a senior citizens' apartment building. Pointing out

17

18

19

20

21

---

[5] *"Jim Crow"*: a term referring to the racial segregation laws in the U.S. South between the late 1800s and the mid-1900s. [Eds.]
[6] *Henry Wadsworth Longfellow* (1807–1882): the most popular American poet of the nineteenth century. [Eds.]

proudly that her building was racially integrated, she reached for two glasses and a pint of bourbon. I was momentarily shocked, because it would have been scandalous in the 1930s and '40s for word to get out that a teacher drank, and nobody had ever raised a rumor that Miss Bessie did.

I felt a new sense of equality as she lifted her glass to mine. Then   22
she revealed a softness and compassion that I had never known as a student.

"I've never forgotten that examination day," she said, "when   23
Buster Martin held up seven fingers, obviously asking you for help with question number seven, 'Name a common carrier.' I can still picture you looking at your exam paper and humming a few bars of 'Chattanooga Choo Choo.' I was so tickled, I couldn't punish either of you."

Miss Bessie was telling me, with bourbon-laced grace, that I   24
never fooled her for a moment.

When Miss Bessie died in 1980, at age 85, hundreds of her for-   25
mer students mourned. They knew the measure of a great teacher: love and motivation. Her wisdom and influence had rippled out across generations.

Some of her students who might normally have been doomed to   26
poverty went on to become doctors, dentists, and college professors. Many, guided by Miss Bessie's example, became public-school teachers.

"The memory of Miss Bessie and how she conducted her class-   27
room did more for me than anything I learned in college," recalls Gladys Wood of Knoxville, Tenn., a highly respected English teacher who spent 43 years in the state's school system. "So many times, when I faced a difficult classroom problem, I asked myself, *How would Miss Bessie deal with this?* And I'd remember that she would handle it with laughter and love."

No child can get all the necessary support at home, and millions   28
of poor children get *no* support at all. This is what makes a wise, ed-ucated, warm-hearted teacher like Miss Bessie so vital to the minds, hearts, and souls of this country's children.

QUESTIONS FOR STUDY AND DISCUSSION

1. In his opening paragraph Rowan states that Miss Bessie "taught me English, history, civics—and a lot more than I realized." What did she teach her students beyond the traditional public

school curriculum? Do you think Rowan's first few paragraphs are an effective introduction for this essay? Explain.

2. At what point in the essay does Rowan give us the details of Miss Bessie's background? Why do you suppose he delays giving us this important information?

3. Throughout the essay Rowan offers details of Miss Bessie's physical appearance. (Glossary: *Details*) What specific details does he give, and in what context does he give them? Did Miss Bessie's physical characteristics match the quality of her character? Explain.

4. Does Miss Bessie's drinking influence your opinion of her? Explain. Why do you think Rowan included this part of her behavior in his essay?

5. How does dialogue serve Rowan's purpose? (Glossary: *Dialogue*)

6. How would you sum up the character of Miss Bessie? Make a list of the key words that Rowan uses that you feel best describe her.

VOCABULARY

Refer to your dictionary to define the following words as they are used in this selection. Then use each word in a sentence of your own.

civics (1)   cajoling (20)
barrios (16)   osmotic (20)
conscience (18)   measure (25)

CLASSROOM ACTIVITY USING BEGINNINGS AND ENDINGS

Rowan uses a series of facts about his teacher, the "unforgettable" Miss Bessie, to begin his essay. Pick two from among the seven other methods for beginning essays discussed in the introduction to this chapter, and use each to write alternative openings for Rowan's essay. Share your beginnings with others in the class, and discuss the effectiveness of each.

SUGGESTED WRITING ASSIGNMENTS

1. In paragraph 18, Rowan writes the following: "'If you don't read, you can't write, and if you can't write, you might as well stop dreaming,' Miss Bessie once told me." Write an essay in

which you explore this theme (which, in essence, is also the theme of *Models for Writers*).

2. Think of all the teachers you have had, and write a description of the one who has had the greatest influence on you. Remember to give some consideration to the balance you want to achieve between physical attributes and personality traits. (Glossary: *Description*)

Paragraphs

Within an essay, the **paragraph** is the most important unit of thought. Like the essay, it has its own main idea, often stated directly in a topic sentence. Like a good essay, a good paragraph is unified: It avoids digressions and develops its main idea. Paragraphs use many of the rhetorical strategies that essays use, strategies like classification, comparison and contrast, and cause and effect. As you read the following three paragraphs, notice how each writer develops his or her topic sentence with explanations, concrete details and statistics, or vivid examples. The topic sentence in each paragraph is italicized.

I've learned from experience that good friendships are based on a delicate balance. When friends are on a par, professionally and personally, it's easier for them to root for one another. It's taken me a long time to realize that not all my "friends" wish me well. Someone who wants what you have may not be able to handle your good fortune: If you find yourself apologizing for your hard-earned raise or soft-pedaling your long-awaited promotion, it's a sure sign that the friendship is off balance. Real friends are secure enough in their own lives to share each other's successes—not begrudge them.

–Stephanie Mansfield

The problem of substance abuse is far more complex and far more pervasive than any of us really knows or is willing to admit. *Most stories of illegal drugs overshadow Americans' struggles with alcohol, tobacco, food, and nonprescription drugs—our so-called legal addictions.* In 1990, for example, 14,000 deaths were attributed to cocaine and heroin. In that same year, 390,000 deaths were attributed to tobacco and 90,000 to alcohol. It's not surprising, then, that many sociologists believe we are a nation of substance abusers—drinkers, smokers, overeaters, and pill poppers. Although the statistics are alarming, they do not begin to suggest the heavy toll of substance abuse on Americans and their families. Loved ones die, relationships are fractured, children are abandoned, job productivity falters, and the dreams of young people are extinguished.

–Alfred Rosa and Paul Eschholz

Photographs have let me know my parents before I was born, as the carefree college students they were, in love and awaiting the rest of their lives. I have seen the light blue Volkswagen van my dad used to take surfing down the coast of California and the silver dress my mom wore to her senior prom. Through pictures I was able to witness their wedding, which showed me that there is much in their relationship that goes beyond their children. I saw the look in their eyes as they held their first, newborn daughter, as well as the jealous expressions of my sister when I was born a few years later. There is something almost magical about viewing images of yourself and your family that you were too young to remember.

–Carrie White, student

Many writers find it helpful to think of the paragraph as a very small, compact essay. Here is a paragraph from an essay on testing:

Multiple-choice questions distort the purposes of education. Picking one answer among four is very different from thinking a question through to an answer of one's own, and far less useful in life. Recognition of vocabulary and isolated facts makes the best kind of multiple-choice questions, so these dominate the tests, rather than questions that test the use of knowledge. Because schools want their children to perform well, they are often tempted to teach the limited sorts of knowledge most useful on the tests.

This paragraph, like all well-written paragraphs, has several distinguishing characteristics: It is unified, coherent, and adequately developed. It is unified in that every sentence and every idea relate to the main idea, stated in the topic sentence, "Multiple-choice questions distort the purposes of education." It is coherent in that the sentences and ideas are arranged logically and the relationships among them are made clear by the use of effective transitions. Finally, the paragraph is adequately developed in that it presents a short but persuasive argument supporting its main idea.

How much development is "adequate" development? The answer depends on many things: how complicated or controversial the main idea is; what readers already know and believe; how much space the writer is permitted. Everyone, or nearly everyone, agrees that the earth circles around the sun; a single sentence would be enough to make that point. A writer trying to argue that affirmative action has outlived its usefulness, however, would need many sentences, indeed many paragraphs, to develop that idea convincingly.

Here is another model of an effective paragraph. As you read this paragraph about the resourcefulness of pigeons in evading attempts to control them, pay particular attention to its main idea, unity, development, and coherence.

> Pigeons (and their human friends) have proved remarkably resourceful in evading nearly all the controls, from birth-control pellets to carbide shells to pigeon apartment complexes, that pigeon-haters have devised. One of New York's leading museums once put large black rubber owls on its wide ledges to discourage the large number of pigeons that roosted there. Within the day the pigeons had gotten over their fear of owls and were back perched on the owls' heads. A few years ago San Francisco put a sticky coating on the ledges of some public buildings, but the pigeons got used to the goop and came back to roost. The city then tried trapping, using electric owls, and periodically exploding carbide shells outside a city building, hoping the noise would scare the pigeons away. It did, but not for long, and the program was abandoned. More frequent explosions probably would have distressed the humans in the area more than the birds. Philadelphia tried a feed that makes pigeons vomit, and then, they hoped, go away. A New York firm claimed it had a feed that made a pigeon's nervous system send "danger signals" to the other members of its flock.

The main idea is stated at the beginning in a topic sentence. Other sentences in the paragraph support this idea with examples. Since all the separate examples illustrate how pigeons have evaded attempts to control them, the paragraph is unified. Since there are enough examples to convince the reader of the truth of the topic statement, the paragraph is adequately developed. Finally, the regular use of transitional words and phrases like *once, within the day, a few years ago,* and *then* lends the paragraph coherence.

How long should a paragraph be? In modern essays, most paragraphs range from 50 to 250 words, but some run a full page or more, and others may be only a few words long. The best answer is that a paragraph should be long enough to develop its main idea adequately. Some writers, when they find a paragraph running very long, break it into two or more paragraphs so that readers can pause and catch their breath. Other writers forge ahead, relying on the unity and coherence of their paragraph to keep their readers from getting lost.

Articles and essays that appear in magazines and newspapers often have relatively short paragraphs, some of only one or two sentences. Short paragraphs are a convention in journalism because of the narrow columns, which make paragraphs of average length appear very long. But often you will find that these journalistic "paragraphs" could be joined together into a few longer paragraphs. Longer, adequately developed paragraphs are the kind you should use in all but journalistic writing.

Simplicity

■ **William Zinsser**

William Zinsser was born in New York City in 1922. After graduating from Princeton University, he worked for the New York Herald Tribune, first as a feature writer and later as its drama editor and film critic. During the 1970s he taught writing at Yale University. A former executive editor of the Book-of-the-Month Club, Zinsser has also served on the Usage Panel of the American Heritage Dictionary. Currently, he is the series editor for the Writer's Craft Series, which publishes talks by writers, and teaches writing at the New School University in New York. Zinsser's own published works cover many aspects of contemporary American culture, but he is best known as the author of lucid and accessible books about writing, including Writing to Learn *(1988),* Inventing the Truth: The Art and Craft of Memoir *(1998), with Russell Baker and Jill Ker Conway, and* On Writing Well, *a perennial favorite for college writing courses as well as the general population, published in a twenty-fifth anniversary edition in 2001. In the following piece, he reminds us, as did Henry David Thoreau before him, to "simplify, simplify." As you read each paragraph, notice the clarity with which Zinsser presents its main idea, and observe how he develops that idea with adequate and logically related supporting information. You should also note that he follows his own advice about simplicity.*

FOR YOUR JOURNAL

Sometimes we get so caught up in what's going on around us that we start to feel frantic, and we lose sight of what is really important or meaningful to us. At such times it's a good idea to take stock of what we are doing and to simplify our lives by dropping activities that are no longer rewarding. Write about a time when you've felt the need to simplify your life.

Clutter is the disease of American writing. We are a society strangling in unnecessary words, circular constructions, pompous frills, and meaningless jargon.   1

Who can understand the clotted language of everyday American 2
commerce: the memo, the corporation report, the business letter, the
notice from the bank explaining its latest "simplified" statement?
What member of an insurance or medical plan can decipher the
brochure explaining his costs and benefits? What father or mother
can put together a child's toy from the instructions on the box? Our
national tendency is to inflate and thereby sound important. The airline pilot who announces that he is presently anticipating experiencing
considerable precipitation wouldn't think of saying it may rain. The
sentence is too simple — there must be something wrong with it.

But the secret of good writing is to strip every sentence to its 3
cleanest components. Every word that serves no function, every long
word that could be a short word, every adverb that carries the same
meaning that's already in the verb, every passive construction that
leaves the reader unsure of who is doing what — these are the thousand and one adulterants that weaken the strength of a sentence. And
they usually occur in proportion to education and rank.

During the 1960s the president of my university wrote a letter to 4
mollify the alumni after a spell of campus unrest. "You are probably
aware," he began, "that we have been experiencing very considerable
potentially explosive expressions of dissatisfaction on issues only
partially related." He meant the students had been hassling them
about different things. I was far more upset by the president's English
than by the students' potentially explosive expressions of dissatisfaction. I would have preferred the presidential approach taken by
Franklin D. Roosevelt when he tried to convert into English his own
government's memos, such as this blackout order of 1942:

> Such preparations shall be made as will completely obscure all
> Federal buildings and non-Federal buildings occupied by the Fed-
> eral government during an air raid for any period of time from visi-
> bility by reason of internal or external illumination.

"Tell them," Roosevelt said, "that in buildings where they have 5
to keep the work going to put something across the windows."

Simplify, simplify. Thoreau[1] said it, as we are so often reminded, 6
and no American writer more consistently practiced what he
preached. Open *Walden* to any page and you will find a man saying
in a plain and orderly way what is on his mind:

---

[1]*Henry David Thoreau* (1817–1862): American essayist, poet, and philosopher-
activist. *Walden*, his masterwork, was published in 1854. [Eds.]

> I went to the woods because I wished to live deliberately, to front only the essential facts of life, and see if I could not learn what it had to teach, and not, when I came to die, discover that I had not lived.

How can the rest of us achieve such enviable freedom from clut- 7 ter? The answer is to clear our heads of clutter. Clear thinking becomes clear writing; one can't exist without the other. It's impossible for a muddy thinker to write good English. He may get away with it for a paragraph or two, but soon the reader will be lost, and there's no sin so grave, for the reader will not easily be lured back.

Who is this elusive creature, the reader? The reader is someone 8 with an attention span of about 30 seconds—a person assailed by other forces competing for attention. At one time those forces were relatively few: newspapers, magazines, radio, spouse, children, pets. Today they also include a "home entertainment center" (television, VCR, tapes, CDs), e-mail, the Internet, the cellular phone, the fax machine, a fitness program, a pool, a lawn, and that most potent of competitors, sleep. The man or woman snoozing in a chair with a magazine or a book is a person who was being given too much unnecessary trouble by the writer.

It won't do to say that the reader is too dumb or too lazy to keep 9 pace with the train of thought. If the reader is lost, it's usually because the writer hasn't been careful enough. The carelessness can take any number of forms. Perhaps a sentence is so excessively cluttered that the reader, hacking through the verbiage, simply doesn't know what it means. Perhaps a sentence has been so shoddily constructed that the reader could read it in several ways. Perhaps the writer has switched pronouns in midsentence, or has switched tenses, so the reader loses track of who is talking or when the action took place. Perhaps Sentence B is not a logical sequel to Sentence A; the writer, in whose head the connection is clear, hasn't bothered to provide the missing link. Perhaps the writer has used a word incorrectly by not taking the trouble to look it up. He or she may think "sanguine" and "sanguinary" mean the same thing, but the difference is a bloody big one. The reader can only infer (speaking of big differences) what the writer is trying to imply.

Faced with such obstacles, readers are at first tenacious. They 10 blame themselves—they obviously missed something, and they go back over the mystifying sentence, or over the whole paragraph, piecing it out like an ancient rune, making guesses and moving on. But they won't do this for long. The writer is making them work too hard, and they will look for one who is better at the craft.

Writers must therefore constantly ask: what am I trying to say? 11
Surprisingly often they don't know. Then they must look at what
they have written and ask: have I said it? Is it clear to someone
encountering the subject for the first time? If it's not, some fuzz
has worked its way into the machinery. The clear writer is someone
clearheaded enough to see this stuff for what it is: fuzz.

I don't mean that some people are born clearheaded and are there- 12
fore natural writers, whereas others are naturally fuzzy and will never
write well. Thinking clearly is a conscious act that writers must force
upon themselves, as if they were working on any other project that requires logic: making a shopping list or doing an algebra problem. Good
writing doesn't come naturally, though most people obviously think it
does. Professional writers are constantly bearded by people who say
they'd like to "try a little writing sometime"—meaning when they retire from their real profession, like insurance or real estate, which is
hard. Or they say, "I could write a book about that." I doubt it.

Writing is hard work. A clear sentence is no accident. Very few 13
sentences come out right the first time, or even the third time. Remember this in moments of despair. If you find that writing is hard,
it's because it *is* hard.

QUESTIONS FOR STUDY AND DISCUSSION

1. What exactly does Zinsser mean by "clutter" (1)? How does
   Zinsser believe we can free ourselves of clutter?
2. Identify the main idea in each of Zinsser's thirteen paragraphs.
   How is each paragraph related to Zinsser's topic and purpose?
3. In what ways do paragraphs 4–6 serve to illustrate the main idea
   of paragraph 3? (Glossary: *Illustration*)
4. In paragraph 11, Zinsser says that writers must constantly ask
   themselves some questions. What are these questions, and why
   are they important?
5. How do Zinsser's first and last paragraphs serve to introduce
   and conclude his essay? (Glossary: *Beginnings and Endings*)
6. What is the relationship between thinking and writing for Zinsser?

VOCABULARY

Refer to your dictionary to define the following words as they are
used in this selection. Then use each word in a sentence of your own.

pompous (1)   enviable (7)

decipher (2)   tenacious (10)

adulterants (3)   bearded (12)

mollify (4)

CLASSROOM ACTIVITY USING PARAGRAPHS

Below you will find a passage from Zinsser's final manuscript of this chapter from the first editon of *On Writing Well.* Zinsser has included these manuscript pages showing his editing for clutter in every edition of his book because he believes they are instructive. He says, "Although they look like a first draft, they had already been rewritten and retyped—like almost every other page—four or five times. With each rewrite I try to make what I have written tighter, stronger, and more precise, eliminating every element that's not doing useful work. Then I go over it once more, reading it aloud, and am always amazed at how much clutter can still be cut. (In later editions I eliminated the sexist pronoun 'he' denoting 'the writer' and 'the reader.')"

Carefully study these manuscript pages and Zinsser's editing, and be prepared to discuss how the changes enhance his paragraphs' unity, coherence, and logical development.

is too dumb or too lazy to keep pace with the ~~writer's~~ train of thought. My sympathies are ~~entirely~~ with him. ~~He's not so dumb.~~ If the reader is lost, it is generally because the writer ~~of the article~~ has not been careful enough to keep him on the ~~proper~~ path.

This carelessness can take any number of ~~different~~ forms. Perhaps a sentence is so excessively ~~long and~~ cluttered that the reader, hacking his way through ~~all~~ the verbiage, simply doesn't know what *it* ~~the writer~~ means. Perhaps a sentence has been so shoddily constructed that the reader could read it in any of *several* ~~two or three different~~ ways. ~~He thinks he knows what the writer is trying to say, but he's not sure.~~ Perhaps the

writer has switched pronouns in midsentence, or ~~perhaps he~~
has switched tenses, so the reader loses track of who is
talking ~~to whom~~ or ~~exactly~~ when the action took place. Perhaps Sentence B is not a logical sequel to Sentence A -- the
writer, in whose head the connection is ~~perfectly~~ clear, has
not **bothered to provide** ~~given enough thought to providing~~ the missing link. Perhaps the writer has used an important word incorrectly by not
taking the trouble to look it up, ~~and make sure.~~ He may think
that "sanguine" and "sanguinary" mean the same thing, but)
~~I can assure you that~~ (the difference is a bloody big one ~~to the
reader.~~ **The reader** ~~He~~ can only ~~try to~~ infer ~~xxxx~~ (speaking of big differences) what the writer is trying to imply.

Faced with **these** ~~such a variety of~~ obstacles, the reader
is at first a remarkably tenacious bird. He ~~tends to~~ blame**s**
himself. ~~He~~ **He** obviously missed something, ~~he thinks,~~ and he goes
back over the mystifying sentence, or over the whole paragraph,
piecing it out like an ancient rune, making guesses and moving
on. But he won't do this for long.) ~~He will soon run out of
patience.~~ (The writer is making him work too hard, ~~harder
than he should have to work~~ (and the reader will look for
~~a writer~~ **one** who is better at his craft.

The writer must therefore constantly ask himself: What am
I trying to say? ~~in this sentence?~~ Surprisingly often, he
doesn't know. ~~And~~ Then he must look at what he has ~~just~~
written and ask: Have I said it? Is it clear to someone
encountering ~~who is coming upon~~ the subject for the first time? If it's not,
~~clear,~~ it is because some fuzz has worked its way into the
machinery. The clear writer is a person ~~who is~~ clear-headed
enough to see this stuff for what it is: fuzz.

I don't mean ~~to suggest~~ that some people are born
clear-headed and are therefore natural writers, whereas

others
~~other people~~ are naturally fuzzy and will ~~therefore~~ never write
well. Thinking clearly is a ~~an entirely~~ conscious act that the
force
writer must ~~keep forcing~~ upon himself, just as if he were
embarking   requires
~~starting out~~ on any other ~~kind of~~ project that ~~calls for~~ logic:
adding up a laundry list or doing an algebra problem ~~or playing~~
~~chess.~~ Good writing doesn't ~~just~~ come naturally, though most
it does.
people obviously think ~~it's as easy as walking.~~

SUGGESTED WRITING ASSIGNMENTS

1. If what Zinsser writes about clutter is an accurate assessment, we should easily be able to find numerous examples of
   clutter all around us. During the next few days, make a point
   of looking for clutter in the written materials you come
   across. Choose one example that you find—an article, an
   essay, a form letter, or a section from a textbook, for example—and write an extended analysis explaining how it
   might have been written more simply. Develop your paragraphs well, make sure they are coherent, and try not to
   "clutter" your own writing.

2. Using some of the ideas you explored in your journal entry
   for this selection, write a brief essay analyzing your need to
   simplify some aspect of your life. For example, are you involved in too many extracurricular activities, taking too
   many courses, working too many hours at an off-campus
   job, or not making sensible choices with regard to your social life?

In Praise of the Humble Comma

■ **Pico Iyer**

Pico Iyer is one of the most popular travel writers at work today. "Travel," writes Iyer, "is how we put a face on the Other and step a little beyond our secondhand images of the alien." Born in 1957 to Indian parents, Iyer graduated from Eton, England's most famous preparatory school, and Oxford University. What is particularly noteworthy about Iyer's travel writing is that he crosses ethnic and cultural barriers with an easy and natural style, taking note of both the borders and the essences of the countries he visits. His books include Video Night in Kathmandu and Other Reports from the Not-So-Distant Far East (1989); The Lady and the Monk: Four Seasons in Kyoto (1991); Falling Off the Map: Some Lonely Places of the World (1993); Cuba and the Night: A Novel (1995); Tropical Classical: Essays from Several Directions (1998); The Global Soul: Jet Lag, Shopping Malls, and the Search for Home (2000); *and the novel* Abandon (2003). *In the following essay, which first appeared in* Time *magazine on June 13, 1988, Iyer takes an apparent detour from his travel writing to offer his take on the nuances and importance of the lowly comma, a mark of punctuation we often take for granted. As you read, however, notice the way that he uses his vast cross-cultural travel experience to inform his analysis of the stylistic messages that the comma can convey. Finally, pay particular attention to the way Iyer constructs his paragraphs and the manner in which he progresses from one to the next.*

FOR YOUR JOURNAL

In "Notes on Punctuation" the late Lewis Thomas had this to say about commas:

> The commas are the most useful and usable of all stops. It is highly important to put them in place as you go along. If you try to come back after doing a paragraph and stick them in the

various spots that tempt you you will discover that they tend to swarm like minnows into all sorts of crevices whose existence you hadn't realized before and before you know it the whole long sentence becomes immobilized and lashed up squirming in commas. Better to use them sparingly, and with affection, precisely when the need for each arises, nicely, by itself.

What has been your experience in using commas? Do commas confuse you, or do you know the rules for their use?

The gods, they say, give breath, and they take it away. But the 1 same could be said—could it not?—of the humble comma. Add it to the present clause, and, of a sudden, the mind is, quite literally, given pause to think; take it out if you wish or forget it and the mind is deprived of a resting place. Yet still the comma gets no respect. It seems just a slip of a thing, a pedant's tick, a blip on the edge of our consciousness, a kind of printer's smudge almost. Small, we claim, is beautiful (especially in the age of the microchip). Yet what is so often used, and so rarely recalled, as the comma—unless it be breath itself?

Punctuation, one is taught, has a point: to keep up law and 2 order. Punctuation marks are the road signs placed along the highway of our communications—to control speeds, provide directions and prevent head-on collisions. A period has the unblinking finality of a red light; the comma is a flashing yellow light that asks us only to slow down; and the semicolon is a stop sign that tells us to ease gradually to a halt, before gradually starting up again. By establishing the relations between words, punctuation establishes the relations between people using words. That may be one reason why schoolteachers exalt it and lovers defy it ("We love each other and belong to each other let's don't ever hurt each other Nicole let's don't ever hurt each other," wrote Gary Gilmore[1] to his girlfriend). A comma, he must have known, "separates inseparables," in the clinching words of H. W. Fowler, King of English Usage.

Punctuation, then, is a civic prop, a pillar that holds society upright. (A run-on sentence, its phrases piling up without division, is as unsightly as a sink piled high with dirty dishes.) Small wonder, then, 3

---

[1]*Gary Gilmore:* convicted murderer whose love letters to and from his girlfriend, Nicole, appear in Norman Mailer's nonfiction account of Gilmore's case, *The Executioner's Song* (1979). [Eds.]

that punctuation was one of the first properties of the Victorian age, the age of the corset, that the modernists threw off: the sexual revolution might be said to have begun when Joyce's Molly Bloom spilled out all her private thoughts in 36 pages of unbridled, almost unperioded, and officially censored prose;[2] and another rebellion was surely marked when E. E. Cummings[3] first felt free to commit "God" to the lower case.

Punctuation thus becomes the signature of cultures. The hot-blooded Spaniard seems to be revealed in the passion and urgency of his doubled exclamation points and question marks *("¡Caramba!" "¿Quien sabe?"),* while the impassive Chinese traditionally added to his so-called inscrutability by omitting directions from his ideograms. The anarchy and commotion of the '60s were given voice in the exploding exclamation marks, riotous capital letters and Day-Glo italics of Tom Wolfe's spray-paint prose; and in Communist societies, where the State is absolute, the dignity—and divinity—of capital letters is reserved for Ministries, Subcommittees, and Secretariats.

Yet punctuation is something more than a culture's birthmark; it scores the music in our minds, gets our thoughts moving to the rhythm of our hearts. Punctuation is the notation in the sheet music of our words, telling us where to rest, or when to raise our voices; it acknowledges that the meaning of our discourse as of any symphonic composition, lies not in the units but in the pauses, the pacing, and the phrasing. Punctuation is the way one bats one's eyes, lowers one's voice, or blushes demurely. Punctuation adjusts the tone and color and volume till the feeling comes into perfect focus, not disgust exactly, but distaste; not lust, or like, but love.

Punctuation, in short, gives us the human voice, and all the meanings that lie between the words. "You aren't young, are you?" loses its innocence when it loses the question mark. Every child knows the menace of a dropped apostrophe (the parent's "Don't do that" shifting to the more enunciated "Do not do that"), and every believer, the ignominy of having his faith reduced to "faith." Add an exclamation point to "To be or not to be . . ." and the gloomy Dane[4]

---

[2]In James Joyce's experimental novel *Ulysses* (1922), the character Molly Bloom's stream-of-consciousness thoughts end the novel in what is often considered the longest sentence in the history of English literature. [Eds.]

[3]*E. E. [Edward Estlin] Cummings* (1894–1962): American poet and painter known for his eccentric punctuation and nonstandard use of lowercase letters. [Eds.]

[4]Iyer is referring to the title character's famous speech in William Shakespeare's tragic drama *Hamlet*. [Eds.]

has all the resolve he needs; add a comma, and the noble sobriety of "God save the Queen" becomes a cry of desperation bordering on double sacrilege.

Sometimes, of course, our markings may be simply a matter of aesthetics. Popping in a comma can be like slipping on the necklace that gives an outfit quiet elegance, or like catching the sound of running water that complements, as it completes, the silence of the Japanese landscape. When V. S. Naipaul,[5] in his latest novel, writes, "He was a middle-aged man, with glasses," the first comma can seem a little precious. Yet it gives the description a spin, as well as a subtlety, that it otherwise lacks, and it shows that the glasses are not part of the middle-agedness, but something else.

Thus all these tiny scratches give us breadth and heft and depth. A world that only has periods is a world without inflections. It is a world without shade. It has a music without sharps and flats. It is a martial music. It has a jackboot rhythm. Words cannot bend and curve. A comma, by comparison, catches the gentle drift of the mind in thought, turning in on itself and back on itself, reversing, redoubling and returning along the course of its own sweet river music; while the semicolon brings clauses and thoughts together with all the silent discretion of a hostess arranging guests around her dinner table.

Punctuation, then, is a matter of care. Care for words, yes, but also, and more important, for what the words imply. Only a lover notices the small things: the way the afternoon light catches the nape of the neck, or how a strand of hair slips out from behind an ear, or the way a finger curls around a cup. And no one scans a letter so closely as a lover, searching for its small print, straining to hear its nuances, its gasps, its sighs and hesitation, poring over the secret messages that lie in every cadence. The difference between "Jane (whom I adore)" and "Jane, whom I adore," and the difference between them both and "Jane—whom I adore—" marks all the distance between ecstasy and heartache. "No iron can pierce the heart with such force as a period put at just the right place," in Isaac Babel's lovely words: a comma can let us hear a voice break, or a heart. Punctuation, in fact, is a labor of love. Which brings us back, in a way, to gods.

---

[5]V. S. [Vidiadhar Surajprasad] Naipaul (b. 1932): Trinidadian writer of Indian descent. The sentence is from *A Bend in the River* (1979). [Eds.]

QUESTIONS FOR STUDY AND DISCUSSION

1. Iyer makes a number of statements that might be considered thesis statements. (Glossary: *Thesis*) What are they, and which one do you think is best qualified as an expression of what his essay is all about?

2. Iyer uses commas in his own sentences as a demonstration of not only their conventional uses, but also how they can be used to achieve stylistic effects. Point out several examples, and explain them.

3. In paragraph 4 Iyer writes, "Punctuation thus becomes the signature of cultures." What does he mean by this, and where does he offer evidence to support this idea?

4. How effective are the beginning and ending of Iyer's essay? What is the relationship between them? How do the beginning and ending support Iyer's thesis? (Glossary: *Beginnings and Endings; Thesis*)

5. Choose any two of Iyer's paragraphs, and examine them for paragraph integrity. Ask yourself the following questions about each one. (Consult the glossary for any terms with which you are unfamiliar.)

   Does the paragraph have a clear topic sentence?

   Has the author developed the paragraph clearly and effectively?

   Is the paragraph unified?

   Is the paragraph coherent?

   Has the author used transitions (repeated key words, references to ideas that come before and after, as well as transitional expressions) to link the paragraph to those before and after it? Be prepared to discuss the two paragraphs you examined and to discuss their integrity.

6. Has Iyer made a good case for the importance of the "humble comma"? Why, or why not? If the comma is as significant as he claims, why has it been so unused and misused?

7. Iyer uses a number of figures of speech in his essay. (Glossary: *Figure of Speech*) Point out three or four examples, and explain how effective they are in furthering his observations about the role commas play in writing.

VOCABULARY

Refer to your dictionary to define the following words as they are used in this selection. Then use each word in a sentence of your own.

pedant (1)   sobriety (6)
unbridled (3)   heft (8)
inscrutability (4)   discretion (8)
riotous (4)   imply (9)
demurely (5)   nuances (9)
ignominy (6)   cadence (9)

CLASSROOM ACTIVITY USING PARAGRAPHS

Rearrange the following sentences to create an effective paragraph. Be ready to explain why you chose the order that you did.

1. PGA golfer Fred Divot leaned the hard way what overtraining could do.

2. Divot's case is typical, and most researchers believe that too much repetition makes it difficult for the athlete to reduce left-hemisphere brain activity.

3. Athletes who overtrain find it very difficult to get in the flow.

4. "Two weeks later, all I could think about was mechanics, and I couldn't hit a fairway to save my life!"

5. Athletes think about mechanics (left hemisphere) rather than feel (right hemisphere), and they lose the ability to achieve peak performance.

6. "I was playing well, so I thought with a bit more practice, I could start winning on tour," Divot recalled.

SUGGESTED WRITING ASSIGNMENTS

1. Iyer has focused his essay on the "humble comma." Write an essay in which you explore some other mark of punctuation, such as the colon or semicolon. Following in Iyer's footsteps, try to use the mark(s) of punctuation you discuss to demonstrate the points you make. Make sure that you carefully develop the content of each paragraph to support its topic sentence. Check that

you have used transitions within each paragraph and between paragraphs to enhance the flow of ideas throughout the essay.

2. Write an essay in which you explore what might be said about the importance of the paragraph as a compositional building block. To what extent can it be a mini-essay in itself? To what extent might it be some other structural device within an essay? What, for example, is a transitional paragraph or group of short related paragraphs? Research in the library or on the Internet to learn about the paragraph, its history, and its purpose as both a thematic and structural device in composition.

"I Just Wanna Be Average"

■ **Mike Rose**

Born in Altoona, Pennsylvania, to Italian American parents, Mike Rose moved to California in the early 1950s. A graduate of Loyola University in Los Angeles, Rose is now a professor at the UCLA Graduate School of Education and Information Studies. He has written a number of books and articles on language and literacy. His best-known book, Lives on the Boundary: The Struggles and Achievements of America's Underprepared, *was recognized by the National Council of Teachers of English with its highest award in 1989. More recently he published* Possible Lives: The Promise of Public Education *(1995). His next book will focus on the relationships between knowledge and perception, skill, and personal identity. In the following selection from* Lives on the Boundary, *Rose explains how his high school English teacher, Jack MacFarland, picked him up out of the doldrums of "scholastic indifference." As you read, notice that although his paragraphs are fairly lengthy, Rose never digresses from the main point of each.*

FOR YOUR JOURNAL

Often our desire to get more out of high school and to go on to college can be traced back to the influence of a single teacher. Which teacher turned you on to learning? Describe what that person did to stimulate change in you.

Jack MacFarland couldn't have come into my life at a better time. 1 My father was dead, and I had logged up too many years of scholastic indifference. Mr. MacFarland had a master's degree from Columbia and decided, at twenty-six, to find a little school and teach his heart out. He never took any credentialing courses, couldn't bear to, he said, so he had to find employment in a private system. He ended up at Our Lady of Mercy teaching five sections of senior English. He was a beatnik who was born too late. His teeth were stained, he tucked his sorry tie in between the third and fourth buttons of his shirt, and his pants were chronically wrinkled. At first, we couldn't believe this guy, thought he slept in his car. But within no time, he had us so startled with work that we didn't much worry about where he slept or if he slept at all. We wrote three or four essays a month. We read a book every two to three weeks, starting with the *Iliad*[1] and ending up with Hemingway. He gave us a quiz on the reading every other day. He brought a prep school curriculum to Mercy High.

MacFarland's lectures were crafted, and as he delivered them he would pace the room jiggling a piece of chalk in his cupped hand, using it to scribble on the board the names of all the writers and philosophers and plays and novels he was weaving into his discussion. He asked questions often, raised everything from Zeno's paradox[2] to the repeated last line of Frost's "Stopping by Woods on a Snowy Evening." He slowly and carefully built up our knowledge of Western intellectual history—with facts, with connections, with speculations. We learned about Greek philosophy, about Dante, the Elizabethan world view, the Age of Reason, existentialism. He analyzed poems with us, had us reading sections from John Ciardi's *How Does a Poem Mean?*, making a potentially difficult book accessible with his own explanations. We gave oral reports on poems Ciardi didn't cover. We imitated the styles of Conrad,[3] Hemingway, and *Time* magazine. We wrote and talked, wrote and talked. The man immersed us in language.

Even MacFarland's barbs were literary. If Jim Fitzsimmons, hung over and irritable, tried to smart-ass him, he'd rejoin with a flourish that would spark the indomitable Skip Madison—who'd lost his front teeth in a hapless tackle—to flick his tongue through the gap and opine, "good chop," drawing out the single "o" in stinging indictment. Jack MacFarland, this tobacco-stained intellectual, brandished linguistic weapons of a kind I hadn't encountered before. Here was this *egghead*, for God's sake, keeping some pretty difficult people in line. And from what I heard, Mike Dweetz and Steve Fusco and all the notorious Voc. Ed. crowd settled down as well when MacFarland took the podium. Though a lot of guys groused in the schoolyard, it just seemed that giving trouble to this particular teacher was a silly thing to do. Tomfoolery, not to mention assault, had no place in the world he was trying to create for us, and instinctively everyone knew

---

[1]*Iliad:* an ancient Greek epic poem attributed to Homer. [Eds.]
[2]*Zeno's paradox:* statements describing a paradox made by the Greek philosopher Zeno of Elea (fifth century B.C.E.). [Eds.]
[3]*Joseph Conrad* (1857–1924): English novelist and short story writer. [Eds.]

that. If nothing else, we all recognized MacFarland's considerable intelligence and respected the hours he put into his work. It came to this: The troublemaker would look foolish rather than daring. Even Jim Fitzsimmons was reading *On the Road*[4] and turning his incipient alcoholism to literary ends.

There were some lives that were already beyond Jack MacFarland's ministrations, but mine was not. I started reading again as I hadn't since elementary school. I would go into our gloomy little bedroom or sit at the dinner table while, on the television, Danny McShane was paralyzing Mr. Moto with the atomic drop, and work slowly back through *Heart of Darkness,* trying to catch the words in Conrad's sentences. I certainly was not MacFarland's best student; most of the other guys in College Prep, even my fellow slackers, had better backgrounds than I did. But I worked very hard, for MacFarland had hooked me. He tapped my old interest in reading and creating stories. He gave me a way to feel special by using my mind. And he provided a role model that wasn't shaped on physical prowess alone, and something inside me that I wasn't quite aware of responded to that. Jack MacFarland established a literacy club, to borrow a phrase of Frank Smith's, and invited me—invited all of us—to join.

There's been a good deal of research and speculation suggesting   5
that the acknowledgment of school performance with extrinsic rewards—smiling faces, stars, numbers, grades—diminishes the intrinsic satisfaction children experience by engaging in reading or writing or problem solving. While it's certainly true that we've created an educational system that encourages our best and brightest to become cynical grade collectors and, in general, have developed an obsession with evaluation and assessment, I must tell you that venal though it may have been, I loved getting good grades from MacFarland. I now know how subjective grades can be, but then they came tucked in the back of essays like bits of scientific data, some sort of spectroscopic readout that said, objectively and publicly, that I had made something of value. I suppose I'd been mediocre for too long and enjoyed a public redefinition. And I suppose the workings of my mind, such as they were, had been private for too long. My linguistic play moved into the world; like the intergalactic stories I told years before on Frank's berry-splattered truck bed, these papers with their circled, red

4

---

[4]*On the Road:* a 1957 novel by American writer Jack Kerouac (1922–1969). [Eds.]

B-pluses and A-minuses linked my mind to something outside it. I carried them around like a club emblem.

One day in the December of my senior year, Mr. MacFarland 6 asked me where I was going to go to college. I hadn't thought much about it. Many of the students I teach today spent their last year in high school with a physics text in one hand and the Stanford catalog in the other, but I wasn't even aware of what "entrance requirements" were. My folks would say that they wanted me to go to college and be a doctor, but I don't know how seriously I ever took that; it seemed a sweet thing to say, a bit of supportive family chatter, like telling a gangly daughter she's graceful. The reality of higher education wasn't in my scheme of things: No one in the family had gone to college; only two of my uncles had completed high school. I figured I'd get a night job and go to the local junior college because I knew that Snyder and Company were going there to play ball. But I hadn't even prepared for that. When I finally said, "I don't know," MacFarland looked down at me—I was seated in his office—and said, "Listen, you can write."

My grades stank. I had A's in biology and a handful of B's in a 7 few English and social science classes. All the rest were C's—or worse. MacFarland said I would do well in his class and laid down the law about doing well in the others. Still, the record for my first three years wouldn't have been acceptable to any four-year school. To nobody's surprise, I was turned down flat by USC and UCLA. But Jack MacFarland was on the case. He had received his bachelor's degree from Loyola University, so he made calls to old professors and talked to somebody in admissions and wrote me a strong letter. Loyola finally accepted me as a probationary student. I would be on trial for the first year, and if I did okay, I would be granted regular status. MacFarland also intervened to get me a loan, for I could never have afforded a private college without it. Four more years of religion classes and four more years of boys at one school, girls at another. But at least I was going to college. Amazing.

QUESTIONS FOR STUDY AND DISCUSSION

1. Why do you think Rose chose the title "I Just Wanna Be Average"? (Glossary: *Title*) How does it relate to the essay?
2. Describe Jack MacFarland. How does his appearance contrast with his ability as a teacher?

3. Rose's paragraphs are long and full of information, but they are very coherent. Summarize the topic of each of the seven paragraphs in separate sentences.

4. How has Rose organized paragraph 2? How does Rose prepare the reader for the concluding sentence: "The man [MacFarland] immersed us in language"?

5. Analyze the transitions between paragraphs 2 and 3 and between 3 and 4. (Glossary: *Transition*) What techniques does Rose use to smoothly introduce the reader to different aspects of his relationship with Jack MacFarland?

6. Rose introduces the reader to some of his classmates, quickly establishes their personalities, and names them in full: Jim Fitzsimmons, Skip Madison, Mike Dweetz. Why does he do this? How does it help him describe MacFarland?

7. Why does Rose have difficulty getting into college? How does he finally make it?

VOCABULARY

Refer to your dictionary to define the following words as they are used in this selection. Then use each word in a sentence of your own.

beatnik (1)	linguistic (3)
curriculum (1)	incipient (3)
paradox (2)	ministrations (4)
existentialism (2)	extrinsic (5)
rejoin (3)	spectroscopic (5)
indomitable (3)	gangly (6)

CLASSROOM ACTIVITY USING PARAGRAPHS

Write a unified, coherent, and adequately developed paragraph using one of the following topic sentences. Be sure to select details that clearly demonstrate or support the general statement you chose. In a classroom discussion students should compare and discuss those paragraphs developed from the same topic sentences as a way to understand the potential for variety in developing a topic sentence.

1. It was the noisiest place I had ever visited.

2. I was terribly frightened.

3. Signs of the sanitation strike were evident everywhere.

4. It was the best meal I've ever eaten.

5. Even though we lost, our team earned an "A" for effort.

SUGGESTED WRITING ASSIGNMENTS

1. Pick a good teacher whom you have had, and describe how he or she influenced your life. Write an essay about the teacher using Rose's essay as a model. Make sure that each paragraph accomplishes a specific purpose and that each is coherent enough to be readily summarized.

2. Write an essay about the process you went through to get into college. Did you visit different schools? Did a parent or relative pressure you to go? Had you always wanted to go to college, or did you make the decision in high school, like Rose, or after high school? Did a particular teacher help you? Make sure that you develop your paragraphs fully and that you have effective transitions between paragraphs.

chapter 8

Transitions

Transitions are words and phrases that are used to signal the relationships among ideas in an essay and to join the various parts of an essay together. Writers use transitions to relate ideas within sentences, between sentences, and between paragraphs. Perhaps the most common type of transition is the so-called transitional expression. Following is a list of transitional expressions categorized according to their functions.

ADDITION: and, again, too, also, in addition, further, furthermore, moreover, besides

CAUSE AND EFFECT: therefore, consequently, thus, accordingly, as a result, hence, then, so

COMPARISON: similarly, likewise, by comparison

CONCESSION: to be sure, granted, of course, it is true, to tell the truth, certainly, with the exception of, although this may be true, even though, naturally

CONTRAST: but, however, in contrast, on the contrary, on the other hand, yet, nevertheless, after all, in spite of

EXAMPLE: for example, for instance

PLACE: elsewhere, here, above, below, farther on, there, beyond, nearby, opposite to, around

RESTATEMENT: that is, as I have said, in other words, in simpler terms, to put it differently, simply stated

SEQUENCE: first, second, third, next, finally

SUMMARY: in conclusion, to conclude, to summarize, in brief, in short

TIME: afterward, later, earlier, subsequently, at the same time, simultaneously, immediately, this time, until now, before, meanwhile, shortly, soon, currently, when, lately, in the meantime, formerly

Besides transitional expressions, there are two other important ways to make transitions: by using pronoun references and by repeating key words, phrases, and ideas. This paragraph begins with the phrase "Besides transitional expressions": The phrase contains the transitional word *besides* and also repeats earlier wording. Thus the reader knows that this discussion is moving toward a new but related idea. Repetition can also give a word or idea emphasis: "Foreigners look to America as a land of freedom. Freedom, however, is not something all Americans enjoy."

Pronoun references avoid monotonous repetition of nouns and phrases. Without pronouns, these two sentences are wordy and tiring to read: "Jim went to the concert, where he heard Beethoven's Ninth Symphony. Afterward, Jim bought a recording of the Ninth Symphony." A more graceful and readable passage results if two pronouns are substituted in the second sentence: "Afterward, he bought a recording of it." The second version has another advantage in that it is now more tightly related to the first sentence. The transition between the two sentences is smoother.

In the following example, notice how Rachel Carson uses transitional expressions, repetition of words and ideas, and pronoun references:

Under primitive agricultural conditions the farmer had few insect problems. *These* arose with the intensification of agriculture—the devotion of immense acreages to a single crop. *Such a system* set the stage for explosive increases in specific insect populations. Single-crop farming does not take advantage of the principles by which nature works; *it* is agriculture as an engineer might conceive it to be. Nature has introduced great variety into the landscape, but man has displayed a passion for simplifying *it*. *Thus he* undoes the built-in checks and balances by which nature holds the species within bounds. One important natural *check* is a limit on the amount of suitable habitat for each species. *Obviously then,* an insect that lives on wheat can build up its population to much higher levels on a farm devoted to wheat than on one in which wheat is intermingled with other crops to which the insect is not adapted.

The same thing happens in other situations. A generation or more ago, the towns of large areas of

[margin annotations: pronoun reference; repeated key idea; pronoun reference; transitional expression; pronoun reference; transitional expression; repeated key word; repeated key idea]

the United States lined their streets with the noble elm tree. *Now* the beauty *they* hopefully created is threatened with complete destruction as disease sweeps through the elms, carried by a beetle that would have only limited chance to build up large populations and to spread from tree to tree if the elms were only occasional trees in a richly diversified planting.

transitional expression; pronoun reference

–Rachel Carson

Carson's transitions in this passage enhance its **coherence**—that quality of good writing that results when all sentences and paragraphs of an essay are effectively and naturally connected.

In the following four-paragraph sequence about a vegetarian's ordeal with her family at Thanksgiving each year, the writer uses transitions effectively to link one paragraph to another.

The holiday that I dread the most is fast approaching. The relatives will gather to gossip and bicker, the house will be filled with the smells of turkey, onions, giblets, and allspice, and I will be pursuing trivial conversations in the hope of avoiding any commentaries upon the state of my plate.

reference to key idea in previous paragraph

Do not misunderstand me: I am not a scrooge. I enjoy the idea of Thanksgiving—the giving of thanks for blessings received in the past year and the opportunity to share an unhurried day with family and friends. The problem for me is that I am one of those freaky, misunderstood people who—as my family jokingly reminds me—eats "rabbit food." Because all traditional Western holidays revolve around food and more specifically around ham, turkey, lamb, or roast beef and their respective starchy accompaniments, it is no picnic for us vegetarians.

repeated key word

The mention of the word *vegetarian* has, at various family get-togethers, caused my Great-Aunt Bertha to rant and rave for what seems like hours about those "liberal conspirators." Other relations cough or groan or simply stare, change the subject or reminisce about somebody they used to know who was "into that," and some proceed either to demand that I defend my position or try to talk me out of it. That is why I try to avoid the subject, but especially during the holidays.

transitional time reference

In years past I have had about as many *successes as failures in steering comments about my food toward other topics.* Politics and religion are the easiest outs, guaranteed to immerse the family in a heated debate lasting until the loudest shouter has been abandoned amidst empty pie plates, wine corks, and rumpled linen napkins. I prefer, however, to use this tactic as a last resort. Holidays are supposed to be for relaxing.

repeated key idea

–Mundy Wilson-Libby, student

How I Got Smart

■ **Steve Brody**

Steve Brody is a retired high school English teacher who enjoys writing about the lighter side of teaching. He was born in Chicago in 1915 and received his bachelor's degree in English from Columbia University. In addition to his articles in educational publications, Brody has published many newspaper articles on travel and a humorous book about golf, How to Break Ninety before You Reach It *(1979). As you read his account of how love made him smart, an essay that first appeared in the* New York Times *in September 1986, notice the way he uses transitional words and expressions to unify his work and to make it a seamless whole.*

FOR YOUR JOURNAL

Motivation is a difficult topic about which to generalize. What motivates one person to act often will not work on another person. How do you get motivated to work, to join extracurricular activities, or to take care of yourself? Are you able to motivate yourself, or do you need to have someone else give you a push?

A common misconception among youngsters attending school is   1
that their teachers were child prodigies. Who else but a bookworm, prowling the libraries and disdaining the normal youngster's propensity for play rather than study, would grow up to be a teacher anyway?

I tried desperately to explain to my students that the image they   2
had of me as an ardent devotee of books and homework during my adolescence was a bit out of focus. Au contraire! I hated compulsory education with a passion. I could never quite accept the notion of having to go to school while the fish were biting.

Consequently, my grades were somewhat bearish. That's how my   3
father, who dabbled in the stock market, described them. Presenting my report card for my father to sign was like serving him a subpoena. At midterm and other sensitive periods, my father kept a low profile.

But in my sophomore year, something beautiful and exciting 4
happened. Cupid aimed his arrow and struck me squarely in the
heart. All at once, I enjoyed going to school, if only to gaze at the
lovely face beneath the raven tresses in English II. My princess sat
near the pencil sharpener, and that year I ground up enough pencils
to fuel a campfire.

Alas, Debbie was far beyond my wildest dreams. We were sepa- 5
rated not only by five rows of desks, but by about 50 I.Q. points. She
was the top student in English II, the apple of Mrs. Larrivee's eye. I
envisioned how eagerly Debbie's father awaited her report card.

Occasionally, Debbie would catch me staring at her, and she 6
would flash a smile — an angelic smile that radiated enlighten-
ment and quickened my heartbeat. It was a smile that signaled hope
and made me temporarily forget the intellectual gulf that sepa-
rated us.

I schemed desperately to bridge that gulf. And one day, as I was 7
passing the supermarket, an idea came to me.

A sign in the window announced that the store was offering the 8
first volume of a set of encyclopedias at the introductory price of 29
cents. The remaining volumes would cost $2.49 each, but it was no
time to be cynical.

I purchased Volume I — Aardvark to Asteroid — and began my 9
venture into the world of knowledge. I would henceforth become a
seeker of facts. I would become chief egghead in English II and sweep
the princess off her feet with a surge of erudition. I had it all planned.

My first opportunity came one day in the cafeteria line. I looked 10
behind me and there she was.

"Hi," she said. 11

After a pause, I wet my lips and said, "Know where anchovies 12
come from?"

She seemed surprised. "No, I don't." 13

I breathed a sigh of relief. "The anchovy lives in salt water and is 14
rarely found in fresh water." I had to talk fast, so that I could get all
the facts in before we reached the cash register. "Fishermen catch anchovies in the Mediterranean Sea and along the Atlantic coast near
Spain and Portugal."

"How fascinating," said Debbie. 15

"The anchovy is closely related to the herring. It is thin and sil- 16
very in color. It has a long snout and a very large mouth."

"Incredible." 17

"Anchovies are good in salads, mixed with eggs, and are often 18
used as appetizers before dinner, but they are salty and cannot be di-
gested too rapidly."

Debbie shook her head in disbelief. It was obvious that I had 19
made quite an impression.

A few days later, during a fire drill, I sidled up to her and asked, 20
"Ever been to the Aleutian Islands?"

"Never have," she replied. 21

"Might be a nice place to visit, but I certainly wouldn't want to 22
live there," I said.

"Why not?" said Debbie, playing right into my hands. 23

"Well, the climate is forbidding. There are no trees on any of the 24
100 or more islands in the group. The ground is rocky and very little
plant life can grow on it."

"I don't think I'd even care to visit," she said. 25

The fire drill was over and we began to file into the building, so I 26
had to step it up to get the natives in. "The Aleuts are short and
sturdy and have dark skin and black hair. They subsist on fish, and
they trap blue fox, seal, and otter for their valuable fur."

Debbie's hazel eyes widened in amazement. She was undoubtedly 27
beginning to realize that she wasn't dealing with an ordinary
lunkhead. She was gaining new and valuable insights instead of engaging in the routine small talk one would expect from most sopho-
mores.

Luck was on my side, too. One day I was browsing through the 28
library during my study period. I spotted Debbie sitting at a table, absorbed in a crossword puzzle. She was frowning, apparently stumped
on a word. I leaned over and asked if I could help.

"Four-letter word for Oriental female servant," Debbie said. 29

"Try *amah*," I said, quick as a flash. 30

Debbie filled in the blanks, then turned to stare at me in amazement. 31
"I don't believe it," she said. "I just don't believe it."

And so it went, that glorious, amorous, joyous sophomore year. 32
Debbie seemed to relish our little conversations and hung on my
every word. Naturally, the more I read, the more my confidence
grew. I expatiated freely on such topics as adenoids, air brakes, and
arthritis.

In the classroom, too, I was gradually making my presence felt. 33
Among my classmates, I was developing a reputation as a wheeler-dealer
in data. One day, during a discussion of Coleridge's "The Ancient
Mariner," we came across the word *albatross*.

"Can anyone tell us what an albatross is?" asked Mrs. Larrivee.   34
My hand shot up. "The albatross is a large bird that lives mostly   35
in the ocean regions below the equator, but may be found in the
north Pacific as well. The albatross measures as long as four feet and
has the greatest wingspread of any bird. It feeds on the surface of the
ocean, where it catches shellfish. The albatross is a very voracious
eater. When it is full it has trouble getting into the air again."

There was a long silence in the room. Mrs. Larrivee couldn't   36
quite believe what she had just heard. I sneaked a peek at Debbie and
gave her a big wink. She beamed proudly and winked back.

It was a great feeling, having Debbie and Mrs. Larrivee and my   37
peers according me respect and paying attention when I spoke.

My grades edged upward and my father no longer tried to avoid me   38
when I brought home my report card. I continued reading the
encyclopedia diligently, packing more and more into my brain.

What I failed to perceive was that Debbie all this while was going   39
steady with a junior from a neighboring school—a hockey player
with a C+ average. The revelation hit me hard, and for a while I felt
like disgorging and forgetting everything I had learned. I had saved
enough money to buy Volume II—Asthma to Bullfinch—but was
strongly tempted to invest in a hockey stick instead.

How could she lead me on like that—smiling and concurring   40
and giving me the impression that I was important?

I felt not only hurt, but betrayed. Like Agamemnon, but with less   41
dire consequences, thank God.

In time I recovered from my wounds. The next year Debbie   42
moved from the neighborhood and transferred to another school.
Soon she became no more than a fleeting memory.

Although the original incentive was gone, I continued poring   43
over the encyclopedias, as well as an increasing number of other
books. Having savored the heady wine of knowledge, I could not
now alter my course. For:

"A little knowledge is a dangerous thing:
   Drink deep, or taste not the Pierian spring."

So wrote Alexander Pope, Volume XIV, Paprika to Pterodactyl.   44

QUESTIONS FOR STUDY AND DISCUSSION

1. How are paragraphs 2 and 3, 3 and 4, 5 and 6, 31 and 32, and
   43 and 44 linked?

2. Brody uses dialogue to tell his story in paragraphs 10–35. (Glossary: *Dialogue*) What does the dialogue add to his story? What would have been lost had he simply told his readers what happened?

3. Why didn't Brody stop reading the encyclopedia when he discovered that Debbie had a steady boyfriend?

4. If you find Brody's narrative humorous, try to explain the sources of his humor. For example, what humor resides in the choice of examples Brody uses?

5. Brody refers to Coleridge's "The Ancient Mariner" in paragraph 33 and to Agamemnon in paragraph 41, and he quotes Alexander Pope in paragraph 43. Use an encyclopedia to explain Brody's allusions. (Glossary: *Allusion*)

6. Comment on the effectiveness of the beginning and ending of Brody's essay. (Glossary: *Beginnings and Endings*)

VOCABULARY

Refer to your dictionary to define the following words as they are used in this selection. Then use each word in a sentence of your own.

misconception (1)	forbidding (24)
prodigies (1)	subsist (26)
devotee (2)	amorous (32)
bearish (3)	expatiated (32)
dabbled (3)	adenoids (32)
surge (9)	voracious (35)
erudition (9)	disgorging (39)
snout (16)	savored (43)
sidled (20)	

CLASSROOM ACTIVITY USING TRANSITIONS

In *The New York Times Complete Manual of Home Repair*, Bernard Gladstone gives directions for applying blacktop sealer to a driveway. His directions appear below in scrambled order. First read all of Gladstone's sentences carefully. Next, arrange the sentences in what seems to you to be the logical sequence. Finally, identify places where

Gladstone has used transitional expressions, the repetition of words and ideas, and pronoun reference to give coherence to his paragraph.

1. A long-handled pushbroom or roofing brush is used to spread the coating evenly over the entire area.
2. Care should be taken to make certain the entire surface is uniformly wet, though puddles should be swept away if water collects in low spots.
3. Greasy areas and oil slicks should be scraped up, then scrubbed thoroughly with a detergent solution.
4. With most brands there are just three steps to follow.
5. In most cases one coat of sealer will be sufficient.
6. The application of blacktop sealer is best done on a day when the weather is dry and warm, preferably while the sun is shining on the surface.
7. This should not be applied until the first coat is completely dry.
8. First sweep the surface absolutely clean to remove all dust, dirt, and foreign material.
9. To simplify spreading and to assure a good bond, the surface of the driveway should be wet down thoroughly by sprinkling with a hose.
10. However, for surfaces in poor condition a second coat may be required.
11. The blacktop sealer is next stirred thoroughly and poured on while the surface is still damp.
12. The sealer should be allowed to dry overnight (or longer if recommended by the manufacturer) before normal traffic is resumed.

SUGGESTED WRITING ASSIGNMENTS

1. One serious thought that arises as a result of reading Brody's essay is that perhaps we learn best when we are sufficiently motivated to do so. And once we are motivated, the desire to learn seems to feed on itself: "Having savored the heady wine of knowledge, I could not now alter my course" (43). Write an essay in which you explore this subject using your own experiences.

2. Relationships can influence our lives either positively or negatively. Even the appearance of a relationship can have an effect, as we saw in Brody's infatuation with Debbie during his sophomore year in high school. By trying to impress Debbie with his knowledge, Brody got hooked on learning and chose a career in education. Write a brief essay in which you explore the effects that a relationship has had on your life.

Becoming a Writer

■ Russell Baker

Russell Baker has had a long and distinguished career as a newspaper reporter and columnist. He was born in Virginia and attended Johns Hopkins University. In 1947, he got his first newspaper job with the Baltimore Sun, *then moved to the* New York Times *in 1954, where he wrote the "Observer" column from 1962 to 1998. His columns have been collected in numerous books over the years. In 1979, he was awarded the Pulitzer Prize, journalism's highest award, as well as the George Polk Award for commentary. Baker's memoir,* Growing Up, *also received a Pulitzer in 1983. His autobiographical follow-up,* The Good Times, *appeared in 1989. His other works include* Russell Baker's Book of American Humor *(1993),* Inventing the Truth: The Art and Craft of Memoir, *with William Zinsser and Jill Ker Conway (revised in 1998), and* Looking Back *(2002), a collection of Baker's essays for the* New York Review of Books. *Since 1992 he has been hosting the distinguished PBS television series* ExxonMobil Masterpiece Theater. *Another essay by Baker appears on pages 427–29. As you read Baker's account of how he discovered his abilities as a writer, note how effectively he uses repetition of key words and ideas to achieve coherence and to emphasize his emotional responses to the events he describes.*

FOR YOUR JOURNAL

Life is full of moments that change us, for better or worse, in major and minor ways. We decide what hobbies we like and dislike, whom we want to date and perhaps eventually marry, what we want to study in school, what career we eventually pursue. Identify an event that changed your life or helped you make an important decision. How did it clarify your situation? How might your life be different if the event had never happened?

The notion of becoming a writer had flickered off and on in my   1
head . . . but it wasn't until my third year in high school that
the possibility took hold. Until then I'd been bored by everything

associated with English courses. I found English grammar dull and baffling. I hated the assignments to turn out "compositions," and went at them like heavy labor, turning out laden, lackluster paragraphs that were agonies for teachers to read and for me to write. The classics thrust on me to read seemed as deadening as chloroform.

When our class was assigned to Mr. Fleagle for third-year English I anticipated another grim year in that dreariest of subjects. Mr. Fleagle was notorious among City students for dullness and inability to inspire. He was said to be stuffy, dull, and hopelessly out of date. To me he looked to be sixty or seventy and prim to a fault. He wore primly severe eyeglasses, his wavy hair was primly cut and primly combed. He wore prim vested suits with neckties blocked primly against the collar buttons of his primly starched white shirts. He had a primly pointed jaw, a primly straight nose, and a prim manner of speaking that was so correct, so gentlemanly, that he seemed a comic antique.

I anticipated a listless, unfruitful year with Mr. Fleagle and for a long time was not disappointed. We read *Macbeth*. Mr. Fleagle loved *Macbeth* and wanted us to love it too, but he lacked the gift of infecting others with his own passion. He tried to convey the murderous ferocity of Lady Macbeth one day by reading aloud the passage that concludes

> . . . I have given suck, and know
> How tender 'tis to love the babe that milks me.
> I would, while it was smiling in my face,
> Have plucked my nipple from his boneless gums . . .

The idea of prim Mr. Fleagle plucking his nipple from boneless gums was too much for the class. We burst into gasps of irrepressible snickering. Mr. Fleagle stopped.

"There is nothing funny, boys, about giving suck to a babe. It is the—the very essence of motherhood, don't you see."

He constantly sprinkled his sentences with "don't you see." It wasn't a question but an exclamation of mild surprise at our ignorance. "Your pronoun needs an antecedent, don't you see," he would say, very primly. "The purpose of the Porter's scene, boys, is to provide comic relief from the horror, don't you see."

Late in the year we tackled the informal essay. "The essay, don't you see, is the . . ." My mind went numb. Of all forms of writing, none seemed so boring as the essay. Naturally we would have to write informal essays. Mr. Fleagle distributed a homework sheet offering us a choice of topics. None was quite so simpleminded as "What I Did on My Summer Vacation," but most seemed to be almost as dull. I took the list home and dawdled until the night before the essay was due. Sprawled on the sofa, I finally faced up to the grim task, took the list out of my notebook, and scanned it. The topic on which my eye stopped was "The Art of Eating Spaghetti."

This title produced an extraordinary sequence of mental images.   7
Surging up from the depths of memory came a vivid recollection of a night in Belleville when all of us were seated around the supper table—Uncle Allen, my mother, Uncle Charlie, Doris, Uncle Hal—and Aunt Pat served spaghetti for supper. Spaghetti was an exotic treat in those days. Neither Doris nor I had ever eaten spaghetti, and none of the adults had enough experience to be good at it. All the good humor of Uncle Allen's house reawoke in my mind as I recalled the laughing arguments we had that night about the socially respectable method for moving spaghetti from plate to mouth.

Suddenly I wanted to write about that, about the warmth and   8
good feeling of it, but I wanted to put it down simply for my own joy, not for Mr. Fleagle. It was a moment I wanted to recapture and hold for myself. I wanted to relive the pleasure of an evening at New Street. To write it as I wanted, however, would violate all the rules of formal composition I'd learned in school, and Mr. Fleagle would surely give it a failing grade. Never mind. I would write something else for Mr. Fleagle after I had written this thing for myself.

When I finished it the night was half gone and there was no time   9
left to compose a proper, respectable essay for Mr. Fleagle. There was no choice next morning but to turn in my private reminiscence of Belleville. Two days passed before Mr. Fleagle returned the graded papers, and he returned everyone's but mine. I was bracing myself for a command to report to Mr. Fleagle immediately after school for discipline when I saw him lift my paper from his desk and rap for the class's attention.

"Now, boys," he said, "I want to read you an essay. This is titled   10
'The Art of Eating Spaghetti.'"

And he started to read. My words! He was reading *my words* out   11
loud to the entire class. What's more, the entire class was listening. Listening attentively. Then somebody laughed, then the entire class was laughing, and not in contempt and ridicule, but with openhearted enjoyment. Even Mr. Fleagle stopped two or three times to repress a small prim smile.

I did my best to avoid showing pleasure, but what I was feeling 12
was pure ecstasy at this startling demonstration that my words had the
power to make people laugh. In the eleventh grade, at the eleventh
hour as it were, I had discovered a calling. It was the happiest moment
of my entire school career. When Mr. Fleagle finished he put the final
seal on my happiness by saying, "Now that, boys, is an essay, don't
you see. It's—don't you see—it's of the very essence of the essay,
don't you see. Congratulations, Mr. Baker."

For the first time, light shone on a possibility. It wasn't a very 13
heartening possibility, to be sure. Writing couldn't lead to a job after
high school, and it was hardly honest work, but Mr. Fleagle had
opened a door for me. After that I ranked Mr. Fleagle among the
finest teachers in the school.

QUESTIONS FOR STUDY AND DISCUSSION

1. Baker makes good use of transitional expressions, repetition of
   words and ideas, and pronoun references in paragraphs 1 and 2.
   Carefully reread the paragraphs, and identify where he employs
   these techniques, using the analysis of Carson's essay in the introduction to this chapter as a model.

2. Examine the transitions Baker uses between paragraphs from
   paragraph 4 to the end of the essay. Explain how these transitions
   work to make the paragraphs flow smoothly from one to another.

3. How does Baker describe his English teacher, Mr. Fleagle, in the
   second paragraph? (Glossary: *Description*) Why does he repeat
   the word *prim* throughout the paragraph? Why is the vivid description important to the essay as a whole? (Glossary: *Dominant Impression*)

4. Baker gives Mr. Fleagle an identifiable voice. What is ironic
   about what Mr. Fleagle says? (Glossary: *Irony*) In what way does
   this irony contribute to Baker's purpose in writing the essay?
   (Glossary: *Purpose*)

5. What does Baker write about in his informal essay for Mr. Fleagle? Why does he write about this subject? Why doesn't he want
   to turn the essay in?

6. Baker's passage about Mr. Fleagle's choosing to read his essay to
   the class is critical to the impact of "Becoming a Writer." Baker
   writes in paragraph 11: "And he started to read. My words! He
   was reading *my words* out loud to the entire class." Why do you

think Baker repeats himself? Why is his wording more effective than a simple "And he started to read my essay to the class" would be?

7. What door had Mr. Fleagle opened for Baker? Why is Baker reluctant to pursue the opportunity that Mr. Fleagle provided to him?

VOCABULARY

Refer to your dictionary to define the following words as they are used in this selection. Then use each word in a sentence of your own.

laden (1)   antecedent (5)
chloroform (1)   reminiscence (9)
irrepressible (3)

CLASSROOM ACTIVITY USING TRANSITIONS

Read the following three paragraphs. Provide transitions between paragraphs so that the narrative flows smoothly.

In the late 1950s, I got lost on a camping trip in the Canadian wilderness. My only thought was to head south, towards warmth and civilization. My perilous journey was exhausting — the cold sapped my strength, and there were few places to find shelter and rest.

There I found friendly faces and a warm fire. As I built my strength, I tried to communicate with the villagers, but they did not understand me. I came to the conclusion that I could stay in the village and wait — perhaps forever — for help to come, or I could strike out on my own again.

I heard a gurgling sound. It was running water. Running water! Spring was here at last. Perhaps I would survive after all. I picked up my pack, squared my shoulders, and marched, the afternoon sun a beautiful sight, still ahead, but starting to drift to my right.

SUGGESTED WRITING ASSIGNMENTS

1. Using as a model Baker's effort to write about eating spaghetti, write something from your own experience that you would like to record for yourself, not necessarily for the teacher. Don't

worry about writing a formal essay; simply use language with which you are comfortable to convey why the event or experience is important to you.

2. Write an essay in which you describe how your perception of someone important in your life changed. How did you feel about the person at first? How do you feel now? What brought about the change? What impact did the transition have on you? Make sure your essay is coherent and flows well—use transitional expressions to help the reader follow the story of *your* transition.

Band of Brothers

■ **Pete Hamill**

Pete Hamill was born in Brooklyn, New York, in 1935, and for more than four decades has been a New York newspaper columnist. After serving in the U.S. Navy in the early fifties, he attended Mexico City College, Pratt Institute, and the School of Visual Arts before starting his career at the New York Post *in 1960. He has been a columnist for the* New York Post, *the* New York Daily News, *and the* Village Voice, *and his articles have appeared in such magazines as* Playboy, Esquire, Conde Nast Traveler, Vanity Fair, *and the* New York Times Magazine. *His distinguished journalism career includes having served as editor-in-chief of both the* New York Post *and the* New York Daily News. *Currently he is on the staff of the* New Yorker. *Hamill is the author of 16 books, including the novels* Snow in August *(1997) and* Forever *(2003), the memoir* A Drinking Life *(1995), and the nonfiction* Why Sinatra Matters *(1998) and* Diego Rivera *(1999). In the following essay, which first appeared in the* Daily News *in the wake of the terrorist attacks on the World Trade Center, Hamill pays tribute to the firefighters who lost their lives on September 11, 2001. As you read his essay, note how Hamill skillfully uses transitions to move readers from one paragraph to the next smoothly.*

FOR YOUR JOURNAL

In his autobiography, Mark Twain wrote, "We find not much in ourselves to admire, we are always wanting to be like someone else. If everybody was satisfied with himself, there would be no heroes." Do you agree? Do you think that it is important for a society to have heroes? Explain. Who are your heroes?

We would see them on summer afternoons, big and brawny or wiry and tough, standing outside the firehouses all over the city. Their denim shirts were often stained with sweat. They had the ease of men who did not need to brag about the work they did. It seemed that they were always laughing.

We would see them when the city leaves turned yellow with autumn, standing in the open doors of those firehouses. Inside, the red fire trucks and engines glistened with the pride of craftsmen who respected their tools. They seemed to love talking with small children. They were all, it seemed, fond of dogs. They sometimes paused and breathed deeply of the crisp air of October, for no men understood better the special beauty of a cleansing breeze. It seemed that they were always laughing.

We would see them inside the closed doors of the New York winter, waiting casually, almost indolently for the sounds of alarms. Upstairs, they talked with passion about food, for they cooked for themselves, and the menu was a kind of democratic choice. In all the places that we ever visited, the job of chef seemed to fall upon the Italian-Americans among them. Lasagna, homemade, with fresh loaves of Italian bread seemed to be the favorite food of Irish-American firemen, and Latinos, and the tough children of the Eastern European Jews, and those whose ancestors went all the way back to Africa. Too often the food went cold as they raced off to practice their dangerous craft. It seemed that they were always laughing.

We would see them in the springtime, the overcoats of winter gone, ballgames playing now on radios, as young women walked by the firehouses to the subways, objects of their admiring collective gaze. They made no rude noises, no crude remarks. Their admiration was always aesthetic, like visitors to museums shocked into silence by the sight of beauty. And after all, most of them were young themselves, their lives filled with the infinite possibilities of youth. They celebrated the multiple beauties of this world because their craft so often took them into horror. And always, always, it seemed that they were laughing.

Now 343 of those firemen are gone. Sept. 11, 2001, was a calamity for thousands of New Yorkers, for its citizens, police, EMS workers. We have all suffered unacceptable losses. But it was also the single worst day in the long history of the New York Fire Department. No other day has even come close.

The firemen were organized as a single unit in 1865 at the command of Albany and became in 1870, at the urgings of an old fireman named Boss Tweed, the Fire Department of New York. That is why the caps and insignias say FDNY, not NYFD. They began when 86th St. was a distant suburb. They began before the five boroughs were joined into one city in 1898. They have been fighting fires and saving lives every since, day after day, night after night, in all seasons.

They have summoned their Celtic pipe band to bury too many of their comrades.

Until Sept. 11, the worst single day for the FDNY took place in 7 October 1966, when a floor collapsed in a burning building on 23d St. That day 12 firemen were killed. That week, New York was shocked and numbed. None of us then alive could have imagined a day when almost 30 times that number would perish in smoke, fire, and exploded steel. No firemen could have been prepared to deal with such murderous ferocity.

It seems to be no accident, in a city of such widespread valor, 8 that in the numbered shorthand of our most terrible day the first three numbers were 911.

Entire fire companies have now disappeared from the landscape 9 of New York. Every living fireman has lost friends or relatives. Even now, the bodies of hundreds of firemen remain entombed under the smoking rubble of Ground Zero. Much of the top brass vanished while serving at the front.

But the heaviest casualties were among the infantry of the FDNY, 10 those who would never pause when asked to take that hill or that town. Men just like them died at Anzio and Omaha Beach, in the Hurtgen Forest and Monte Cassino, on Tarawa, Iwo Jima, and Okinawa, and too many other godforsaken places from the Yalu Reservoir to Anh Khe.[1] In all those places, and in the towers of lower Manhattan, decent men became young forever.

Many were married, with wives and children now scattered all 11 over the metropolitan area, orphaned by the heartless storm of fanaticism. Many were single, in the first sweet stages of maturity. Some were veterans, gnarled but not hardened by repeated exposure to human suffering, bearers of the department's memory, teachers of their dangerous craft. Many were the children of firemen, or had their own children assigned to our firehouses. Not one of them woke up that morning thinking it might be their last.

An old reporter visiting the site on the night of the disaster said 12 to a middle-aged policeman: "Thank you. You guys are real heroes."

"No, no, we're not," he said, heavy with exhaustion and sorrow. 13 "We're here, two blocks away. The cops on the scene, they're heroes. The ambulance guys, heroes." Then he shook his head and smothered a sob. "But those firemen, those crazy goddamned firemen . . ."

---

[1]*Anzio and Omaha Beach . . . :* various battlefields and sites from World War II, the Korean War, and the Vietnam War. [Eds.]

Those crazy goddamned firemen were all part of the same band   14
of brothers, transcending the petty differences of race or religion.
Such differences were most often dissolved in jokes and laughter. The
fraternity itself, like that of combat soldiers, was forged in shared
adversity.

Some could trace their FDNY lineage back through the genera-   15
tions. Sons honored fathers and grandfathers by taking their own
places in the fire companies of New York. Some, of course, were the
first in their families to lug hose into burning buildings. But Irishness
was there from the beginning, when the children of the Irish devastated by the famine[2] climbed upon horse-drawn trucks to race to the
rescue. In some old FDNY families, where Mayo and Galway[3] were
the countries of origin, one son was a cop, one was a fireman, and
the third was a priest. In firehouses, there were jokes about the new
recruits, whose names were transformed into O'Morales or McLevin.
Nobody at Ground Zero on Sept. 11 can ever forget that black fireman weeping for "my brothers"—who were, of course, the bearers
of Irish, Italian, Hispanic, and Jewish names.

Nor should anybody ever forget the multiple images of firemen in   16
helmets and rubbery raincoats, carrying equipment into the towers
while frantic civilians moved past them in the direction of open
streets, cobalt skies, and breathable air. At an improvised firehouse
altar on Lafayette St., one sign, hand-lettered by a citizen, said: "You
ran in when we ran out. We are grateful forever." That firehouse lost
14 men.

Everyone in the city seemed to understand that the primary mis-   17
sion of those firemen was to save human life. That is the job. Life
first, property second. Firemen don't pack guns. They are not asked
to face criminals or madmen. They don't ever confront fellow citizens
the way police officers sometimes must: to impose order on chaos.
They don't make arrests. They don't need to make split-second judgments about innocence or guilt. They are simply there to save human
life.

. . . In the days and years to come, their lives will be memorial-   18
ized by historians. We hope they will emerge as complete individuals,
who lived dense, rounded lives. We hope they will flower as human

---

[2]*The famine:* the Irish Famine of 1846 to 1850, which began with the blight of the
potato crop, took one million lives from hunger and disease, and spurred new waves of
immigration to the United States. [Eds.]
[3]*Mayo and Galway:* major regions of Ireland. [Eds.]

beings full of hopes, ambitions, desires, and the usual human imperfections. . . . And remember: these men ennobled our race, which is, of course, the human race.

Remember, too, that these men—the firemen of Sept. 11—were   19
extraordinary human beings. They went where most human beings never go. They kept climbing and climbing and climbing, into the smoke-fouled air, looking for living human beings. They went toward the fire, which so terrified the trapped people of the upper floors that they preferred leaping to their deaths. These firemen died while climbing toward the fearful sky.

Now, and in all the days to come, for all of us who remain   20
among the living, we must honor them each time we pass a firehouse. With a tip of a hat. A nod. A word of thanks. We must honor what they did, and what their brothers keep on doing. They will, of course, honor us in the coming days with their courage, their tenacity, and their laughter.

QUESTIONS FOR STUDY AND DISCUSSION

1. What is Hamill's purpose in this essay? (Glossary: *Purpose*) Does he ask readers to take any action?

2. According to Hamill, how are firefighters different from police officers? (Glossary: *Comparison and Contrast*) What point does Hamill make in pointing out these differences?

3. Hamill uses repeated words and phrases, transitional expressions, pronouns, and repeated key ideas to connect one paragraph to another. Identify examples of each of these transitional devices in Hamill's essay.

4. In paragraphs 6, 7, and 15 Hamill provides readers with a brief history of the Fire Department of New York. And in paragraph 10 he compares New York firefighters to soldiers who died in war. What do these historical references add to Hamill's tribute to the firefighters who lost their lives on September 11, 2001?

5. Hamill concludes each of the first four paragraphs with the refrain, "It seemed that they were always laughing." How did this refrain strike you when you first read it? What does it tell you about the New York firefighters? How has Hamill tied his conclusion to the opening refrain? (Glossary: *Beginnings and Endings*)

VOCABULARY

Refer to your dictionary to define each of the following words as they are used in this selection. Then use each word in a sentence of your own.

wiry (1)   ferocity (8)
indolently (3)   gnarled (12)
aesthetic (5)   forged (15)
calamity (6)

CLASSROOM ACTIVITY USING TRANSITIONS

The following sentences, which make up the first paragraph of E. B. White's essay "Once More to the Lake," have been rearranged. Place the sentences in what seems to you to be a coherent sequence by relying on language signals like transitions, repeated words, pronouns, and temporal references. Be prepared to explain your reasons for the placement of each sentence.

1. I have since become a salt-water man, but sometimes in summer there are days when the restlessness of the tides and the fearful cold of the sea water and the incessant wind which blows across the afternoon and into the evening make me wish for the placidity of a lake in the woods.

2. We all got ringworm from some kittens and had to rub Pond's Extract on our arms and legs night and morning, and my father rolled over in a canoe with all his clothes on; but outside of that the vacation was a success and from then on none of us ever thought there was any place in the world like that lake in Maine.

3. A few weeks ago this feeling got so strong I bought myself a couple of bass hooks and a spinner and returned to the lake where we used to go for a week's fishing and to revisit old haunts.

4. One summer, along about 1904, my father rented a camp on a lake in Maine and took us all there for the month of August.

5. We returned there summer after summer — always on August 1st for one month.

SUGGESTED WRITING ASSIGNMENTS

1. Using your response to the journal prompt for this selection as a starting point, write an essay about one of your heroes. What about this person qualifies him or her to be your hero? In what ways do you benefit from having this person as your hero? Does the person serve as a role model for you?

2. Hamill observes that in times of "shared adversity," people are able to transcend "the petty differences of race or religion" (14). Write an essay in which you tell about how an adversity brought a community you were part of closer together.

Effective Sentences

Each of the following paragraphs describes the city of Vancouver. Although the content of both paragraphs is essentially the same, the first paragraph is written in sentences of nearly the same length and pattern, and the second paragraph in sentences of varying length and pattern.

UNVARIED SENTENCES

Water surrounds Vancouver on three sides. The snow-crowned Coast Mountains ring the city on the northeast. Vancouver has a floating quality of natural loveliness. There is a curved beach at English Bay. This beach is in the shape of a half moon. Residential high rises stand behind the beach. They are in pale tones of beige, blue, and ice-cream pink. Turn-of-the-century houses of painted wood frown upward at the glitter of office towers. Any urban glare is softened by folds of green lawns, flowers, fountains, and trees. Such landscaping appears to be unplanned. It links Vancouver to her ultimate treasure of greenness. That treasure is thousand-acre Stanley Park. Surrounding stretches of water dominate. They have image-evoking names like False Creek and Lost Lagoon. Sailboats and pleasure craft skim blithely across Burrard Inlet. Foreign freighters are out in English Bay. They await their turn to take on cargoes of grain.

VARIED SENTENCES

Surrounded by water on three sides and ringed to the northeast by the snow-crowned Coast Mountains, Vancouver has a floating quality of natural loveliness. At English Bay, the half-moon curve of beach is backed by high rises in pale tones of beige, blue, and ice-cream pink. Turn-of-the-century houses of painted wood frown up-ward at the glitter of office towers. Yet any urban glare is quickly softened by folds of green lawns, flowers, fountains, and trees that in a seemingly unplanned fashion link Vancouver to her ultimate treasure of greenness—thousand-acre Stanley Park. And always it is the surrounding stretches of water that dominate, with their image-evoking names like False Creek and Lost Lagoon. Sailboats and pleasure craft skim blithely across Burrard Inlet, while out in English Bay foreign freighters await their turn to take on cargoes of grain.

The difference between these two paragraphs is dramatic. The first is monotonous because of the sameness of the sentences and because the ideas are not related to one another in a meaningful way. The second paragraph is much more interesting and readable; its sentences vary in length and are structured to clarify the relationships among the ideas. Sentence variety, an important aspect of all good writing, should not be used for its own sake, but rather to express ideas precisely and to emphasize the most important ideas within each sentence. Sentence variety includes the use of subordination, periodic and loose sentences, dramatically short sentences, active and passive voice, and coordination.

■ Sentence Variety

SUBORDINATION

Subordination, the process of giving one idea less emphasis than another in a sentence, is one of the most important characteristics of an effective sentence and a mature prose style. Writers subordinate ideas by introducing them either with subordinating conjunctions *(because, if, as though, while, when, after, in order that)* or with relative pronouns *(that, which, who, whomever, what)*. Subordination not only deemphasizes some ideas, but also highlights others that the writer feels are more important.

Of course, there is nothing about an idea—*any* idea—that automatically makes it primary or secondary in importance. The writer decides what to emphasize, and he or she may choose to emphasize the less profound or noteworthy of two ideas. Consider, for example, the following sentence: "Melissa was reading a detective story while the national election results were televised." Everyone, including the author of the sentence, knows that the national election is a more noteworthy event than Melissa's reading the detective story. But the sentence concerns Melissa, not the election, and so the fact that she was reading is stated in the main clause, while the election news is subordinated in a dependent clause.

Generally, writers place the ideas they consider important in main clauses, and other ideas go into dependent clauses. For example:

When she was thirty years old, she made her first solo flight across the Atlantic.

When she made her first solo flight across the Atlantic, she was thirty years old.

The first sentence emphasizes the solo flight; in the second, the emphasis is on the pilot's age.

PERIODIC AND LOOSE SENTENCES

Another way to achieve emphasis is to place the most important words, phrases, and clauses at the beginning or end of a sentence. The ending is the most emphatic part of a sentence; the beginning is less emphatic; and the middle is the least emphatic of all. The two sentences about the pilot put the main clause at the end, achieving special emphasis. The same thing occurs in a much longer kind of sentence, called a *periodic sentence,* in which the main idea is placed at the end, closest to the period. Here is an example:

On the afternoon of the first day of spring, when the gutters were still heaped high with Monday's snow but the sky itself had been swept clean, we put on our galoshes and walked up the sunny side of Fifth Avenue to Central Park.

–John Updike

By holding the main clause back, Updike keeps his readers in suspense and so puts the most emphasis possible on his main idea.

A *loose sentence,* on the other hand, states its main idea at the beginning and then adds details in subsequent phrases and clauses. Rewritten as a loose sentence, Updike's sentence might read like this:

We put on our galoshes and walked up the sunny side of Fifth Avenue to Central Park on the afternoon of the first day of spring, when the gutters were still heaped high with Monday's snow but the sky itself had been swept clean.

The main idea still gets plenty of emphasis, since it is contained in a main clause at the beginning of the sentence. A loose sentence resembles the way people talk: it flows naturally and is easy to understand.

DRAMATICALLY SHORT SENTENCES

Another way to create emphasis is to use a *dramatically short sentence.* Especially following a long and involved sentence, a short declarative sentence helps drive a point home. Here are two examples:

> The qualities that Barbie promotes (slimness, youth, and beauty) allow no tolerance of gray hair, wrinkles, sloping posture, or failing eyesight and hearing. Barbie's perfect body is eternal.
>
> –Danielle Kuykendall, student

> The executive suite on the thirty-fifth floor of the Columbia Broadcasting System skyscraper in Manhattan is a tasteful blend of dark wood paneling, expensive abstract paintings, thick carpets, and pleasing colors. It has the quiet look of power.
>
> –David Wise

ACTIVE AND PASSIVE VOICE

Finally, since the subject of a sentence is automatically emphasized, writers may choose to use the *active voice* when they want to emphasize the doer of an action and the *passive voice* when they want to downplay or omit the doer completely. Here are two examples:

> High winds pushed our sailboat onto the rocks, where the force of the waves tore it to pieces.

> Our sailboat was pushed by high winds onto the rocks, where it was torn to pieces by the force of the waves.
>
> –Liz Coughlan, student

The first sentence emphasizes the natural forces that destroyed the boat, while the second sentence focuses attention on the boat itself. The passive voice may be useful in placing emphasis, but it has important disadvantages. As the examples show, and as the terms suggest, active-voice verbs are more vigorous and vivid than the same verbs in the passive voice. Then, too, some writers use the passive voice to hide or evade responsibility. "It has been decided" conceals who did the deciding, whereas "I have decided" makes all clear. So the passive voice should be used only when necessary—as it is in this sentence.

■ Sentence Emphasis

COORDINATION

Often, a writer wants to place equal emphasis on several facts or ideas. One way to do this is to give each its own sentence. For example, consider these three sentences about golfer Nancy Lopez.

> Nancy Lopez selected her club. She lined up her shot. She chipped the ball to within a foot of the pin.

But a long series of short, simple sentences quickly becomes tedious. Many writers would combine these three sentences by using **coordination.** The coordinating conjunctions *and, but, or, nor, for, so,* and *yet* connect words, phrases, and clauses of equal importance:

> Nancy Lopez selected her club, lined up her shot, *and* chipped the ball to within a foot of the pin.
>
> –Will Briggs, student

By coordinating three sentences into one, the writer not only makes the same words easier to read, but also shows that Lopez's three actions are equally important parts of a single process.

PARALLELISM

When parts of a sentence are not only coordinated but also grammatically the same, they are parallel. **Parallelism** in a sentence is created by balancing a word with a word, a phrase with a phrase, or a clause with a clause. Here is a humorous example from the beginning of Mark Twain's *Adventures of Huckleberry Finn:*

> Persons attempting to find a motive in this narrative will be prosecuted; persons attempting to find a moral in it will be banished; persons attempting to find a plot in it will be shot.
>
> –Mark Twain

Parallelism is also often found in speeches. For example, in the last sentence of the Gettysburg Address Lincoln proclaims his hope that "government of the people, by the people, for the people, shall not perish from the earth."

Hitting Pay Dirt

■ **Annie Dillard**

Annie Dillard was born in 1945 in Pennsylvania and attended Hollins College in Virginia. Although she is known primarily as an essayist for such works as Pilgrim at Tinker Creek *(1974), which won a Pulitzer Prize,* Teaching a Stone to Talk *(1982), and* For the Time Being *(2000), she has demonstrated an impressive versatility in her publications:* Tickets for a Prayer Wheel *(1974) and* Mornings Like This: Found Poems *(1995), poetry;* Holy the Firm *(1977), a prose narrative;* Living by Fiction *(1982), literary theory;* An American Childhood *(1987), autobiography; and* The Living *(1992), a novel. In* The Writing Life *(1989), Dillard explores the processes of writing itself. She is currently Adjunct Professor of English and Writer in Residence at Wesleyan University. As you read the selection below, taken from* An American Childhood, *pay particular attention to the way Dillard's active verbs give her sentences strength and emphasis. There is also a good example of parallel sentence structure in paragraph 5.*

FOR YOUR JOURNAL

What was your favorite possession in your preteen years? How did you get it? Why was it special to you?

A fter I read *The Field Book of Ponds and Streams* several times, I 1
longed for a microscope. Everybody needed a microscope. Detectives used microscopes, both for the FBI and at Scotland Yard. Although usually I had to save my tiny allowance for things I wanted, that year for Christmas my parents gave me a microscope kit.

In a dark basement corner, on a white enamel table, I set up the 2
microscope kit. I supplied a chair, a lamp, a batch of jars, a candle, and a pile of library books. The microscope kit supplied a blunt black three-speed microscope, a booklet, a scalpel, a dropper, an ingenious device for cutting thin segments of fragile tissue, a pile of clean slides and cover slips, and a dandy array of corked test tubes.

One of the test tubes contained "hay infusion." Hay infusion was 3
a wee brown chip of grass blade. You added water to it, and after a

week it became a jungle in a drop, full of one-celled animals. This did not work for me. All I saw in the microscope after a week was a wet chip of dried grass, much enlarged.

Another test tube contained "diatomaceous earth." This was, I believed, an actual pinch of the white cliffs of Dover.[1] On my palm it was an airy, friable chalk. The booklet said it was composed of the siliceous bodies of diatoms—one-celled creatures that lived in, as it were, small glass jewelry boxes with fitted lids. Diatoms, I read, come in a variety of transparent geometrical shapes. Broken and dead and dug out of geological deposits, they made chalk, and a fine abrasive used in silver polish and toothpaste. What I saw in the microscope must have been the fine abrasive—grit enlarged. It was years before I saw a recognizable, whole diatom. The kit's diatomaceous earth was a bust.

All that winter I played with the microscope. I prepared slides from things at hand, as the books suggested. I looked at the transparent membrane inside an onion's skin and saw the cell. I looked at a section of cork and saw the cells, and at scrapings from the inside of my cheek, ditto. I looked at my blood and saw not much; I looked at my urine and saw a long iridescent crystal, for the drop had dried.

All this was very well, but I wanted to see the wildlife I had read about. I wanted especially to see the famous amoeba, who had eluded me. He was supposed to live in the hay infusion, but I hadn't found him there. He lived outside in warm ponds and streams, too, but I lived in Pittsburgh, and it had been a cold winter.

Finally late that spring I saw an amoeba. The week before, I had gathered puddle water from Frick Park; it had been festering in a jar in the basement. This June night after dinner I figured I had waited long enough. In the basement at my microscope table I spread a scummy drop of Frick Park puddle water on a slide, peeked in, and lo, there was the famous amoeba. He was as blobby and grainy as his picture; I would have known him anywhere.

Before I had watched him at all, I ran upstairs. My parents were still at the table, drinking coffee. They, too, could see the famous amoeba. I told them, bursting, that he was all set up, that they should hurry before his water dried. It was the chance of a lifetime.

Father had stretched out his long legs and was tilting back in his chair. Mother sat with her knees crossed, in blue slacks, smoking a

---

[1]*Dover:* Harbor city situated on the southeast coast of England, known for its fabled White Cliffs [Eds.]

Chesterfield. The dessert dishes were still on the table. My sisters were nowhere in evidence. It was a warm evening; the big dining-room windows gave onto blooming rhododendrons. Mother regarded me warmly. She gave me to understand that she 10 was glad I had found what I had been looking for, but that she and Father were happy to sit with their coffee, and would not be coming down.

She did not say, but I understood at once, that they had their 11 pursuits (coffee?) and I had mine. She did not say, but I began to understand then, that you do what you do out of your private passion for the thing itself.

I had essentially been handed my own life. In subsequent years 12 my parents would praise my drawings and poems, and supply me with books, art supplies, and sports equipment, and listen to my troubles and enthusiasms, and supervise my hours, and discuss and inform, but they would not get involved with my detective work, nor hear about my reading, nor inquire about my homework or term papers or exams, nor visit the salamanders I caught, nor listen to me play the piano, nor attend my field hockey games, nor fuss over my insect collection with me, or my poetry collection or stamp collection or rock collection. My days and nights were my own to plan and fill.

When I left the dining room that evening and started down the 13 dark basement stairs, I had a life. I sat down to my wonderful amoeba, and there he was, rolling his grains more slowly now, extending an arc of his edge for a foot and drawing himself along by that foot, and absorbing it again and rolling on. I gave him some more pond water.

I had hit pay dirt. For all I knew, there were paramecia, too, in 14 that pond water, or daphniae, or stentors, or any of the many other creatures I had read about and never seen: volvox, the spherical algal colony; euglena with its one red eye; the elusive, glassy diatom; hydra, rotifers, water bears, worms. Anything was possible. The sky was the limit.

QUESTIONS FOR STUDY AND DISCUSSION

1. In her second sentence, Dillard says, "Everybody needed a microscope." This confident yet naive statement indicates that she is writing from the point of view of herself as a child. (Glossary: *Point of View*) Why does she write her essay from this point of view?

2. Analyze the sentences in the first four paragraphs. How would you describe Dillard's use of sentence variety? Identify her very short sentences—those with eight or fewer words. What does each contribute to the essay?

3. Why does the microscope appeal to Dillard? How does she react to her early disappointments?

4. Is Dillard's diction appropriate for the essay's content and point of view? (Glossary: *Diction*) Defend your answer with specific examples from the essay.

5. Reread paragraph 12, noting Dillard's sentence constructions. In what way does their construction reinforce Dillard's content? Explain.

6. Three of the four sentences in Dillard's concluding paragraph are five words or less. What impact do these short sentences have on readers? Explain.

VOCABULARY

Refer to your dictionary to define the following words as they are used in this selection. Then use each word in a sentence of your own.

infusion (3)   iridescent (5)
friable (4)   festering (7)
siliceous (4)

CLASSROOM ACTIVITY USING EFFECTIVE SENTENCES

Rewrite the following paragraph, presenting the information in any order you choose. Use sentence variety and subordination, as discussed in the chapter introduction, to make the paragraph more interesting to read.

When Billy saw the crime, he was in a grocery store buying hot dog buns for the barbecue he had scheduled for the next weekend. The crime was a burglary, and the criminal was someone you would never expect to see commit a crime. His basketball shoes squeaked as he ran away, and he looked no more than fifteen years old with a fresh, eager face that was the picture of innocence. Billy watched the youth steal a purse right off a woman's shoulder, and the bright sun reflected off the thief's forehead as he ran away, although the weather was quite chilly and had been for a week. The police officer who caught the thief tripped him and handcuffed him as Billy paid for the hot dog buns, got in his car, and drove away.

SUGGESTED WRITING ASSIGNMENTS

1. Dillard learned an important life lesson from her parents' reaction to her news of the amoeba. How would you describe that lesson? Use your description as the basis for a brief essay in which you discuss the role of parents in fostering children's creativity and desire for knowledge. (Glossary: *Description*) Pay close attention to your sentences, and use them to emphasize the most important parts of your discussion.

2. Write a brief essay using one of the following sentences to focus and control the descriptive details you select. Place the sentence in the essay wherever it will have the greatest emphasis.

The music stopped.

It was broken glass.

I started to sweat.

She had convinced me.

It was my turn to step forward.

Now I understood.

Salvation

■ **Langston Hughes**

*Born in Joplin, Missouri, Langston Hughes (1902–1967) be-
came an important figure in the African American cultural
movement of the 1920s known as the Harlem Renaissance. He
wrote poetry, fiction, and plays and contributed columns to the*
New York Post *and an African American weekly, the* Chicago
Defender. *He is best known for* The Weary Blues *(1926) and
other books of poetry that express his racial pride, his familiar-
ity with African American traditions, and his understanding of
blues and jazz rhythms. In his memory, New York City desig-
nated his residence at 20 East 127th Street in Harlem as a landmark, and his street was renamed "Langston Hughes Place." In
the following selection from his autobiography,* The Big Sea
*(1940), note how, for the sake of emphasis, Hughes varies the
length and types of sentences he uses. The impact of the dramatically short sentence in paragraph 12, for instance, derives from
the variety of sentences preceding it.*

FOR YOUR JOURNAL

What role does religion play in your family? Do you consider
yourself a religious person? Have you ever felt pressure from
others to participate in religious activities? How did that make
you feel?

I was saved from sin when I was going on thirteen. But not really   1
saved. It happened like this. There was a big revival at my Auntie
Reed's church. Every night for weeks there had been much preaching,
singing, praying, and shouting, and some very hardened sinners had
been brought to Christ, and the membership of the church had grown
by leaps and bounds. Then just before the revival ended, they held a
special meeting for children, "to bring the young lambs to the fold."
My aunt spoke of it for days ahead. That night I was escorted to the
front row and placed on the mourners' bench with all the other
young sinners, who had not yet been brought to Jesus.

My aunt told me that when you were saved you saw a light, and 2 something happened to you inside! And Jesus came into your life! And God was with you from then on! She said you could see and hear and feel Jesus in your soul. I believed her. I had heard a great many old people say the same thing and it seemed to me they ought to know. So I sat there calmly in the hot, crowded church, waiting for Jesus to come to me.

The preacher preached a wonderful rhythmical sermon, all 3 moans and shouts and lonely cries and dire pictures of hell, and then he sang a song about the ninety and nine safe in the fold, but one little lamb was left out in the cold. Then he said: "Won't you come? Won't you come to Jesus? Young lambs, won't you come?" And he held out his arms to all us young sinners there on the mourners' bench. And the little girls cried. And some of them jumped up and went to Jesus right away. But most of us just sat there.

A great many old people came and knelt around us and prayed, 4 old women with jet-black faces and braided hair, old men with work-gnarled hands. And the church sang a song about the lower lights are burning, some poor sinners to be saved. And the whole building rocked with prayer and song.

Still I kept waiting to *see* Jesus. 5

Finally all the young people had gone to the altar and were saved, 6 but one boy and me. He was a rounder's son named Westley. Westley and I were surrounded by sisters and deacons praying. It was very hot in the church, and getting late now. Finally Westley said to me in a whisper: "God damn! I'm tired o' sitting here. Let's get up and be saved." So he got up and was saved.

Then I was left all alone on the mourners' bench. My aunt came 7 and knelt at my knees and cried, while prayers and songs swirled all around me in the little church. The whole congregation prayed for me alone, in a mighty wail of moans and voices. And I kept waiting serenely for Jesus, waiting, waiting—but he didn't come. I wanted to see him, but nothing happened to me. Nothing! I wanted something to happen to me, but nothing happened.

I heard the songs and the minister saying: "Why don't you come? 8 My dear child, why don't you come to Jesus? Jesus is waiting for you. He wants you. Why don't you come? Sister Reed, what is this child's name?"

"Langston," my aunt sobbed. 9

"Langston, why don't you come? Why don't you come and be 10 saved? Oh, Lamb of God! Why don't you come?"

Now it was really getting late. I began to be ashamed of myself,   11
holding everything up so long. I began to wonder what God thought
about Westley, who certainly hadn't seen Jesus either, but who was
now sitting proudly on the platform, swinging his knickerbockered
legs and grinning down at me, surrounded by deacons and old
women on their knees praying. God had not struck Westley dead for
taking his name in vain or for lying in the temple. So I decided that
maybe to save further trouble, I'd better lie, too, and say that Jesus
had come, and get up and be saved.

So I got up.   12

Suddenly the whole room broke into a sea of shouting, as they   13
saw me rise. Waves of rejoicing swept the place. Women leaped in the
air. My aunt threw her arms around me. The minister took me by the
hand and led me to the platform.

When things quieted down, in a hushed silence, punctuated by a   14
few ecstatic "Amens," all the new young lambs were blessed in the
name of God. Then joyous singing filled the room.

That night, for the last time in my life but one — for I was a big boy   15
twelve years old — I cried. I cried, in bed alone, and couldn't stop. I
buried my head under the quilts, but my aunt heard me. She woke up
and told my uncle I was crying because the Holy Ghost had come into
my life, and because I had seen Jesus. But I was really crying because I
couldn't bear to tell her that I had lied, that I had deceived everybody in
the church, that I hadn't seen Jesus, and that now I didn't believe there
was a Jesus any more, since he didn't come to help me.

QUESTIONS FOR STUDY AND DISCUSSION

1. What is salvation? Is it important to young Langston Hughes that he
   be saved? Why does he expect to be saved at the revival meeting?

2. Hughes varies the length and structure of his sentences throughout the essay. How does this variety capture and reinforce the
   rhythms and drama of the evening's events? Explain.

3. What would be gained or lost if the essay began with the first
   two sentences combined as follows: "I was saved from sin when I
   was going on thirteen, but I was not really saved"?

4. Identify the coordinating conjunctions in paragraph 3. (Glossary:
   Coordination) Rewrite the paragraph without them. Compare
   your paragraph with the original, and explain what Hughes
   gains by using coordinating conjunctions.

5. Identify the subordinating conjunctions in paragraph 15. (Glossary: *Subordination*) What is it about the ideas in this last paragraph that makes it necessary for Hughes to use these subordinating conjunctions?
6. How does Hughes's choice of words, or diction, help to establish a realistic atmosphere for a religious revival meeting? (Glossary: *Diction*)
7. Why does young Langston cry on the night of his being "saved"? Why is the story of his being saved so ironic? (Glossary: *Irony*)

VOCABULARY

Refer to your dictionary to define the following words as they are used in this selection. Then use each word in a sentence of your own.

dire (3)   punctuated (14)
gnarled (4)   ecstatic (14)
vain (11)

CLASSROOM ACTIVITY USING EFFECTIVE SENTENCES

Using coordination or subordination, rewrite each set of short sentences as a single sentence. Here is an example:

ORIGINAL: This snow is good for Colorado's economy. Tourists are now flocking to ski resorts.

REVISED: This snow is good for Colorado's economy because tourists are now flocking to ski resorts.

1. I can take the 6:30 express train. I can catch the 7:00 bus.
2. Miriam worked on her research paper. She interviewed five people for the paper. She worked all weekend. She was tired.
3. Juan's new job kept him busy every day. He did not have time to work out at the gym for over a month.
4. The Statue of Liberty welcomes newcomers to America. It was a gift of the French government. It was completely restored for the nation's two hundredth birthday. It is over 120 years old.
5. Carla is tall. She is strong. She is a team player. She was the starting center on the basketball team.
6. Betsy loves Bach's music. She also likes Scott Joplin.

SUGGESTED WRITING ASSIGNMENTS

1. Like the young Langston Hughes, we sometimes find ourselves in situations in which, for the sake of conformity, we do things we do not believe in. Consider one such experience you have had, and write an essay about it. What is it about human nature that makes us act occasionally in ways that contradict our inner feelings? As you write, pay particular attention to your sentence variety.

2. Reread the introduction to this chapter. Then review one of the essays that you have written, paying particular attention to sentence structure. Recast sentences as necessary to make your writing more interesting and effective.

The Good Daughter

■ Caroline Hwang

Freelance writer and editor Caroline Hwang was born in Milwaukee, Wisconsin. After graduating from the University of Pennsylvania in 1991, she entered the world of popular magazines, holding editorial positions at Glamour, Mademoiselle, *and* Redbook. *She later earned an M.F.A. from New York University. She recently published her first novel,* In Full Bloom *(2003), and was a featured reader during the Asian American Writers' Workshop event series in New York City. In the following essay, which first appeared in* Newsweek *in 1998, Hwang illuminates the difficulty of growing up as the daughter of Korean immigrant parents. Notice how Hwang uses sentence variety for emphasis and dramatic effect in recounting how she has been torn between her parents' dreams for her and her own dreams.*

FOR YOUR JOURNAL

What is your cultural identity? Do you consider yourself an American, or do you identify with another culture? How comfortable do you feel with this identity? Explain why you feel as you do.

The moment I walked into the dry-cleaning store, I knew the woman behind the counter was from Korea, like my parents. To show her that we shared a heritage, and possibly get a fellow countryman's discount, I tilted my head forward, in shy imitation of a traditional bow. 1

"Name?" she asked, not noticing my attempted obeisance. 2

"Hwang," I answered. 3

"Hwang? Are you Chinese?" 4

Her question caught me off-guard. I was used to hearing such queries from non-Asians who think Asians all look alike, but never from one of my own people. Of course, the only Koreans I knew were my parents and their friends, people who've never asked me where I came from, since they knew better than I. 5

I ransacked my mind for the Korean words that would tell her who I was. It's always struck me as funny (in a mirthless sort of way) that I can more readily say "I am Korean" in Spanish, German, and 6 even Latin than I can in the language of my ancestry. In the end, I told her in English.

The dry-cleaning woman squinted as though trying to see past the glare of my strangeness, repeating my surname under her breath. "Oh, *Fxuang*," she said, doubling over with laughter. "You don't know how to speak your name." 7

I flinched. Perhaps I was particularly sensitive at the time, having just dropped out of graduate school. I had torn up my map for the future, the one that said not only where I was going but who I was. My sense of identity was already disintegrating. 8

When I got home, I called my parents to ask why they had never bothered to correct me. "Big deal," my mother said, sounding more flippant than I knew she intended. (Like many people who learn English in a classroom, she uses idioms that don't always fit the occasion.) "So what if you can't pronounce your name? You are American," she said. 9

Though I didn't challenge her explanation, it left me unsatisfied. The fact is, my cultural identity is hardly that clear-cut. 10

My parents immigrated to this country 30 years ago, two years before I was born. They told me often, while I was growing up, that, if I wanted to, I could be president someday, that here my grasp would be as long as my reach. 11

To ensure that I reaped all the advantages of this country, my parents saw to it that I became fully assimilated. So, like any American of my generation, I whiled away my youth strolling malls and talking on the phone, rhapsodizing over Andrew McCarthy's blue eyes, or analyzing the meaning of a certain upperclassman's offer of a ride to the Homecoming football game. 12

To my parents, I am all American, and the sacrifices they made in leaving Korea — including my mispronounced name — pale in comparison to the opportunities those sacrifices gave me. They do not see that I straddle two cultures, nor that I feel displaced in the only country I know. I identify with Americans, but Americans do not identify with me. I've never known what it's like to belong to a community — neither one at large, nor of an extended family. I know more about Europe than the continent my ancestors unmistakably come from. I sometimes wonder, as I did that day in the dry cleaner's, if I would be a happier person had my parents stayed in Korea. 13

I first began to consider this thought around the time I decided to go to graduate school. It had been a compromise: my parents wanted me to go to law school; I wanted to skip the starched-collar track and 14 be a writer—the hungrier the better. But after 20-some years of following their wishes and meeting all of their expectations, I couldn't bring myself to disobey or disappoint. A writing career is riskier than law, I remember thinking. If I'm a failure and my life is a washout, then what does that make my parents' lives?

I know that many of my friends had to choose between pleasing 15 their parents and being true to themselves. But for the children of immigrants, the choice seems more complicated, a happy outcome impossible. By making the biggest move of their lives for me, my parents indentured me to the largest debt imaginable—I owe them the fulfillment of their hopes for me.

It tore me up inside to suppress my dream, but I went to school 16 for a Ph.D. in English literature, thinking I had found the perfect compromise. I would be able to write at least about books while pursuing a graduate degree. Predictably, it didn't work out. How could I labor for five years in a program I had no passion for? When I finally left school, my parents were disappointed, but since it wasn't what they wanted me to do, they weren't devastated. I, on the other hand, felt I was staring at the bottom of the abyss. I had seen the flaw in my life of halfwayness, in my planned life of compromises.

I hadn't thought about my love life, but I had a vague plan to 17 make concessions there, too. Though they raised me as an American, my parents expect me to marry someone Korean and give them grandchildren who look like them. This didn't seem like such a huge request when I was 14, but now I don't know what I'm going to do. I've never been in love with someone I dated, or dated someone I loved. (Since I can't bring myself even to entertain the thought of marrying the non-Korean men I'm attracted to, I've been dating only those I know I can stay clearheaded about.) And as I near that age when the question of marriage stalks every relationship, I can't help but wonder if my parents' expectations are responsible for the lack of passion in my life.

My parents didn't want their daughter to be Korean, but they 18 don't want her fully American, either. Children of immigrants are living paradoxes. We are the first generation and the last. We are in this country for its opportunities, yet filial duty binds us. When my parents boarded the plane, they knew they were embarking on a rough trip. I don't think they imagined the rocks in the path of their daughter who can't even pronounce her own name.

QUESTIONS FOR STUDY AND DISCUSSION

1. What is Hwang's thesis, and where is it most clearly stated? (Glossary: *Thesis*)
2. Hwang begins her essay by recounting an unsettling incident in a dry-cleaning store. How effective did you find this opening? (Glossary: *Beginnings and Endings*) What contribution does dialogue make to her telling of this story? Where else does she use dialogue in her essay? (Glossary: *Dialogue*)
3. Hwang starts paragraphs 5 and 8 with short sentences. How does each of these sentences enhance the drama between Hwang and the Korean woman at the dry cleaner's?
4. Analyze the sentences in paragraph 13. In what ways does the structure of these sentences reinforce Hwang's uncertainty about her own identity? Explain.
5. What does Hwang mean when she says, "Children of immigrants are living paradoxes. We are the first generation and the last" (18)?

VOCABULARY

Refer to your dictionary to define the following words as they are used in this selection. Then use each word in a sentence of your own.

obeisance (2)	rhapsodizing (12)
ransacked (6)	concessions (17)
flippant (9)	paradoxes (18)
assimilated (12)	filial (18)

CLASSROOM ACTIVITY USING EFFECTIVE SENTENCES

Rewrite the following sets of sentences to combine short, simple sentences and to reduce repetition wherever possible. Here is an example:

ORIGINAL: Angelo's team won the championship. He pitched a two-hitter. He struck out ten batters. He hit a home run.

REVISED: Angelo's team won the championship because he pitched a two-hitter, struck out ten batters, and hit a home run.

1. Bonnie wore shorts. The shorts were red. The shorts had pockets.
2. The deer hunter awoke at 5:00 A.M. He ate a quick breakfast.

The breakfast consisted of coffee, juice, and cereal. He was in the woods before the sun came up.

3. My grandparents played golf every weekend for years. Last year they stopped playing. They miss the game now.

4. Fly over any major city. Look out the airplane's window. You will be appalled at the number of tall smokestacks you will see.

5. It did not rain for over three months. Most crops in the region failed. Some farmers were on the brink of declaring bankruptcy.

6. Every weekday I go to work. I exercise. I shower and relax. I eat a light, low-fat dinner.

SUGGESTED WRITING ASSIGNMENTS

1. Hwang reveals that her passion is to become a writer. In deciding to go to graduate school for a Ph.D. in English literature, she thought that she had "found the perfect compromise" between her dream to be a writer and her parents' dream for her to become a lawyer. Write an essay describing your own dream, if you have one, and explain what you will need to do to fulfill it. Does your family support you in this pursuit?

2. Choose a country that you have studied, visited, or at least read about. Compare who you are now with who you think you would be if you had been born in that country. How would you be different? Why?

38 Who Saw Murder Didn't Call Police

■ **Martin Gansberg**

Reporter Martin Gansberg (1920–1995) was born in Brooklyn, New York, and graduated from St. John's University. Gansberg was an experienced copy editor completing one of his first reporting assignments when he wrote the following essay for the New York Times in 1964, two weeks after the events he so poignantly narrates. Once you've finished reading the essay, you will understand why it has been reprinted so often and why the name Kitty Genovese is still invoked whenever questions of public apathy arise. Gansberg uses dialogue effectively to emphasize his point. Pay particular attention to how he constructs the sentences that incorporate dialogue and to how subordination and coordination often determine where quoted material appears.

FOR YOUR JOURNAL

Have you ever witnessed an accident or a crime? How did you react to the situation—did you come forward and testify, or did you choose not to get involved? Why do you think you reacted the way you did? How do you feel about your behavior?

For more than half an hour 38 respectable, law-abiding citizens in Queens[1] watched a killer stalk and stab a woman in three separate attacks in Kew Gardens.

Twice their chatter and the sudden glow of their bedroom lights interrupted him and frightened him off. Each time he returned, sought her out, and stabbed her again. Not one person telephoned the police during the assault; one witness called after the woman was dead.

That was two weeks ago today.

Still shocked is Assistant Chief Inspector Frederick M. Lussen, in charge of the borough's detectives and a veteran of 25 years of homi-

---

[1]*Queens:* one of New York City's five boroughs. [Eds.]

cide investigations. He can give a matter-of-fact recitation on many murders. But the Kew Gardens slaying baffles him—not because it is a murder, but because the "good people" failed to call the police.

"As we have reconstructed the crime," he said, "the assailant had three chances to kill this woman during a 35-minute period. He returned twice to complete the job. If we had been called when he first attacked, the woman might not be dead now."

This is what the police say happened beginning at 3:20 A.M. in the staid, middle-class, tree-lined Austin Street area:

Twenty-eight-year-old Catherine Genovese, who was called Kitty by almost everyone in the neighborhood, was returning home from her job as manager of a bar in Hollis. She parked her red Fiat in a lot adjacent to the Kew Gardens Long Island Rail Road Station, facing Mowbray Place. Like many residents of the neighborhood, she had parked there day after day since her arrival from Connecticut a year ago, although the railroad frowns on the practice.

She turned off the lights of her car, locked the door, and started to walk the 100 feet to the entrance of her apartment at 82-70 Austin Street, which is in a Tudor building, with stores in the first floor and apartments on the second.

The entrance to the apartment is in the rear of the building because the front is rented to retail stores. At night the quiet neighborhood is shrouded in the slumbering darkness that marks most residential areas.

Miss Genovese noticed a man at the far end of the lot, near a seven-story apartment house at 82-40 Austin Street. She halted. Then, nervously, she headed up Austin Street toward Lefferts Boulevard, where there is a call box to the 102nd Police Precinct in nearby Richmond Hill.

She got as far as a street light in front of a bookstore before the man grabbed her. She screamed. Lights went on in the 10-story apartment house at 82-67 Austin Street, which faces the bookstore. Windows slid open and voices punctuated the early-morning stillness.

Miss Genovese screamed: "Oh, my God, he stabbed me! Please help me! Please help me!"

From one of the upper windows in the apartment house, a man called down: "Let that girl alone!"

The assailant looked up at him, shrugged, and walked down Austin Street toward a white sedan parked a short distance away. Miss Genovese struggled to her feet.

Lights went out. The killer returned to Miss Genovese, now try- 15
ing to make her way around the side of the building by the parking
lot to get to her apartment. The assailant stabbed her again.

"I'm dying!" she shrieked. "I'm dying!" 16

Windows were opened again, and lights went on in many apart- 17
ments. The assailant got into his car and drove away. Miss Genovese
staggered to her feet. A city bus, O-10, the Lefferts Boulevard line to
Kennedy International Airport, passed. It was 3:35 A.M.

The assailant returned. By then, Miss Genovese had crawled to 18
the back of the building, where the freshly painted brown doors to
the apartment house held out hope for safety. The killer tried the first
door; she wasn't there. At the second door, 82-62 Austin Street, he
saw her slumped on the floor at the foot of the stairs. He stabbed her
a third time — fatally.

It was 3:50 by the time the police received their first call, from a 19
man who was a neighbor of Miss Genovese. In two minutes they were
at the scene. The neighbor, a 70-year-old woman, and another woman
were the only persons on the street. Nobody else came forward.

The man explained that he had called the police after much delib- 20
eration. He had phoned a friend in Nassau County for advice and
then he had crossed the roof of the building to the apartment of the
elderly woman to get her to make the call.

"I didn't want to get involved," he sheepishly told the police. 21

Six days later, the police arrested Winston Moseley, a 29-year- 22
old business-machine operator, and charged him with homicide.
Moseley had no previous record. He is married, has two children and
owns a home at 133-19 Sutter Avenue, South Ozone Park, Queens.
On Wednesday, a court committed him to Kings County Hospital for
psychiatric observation.

When questioned by the police, Moseley also said that he had 23
slain Mrs. Annie May Johnson, 24, of 146-12 133d Avenue, Jamaica,
on Feb. 29 and Barbara Kralik, 15, of 174-17 140th Avenue, Spring-
field Gardens, last July. In the Kralik case, the police are holding
Alvin L. Mitchell, who is said to have confessed to that slaying.

The police stressed how simple it would have been to have gotten 24
in touch with them. "A phone call," said one of the detectives,
"would have done it." The police may be reached by dialing "O" for
operator or SPring 7-3100.[2]

---

[2]This mid-twentieth century phone number uses a combination of both letters (the *SP*
of *spring*) and numbers. [Eds.]

Today witnesses from the neighborhood, which is made up of 25 one-family homes in the $35,000 to $60,000 range with the exception of the two apartment houses near the railroad station, find it difficult to explain why they didn't call the police.

A housewife, knowingly if quite casually, said, "We thought it 26 was a lovers' quarrel." A husband and wife both said, "Frankly, we were afraid." They seemed aware of the fact that events might have been different. A distraught woman, wiping her hands in her apron, said, "I didn't want my husband to get involved."

One couple, now willing to talk about that night, said they heard the 27 first screams. The husband looked thoughtfully at the bookstore where the killer first grabbed Miss Genovese.

"We went to the window to see what was happening," he said, 28 "but the light from our bedroom made it difficult to see the street." The wife, still apprehensive, added: "I put out the light and we were able to see better."

Asked why they hadn't called the police, she shrugged and 29 replied: "I don't know."

A man peeked out from a slight opening in the doorway to his 30 apartment and rattled off an account of the killer's second attack. Why hadn't he called the police at the time? "I was tired," he said without emotion. "I went back to bed."

It was 4:25 A.M. when the ambulance arrived to take the body of 31 Miss Genovese. It drove off. "Then," a solemn police detective said, "the people came out."

QUESTIONS FOR STUDY AND DISCUSSION

1. What is the author's purpose in this selection? (Glossary: *Purpose*) What are the advantages or disadvantages in using narration to accomplish this purpose? Explain.

2. Where does the narrative actually begin? (Glossary: *Narration*) What is the function of the material that precedes the beginning of the narrative?

3. Analyze Gansberg's sentences in paragraphs 7–9. How does he use subordination to highlight what he believes is essential information?

4. Gansberg uses a number of two- and three-word sentences in his narrative. Identify several of these sentences, and explain how they serve to punctuate and to add drama to this story. Which short sentences have the greatest impact on you? Explain why.

5. Gansberg uses dialogue throughout his essay. (Glossary: *Dialogue*) How many people does he quote? What does he accomplish by using dialogue?

6. How would you describe Gansberg's tone? (Glossary: *Tone*) Is the tone appropriate for the story Gansberg narrates? Explain.

7. Reflect on Gansberg's ending. (Glossary: *Beginnings and Endings*) What would be lost or gained by adding a paragraph that analyzed the meaning of the narrative for the reader?

VOCABULARY

Refer to your dictionary to define the following words as they are used in this selection. Then use each word in a sentence of your own.

stalk (1)	shrouded (9)
recitation (4)	sheepishly (21)
assailant (5)	apprehensive (28)
staid (6)	

CLASSROOM ACTIVITY USING EFFECTIVE SENTENCES

Repetition can be an effective writing device to emphasize important points and to enhance coherence. Unless it is handled carefully, however, it can often result in a tedious piece of writing. Rewrite the following paragraph, either eliminating repetition or reworking the repetitions to improve coherence and to emphasize important information.

Daycare centers should be available to all women who work and have no one to care for their children. Daycare centers should not be available only to women who are raising their children alone or to families whose income is below the poverty level. All women who work should have available to them care for their children that is reliable, responsible, convenient, and does not cost an exorbitant amount. Women who work need and must demand more daycare centers. No woman should be prevented from working because of the lack of convenient and reliable facilities for child care.

SUGGESTED WRITING ASSIGNMENTS

1. Gansberg's essay is about public apathy and fear. What reasons did Kitty Genovese's neighbors give for not calling the police when they first heard her calls for help? How do these reasons

reflect on human nature, particularly as it manifests itself in contemporary American society? Modeling your essay after Gansberg's, narrate another event or series of events you know about that demonstrates either public involvement or public apathy.

2. It is common when using narration to tell about firsthand experience and to tell the story in the first person. It is good practice, however, to try writing a narration about something you don't know about firsthand but must learn about, much as a newspaper reporter gathers information for a story. For several days, be attentive to events occurring around you—in your neighborhood, school, community, region—events that would be appropriate for a narrative essay. Interview the principal characters involved in your story, take detailed notes, and then write your narration.

The Language
of the Essay

chapter 10

Diction and Tone

■ Diction

Diction refers to a writer's choice and use of words. Good diction is precise and appropriate — the words mean exactly what the writer intends, and the words are well suited to the writer's subject, purpose, and intended audience.

For careful writers it is not enough merely to come close to saying what they want to say; they select words that convey their exact meaning. Perhaps Mark Twain put this best when he said, "The difference between the right word and the almost right word is the difference between lightning and the lightning bug." Inaccurate, imprecise, or inappropriate diction not only fails to convey the writer's intended meaning but also may cause confusion and misunderstanding for the reader.

CONNOTATION AND DENOTATION

Both **connotation** and **denotation** refer to the meanings of words. Denotation is the dictionary meaning of a word, the literal meaning. Connotative meanings are the associations or emotional overtones that words have acquired. For example, the word *home* denotes a place where someone lives, but it connotes warmth, security, family, comfort, affection, and other more private thoughts and images. The word *residence* also denotes a place where someone lives, but its connotations are colder and more formal.

Many words in English have synonyms, words with very similar denotations — for example, *mob, crowd, multitude,* and *bunch.* Deciding which to use depends largely on the connotations that each synonym has and the context in which the word is to be used. For example, you might say, "There was a crowd at the lecture," but not

"There was a mob at the lecture." Good writers are sensitive to both the denotations and the connotations of words.

ABSTRACT AND CONCRETE WORDS

Abstract words name ideas, conditions, emotions—things nobody can touch, see, or hear. Some abstract words are *love, wisdom, cowardice, beauty, fear,* and *liberty.* People often disagree about abstract things. You may find a forest beautiful, while someone else might find it frightening, and neither of you would be wrong. Beauty and fear are abstract ideas; they exist in your mind, not in the forest along with the trees and the owls. **Concrete** words refer to things we can touch, see, hear, smell, and taste, such as *sandpaper, soda, birch tree, smog, cow, sailboat, rocking chair,* and *pancake.* If you disagree with someone on a concrete issue—say, you claim that the forest is mostly birch trees, while the other person says it is mostly pine—only one of you can be right, and both of you can be wrong; the kinds of trees that grow in the forest is a concrete fact, not an abstract idea.

Good writing balances ideas and facts, and it also balances abstract and concrete diction. If the writing is too abstract, with too few concrete facts and details, it will be unconvincing and tiresome. If the writing is too concrete, devoid of abstract ideas and emotions, it can seem mundane and dry.

GENERAL AND SPECIFIC WORDS

General and **specific** do not necessarily refer to opposites. The same word can often be either general or specific, depending on the context: *Dessert* is more specific than *food,* but more general than *chocolate cream pie.* Being very specific is like being concrete: Chocolate cream pie is something you can see and taste. Being general, on the other hand, is like being abstract. Food, dessert, and even pie are large classes of things that bring only very general tastes or images to mind.

Good writing moves back and forth from the general to the specific. Without specific words, generalities can be unconvincing and even confusing: The writer's idea of "good food" may be very different from the reader's. But writing that does not relate specifics to each other by generalization often lacks focus and direction.

CLICHÉS

Words, phrases, and expressions that have become trite through overuse are called clichés. Let's assume your roommate has just returned from an evening out. You ask her, "How was the concert?" She responds, "The concert was okay, but they had us *packed in* there *like sardines.* How was your evening?" And you reply, "Well, I finished my term paper, but the noise here is enough to *drive me crazy. The dorm is a real zoo."* At one time the italicized expressions were vivid and colorful, but through constant use they have grown stale and ineffective. Experienced writers always try to avoid such clichés as *believe it or not, doomed to failure, hit the spot, let's face it, sneaking suspicion, step in the right direction,* and *went to great lengths.* They strive to use fresh language.

JARGON

Jargon, or technical language, is the special vocabulary of a trade or profession. Writers who use jargon do so with an awareness of their audience. If their audience is a group of coworkers or professionals, jargon may be used freely. If the audience is more general, jargon should be used sparingly and carefully so that readers can understand it. Jargon becomes inappropriate when it is overused, used out of context, or used pretentiously. For example, computer terms like *input, output,* and *feedback* are sometimes used in place of *contribution, result,* and *response* in other fields, especially in business. If you think about it, the terms suggest that people are machines, receiving and processing information according to a program imposed by someone else.

FORMAL AND INFORMAL DICTION

Diction is appropriate when it suits the occasion for which it is intended. If the situation is informal—a friendly letter, for example— the writing may be colloquial; that is, its words may be chosen to suggest the way people talk with each other. If, on the other hand, the situation is formal—a term paper or a research report, for example—then the words should reflect this formality. Informal writing tends to be characterized by slang, contractions, references to the reader, and concrete nouns. Formal writing tends to be impersonal, abstract, and free of contractions and references to the reader. Formal writing and informal writing are, of course, the extremes. Most writing falls between these two extremes and is a blend of those formal and informal elements that best fit the context.

▪ Tone

Tone is the attitude a writer takes toward the subject and the audience. The tone may be friendly or hostile, serious or humorous, intimate or distant, enthusiastic or skeptical.

As you read the following paragraphs, notice how each writer has created a different tone and how that tone is supported by the diction — the writer's particular choice and use of words.

NOSTALGIC

When I was six years old, I thought I knew a lot. How to jump rope, how to skip a rock across a pond, and how to color and stay between the lines — these were all things I took great pride in. Nothing was difficult, and my days were carefree. That is, until the summer when everything became complicated and I suddenly realized I didn't know that much.

–Heather C. Blue, student

ANGRY

Cans. Beer cans. Glinting on the verges of a million miles of roadways, lying in scrub, grass, dirt, leaves, sand, mud, but never hidden. Piels, Rheingold, Ballantine, Schaefer, Schlitz, shining in the sun or picked by moon or the beams of headlights at night; washed by rain or flattened by wheels, but never dulled, never buried, never destroyed. Here is the mark of savages, the testament of wasters, the stain of prosperity.

–Marya Mannes

HUMOROUS

In perpetrating a revolution, there are two requirements: someone or something to revolt against and someone to actually show up and do the revolting. Dress is usually casual and both parties may be flexible about time and place but if either faction fails to attend the whole enterprise is likely to come off badly. In the Chinese

Revolution of 1650 neither party showed up and the deposit on the hall was forfeited.

–Woody Allen

RESIGNED

I make my living humping cargo for Seaboard World Airlines, one of the big international airlines at Kennedy Airport. They handle strictly all cargo. I was once told that one of the Rockefellers is the major stockholder for the airline, but I don't really think about that too much. I don't get paid to think. The big thing is to beat that race with the time clock every morning of your life so the airline will be happy. The worst thing a man could ever do is to make suggestions about building a better airline. They pay people $40,000 a year to come up with better ideas. It doesn't matter that these ideas never work; it's just that they get nervous when a guy from South Brooklyn or Ozone Park acts like he has a brain.

–Patrick Fenton

IRONIC

Once upon a time there was a small, beautiful, green and graceful country called Vietnam. It needed to be saved. (In later years no one could remember exactly what it needed to be saved from, but that is another story.) For many years Vietnam was in the process of being saved by France, but the French eventually tired of their labors and left. Then America took on the job. America was well equipped for country-saving. It was the richest and most powerful nation on earth. It had, for example, nuclear explosives on hand and ready to use equal to six tons of TNT for every man, woman, and child in the world. It had huge and very efficient factories, brilliant and dedicated scientists, and most (but not everybody) would agree, it had good intentions. Sadly, America had one fatal flaw—its inhabitants were in love with technology and thought it could do no wrong. A visitor to America during the time of this story would probably have guessed its outcome after seeing how its inhabitants were treating their own country. The air was mostly foul, the water putrid, and most of the land was either covered with concrete or garbage. But Americans were never much on introspection, and they didn't foresee the result of their loving embrace on the small country. They set out to save Vietnam with the same enthusiasm and determination their forefathers had displayed in conquering the frontier.

–The Sierra Club

The diction and tone of an essay are subtle forces, but they exert a tremendous influence on readers. They are instrumental in determining how we will feel while reading the essay and what attitude we will have toward its argument or the points that it makes. Of course, readers react in a variety of ways. An essay written informally but with a largely angry tone may make one reader defensive and unsympathetic; another may feel that the author is being unusually honest and courageous and may admire these qualities and feel moved by them. Either way, the diction and tone of the piece have made a strong emotional impression. As you read the essays in this chapter and throughout this book, see if you can analyze how the diction and tone are shaping your reactions.

Does a Finger Fing?

■ **Nedra Newkirk Lamar**

Freelance writer Nedra Newkirk Lamar writes extensively on the English language and on matters of effective communication. She has authored a number of books on writing and speaking, including How to Speak the Written Word, Pronunciation of Bible Names and Places, *and* 1,000 Hard and Easy Words Frequently Mispronounced. *Lamar knows that people learn how to form new words in English in many different ways. They add* -ment *to some verbs, for example, to form nouns like* excitement *and* development. *Or they combine words like* snow *and* board *to create* snowboard, *or they shorten words like* referee, laboratory, *and* mathematics *to* ref, lab, *and* math. *As you may have expected, the rules for word formation are not always consistent. In the following essay, which first appeared in* The Christian Science Monitor *in February 1970, Lamar takes a close look at what happens when we add the suffix* -er *to words. Experience tells us that when we add* -er *to a word like* teach *we create the new word* teacher, *meaning "one who teaches." But as Lamar points out, this is not always the case. With a twinkle in her eye, she reveals the incongruities that result when "rules" are applied mechanically.*

FOR YOUR JOURNAL

Many of us grew up memorizing the following traditional rhyme for *ie* and *ei* spellings:

Write *i* before *e*
Except after *c*
Or when sounded like *ay*
As in neighbor or weigh.

But remember the exceptions? Does this little rhyme remind you of other "rules" you learned in school? What do you remember about learning to speak and write in English?

Everybody knows that a tongue-twister is something that twists the tongue, and a skyscraper is something that scrapes the sky, but is an eavesdropper someone who drops eaves? A thinker is someone who thinks but is a tinker someone who tinks? Is a clabber something that goes around clabbing?

Somewhere along the way we all must have had an English teacher who gave us the fascinating information that words that end in ER mean something or somebody who *does* something, like trapper, designer, or stopper.

A stinger is something that stings, but is a finger something that fings? Fing fang fung. Today I fing. Yesterday I fang. Day before yesterday I had already fung.

You'd expect eyes, then, to be called seers and ears to be hearers. We'd wear our shoes on our walkers and our sleeves on our reachers. But we don't. The only parts of the body that sound as if they might indicate what they're supposed to do are our fingers, which we've already counted out, our livers, and our shoulders. And they don't do what they sound as if they might. At least, I've never seen anyone use his shoulders for shoulding. You shoulder your way through a crowd, but you don't should your way. It's only in slang that we follow the pattern, when we smell with our smellers and kiss with our kissers.

The animal pattern seems to have more of a feeling for this formation than people do, because insects actually do feel with their feelers. But do cats use their whiskers for whisking?

I've seen people mend socks and knit socks, but I've never seen anyone dolage a sock. Yet there must be people who do, else how could we have sock-dolagers?

Is a humdinger one who dings hums? And what is a hum anyway, and how would one go about dinging it? Maybe Winnie the Pooh could have told us. He was always humming hums, but A. A. Milne never tells us whether he also was fond of dinging them. He sang them but do you suppose he ever dang them?

Sometimes occupational names do reveal what the worker does, though. Manufacturers manufacture, miners mine, adjusters adjust— or at least try to. But does a grocer groce? Does a fruiterer fruiter? Does a butler buttle?

No, you just can't trust the English language. You can love it because it's your mother tongue. You can take pride in it because it's the language Shakespeare was dramatic in. You can thrill to it because it's the language Browning and Tennyson were poetic in. You can have fun with it because it's the language Dickens and Mark

Twain and Lewis Carroll were funny in. You can revere it because it's the language Milton[1] was majestic in. You can be grateful to it because it's the language the Magna Carta[2] and the Declaration of Independence were expressed in.

But you just can't trust it! 10

QUESTIONS FOR STUDY AND DISCUSSION

1. What is Lamar's thesis in this essay, and where does she state it? (Glossary: *Thesis*)
2. What is Lamar's purpose—to tell, to describe, to explain, or to convince? (Glossary: *Purpose*) Explain.
3. Lamar's tone in this essay can best be described as playful. In what ways is this tone appropriate for her subject and purpose?
4. Lamar's opening paragraph consists of three rhetorical questions that focus on words that end in the suffix -*er*. (Glossary: *Rhetorical Question*) Did these questions engage you and start you thinking about the incongruities of the English language? How effective did you find this strategy for beginning an essay? Where else does Lamar use rhetorical questions in her essay?
5. One of the real strengths of Lamar's essay is her examples. (Glossary: *Example*) What specifically do these well-chosen examples add to her essay? Which examples worked best for you? Why?
6. In paragraph 9 Lamar uses a number of strong verbs to explain all that there is to like about the English language. (Glossary: *Verb*) Identify the strong verbs, and then substitute the verb *like* for each of the verbs you identified. What is lost when you make this substitution?

VOCABULARY

Refer to your dictionary to define the following words as they are used in this selection. Then use each word in a sentence of your own.

tinker (1)   sock-dolagers (6)
slang (4)   occupational (8)

---

[1]*John Milton* (1608–1674): English poet. [Eds.]
[2]*Magna Carta*: the charter of English liberties granted by King John in 1215 under threat of civil war. [Eds.]

CLASSROOM ACTIVITY USING TONE AND DICTION

Good writers rely on strong verbs—verbs that contribute significantly to what is being said. Because they must repeatedly describe similar situations, sportswriters, for example, are acutely aware of the need for strong action verbs. It is not enough for them to say that a team wins or loses; they must describe the type of win or loss more precisely. As a result, such verbs as *beat, bury, edge, shock,* and *trounce* are common in the headlines on the sports page. In addition to describing the act of winning, each of these verbs makes a statement about the quality of the victory. Like sportswriters, all of us write about actions that are performed daily. If we were restricted only to the verbs *eat, drink, sleep,* and *work* for each of these activities, for example, our writing would be repetitious, monotonous, and most likely wordy. List as many verbs as you can that you could use in place of these four. What connotative differences do you find in your lists of alternatives? What is the importance of these connotative differences for you as a writer?

SUGGESTED WRITING ASSIGNMENTS

1. Using Lamar's statement "You just can't trust the English language" as a starting point, write an essay in which you recount one or more of your own frustrating experiences with the English language. In what ways did you believe that the language had let you down? You may find it helpful to read what you wrote in response to the journal prompt for this selection before starting to write your essay.

2. In paragraph 9 Lamar lists many of the reasons why we can love or take pride in the English language. Do you agree with the reasons she lists? Why, or why not? What reasons of your own can you add to Lamar's list? What do all these reasons say about the power of language in our lives? Write an essay in which you discuss the importance of language in your own life.

On Being 17, Bright, and Unable to Read

■ **David Raymond**

When the following article appeared in the New York Times *in 1976, David Raymond was a high school student in Connecticut. In 1981, Raymond graduated from Curry College outside of Boston, one of the few colleges with learning-disability programs at the time. He and his family now live in Fairfield, Connecticut, where he works as a builder. In his essay, he poignantly discusses the great difficulties he had with reading because of his dyslexia and the many problems he experienced in school as a result. As you read, pay particular attention to the natural quality of the words he uses to convey his ideas and how that naturalness of diction contributes to the essay's informal yet sincere tone.*

FOR YOUR JOURNAL

One of the fundamental skills that we are supposed to learn in school is how to read. How would you rate yourself as a reader? Would you like to be able to read better? How important is reading in your everyday life?

O ne day a substitute teacher picked me to read aloud from the textbook. When I told her "No, thank you," she came unhinged. She thought I was acting smart, and told me so. I kept calm, and that got her madder and madder. We must have spent 10 minutes trying to solve the problem, and finally she got so red in the face I thought she'd blow up. She told me she'd see me after class.

Maybe someone like me was a new thing for that teacher. But she wasn't new to me. I've been through scenes like that all my life. You see, even though I'm 17 and a junior in high school, I can't read because I have dyslexia. I'm told I read "at a fourth-grade level," but from where I sit, that's not reading. You can't know what that means unless you've been there. It's not easy to tell how it feels when you can't read your homework assignments or the newspaper or a menu in a restaurant or even notes from your own friends.

My family began to suspect I was having problems almost from the first day I started school. My father says my early years in school were the worst years of his life. They weren't so good for me, either. As I look back on it now, I can't find the words to express how bad it really was. I wanted to die. I'd come home from school screaming, "I'm dumb. I'm dumb—I wish I were dead!"

I guess I couldn't read anything at all then—not even my own name—and they tell me I didn't talk as good as other kids. But what I remember about those days is that I couldn't throw a ball where it was supposed to go, I couldn't learn to swim, and I wouldn't learn to ride a bike, because no matter what anyone told me, I knew I'd fail.

Sometimes my teachers would try to be encouraging. When I couldn't read the words on the board they'd say, "Come on, David, you know that word." Only I didn't. And it was embarrassing. I just felt dumb. And dumb was how the kids treated me. They'd make fun of me every chance they got, asking me to spell "cat" or something like that. Even if I knew how to spell it, I wouldn't; they'd only give me another word. Anyway, it was awful, because more than anything I wanted friends. On my birthday when I blew out the candles I didn't wish I could learn to read; what I wished for was that the kids would like me.

With the bad reports coming from school, and with me moaning about wanting to die and how everybody hated me, my parents began looking for help. That's when the testing started. The school tested me, the child-guidance center tested me, private psychiatrists tested me. Everybody knew something was wrong—especially me.

It didn't help much when they stuck a fancy name onto it. I couldn't pronounce it then—I was only in second grade—and I was ashamed to talk about it. Now it rolls off my tongue, because I've been living with it for a lot of years—dyslexia.

All through elementary school it wasn't easy. I was always having to do things that were "different," things the other kids didn't have to do. I had to go to a child psychiatrist, for instance.

One summer my family forced me to go to a camp for children with reading problems. I hated the idea, but the camp turned out pretty good, and I had a good time. I met a lot of kids who couldn't read and somehow that helped. The director of the camp said I had a higher I.Q. than 90 percent of the population. I didn't believe him.

About the worst thing I had to do in fifth and sixth grade was go   10
to a special education class in another school in our town. A bus
picked me up, and I didn't like that at all. The bus also picked up
emotionally disturbed kids and retarded kids. It was like going to a
school for the retarded. I always worried that someone I knew would
see me on that bus. It was a relief to go to the regular junior high
school.

Life began to change a little for me then, because I began to feel   11
better about myself. I found the teachers cared; they had meetings
about me and I worked harder for them for a while. I began to work
on the potter's wheel, making vases and pots that the teachers said
were pretty good. Also, I got a letter for being on the track team. I
could always run pretty fast.

At high school the teachers are good and everyone is trying to   12
help me. I've gotten honors some marking periods and I've won a letter on the cross-country team. Next quarter I think the school might
hold a show of my pottery. I've got some friends. But there are still
some embarrassing times. For instance, every time there is writing in
the class, I get up and go to the special education room. Kids ask me
where I go all the time. Sometimes I say, "to Mars."

Homework is a real problem. During free periods in school I go   13
into the special ed room and staff members read assignments to me.
When I get home my mother reads to me. Sometimes she reads an assignment into a tape recorder, and then I go into my room and listen
to it. If we have a novel or something like that to read, she reads it
out loud to me. Then I sit down with her and we do the assignment.
She'll write, while I talk my answers to her. Lately I've taken to dic-
tating into a tape recorder, and then someone — my father, a private
tutor or my mother — types up what I've dictated. Whatever homework I do takes someone else's time, too. That makes me feel bad.

We had a big meeting in school the other day — eight of us, four   14
from the guidance department, my private tutor, my parents and me.
The subject was me. I said I wanted to go to college, and they told
me about colleges that have facilities and staff to handle people like
me. That's nice to hear.

As for what happens after college, I don't know and I'm worried   15
about that. How can I make a living if I can't read? Who will hire me?
How will I fill out the application form? The only thing that gives me
any courage is the fact that I've learned about well-known people who
couldn't read or had other problems and still made it. Like Albert

Einstein,[1] who didn't talk until he was 4 and flunked math. Like Leonardo da Vinci,[2] who everyone seems to think had dyslexia.

I've told this story because maybe some teacher will read it and [16] go easy on a kid in the classroom who has what I've got. Or, maybe some parent will stop nagging his kid, and stop calling him lazy. Maybe he's not lazy or dumb. Maybe he just can't read and doesn't know what's wrong. Maybe he's scared, like I was.

QUESTIONS FOR STUDY AND DISCUSSION

1. Raymond uses many colloquial and idiomatic expressions, such as "she came unhinged" and "she got so red in the face I thought she'd blow up" (1). (Glossary: *Colloquial Expression*) Identify other examples of such diction, and tell how they affect your reaction to the essay.

2. In the context of the essay, comment on the appropriateness of each of the following possible choices of diction. Which word is better in each case? Why?
   a. *selected* for *picked* (1)
   b. *experience* for *thing* (2)
   c. *speak as well* for *talk as good* (4)
   d. *negative* for *bad* (6)
   e. *important* for *big* (14)
   f. *failed* for *flunked* (15)
   g. *frightened* for *scared* (16)

3. How would you describe Raymond's tone in this essay?

4. What is dyslexia? Is it essential for an understanding of the essay that we know more about dyslexia than Raymond tells us? Explain.

5. What does Raymond say his purpose is in telling his story? (Glossary: *Purpose*)

6. What does Raymond's story tell us about the importance of our early childhood experiences, especially within our educational system?

---

[1]*Albert Einstein* (1879–1955): German American physicist.
[2]*Leonardo da Vinci* (1452–1519): Italian painter, draftsman, sculptor, architect, and engineer.

VOCABULARY

Refer to your dictionary to define the following words as they are used in this selection. Then use each word in a sentence of your own.

dyslexia (2)   psychiatrists (6)

CLASSROOM ACTIVITY USING DICTION AND TONE

Many menus use connotative language to persuade customers that they are about to have an exceptional eating experience. Phrases like the following are commonplace: "skillfully seasoned and basted with lime juice," "festive red cranberry sauce," "a bed of crisp baby vegetables," and "freshly ground coffee." Imagine that you are creating a menu. Use connotative language to describe the following basic foods. Try to make them sound as attractive and inviting as possible.

1. tomato juice
2. onion soup
3. ground beef
4. chicken
5. peas

6. potatoes
7. salad
8. bread and butter
9. teas
10. cake

SUGGESTED WRITING ASSIGNMENTS

1. Imagine that you are away at school. Recently you were caught in a speed trap — you were going 70 miles per hour in a 55-mile-per-hour zone — and have just lost your license; you will not be able to go home this coming weekend, as you had planned. Write two letters in which you explain why you will not be able to go home, one to your parents and the other to your best friend. Your audience is different in each case, so be sure to choose your diction accordingly. Try to imitate Raymond's informal yet serious tone in one of your letters.

2. Select an essay you have already completed for this course. Who was your intended audience for this essay? Rewrite the essay with a different audience in mind. For example, if your intended audience was originally your teacher and you wrote in a formal, serious tone, rewrite your essay for your sister, altering your tone accordingly. You might also choose as your intended audience your classmates, your religious leader, or the state environmental board. Reshape your essay as necessary.

Pop-A-Shot

■ **Sarah Vowell**

*Author and cultural observer, Sarah Vowell was born in Okla-
homa in 1969 and raised in Oklahoma and Montana. She now
lives in New York City. She is perhaps best known for the witty
and sometimes quirky monologues and documentaries that she's
done for National Public Radio's* This American Life *since
1996. A guest of late-night television hosts David Letterman
and Conan O'Brien, Vowell has performed her comic routines
at the Aspen Comedy Festival, Amsterdam's Crossing Borders
Festival, and Seattle's Foolproof Comedy Festival. Vowell's essays have appeared in* Esquire, the Los Angeles Times, *the* Village Voice, Spin, *and* Salon. *Many of her most popular essays
have been gathered in two books,* Take the Cannoli: Stories
from the New World *(2000) and* The Partly Cloudy Patriot
(2002). Her first book was Radio On: A Listener's Diary
*(1997), a commentary on AM and FM radio in America. In the
following essay, taken from* The Partly Cloudy Patriot, *Vowell reflects on her own fascination with the arcade game Pop-A-Shot.
As you read, notice how she uses her humorous, off-beat perspective to make a point about what she does to find happiness.*

FOR YOUR JOURNAL

What does it mean to "goof off"? What kinds of things do you
and your friends do when goofing off? For example, do you play
arcade games or video games when you want to escape the stresses
of everyday life? What, for you, are the benefits of goofing off?

Along with voting, jury duty, and paying taxes, goofing off is one   1
of the central obligations of American citizenship. So when my
friends Joel and Stephen and I play hooky from our jobs in the middle of the afternoon to play Pop-A-Shot in a room full of children, I
like to think we are not procrastinators; we are patriots pursuing
happiness.

Pop-A-Shot is not a video game. It involves shooting real, if   2
miniature, basketballs for forty seconds. It's embarrassing how giddy

the three of us get when it's our turn to put money into the machine. (Often, we have to stand behind some six-year-old girl who bogarts[1] the game and whose father keeps dropping in quarters even though the kid makes only about 4 points if she's lucky and we are forced to glare at the back of her pigtailed head, waiting just long enough to start questioning our adulthood and how by the time our parents were our age they were beholden to mortgages and PTA meetings and here we are, stuck in an episode of *Friends*.)

Finally it's my turn. A wave of balls slide toward me and I shoot, making my first basket. I'm good at this. I'm not great. The machine I usually play on has a high score of 72, and my highest score is 56. But considering that I am five foot four, that I used to get C's in gym, and that I campaigned for Dukakis, the fact that I am capable of scoring 56 points in forty seconds is a source of no small amount of pride. Plus, even though these modern men won't admit it, it really bugs Joel and Steve to get topped by a girl.

There are two reasons I can shoot a basketball: black-eyed peas and Uncle Hoy. I was a forward on my elementary school team. This was in Oklahoma, back when girls played half-court basketball, which meant I never crossed over to the other team's side, which meant all I ever had to do was shoot, a bonus considering that I cannot run, pass, or dribble. Blessed with one solitary athletic skill, I was going to make the most of it. I shot baskets in the backyard every night after dinner. We lived out in the country, and my backboard was nailed to an oak tree that grew on top of a hill. If I missed a shot, the ball would roll downhill into the drainage ditch for the kitchen sink, a muddy rivulet flecked with corn and black-eyed peas. So if the ball bounced willy-nilly off the rim, I had to run after it, retrieve it from the gross black-eyed pea mud, then hose it off. So I learned not to miss.

My mother's brother, Hoy, was a girls' basketball coach. Once he saw I had a knack for shooting, he used to drill me on free throws, standing under the hoop at my grandmother's house, where he himself learned to play. And Hoy, who was also a math teacher—he had gone to college on a dual math-basketball scholarship—revered the geometrical arc of the swish. Hoy hated the backboard, and thought players who used it to make anything other than layups lacked elegance. And so, if I made a free throw that bounced off the backboard before gliding through the basket, he'd yell, "Doesn't count."

---

[1]*bogart:* to be selfish, to take more than one's share of.

Sometimes, trash-talking at Pop-A-Shot, I bark that at Joel and Stephen when they score their messy bank shots. "Doesn't count!" The electronic scoreboard, unfortunately, makes no distinction for grace and beauty.

I watch the NBA. I lived in Chicago during the heyday of the   6
Bulls. And I have noticed that in, as I like to call it, the moving-around-basketball, the players spend the whole game trying to shoot. There's all that wasted running and throwing and falling down on cameramen in between baskets. But Pop-A-Shot is basketball concentrate. I've made 56 points in forty seconds. Michael Jordan never did that. When Michael Jordan would make even 40 points in a game it was the lead in the eleven o'clock news. It takes a couple of hours to play a moving-around-basketball game. Pop-A-Shot distills this down to less than a minute. It is the crack cocaine of basketball. I can make twenty-eight baskets at a rate of less than two seconds per.

Joel, an excellent shot, also appreciates this about Pop-A-Shot.   7
He likes the way it feels, but he's embarrassed by how it sounds stupid when he describes it to other people. (He spent part of last year working in Canada, and I think it rubbed off on him, diminishing his innate American ability to celebrate the civic virtue of idiocy.) Joel plays in a fairly serious adult basketball league in New York. One night, he left Stephen and me in the arcade and rushed off to a—this hurt my feelings—"real" game. That night, he missed a foul shot by two feet and made the mistake of admitting to the other players that his arms were tired from throwing miniature balls at a shortened hoop all afternoon. They laughed and laughed. "In the second over-time," Joel told me, "when the opposing team fouled me with four seconds left and gave me the opportunity to shoot from the line for the game, they looked mighty smug as they took their positions along the key. Oh, Pop-A-Shot guy, I could hear them thinking to their smug selves. He'll never make a foul shot. He plays baby games. Wa-wa-wa, little Pop-A-Shot baby, would you like a zwieback biscuit? But you know what? I made those shots, and those sons of bitches had to wipe their smug grins off their smug faces and go home thinking that maybe Pop-A-Shot wasn't just a baby game after all."

I think Pop-A-Shot's a baby game. That's why I love it. Unlike   8
the game of basketball itself, Pop-A-Shot has no standard socially re-deeming value whatsoever. Pop-A-Shot is not about teamwork or getting along or working together. Pop-A-Shot is not about getting exercise or fresh air. It takes place in fluorescent-lit bowling alleys or darkened bars. It costs money. At the end of a game, one does not

swig Gatorade. One sips bourbon or margaritas or munches cupcakes. Unless one is playing the Super Shot version at the ESPN Zone in Times Square,[2] in which case, one orders the greatest appetizer ever invented on this continent — a plate of cheeseburgers.

In other words, Pop-A-Shot has no point at all. And that, for me, is the point. My life is full of points — the deadlines and bills and recycling and phone calls. I have come to appreciate, to depend on, this one dumb-ass little passion. Because every time a basketball slides off my fingertips and drops perfectly, flawlessly, into that hole, well, swish, happiness found.

9

QUESTIONS FOR STUDY AND DISCUSSION

1. In the opening paragraph, Vowell announces that "goofing off is one of the central obligations of American citizenship." How serious do you think she is in making this claim? How does she support this claim?

2. How does Vowell account for her success at Pop-A-Shot?

3. How would you describe Vowell's tone in this essay? How did her choice of words lead you to this conclusion?

4. What does Vowell mean when she says that "Pop-A-Shot is basketball concentrate" (6)?

5. In paragraph 7, Vowell relates a story about her friend Joel's experience in a "real" basketball game. How is this paragraph about Joel related to Vowell's main idea, or is this paragraph a digression in the essay? (Glossary: *Unity*)

6. What do you know about the writer as a result of reading this essay? How would you describe her?

7. What, for Vowell, is the point of Pop-A-Shot? Why does she love this game?

VOCABULARY

Refer to your dictionary to define the following words as they are used in this selection. Then use each word in a sentence of your own.

procrastinators (1)   rivulet (4)
patriots (1)   knack (5)

---

[2]*Times Square:* a major entertainment district in New York City. [Eds.]

CLASSROOM ACTIVITY USING DICTION AND TONE

Writers use different levels of diction to communicate with different audiences of readers. For example, a writer might use the formal label *police officer* in an article for law enforcement professionals and the more informal word *cop* in a humorous piece for a general audience. Recall a fairground activity, an amusement park ride, or a video game that you have enjoyed. Write a paragraph in which you describe this activity, ride, or game to an older relative. Then rewrite the paragraph to appeal to a ten-year-old.

SUGGESTED WRITING ASSIGNMENTS

1. Vowell states that Americans like her friend Joel have the "innate . . . ability to celebrate the civic virtue of idiocy" (7). What do you think? Has the world gotten so serious and stressful that we all need "one dumb-ass little passion" (9) like Pop-A-Shot to make life tolerable? Write an essay in which you present your views on mindless or pointless games in our culture.

2. What makes you happy? For example, do you find happiness when you are with other people or while you are doing a particular activity? Write an essay in which you explain what makes you happy.

And May He Be Bilingual

■ **Judith Ortiz Cofer**

*Author and educator Judith Ortiz Cofer was born in Hormi-gueros, Puerto Rico, in 1952, but her family immigrated to the United States in 1954, settling first in Paterson, New Jersey, and later in Augusta, Georgia. She earned her B.A. at Augusta Col-lege in 1974 and her M.A. from Florida Atlantic University in 1977. Currently, she is Franklin Professor of English and Cre-ative Writing at the University of Georgia. She has published a novel and collections of poetry, essays, and short fiction, includ-*ing Terms of Survival *(1987),* Reaching for the Mainland *(1987),* The Line of the Sun *(1989),* Silent Dancing: A Partial Remembrance of a Puerto Rican Childhood *(1990),* The Latin Deli *(1993),* An Island Like You: Stories of the Barrio *(1995),* and The Year of Our Revolution *(1998). Much of Cofer's writ-ing focuses on Hispanic issues and the culture clashes that occur between the Anglo and Hispanic communities. In the following autobiographical essay, which first appeared in her most recent book,* Woman in Front of the Sun: On Becoming a Writer *(2000), Cofer explores the "coalescing of languages and cul-tures" in a culturally diverse country like America. Cofer's straightforward, almost conversational, tone engages readers at once and draws them into her reflections about teaching and writing in her second language.*

FOR YOUR JOURNAL

Today most colleges and universities are trying to create cultur-ally diverse campuses. What is the value of living and learning within a culturally diverse community? Explain.

Latin Women Pray

Latin women pray
In incense sweet churches
They pray in Spanish
To an Anglo God
With a Jewish heritage.

And this Great White Father
Imperturbable
In his marble pedestal
Looks down upon
His brown daughters
Votive candles shining like lust
In his all seeing eyes
Unmoved
By their persistent prayers.
Yet year after year
Before his image they kneel
Margarita, Josefina, Maria, and Isabel
All fervently hoping
That if not omnipotent
At least He be bilingual.

In this early poem I express the sense of powerlessness I felt as a 1
non-native speaker of English in the United States. Non-native.
Non-participant in the mainstream culture. *Non,* as in no, not, nothing. This little poem is about the non-ness of the non-speakers of the
ruling language making a pilgrimage to the only One who can help,
hopeful in their faith that someone is listening, yet still suspicious
that even He doesn't understand their language. I grew up in the tight
little world of the Puerto Rican community in Paterson, New Jersey,
and later moved to Augusta, Georgia, where my "native" universe
shrank even further to a tiny group of us who were brought to the
Deep South through the military channels our fathers had chosen out
of economic necessity. I wrote this ironic poem years ago, out of a
need to explore the loneliness, the almost hopelessness, I had felt and
observed in the other non-native speakers, many my own relatives,
who would never master the English language well enough to be able
to connect with the native speakers in as significant ways as I did.

Having come to age within the boundaries of language exiles, 2
and making only brief forays out into the vast and often frightening
landscape called *the mainstream,* it's easy for the newcomer to
become ethnocentric. That's what Little Italy, Little Korea, Little
Havana, Chinatown, and barrios are, centers of ethnic concerns.
After all, it's a natural human response to believe that there is safety
only within the walls around the circle of others who look like us,
speak like us, behave like us: it is the animal kingdom's basic rule of

survival—if whatever is coming toward you does not look like you or your kin, either fight or fly.

It is this primal fear of the unfamiliar that I have conquered 3 through education, travel, and my art. I am an English teacher by profession and a writer by vocation. I have written several books of prose and poetry based mainly on my experiences in growing up Latina in the United States. Until a few years ago, when multiculturalism became part of the American political agenda, no one seemed to notice my work; suddenly I find myself a Puerto Rican/American (Latina)/Woman writer. Not only am I supposed to share my particular vision of American life, but I am also supposed to be a role model for a new generation of Latino students who expect me to teach them how to get a piece of the proverbial English language pie. I actually enjoy both of these public roles, in moderation. I love teaching literature. Not my own work, but the work of my literary ancestors in English and American literature—my field, that is, the main source of my models as a writer. I also like going into my classrooms at the University of Georgia, where my English classes at this point are still composed mainly of white American students, with a sprinkling of African American and Asian American, and only occasionally a Latino, and sharing my bicultural, bilingual views with them. It is a fresh audience. I am not always speaking to converts.

I teach American literature as an outsider in love with the 4 Word—whatever language it is written in. They, at least some of them, come to understand that my main criterion when I teach is excellence and that I will talk to them about so-called minority writers whom I admire in the same terms as I will the old standards they know they are supposed to honor and study. I show them why they should admire them, not blindly, but with a critical eye. I speak English with my Spanish accent to these native speakers. I tell them about my passion for the genius of humankind, demonstrated through literature: the power of language to affect, to enrich, or to diminish and destroy lives, its potential to empower someone like me, someone like them. The fact that English is my second language does not seem to matter beyond the first few lectures, when the students sometimes look askance at one another, perhaps wondering whether they have walked into the wrong classroom and at any moment this obviously "Spanish" professor will ask them to start conjugating regular and irregular verbs. They can't possibly know this about me: in my classes, everyone is safe from Spanish grammar recitation. Because almost all of my formal education has been in English, I avoid all possible risk of falling into a discussion of the uses of the conditional or of the merits of the subjunctive tense in the Spanish language: Hey, I just *do* Spanish, I don't explain it.

Likewise, when I *do* use my Spanish and allude to my Puerto   5
Rican heritage, it comes from deep inside me where my imagination and memory reside, and I do it through my writing. My poetry, my stories, and my essays concern themselves with the coalescing of languages and cultures into a vision that has meaning first of all for me; then, if I am served well by my craft and the transformation occurs, it will also have meaning for others as art.

My life as a child and teenager was one of constant dislocation.   6
My father was in the U.S. Navy, and we moved back to Puerto Rico during his long tours of duty abroad. On the Island, my brother and I attended a Catholic school run by American nuns. Then it was back to Paterson, New Jersey, to try to catch up, and sometimes we did, academically, but socially it was a different story altogether. We were the perennial new kids on the block. Yet when I write about these gypsy days, I construct a continuity that allows me to see my life as equal to any other, with its share of chaos, with its own system of order. This is what I have learned from writing as a minority person in America that I can teach my students: Literature is the human search for meaning. It is as simple and as profound as that. And we are all, if we are thinking people, involved in the process. It is both a privilege and a burden.

Although as a child I often felt resentful of my rootlessness, de-   7
prived of a stable home, lasting friendships, the security of one house, one country, I now realize that these same circumstances taught me some skills that I use today to adapt in a constantly changing world, a place where you can remain in one spot for years and still wake up every day to strangeness wrought by technology and politics. We can stand still and find ourselves in a different nation created overnight by decisions we did not participate in making. I submit that we are all becoming more like the immigrant and can learn from her experiences as a stranger in a strange land. I know I am a survivor in language. I learned early that possessing the secret of words was to be my passport into mainstream life. Notice I did not say "assimilation" into mainstream life. This is a word that has come to mean the acceptance of loss of native culture. Although I know for a fact that to survive everyone "assimilates" what they need out of many different cultures, especially in America, I prefer to use the term "adapt" instead. Just as I acquired the skills to adapt to American life, I have

now come to terms with a high-tech world. It is not that different. I learned English to communicate, but now I know computer language. I have been greedy in my grasping and hoarding of words. I own enough stock in English to feel secure in almost any situation where my language skills have to serve me; and I have claimed my rich Puerto Rican culture to give scope and depth to my personal search for meaning.

As I travel around this country I am constantly surprised by the di-   8
versity of its peoples and cultures. It is like a huge, colorful puzzle. And the beauty is in its complexity. Yet there are some things that transcend the obvious differences: great literature, great ideas, and great idealists, for example. I find Don Quixote[1] plays almost universal; after all, who among us does not have an Impossible Dream? Shakespeare's wisdom is planetary in its appeal; Ghandi's[2] and King's[3] message is basic to the survival of our civilization, and most people know it; and other voices that are like a human racial memory speak in a language that can almost always be translated into meaning.

And genius doesn't come in only one package. The Bard[4] hap-   9
pened to be a white gentleman from England, but what about our timid Emily Dickinson? Would we call on her in our class, that mousy little girl in the back of the room squinting at the chalkboard and blushing at everything? We almost lost her art to neglect. Thank God poetry is stronger than time and prejudices.

This is where my idealism as a teacher kicks in: I ask myself, who   10
is to say that at this very moment there isn't a Native American teenager gazing dreamily at the desert outside her window as she works on today's assignment, seeing the universe in a grain of sand,[5] preparing herself to share her unique vision with the world. It may all depend on the next words she hears, which may come out of my mouth, or yours. And what about the African American boy in a rural high school in Georgia who showed me he could rhyme for as

---

[1]*Don Quixote:* the title character in a widely translated and adapted Spanish novel by Miguel de Cervantes (1547–1616) about a quest motivated by the "impossible dream." [Eds.]

[2]*Mahatma Gandhi* (1869–1948): leader of the nonviolent Indian nationalist movement against British rule. [Eds.]

[3]*Dr. Martin Luther King Jr.* (1929–1968): civil rights leader and Nobel Peace Prize recipient. [Eds.]

[4]*The Bard:* William Shakespeare. [Eds.]

[5]Cofer is referring to a line from a poem by English poet, artist, and visionary mystic William Blake (1757–1827). [Eds.]

long as I let him talk. His teachers had not been able to get him to respond to literature. Now they listened in respectful silence while he composed an ode to his girl and his car extemporaneously, in a form so tight and so right (contagious too) that when we discuss the exalted Alexander Pope's oeuvre, we call it heroic couplets. But he was intimidated by the manner in which Pope and his worthy comrades in the canon had been presented to him and his classmates, as gods from Mt. Olympus, inimitable and incomprehensible to mere mortals like himself. He was in turn surprised to see, when it was finally brought to his attention, that Alexander Pope and he shared a good ear.

What I'm trying to say is that the phenomenon we call culture in 11
a society is organic, not manufactured. It grows where we plant it. Culture is our garden, and we may neglect it, trample on it, or we may choose to cultivate it. In America we are dealing with varieties we have imported, grafted, cross-pollinated. I can only hope the experts who say that the land is replenished in this way are right. It is the ongoing American experiment, and it has to take root in the classroom first. If it doesn't succeed, then we will be back to praying and hoping that at least He be bilingual.

QUESTIONS FOR STUDY AND DISCUSSION

1. When she was young, how did Cofer feel as a non-native speaker of English living in the United States? What did she observe in other non-native speakers? How is her poem "Latin Women Pray" related to these experiences? What is ironic about the poem?

2. According to Cofer, why do non-English-speaking immigrants to the United States find mainstream culture frightening? How did Cofer conquer her own fear of the mainstream?

3. How did the rise of multiculturalism in the United States affect Cofer as a teacher and a writer?

4. According to Cofer, what is the power of language? And how is language related to culture? How would you describe Cofer's diction in this essay?

5. What do you think Cofer means when she says, "This is what I have learned from writing as a minority person in America that I can teach my students: Literature is the human search for meaning" (6)? In what ways can most writing be called a "human search for meaning"? Explain.

6. What does Cofer believe all Americans can learn from the immigrant experience? What do you think she means when she says, "I know I am a survivor in language" (7)?

7. In paragraph 7, Cofer states that she prefers to use the word *adapt* instead of *assimilate*. What, for her, are the differences between these two words? Do you agree with her position? Why, or why not? What does Cofer see as the promise of America's ongoing experiment with multiculturalism?

8. How would you describe Cofer's tone in this essay?

VOCABULARY

Refer to your dictionary to define the following words as they are used in this selection. Then use each word in a sentence of your own.

forays (2)	assimilation (7)
ethnocentric (2)	hoarding (7)
vocation (3)	transcend (8)
proverbial (3)	extemporaneously (10)
criterion (4)	contagious (10)
allude (5)	inimitable (10)
coalescing (5)	grafted (11)
perennial (6)	

CLASSROOM ACTIVITY USING DICTION AND TONE

Writers create and control tone in their writing in part through the words they choose. For example, words like *laugh, cheery, dance,* and *melody* help to create a tone of celebration. Make a list of the words that come to mind for each of the following tones:

humorous	tentative
angry	triumphant
authoritative	repentant

Compare your lists of words with those of others in the class. What generalizations can you make about the connotations associated with each of these tones?

SUGGESTED WRITING ASSIGNMENTS

1. Put yourself in Cofer's place and imagine you were to emigrate somewhere where they speak another language. How hard would you work to learn the predominate language of your chosen country? What advantages would there be in learning that language? How would you feel if the country had a law that forced you to learn its language as quickly as possible? Write an essay in which you explore the advantages of being multilingual.

2. Using your response to the journal prompt for this selection as a starting point, write an essay in which you discuss cultural diversity at your college or university. How would you characterize your school? Are the faculty and student body culturally diverse? What still needs to be done? Is the administration at your school actively trying to promote cultural diversity? What have been the benefits of diversity for you and other students both in and out of the classroom? You may find it helpful to talk with several faculty members and with other students about their views on campus diversity before you start to write.

chapter 11

Figurative Language

Figurative language is language used in an imaginative rather than a literal sense. Although it is most often associated with poetry, figurative language is used widely in our daily speech and in our writing. Prose writers have long known that figurative language not only brings freshness and color to writing, but also helps to clarify ideas. For example, when asked by his teacher to explain the concept of brainstorming, one student replied, "Well, brainstorming is like having a tornado in your head." This figurative language helps others imagine the whirl of ideas in this young writer's head as he brainstorms a topic for writing.

Two of the most commonly used **figures of speech** are the simile and the metaphor. A *simile* is an explicit comparison between two essentially different ideas or things that uses the words *like* or *as* to link them.

> Canada geese sweep across the hills and valleys like a formation of strategic bombers.
>
> –Benjamin B. Bachman

> I walked toward her and hailed her as a visitor to the moon might salute a survivor of a previous expedition.
>
> –John Updike

A *metaphor,* on the other hand, makes an implicit comparison between dissimilar ideas or things without using *like* or *as.*

> She was very old and small and she walked slowly in the dark pine shadows, moving a little from side to side in her steps, with the balanced heaviness and lightness of a pendulum in a grandfather clock.
>
> –Eudora Welty

Charm is the ultimate weapon, the supreme seduction, against which there are few defenses.

–Laurie Lee

To take full advantage of the richness of a particular comparison, writers sometimes use several sentences or even a whole paragraph to develop a metaphor. Such a comparison is called an *extended metaphor.*

The point is that you have to strip down your writing before you can build it back up. You must know what the essential tools are and what job they were designed to do. If I may belabor the metaphor on carpentry, it is first necessary to be able to saw wood neatly and to drive nails. Later you can bevel the edges or add elegant finials, if that is your taste. But you can never forget that you are practicing a craft that is based on certain principles. If the nails are weak, your house will collapse. If your verbs are weak and your syntax is rickety, your sentences will fall apart.

–William Zinsser

Another frequently used figure of speech is *personification.* In personification, the writer attributes human qualities to animals or inanimate objects.

The moon bathed the valley in a soft, golden light.

–Corey Davis, student

Blond October comes striding over the hills wearing a crimson shirt and faded green trousers.

–Hal Borland

Indeed, haste can be the assassin of elegance.

–T. H. White

In the preceding examples, the writers have, through the use of figurative language, both enlivened their prose and emphasized their ideas. Each has vividly communicated an idea or the essence of an object by comparing it to something concrete and familiar. In each case, too, the figurative language grows out of the writer's thinking, reflecting the way he or she sees the material. Be similarly honest in your use of figurative language, and keep in mind that figurative language should never be used merely to "dress up" writing; above all, it should help you develop your ideas and clarify your meaning for the reader.

The Barrio

■ Robert Ramirez

Robert Ramirez has worked as a cameraman, reporter, anchorman, and producer for the news team at KGBT-TV in Edinburg, Texas, and in the Latin American division of the Northern Trust Bank in Chicago. In the following essay, Ramirez uses figurative language, particularly metaphors, to awaken the reader's senses to the sights, smells, and sounds that are the essense of the barrio.

FOR YOUR JOURNAL

Where did you grow up? What do you remember most about your childhood neighborhood? How did it feel as a young person to live in this world? Do you still call this neighborhood "home"? Explain.

The train, its metal wheels squealing as they spin along the silvery   1
tracks, rolls slower now. Through the gaps between the cars blinks a streetlamp, and this pulsing light on a barrio streetcorner beats slower, like a weary heartbeat, until the train shudders to a halt, the light goes out, and the barrio is deep asleep.

Throughout Aztlán[1] (the Nahuatl term meaning "land to the   2
north"), trains grumble along the edges of a sleeping people. From Lower California, through the blistering Southwest, down the Rio Grande[2] to the muddy Gulf, the darkness and mystery of dreams engulf communities fenced off by railroads, canals, and expressways. Paradoxical communities, isolated from the rest of the town by concrete columned monuments of progress, and yet stranded in the past. They are surrounded by change. It eludes their reach, in their own backyards, and the people, unable and unwilling to see the future, or even touch the present, perpetuate the past.

---

[1]*Aztlán:* the mythical place of origin of the Aztec peoples. [Eds.]
[2]*Rio Grande:* a river flowing from southwest Colorado to Texas and Mexico and into the Gulf of Mexico. [Eds.]

Leaning from the expressway or jolting across the tracks, one enters a different physical world permeated by a different attitude. The physical dimensions are impressive. It is a large section of town which extends for fifteen blocks north and south along the tracks, and then advances eastward, thinning into nothingness beyond the city limits. Within the invisible (yet sensible) walls of the barrio are many, many people living in too few houses. The homes, however, are much more numerous than on the outside.

Members of the barrio describe the entire area as their home. It is a home, but it is more than this. The barrio is a refuge from the harshness and the coldness of the Anglo world. It is a forced refuge. The leprous people are isolated from the rest of the community and contained in their section of town. The stoical pariahs of the barrio accept their fate, and from the angry seeds of rejection grow the flowers of closeness between outcasts, not the thorns of bitterness and the mad desire to flee. There is no want to escape, for the feeling of the barrio is known only to its inhabitants, and the material needs of life can also be found here.

The *tortillería* [tortilla factory] fires up its machinery three times a day, producing steaming, round, flat slices of barrio bread. In the winter, the warmth of the tortilla factory is a wool *sarape* [blanket] in the chilly morning hours, but in the summer, it unbearably toasts every noontime customer.

The *panadería* [bakery] sends its sweet messenger aroma down the dimly lit street, announcing the arrival of fresh, hot sugary *pan dulce* [sweet rolls].

The small corner grocery serves the meal-to-meal needs of customers, and the owner, a part of the neighborhood, willingly gives credit to people unable to pay cash for foodstuffs.

The barbershop is a living room with hydraulic chairs, radio, and television, where old friends meet and speak of life as their salted hair falls aimlessly about them.

The pool hall is a junior level country club where *'chucos* [young men], strangers in their own land, get together to shoot pool and rap, while veterans, unaware of the cracking, popping balls on the green felt, complacently play dominoes beneath rudely hung *Playboy* foldouts.

The *cantina* [canteen or snackbar] is the night spot of the barrio. It is the country club and the den where the rites of puberty are enacted. Here the young become men. It is in the taverns that a young dude shows his *machismo* through the quantity of beer he can hold, the stories of *rucas* [women] he has had, and his willingness and ability to defend his image against hardened and scarred old lions.

No, there is no frantic wish to flee. It would be absurd to leave the familiar and nervously step into the strange and cold Anglo community when the needs of the Chicano can be met in the barrio.   11

The barrio is closeness. From the family living unit, familial relationships stretch out to immediate neighbors, down the block, around the corner, and to all parts of the barrio. The feeling of family, a rare and treasurable sentiment, pervades and accounts for the inability of the people to leave. The barrio is this attitude manifested on the countenances of the people, on the faces of their homes, and in the gaiety of their gardens.   12

The color-splashed homes arrest your eyes, arouse your curiosity, and make you wonder what life scenes are being played out in them. The flimsy, brightly colored, wood-frame houses ignore no neon-brilliant color. Houses trimmed in orange, chartreuse, lime-green, yellow, and mixtures of these and other hues beckon the beholder to reflect on the peculiarity of each home. Passing through this land is refreshing like Brubeck,[3] not narcoticizing like revolting rows of similar houses, which neither offend nor please.   13

In the evenings, the porches and front yards are occupied with men calmly talking over the noise of children playing baseball in the unpaved extension of the living room, while the women cook supper or gossip with female neighbors as they water the *jardines* [gardens]. The gardens mutely echo the expressive verses of the colorful houses. The denseness of multicolored plants and trees gives the house the appearance of an oasis or a tropical island hideaway, sheltered from the rest of the world.   14

Fences are common in the barrio, but they are fences and not the walls of the Anglo community. On the western side of town, the high wooden fences between houses are thick, impenetrable walls, built to keep the neighbors at bay. In the barrio, the fences may be rusty, wire contraptions or thick green shrubs. In either case you can see through them and feel no sense of intrusion when you cross them.   15

Many lower-income families of the barrio manage to maintain a comfortable standard of living through the communal action of family members who contribute their wages to the head of the family. Economic need creates interdependence and closeness. Small bare-footed boys sell papers on cool, dark Sunday mornings, deny them-   16

---

[3]*Dave Brubeck:* pianist, composer, and conductor of "cool" modern jazz. [Eds.]

selves pleasantries, and give their earnings to *mamá*. The older the child, the greater the responsibility to help the head of the household provide for the rest of the family.

There are those, too, who for a number of reasons have not 17
achieved a relative sense of financial security. Perhaps it results from too many children too soon, but it is the homes of these people and their situation that numbs rather than charms. Their houses, aged and bent, oozing children, are fissures in the horn of plenty. Their wooden homes may have brick-pattern asbestos tile on the outer walls, but the tile is not convincing.

Unable to pay city taxes or incapable of influencing the city to 18
live up to its duty to serve all the citizens, the poorer barrio families remain trapped in the nineteenth century and survive as best they can. The backyards have well-worn paths to the outhouses, which sit near the alley. Running water is considered a luxury in some parts of the barrio. Decent drainage is usually unknown, and when it rains, the water stands for days, an incubator of health hazards and an avoidable nuisance. Streets, costly to pave, remain rough, rocky trails. Tires do not last long, and the constant rattling and shaking grind away a car's life and spread dust through screen windows.

The houses and their *jardines*, the jollity of the people in an adverse 19
world, the brightly feathered alarm clock pecking away at supper and cautiously eyeing the children playing nearby, produce a mystifying sensation at finding the noble savage[4] alive in the twentieth century. It is easy to look at the positive qualities of life in the barrio, and look at them with a distantly envious feeling. One wishes to experience the feelings of the barrio and not the hardships. Remembering the illness, the hunger, the feeling of time running out on you, the walls, both real and imagined, reflecting on living in the past, one finds his envy becoming more elusive, until it has vanished altogether.

Back now beyond the tracks, the train creaks and groans, the 20
cars jostle each other down the track, and as the light begins its pulsing, the barrio, with all its meanings, greets a new dawn with yawns and restless stretchings.

QUESTIONS FOR STUDY AND DISCUSSION

1. What is the barrio? Where is it? What does Ramirez mean when he says, "There is no want to escape, for the feeling of the barrio

---

[4]*Noble savage:* in literature, an idealized concept of uncivilized man. [Eds.]

is known only to its inhabitants, and the material needs of life can also be found here" (4)?

2. Ramirez uses Spanish phrases throughout his essay. Why do you suppose he uses them? What is their effect on the reader? He also uses the words *home, refuge, family,* and *closeness.* What do they connote in the context of this essay? (Glossary: *Connotation/Denotation*) In what ways, if any, are they essential to the writer's purpose? (Glossary: *Purpose*)

3. Identify several of the metaphors and similes that Ramirez uses in his essay, and explain why they are particularly appropriate.

4. In paragraph 6, Ramirez uses personification when he calls the aroma of freshly baked sweet rolls a "messenger" who announces the arrival of the baked goods. Cite other words or phrases that Ramirez uses to give human characteristics to the barrio.

5. Explain Ramirez's use of the imagery of walls and fences to describe a sense of cultural isolation. What might this imagery be symbolic of? (Glossary: *Symbol*)

6. Ramirez begins his essay with a relatively positive picture of the barrio, but ends on a more disheartening note. Why has he organized his essay this way? What might the effect have been if he had reversed these images? (Glossary: *Beginnings and Endings*)

VOCABULARY

Refer to your dictionary to define the following words as they are used in this selection. Then use each word in a sentence of your own.

paradoxical (2)	Chicano (11)
eludes (2)	countenances (12)
permeated (3)	fissures (17)
stoical (4)	adverse (19)
pariahs (4)	elusive (19)
complacently (9)	

CLASSROOM ACTIVITY USING FIGURATIVE LANGUAGE

Create a metaphor or simile that would be helpful in describing each item in the following list. The first one has been completed for you to illustrate the process.

1. skyscraper: The skyscraper sparkled like a huge glass needle.
2. sound of an explosion
3. intelligent student
4. crowded bus
5. slow-moving car
6. pillow
7. narrow alley
8. greasy french fries
9. hot sun
10. dull knife

Compare your metaphors and similes with those written by other members of your class. Which metaphors and similes for each item on the list seem to work best? Why? Do any seem tired or clichéd?

SUGGESTED WRITING ASSIGNMENTS

1. In paragraph 19 Ramirez says, "One wishes to experience the feelings of the barrio and not the hardships." Explore his meaning in light of what you have just read and of other experience or knowledge you may have of "ghetto" living. In what way can it be said that the hardships of such living are a necessary part of its "feelings"? How might barrio life change, for better or for worse, if the city were to "live up to its duty to serve all the citizens" (18)?

2. Write a brief essay in which you describe your own neighborhood. You may find it helpful to review what you wrote in response to the journal prompt for this selection.

The Jacket

■ **Gary Soto**

*Born in Fresno, California, in 1952 to working-class Mexican American parents, Gary Soto is an award-winning author of poetry and fiction for readers of all ages, as well as an opera librettist and film producer. After laboring as a migrant farm worker in the San Joaquin Valley during the 1960s, he studied geography at the California State University at Fresno and at the University of California at Irvine before turning his hand to poetry. In his first two collections of poetry—*The Elements of San Joaquin *(1977) and* The Tale of Sunlight *(1978)—Soto draws heavily on his childhood experiences as a Mexican American growing up in the central valley of California. As critics have noted, his poetry captures the violent reality of city life and the backbreaking work of the migrant worker, together with the frustration of lost innocence. To date he has published four other volumes of poetry, a collection of short stories, and four works of nonfiction, including* Living Up the Street: Narrative Recollections *(1985) and* A Summer Life *(1991). His latest novel,* Amnesia in a Republican County *(2003) is a satire on political correctness. "The Jacket" is taken from Soto's very popular collection of essays,* The Effects of Knut Hamsun on a Fresno Boy *(2000). As you read, notice how Soto makes the intensity of his feelings for his jacket known through his extensive use of figurative language—simile, personification, and metaphor.*

FOR YOUR JOURNAL

Do you remember an article of clothing that took on special significance for you as you were growing up? It might have been a pair of beautiful cowboy boots, a dress that made you feel like a princess, a sweater you were forced to wear that brought the wrong kinds of attention, a hat that was your signature piece of clothing, a T-shirt you couldn't bear to be without. Recall the emotions that arose when you wore that special article of clothing. Reflect on the relationship between clothes and one's identity.

My clothes have failed me. I remember the green coat that I wore   1
in fifth and sixth grades when you either danced like a champ
or pressed yourself against a greasy wall, bitter as a penny toward the
happy couples.

When I needed a new jacket and my mother asked what kind I   2
wanted, I described something like bikers wear: black leather and silver studs with enough belts to hold down a small town. We were in
the kitchen, steam on the windows from her cooking. She listened so
long while stirring dinner that I thought she understood for sure the
kind I wanted. The next day when I got home from school, I discovered draped on my bedpost a jacket the color of day-old guacamole. I
threw my books on the bed and approached the jacket slowly, as if it
were a stranger whose hand I had to shake. I touched the vinyl sleeve,
the collar, and peeked at the mustard-colored lining.

From the kitchen mother yelled that my jacket was in the closet. I   3
closed the door to her voice and pulled at the rack of clothes in the
closet, hoping the jacket on the bedpost wasn't for me but my mean
brother. No luck. I gave up. From my bed, I stared at the jacket. I
wanted to cry because it was so ugly and so big that I knew I'd have
to wear it a long time. I was a small kid, thin as a young tree, and it
would be years before I'd have a new one. I stared at the jacket, like
an enemy, thinking bad things before I took off my old jacket whose
sleeves climbed halfway to my elbow.

I put the big jacket on. I zipped it up and down several times, and   4
rolled the cuffs up so they didn't cover my hands. I put my hands in
the pockets and flapped the jacket like a bird's wings. I stood in front
of the mirror, full face, then profile, and then looked over my shoulder as if someone had called me. I sat on the bed, stood against the
bed, and combed my hair to see what I would look like doing something natural. I looked ugly. I threw it on my brother's bed and
looked at it for a long time before I slipped it on and went out to the
backyard, smiling a "thank you" to my mom as I passed her in
the kitchen. With my hands in my pockets I kicked a ball against the
fence, and then climbed it to sit looking into the alley. I hurled orange
peels at the mouth of an open garbage can and when the peels were
gone I watched the white puffs of my breath thin to nothing.

I jumped down, hands in my pockets, and in the backyard on my   5
knees I teased my dog, Brownie, by swooping my arms while making
bird calls. He jumped at me and missed. He jumped again and again,
until a tooth sunk deep, ripping an L-shaped tear on my left sleeve. I
pushed Brownie away to study the tear as I would a cut on my arm.

There was no blood, only a few loose pieces of fuzz. Damn dog, I thought, and pushed him away hard when he tried to bite again. I got up from my knees and went to my bedroom to sit with my jacket on my lap, with the lights out.

That was the first afternoon with my new jacket. The next day I wore it to sixth grade and got a D on a math quiz. During the morning recess Frankie T., the playground terrorist, pushed me to the ground and told me to stay there until recess was over. My best friend, Steve Negrete, ate an apple while looking at me, and the girls turned away to whisper on the monkey bars. The teachers were no help: they looked my way and talked about how foolish I looked in my new jacket. I saw their heads bob with laughter, their hands half-covering their mouths.

Even though it was cold, I took off the jacket during lunch and played kickball in a thin shirt, my arm feeling like braille from the goose bumps. But when I returned to class I slipped the jacket on and shivered until I was warm. I sat on my hands, heating them up, while my teeth chattered like a cup of crooked dice. Finally warm, I slid out of the jacket but a few minutes later put it back on when the fire bell rang. We paraded out into the yard where we, the sixth graders, walked past all the other grades to stand against the back fence. Everybody saw me. Although they didn't say out loud, "Man, that's ugly," I heard the buzz-buzz of gossip and even laughter that I knew was meant for me.

And so I went, in my guacamole-colored jacket. So embarrassed, so hurt, I couldn't even do my homework. I received Cs on quizzes, and forgot the state capitals and rivers of South America, our friendly neighbor. Even the girls who had been friendly blew away like loose flowers to follow the boys in neat jackets.

I wore that thing for three years until the sleeves grew short and my forearms stuck out like the necks of turtles. All during that time no love came to me—no little dark girl in a Sunday dress she wore on Monday. At lunchtime I stayed with the ugly boys who leaned against the chainlink fence and looked around with propellers of grass spinning in our mouths. We saw girls walk by alone, saw couples, hand in hand, their heads like bookends pressing air together. We saw them and spun our propellers so fast our faces were blurs.

I blame that jacket for those bad years. I blame my mother for her bad taste and her cheap ways. It was a sad time for the heart. With a friend I spent my sixth-grade year in a tree in the alley, waiting for something good to happen to me in that jacket, which had become the ugly brother who tagged along wherever I went. And it was about that time that I began to grow. My chest puffed up with muscle and, strangely, a few more ribs. Even my hands, those fleshy hammers, showed bravely through the cuffs, the fingers already hardening for the coming fights. But that L-shaped rip on the left sleeve got bigger, bits of stuffing coughed out from its wound after a hard day of play. I finally Scotch-taped it closed, but in rain or cold weather the tape peeled off like a scab and more stuffing fell out until that sleeve shriveled into a palsied arm. That winter the elbows began to crack and whole chunks of green began to fall off. I showed the cracks to my mother, who always seemed to be at the stove with steamed-up glasses, and she said that there were children in Mexico who would love that jacket. I told her that this was America and yelled that Debbie, my sister, didn't have a jacket like mine. I ran outside, ready to cry, and climbed the tree by the alley to think bad thoughts and watch my breath puff white and disappear.

But whole pieces still casually flew off my jacket when I played 11 hard, read quietly, or took vicious spelling tests at school. When it became so spotted that my brother began to call me "camouflage," I flung it over the fence into the alley. Later, however, I swiped the jacket off the ground and went inside to drape it across my lap and mope.

I was called to dinner: steam silvered my mother's glasses as she 12 said grace; my brother and sister with their heads bowed made ugly faces at their glasses of powdered milk. I gagged too, but eagerly ate big rips of buttered tortilla that held scooped-up beans. Finished, I went outside with my jacket across my arm. It was a cold sky. The faces of clouds were piled up, hurting. I climbed the fence, jumping down with a grunt. I started up the alley and soon slipped into my jacket, that green ugly brother who breathed over my shoulder that day and ever since.

QUESTIONS FOR STUDY AND DISCUSSION

1. Explain the relationship between Soto and the jacket. What does the jacket symbolize for him? In what sense might the jacket be something more than the cause of his failures and embarrassments? What is the jacket's role in Soto's essay? Explain.
2. What does the tree in the backyard symbolize? (Glossary: *Symbol*)

3. Why do you suppose that Soto's mother did not buy him the black leather jacket he wanted so badly? Was she trying to embarrass him or punish him in some way? What other reason might explain her decision to buy a jacket that was the color of "day-old guacamole" (2)?

4. Soto includes a rich range of figures of speech in his narrative. Identify at least a half dozen such figures. What purpose does each serve for him? What effect does each have on you as a reader? Would his story have been as effective had he not used them? Explain.

5. Soto refers to his brother when explaining how much he disliked the new jacket. What is the relationship between the new jacket and the brother?

6. Did Soto's new jacket cause his grades to suffer? Explain. (Glossary: *Cause and Effect*) Did the jacket cause Soto to miss out on any friendships with girls? Explain.

VOCABULARY

Refer to your dictionary to define the following words as they are used in this selection. Then use each word in a sentence of your own.

guacamole (2) chattered (7)
swooping (5) mope (11)
braille (7)

CLASSROOM ACTIVITY USING FIGURATIVE LANGUAGE

Soto makes use of a variety of figures of speech, including personification. For example, the essay begins, "My clothes have failed me" (1), and in the end, Soto refers to his jacket as "that green ugly brother who breathed over my shoulder that day and ever since" (12). Select an article of your own clothing, and personify it in a brief description or narrative.

SUGGESTED WRITING ASSIGNMENTS

1. It might be argued that in times of crisis everything becomes symbolic. So it is with this essay. Soto is going through a rough period in his life as he tries to negotiate the stresses of approach-

ing adolescence. The jacket becomes symbolic of all the difficulties he is having, or perceives himself to be having, with his circumstances and everyone around him. His situation is not unlike our own at times. That Soto is able to make us understand and feel for the narrator is the product of his expertise as a writer. Write an essay about a dilemma or crisis, real or perceived, in your life that is similar to what the narrator experiences in "The Jacket." Try to include as many other figures of speech as you can but only if they are natural and occasioned by the context of your narrative.

2. In a recent interview in *Esquire* magazine, Hollywood producer Bob Evans said the following: "Background makes foreground. This goes for the movies, it goes for dressing, it goes for living. Here's an example: If I go to a party and eight different people come over and say, 'Gee, that's a great-looking tie,' as soon as I get home, I take the tie off and put it in the shredder. Screw the tie! I'm not there to make the *tie* look good. The tie is there to make *me* look good. That's what I mean by background makes foreground." Write an essay on the relationship between people and clothes. Do clothes make the person? If not, why are so many people clothes-conscious? Use as many types of figurative language as you can to enliven your prose and make your point.

A Hanging

■ **George Orwell**

Although probably best known for his novels Animal Farm
(1945) and 1984 *(1949), George Orwell (1903–1950) was also
a renowned essayist on language and politics. Two of his most
famous essays, "Shooting an Elephant" and "Politics and the
English Language," are among the most frequently reprinted.
Orwell was born in Bengal, India, and was educated in
England. He traveled a great deal during his life and spent five
years serving with the British colonial police in Burma. The following essay is a product of that experience. In it, Orwell relies
consistently on similes to help convey and emphasize his attitude
about the events he describes, events in which he is both an observer and a participant.*

FOR YOUR JOURNAL

Throughout history, people have gone out of their way to witness events in which someone was certain to be killed, such as
fights between gladiators, jousting tournaments, and public exe-
cutions. Why do you think such events fascinate people?

It was in Burma,[1] a sodden morning of the rains. A sickly light, like   1
yellow tinfoil, was slanting over the high walls into the jail yard.
We were waiting outside the condemned cells, a row of sheds fronted
with double bars, like small animal cages. Each cell measured about
ten feet by ten and was quite bare within except for a plank bed and
a pot of drinking water. In some of them brown silent men were
squatting at the inner bars, with their blankets draped round them.
These were the condemned men, due to be hanged within the next
week or two.

One prisoner had been brought out of his cell. He was a Hindu,[2]   2
a puny wisp of a man, with a shaven head and vague liquid eyes. He

---

[1]*Burma:* a country in Southeast Asia, formerly part of Britain's Indian Empire. [Eds.]
[2]*Hindu:* a person whose beliefs and practices are rooted in the philosophical and religious tenets of Hinduism, which originated in India. [Eds.]

had a thick, sprouting moustache, absurdly too big for his body, rather like the moustache of a comic man in the films. Six tall Indian warders were guarding him and getting him ready for the gallows. Two of them stood by with rifles with fixed bayonets, while the others handcuffed him, passed a chain through his handcuffs and fixed it to their belts, and lashed his arms tight to his sides. They crowded very close about him, with their hands always on him in a careful, caressing grip, as though all the while feeling him to make sure he was there. It was like men handling a fish which is still alive and may jump back into the water. But he stood quite unresisting, yielding his arms limply to the ropes, as though he hardly noticed what was happening.

Eight o'clock struck and a bugle call, desolately thin in the wet air, floated from the distant barracks. The superintendent of the jail, who was standing apart from the rest of us, moodily prodding the gravel with his stick, raised his head at the sound. He was an army doctor, with a grey toothbrush moustache and a gruff voice. "For God's sake hurry up, Francis," he said irritably. "The man ought to have been dead by this time. Aren't you ready yet?" ₃

Francis, the head jailer, a fat Dravidian[3] in a white drill suit and gold spectacles, waved his black hand. "Yes sir, yes sir," he bubbled. "All iss satisfactorily prepared. The hangman iss waiting. We shall proceed." ₄

"Well, quick march, then. The prisoners can't get their breakfast till this job's over." ₅

We set out for the gallows. Two warders marched on either side of the prisoner, with their files at the slope; two others marched close against him, gripping him by arm and shoulder, as though at once pushing and supporting him. The rest of us, magistrates and the like, followed behind. Suddenly, when we had gone ten yards, the procession stopped short without any order or warning. A dreadful thing had happened—a dog, come goodness knows whence, had appeared in the yard. It came bounding among us with a loud volley of barks, and leapt round us wagging its whole body, wild with glee at finding so many human beings together. It was a large woolly dog, half Airedale, half pariah. For a moment it pranced round us, and then, before anyone could stop it, it had made a dash for the prisoner, and ₆

---

[3]*Dravidian:* someone who speaks one of the twenty-three languages belonging to the family of languages known as Dravidian, which is spoken in South Asia. [Eds.]

jumping up tried to lick his face. Everyone stood aghast, too taken aback even to grab at the dog.

"Who let that bloody brute in here?" said the superintendent angrily. "Catch it, someone!"   7

A warder, detached from the escort, charged clumsily after the   8
dog, but it danced and gamboled just out of his reach, taking everything as part of the game. A young Eurasian jailer picked up a handful of gravel and tried to stone the dog away, but it dodged the stones and came after us again. Its yaps echoed from the jail walls. The prisoner, in the grasp of the two warders, looked on incuriously, as though this was another formality of the hanging. It was several minutes before someone managed to catch the dog. Then we put my handkerchief through its collar and moved off once more, with the dog still straining and whimpering.

It was about forty yards to the gallows. I watched the bare   9
brown back of the prisoner marching in front of me. He walked clumsily with his bound arms, but quite steadily, with that bobbing gait of the Indian who never straightens his knees. At each step his muscles slid neatly into place, the lock of hair on his scalp danced up and down, his feet printed themselves on the wet gravel. And once, in spite of the men who gripped him by each shoulder, he stepped slightly aside to avoid a puddle on the path.

It is curious, but till that moment I had never realized what it   10
means to destroy a healthy, conscious man. When I saw the prisoner step aside to avoid the puddle, I saw the mystery, the unspeakable wrongness, of cutting a life short when it is in full tide. This man was not dying, he was alive just as we were alive. All the organs of his body were working—bowels digesting food, skin renewing itself, nails growing, tissues forming—all toiling away in solemn foolery. His nails would still be growing when he stood on the drop, when he was falling through the air with a tenth of a second to live. His eyes saw the yellow gravel and the gray walls, and his brain still remembered, foresaw, reasoned—reasoned even about puddles. He and we were a party of men walking together, seeing, hearing, feeling, understanding the same world; and in two minutes, with a sudden snap, one of us would be gone—one mind less, one world less.

The gallows stood in a small yard, separate from the main   11
grounds of the prison, and overgrown with tall prickly weeds. It was a brick erection like three sides of a shed, with planking on top, and above that two beams and a crossbar with the rope dangling. The hangman, a grey-haired convict in the white uniform of the prison,

was waiting beside his machine. He greeted us with a servile crouch as we entered. At a word from Francis the two warders, gripping the prisoner more closely than ever, half led, half pushed him to the gallows and helped him clumsily up the ladder. Then the hangman climbed up and fixed the rope round the prisoner's neck.

We stood waiting, five yards away. The warders had formed in a 12 rough circle round the gallows. And then, when the noose was fixed, the prisoner began crying out to his god. It was a high, reiterated cry of "Ram! Ram! Ram! Ram!," not urgent and fearful like a prayer or a cry for help, but steady, rhythmical, almost like the tolling of a bell. The dog answered the sound with a whine. The hangman, still standing on the gallows, produced a small cotton bag like a flour bag and drew it down over the prisoner's face. But the sound, muffled by the cloth, still persisted, over and over again: "Ram! Ram! Ram! Ram! Ram!"

The hangman climbed down and stood ready, holding the lever. 13 Minutes seemed to pass. The steady, muffled crying from the prisoner went on and on, "Ram! Ram! Ram!" never faltering for an instant. The superintendent, his head on his chest, was slowly poking the ground with his stick; perhaps he was counting the cries, allowing the prisoner a fixed number — fifty, perhaps, or a hundred. Everyone had changed color. The Indians had gone gray like bad coffee, and one or two of the bayonets were wavering. We looked at the lashed, hooded man on the drop, and listened to his cries — each cry another second of life; the same thought was in all our minds: oh, kill him quickly, get it over, stop that abominable noise!

Suddenly the superintendent made up his mind. Throwing up his 14 head he made a swift motion with his stick. "Chalo!" he shouted almost fiercely.

There was a clanking noise, and then dead silence. The prisoner 15 had vanished, and the rope was twisting on itself. I let go of the dog, and it galloped immediately to the back of the gallows; but when it got there it stopped short, barked, and then retreated into the corner of the yard, where it stood among the weeds, looking timorously out at us. We went round the gallows to inspect the prisoner's body. He was dangling with his toes pointed straight downwards, very slowly revolving, as dead as a stone.

The superintendent reached out with his stick and poked the bare 16 body; it oscillated, slightly. "*He's* all right," said the superintendent. He backed out from under the gallows, and blew out a deep breath. The moody look had gone out of his face quite suddenly. He glanced at his wristwatch. "Eight minutes past eight. Well, that's all for this morning, thank God."

The warders unfixed bayonets and marched away. The dog, 17 sobered and conscious of having misbehaved itself, slipped after them. We walked out of the gallows yard, past the condemned cells with their waiting prisoners, into the big central yard of the prison. The convicts, under the command of warders armed with lathis,[4] were already receiving their breakfast. They squatted in long rows, each man holding a tin pannikin, while two warders with buckets marched round ladling out rice; it seemed quite a homely, jolly scene, after the hanging. An enormous relief had come upon us now that the job was done. One felt an impulse to sing, to break into a run, to snigger. All at once everyone began chattering gaily.

The Eurasian boy walking beside me nodded towards the way we 18 had come, with a knowing smile: "Do you know, sir, our friend (he meant the dead man), when he heard his appeal had been dismissed, he pissed on the floor of his cell. From fright.—Kindly take one of my cigarettes, sir. Do you not admire my new silver case, sir? From the boxwallah,[5] two rupees eight annas. Classy European style."

Several people laughed—at what, nobody seemed certain. 19

Francis was walking by the superintendent, talking garrulously: 20 "Well, sir, all hass passed off with the utmost satisfactoriness. It wass all finished—flick! like that. It iss not always so—oah, no! I have known cases where the doctor wass obliged to go beneath the gallows and pull the prisoner's legs to ensure decease. Most disagreeable!"

"Wriggling about, eh? That's bad," said the superintendent. 21

"Ach, sir, it iss worse when they become refractory! One man, I 22 recall, clung to the bars of hiss cage when we went to take him out. You will scarcely credit, sir, that it took six warders to dislodge him, three pulling at each leg. We reasoned with him. 'My dear fellow,' we said, 'think of all the pain and trouble you are causing to us!' But no, he would not listen! Ach, he wass very troublesome!"

I found that I was laughing quite loudly. Everyone was laughing. 23 Even the superintendent grinned in a tolerant way. "You'd better all come out and have a drink," he said quite genially. "I've got a bottle of whisky in the car. We could do with it."

We went through the big double gates of the prison, into the 24 road. "Pulling at his legs!" exclaimed a Burmese magistrate suddenly,

---

[4]*Lathis:* wooden or metal baton. [Eds.]
[5]*Boxwallah:* A trader or peddler. [Eds.]

and burst into a loud chuckling. We all began laughing again. At that moment Francis's anecdote seemed extraordinarily funny. We all had a drink together, native and European alike, quite amicably. The dead man was a hundred yards away.

QUESTIONS FOR STUDY AND DISCUSSION

1. In paragraph 6, why is the appearance of the dog "a dreadful thing"? From whose point of view is it dreadful? Why?

2. The role of the narrator of this essay (Glossary: *Narration*) is never clearly defined, nor is the nature of the prisoner's transgression. Why does Orwell deliberately withhold this information?

3. In paragraphs 9 and 10, the prisoner steps aside to avoid a puddle, and Orwell considers the implications of this action. What understanding does he reach? In paragraph 10, what is the meaning of the phrase "one mind less, one world less"?

4. In paragraph 22, what is ironic about Francis's story of the "troublesome" prisoner? (Glossary: *Irony*)

5. Throughout this essay, Orwell uses figurative language, primarily similes, to bring a foreign experience closer to the reader's understanding. Find and explain three or four similes that clarify the event for a modern American reader.

6. Orwell goes to some pains to identify the multicultural nature of the group participating in the hanging scene: Hindu, Dravidian, Eurasian, European, Burmese. Why is the variety of backgrounds of the participants important to the central idea of the essay? Even the dog is "half Airedale, half pariah." What is a pariah, and why is the inclusion of this description appropriate?

7. What words would you use to describe the mood of the group that observed the hanging before the event? Afterward? Cite specific details to support your word choice. Why are the moods so extreme?

VOCABULARY

Refer to your dictionary to define the following words as they are used in this selection. Then use each word in a sentence of your own.

magistrates (6)	gamboled (8)
volley (6)	erection (11)

servile (11)   garrulously (20)
abominable (13)   refractory (22)
timorously (15)   genially (23)
oscillated (16)   amicably (24)

CLASSROOM ACTIVITY USING FIGURATIVE LANGUAGE

Think of a time when you were one of a group of people assembled to do something most or all of you didn't really want to do. People in such a situation behave in various ways, showing their discomfort. One might stare steadily at the ground, for example. A writer describing the scene could use a metaphor to make it more vivid for the reader: "With his gaze he drilled a hole in the ground between his feet." Other people in an uncomfortable situation might fidget, lace their fingers together, breathe rapidly, squirm, or tap an object, such as a pen or a key. Create a simile or a metaphor to describe each of these behaviors.

SUGGESTED WRITING ASSIGNMENTS

1. Are the men who carry out the hanging in Orwell's essay cruel? Are they justified in their actions, following orders from others better able to judge? Or should they question their assigned role as executioners? Who has the right to take the life of another? Write an essay in which you either condemn or support Orwell's role in the hanging of the Hindu. Was it appropriate for him to have participated, even as a spectator? What, if anything, should or could he have done when he "saw the mystery, the unspeakable wrongness, of cutting a life short when it is in full tide" (10)?

2. Recall and narrate an event in your life when you or someone you know underwent some sort of punishment. You may have been a participant or a spectator in the event. How did you react when you learned what the punishment was to be? When it was administered? After it was over? Use figurative language to make vivid the scene during which the punishment was imposed.

Types
of Essays

chapter 12

Illustration

Illustration is the use of **examples**—facts, opinions, samples, and anecdotes or stories—to make ideas more concrete and to make generalizations more specific and detailed. Examples enable writers not just to tell, but also to show what they mean. The more specific the example, the more effective it is. For instance, in an essay about alternative sources of energy, a writer might offer an example of how a local architecture firm designed a home heated by solar collectors instead of a conventional oil, gas, or electric system.

In an essay, a writer uses examples to clarify or support the thesis; in a paragraph, to clarify or support the main idea. Sometimes a single striking example suffices; sometimes a whole series of related examples is necessary. The following paragraph presents a single extended example—an anecdote that illustrates the writer's point about cultural differences:

> Whenever there is a great cultural distance between two people, there are bound to be problems arising from differences in behavior and expectations. An example is the American couple who consulted a psychiatrist about their marital problems. The husband was from New England and had been brought up by reserved parents who taught him to control his emotions and to respect the need for privacy. His wife was from an Italian family and had been brought up in close contact with all the members of her large family, who were extremely warm, volatile, and demonstrative. When the husband came home after a hard day at the office, dragging his feet and longing for peace and quiet, his wife would rush to him and smother him. Clasping his hands, rubbing his brow, crooning over his weary head, she never left him alone. But when the wife was upset or anxious about her day, the husband's response was to withdraw completely and leave her alone. No comforting, no affectionate embrace, no attention—just solitude. The woman became convinced her husband didn't love her and, in desperation, she

consulted a psychiatrist. Their problem wasn't basically psychological but cultural.

—Edward T. Hall

This single example is effective because it is *representative*—that is, essentially similar to other such problems Hall might have described and familiar to many readers. Hall tells the story with enough detail that readers can understand the couple's feelings and so better understand the point he is trying to make.

In contrast, another writer supports his topic sentence about country superstitions with ten examples:

> In the folklore of the country, numerous superstitions relate to winter weather. Back-country farmers examine their corn husks—the thicker the husk, the colder the winter. They watch the acorn crop—the more acorns, the more severe the season. They observe where white-faced hornets place their paper nests—the higher they are, the deeper will be the snow. They examine the size and shape and color of the spleens of butchered hogs for clues to the severity of the season. They keep track of the blooming of dogwood in the spring—the more abundant the blooms, the more bitter the cold in January. When chipmunks carry their tails high and squirrels have heavier fur and mice come into country houses early in the fall, the superstitious gird themselves for a long, hard winter. Without any scientific basis, a wider-than-usual black band on a woolly-bear caterpillar is accepted as a sign that winter will arrive early and stay late. Even the way a cat sits beside the stove carries its message to the credulous. According to a belief once widely held in the Ozarks, a cat sitting with its tail to the fire indicates very cold weather is on the way.
>
> —Edwin Way Teale

Teale uses numerous examples because he is writing about various superstitions. Also, putting all those strange beliefs side by side in a kind of catalog makes the paragraph fun to read as well as convincing and informative.

To use illustration effectively, begin by thinking of ideas and generalizations about your topic that you can make clearer and more persuasive by illustrating them with facts, anecdotes, or specific details. You should focus primarily on your main point, the central generalization that you will develop in your essay. Also be alert for other statements or references that may benefit from illustration. Points that are already clear and uncontroversial, that your readers will understand and immediately agree with, can stand on their own as you pass along quickly to your next idea; belaboring the obvious wastes your time and energy, as well as your reader's. Often, however, you will find that examples add clarity, color, and weight to what you say.

Consider the following generalization:

> Americans are a pain-conscious people who would rather get rid of pain than seek and cure its root causes.

This assertion is broad and general; it raises the following questions: How so? What does this mean exactly? Why does the writer think so? The statement could be the topic sentence of a paragraph or perhaps even the thesis of an essay or of an entire book. As a writer, you could make the generalization stronger and more meaningful through illustration. You might support this statement by citing specific situations or specific cases in which Americans have gone to the drugstore instead of to a doctor, as well as by supplying sales figures per capita of painkillers in the United States as compared with other countries.

Illustration is so useful and versatile a strategy that it is found in all kinds of writing. It is essential, for example, in writing a successful argument essay. In an essay arguing that non-English-speaking students starting school in the United States should be taught English as a second language, a writer supported her argument with the following illustration, drawn from her own experience as a Spanish-speaking child in an English-only school:

> Without the use of Spanish, unable to communicate with the teacher or students, for six long weeks we guessed at everything we did. When we lined up to go anywhere, neither my sister nor I knew what to expect. Once, the teacher took the class on a bathroom break, and I mistakenly thought we were on our way to the cafeteria for lunch. Before we left, I grabbed our lunch money, and one of the girls in line began sneering and pointing. Somehow she figured out my mistake before I did. When I realized why she was laughing, I became embarrassed and threw the money into my sister's desk as we walked out of the classroom.
>
> –Hilda Alvarado, student

Alvarado could have summarized her point in the preceding paragraph in fewer words:

Not only are non-English-speaking students in English-only schools unable to understand the information they are supposed to be learning, but they are subject to frequent embarrassment and teasing from their classmates.

By offering an illustration, however, Alvarado makes her point more vividly and effectively.

A Crime of Compassion

■ **Barbara Huttmann**

Barbara Huttmann, who lives in the San Francisco Bay Area, received her nursing degree in 1976. After obtaining a master's degree in nursing administration, she cofounded a health-care consulting firm for hospitals, nursing organizations, and consumers. Her interest in patients' rights is clearly evident in her two books, The Patient's Advocate *(1981) and* Code Blue *(1982). In the following essay, which first appeared in* Newsweek *in 1983, Huttmann narrates the final months of the life of Mac, one of her favorite patients. By using emotional and graphic detail, Huttmann hopes Mac's example will convince her audience of the need for new legislation that would permit terminally ill patients to choose to die rather than suffer great pain and indignity. As you read about Mac, consider the degree to which his experience seems representative of what patients often endure because medical technology is now able to keep them alive longer than they would be able to survive on their own.*

FOR YOUR JOURNAL

For most people, being sick is at best an unpleasant experience. Reflect on an illness you have had, whether you were sick with a simple common cold or with an affliction that required you to be hospitalized for a time. What were your concerns, your fears? For what were you most thankful?

"Murderer," a man shouted. "God help patients who get *you* for a nurse."   1

"What gives you the right to play God?" another one asked.   2

It was the Phil Donahue show[1] where the guest is a fatted calf   3
and the audience a 200-strong flock of vultures hungering to pick at
the bones. I had told them about Mac, one of my favorite cancer

---

[1]*Phil Donahue show:* the first daytime TV talk show that got the audience involved. It was in syndication from 1970 to 1996. [Eds.]

patients. "We resuscitated him 52 times in just one month. I refused to resuscitate him again. I simply sat there and held his hand while he died."

There wasn't time to explain that Mac was a young, witty, 4 macho cop who walked into the hospital with 32 pounds of attack equipment, looking as if he could single-handedly protect the whole city, if not the entire state. "Can't get rid of this cough," he said. Otherwise, he felt great.

Before the day was over, tests confirmed that he had lung cancer. 5 And before the year was over, I loved him, his wife, Maura, and their three kids as if they were my own. All the nurses loved him. And we all battled his disease for six months without ever giving death a thought. Six months isn't such a long time in the whole scheme of things, but it was long enough to see him lose his youth, his wit, his macho, his hair, his bowel and bladder control, his sense of taste and smell, and his ability to do the slightest thing for himself. It was also long enough to watch Maura's transformation from a young woman into a haggard, beaten old lady.

When Mac had wasted away to a 60-pound skeleton kept alive 6 by liquid food we poured down a tube, IV solutions we dripped into his veins, and oxygen we piped to a mask on his face, he begged us: "Mercy . . . for God's sake, please just let me go."

The first time he stopped breathing, the nurse pushed the button 7 that calls a "code blue" throughout the hospital and sends a team rushing to resuscitate the patient. Each time he stopped breathing, sometimes two or three times in one day, the code team came again. The doctors and technicians worked their miracles and walked away. The nurses stayed to wipe the saliva that drooled from his mouth, irrigate the big craters of bedsores that covered his hips, suction the lung fluids that threatened to drown him, clean the feces that burned his skin like lye, pour the liquid food down the tube attached to his stomach, put pillows between his knees to ease the bone-on-bone pain, turn him every hour to keep the bedsores from getting worse, and change his gown and linen every two hours to keep him from being soaked in perspiration.

At night I went home and tried to scrub away the smell of decay- 8 ing flesh that seemed woven into the fabric of my uniform. It was in my hair, the upholstery of my car—there was no washing it away. And every night I prayed that Mac would die, that his agonized eyes would never again plead with me to let him die.

Every morning I asked his doctor for a "no-code" order. Without 9 that order, we had to resuscitate every patient who stopped breathing.

His doctor was one of several who believe we must extend life as long as we have the means and knowledge to do it. To not do it is to be liable for negligence, at least in the eyes of many people, including some nurses. I thought about what it would be like to stand before a judge, accused of murder, if Mac stopped breathing and I didn't call a code.

And after the fifty-second code, when Mac was still lucid 10 enough to beg for death again, and Maura was crumbled in my arms again, and when no amount of pain medication stilled his moaning and agony, I wondered about a spiritual judge. Was all this misery and suffering supposed to be building character or infusing us all with the sense of humility that comes from impotence?

Had we, the whole medical community, become so arrogant that 11 we believed in the illusion of salvation through science? Had we become so self-righteous that we thought meddling in God's work was our duty, our moral imperative, and our legal obligation? Did we really believe that we had the right to force "life" on a suffering man who had begged for the right to die?

Such questions haunted me more than ever early one morning 12 when Maura went home to change her clothes and I was bathing Mac. He had been still for so long, I thought he at last had the blessed relief of coma. Then he opened his eyes and moaned, "Pain . . . no more . . . Barbara . . . do something . . . God, let me go."

The desperation in his eyes and voice riddled me with guilt. "I'll 13 stop," I told him as I injected the pain medication.

I sat on the bed and held Mac's hands in mine. He pressed his 14 bony fingers against my hand and muttered, "Thanks." Then there was one soft sigh and I felt his hands go cold in mine. "Mac?" I whispered, as I waited for his chest to rise and fall again.

A clutch of panic banded my chest, drew my finger to the code 15 button, urged me to do something, anything . . . but sit there alone with death. I kept one finger on the button, without pressing it, as a waxen pallor slowly transformed his face from person to empty shell. Nothing I've ever done in my 47 years has taken so much effort as it took *not* to press that code button.

Eventually, when I was as sure as I could be that the code team 16 would fail to bring him back, I entered the legal twilight zone and pushed the button. The team tried. And while they were trying, Maura walked into the room and shrieked, "No . . . don't let them do this to him . . . for God's sake . . . please, no more."

Cradling her in my arms was like cradling myself, Mac, and all 17 those patients and nurses who had been in this place before, who do the best they can in a death-denying society.

So a TV audience accused me of murder. Perhaps I am guilty. If a 18 doctor had written a no-code order, which is the only *legal* alternative, would he have felt any less guilty? Until there is legislation making it a criminal act to code a patient who has requested the right to die, we will all of us risk the same fate as Mac. For whatever reason, we developed the means to prolong life, and now we are forced to use it. We do not have the right to die.

QUESTIONS FOR STUDY AND DISCUSSION

1. Why did people in the audience of the *Phil Donahue Show* call Huttmann a "murderer"? Is there any sense in which their accusation is justified? In what ways do you think Huttmann might agree with them?

2. In paragraph 15, Huttmann says, "Nothing I've ever done in my 47 years has taken so much effort as it took *not* to press that code button." How effectively does she describe her struggle against pressing the button? What steps led to her ultimate decision not to press the code button?

3. What, according to Huttmann, is the "only *legal* alternative" to her action? What does she find hypocritical about that choice?

4. Huttmann makes a powerfully emotional appeal for a patient's right to die. Some readers might even find some of her story shocking or offensive. Cite examples of some of the graphic scenes Huttmann describes, and discuss their impact on you as a reader. (Glossary: *Example*) Did they help persuade you to Huttmann's point of view, or did you find them overly unnerving? What would have been gained or lost had she left them out?

5. The story in Huttmann's example covers a period of six months. In paragraphs 4–6, she describes the first five months of Mac's illness; in paragraphs 7–10, the sixth month; and in paragraphs 12–17, the final morning. What important point about narration does her use of time in this sequence demonstrate? (Glossary: *Narration*)

6. Huttmann concludes her essay with the statement, "We do not have the right to die." What does she mean by this? In your

opinion, is she exaggerating or simply stating the facts? Does her example of Mac adequately illustrate Huttmann's concluding point?

VOCABULARY

Refer to your dictionary to define the following words as they are used in this selection. Then use each word in a sentence of your own.

resuscitated (3)   imperative (11)
irrigate (7)   waxen (15)
lucid (10)   pallor (15)

CLASSROOM ACTIVITY USING ILLUSTRATION

Barbara Huttmann illustrates her thesis by using the single example of Mac's experience in the hospital. Using the first statement as a model, find a single example that might be used to best illustrate each of the following potential thesis statements:

Seat belts save lives. (*Possible answer:* an automobile accident in which a relative's life was saved because she was wearing her seat belt.)

Friends can be very handy.

Having good study skills can improve a student's grades.

Loud music can damage your hearing.

Reading the directions for a new product you have just purchased can save time and aggravation.

Humor can often make a bad situation more tolerable.

American manufacturers can make their products safer.

SUGGESTED WRITING ASSIGNMENTS

1. Write a letter to the editor of *Newsweek* in which you respond to Huttmann's essay. Would you be for or against legislation that would give terminally ill patients the right to die? Give examples from your personal experience or from your reading to support your opinion.

2. Using one of the following sentences as your thesis statement, write an essay giving examples from personal experience or from reading to support your opinion.

Consumers have more power than they realize.

Most products do (do not) measure up to the claims of their advertisements.

Religion is (is not) alive and well in America.

Our government works far better than its critics claim.

Being able to write well is more than a basic skill.

The seasons for professional sports are too long.

Today's college students are (are not) serious minded when it comes to academics.

Be Specific

■ **Natalie Goldberg**

Natalie Goldberg has made a specialty of writing about writing. Her first and best-known work, Writing Down the Bones: Freeing the Writer Within, *was published in 1986. Goldberg's advice to would-be writers is, on the one hand, practical and pithy; on the other, it is almost mystical in its call to know and appreciate the world.* Writing Down the Bones *was followed by three more successful books about writing:* Wild Mind: Living the Writer's Life *(1990),* Living Color *(1996), and* Thunder and Lightning: Cracking Open the Writer's Craft *(2000). Goldberg has also written fiction. Her first novel,* Banana Rose, *was published in 1994. She is also a painter whose work is exhibited in Taos, New Mexico, and she has recently published* Living Color: A Writer Paints Her World *(1997), about painting as her second art form, and* Top of My Lungs *(2002), a collection of poetry and paintings. Altogether, more than a million copies of Goldberg's books are now in print. "Be Specific," the excerpt from* Writing Down the Bones *that appears here, is representative of the work as a whole. Amid widespread acclaim for the book, one critic commented, "Goldberg teaches us not only how to write better, but how to live better." Notice the way in which Goldberg demonstrates her advice to be specific in the following selection.*

FOR YOUR JOURNAL

Suppose someone says to you, "I walked in the woods." What do you envision? Write down what you see in your mind's eye. Now suppose someone says, "I walked in the redwood forest." Again, write what you see. How are the two descriptions different, and why?

Be specific. Don't say "fruit." Tell what kind of fruit—"It is a   1
pomegranate." Give things the dignity of their names. Just as with human beings, it is rude to say, "Hey, girl, get in line." That "girl" has a name. (As a matter of fact, if she's at least twenty years

old, she's a woman, not a "girl" at all.) Things, too, have names. It is much better to say "the geranium in the window" than "the flower in the window." "Geranium"—that one word gives us a much more specific picture. It penetrates more deeply into the beingness of that flower. It immediately gives us the scene by the window—red petals, green circular leaves, all straining toward sunlight.

About ten years ago I decided I had to learn the names of plants 2 and flowers in my environment. I bought a book on them and walked down the tree-lined streets of Boulder,[1] examining leaf, bark, and seed, trying to match them up with their descriptions and names in the book. Maple, elm, oak, locust. I usually tried to cheat by asking people working in their yards the names of the flowers and trees growing there. I was amazed how few people had any idea of the names of the live beings inhabiting their little plot of land.

When we know the name of something, it brings us closer to the 3 ground. It takes the blur out of our mind; it connects us to the earth. If I walk down the street and see "dogwood," "forsythia," I feel more friendly toward the environment. I am noticing what is around me and can name it. It makes me more awake.

If you read the poems of William Carlos Williams,[2] you will see 4 how specific he is about plants, trees, flowers—chicory, daisy, locust, poplar, quince, primrose, black-eyed Susan, lilacs—each has its own integrity. Williams says, "Write what's in front of your nose." It's good for us to know what is in front of our nose. Not just "daisy," but how the flower is in the season we are looking at it—"The days-eye hugging the earth / in August . . . brownedged, / green and pointed scales / armor his yellow.* Continue to hone your awareness: to the name, to the month, to the day, and finally to the moment.

Williams also says: "No idea, but in things." Study what is "in 5 front of your nose." By saying "geranium" instead of "flower," you are penetrating more deeply into the present and being there. The closer we can get to what's in front of our nose, the more it can teach us everything. "To see the World in a Grain of Sand, and a heaven in a Wild Flower . . .**

---

[1]*Boulder:* a city in Colorado. [Eds.]
[2]*William Carlos Williams* (1883–1963): American poet. [Eds.]
* William Carlos Williams, "Daisy," in *The Collected Earlier Poems* (New York: New Directions, 1938).
** William Blake, "The Auguries of Innocence."

In writing groups and classes too, it is good to quickly learn the ⁶ names of all the other group members. It helps to ground you in the group and make you more attentive to each other's work.

Learn the names of everything: birds, cheese, tractors, cars, ⁷ buildings. A writer is all at once everything—an architect, French cook, farmer—and at the same time, a writer is none of these things.

QUESTIONS FOR STUDY AND DISCUSSION

1. How does Goldberg "specifically" follow the advice she gives writers in this essay?

2. Goldberg makes several lists of the names of things. What purpose do these lists serve? (Glossary: *Purpose*)

3. Throughout the essay, Goldberg instructs the reader to be specific and to be aware of the physical world. Of what besides names is the reader advised to be aware? Why?

4. In paragraphs 3, 5, and 6, Goldberg cites a number of advantages to be gained by knowing the names of things. What are these advantages? Do they ring true to you?

5. Goldberg says that to name an object gives it dignity (1) and integrity (4). What does she mean in each case?

6. What specific audience is Goldberg addressing in this essay? (Glossary: *Audience*) How do you know?

VOCABULARY

Refer to your dictionary to define the following words as they are used in this selection. Then use each word in a sentence of your own.

pomegranate (1)

integrity (4)

CLASSROOM ACTIVITY USING ILLUSTRATION

A useful exercise in learning to be specific is to see the words we use for people, places, things, and ideas as being positioned somewhere on a "ladder of abstraction." In the following chart, notice how the words progress from more general to more specific.

More General	General	Specific	More Specific
organism	plant	flower	Alstrumaria
vehicle	car	Chevrolet	'58 Chevrolet Impala

Try to fill in the missing parts of the following ladder of abstraction:

More General	General	Specific	More Specific
writing instrument	_____	fountain pen	Waterman fountain pen
_____	sandwich	corned beef sandwich	Reuben
American	_____	Navaho	Laguna Pueblo
book	reference book	dictionary	_____
school	high school	technical high school	_____
medicine	oral medicine	gel capsule	_____

SUGGESTED WRITING ASSIGNMENTS

1. Goldberg likes William Carlos Williams's statement, "No idea, but in things." Using this line as both a title and a thesis, write your own argument for the use of the specific over the general in a certain field — news reporting, poetry, or airport traffic control, for example. Be sure to support your argument with examples.

2. Write a brief essay advising your readers of something they should do. Title your essay, as Goldberg does, with a directive ("Be Specific"). Tell your readers how they can improve their lives by taking your advice, and give strong examples of the behavior you are recommending.

The Case for Short Words

■ **Richard Lederer**

Born in 1938, Richard Lederer holds degrees from Haverford College, Harvard, and the University of New Hampshire. He has been a prolific and popular writer about language. A former high school English teacher, he is the vice president of S.P.E.L.L. (the Society for the Preservation of English Literature and Language). Lederer has written numerous books about how Americans use language, including Anguished English *(1987),* Crazy English: The Ultimate Joy Ride through Our Language *(1989),* The Play of Words *(1990),* The Miracle of Language *(1991),* More Anguished English *(1993),* Adventures of a Verbivore *(1994), and* Fractured English *(1996). He cowrote* The Write Way: The S.P.E.L.L. Guide to Real-Life Writing *(1995) and* The Dictionary of Concise Writing: 10,000 Alternatives to Wordy Phrases *(2002). In addition to writing books, Lederer pens a weekly column called "Looking at Language" for newspapers and magazines all over the United States. He is also the Grammar Grappler for* Writer's Digest, *the language commentator for National Public Radio, and an award-winning public speaker who makes approximately 200 appearances each year. In the essay below, taken from* The Miracle of Language, *pay particular attention to the different ways Lederer uses examples to illustrate. The title and first four paragraphs serve as an extended example of his point about small words, while later in the essay he incorporates examples from his students' writing to illustrate that point more deliberately.*

FOR YOUR JOURNAL

We all carry with us a vocabulary of short, simple-looking words that possess a special personal meaning. For example, to some the word *rose* represents not just a flower, but a whole array of gardens, ceremonies, and romantic occasions. What little words have special meaning for you? What images do they bring to mind?

When you speak and write, there is no law that says you have to use big words. Short words are as good as long ones, and short, old words—like *sun* and *grass* and *home*—are best of all. A lot of small words, more than you might think, can meet your needs with a strength, grace, and charm that large words do not have. 1

Big words can make the way dark for those who read what you write and hear what you say. Small words cast their clear light on big things—night and day, love and hate, war and peace, and life and death. Big words at times seem strange to the eye and the ear and the mind and the heart. Small words are the ones we seem to have known from the time we were born, like the hearth fire that warms the home. 2

Short words are bright like sparks that glow in the night, prompt like the dawn that greets the day, sharp like the blade of a knife, hot like salt tears that scald the cheek, quick like moths that flit from flame to flame, and terse like the dart and sting of a bee. 3

Here is a sound rule: Use small, old words where you can. If a long word says just what you want to say, do not fear to use it. But know that our tongue is rich in crisp, brisk, swift, short words. Make them the spine and the heart of what you speak and write. Short words are like fast friends. They will not let you down. 4

The title of this chapter and the four paragraphs that you have just read are wrought entirely of words of one syllable. In setting myself this task, I did not feel especially cabined, cribbed, or confined. In fact, the structure helped me to focus on the power of the message I was trying to put across. 5

One study shows that twenty words account for twenty-five percent of all spoken English words, and all twenty are monosyllabic. In order of frequency they are: *I, you, the, a, to, is, it, that, of, and, in, what, he, this, have, do, she, not, on,* and *they.* Other studies indicate that the fifty most common words in written English are each made of a single syllable. 6

For centuries our finest poets and orators have recognized and employed the power of small words to make a straight point between two minds. A great many of our proverbs punch home their points with pithy monosyllables: "Where there's a will, there's a way," "A stitch in time saves nine," "Spare the rod and spoil the child," "A bird in the hand is worth two in the bush." 7

Nobody used the short word more skillfully than William Shakespeare,[1] whose dying King Lear laments: 8

---

[1]William Shakespeare (1564–1616): English poet, dramatist, and actor. [Eds.]

> And my poor fool is hang'd! No, no, no life!
> Why should a dog, a horse, a rat have life,
> And thou no breath at all? . . .
> Do you see this? Look on her, look, her lips.
> Look there, look there!

Shakespeare's contemporaries made the King James Bible a cen-   9
terpiece of short words — "And God said, Let there be light: and
there was light. And God saw the light, that it was good." The descendants of such mighty lines live on in the twentieth century. When
asked to explain his policy to Parliament, Winston Churchill[2] responded with these ringing monosyllables: "I will say: it is to wage
war, by sea, land, and air, with all our might and with all the strength
that God can give us." In his "Death of the Hired Man" Robert
Frost[3] observes that "Home is the place where, when you have to go
there, / They have to take you in." And William H. Johnson[4] uses
ten two-letter words to explain his secret of success: "If it is to be, / It
is up to me."

You don't have to be a great author, statesman, or philosopher   10
to tap the energy and eloquence of small words. Each winter I ask my
ninth graders at St. Paul's School to write a composition composed
entirely of one-syllable words. My students greet my request with
obligatory moans and groans, but, when they return to class with
their essays, most feel that, with the pressure to produce high-
sounding polysyllables relieved, they have created some of their most
powerful and luminous prose. Here are submissions from two of my
ninth graders:

> What can you say to a boy who has left home? You can say
> that he has done wrong, but he does not care. He has left home so
> that he will not have to deal with what you say. He wants to go as
> far as he can. He will do what he wants to do.
>   This boy does not want to be forced to go to church, to comb
> his hair, or to be on time. A good time for this boy does not lie in
> your reach, for what you have he does not want. He dreams of
> ripped jeans, shorts with no starch, and old socks.
>   So now this boy is on a bus to a place he dreams of, a place
> with no rules. This boy now walks a strange street, his long hair

---

[2]Sir Winston Churchill (1874–1965): British orator, author, and statesman. [Eds.]
[3]Robert Frost (1874–1963): American poet. [Eds.]
[4]William H. Johnson: associate justice of the U.S. Supreme Court, 1771–1934. [Eds.]

blown back by the wind. He wears no coat or tie, just jeans and an old shirt. He hates your world, and he has left it.

–Charles Shaffer

For a long time we cruised by the coast and at last came to a wide bay past the curve of a hill, at the end of which lay a small town. Our long boat ride at an end, we all stretched and stood up to watch as the boat nosed its way in.

The town climbed up the hill that rose from the shore, a space in front of it left bare for the port. Each house was a clean white with sky blue or gray trim; in front of each one was a small yard, edged by a white stone wall strewn with green vines.

As the town basked in the heat of noon, not a thing stirred in the streets or by the shore. The sun beat down on the sea, the land, and the back of our necks, so that, in spite of the breeze that made the vines sway, we all wished we could hide from the glare in a cool, white house. But, as there was no one to help dock the boat, we had to stand and wait.

At last the head of the crew leaped from the side and strode to a large house on the right. He shoved the door wide, poked his head through the gloom, and roared with a fierce voice. Five or six men came out, and soon the port was loud with the clank of chains and creak of planks as the men caught ropes thrown by the crew, pulled them taut, and tied them to posts. Then they set up a rough plank so we could cross from the deck to the shore. We all made for the large house while the crew watched, glad to be rid of us.

–Celia Wren

You too can tap into the vitality and vigor of compact expres-   11
sion. Take a suggestion from the highway department. At the boundaries of your speech and prose place a sign that reads "Caution: Small Words at Work."

QUESTIONS FOR STUDY AND DISCUSSION

1. Lederer says in paragraph 1 that "short, old words—like *sun* and *grass* and *home*—are best of all." What are the attributes of these words that make them "best"? Why are short old words superior to short newer words? (Glossary: *Connotation/Denotation*)

2. In this essay, written to encourage the use of short words, Lederer himself employs many polysyllabic words, especially in paragraphs 5–9. What is his purpose in doing so? (Glossary: *Purpose*)

3. Lederer quotes a wide variety of passages to illustrate the effectiveness of short words. For example, he quotes from famous, universally familiar old sources such as Shakespeare and the King James Bible, and from unknown contemporary sources such as his own ninth-grade students. How does the variety of his illustrations serve to inform his readers? (Glossary: *Exposition*) How does each example gain impact from the inclusion of the others?

4. To make clear to the reader why short words are effective, Lederer relies heavily on metaphor and simile, especially in the first four paragraphs. (Glossary: *Figure of Speech*) Choose at least one metaphor and one simile from these paragraphs, and explain the comparison implicit in each.

5. In paragraph 10, Lederer refers to the relief his students feel when released from "the pressure to produce high-sounding polysyllables." Where does this pressure come from? How does it relate to the central purpose of this essay?

6. How does the final paragraph serve to close the essay effectively? (Glossary: *Beginnings and Endings*)

7. This essay abounds with examples of striking sentences and passages consisting entirely of words of one syllable. Choose four of the single-sentence examples or a section of several sentences from one of the longer examples, and rewrite them, using primarily words of two or more syllables. Notice how the effect differs from the original.

VOCABULARY

Refer to your dictionary to define the following words as they are used in this selection. Then use each word in a sentence of your own.

cabined (5)	eloquence (10)
cribbed (5)	obligatory (10)
monosyllabic (6)	vitality (11)
proverbs (7)	

CLASSROOM ACTIVITY USING ILLUSTRATION

In your opinion, what is the finest sort of present to give or receive? Why? Define the ideal gift. Illustrate by describing one or more of the best gifts you have received or given, making it clear how each fits the ideal.

SUGGESTED WRITING ASSIGNMENTS

1. Follow the assignment Lederer gives his own students, and write a composition composed entirely of one-syllable words. Make your piece about the length of his student examples or of his own four-paragraph opening.

2. A chief strength of Lederer's essay is his use of a broad variety of examples to illustrate his thesis that short words are the most effective. Choose a subject about which you are knowledgeable, and find as wide a range of examples as you can to illustrate its appeal. For example, if you are enthusiastic about water, you could explore the relative attractions of puddles, ponds, lakes, and oceans; if a music lover, you might consider why Bach or the Beatles remain popular today.

Three Days to See

■ **Helen Keller**

At the age of eighteen months, Helen Keller (1880–1968) was afflicted by a disease that left her blind and deaf. With the aid of her teacher, Anne Sullivan, she was able to overcome her severe disabilities, graduate from Radcliffe College, and lead a productive and challenging adult life. More biographical information appears on p. 70. In the following essay, first published in the Atlantic Monthly *in January 1933, Keller answers the question, "What would you look at if you had just three days of sight?" As you read Keller's essay, notice how she has organized it in terms of what she would like to see during each of the three days and how she uses specific examples that appeal to the senses.*

FOR YOUR JOURNAL

Which of your five senses—sight, sound, touch, taste, or smell—do you depend on most? Imagine for a moment what your life would be like without that sense.

I have often thought it would be a blessing if each human being were stricken blind and deaf for a few days at some time during his early adult life. Darkness would make him more appreciative of sight; silence would teach him the joys of sound. 1

Now and then I have tested my seeing friends to discover what they see. Recently I asked a friend, who had just returned from a long walk in the woods, what she had observed. "Nothing in particular," she replied. 2

How was it possible, I asked myself, to walk for an hour through the woods and see nothing worthy of note? I who cannot see find hundreds of things to interest me through mere touch. I feel the delicate symmetry of a leaf. I pass my hands lovingly about the smooth skin of a silver birch, or the rough, shaggy bark of a pine. In spring I touch the branches of trees hopefully in search of a bud, the first sign of awakening Nature after her winter's sleep. Occasionally, if I am very fortunate, I place my hand gently on a small tree and feel the happy quiver of a bird in full song. 3

At times my heart cries out with longing to see all these things. If   4
I can get so much pleasure from mere touch, how much more beauty
must be revealed by sight. And I have imagined what I should most
like to see if I were given the use of my eyes, say, for just three days.

I should divide the period into three parts. On the first day, I   5
should want to see the people whose kindness and companionship
have made my life worth living. I do not know what it is to see into
the heart of a friend through that "window of the soul," the eye. I
can only "see" through my finger tips the outline of a face. I can detect laughter, sorrow, and many other obvious emotions. I know my
friends from the feel of their faces.

How much easier, how much more satisfying it is for you who   6
can see to grasp quickly the essential qualities of another person by
watching the subtleties of expression, the quiver of a muscle, the
flutter of a hand. But does it ever occur to you to use your sight to see
into the inner nature of a friend? Do not most of you seeing people
grasp casually the outward features of a face and let it go at that?

For instance, can you describe accurately the faces of five good   7
friends? As an experiment, I have questioned husbands about the
color of their wives' eyes, and often they express embarrassed confusion and admit that they do not know.

Oh, the things that I should see if I had the power of sight for just   8
three days!

The first day would be a busy one. I should call to me all my dear   9
friends and look long into their faces, imprinting upon my mind the
outward evidences of the beauty that is within them. I should let my
eyes rest, too, on the face of a baby, so that I could catch a vision of
the eager, innocent beauty which precedes the individual's consciousness of the conflicts which life develops. I should like to see the books
which have been read to me, and which have revealed to me the deepest channels of human life. And I should like to look into the loyal,
trusting eyes of my dogs, the little Scottie and the stalwart Great
Dane.

In the afternoon I should take a long walk in the woods and in-   10
toxicate my eyes on the beauties of the world of Nature. And I should
pray for the glory of a colorful sunset. That night, I think, I should
not be able to sleep.

The next day I should arise with the dawn and see the thrilling mir-   11
acle by which night is transformed into day. I should behold with

awe the magnificent panorama of light with which the sun awakens the sleeping earth.

This day I should devote to a hasty glimpse of the world, past 12 and present. I should want to see the pageant of man's progress, and so I should go to the museums. There my eyes would see the condensed history of the earth—animals and the races of men pictured in their native environment; gigantic carcasses of dinosaurs and mastodons which roamed the earth before man appeared, with his tiny stature and powerful brain, to conquer the animal kingdom.

My next stop would be the Museum of Art. I know well through 13 my hands the sculptured gods and goddesses of the ancient Nile-land. I have felt copies of Parthenon friezes, and I have sensed the rhythmic beauty of charging Athenian warriors. The gnarled, bearded features of Homer are dear to me, for he, too, knew blindness.

So on this, my second day, I should try to probe into the soul of 14 man through his art. The things I knew through touch I should now see. More splendid still, the whole magnificent world of painting would be opened to me. I should be able to get only a superficial impression. Artists tell me that for a deep and true appreciation of art one must educate the eye. One must learn through experience to weigh the merits of line, of composition, of form and color. If I had eyes, how happily would I embark on so fascinating a study!

The evening of my second day I should spend at a theater or at 15 the movies. How I should like to see the fascinating figure of Hamlet, or the gusty Falstaff amid colorful Elizabethan trappings! I cannot enjoy the beauty of rhythmic movement except in a sphere restricted to the touch of my hands. I can vision only dimly the grace of a Pavlova, although I know something of the delight of rhythm, for often I can sense the beat of music as it vibrates through the floor. I can well imagine that cadenced motion must be one of the most pleasing sights in the world. I have been able to gather something of this by tracing with my fingers the lines in sculptured marble; if this static grace can be so lovely, how much more acute must be the thrill of seeing grace in motion.

The following morning, I should again greet the dawn, anxious to 16 discover new delights, new revelations of beauty. Today, this third day, I shall spend in the workaday world, amid the haunts of men going about the business of life. The city becomes my destination.

First, I stand at a busy corner, merely looking at people, trying by 17 sight of them to understand something of their daily lives. I see smiles, and I am happy. I see serious determination, and I am proud. I see suffering, and I am compassionate.

I stroll down Fifth Avenue. I throw my eyes out of focus, so that I 18
see no particular object but only a seething kaleidoscope of color. I am certain that the colors of women's dresses moving in a throng must be a gorgeous spectacle of which I should never tire. But perhaps if I had sight I should be like most other women — too interested in styles to give much attention to the splendor of color in the mass.

From Fifth Avenue I make a tour of the city — to the slums, to fac- 19
tories, to parks where children play. I take a stay-at-home trip abroad by visiting the foreign quarters. Always my eyes are open wide to all the sights of both happiness and misery so that I may probe deep and add to my understanding of how people work and live.

My third day of sight is drawing to an end. Perhaps there are 20
many serious pursuits to which I should devote the few remaining hours, but I am afraid that on the evening of that last day I should again run away to the theater, to a hilariously funny play, so that I might appreciate the overtones of comedy in the human spirit.

At midnight permanent night would close in on me again. Natu- 21
rally in those three short days I should not have seen all I wanted to see. Only when darkness had again descended upon me should I realize how much I had left unseen.

Perhaps this short outline does not agree with the program you 22
might set for yourself if you knew that you were about to be stricken blind. I am, however, sure that if you faced that fate you would use your eyes as never before. Everything you saw would become dear to you. Your eyes would touch and embrace every object that came within your range of vision. Then, at last, you would really see, and a new world of beauty would open itself before you.

I who am blind can give one hint to those who see: Use your eyes as if 23
tomorrow you would be stricken blind. And the same method can be applied to the other senses. Hear the music of voices, the song of a bird, the mighty strains of an orchestra, as if you would be stricken deaf tomorrow. Touch each object as if tomorrow your tactile sense would fail. Smell the perfume of flowers, taste with relish each morsel, as if tomorrow you could never smell and taste again. Make the most of every sense; glory in all the facets of pleasure and beauty which the world reveals to you through the several means of contact which Nature provides. But of all the senses, I am sure that sight must be the most delightful.

QUESTIONS FOR STUDY AND DISCUSSION

1. Why does Keller believe that "it would be a blessing if each human being were stricken blind and deaf for a few days at some time during his early adult life" (1)? Do you think that this would be a good idea? Explain.

2. Why does Keller become upset with her friend who reports that she observed "nothing in particular" (2) while on a long walk in the woods? What examples does Keller use to illustrate how she can find hundreds of things of interest in the woods? What senses does she appeal to?

3. Keller challenges her readers by claiming that most sighted people take their vision for granted. She asks, "But does it ever occur to you to use your sight to see into the inner nature of a friend?" (6) How would you answer her question? Explain your answer with examples.

4. Paragraph 8 is a one-sentence paragraph. How does it function in the context of this essay? (Glossary: *Paragraph*)

5. So as not to waste any of her allotted time, Keller carefully structures each of her three days. What does she want to see on each day? Why do you think she planned her three days in the way she did? Explain.

6. What, if anything, did you learn after reading about what Keller would choose to see if she were granted the use of her eyes for three days? Did any of her choices surprise you? If so, which ones? Do you think you now have a greater appreciation of what it is like to live in a world of "permanent night" (21)?

7. What advice does Keller leave with her readers? How difficult would it be for you to do what she asks?

VOCABULARY

Refer to your dictionary to define the following words as they are used in this selection. Then use each word in a sentence of your own.

quiver (3)	pageant (12)
subtleties (6)	friezes (13)
imprinting (9)	embark (14)
channels (9)	cadenced (15)
intoxicate (10)	overtones (20)
panorama (11)	

CLASSROOM ACTIVITY USING ILLUSTRATION

To present a good example you need to provide details that appeal to the senses, and to do this you must be observant. To test your powers of observation, try listing the features of an ordinary object—a water bottle, a ballpoint pen, a backpack—something everyone in class has access to. Compare your list of characteristics with those of other members of the class. Discuss whether having a name for the object is a help or a hindrance in describing it.

SUGGESTED WRITING ASSIGNMENTS

1. Using Keller's essay as a model, write an essay in which you lay out "the program you might set for yourself if you knew that you were about to be stricken blind" (22). Be sure to use specific examples to illustrate the things that you would choose to see.

2. Because most of us have eyes that work, it is easy to assume that we can really see. All too often, however, like Keller's friend, we report that we've seen "nothing in particular" after taking a walk, visiting a friend, or attending an event. Occasionally, we find ourselves in situations where others "see" more in an object or in a situation than we do. Have you ever wondered what makes others more observant than you are? In preparation for writing an essay about "seeing," read "Learning to See" (pp. 98–102) by Samuel H. Scudder and "A View from the Bridge" (pp. 111–14) by Cherokee Paul McDonald. Using examples from your own experience as well as examples from the essays by Keller, Scudder, and McDonald, write an essay in which you explore the reasons why people have difficulty really seeing the world around them. What must people do to train themselves to see beyond the superficial?

Narration

To *narrate* is to tell a story or to recount a series of events. Whenever you relate an incident or use an **anecdote** (a very brief story) to make a point, you use narration. In its broadest sense, **narration** is any account of any event or series of events. We all love to hear stories; some people believe that sharing stories is a part of what defines us as human beings. Good stories are interesting, sometimes suspenseful, and always instructive because they give us insights into the human condition. Although most often associated with fiction, narration is effective and useful in all kinds of writing. For example, in "How I Got Smart" (188–91), retired high school English teacher Steve Brody narrates the humorous story of how an infatuation with a classmate, Debbie, motivated him to hit the books. In "As They Say, Drugs Kill" (507–10), writer Laura Rowley recounts a particularly poignant experience to argue against substance abuse.

Good narration has five essential features: a clear context; well-chosen and thoughtfully emphasized details; a logical, often chronological organization; an appropriate and consistent point of view; and a meaningful point or purpose. Consider, for example, the following narrative, entitled "Is Your Jar Full?"

> One day, an expert in time management was speaking to a group of business students and, to drive home a point, used an illustration those students will never forget. As he stood in front of the group of high-powered overachievers he said, "Okay, time for a quiz" and he pulled out a one-gallon mason jar and set it on the table in front of him. He also produced about a dozen fist-sized rocks and carefully placed them, one at a time, into the jar. When the jar was filled to the top and no more rocks would fit inside, he asked, "Is this jar full?"
>
> Everyone in the class yelled, "Yes."
>
> The time management expert replied, "Really?" He reached under the table and pulled out a bucket of gravel. He dumped some

gravel in and shook the jar causing pieces of gravel to work themselves down into the spaces between the big rocks. He then asked
the group once more, "Is the jar full?" By this time the class was on
to him.

"Probably not," one of them answered.

"Good!" he replied. He reached under the table and brought
out a bucket of sand. He started dumping the sand in the jar and it
went into all of the spaces left between the rocks and the gravel.

Once more he asked the question, "Is this jar full?"

"No!" the class shouted.

Once again he said, "Good." Then he grabbed a pitcher of
water and began to pour it in until the jar was filled to the brim.
Then he looked at the class and asked, "What is the point of this
illustration?"

One eager beaver raised his hand and said, "The point is, no
matter how full your schedule is, if you try really hard you can always fit some more things in it!"

"No," the speaker replied, "that's not the point. The truth this
illustration teaches us is: If you don't put the big rocks in first,
you'll never get them in at all. What are the 'big rocks' in your
life—time with your loved ones, your faith, your education, your
dreams, a worthy cause, teaching or mentoring others? Remember
to put these BIG ROCKS in first or you'll never get them in at all."

So, tonight, or in the morning, when you are reflecting on this
short story, ask yourself this question: What are the "big rocks" in
my life? Then, put those in your jar first.

This story contains all the elements of good narration. The writer
begins by establishing a clear context for her narrative, telling when,
where, and to whom the action happened. She has chosen details well,
including enough detail so that we know what is happening but not so
much that we become overwhelmed, confused, or bored. The writer or-
ganizes her narration logically, with a beginning that sets the scene, a
middle that relates the exchange between the time-management expert
and the students, and an end that makes her point, all arranged chronologically. She tells the story from the third-person point of view.
Finally, she reveals the point of her narration: People need to think
about what's important in their lives and put these activities first.

The writer could have told her story from the first-person point of
view. In this point of view, the narrator is a participant in the action and
uses the pronoun *I*. In the following example, Willie Morris tells a story
of how the comfortably well-off respond coolly to the tragedies of the

ghetto. We experience the event directly through the writer's eyes and ears, as if we too had been on the scene of the action.

> One afternoon in late August, as the summer's sun streamed into the [railroad] car and made little jumping shadows on the windows, I sat gazing out at the tenement-dwellers, who were themselves looking out of their windows from the gray crumbling buildings along the tracks of upper Manhattan. As we crossed into the Bronx, the train unexpectedly slowed down for a few miles. Suddenly from out of my window I saw a large crowd near the tracks, held back by two policemen. Then, on the other side from my window, I saw a sight I would never be able to forget: a little boy almost severed in halves, lying at an incredible angle near the track. The ground was covered with blood, and the boy's eyes were opened wide, strained and disbelieving in his sudden oblivion. A policeman stood next to him, his arms folded, staring straight ahead at the windows of our train. In the orange glow of late afternoon the policemen, the crowd, the corpse of the boy were for a brief moment immobile, motionless, a small tableau to violence and death in the city. Behind me, in the next row of seats, there was a game of bridge. I heard one of the four men say as he looked out at the sight, "God, that's horrible." Another said, in a whisper, "Terrible, terrible." There was a momentary silence, punctuated only by the clicking of the wheels on the track. Then, after the pause, I heard the first man say: "Two hearts."
>
> —Willie Morris

As you begin to write your own narration, take time to ask yourself why you are telling your story. Your purpose in writing will influence which events and details you include and which you leave out. You should include enough detail about the action and its context so that your readers can understand what's going on. You should not get so carried away with details that your readers become confused or bored by an excess of information, however. In good storytelling, deciding what to leave out is as important as deciding what to include.

Be sure to give some thought to the organization of your narrative. While chronological organization is natural in narration because it is a reconstruction of the original order of events, it is not always the most interesting. To add interest to your storytelling, try using a technique common in the movies and theater called *flashback*. Begin your narration midway through the story with an important or exciting event and then use flashback to fill in what happened earlier.

Notice how one of our students uses this very technique. She disrupts the chronological organization of her narrative by beginning in the recent past and then uses a flashback to take us back to when she was a youngster:

It was a Monday afternoon, and I was finally home from track practice. The coach had just told me that I had a negative attitude and should contemplate why I was on the team. My father greeted me in the living room.

Essay opens in recent past

"Hi, honey. How was practice?"

"Not good, Dad. Listen, I don't want to do this anymore. I hate the track team."

"What do you mean *hate?*"

"The constant pressure is making me crazy."

"How so?"

"It's just not fun anymore."

"Well, I'll have to talk to the coach — "

"No! You're supposed to be my father, not my coach."

"I am your father, but I'm sure . . ."

"Just let me do what I want. You've had your turn."

Dialogue creates historical present

He just let out a sigh and left the room. Later he told me that I was wasting my "God-given abilities." The funny part was that none of my father's anger hit me at first. All I knew was that I was free.

My troubles began the summer I was five years old. It was late June. . . .

Essay returns in time to when troubles began

–Trena Isley, student

What's in a Name?

■ **Henry Louis Gates Jr.**

The preeminent African American scholar of our time, Henry Louis Gates Jr. is the W. E. B. Du Bois Professor of the Humanities, chair of Afro-American Studies, and director of the W. E. B. Du Bois Institute of Afro-American Research at Harvard University. Among his impressive list of publications are Figures in Black: Words, Signs and the "Racial" Self *(1987),* The Signifying Monkey: A Theory of Afro-American Literary Criticism *(1988),* Loose Canons: Notes on Culture Wars *(1992),* The Future of the Race *(1997), and* Thirteen Ways of Looking at a Black Man *(1999). His most recent book is* Mr. Jefferson and Miss Wheatley *(2003). His* Colored People: A Memoir *(1994) recollects in a wonderful prose style his youth growing up in Piedmont, West Virginia, and his emerging sexual and racial awareness. Gates graduated from Yale and took his advanced degrees at Clare College at the University of Cambridge. He has been honored with a MacArthur Foundation Fellowship, inclusion in* Time *magazine's "25 Most Influential Americans" list, a National Humanities Medal, and election to the American Academy of Arts and Letters. "What's in a Name?," excerpted from a longer article published in the fall 1989 issue of* Dissent *magazine, tells the story of Gates's first encounter with one of the "bynames" used by white people to refer to African Americans.*

FOR YOUR JOURNAL

Reflect on the use of racially charged language. For example, has anyone ever used a racial epithet or name to refer to you? When did you first become aware that such names existed? How do you feel about being characterized by your race? If you yourself have ever used such names, what was your intent in using them? What was the response of others?

The question of color takes up much space in these pages, but the question of color, especially in this country, operates to hide the graver questions of the self.

–James Baldwin, 1961

. . . blood, darky, Tar Baby, Kaffir, shine . . . moor, blackamoor, Jim Crow, spook . . . quadroon, meriney, red bone, high yellow . . . Mammy, porch monkey, home, homeboy, George . . . spearchucker, schwarze, Leroy, Smokey . . . mouli, buck, Ethiopian, brother, sistah. . . .

–Trey Ellis, 1989

I had forgotten the incident completely, until I read Trey Ellis's   1
essay, "Remember My Name," in a recent issue of the *Village Voice*[1] (June 13, 1989). But there, in the middle of an extended itali-cized list of the bynames of "the race" ("the race" or "our people" being the terms my parents used in polite or reverential discourse, "ji-gaboo" or "nigger" more commonly used in anger, jest, or pure dis-gust) it was: "George." Now the events of that very brief exchange return to mind so vividly that I wonder why I had forgotten it.

My father and I were walking home at dusk from his second job.   2
He "moonlighted" as a janitor in the evenings for the telephone com-pany. Every day but Saturday, he would come home at 3:30 from his regular job at the paper mill, wash up, eat supper, then at 4:30 head downtown to his second job. He used to make jokes frequently about a union official who moonlighted. I never got the joke, but he and his friends thought it was hilarious. All I knew was that my family al-ways ate well, that my brother and I had new clothes to wear, and that all of the white people in Piedmont, West Virginia, treated my parents with an odd mixture of resentment and respect that even we understood at the time had something directly to do with a small but certain measure of financial security.

He had left a little early that evening because I was with him and   3
I had to be in bed early. I could not have been more than five or six, and we had stopped off at the Cut-Rate Drug Store (where no black person in town but my father could sit down to eat, and eat off real plates with real silverware) so that I could buy some caramel ice cream, two scoops in a wafer cone, please, which I was busy licking when Mr. Wilson walked by.

Mr. Wilson was a very quiet man, whose stony, brooding, silent   4
manner seemed designed to scare off any overtures of friendship, even from white people. He was Irish, as was one-third of our village (an-other third being Italian), the more affluent among whom sent their children to "Catholic School" across the bridge in Maryland. He had

---

[1]*Village Voice:* a nationally distributed weekly newspaper published in New York City. [Eds.]

white straight hair, like my Uncle Joe, whom he uncannily resembled, and he carried a back worn metal lunch pail, the kind that Riley[2] carried on the television show. My father always spoke to him, and for reasons that we never did understand, he always spoke to my father.

"Hello, Mr. Wilson," I heard my father say.   5

"Hello, George."   6

I stopped licking my ice cream cone, and asked my Dad in a loud   7
voice why Mr. Wilson had called him "George."

"Doesn't he know your name, Daddy? Why don't you tell him   8
your name? Your name isn't George."

For a moment I tried to think of who Mr. Wilson was mixing   9
Pop up with. But we didn't have any Georges among the colored people in Piedmont; nor were there colored Georges living in the neighboring towns and working at the mill.

"Tell him your name, Daddy."   10

"He knows my name, boy," my father said after a long pause.   11
"He calls all colored people George."

A long silence ensued. It was "one of those things," as my Mom   12
would put it. Even then, that early, I knew when I was in the presence of "one of those things," one of those things that provided a glimpse, through a rent curtain, at another world that we could not affect but that affected us. There would be a painful moment of silence, and you would wait for it to give way to a discussion of a black superstar such as Sugar Ray[3] or Jackie Robinson.[4]

"Nobody hits better in a clutch than Jackie Robinson."   13

"That's right. Nobody."   14

I never again looked Mr. Wilson in the eye.   15

QUESTIONS FOR STUDY AND DISCUSSION

1. Gates prefaces his essay with two quotations. What is the meaning of each quotation? Why do you suppose Gates uses both quotations? How does each relate to his purpose in the essay as a whole? (Glossary: *Purpose*)

---

[2]*Riley:* a character on the U.S. television show *The Life of Riley,* a blue-collar, ethnic sitcom popular in the 1950s. [Eds.]
[3]*Sugar Ray:* Walker Smith Jr. (1921–1989), American professional boxer and six-time world champion. [Eds.]
[4]*Jackie Robinson* (1919–1972): the first black baseball player in the National Baseball League. [Eds.]

2. Gates begins his essay by explaining where he got the idea for it. How well does this approach work? Is it an approach that you could see yourself using often? Explain.

3. Explain what happens in paragraph 12. What is "one of those things," as Gates's mom put it? In what ways is "one of those things" really Gates's purpose in telling his story? Why does Gates say, "I never again looked Mr. Wilson in the eye" (15)?

4. Gates sets the context for his narrative in his first paragraph. He also reveals that his parents used terms of racial abuse among themselves. Why does Gates make so much of Mr. Wilson's use of *George* when his own parents used words so much more obviously offensive?

5. Gates describes and provides some background information about Mr. Wilson in paragraph 4. What is Gates's purpose in providing this information? (Glossary: *Description*)

VOCABULARY

Refer to your dictionary to define the following words as they are used in this selection. Then use each word in a sentence of your own.

bynames (1)	uncannily (4)
reverential (1)	rent (12)
moonlighted (2)	clutch (13)

CLASSROOM ACTIVITY USING NARRATION

Beginning at the beginning and ending at the end is not the only way to tell a story. Think of the events in a story that you would like to tell. Don't write the story, but simply list the events that need to be included. Be sure to include at least ten major events in your story. Now play with the arrangement of those events so as to avoid the chronological sequencing of them that would naturally come to mind. Try to develop as many patterns as you can, but be careful that you have a purpose in developing each sequence and that you create nothing that might confuse a listener or reader. Discuss your results with your classmates.

SUGGESTED WRITING ASSIGNMENTS

1. Using Gates's essay as a model, identify something that you have recently read that triggers in you a story from the past. Perhaps a newspaper article about how local high school students helped the community reminds you of a community project you and your classmates were involved in. Or perhaps reading about some act of heroism reminds you of a situation in which you performed (or failed to perform) a similar deed. Make sure that you have a purpose in telling the story, that you establish a clear context for it, and that you have enough supporting details to enrich your story. Think, as well, about how to begin and end your story and about the narrative sequence you will use in narrating it.

2. Charlotte Montgomery wrote, "The one thing you feel strongly about is your name." How do you feel about your name? Do you like it? Does it sound pleasant? Do you think your name shapes your self-identity in a positive or negative way, or do you think it has no effect on your sense of who you are? Write an essay about your name and the way it helps or fails to help you present yourself to the world. Be sure to develop your essay using narration by including several anecdotes or a longer story involving your name.

The Dare

■ **Roger Hoffmann**

Born in 1948, Roger Hoffmann is a freelance writer and the author of The Complete Software Marketplace *(1984). In "The Dare," first published in the* New York Times Magazine *in 1986, Hoffmann recounts how in his youth he accepted a friend's challenge to dive under a moving freight train and to roll out on the other side. As an adult, Hoffmann appreciates the act for what it was—a crazy, dangerous childhood stunt. But he also remembers what the episode meant to him as a seventh-grader trying to prove himself to his peers. As you read the essay, pay particular attention to how Hoffman incorporates both of these perspectives into his point of view concerning "I-dare-you's."*

FOR YOUR JOURNAL

When we are growing up, most of us want more than anything to be a part of a group. Was being part of a group something you cherished as a youngster? Or did you have a desire to be independent, to be your own person? Why do you think young people in particular worry about the issue of independence versus belonging?

The secret to diving under a moving freight train and rolling out the other side with all your parts attached lies in picking the right spot between the tracks to hit with your back. Ideally, you want soft dirt or pea gravel, clear of glass shards and railroad spikes that could cause you instinctively, and fatally, to sit up. Today, at thirty-eight, I couldn't be threatened or baited enough to attempt that dive. But as a seventh grader struggling to make the cut in a tough Atlanta grammar school, all it took was a dare.

I coasted through my first years of school as a fussed-over smart kid, the teacher's pet who finished his work first and then strutted around the room tutoring other students. By the seventh grade, I had more A's than friends. Even my old cronies, Dwayne and O.T., made it clear I'd never be one of the guys in junior high if I didn't dirty up my act. They challenged me to break the rules, and I did. The I-dare-you's escalated: shoplifting, sugaring teachers' gas tanks, dropping lighted matches into public mailboxes. Each guerrilla act won me the approval I never got for just being smart.

Walking home by the railroad tracks after school, we started 3 playing chicken with oncoming trains. O.T., who was failing that year, always won. One afternoon he charged a boxcar from the side, stopping just short of throwing himself between the wheels. I was stunned. After the train disappeared, we debated whether someone could dive under a moving car, stay put for a 10-count, then scramble out the other side. I thought it could be done and said so. O.T. immediately stepped in front of me and smiled. Not by me, I added quickly, I certainly didn't mean that I could do it. "A smart guy like you," he said, his smile evaporating, "you could figure it out easy." And then, squeezing each word for effect, "I . . . DARE . . . you." I'd just turned twelve. The monkey clawing my back was Teacher's Pet. And I'd been dared.

As an adult, I've been on both ends of life's implicit business and 4 social I-dare-you's, although adults don't use those words. We pro-voke with body language, tone of voice, ambiguous phrases. I dare you to: argue with the boss, tell Fred what you think of him, send the wine back. Only rarely are the risks physical. How we respond to dares when we are young may have something to do with which of the truly hazardous male inner dares—attacking mountains, tempt-ing bulls at Pamplona[1]—we embrace or ignore as men.

For two weeks, I scouted trains and tracks. I studied moving box-5 cars close up, memorizing how they squatted on their axles, never getting used to the squeal or the way the air fell hot from the sides. I created an imaginary, friendly train and ran next to it. I mastered a shallow, head-first dive with a simple half-twist. I'd land on my back, count to ten, imagine wheels and, locking both hands on the rail to my left, heave myself over and out. Even under pure sky, though, I had to fight to keep my eyes open and my shoulders between the rails.

The next Saturday, O.T., Dwayne and three eighth graders met 6 me below the hill that backed up to the lumberyard. The track fol-lowed a slow bend there and opened to a straight, slightly uphill

---

[1]*Pamplona, Spain:* site of La Fiesta de San Fermin and the annual Running of the Bulls, in which people run with bulls set free in the city's narrow streets. [Eds.]

climb for a solid third of a mile. My run started two hundred yards after the bend. The train would have its tongue hanging out.

The other boys huddled off to one side, a circle on another 7 planet, and watched quietly as I double-knotted my shoelaces. My hands trembled. O.T. broke the circle and came over to me. He kept his hands hidden in the pockets of his jacket. We looked at each other. BB's of sweat appeared beneath his nose. I stuffed my wallet in one of his pockets, rubbing it against his knuckles on the way in, and slid my house key, wired to a red-and-white fishing bobber, into the other. We backed away from each other, and he turned and ran to join the four already climbing up the hill.

I watched them all the way to the top. They clustered together as 8 if I were taking their picture. Their silhouette resembled a round-shouldered tombstone. They waved down to me, and I dropped them from my mind and sat down on the rail. Immediately, I jumped back. The steel was vibrating.

The train sounded like a cow going short of breath. I pulled my 9 shirttail out and looked down at my spot, then up the incline of track ahead of me. Suddenly the air went hot, and the engine was by me. I hadn't pictured it moving that fast. A man's bare head leaned out and stared at me. I waved to him with my left hand and turned into the train, burying my face in the incredible noise. When I looked up, the head was gone.

I started running alongside the boxcars. Quickly, I found their 10 pace, held it, and then eased off, concentrating on each thick wheel that cut past me. I slowed another notch. Over my shoulder, I picked my car as it came off the bend, locking in the image of the white mountain goat painted on its side. I waited, leaning forward like the anchor in a 440-relay, wishing the baton up the track behind me. Then the big goat fired by me, and I was flying and then tucking my shoulder as I dipped under the train.

A heavy blanket of red dust settled over me. I felt bolted to the 11 earth. Sheet-metal bellies thundered and shook above my face. Count to ten, a voice said, watch the axles and look to your left for daylight. But I couldn't count, and I couldn't find left if my life depended on it, which it did. The colors overhead went from brown to red to black to red again. Finally, I ripped my hands free, forced them to the rail, and, in one convulsive jerk, threw myself into the blue light.

I lay there face down until there was no more noise, and I could 12 feel the sun against the back of my neck. I sat up. The last ribbon of train was slipping away in the distance. Across the tracks, O.T. was leading a cavalry charge down the hill, five very small, galloping boys, their fists whirling above them. I pulled my knees to my chest. My corduroy pants puckered wet across my thighs. I didn't care.

QUESTIONS FOR STUDY AND DISCUSSION

1. Why did Hoffmann accept O.T.'s dare when he was twelve years old? Would he accept the same dare today? Explain.
2. How does paragraph 4 function in the context of Hoffmann's narrative?
3. How has Hoffmann organized his essay? (Glossary: *Organization*) What period of time is covered in paragraphs 2–5? In paragraphs 6–12? What conclusions about narrative time can you draw from what Hoffmann has done?
4. What were Hoffmann's feelings on the day of his dive under the moving freight train? Do you think he was afraid? How do you know?
5. Identify four figures of speech that Hoffmann uses in his essay. (Glossary: *Figure of Speech*) What does each figure add to his narrative?
6. Hoffmann tells his story in the first person: The narrator is the principal actor. (Glossary: *Point of View*) What would have been gained or lost had Hoffmann used either O.T. or Dwayne to tell the story as third-person observers? Explain.

VOCABULARY

Refer to your dictionary to define the following words as they are used in this selection. Then use each word in a sentence of your own.

shards (1)	evaporating (3)
baited (1)	implicit (4)
cronies (2)	ambiguous (4)
escalated (2)	convulsive (11)
guerrilla (2)	

CLASSROOM ACTIVITY USING NARRATION

At the heart of Hoffmann's narrative in paragraphs 10 and 11 is a very detailed depiction of the precise movements he made as he threw himself under the train and swung himself out to the other side of the tracks. Using these paragraphs as a model, spend 10 or 15 minutes narrating a simple sequence of movements. You might, for example, capture a movement in gymnastics, a classic ballet step, a turn at bat in baseball, a skateboarding stunt, or any action of your own choosing. Share your narration with classmates to see how successful you have been.

SUGGESTED WRITING ASSIGNMENTS

1. Can you remember any dares that you made or accepted while growing up? What were the consequences of those dares? Did you and your peers find dares a way to test or prove yourselves? Using Hoffmann's essay as a model, write a narrative essay about a dare that you made, accepted, or simply witnessed.

2. Each of us can tell of an experience, like the one narrated by Hoffmann, that has been unusually significant for us. Think about your past, identify one experience that has been especially important for you, and write an essay about it. In preparing to write your narrative, you may find it helpful to ask yourself: Why is the experience important for me? What details do I need to re-create the experience in an interesting and engaging way? How can I most effectively organize my narrative of the experience? Over what period of time did the experience occur? What point of view will work best? What did I learn from this experience?

Momma, the Dentist, and Me

■ **Maya Angelou**

Best-selling author and poet Maya Angelou is an educator, historian, actress, playwright, civil rights activist, producer, and director. She is best known as the author of I Know Why the Caged Bird Sings *(1970), the first book in a series that constitutes her recently completed autobiography, and for "On the Pulse of the Morning," a characteristically optimistic poem on the need for personal and national renewal that she read at President Bill Clinton's inauguration in 1993. Starting with her beginnings in St. Louis in 1928, Angelou's autobiography presents a life of joyful triumph over hardships that test her courage and threaten her spirit. It includes the titles* All God's Children Need Traveling Shoes *(1986),* Wouldn't Take Nothing for My Journey Now *(1993), and* Heart of a Woman *(1997). The sixth and final book in the series,* A Song Flung Up to Heaven, *was published in 2002. Several volumes of her poetry were collected in* Complete Collected Poems of Maya Angelou *in 1994. In the following excerpt from* I Know Why the Caged Bird Sings, *Angelou narrates what happened, and what might have happened, when her grandmother, the "Momma" of the story, took her to the local dentist. As you read, consider how vital first-person narration is to the essay's success, particularly as you gauge the effect of the italicized paragraphs.*

FOR YOUR JOURNAL

When you were growing up, were you ever present when one or both of your parents were arguing with another adult about a matter concerning you? What were the circumstances? Perhaps, for example, you saw your parents criticizing a babysitter for letting you stay up past your bedtime or arguing with school officials about the school's dress code or a class activity that they found objectionable. Narrate the events that brought about the controversy, and show how it was resolved. Were you embarrassed by your parents' actions or happy that they stood up for you?

The angel of the candy counter had found me out at last, and was ex- 1
acting excruciating penance for all the stolen Milky Ways, Mounds, Mr. Goodbars and Hersheys with Almonds. I had two cavities that were rotten to the gums. The pain was beyond the bailiwick of crushed aspirins or oil of cloves. Only one thing could help me, so I prayed earnestly that I'd be allowed to sit under the house and have the building collapse on my left jaw. Since there was no Negro dentist in Stamps, nor doctor either, for that matter, Momma had dealt with previous toothaches by pulling them out (a string tied to the tooth with the other end looped over her fist), pain killers and prayer. In this particular instance the medicine had proved ineffective; there wasn't enough enamel left to hook a string on, and the prayers were being ignored because the Balancing Angel was blocking their passage.

I lived a few days and nights in blinding pain, not so much toying 2
with as seriously considering the idea of jumping in the well, and Momma decided I had to be taken to a dentist. The nearest Negro dentist was in Texarkana, twenty-five miles away, and I was certain that I'd be dead long before we reached half the distance. Momma said we'd go to Dr. Lincoln, right in Stamps, and he'd take care of me. She said he owed her a favor.

I knew there were a number of whitefolks in town that owed her 3
favors. Bailey and I had seen the books which showed how she had lent money to Blacks and whites alike during the Depression, and most still owed her. But I couldn't aptly remember seeing Dr. Lincoln's name, nor had I ever heard of a Negro's going to him as a patient. However, Momma said we were going, and put water on the stove for our baths. I had never been to a doctor, so she told me that after the bath (which would make my mouth feel better) I had to put on freshly starched and ironed underclothes from inside out. The ache failed to respond to the bath, and I knew then that the pain was more serious than that which anyone had ever suffered.

Before we left the Store, she ordered me to brush my teeth and 4
then wash my mouth with Listerine. The idea of even opening my clamped jaws increased the pain, but upon her explanation that when you go to a doctor you have to clean yourself all over, but most especially the part that's to be examined, I screwed up my courage and unlocked my teeth. The cool air in my mouth and the jarring of my molars dislodged what little remained of my reason. I had frozen to the pain, my family nearly had to tie me down to take the toothbrush away. It was no small effort to get me started on the road to the dentist. Momma spoke to all the passers-by, but didn't stop to chat.

She explained over her shoulder that we were going to the doctor and she'd "pass the time of day" on our way home.

Until we reached the pond the pain was my world, an aura that haloed me for three feet around. Crossing the bridge into whitefolks' country, pieces of sanity pushed themselves forward. I had to stop moaning and start walking straight. The white towel, which was drawn under my chin and tied over my head, had to be arranged. If one was dying, it had to be done in style if the dying took place in whitefolks' part of town.

On the other side of the bridge the ache seemed to lessen as if a whitebreeze blew off the whitefolks and cushioned everything in their neighborhood—including my jaw. The gravel road was smoother, the stones smaller and the tree branches hung down around the path and nearly covered us. If the pain didn't diminish then, the familiar yet strange sights hypnotized me into believing that it had.

But my head continued to throb with the measured insistence of a bass drum, and how could a toothache pass the calaboose, hear the songs of the prisoners, their blues and laughter, and not be changed? How could one or two or even a mouthful of angry tooth roots meet a wagonload of powhitetrash children, endure their idiotic snobbery and not feel less important?

Behind the building which housed the dentist's office ran a small path used by servants and those tradespeople who catered to the butcher and Stamps' one restaurant. Momma and I followed that lane to the backstairs of Dentist Lincoln's office. The sun was bright and gave the day a hard reality as we climbed up the steps to the second floor.

Momma knocked on the back door and a young white girl opened it to show surprise at seeing us there. Momma said she wanted to see Dentist Lincoln and to tell him Annie was there. The girl closed the door firmly. Now the humiliation of hearing Momma describe herself as if she had no last name to the young white girl was equal to the physical pain. It seemed terribly unfair to have a toothache and a headache and have to bear at the same time the heavy burden of Blackness.

It was always possible that the teeth would quiet down and maybe drop out of their own accord. Momma said we would wait. We leaned in the harsh sunlight on the shaky railings of the dentist's back porch for over an hour.

He opened the door and looked at Momma. "Well, Annie, what can I do for you?"

He didn't see the towel around my jaw or notice my swollen face.   12

Momma said, "Dentist Lincoln. It's my grandbaby here. She got   13
two rotten teeth that's giving her a fit."

She waited for him to acknowledge the truth of her statement.   14
He made no comment, orally or facially.

"She had this toothache purt' near four days now, and today I   15
said, 'Young lady, you going to the Dentist.'"

"Annie?"   16

"Yes, sir, Dentist Lincoln."   17

He was choosing words the way people hunt for shells. "Annie,   18
you know I don't treat nigra, colored people."

"I know, Dentist Lincoln. But this here is just my little grand-   19
baby, and she ain't gone be no trouble to you . . ."

"Annie, everybody has a policy. In this world you have to have a   20
policy. Now, my policy is I don't treat colored people."

The sun had baked the oil out of Momma's skin and melted the   21
Vaseline in her hair. She shone greasily as she leaned out of the dentist's shadow.

"Seem like to me, Dentist Lincoln, you might look after her, she   22
ain't nothing but a little mite. And seems like maybe you owe me a
favor or two."

He reddened slightly. "Favor or no favor. The money has all   23
been repaid to you and that's the end of it. Sorry, Annie." He had his
hand on the doorknob. "Sorry." His voice was a bit kinder on the
second "Sorry," as if he really was.

Momma said, "I wouldn't press on you like this for myself but I   24
can't take No. Not for my grandbaby. When you come to borrow my
money you didn't have to beg. You asked me, and I lent it. Now, it
wasn't my policy. I ain't no moneylender, but you stood to lose this
building and I tried to help you out."

"It's been paid, and raising your voice won't make me change my   25
mind. My policy . . ." He let go of the door and stepped nearer Momma.
The three of us were crowded on the small landing. "Annie, my policy
is I'd rather stick my hand in a dog's mouth than in a nigger's."

He had never once looked at me. He turned his back and went   26
through the door into the cool beyond. Momma backed up inside
herself for a few minutes. I forgot everything except her face which
was almost a new one to me. She leaned over and took the doorknob,
and in her everyday soft voice she said, "Sister, go on downstairs.
Wait for me. I'll be there directly."

Under the most common of circumstances I knew it did no good 27
to argue with Momma. So I walked down the steep stairs, afraid to
look back and afraid not to do so. I turned as the door slammed, and
she was gone.

Momma walked in that room as if she owned it. She shoved that 28
silly nurse aside with one hand and strode into the dentist's office. He
was sitting in his chair, sharpening his mean instruments and putting
extra sting into his medicines. Her eyes were blazing like live coals
and her arms had doubled themselves in length. He looked up at her
just before she caught him by the collar of his white jacket.

"Stand up when you see a lady, you contemptuous scoundrel." 29
Her tongue had thinned and the words rolled off well enunciated.
Enunciated and sharp like little claps of thunder.

The dentist had no choice but to stand at R.O.T.C.[1] attention. 30
His head dropped after a minute and his voice was humble. "Yes,
ma'am, Mrs. Henderson."

"You knave, do you think you acted like a gentleman, speaking 31
to me like that in front of my granddaughter?" She didn't shake him,
although she had the power. She simply held him upright.

"No, ma'am, Mrs. Henderson." 32

"No, ma'am, Mrs. Henderson, what?" Then she did give him the 33
tiniest of shakes, but because of her strength the action set his head
and arms to shaking loose on the ends of his body. He stuttered much
worse than Uncle Willie. "No, ma'am, Mrs. Henderson, I'm sorry."

With just an edge of her disgust showing, Momma slung him back 34
in his dentist's chair. "Sorry is as sorry does, and you're about the sor-
riest dentist I ever laid my eyes on." (She could afford to slip into the
vernacular because she had such eloquent command of English.)

"I didn't ask you to apologize in front of Marguerite, because I 35
don't want her to know my power, but I order you, now and here-
with. Leave Stamps by sundown."

"Mrs. Henderson, I can't get my equipment . . ." He was shaking 36
terribly now.

"Now, that brings me to my second order. You will never again 37
practice dentistry. Never! When you get settled in your next place,
you will be a vegetarian caring for dogs with the mange, cats with the
cholera and cows with the epizootic. Is that clear?"

---

[1]*R.O.T.C.:* Reserve Officers Training Corps of the U.S. military. [Eds.]

The saliva ran down his chin and his eyes filled with tears. "Yes,   38
ma'am. Thank you for not killing me. Thank you, Mrs. Henderson."

Momma pulled herself back from being ten feet tall with eight-   39
foot arms and said, "You're welcome for nothing, you varlet, I
wouldn't waste a killing on the likes of you."

On her way out she waved her handkerchief at the nurse and   40
turned her into a crocus sack of chicken feed.

Momma looked tired when she came down the stairs, but who   41
wouldn't be tired if they had gone through what she had. She came
close to me and adjusted the towel under my jaw (I had forgotten the
toothache; I only knew that she made her hands gentle in order not to
awaken the pain). She took my hand. Her voice never changed.
"Come on, Sister."

I reckoned we were going home where she would concoct a brew   42
to eliminate the pain and maybe give me new teeth too. New teeth
that would grow overnight out of my gums. She led me toward the
drugstore, which was in the opposite direction from the Store. "I'm
taking you to Dentist Baker in Texarkana."

I was glad after all that I had bathed and put on Mum[2] and   43
Cashmere Bouquet talcum powder. It was a wonderful surprise. My
toothache had quieted to solemn pain, Momma had obliterated the
evil white man, and we were going on a trip to Texarkana, just the
two of us.

On the Greyhound she took an inside seat in the back, and I sat   44
beside her. I was so proud of being her granddaughter and sure that
some of her magic must have come down to me. She asked if I was
scared. I only shook my head and leaned over on her cool brown
upper arm. There was no chance that a dentist, especially a Negro
dentist, would dare hurt me then. Not with Momma there. The trip
was uneventful, except that she put her arm around me, which was
very unusual for Momma to do.

The dentist showed me the medicine and the needle before he   45
deadened my gums, but if he hadn't I wouldn't have worried.
Momma stood right behind him. Her arms were folded and she
checked on everything he did. The teeth were extracted and she
bought me an ice cream cone from the side window of a drug
counter. The trip back to Stamps was quiet, except that I had to spit
into a very small empty snuff can which she had gotten for me and it
was difficult with the bus humping and jerking on our country roads.

---

[2]*Mum:* name of a brand of deodorant. [Eds.]

At home, I was given a warm salt solution, and when I washed 46
out my mouth I showed Bailey the empty holes, where the clotted
blood sat like filling in a pie crust. He said I was quite brave, and that
was my cue to reveal our confrontation with the peckerwood dentist
and Momma's incredible powers.

I had to admit that I didn't hear the conversation, but what else 47
could she have said than what I said she said? What else done? He
agreed with my analysis in a lukewarm way, and I happily (after all,
I'd been sick) flounced into the Store. Momma was preparing our
evening meal and Uncle Willie leaned on the door sill. She gave her
version.

"Dentist Lincoln got right uppity. Said he'd rather put his hand 48
in a dog's mouth. And when I reminded him of the favor, he brushed
it off like a piece of lint. Well, I sent Sister downstairs and went inside. I hadn't never been in his office before, but I found the door to
where he takes out teeth, and him and the nurse was in there thick as
thieves. I just stood there till he caught sight of me." Crash bang the
pots on the stove. "He jumped just like he was sitting on a pin. He
said, 'Annie, I done tole you, I ain't gonna mess around in no nig-
gah's mouth.' I said, 'Somebody's got to do it then,' and he said,
'Take her to Texarkana to the colored dentist' and that's when I said,
'If you paid me my money I could afford to take her.' He said, 'It's all
been paid.' I tole him everything but the interest been paid. He said,
''Twasn't no interest.' I said, ''Tis now. I'll take ten dollars as payment in full.' You know, Willie, it wasn't no right thing to do, 'cause
I lent that money without thinking about it.

"He tole that little snippety nurse of his'n to give me ten dollars 49
and make me sign a 'paid in full' receipt. She gave it to me and I
signed the papers. Even though by rights he was paid up before, I
figger, he gonna be that kind of nasty, he gonna have to pay for it."

Momma and her son laughed and laughed over the white man's 50
evilness and her retributive sin.

I preferred, much preferred, my version. 51

QUESTIONS FOR STUDY AND DISCUSSION

1. What is Angelou's purpose in narrating the story she tells? (Glossary: *Purpose*)
2. Compare and contrast the content and style of the interaction between Momma and the dentist that is given in italics with the

one given at the end of the narrative. (Glossary: *Comparison and Contrast*)

3. Angelou tells her story chronologically and in the first person. (Glossary: *Point of View*) What are the advantages of the first-person narrative?

4. Identify three similes that Angelou uses in her narrative. (Glossary: *Figure of Speech*) Explain how each simile serves her purpose.

5. Why do you suppose Angelou says she prefers her own version of the episode to that of her grandmother?

6. This story is a story of pain and not just the pain of a toothache. How does Angelou describe the pain of the toothache? What other pain does Angelou tell of in this autobiographical narrative?

VOCABULARY

Refer to your dictionary to define the following words as they are used in this selection. Then use each word in a sentence of your own.

bailiwick (1)	varlet (39)
calaboose (7)	concoct (42)
mite (22)	snippety (49)
vernacular (34)	retributive (50)

CLASSROOM ACTIVITY USING NARRATION

One of Angelou's themes in "Momma, the Dentist, and Me" is that cruelty, whether racial, social, professional, or personal, is very difficult to endure and leaves a lasting impression on a person. As a way of practicing chronological order, consider a situation in which an unthinking or insensitive person made you feel inferior. Rather than write a draft of an essay at this point, simply list the sequence of events that occurred, in chronological order. Once you have completed this step, consider whether there is a more dramatic order you might use if you were actually to write an essay.

SUGGESTED WRITING ASSIGNMENTS

1. Using Angelou's essay as a model, give two versions of an actual event—one the way you thought or wished it had happened, and the other the way events actually took place. You may want to refer to your journal entry for this reading.

2. Every person who tells a story does so by putting his or her signature on it in some way—by the sequencing of events, the amount and type of details used, and the tone the teller of the story employs. If you and a relative or friend experienced the same interesting sequence of events, try telling the story of those events from your unique perspective. Once you have done so, try telling the story from what you imagine the other person's perspective to be. Perhaps you even heard the other person actually tell the story. What is the same in both versions? How do the renditions differ?

The Story of an Hour

■ Kate Chopin

Kate Chopin (1851–1904) was born in St. Louis, of Creole Irish descent. After her marriage she lived in Louisiana, where she acquired the intimate knowledge of Creole Cajun culture that provided the impetus for much of her work and earned her a reputation as a writer who captured the ambience of the bayou region. When her first novel, The Awakening *(1899), was published, however, it generated scorn and outrage for its explicit depiction of a southern woman's sexual awakening. Only recently has Chopin been recognized for her literary talent and originality. Besides* The Awakening, *her works include two collections of short fiction,* Bayou Folk *(1894) and* A Night in Acadie *(1897). In 1969,* The Complete Works of Kate Chopin *was published by Louisiana State University Press, and the Library of America published* Kate Chopin: Complete Novels and Stories *in 2002. As you read the selection below, try to gauge how your reactions to Mrs. Mallard are influenced by Chopin's use of third-person narration.*

FOR YOUR JOURNAL

How do you react to the idea of marriage—committing to someone for life? What are the advantages of such a union? What are the disadvantages?

Knowing that Mrs. Mallard was afflicted with a heart trouble, 1
great care was taken to break to her as gently as possible the news of her husband's death.

It was her sister Josephine who told her, in broken sentences; 2
veiled hints that revealed in half concealing. Her husband's friend Richards was there, too, near her. It was he who had been in the newspaper office when intelligence of the railroad disaster was received, with Brently Mallard's name leading the list of "killed." He had only taken the time to assure himself of its truth by a second telegram, and had hastened to forestall any less careful, less tender friend in bearing the sad message.

She did not hear the story as many women have heard the same,   3
with a paralyzed inability to accept its significance. She wept at once,
with sudden, wild abandonment, in her sister's arms. When the storm
of grief had spent itself she went away to her room alone. She would
have no one follow her.

There stood, facing the open window, a comfortable, roomy   4
armchair. Into this she sank, pressed down by a physical exhaustion
that haunted her body and seemed to reach into her soul.

She could see in the open square before her house the tops of   5
trees that were all aquiver with the new spring life. The delicious
breath of rain was in the air. In the street below a peddler was crying
his wares. The notes of a distant song which someone was singing
reached her faintly, and countless sparrows were twittering in the
eaves.

There were patches of blue sky showing here and there through   6
the clouds that had met and piled one above the other in the west facing her window.

She sat with her head thrown back upon the cushion of the chair,   7
quite motionless, except when a sob came up into her throat and
shook her, as a child who has cried itself to sleep continues to sob in
its dreams.

She was young, with a fair, calm face, whose lines bespoke re-   8
pression and even a certain strength. But now there was a dull stare
in her eyes, whose gaze was fixed away off yonder on one of those
patches of blue sky. It was not a glance of reflection, but rather indi-
cated a suspension of intelligent thought.

There was something coming to her and she was waiting for it,   9
fearfully. What was it? She did not know; it was too subtle and elusive to name. But she felt it, creeping out of the sky, reaching toward
her through the sounds, the scents, the color that filled the air.

Now her bosom rose and fell tumultuously. She was beginning to   10
recognize this thing that was approaching to possess her, and she was
striving to beat it back with her will—as powerless as her two white
slender hands would have been.

When she abandoned herself a little whispered word escaped her   11
slightly parted lips. She said it over and over under her breath: "free,
free, free!" The vacant stare and the look of terror that had followed
it went from her eyes. They stayed keen and bright. Her pulses beat
fast, and the coursing blood warmed and relaxed every inch of her
body.

She did not stop to ask if it were or were not a monstrous joy   12
that held her. A clear and exalted perception enabled her to dismiss
the suggestion as trivial.

She knew that she would weep again when she saw the kind, ten-   13
der hands folded in death; the face that had never looked save with
love upon her, fixed and gray and dead. But she saw beyond that bitter moment a long procession of years to come that would belong to
her absolutely. And she opened and spread her arms out to them in
welcome.

There would be no one to live for her during those coming years;   14
she would live for herself. There would be no powerful will bending
hers in that blind persistence with which men and women believe
they have a right to impose a private will upon a fellow-creature. A
kind intention or a cruel intention made the act seem no less a crime
as she looked upon it in that brief moment of illumination.

And yet she had loved him—sometimes. Often she had not.   15
What did it matter! What could love, the unsolved mystery, count for
in face of this possession of self-assertion which she suddenly recognized as the strongest impulse of her being!

"Free! Body and soul free!" she kept whispering.   16

Josephine was kneeling before the closed door with her lips to the   17
keyhole, imploring for admission. "Louise, open the door! I beg;
open the door—you will make yourself ill. What are you doing,
Louise? For heaven's sake open the door."

"Go away. I am not making myself ill." No; she was drinking in   18
a very elixir of life through that open window.

Her fancy was running riot along those days ahead of her. Spring   19
days, and summer days, and all sorts of days that would be her own.
She breathed a quick prayer that life might be long. It was only yesterday she had thought with a shudder that life might be long.

She arose at length and opened the door to her sister's importuni-   20
ties. There was a feverish triumph in her eyes, and she carried herself
unwittingly like a goddess of Victory. She clasped her sister's waist,
and together they descended the stairs. Richards stood waiting for
them at the bottom.

Some one was opening the front door with a latchkey. It was   21
Brently Mallard who entered, a little travel-stained, composedly carrying his grip-sack and umbrella. He had been far from the scene of
the accident, and did not even know there had been one. He stood
amazed at Josephine's piercing cry; at Richards' quick motion to
screen him from the view of his wife.

But Richards was too late.   22

When the doctors came they said she had died of heart disease —   23
of joy that kills.

QUESTIONS FOR STUDY AND DISCUSSION

1. What assumptions do Mrs. Mallard's relatives and friends make about her feelings toward her husband? How would you describe her true feelings?

2. Reread paragraphs 5–9. What is Chopin's purpose in this section of the story? (Glossary: *Purpose*) Do these paragraphs add to the story's effectiveness? Explain.

3. Why does Mrs. Mallard fight her feeling of freedom, however briefly?

4. All of the events of this story take place in an hour. Would the story be as poignant if they had taken place over the course of a day, or even several days? Explain. Why do you suppose the author selected the time frame as a title for her story? (Glossary: *Title*)

5. Chopin could have written an essay detailing the oppression of women in marriage, but she chose instead to write a fictional narrative. This allows her to show readers the type of situation that can arise in an outwardly happy marriage, rather than tell them about it. Why else do you think she chose to write a fictional narrative? What other advantages does it give her over nonfiction?

6. Why do you suppose Chopin chose to narrate her story in the third person? (Glossary: *Point of View*)

VOCABULARY

Refer to your dictionary to define the following words as they are used in this selection. Then use each word in a sentence of your own.

afflicted (1)   exalted (12)
aquiver (5)   imploring (17)
bespoke (8)   elixir (18)
tumultuously (10)   importunities (20)

CLASSROOM ACTIVITY USING NARRATION

Using cues in the following sentences, rearrange them in chronological order.

1. The sky was gray and gloomy for as far as she could see, and sleet hissed off the glass.
2. "Oh, hi, I'm glad you called," she said happily, but her smile dimmed when she looked outside.
3. As Betty crossed the room, the phone rang, startling her.
4. "No, the weather's awful, so I don't think I'll get out to visit you today," she sighed.
5. "Hello," she said, and she wandered over to the window, dragging the phone cord behind her.

Write five sentences of your own that cover a progression of events. Try to include dialogue. Then scramble them, and see if a classmate can put them back in the correct order.

SUGGESTED WRITING ASSIGNMENTS

1. Using Chopin's story as a model, write a short piece of narrative fiction in which your main character reacts to a specific, dramatic event. Portray the character's emotional response, as well as how the character perceives his or her surroundings. What does the character see, hear, touch? How are these senses affected by the situation?

2. Write a narrative essay in which you describe your reaction to a piece of news that you once received—good or bad—that provoked a strong emotional response. What were your emotions? What did you do in the couple of hours after you received the news? How did your perceptions of the world around you change? What made the experience memorable?

Description

To describe is to create a verbal picture. A person, a place, a thing—even an idea or a state of mind—can be made vividly concrete through **description**. Here, for example, is a brief description of a delicatessen:

> It was a narrow room, with a rather high ceiling, and crowded from floor to ceiling with goodies. There were rows and rows of hams and sausages of all shapes and colors—white, yellow, red, and black; fat and lean and round and long—rows of canned preserves, cocoa and tea, bright translucent glass bottles of honey, marmalade, and jam; round bottles and slender bottles, filled with liqueurs and punch—all these things crowded every inch of the shelves from top to bottom.
>
> –Thomas Mann

Writing any description requires, first of all, that the writer gather many details about a subject, relying not only on what the eyes see but on the other sense impressions—touch, taste, smell, hearing—as well. From this catalog of details the writer selects those that will most effectively create a **dominant impression**—the single quality, mood, or atmosphere that the writer wishes to emphasize. Consider, for example, the details that Mary McCarthy uses to evoke the dominant impression in the following passage, and contrast them with those in the subsequent example by student Dan Bubany:

> Whenever we children came to stay at my grandmother's house, we were put to sleep in the sewing room, a bleak, shabby, utilitarian rectangle, more office than bedroom, more attic than office, that played to the hierarchy of chambers the role of poor relation. It was a room without pride: the old sewing machine, some cast-off chairs, a shadeless lamp, rolls of wrapping paper, piles of cardboard boxes that might someday come in handy, papers of

pins, and remnants of a material united with the iron folding cots put out for our use and the bare floor boards to give an impression of intense and ruthless temporality. Thin white spreads, of the kind used in hospitals and charity institutions, and naked blinds at the windows reminded us of our orphaned condition and of the ephemeral character of our visit; there was nothing here to encourage us to consider this our home.

–Mary McCarthy

For this particular Thursday game against Stanford, Fleming wears white gloves, a maroon sport coat with brass buttons, and gray slacks. Shiny silver-framed bifocals match the whistle pressed between the lips on his slightly wrinkled face, and he wears freshly polished black shoes so glossy that they reflect the grass he stands on. He is not fat, but his coat neatly conceals a small, round pot belly.

–Dan Bubany, student

The dominant impression that McCarthy creates is one of clutter, bleakness, and shabbiness. There is nothing in the sewing room that suggests permanence or warmth. Bubany, on the other hand, creates a dominant impression of a neat, polished kindly man.

Writers must also carefully plan the order in which to present their descriptive details. The pattern of organization must fit the subject of the description logically and naturally and must also be easy to follow. For example, visual details can be arranged spatially — from left to right, top to bottom, near to far, or in any other logical order. Other patterns include smallest to largest, softest to loudest, least significant to most significant, most unusual to least unusual. McCarthy, for example, suggests a jumble of junk not only by her choice of details but by the apparently random order in which she presents them.

How much detail is enough? There is no fixed answer. A good description includes enough vivid details to create a dominant impression and to bring a scene to life, but not so many that readers are distracted, confused, or bored. In an essay that is purely descriptive, there is room for much detail. Usually, however, writers use description to create the setting for a story, to illustrate ideas, to help clarify a definition or a comparison, or to make the complexities of a process more understandable. Such descriptions should be kept short and should include just enough detail to make them clear and helpful.

Subway Station

■ **Gilbert Highet**

Gilbert Highet (1906–1978) was born in Scotland and became a naturalized U.S. citizen in 1951. A prolific writer and translator, distinguished scholar, and critic, Highet was for many years a professor of classics at Columbia University, as well as a popular radio essayist. His Art of Teaching, *a classic in education, was reissued in paperback and is still available. Another of his books,* The Classical Tradition: Greek and Roman Influences on Western Literature, *was reissued in paperback in 1992. The following selection is from his book* Talents and Geniuses (1957). *Take note of Highet's keen eye for detail as you read. Concrete and vivid images help him re-create the unseemly world of a subway station.*

FOR YOUR JOURNAL

Try to remember what it is like to be in a subway station, airport, or bus station. What are the sights, sounds, and smells you recall? What do you remember most about any of these crowded, transient places? What was your overall impression of the place?

Standing in a subway station, I began to appreciate the place—almost to enjoy it. First of all, I looked at the lighting: a row of meager electric bulbs, unscreened, yellow, and coated with filth, stretched toward the black mouth of the tunnel, as though it were a bolt hole in an abandoned coal mine. Then I lingered, with zest, on the walls and ceiling: lavatory tiles which had been white about fifty years ago, and were now encrusted with soot, coated with the remains of a dirty liquid which might be either atmospheric humidity mingled with smog or the result of a perfunctory attempt to clean them with cold water; and, above them, gloomy vaulting from which dingy paint was peeling off like scabs from an old wound, sick black paint leaving a leprous white undersurface. Beneath my feet, the floor was a nauseating dark brown with black stains upon it which might be stale oil or dry chewing gum or some worse defilement; it looked like the hallway of a condemned slum building. Then my eye traveled to the tracks, where two lines of glittering steel—the only positively clean objects in the whole place—ran out of darkness into darkness above an unspeakable mass of congealed oil, puddles of dubious liquid, and a mishmash of old cigarette packets, mutilated and filthy newspapers, and the débris that filtered down from the street above through a barred grating in the roof. As I looked up toward the sunlight, I could see more débris sifting slowly downward, and making an abominable pattern in the slanting beam of dirt-laden sunlight. I was going on to relish more features of this unique scene: such as the advertisement posters on the walls—here a text from the Bible, there a half-naked girl, here a woman wearing a hat consisting of a hen sitting on a nest full of eggs, and there a pair of girl's legs walking up the keys of a cash register—all scribbled over with unknown names and well-known obscenities in black crayon and red lipstick; but then my train came in at last, I boarded it, and began to read. The experience was over for the time.

QUESTIONS FOR STUDY AND DISCUSSION

1. What dominant impression does Highet create in his description? (Glossary: *Dominant Impression*) List the details that help Highet create his dominant impression.

2. Why do you think Highet observes the subway station with "zest" and "relish"? What does he find appealing about the experience?

3. What similes and metaphors can you find in Highet's description? (Glossary: *Figure of Speech*) How do they help make the description vivid?

4. What mix of advertisements does Highet observe? Based on Highet's description of what they depict, their current appearance, and the atmosphere of their surroundings, suggest what product each poster might be advertising. Explain your suggestions.

5. Highet has an eye for detail that is usually displayed by those who are seeing something for the first time. Do you think it is his first time in a subway station, or is he a regular rider who is taking time out to "relish" his physical surroundings? What in the essay leads you to your conclusion?

VOCABULARY

Refer to your dictionary to define the following words as they are used in this selection. Then use each word in a sentence of your own.

perfunctory   dubious
leprous   abominable
defilement

CLASSROOM ACTIVITY USING DESCRIPTION

Make a long list of the objects and people in your classroom as well as the physical features of the classroom—desks, windows, chalkboard, students, professor, dirty walls, burned-out lightbulb, a clock that is always ten minutes fast, and so on. Determine a dominant impression that you would like to create in describing the classroom. Now choose from your list those items that would best illustrate the dominant impression you have chosen. Your instructor may wish to have students compare their responses.

SUGGESTED WRITING ASSIGNMENTS

1. Using Highet's essay as a model, write an extended one-paragraph description of a room in your house or apartment where you do not spend much time. Take your time observing the details in the room. Before you write, decide on the dominant impression you wish to communicate to the reader.

2. Write a short essay in which you describe one of the following places (or another place of your choice). Arrange the details of your description from top to bottom, left to right, near to far, or according to some other spatial organization.

   a closet   a barbershop or beauty salon
   a pizza parlor   a bookstore
   a locker room   a campus dining hall

The Sounds of the City

■ **James Tuite**

James Tuite had a long career at the New York Times, *where he once served as sports editor. As a freelance writer he has contributed to all of the major sports magazines and has written* Snowmobiles and Snowmobiling *(1969) and* How to Enjoy Sports on TV *(1976). The following selection is a model of how a place can be described by using a sense other than sight. Tuite describes New York City by its sounds, which for him comprise the very life of the city.*

FOR YOUR JOURNAL

Sit in a relatively busy place—your dormitory lounge, a campus eatery, a science laboratory, a classroom as it begins to fill with students for your next class. Close your eyes, and try to take in all the sounds you hear for approximately 20 seconds. Record in your journal what you have heard. Then listen again for another 20 seconds and record again. Repeat this process five or six times. Finally, make a journal entry describing the place you chose, using only the sounds that you have heard.

New York is a city of sounds: muted sounds and shrill sounds; 1 shattering sounds and soothing sounds; urgent sounds and aimless sounds. The cliff dwellers of Manhattan—who would be racked by the silence of the lonely woods—do not hear these sounds because they are constant and eternally urban.

The visitor to the city can hear them, though, just as some ani- 2 mals can hear a high-pitched whistle inaudible to humans. To the casual caller to Manhattan, lying restive and sleepless in a hotel twenty or thirty floors above the street, they tell a story as fascinating as life itself. And back of the sounds broods the silence.

Night in midtown is the noise of tinseled honky-tonk and vio- 3 lence. Thin strains of music, usually the firm beat of rock 'n' roll or the frenzied outbursts of the discotheque, rise from ground level. This is the cacophony, the discordance of youth, and it comes on strongest when nights are hot and young blood restless.

Somewhere in the canyons below there is shrill laughter or rau- 4
cous shouting. A bottle shatters against concrete. The whine of a police siren slices through the night, moving ever closer, until an eerie
Doppler effect[1] brings it to a guttural halt.

There are few sounds so exciting in Manhattan as those of fire 5
apparatus dashing through the night. At the outset there is the tentative hint of the first-due company bullying his way through midtown
traffic. Now a fire whistle from the opposite direction affirms that
trouble is, indeed, afoot. In seconds, other sirens converging from
other streets help the skytop listener focus on the scene of excitement.

But he can only hear and not see, and imagination takes flight. 6
Are the flames and smoke gushing from windows not far away? Are
victims trapped there, crying out for help? Is it a conflagration, or
only a trash-basket fire? Or, perhaps, it is merely a false alarm.

The questions go unanswered and the urgency of the moment 7
dissolves. Now the mind and the ear detect the snarling, arrogant
bickering of automobile horns. People in a hurry. Taxicabs blaring,
insisting on their checkered[2] priority.

Even the taxi horns dwindle down to a precocious few in the 8
gray and pink moments of dawn. Suddenly there is another sound, a
morning sound that taunts the memory for recognition. The growl of
a predatory monster? No, just garbage trucks that have begun a day
of scavenging.

Trash cans rattle outside restaurants. Metallic jaws on sanitation 9
trucks gulp and masticate the residue of daily living, then digest it
with a satisfied groan of gears. The sounds of the new day are busi-
nesslike. The growl of buses, so scattered and distant at night, becomes a demanding part of the traffic bedlam. An occasional jet or
helicopter injects an exclamation point from an unexpected quarter.
When the wind is right, the vibrant bellow of an ocean liner can be
heard.

The sounds of the day are as jarring as the glare of a sun that 10
outlines the canyons of midtown in drab relief. A pneumatic drill
frays countless nerves with its rat-a-tat-tat, for dig they must to perpetuate the city's dizzy motion. After each screech of brakes there is a

---

[1]*Doppler effect:* the drop in pitch that occurs as a source of sound quickly passes by a
listener. [Eds.]
[2]This reference is to the checkered paint jobs of taxis belonging to the Checker Cab
Company. [Eds.]

moment of suspension, of waiting for the thud or crash that never seems to follow.

The whistles of traffic policemen and hotel doormen chirp from all sides, like birds calling for their mates across a frenzied aviary. And all of these sounds are adult sounds, for childish laughter has no place in these canyons. 11

Night falls again, the cycle is complete, but there is no surcease from sound. For the beautiful dreamers, perhaps, the "sounds of the rude world heard in the day, lulled by the moonlight have all passed away,"[3] but this is not so in the city. 12

Too many New Yorkers accept the sounds about them as bland parts of everyday existence. They seldom stop to listen to the sounds, to think about them, to be appalled or enchanted by them. In the big city, sounds are life. 13

QUESTIONS FOR STUDY AND DISCUSSION

1. In your opinion, what is Tuite's main purpose in describing the sounds of New York City? (Glossary: *Purpose*)

2. What dominant impression of New York City does Tuite create in his essay? (Glossary: *Dominant Impression*)

3. Tuite describes "raucous shouting" (4) and the "screech of brakes" (10). Make a list of the various sounds that he describes in his essay. How do the varied adjectives and verbs Tuite uses to capture the essence of each sound enhance his description? (Glossary: *Diction*)

4. According to Tuite, why are visitors to New York City more sensitive to or aware of the multitude of sounds than the "cliff dwellers of Manhattan" (1)? What does he believe that New Yorkers have missed when they fail to take notice of these sounds?

5. Locate several metaphors and similes in the essay. What picture of the city does each give you? (Glossary: *Figure of Speech*)

6. How does Tuite organize his essay? Do you think the organization is effective? (Glossary: *Organization*)

---

[3]Lines from "Beautiful Dreamer," by Stephen Collins Foster (1826–1864), American songwriter. [Eds.]

VOCABULARY

Refer to your dictionary to define the following words as they are used in this selection. Then use each word in a sentence of your own.

muted (1)	precocious (8)
inaudible (2)	taunts (8)
restive (2)	vibrant (9)
raucous (4)	perpetuate (10)
tentative (5)	

CLASSROOM ACTIVITY USING DESCRIPTION

Write five sentences describing the place you would most like to go. What details about the place do you want to include? Choose your words carefully so that you create the dominant impression that you have of that place — beautiful, dangerous, serene, fun, relaxing, etc.

SUGGESTED WRITING ASSIGNMENTS

1. As Tuite has done, write a short composition describing a city you know well. Try to include as many sights, sounds, and smells as you can in your description. Your goal should be to create a single dominant impression of the city.

2. Describe a familiar inanimate object in a way that brings out its character and makes it interesting to the reader. First, determine your purpose in describing the object. Suppose, for example, your family has had the same dining table for as long as you can remember. Think of what that table has been a part of over the years — the birthday parties, the fights, the holiday meals, the long hours of studying and doing homework. A description of such a table would give your reader a sense of the history of your family. Next, make an exhaustive list of the object's physical features, and include in your descriptive essay the features that contribute to a dominant impression and support your purpose in writing the essay.

I Love Washington

■ **David McCullough**

Pulitzer Prize–winning historian David McCullough was born in Pittsburgh, Pennsylvania, in 1933 and graduated from Yale University. He has enjoyed a full and varied career as a writer, teacher, and lecturer. He taught at Cornell University, Dartmouth College, and Wesleyan University and has spoken as part of the White House presidential lecture series. Critics have called McCullough "a master of the art of narrative history," and his many books show that he is deserving of the acclaim. His presidential biographies Truman *(1992) and* John Adams *(2001) each earned McCullough a Pulitzer Prize. He is a familiar presence on public television, hosting the popular* Smithsonian World *and* The American Experience *and narrating documentaries like* The Civil War. *In the following essay, first published in the April/May 1986 issue of* American Heritage *magazine, McCullough describes what he believes is "our most civilized city." Pay particular attention to the descriptive details he chooses to explain his feelings about our nation's capital.*

FOR YOUR JOURNAL

What are your impressions of Washington, D.C.? Were your impressions formed firsthand while visiting the city, or were they formed from something you have read or seen on television or in the movies? When you hear the name of our country's capital mentioned, where do your thoughts go? If you have never been to Washington, what sights would you like most to see? Why?

Washington is a wonderful city. The scale seems right, more hu- 1
mane than other places. I like all the white marble and green trees, the ideals celebrated by the great monuments and memorials. I like the climate, the slow shift of the seasons here. Spring, so Southern in feeling, comes early and the long, sweet autumns can last into December. Summers are murder, equatorial—no question; the compensation is that Congress adjourns, the city empties out, eases off.

Winter evenings in Georgetown with the snow falling and the lights just coming on are as beautiful as any I've known.

I like the elegant old landmark hotels—the Willard, now re-   2
stored to its former glory, the Mayflower, with its long, glittering, palm-lined lobby, the Hay-Adams on Lafayette Square, overlooking the White House. And Massachusetts Avenue, as you drive down past the British Embassy and over Rock Creek Park, past the Mosque and around Sheridan Circle. This is an avenue in the grand tradition, befitting a world capital.

The presence of the National Gallery, it seems to me, would be   3
reason enough in itself to wish to live here.

In many ways it is our most civilized city. It accommodates its   4
river, accommodates trees and grass, makes room for nature as other cities don't. There are parks everywhere and two great, unspoiled, green corridors running beside the Potomac and out Rock Creek where Theodore Roosevelt liked to take his rough cross-country walks. There is no more beautiful entrance to any of our cities than the George Washington Parkway which comes sweeping down the Virginia side of the Potomac. The views of the river gorge are hardly changed from Jefferson's time. Across the river, on the towpath of the old C&O Canal, you can start at Georgetown and walk for miles with never a sense of being in a city. You can walk right out of town, ten, twenty, fifty miles if you like, more, all the way to Harpers Ferry[1] where you can pick up the Appalachian Trail going north or south.

Some mornings along the towpath it is as if you are walking   5
through a Monet.[2] Blue herons stalk the water. You see deer prints. Once, in Glover Park, in the heart of the city, I saw a red fox. He stopped right in front of me, not more than thirty feet down the path, and waited a count or two before vanishing into the woods, as if giving me time to look him over, as if he wanted me never to wonder whether my eyes had played tricks.

Even the famous National Zoo is a "zoological park," a place to   6
walk, as specifically intended in the original plan by Frederick Law Olmsted.

It was Olmsted also who did the magnificent Capitol grounds   7
and who had the nice idea of putting identifying tags on the trees,

---

[1]*Harpers Ferry:* a town in northeastern West Virginia. [Eds.]
[2]*Claude Monet* (1840–1926): French painter. [Eds.]

giving their places of origin and Latin names. I like particularly the tulip trees (*Liriodendron tulipifera*); the tulip is one of the common trees of Washington, and it lines the main drive to the east front of the Capitol. There are red oak, white oak, silver linden, a tremendous spreading white ash, sugar maples, five kinds of American magnolias, a huge Japanese pagoda tree. A spectacular willow oak on the west side has a trunk three men couldn't put their arms around. In spring the dogwood in bloom all around the Capitol are enough to take your breath away.

There are trees and there is sky, the immense, blessed overarching   8
sky of the Mall.[3] What city has anything to compare to the Mall? At first light on a summer morning, before the rush hour, before the first jets come roaring out of National, the dominant sound is of crows and the crunch of your own feet along the gravel pathways. The air, still cool from the night, smells of trees and damp grass, like a country town. Floodlights are still on at the old red Smithsonian castle, bathing it in a soft theatrical glow, like the backdrop for some nineteenth century Gothic fantasy. The moon is up still, hanging in a pale, clear sky beyond the Monument,[4] which for the moment is a very pale pink.

QUESTIONS FOR STUDY AND DISCUSSION

1. McCullough begins by announcing his affection for our nation's capital. What specifically does he like about the city?

2. How well does McCullough know Washington, D.C.? How does he reveal his authority on the subject?

3. McCullough creates for Washington a dominant impression of quiet grandeur and balance, a place where "the scale seems right, more humane than other places" (1). Which descriptive details help him create this impression? (Glossary: *Dominant Impression*) Which details were most effective for you? Explain why.

4. How does McCullough support his claim that Washington "makes room for nature as other cities don't" (4)? Were you surprised to discover blue herons, deer prints, and even a fox "in the heart of the city" (5)?

---

[3]*The Mall:* the wide open green space and walkway in Washington, D.C. that extends from the Capitol to the Potomac River. [Eds.]

[4]*The Monument:* an obelisk in Washington, D.C., honoring George Washington. [Eds.]

5. Which of your senses does McCullough's description appeal to? Why do you think he chose to describe the Washington Mall "at first light on a summer morning" (8)?

VOCABULARY

Refer to your dictionary to define the following words as they are used in this selection. Then use each word in a sentence of your own.

humane (1)   corridors (4)
equatorial (1)   backdrop (8)
accommodates (4)   fantasy (8)

CLASSROOM ACTIVITY USING DESCRIPTION

The verbs you use in writing a description can themselves convey much descriptive information. Take, for example, the verb *walk*. This word actually tells us little more than the general sense "to move on foot." Using more precise and descriptive alternatives—*hike, slink, saunter, stalk, step, stride, stroll, tramp, wander*—enhances your descriptive powers and enlivens your writing. For each of the following verbs, make a list of at least four descriptive alternatives:

go   throw   exercise
see   take   study
say   drink

Compare your lists of descriptive alternatives with those of others in the class.

SUGGESTED WRITING ASSIGNMENTS

1. What is your favorite city and what are your favorite places in that city? For example, if New York is your favorite city, the Metropolitan Museum of Art, Central Park, the Empire State Building, Broadway, and Yankee Stadium might be among your favorite places. Using McCullough's essay as a model, write an essay in which you describe the city you love.

2. Write a brief report about American landscape architect Frederick Law Olmsted (1822–1903). In addition to the National Zoo

and the Capitol grounds, what other public places did Olmsted design? What are the hallmarks of an Olmsted-designed landscape? In what ways and to what extent do you think Olmsted's design for Washington is responsible for McCullough's favorable reaction to the city? Explain.

My Favorite Teacher

■ **Thomas L. Friedman**

New York Times *foreign affairs columnist Thomas L. Friedman was born in Minneapolis, Minnesota, in 1953. He graduated from Brandeis University in 1975 and received a Marshall Scholarship to study Modern Middle East Studies at St. Antony's College, Oxford University, where he earned a master's degree. He has worked for the* New York Times *since 1981, first in Lebanon, then in Israel, and since 1989 in Washington, D.C. He was awarded the Pulitzer Prize for reporting in 1983 and again in 1988, and recently, his column won him his third Pulitzer Prize. His 1989 bestseller,* From Beirut to Jerusalem, *received the National Book Award for nonfiction. Friedman's most recent books are* The Lexus and the Olive Tree: Understanding Globalization *(2000) and* Longitudes and Attitudes: Exploring the World after September 11 *(2002). In the following essay, which first appeared in the* New York Times *on January 9, 2001, Friedman pays tribute to his tenth-grade journalism teacher. As you read Friedman's profile of Hattie M. Steinberg, note the descriptive detail he selects to create the dominant impression of "a woman of clarity in an age of uncertainty."*

FOR YOUR JOURNAL

If you had to name your three favorite teachers to date, who would be on your list? Why do you consider each of the teachers a favorite? Which one, if any, are you likely to remember twenty-five years from now? Why?

Last Sunday's *New York Times Magazine* published its annual review of people who died last year who left a particular mark on the world. I am sure all readers have their own such list. I certainly do. Indeed, someone who made the most important difference in my life died last year—my high school journalism teacher, Hattie M. Steinberg.

1

I grew up in a small suburb of Minneapolis, and Hattie was the 2
legendary journalism teacher at St. Louis Park High School, Room
313. I took her intro to journalism course in 10th grade, back in
1969, and have never needed, or taken, another course in journalism
since. She was that good.

Hattie was a woman who believed that the secret for success in 3
life was getting the fundamentals right. And boy, she pounded the
fundamentals of journalism into her students—not simply how to
write a lead or accurately transcribe a quote, but, more important,
how to comport yourself in a professional way and to always do
quality work. To this day, when I forget to wear a tie on assignment,
I think of Hattie scolding me. I once interviewed an ad exec for our
high school paper who used a four-letter word. We debated whether
to run it. Hattie ruled yes. That ad man almost lost his job when it
appeared. She wanted to teach us about consequences.

Hattie was the toughest teacher I ever had. After you took her 4
journalism course in 10th grade, you tried out for the paper, The
Echo, which she supervised. Competition was fierce. In 11th grade, I
didn't quite come up to her writing standards, so she made me business manager, selling ads to the local pizza parlors. That year,
though, she let me write one story. It was about an Israeli general
who had been a hero in the Six-Day War,[1] who was giving a lecture
at the University of Minnesota. I covered his lecture and interviewed
him briefly. His name was Ariel Sharon.[2] First story I ever got published.

Those of us on the paper, and the yearbook that she also super- 5
vised, lived in Hattie's classroom. We hung out there before and after
school. Now, you have to understand, Hattie was a single woman,
nearing 60 at the time, and this was the 1960's. She was the polar opposite of "cool," but we hung around her classroom like it was a
malt shop and she was Wolfman Jack.[3] None of us could have articulated it then, but it was because we enjoyed being harangued by her,
disciplined by her, and taught by her. She was a woman of clarity in
an age of uncertainty.

---

[1]*Six-Day War:* the short but pivotal war in June 1967 between Israel and the allied
countries of Egypt, Syria, and Jordan. [Eds.]
[2]*Ariel Sharon* (b. 1928): Israeli general and politician, elected prime minister of Israel
in 2001. [Eds.]
[3]*Wolfman Jack:* pseudonym of Robert Weston Smith (1938–1995), a famous American rock-and-roll radio disc jockey. [Eds.]

We remained friends for 30 years, and she followed, bragged   6
about, and critiqued every twist in my career. After she died, her
friends sent me a pile of my stories that she had saved over the years.
Indeed, her students were her family—only closer. Judy Harrington,
one of Hattie's former students, remarked about other friends who
were on Hattie's newspapers and yearbooks: "We all graduated 41
years ago; and yet nearly each day in our lives something comes up—
some mental image, some admonition that makes us think of Hattie."

Judy also told the story of one of Hattie's last birthday parties,   7
when one man said he had to leave early to take his daughter somewhere. "Sit down," said Hattie. "You're not leaving yet. She can just
be a little late."

That was my teacher! I sit up straight just thinkin' about her.   8

Among the fundamentals Hattie introduced me to was The New   9
York Times. Every morning it was delivered to Room 313. I had
never seen it before then. Real journalists, she taught us, start their
day by reading The Times and columnists like Anthony Lewis and
James Reston.

I have been thinking about Hattie a lot this year, not just because   10
she died on July 31, but because the lessons she imparted seem so relevant now. We've just gone through this huge dot-com-Internet-
globalization bubble—during which a lot of smart people got carried
away and forgot the fundamentals of how you build a profitable
company, a lasting portfolio, a nation state, or a thriving student. It
turns out that the real secret of success in the information age is what
it always was: fundamentals—reading, writing and arithmetic,
church, synagogue and mosque, the rule of law, and good governance.

The Internet can make you smarter, but it can't make you smart.   11
It can extend your reach, but it will never tell you what to say at a
P.T.A. meeting. These fundamentals cannot be downloaded. You can
only upload them, the old-fashioned way, one by one, in places like
Room 313 at St. Louis Park High. I only regret that I didn't write this
column when the woman who taught me all that was still alive.

QUESTIONS FOR STUDY AND DISCUSSION

1. Friedman claims that his high school journalism teacher, Hattie
   M. Steinberg, was "someone who made the most important difference in my life" (1). What descriptive details does Friedman
   use to support this thesis? (Glossary: *Thesis*)

2. Hattie Steinberg taught her students the fundamentals of journalism — "not simply how to write a lead or accurately transcribe a quote, but, more important, how to comport yourself in a professional way and to always do quality work" (3). According to Friedman, what other fundamentals did she introduce to her students? Why do you think he values these fundamentals so much?

3. Friedman punctuates his description of Steinberg's teaching with short, pithy sentences. For example, he ends paragraph 2 with the sentence "She was that good" and paragraph 3 with "She wanted to teach us about consequences." Paragraph 8 is made up of two short sentences: "That was my teacher! I sit up straight just thinkin' about her." Identify several other short sentences that he uses. What do these sentences have in common? How do short sentences like these affect you as a reader? Explain.

4. Why do you think that Friedman tells us three times that Hattie's classroom was number 313 at St. Louis Park High School? Details such as this give authority to a piece of writing as well as make it come alive. What details in Friedman's portrait of his teacher stand out for you? Why do you suppose Friedman chose the details that he did? What dominant impression of Hattie M. Steinberg do they collectively create?

5. According to Friedman, what went wrong when the "huge dot-com-Internet-globalization bubble" (10) of the late 1990s burst? Do you agree?

6. What does Friedman mean when he says, "The Internet can make you smarter, but it can't make you smart"(11)?

VOCABULARY

Refer to your dictionary to define the following words as they are used in this selection. Then use each word in a sentence of your own.

transcribe (3)   harangued (5)
consequences (3)   admonition (6)
articulated (5)

CLASSROOM ACTIVITY USING DESCRIPTION

Important advice for writing well is to show rather than tell. Let's assume that your task is to reveal a person's character. What activities might you show the person doing to give your readers the correct impression of his or her character? For example, to indicate that someone is concerned about current events without coming out and saying so, you might show her reading the morning newspaper. Or you might show a character's degree of formality by including his typical greeting: *How ya doing?* In other words, the things a person says and does are often important indicators of personality. Choose one of the following traits, and make a list of at least four ways to show that someone possesses that trait.

simple but good	politically involved
reckless	irresponsible
sensitive to the arts	independent
a sports lover	quick-witted
thoughtful	public spirited

Share your list with the class, and discuss the "show-not-tell" strategies you have used.

SUGGESTED WRITING ASSIGNMENTS

1. Friedman believes that "the real secret of success in the information age is what it always was: fundamentals — reading, writing and arithmetic, church, synagogue and mosque, the rule of law, and good governance" (10). Do you agree? What are the fundamentals that you value most? Write an essay in which you discuss what you believe to be the secret of success today.

2. Who are your favorite teachers? What important differences did these people make in your life? What characteristics do these teachers share with Hattie M. Steinberg in this essay, Miss Bessie in Carl T. Rowan's "Unforgettable Miss Bessie" (pp. 153–57), or Professor Louis Agassiz in Samuel H. Scudder's "Learning to See" (pp. 98–102)? Using examples from your own school experience as well as from one or more of the essays above, write an essay in which you explore what makes a great teacher. Be sure that you choose examples that clearly illustrate each of your points.

chapter 15

Process Analysis

When you give someone directions to your home, tell how to make ice cream, or explain how a president is elected, you are using **process analysis.**

Process analysis usually arranges a series of events in order and relates them to one another, as narration and cause and effect do, but process analysis has a different emphasis. Whereas narration tells mainly *what* happens and cause and effect focuses on *why* it happens, process analysis tries to explain—in detail—*how* it happens.

There are two types of process analysis: directional and informational. The *directional* type provides instructions on how to do something. These instructions can be as brief as the directions for making instant coffee printed on the label or as complex as the directions in a manual for assembling a new gas grill. The purpose of directional process analysis is simple: to give the reader directions to follow that will lead to the desired results.

Consider these directions for sharpening a knife:

> If you have never done any whittling or wood carving before, the first skill to learn is how to sharpen your knife. You may be surprised to learn that even a brand-new knife needs sharpening. Knives are never sold honed (finely sharpened), although some gouges and chisels are. It is essential to learn the firm stroke on the stone that will keep your blades sharp. The sharpening stone must be fixed in place on the table, so that it will not move around. You can do this by placing a piece of rubber inner tube or a thin piece of foam rubber under it. Or you can tack four strips of wood, if you have a rough worktable, to frame the stone and hold it in place. Put a generous puddle of oil on the stone—this will soon disappear into the surface of a new stone, and you will need to keep adding more oil. Press the knife blade flat against the stone in the puddle of oil, using your index finger. Whichever way the cutting edge of the knife faces is the side of the blade that should get a little more

pressure. Move the blade around three or four times in a narrow oval about the size of your fingernail, going *counterclockwise* when the sharp edge is facing right. Now turn the blade over in the same spot on the stone, press hard, and move it around the small oval *clockwise*, with more pressure on the cutting edge that faces left. Repeat the ovals, flipping the knife blade over six or seven times, and applying lighter pressure to the blade the last two times. Wipe the blade clean with a piece of rag or tissue and rub it flat on the piece of leather strop at least twice on each side. Stroke *away* from the cutting edge to remove the little burr of metal that may be left on the blade.

–Florence H. Pettit

After first establishing her context and purpose, Pettit presents step-by-step directions for sharpening a knife, selecting details that a novice would understand.

After explaining in two previous paragraphs the first two steps in his article on juggling, a student writer moves to the important third step. Notice here how he explains the third step, offers advice on what to do if things go wrong, and encourages your efforts—all useful in directional process writing:

Step three is merely a continum of "the exchange" with the addition of the third ball. Don't worry if you are confused—I will explain. Hold two balls in your right hand and one in your left. Make a perfect toss with one of your balls in your right hand and then an exchange with the one in your left hand. The ball coming from your left hand should now be exchanged with the, as of now, unused ball in your right hand. This process should be continued until you find yourself reaching under nearby chairs for bouncing tennis balls. It is true that many persons' backs and legs become sore when learning how to juggle because they've been picking up balls that they've inadvertently tossed around the room. Try practicing over a bed; you won't have to reach down so far. Don't get too upset if things aren't going well; you're probably keeping the same pace as everyone else at this stage.

–William Peterson, student

The *informational* type of process analysis, on the other hand, tells how something works, how something is made, or how something occurs. You would use informational process analysis if you wanted to explain how the human heart functions, how an atomic bomb works, how hailstones are formed, how you selected the college you are attending, or how the polio vaccine was developed. Rather than giving specific directions, informational process analysis explains and informs.

In the illustration by Nigel Holmes on page 365, Jim Collins uses informational process analysis to explain a basic legislative procedure: how a bill becomes a law.

Clarity is crucial for successful process analysis. The most effective way to explain a process is to divide it into steps and to present those steps in a clear (usually chronological) sequence. Transitional words and phrases such as *first, next, after,* and *before* help to connect steps to one another. Naturally, you must be sure that no step is omitted or given out of order. Also, you may sometimes have to explain *why* a certain step is necessary, especially if it is not obvious. With intricate, abstract, or particularly difficult steps, you might use analogy or comparison to clarify the steps for your reader.

Illustration by Nigel Holmes

How to Write a Personal Letter

■ **Garrison Keillor**

Writer and broadcaster Garrison Keillor was born in Anoka, Minnesota, in 1942. After graduating from the University of Minnesota, he became a successful writer of humorous stories, many of which appeared in the New Yorker. *He is perhaps best known for his radio program,* A Prairie Home Companion, *which is broadcast on National Public Radio. Keillor has written many books, including* Lake Wobegon Days *(1985),* Leaving Home: A Collection of Lake Wobegon Stories *(1987),* Me: By Jimmy (Big Boy) Valente *(1999), and* A Prairie Home Companion: Pretty Good Joke Book *(2000). In 2002, he published a book of poetry titled* Good Poems *that he compiled and introduces. He has also produced a wide selection of recordings featuring his stories and radio shows. In this selection, written as part of a popular and highly successful advertising campaign for the International Paper Company, the sage of Lake Wobegon offers some sound and practical directions for writing personal letters.*

FOR YOUR JOURNAL

How do you feel when you receive a letter from a relative or friend? Do you feel the same way about telephone calls or email messages? To you, what does a letter say about the person who wrote it?

We shy persons need to write a letter now and then, or else we'll dry up and blow away. It's true. And I speak as one who loves to reach for the phone and talk. The telephone is to shyness what Hawaii is to February; it's a way out of the woods. *And yet:* a letter is better.

Such a sweet gift—a piece of handmade writing, in an envelope that is not a bill, sitting in our friend's path when she trudges home from a long day spent among wahoos and savages, a day our words will help repair. They don't need to be immortal, just sincere. She can read them twice and again tomorrow: *You're someone I care about, Corinne, and think of often, and every time I do, you make me smile.*

We need to write, otherwise nobody will know who we are. They will have only a vague impression of us as A Nice Person, because, frankly, we don't shine at conversation, we lack the confidence to thrust our faces forward and say, "Hi, I'm Heather Hooten, let me tell you about my week." Mostly we say "Uh-huh" and "Oh really." People smile and look over our shoulder, looking for someone else to talk to.

So a shy person sits down and writes a letter. To be known by another person—to meet and talk freely on the page—to be close despite distance. To escape from anonymity and be our own sweet selves and express the music of our souls.

We want our dear Aunt Eleanor to know that we have fallen in love, that we quit our job, that we're moving to New York, and we want to say a few things that might not get said in casual conversation: *Thank you for what you've meant to me. I am very happy right now.*

The first step in writing letters is to get over the guilt of *not* writing. You don't "owe" anybody a letter. Letters are a gift. The burning shame you feel when you see unanswered mail makes it harder to pick up a pen and makes for a cheerless letter when you finally do. *I feel bad about not writing, but I've been so busy,* etc. Skip this. Few letters are obligatory, and they are *Thanks for the wonderful gift* and *I am terribly sorry to hear about George's death.* Write these promptly if you want to keep your friends. Don't worry about the others, except love letters, of course. When your true love writes *Dear Light of My Life, Joy of My Heart,* some response is called for.

Some of the best letters are tossed off in a burst of inspiration, so keep your writing stuff in one place where you can sit down for a few minutes and—*Dear Roy, I am in the middle of an essay but thought I'd drop you a line. Hi to your sweetie too*—dash off a note to a pal. Envelopes, stamps, address book, everything in a drawer so you can write fast when the pen is hot.

A blank white 8 × 11 sheet can look as big as Montana if the pen's not so hot—try a smaller page and write boldly. Get a pen that makes a sensuous line, get a comfortable typewriter, a friendly word processor—whichever feels easy to the hand.

Sit for a few minutes with the blank sheet of paper in front of you, and let your friend come in mind. Remember the last time you saw each other and how your friend looked and what you said and

what perhaps was unsaid between you; when your friend becomes
real to you, start to write.

Write the salutation—*Dear You*—and take a deep breath and
plunge in. A simple declarative sentence will do, followed by another
and another. As if you were talking to us. Don't think about grammar, don't think about style, just give us your news. Where did you
go, who did you see, what did they say, what do you think?

If you don't know where to begin, start with the present: *I'm sit-*
ting at the kitchen table on a rainy Saturday morning. Everyone is
gone and the house is quiet. Let the letter drift along. The toughest
letter to crank out is one that is meant to impress, as we all know
from writing job applications; if it's hard work to slip off a letter to a
friend, maybe you're trying too hard to be terrific. A letter is only a
report to someone who already likes you for reasons other than your
brilliance. Take it easy.

Don't worry about form. It's not a term paper. When you come
to the end of one episode, just start a new paragraph. You can go
from a few lines about the sad state of rock 'n' roll to the fight with
your mother to your fond memories of Mexico to the kitchen sink
and what's in it. The more you write, the easier it gets, and when you
have a True True Friend to write to, a soul sibling, then it's like
driving a car; you just press on the gas.

Don't tear up the page and start over when you write a bad
line—try to write your way out of it. Make mistakes and plunge on.
Let the letter cook along and let yourself be bold. Outrage, confusion, love—whatever is in your mind, let it find a way to the page.
Writing is a means of discovery, always, and when you come to the
end and write *Yours ever* or *Hugs and Kisses,* you'll know something
you didn't when you wrote *Dear Pal.*

Probably your friend will put your letter away, and it'll be read
again a few years from now—and it will improve with age.

And forty years from now, your friend's grandkids will dig it out
of the attic and read it, a sweet and precious relic of the [early
twenty-first century] that gives them a sudden clear glimpse of the
world we old-timers knew. You will have then created an object of
art. Your simple lines about where you went, who you saw, what
they said, will speak to those children and they will feel in their hearts
the humanity of our times.

You can't pick up a phone and call the future and tell them about
our times. You have to pick up a piece of paper.

QUESTIONS FOR STUDY AND DISCUSSION

1. Keillor calls a personal letter a "gift" (2). Why do you suppose he thinks of a letter in this way?
2. What advice does Keillor have for people before they start writing? In what ways is this advice part of his process analysis? Why does he suggest small stationery instead of 8 × 11 sheets of paper?
3. Is Keillor's process analysis directional or informational? What leads you to this conclusion?
4. Keillor suggests that before starting to write a friend, you think about that friend for a while until he or she becomes real to you. At that point you're ready to write. What should happen next in the process?
5. What do you think Keillor means when he says, "We need to write, otherwise nobody will know who we are" (3)?
6. Instead of taking us step-by-step through a personal letter in paragraphs 12–14, Keillor anticipates the problems that a letter writer is likely to encounter and offers his own advice. What are the most common problems? What solutions does Keillor offer? (Glossary: *Example*) How has he organized his advice? (Glossary: *Organization*)
7. By the time you have come to the end of a letter, what, according to Keillor, should have happened? Why?

VOCABULARY

Refer to your dictionary to define the following words as they are used in this selection. Then use each word in a sentence of your own.

trudges (2)   crank (11)
wahoos (2)   episode (12)
anonymity (4)   relic (15)
sensuous (8)

CLASSROOM ACTIVITY USING PROCESS ANALYSIS

Most do-it-yourself jobs require that you follow a set process to achieve the best results. Make a list of the steps involved in doing one of the following household activities:

cleaning windows
repotting a plant
doing laundry
baking chocolate chip cookies
changing a flat tire
unclogging a drain

SUGGESTED WRITING ASSIGNMENTS

1. What does Keillor see as the advantages of a letter over a telephone call? Can you think of times when a telephone call or email is preferable? Write an essay in which you agree or disagree with Keillor's position on the importance of personal letters. Before starting to write, you may find it helpful to review what you wrote in your journal for this selection.

2. Write an essay in which you give directions or advice for finding a summer job or part-time employment during the school year. In what ways is looking for such jobs different from looking for permanent positions? You can use Keillor's essay as a model for your own.

A Tricky Stick

■ **Manny Howard**

*Born in Brooklyn, New York, in 1966, Manny Howard received
his bachelor's degree in African American History and Politics
from Vassar College in Poughkeepsie, New York. He worked on
several political campaigns before beginning a career in magazine publishing. He has been an editor at* American Lawyer,
Worth, New York, George, Gourmet, *and* Lucky *magazines.
His freelance work has appeared in the* New York Times, GQ,
Esquire, Harper's, Elle, Rolling Stone, Cosmopolitan, Travel &
Leisure, *and many other popular magazines. Asked to give some
advice to young writers, Howard said, "Write something every
day (much, much more difficult than it sounds, so reward yourself—any way you like—when you have managed to do that
for a month). Even if you do manage to write every day always
read more than you write." And on editing he had this practical
advice to offer: "Always edit your own work before you hand it
off, but never dare to do that until twenty-four hours has
passed. Read your work out loud. If it doesn't sound right, it
isn't. If it doesn't sound like you, it isn't." In "A Tricky Stick,"
which first appeared in the* New York Times Magazine *on
December 30, 2001, Howard delves into the secret composition
of one of America's popular snacks.*

FOR YOUR JOURNAL

Do you wonder what is in the food you eat? One might say,
"You are what you eat," but do we really know what we are
eating? Even something as simple and pure as an apple might be
problematic. Has it been sprayed with chemicals? Has it been
washed or coated? Reflect on the appearance and reality of
what you, the modern consumer, are eating these days.

The Slim Jim was created by Adolph Levis in Philadelphia in the
1940's. After an unsuccessful early career as a violinist and a failed
effort to operate a string of tobacco shops, Levis and a partner had
turned to the pickled-food trade, hawking pig's feet, cabbage, and

cucumbers to bars and taverns in and around Philadelphia. Pepperoni, he noticed, was becoming popular among his clientele, and he made an end run around the fad by creating a preserved meat product that, rather than curing for weeks, could be manufactured in a matter of days by a process of fermentation and hot smoking.

The snack sold well in the bars, first in Philadelphia and then up   2
and down the East Coast. Eventually, a bidding war broke out over Slim Jim's name and recipe, and in 1967, Levis (pronounced LEV-iss) and his partner sold out to General Mills, for $20 million. The brand would pass through three other companies in the ensuing years, and each time it did, the recipe changed a little, to make production cheaper and more efficient. They even started putting chicken into the original all-beef formula. What at first required just 10 common ingredients now calls for 31. But the taste, everyone agrees, remains true to Levis's original.

The sale of anything, even a stick of dried meat, to a company   3
like General Mills pretty much assures that the instructions for making it become an industrial secret. So when we decided to make a Levis-era Slim Jim, as a salute to its inventor who died this year, we got no help from its current owner, Con-Agra. They wished us luck and sent us on our way.

Undeterred, we went to Harvey Brodsky, Levis's son-in-law, who   4
told us he didn't know the original recipe. "It's not like we've got it written down in family scrapbooks," he said good-naturedly. He supplied one critical clue, however: the use of lactic acid is crucial in the fermentation process because it lowers the pH and imparts a unique tanginess.

We realized that we would have to go freelance, and so our next   5
stop was Wade Moises, the sous-chef and butcher at Lupa restaurant in New York. He is that rare breed, a sausage geek, and he was certain that he could help us reverse-engineer a Slim Jim. Though he did have some reservations. Before settling down to work, he snapped off a piece of a Slim Jim, chewed it and winced. "You sure you want to do this?"

From Bruce Aidells, the man who restored the good name of   6
mass-produced sausage in America, we learned that Levis's original recipe was probably based on an Eastern European thin rope sausage, usually made with pork and beef, because "its spices are mild and it takes the smoke well."

A recipe for rope sausage, provided by Aidells,[1] has 10 ingredi-   7
ents (not counting the meat and the fat), like the original Slim Jim.

---

[1]*Aidells:* a sausage company founded in 1983 in the San Francisco Bay Area. [Eds.]

The heat comes from white and black pepper; Moises suggested using cayenne instead and doubling the salt. "The meat-to-fat ratio is very important and so is the amount of lactic acid," he says, dropping pieces of top-round chuck and beef fat into a meat grinder. "After that, it's a question of adjusting the spices."

Making sausage is really quite straightforward. The meat is 8 ground, then kneaded together with spices, lactic-acid starter (freeze-dried milk, essentially), and a pink curing salt. The meat-and-spice mixture has to be kneaded until it is doughy and can be squeezed through the sausage press and into the sheathing. Slim Jims are now cased in collagen, but we figure that the originals were natural. So we go with lamb intestines, which are properly narrow.

A sausage maker close to the Slim Jim production process, speak- 9 ing on the condition of anonymity, revealed to us that a Slim Jim is smoked at between 110 and 140 degrees for 22 hours and then allowed to cool at 50 degrees with next to no humidity. So that's what we do.

After tasting the first batch, we decide it needs an additional two 10 tablespoons of salt and eight more ounces of fat to make it into Slim Jim territory. By the third generation, we think we have something close, so we let it dry overnight in a refrigerator and then smoke it. "I think we got it," says Moises, looking up from his prep work on the fifth day of our project. "It could be a bit greasier, but the spice and the tanginess is there."

We send a package of our homemade Slim Jims overnight to 11 Brodsky. He is defensive and not at all complimentary. "The samples are way off," he says in a voice-mail message. "The color is wrong, the chop is wrong, the consistency of the casing is wrong. The spicing just doesn't seem to be there, and the lactic-acid starter culture? Didn't taste any."

We decide not to take his word for it, and as his father-in-law 12 might have done, we head out to a local tavern. At Montero's, hard by the Brooklyn docks, a regular sits at the bar. "You made your own Slim Jim?" he says, as if he has heard this one already too. When I ask if he'd try one and tell me if it tastes like the Slim Jims of old, he wrinkles up his face and says, "Why not?"

He chews for a moment, then shrugs. "Sure," he says. "You 13 made a Slim Jim. Good for you."

WADE MOISES'S TAKE ON THE ORIGINAL SLIM JIM
(Adapted from Bruce Aidells)

1 lamb intestine casing (4 feet long)
2½ pounds top round chuck, cubed
1 pound beef fat, cubed
3 tablespoons paprika
2 teaspoons black pepper
2 teaspoons cayenne pepper
½ teaspoon ground coriander
1 teaspoon ground fennel seeds
1 teaspoon No. 1 curing salt
4 tablespoons kosher salt
2 teaspoons sugar
1 clove garlic, peeled and smashed
⅓ cup lactic-acid starter culture

1. Rinse salt off the sausage casing. Soak in ice water for at least 1 hour.

2. Combine meat and fat. Run the mixture through a meat grinder into a large bowl, using the finest setting. Add all ingredients, along with one cup of ice water. Knead vigorously until mixture is the consistency of bread dough (about 8 minutes).

3. Rinse casing one last time. Choose the narrowest gauge tube of your sausage press. Splash the tube with ice water, then pull the casing over it. Transfer the mixture, about two fistfuls at a time, to the sausage press and then pump the meat into the casing, splashing more water on the tubing as needed to stop the casing from tearing.

4. Preheat an electric smoker to 100 degrees. Hang sausage in the smoker for 22 hours. Temperature should never dip below 90 degrees or go above 110 degrees. After 22 hours, raise the temperature to 150 degrees and cook until the internal temperature reaches 150 to 155 degrees (about 30 minutes).

5. Remove from smoker and let cool at about 50 degrees in a dry place for 4 hours. Cut sausage into 4-inch lengths.

Yield: 16 servings.

QUESTIONS FOR STUDY AND DISCUSSION

1. Why is it so hard for Howard and his associates to determine the ingredients of the original Slim Jim? Why does he say he wants to "reverse-engineer" (5) this product? What does this mean? (Glossary: *Cause and Effect*)

2. Why doesn't Howard accept the negative assessment of the product offered by Brodsky (the son-in-law of the inventor of the Slim Jim) and start over? Whose judgment does Howard value the most?

3. What kind of process analysis does Manny Howard use in "A Tricky Stick"? Is the recipe that he includes at the end of the essay also a process analysis?

4. Howard says, "Making sausage is really quite straightforward" (8). What are the steps? While the process of following a recipe may be straightforward, other processes are taking place in order to get to the final product. What are those processes, and how do they occur? In other words, what is happening to the physical and chemical properties of the ingredients?

5. Assess the recipe that follows the essay. Is it an effective directional process analysis? Do you think you can make a Slim Jim using the recipe? In your estimation, what would be the most difficult part of following the recipe?

VOCABULARY

Refer to your dictionary to define the following words as they are used in this selection. Then use each word in a sentence of your own.

hawking (1)	sous-chef (5)
pepperoni (1)	winced (5)
fermentation (1)	sheathing (8)
salute (3)	anonymity (9)
undeterred (4)	shrugs (3)
tanginess (4)	

CLASSROOM ACTIVITY USING PROCESS ANALYSIS

1. Howard's essay ends with a recipe, the classic directional process writing exercise. The writing of even the simplest recipe takes a lot of thought, and the recipe needs to be tested to make sure all

376 ■ PROCESS ANALYSIS

the ingredients are listed, that they are identified fully, and that they are added in the proper sequence. In addition, the directions for how long to mix, stir, and cook, bake, or boil, as well as the cooking and baking temperatures, need to be given in precise language. Try your hand at writing the recipe for a food you like to eat and have already made a number of times. Exchange your recipe with a classmate, and identify any revisions that need to be made.

2. Carefully read the directions for constructing an astro tube — a cylindrical airfoil made from a sheet of heavy writing paper — that appear on page 377. Now construct your own astro tube, and fly it. How helpful did you find the illustrations that accompany the written instructions?

SUGGESTED WRITING ASSIGNMENTS

1. Use the illustration on p. 365 as a preliminary outline of how a bill becomes law, and research the topic more thoroughly through reading and, if possible, discussing the process with a political science instructor at your school. The illustration ends with the question, "Does it EVER go as smoothly as this?" and the answer, "Nope." What kinds of situations can and often do alter the process?

2. Think about a process that you are familiar with that you believe needs improvement. After choosing your topic, you might want to do a little background research in the library. Make sure that you are able to put the process in your own words, and then write a process analysis in which you argue for a revision of the existing process. For example, are you happy with the process for dealing with recyclables where you live, the process for registering for classes, or the way dorm rooms are assigned on your campus?

Making an Astro Tube

Start with an 8.5-inch by 11-inch sheet of heavy writing paper. (Never use newspaper in making paper models because it isn't strongly bonded and can't hold a crease.) Follow these numbered steps, corresponding to the illustrations.
1. With the long side of the sheet toward you, fold up one third of the paper.
2. Fold the doubled section in half.
3. Fold the section in half once more and crease well.
4. Unfold preceding crease.
5. Curve the ends together to form a tube, as shown in the illustration.

6. Insert the right end inside the left end between the single outer layer and the doubled layers. Overlap the ends about an inch and a half. (This makes a tube for right-handers, to be used with an underhand throw. For an overhand tube, or an underhand version to be thrown by a lefty, reverse the directions, and insert the left end inside the right end at this step.)
7. Hold the tube at the seam with one hand, where shown by the dot in the illustration, and turn the rim inward along the crease made in step 3. Start turning in at the seam and roll the rim under, moving around the circumference in a circular manner. Then

round out the rim.
8. Fold the fin to the left, as shown, then raise it so that it's perpendicular to the tube. Be careful not to tear the paper at the front.
9. Hold the tube from above, near the rim. Hold it between the thumb and fingers. The rim end should be forward, with the fin on the bottom. Throw the tube underhanded, with a motion like throwing a bowling ball, letting it spin off the fingers as it is released. The tube will float through the air, spinning as it goes. Indoor flights of 30 feet or more are easy. With practice you can achieve remarkable accuracy.

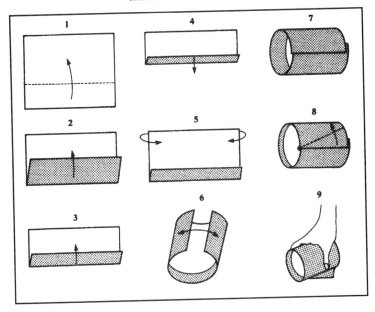

Built by Fire

■ **Janisse Ray**

Poet, nonfiction writer, and winner of the 1996 Merriam Frontier Award, Janisse Ray burst onto the literary scene as a nature writer in 1999 with the publication of her Ecology of a Cracker Childhood. *Ray, a native of the coastal plains of southern Georgia, grew up in her father's junkyard along U.S. Highway 1 amidst the leftover rubble of our modern civilization. Her life of rural isolation instilled in her the intense desire to save the endangered longleaf pine ecosystem that existed before Georgia's poor first settlers, known as Crackers, ever entered the area. Ray's portrait of the region is as much about people as the ecosystem, however, and their interconnection is reflected in her own intensely personal depiction of her home. A series of interlocking chapters that weave portraits of her family members and her understanding of the unnatural history of her home,* Ecology of a Cracker Childhood *is critical but not unsympathetic. As she says, "When getting by meant using the land, we used it. When getting by meant ignoring the land, we ignored it." Now living on a farm in rural Georgia, Ray has been published in* Wild Earth, Orion, Florida Naturalist, *and* Georgia Wildlife *and is a nature commentator for Georgia Public Radio. Her second book,* Wild Card Quilt: Taking a Chance on Home, *was published in 2003. In "Built by Fire," a chapter taken from* Ecology of a Cracker Childhood, *Ray paints a wonderful picture of how the longleaf pine forest was built by fires that occurred naturally over the years.*

FOR YOUR JOURNAL

What do you know about the ecology of the area where you spent most of your time growing up? Who were the native inhabitants, and what was their relationship to the land? Did commercial forces come into conflict with nature in your area? How have the practical needs of the current inhabitants affected the unique ecosystems at work in your area? If you do not know anything about these issues, brainstorm on how you might find more information. Finally, why do you think it is important to know about such matters? What influence does our knowledge of the past have on the future when it comes to our ability to be effective stewards of the land we inhabit?

A couple of million years ago a pine fell in love with a place that belonged to lightning. Flying past, a pine seed saw the open, flat land and grew covetous. The land was veined with runs of water — some bold, some fine as a reed. Seeing it unoccupied, the pine imperiously took root and started to grow there, in the coastal plains of the southern United States, and every day praised its luck. The place was broadly beautiful with clean and plentiful water sources, the sun always within reach. In the afternoons and evenings, thunderstorms lumbered across the land, lashing out rods of lightning that emptied the goatskin clouds; in those times the pine lay low.

The lightning announced itself lightly to the pine one summer evening, "I reign over this land," it said. "You must leave immediately."

"There was nothing here when I came," said the pine.

"I was here," said lightning. "I am always here. I am here more than any other place in the world." The clouds nodded, knowing that lightning spoke true.

In that short time, however, the pine had begun to love the place and called out, "Please. You live in the sky. Let me have the earth." The clouds glowered and began to thicken.

Lightning was extremely possessive and would not agree to divide.

"Then do what you will," said the pine. For years they warred. The lightning would fling as many as forty million bolts a year at the tree, striking when it could, the pine dodging and ducking. A single thunderstorm might raise thousands of bolts. Wind helped the tree, and although it was struck a few times, the damage was never serious.

After the tree had reached a fair age — old enough for government work, as they say — on the hottest of summer afternoons lightning crept close, hidden by towering maroon thunderheads, and aimed for the tree, sundering its bole crown to roots. When the lightning glanced the ground, such was its ferocity that it dug a trench wide enough to bury a horse before its force subsided. Needles from the pine had fallen about, like a woman's long brown hairs, and they began to smoke and then to flame, and from them fire spread outward, burning easy and slow.

In its dying, the pine sprang forth a mast of cones filled with   9
seeds. The wind played with the seeds and scattered them for miles.
And because the mineral soil was laid bare by fire, they could germi-
nate.

But lightning was not worried. Kindling the whole place didn't   10
take much effort. Once lightning struck, the fire might burn slowly
through the grasses for weeks, miles at a time, arrested only by rivers,
lakes, creeks, and ponds. So if the seeds began to grow, lightning
would burn them.

Over the decades the fury and constancy of lightning knew no   11
end — every few years it would burn the place again — and the green-
horn pines learned to lay low, sometimes for five or six years, drilling
a taproot farther and farther into the moist earth, surviving the fast-
burning, low-intensity fires of lightning's wrath by huddling, covering their terminal buds with a tuft of long needles. Sometimes the
buds steamed and crackled inside their bonnets.

Young trees that mimicked grass survived fire. That low, they   12
didn't look like trees.

The grass-trees began to learn that if they waited until the light-   13
ning went to sleep in the rainy springs and suddenly cast themselves
upward, to the height of a yard or more in one season, drawing nu-
trient reserves from their long, patient roots, and if they hurriedly
thickened the bark of their trunks, a lamination, then when the fires
came again they could withstand the heat and their terminal bud
would be out of flame's reach.

Only then would the trees dare to branch.   14

Lightning was nonplussed. No matter what it did, the trees flour-   15
ished and multiplied. Admiring the courage of the longleaf pine,
other trees, hardwoods — sweet gum and sumac and oak — tried to
settle. Always, not knowing the secret history of longleaf's adaptation, they burned.

And then lightning realized the pine tree was plugging its needles   16
with volatile resins and oils, rendering them highly flammable. The
tree, of course, only thought to make the fires burn rapidly so danger
would pass quickly. Flammability was important in driving wildfire
through the forest, in order to leave older trees unharmed. The longleaf grew taller, spread farther.

The lightning saw volatility as an act of remuneration.   17

Longleaf and lightning began to depend on each other and other   18
plants — the ground cover grasses and forbs, or flowering herbs —
evolved to survive and welcome fire as well. Wiregrass, for instance,

would not reproduce sexually in lightning's absence. The animals learned to expect fire and to adapt. They scrambled off or took cover: down into tortoise burrows, up into tree crowns. During a fire, exotic insects never otherwise seen would scurry from the plates of bark, scooting up the tree. Snakes and tortoises would dash for their holes.

Longleaf became known as the pine that fire built. 19

QUESTIONS FOR STUDY AND DISCUSSION

1. In your own words, describe the informational process by which a longleaf pine and hence an entire forest of longleaf pine trees grew, according to Ray. Is her description of the process easy to follow? Explain.

2. Why do you suppose Ray chose to personify the pine seed and lightning, as well as other elements in the forest, and to give them dialogue? (Glossary: *Figure of Speech*) How effective do you find this technique? Explain.

3. In personifying the tree and the various other elements in the forest, Ray attributes motive and emotions to them. For example, she writes, "But lightning was not worried" (10). How does the attribution of such motives and emotions to her "characters" sit with your understanding of the evolution of natural processes?

4. What precisely does Ray mean in paragraph 17 when she says, "The lightning saw volatility as an act of remuneration"? What does lightning gain, and what does the tree gain?

5. In paragraph 18, Ray says that longleaf and lightning began to depend on each other. How did the pine, the animals, and the insects learn to adapt to fire, and what was gained from this adaptation?

6. Ray describes the battle between the longleaf and the lightning in almost epic proportion and tone. (Glossary: *Tone*) How does she achieve this particular stylistic effect in her writing?

VOCABULARY

Refer to your dictionary to define the following words as they are used in this selection. Then use each word in a sentence of your own.

covetous (1)   lumbered (1)
imperiously (1)   sundering (8)

bole (8)	wrath (11)
germinate (9)	nonplussed (15)
greenhorn (11)	volatility (17)
taproot (11)	remuneration (17)

CLASSROOM ACTIVITY USING PROCESS ANALYSIS

To give another person clear directions about how to do something, you need to have a thorough understanding of the process yourself. Analyze one of the following activities by listing the materials you might need and the steps you would follow in completing it:

studying for an exam

determining miles per gallon for an automobile

finding a person's street address (or email address) on the Internet

getting from where your writing class normally meets to where you normally have lunch

installing new software on your computer

buying a DVD player on the Internet

adding or dropping a class from your schedule

SUGGESTED WRITING ASSIGNMENTS

1. Our world is filled with countless natural processes—for example, the cycle of the moon, the rising and the setting of the sun, the germination of a seed, the movement of the tides, the formation of a tornado, the transformation of a caterpillar into a butterfly or moth, and the flowering of a tree. Using Ray's essay as a model, write an informational process analysis explaining a natural process.

2. Select one of the tasks listed in the Classroom Activity, and write a brief essay in which you give directions for successfully performing the task.

On Dumpster Diving

■ **Lars Eighner**

Born in Texas in 1948, Lars Eighner attended the University of Texas at Austin. After graduation, he launched a career writing essays and fiction. A volume of his short stories, Bayou Boy *and* Other Stories, *was published in 1985. Eighner became homeless in 1988 when he left his job as an attendant at a mental hospital. The following piece, which appeared in the* Utne Reader, *is an abridged version of an essay that first appeared in* Three-penny Review. *The piece eventually became part of Eighner's startling account of the three years he spent as a homeless person,* Travels with Lizbeth *(1993). Since then he has written two novels,* Pawn to Queen Four *(1995) and* Whispered in the Dark *(1996), and a collection of essays,* Gay Cosmos *(1995). Eighner uses a number of rhetorical strategies in "On Dumpster Diving," but pay particular attention to the importance of process analysis in the success of the essay overall as he delineates the "stages a person goes through in learning to scavenge."*

FOR YOUR JOURNAL

Some people believe that acquiring material objects is what life is all about and that the measure of their own "worth" is in the inventory of their possessions. Comment on the role that material objects play in your life and on whether your view of their importance has changed as you have grown older.

I began Dumpster diving about a year before I became homeless.   1

I prefer the term *scavenging*. I have heard people, evidently   2
meaning to be polite, use the word *foraging*, but I prefer to reserve
that word for gathering nuts and berries and such, which I also do,
according to the season and opportunity.

I like the frankness of the word *scavenging*. I live from the refuse   3
of others. I am a scavenger. I think it a sound and honorable niche,
although if I could I would naturally prefer to live the comfortable
consumer life, perhaps—and only perhaps—as a slightly less wasteful consumer owing to what I have learned as a scavenger.

Except for jeans, all my clothes come from Dumpsters. Boom   4
boxes, candles, bedding, toilet paper, medicine, books, a typewriter, a
virgin male love doll, coins sometimes amounting to many dollars: all
came from Dumpsters. And, yes, I eat from Dumpsters, too.

There is a predictable series of stages that a person goes through   5
in learning to scavenge. At first the new scavenger is filled with dis-
gust and self-loathing. He is ashamed of being seen.

This stage passes with experience. The scavenger finds a pair of   6
running shoes that fit and look and smell brand-new. He finds a pocket
calculator in perfect working order. He finds pristine ice cream, still
frozen, more than he can eat or keep. He begins to understand: people
do throw away perfectly good stuff, a lot of perfectly good stuff.

At this stage he may become lost and never recover. All the   7
Dumpster divers I have known come to the point of trying to acquire
everything they touch. Why not take it, they reason, it is all free. This
is, of course, hopeless, and most divers come to realize that they must
restrict themselves to items of relatively immediate utility.

The finding of objects is becoming something of an urban art.   8
Even respectable, employed people will sometimes find something
tempting sticking out of a Dumpster or standing beside one. Quite a
number of people, not all of them of the bohemian type, are willing
to brag that they found this or that piece in the trash.

But eating from Dumpsters is the thing that separates the dilet-   9
tanti from the professionals. Eating safely involves three principles:
using the senses and common sense to evaluate the condition of the
found materials; knowing the Dumpsters of a given area and check-
ing them regularly; and seeking always to answer the question "Why
was this discarded?"

Yet perfectly good food can be found in Dumpsters. Canned   10
goods, for example, turn up fairly often in the Dumpsters I frequent. I
also have few qualms about dry foods such as crackers, cookies, cereal, chips, and pasta if they are free of visible contaminants and still
dry and crisp. Raw fruits and vegetables with intact skins seem perfectly safe to me, excluding, of course, the obviously rotten. Many
are discarded for minor imperfections that can be pared away.

A typical discard is a half jar of peanut butter—though non-   11
organic peanut butter does not require refrigeration and is unlikely
to spoil in any reasonable time. One of my favorite finds is
yogurt—often discarded, still sealed, when the expiration date has
passed—because it will keep for several days, even in warm weather.

No matter how careful I am I still get dysentery at least once 12
a month, oftener in warm weather. I do not want to paint too romantic a picture. Dumpster diving has serious drawbacks as a way of
life.

I find from the experience of scavenging two rather deep lessons. 13
The first is to take what I can use and let the rest go. I have come to
think that there is no value in the abstract. A thing I cannot use or
make useful, perhaps by trading, has no value, however fine or rare it
may be.

The second lesson is the transience of material being. I do not 14
suppose that ideas are immortal, but certainly they are longer-lived
than material objects.

The things I find in Dumpsters, the love letters and rag dolls of so 15
many lives, remind me of this lesson. Now I hardly pick up a thing
without envisioning the time I will cast it away. This, I think, is a
healthy state of mind. Almost everything I have now has already been
cast out at least once, proving that what I own is valueless to
someone.

I find that my desire to grab for the gaudy bauble has been largely 16
sated. I think this is an attitude I share with the very wealthy — we both
know there is plenty more where whatever we have came from. Between us are the rat-race millions who have confounded their selves
with the objects they grasp and who nightly scavenge the cable channels
for they know not what.

I am sorry for them. 17

QUESTIONS FOR STUDY AND DISCUSSION

1. What is "Dumpster diving"? Why does Eighner prefer the word
   scavenging to *foraging* or *Dumpster diving?* What do these three
   terms mean to him? What does his discussion of these terms at
   the beginning of his essay tell you about Eighner himself?

2. What stages do beginning scavengers go through before they become what Eighner terms "professionals"? What examples does
   Eighner use to illustrate the passage through these stages? What
   "separates the dilettanti from the professionals" (9)?

3. Summarize the various steps in Eighner's explanation of the
   process of Dumpster diving. Why do you think Eighner did not
   title the essay "How to Dumpster Dive"?

4. What are the two lessons Eighner learns from scavenging? Why are they important to him? In what ways has scavenging benefited Eighner? In what ways has it harmed him?

5. Eighner's essay deals with both the immediate, physical aspects of Dumpster diving, such as what can be found in a typical Dumpster and the physical price one pays for eating out of them, and the larger, abstract issues that Dumpster diving raises, such as materialism and the transience of material objects. (Glossary: *Concrete/Abstract*) Why do you suppose he describes the concrete details before he discusses the abstract issues? What does he achieve by using both types of elements?

6. Writers often use process analysis in conjunction with another strategy—especially argument—to try to improve the way a process is carried out or to comment on issues exposed by the process analysis. (Glossary: *Argumentation*) In this essay, for example, Eighner uses a full process analysis to present his views on American values and materialism. In what ways does Eighner's process analysis support his opinions about our society?

VOCABULARY

Refer to your dictionary to define the following words as they are used in this selection. Then use each word in a sentence of your own.

refuse (3)   qualms (10)
niche (3)   transience (14)
pristine (6)   sated (16)
bohemian (8)

CLASSROOM ACTIVITY USING PROCESS ANALYSIS

In her best-selling Italian memoir *Under the Tuscan Sun,* Frances Mayes shares a number of her favorite recipes, including this one for Lemon Cake. Carefully read her directions as you imagine yourself making this cake. Did you find her recipe interesting to read? How clear did you find her directions? Were there any parts of the recipe that you felt needed clarification? Is it necessary to be familiar with the world of baking to read or appreciate Mayes's recipe? Explain.

LEMON CAKE

A family import, this Southern cake is one I've made a hundred times. Thin slices seem at home here with summer strawberries and cherries or winter pears. . . .

> *Cream together 1 cup of sweet butter and 2 cups of sugar. Beat in 3 eggs, one at a time. The mixture should be light. Mix together 3 cups of flour, 1 teaspoon of baking powder, 1/4 teaspoon of salt, and incorporate this with the butter mixture alternately with 1 cup buttermilk. (In Italy, I use one cup of cream since buttermilk is not available.) Begin and end with the flour mixture. Add 3 tablespoons of lemon juice and the grated zest of the lemon. Bake in a nonstick tube pan at 300° for 50 minutes. Test for doneness with a toothpick. The cake can be glazed with 1/4 cup of soft butter into which 1-1/2 cups of powdered sugar and 3 tablespoons of lemon juice have been beaten. Decorate with tiny curls of lemon rind.*

SUGGESTED WRITING ASSIGNMENTS

1. How important are material objects to you? Eighner emphasizes the transience of material objects and thinks that all of us delude ourselves with the objects we strive to acquire. Is there anything wrong with desiring material goods? Write an essay in which you react to Eighner's position on materialism.

2. Write a process analysis in which you explain the steps you usually follow when deciding to make a purchase of some importance or expense to you. Hint: It's best to analyze your process with a specific product or products in mind. Do you compare brands, store prices, and so on? What are your priorities — must the item be stylish, durable, offer good overall value, give high performance?

chapter 16

Definition

Definition allows you to communicate precisely what you want to say. At the most basic level, you will frequently need to define key words. Your reader needs to know just what you mean when you use unfamiliar words, such as *accoutrement,* or words that are open to various interpretations, such as *liberal,* or words that, while generally familiar, are used in a particular sense. Failure to define important terms, or to define them accurately, confuses readers and hampers communication.

Consider the opening paragraph from an essay entitled "Secular Mantras":

> Remember *The Little Engine That Could?* That's the story about the tiny locomotive that hauled the train over the mountain when the big, rugged locomotives wouldn't. Remember how the Little Engine strained and heaved and chugged, "I think I can — I think I can — I think I can" until she reached the top of the mountain? That's a perfect example of a secular mantra in action. You probably have used a secular mantra (pronounce it "mantruh") already today. It's any word or group of words that helps you use your energy when you consciously repeat it to yourself. You must understand two qualities about secular mantras to be able to recognize one.
>
> –Keith Eldred, student

Eldred engages his readers with the story of the Little Engine and then uses that example to lead into a definition of *secular mantras.* He concludes the paragraph with a sentence that clearly tells readers what is coming next.

There are three basic ways to define a word; each is useful in its own way. The first method is to give a *synonym,* a word that has nearly the same meaning as the word you wish to define: *face* for *countenance, nervousness* for *anxiety.* No two words ever have exactly the same meaning, but you can nevertheless pair an unfamiliar word with a familiar one and thereby clarify your meaning.

Another way to define a word quickly, often within a single sentence, is to give a *formal definition;* that is, to place the term to be defined in a general class and then to distinguish it from other members of that class by describing its particular characteristics. For example:

Word	*Class*	*Characteristics*
A watch	is a mechanical device	for telling time and is usually carried or worn.
Semantics	is an area of linguistics	concerned with the study of the meaning of words.

The third method is known as *extended definition.* While some extended definitions require only a single paragraph, more often than not you will need several paragraphs or even an entire essay to define a new or difficult term or to rescue a controversial word from misconceptions and associations that may obscure its meaning.

In an essay-length extended definition, you provide your readers with far more information than you would when using a synonym or a formal definition. You are, in most cases, exploring the meaning of your topic, whether it be a single word, a concept, or an object. In many cases, you must consider what your readers already know, or think they know, about your topic. Are there popular misconceptions that need to be done away with? Are there aspects of the topic that are seldom considered? Have particular experiences helped you understand the topic? You can use synonyms or formal definitions to help you define your topic, but you must convince your readers to accept your particular understanding of it.

In the following four-paragraph sequence, the writers provide an extended definition of *freedom,* an important but elusive concept.

Choosing between negative alternatives often seems like no choice at all. Take the case of a woman trying to decide whether to stay married to her inconsiderate, incompetent husband, or get a divorce. She doesn't want to stay with him, but she feels divorce is a sign of failure and will stigmatize her socially. Or think of the decision faced by many young men [more than thirty] years ago, when they were forced to choose between leaving their country and family or being sent to Vietnam.

When we face decisions involving only alternatives we see as negatives, we feel so little freedom that we twist and turn searching for another choice with some positive characteristics.

Freedom is a popular word. Individuals talk about how they feel free with one person and not with another, or how their bosses encourage or discourage freedom on the job. We hear about civil wars and revolutions being fought for greater freedom, with both sides righteously making the claim. The feeling of freedom is so important that people say they're ready to die for it, and supposedly have.

Still, most people have trouble coming up with a precise definition of freedom. They give answers describing specific situations — "Freedom means doing what I want to do, not what the Government wants me to do," or "Freedom means not having my mother tell me when to come home from a party" — rather than a general definition covering many situations. The idea they seem to be expressing is that freedom is associated with making decisions, and that other people sometimes limit the number of alternatives from which they can select.

–Jerald M. Jellison and John H. Harvey

Another term that illustrates the need for extended definition is *obscene*. What is obscene? Books that are banned in one school system are considered perfectly acceptable in another. Movies that are shown in one town cannot be shown in a neighboring town. Clearly, the meaning of *obscene* has been clouded by contrasting personal opinions as well as by conflicting social norms. Therefore, if you use the term *obscene* (and especially if you tackle the issue of obscenity itself), you must be careful to define clearly and thoroughly what you mean by that term — that is, you have to give an extended definition. There are a number of methods you might use to develop such a definition. You could define *obscene* by explaining what it does not mean. You could also make your meaning clear by narrating an experience, by comparing and contrasting it to related terms such as *pornographic* or *exotic,* by citing specific examples, or by classifying the various types of obscenity. Any of these methods could provide an effective definition.

Intelligence

■ Isaac Asimov

Born in the Soviet Union, Isaac Asimov immigrated to the United States in 1923. His death in 1992 ended a long, prolific career as a science-fiction and nonfiction writer. Asimov was uniquely talented at making a diverse range of topics, from Shakespeare to atomic physics, not only comprehensible but also entertaining to the general reader. Asimov earned three degrees at Columbia University and later taught biochemistry at Boston University. At the time of his death, he had published more than five hundred books. It's Been a Good Life, *published in 2002, was compiled from selections made from Asimov's three previous autobiographical volumes:* In Memory Yet Green *(1979),* In Joy Still Felt *(1980), and* I. Asimov: A Memoir *(1994). Edited by Janet Jeppson Asimov, the book also features "A Way of Thinking," Asimov's four hundredth essay for the* Magazine of Fantasy and Science Fiction. *In the following essay, Asimov, an intellectually gifted man, ponders the nature of intelligence. His academic brilliance, he concedes, would mean little or nothing if like-minded intellectuals had not established the standards for intelligence in our society.*

FOR YOUR JOURNAL

Our society defines the academically gifted as intelligent, but perhaps *book smart* would be a better term. IQ tests don't take into account common sense or experience, attributes that the academically gifted sometimes lack outside of a scholarly setting. Who's the smartest person you know? Is he or she academically gifted or smart in some way that would not be readily recognized as a form of intelligence?

What is intelligence, anyway? When I was in the army I received a kind of aptitude test that soldiers took and, against a norm of 100, scored 160. No one at the base had ever seen a figure like that, and for two hours they made a big fuss over me. (It didn't mean anything. The next day I was still a buck private with KP[1] as my highest duty.)

All my life I've been registering scores like that, so that I have the complacent feeling that I'm highly intelligent, and I expect other people to think so, too. Actually, though, don't such scores simply mean that I am very good at answering the type of academic questions that are considered worthy of answers by the people who make up the intelligence tests—people with intellectual bents similar to mine? 2

For instance, I had an auto-repair man once, who, on these intelligence tests, could not possibly have scored more than 80, by my estimate. I always took it for granted that I was far more intelligent than he was. Yet, when anything went wrong with my car I hastened to him with it, watched him anxiously as he explored its vitals, and listened to his pronouncements as though they were divine oracles—and he always fixed my car. 3

Well, then, suppose my auto-repair man devised questions for an intelligence test. Or suppose a carpenter did, or a farmer, or, indeed, almost anyone but an academician. By every one of those tests, I'd prove myself a moron. And I'd *be* a moron, too. In a world where I could not use my academic training and my verbal talents but had to do something intricate or hard, working with my hands, I would do poorly. My intelligence, then, is not absolute but is a function of the society I live in and of the fact that a small subsection of that society has managed to foist itself on the rest as an arbiter of such matters. 4

Consider my auto-repair man, again. He had a habit of telling me jokes whenever he saw me. One time he raised his head from under the automobile hood to say: "Doc, a deaf-and-dumb guy went into a hardware store to ask for some nails. He put two fingers together on the counter and made hammering motions with the other hand. The clerk brought him a hammer. He shook his head and pointed to the two fingers he was hammering. The clerk brought him nails. He picked out the sizes he wanted, and left. Well doc, the next guy who came in was a blind man. He wanted scissors. How do you suppose he asked for them? 5

Indulgently, I lifted my right hand and made scissoring motions with my first two fingers. Whereupon my auto-repair man laughed raucously and said, "Why you dumb jerk, he used his *voice* and asked for them." Then he said, smugly, "I've been trying that on all my customers today." "Did you catch many?" I asked. "Quite a few," he said, "but I knew for sure I'd catch *you*." "Why is that?" I 6

---

[1]*KP:* abbreviation for the military term *kitchen police.* [Eds.]

asked. "Because you're so goddamned educated, doc, I *knew* you couldn't be very smart."

And I have an uneasy feeling he had something there.   7

QUESTIONS FOR STUDY AND DISCUSSION

1. Why does Asimov begin his essay with a rhetorical question? (Glossary: *Rhetorical Question*) What does he emphasize by asking the question? How does the rest of his first paragraph relate to the question?
2. What is Asimov's thesis? (Glossary: *Thesis*) Where does he state it? How do his interactions with his auto-repair man serve to illustrate the thesis?
3. Analyze how Asimov transitions from one paragraph to the next. What transitional expressions or devices does he use? (Glossary: *Transition*)
4. Asimov refers to himself as a "moron" in most fields outside academics. What does the term *moron* connote to you? (Glossary: *Connotation/Denotation*) Why do you think Asimov uses the term, rather than simply stating that he would not do well in other fields?
5. How does Asimov's conclusion, although concise and ambiguous, serve to expand upon his thesis? (Glossary: *Beginnings and Endings*) Why do you think he chose ambiguity instead of a strong statement?

VOCABULARY

Refer to your dictionary to define the following words as they are used in this selection. Then use each word in a sentence of your own.

aptitude (1)   foist (4)

complacent (2)   arbiter (4)

intellectual (2)   indulgently (6)

oracles (3)   raucously (6)

academician (4)

CLASSROOM ACTIVITY USING DEFINITION

Definitions are often dependent on perspective. In Asimov's essay, for example, we have the writer's perspective as well as the auto-repair man's perspective on intelligence. Discuss with your classmates other words or terms—such as *competition, wealth, success, failure, food*—whose definitions are dependent on one's perspective. Choose several of these words and write definitions for them from your perspective. Discuss your definitions with your classmates. What perspective differences, if any, are apparent in the definitions?

SUGGESTED WRITING ASSIGNMENTS

1. Write an essay in which you address Asimov's opening question: "What is intelligence, anyway?" Define what intelligence means to you, both in yourself and in those around you. Is intelligence a reflection of how well you can function in your environment, or can someone be simultaneously intelligent and inept? Be sure to avoid beginning your essay with a dictionary definition or a platitude, both of which may be tempting to use.

2. Think about people you know well whose "book smarts" are exceeded by another attribute or a different kind of intelligence. They need not be academically challenged—indeed, they may be gifted—but perhaps they left their studies to pursue music, art, crafts, or another field. Write an essay in which you describe one such person's situation. Has he or she benefited from a "different" intelligence? Explain. Has this person's lack of academic achievement hindered him or her in any way? If so, in what ways? How has this person influenced your thinking about your studies and your career goals? Craft both your beginning and your ending to create and enhance the dominant impression you wish the reader to have about this person. You may wish to review what you wrote in your journal exercise for this selection before starting to write.

The Hoax

■ **John Berendt**

Born in Syracuse, New York, in 1939, John Berendt earned a bachelor's degree in English from Harvard University in 1961, where he worked on the Harvard Lampoon. Esquire *magazine hired him out of Harvard, and it was at* Esquire, *according to Berendt, that he "learned to write." Later he edited* Holiday *magazine, wrote television programs, and edited* New York *magazine. Berendt became a household name in 1993 when his novel* Midnight in the Garden of Good and Evil *was nominated for a Pulitzer Prize. Based on a murder in Savannah, Georgia, Berendt's novel spent more time on the* New York Times *bestseller list than any previous fiction or nonfiction title and was later made into a movie. As you read this selection, which first appeared in* Esquire *in 1994, notice how Berendt uses examples to help him define what a hoax is.*

FOR YOUR JOURNAL

Have you ever played a practical joke on someone or had one played on you? Retell what happened as best you can. What were the consequences of the practical joke?

When the humorist Robert Benchley was an undergraduate at 1
Harvard eight years ago, he and a couple of friends showed up one morning at the door of an elegant Beacon Hill[1] mansion, dressed as furniture repairmen. They told the housekeeper they had come to pick up the sofa. Five minutes later they carried the sofa out the door, put it on a truck, and drove it three blocks away to another house, where, posing as deliverymen, they plunked it down in the parlor. That evening, as Benchley well knew, the couple living in house A were due to attend a party in house B. Whatever the outcome—and I'll get to that shortly—it was guaranteed to be a defining example of how proper Bostonians handle social crises. The wit

---

[1]*Beacon Hill:* a historic, upscale neighborhood of Boston, Massachusetts. [Eds.]

inherent in Benchley's practical joke elevated it from the level of prank to the more respectable realm of hoax.

To qualify as a hoax, a prank must have magic in it—the word is derived from *hocus-pocus*, after all. Daring and irony are useful ingredients, too. A good example of a hoax is the ruse perpetrated by David Hampton, the young black man whose pretense of being Sidney Poitier's son inspired John Guare's *Six Degrees of Separation*. Hampton managed to insinuate himself into two of New York's most sophisticated households—one headed by the president of the public-television station WNET, the other by the dean of the Columbia School of Journalism. Hampton's hoax touched a number of sensitive themes: snobbery, class, race, and sex, all of which playwright Guare deftly exploited.

Hampton is a member of an elite band of famous impostors that includes a half-mad woman who for fifty years claimed to be Anastasia, the lost daughter of the assassinated czar Nicholas II; and a man named Harry Gerguson, who became a Hollywood restaurateur and darling of society in the 1930s and 1940s as the ersatz Russian prince Mike Romanoff.

Forgeries have been among the better hoaxes. Fake Vermeers[2] painted by an obscure Dutch artist, Hans van Meegeren, were so convincing that they fooled art dealers, collectors, and museums. The hoax came to light when Van Meegeren was arrested as a Nazi[3] collaborator after the war. To prove he was not a Nazi, he admitted he had sold a fake Vermeer to Hermann Göring for $256,000. Then he owned up to having created other "Vermeers," and to prove he could do it, he painted *Jesus in the Temple* in the style of Vermeer while under guard in jail.

In a bizarre twist, a story much like Van Meegeren's became the subject of the book *Fake!*, by Clifford Irving, who in 1972 attempted to pull off a spectacular hoax of his own: a wholly fraudulent "authorized" biography of Howard Hughes.[4] Irving claimed to have

---

[2]*Fake Vermeers*: paintings falsely presented as the work of Dutch painter Jan Vermeer (1632–1675). [Eds.]

[3]*Nazi*: the short name of the National Socialist German Workers' Party, the political party of Adolf Hitler and Hermann Göring, which controlled Germany from 1933 to 1945. [Eds.]

[4]*Howard Hughes* (1905–1976): vastly wealthy, eccentric U.S. manufacturer, aviator, and film producer known for his aversion to publicity. [Eds.]

conducted secret interviews with the reclusive Hughes, and McGraw-Hill gave him a big advance. Shortly before publication, Hughes surfaced by telephone and denied that he had ever spoken with Irving. Irving had already spent $100,000 of the advance; he was convicted of fraud and sent to jail.

As it happens, we are used to hoaxes where I come from. I grew   6
up just a few miles down the road from Cardiff, New York—a town made famous by the Cardiff Giant. As we learned in school, a farmer named Newell complained, back in 1889, that his well was running dry, and while he and his neighbors were digging a new one, they came upon what appeared to be the fossilized remains of a man twelve feet tall. Before the day was out, Newell had erected a tent and posted a sign charging a dollar for a glimpse of the "giant"—three dollars for a longer look. Throngs descended on Cardiff. It wasn't long before scientists determined that the giant had been carved from a block of gypsum. The hoax came undone fairly quickly after that, but even so—as often happens with hoaxes—the giant became an even bigger attraction *because* it was a hoax. P. T. Barnum offered Newell a fortune for the giant, but Newell refused, and it was then that he got his comeuppance. Barnum simply made a replica and put it on display as the genuine Cardiff giant. Newell's gig was ruined.

The consequences of hoaxes are what give them spice. Orson   7
Welles's lifelike 1938 radio broadcast of H. G. Wells's *War of the Worlds* panicked millions of Americans, who were convinced that Martians had landed in New Jersey. The forged diary of Adolf Hitler embarrassed historian Hugh Trevor-Roper, who had vouched for its authenticity, and *Newsweek* and *The Sunday Times* of London, both of which published excerpts in 1983 shortly before forensic tests proved that there were nylon fibers in the paper it was written on, which wouldn't have been possible had it originated before 1950. The five-hundred-thousand-year-old remains of Piltdown man,[5] found in 1912, had anthropologists confused about human evolution until 1953, when fluoride tests exposed the bones as an elaborate modern hoax. And as for Robert Benchley's game on Beacon Hill, no one said a word about the sofa all evening, although there it sat in plain sight. One week later, however, couple A sent an anonymous package to couple B. It contained the sofa's slipcovers.

---

[5]*Piltdown man:* the first of two skulls discovered by Charles Dawson in the Piltdown quarry in Sussex, England. [Eds.]

QUESTIONS FOR STUDY AND DISCUSSION

1. According to Berendt, what is a hoax? How does a hoax differ from a prank? Explain.
2. Berendt uses the story of humorist Robert Benchley's sofa hoax in the Beacon Hill section of Boston to both begin and end his essay. (Glossary: *Beginnings and Endings*) How well does this tactic work?
3. In what ways was the outcome of the sofa hoax "a defining example of how proper Bostonians handle social crises" (1)?
4. To define what he means by *hoax*, Berendt uses numerous examples. (Glossary: *Example*) How does he organize his examples? What are the three main types of hoaxes that he discusses? Which of the examples did you find most illuminating? Most interesting? Why?
5. What does Berendt mean when he says, "The consequences of hoaxes are what give them spice" (7)?
6. Structurally, how is paragraph 7 related to the first six paragraphs? Explain how the concluding paragraph gives Berendt's essay unity and coherence. (Glossary: *Unity; Coherence*)

VOCABULARY

Refer to your dictionary to define the following words as they are used in this selection. Then use each word in a sentence of your own.

wit (1)
prank (1)
irony (2)
ruse (2)
insinuate (2)
deftly (2)

ersatz (3)
reclusive (5)
comeuppance (6)
vouched (7)
forensic (7)

CLASSROOM ACTIVITY USING DEFINITION

Try formally defining one of the following terms by putting it in a class and then differentiating it from other words in the class. (See p. 389.)

potato chips   tenor saxophone   sociology   Monopoly (the game)
love   physical therapy   chickadee   Buddhism

SUGGESTED WRITING ASSIGNMENTS

1. For you, when is a hoax not a hoax? Is it possible for a person to cross some line when a hoax is no longer fun or decent? Several of Berendt's examples involve criminal fraud, yet he still considers them hoaxes. Do you agree with him? Write an essay in which you explain where you draw the line between hoax and crime.

2. Every generation develops its own slang, which generally enlivens the speech and writing of those who use it. Ironically, however, no generation can arrive at a consensus definition of even its most popular slang terms—for example, *dork, funky, cool.* Select a slang term that you use frequently, and write an essay in which you define the term. As Berendt does in his essay, use examples to illustrate your definition. When you have finished your first draft, read your definition aloud to a group from your class. Do they agree with your definition? Using their suggestions, revise your essay.

The Company Man

■ **Ellen Goodman**

Ellen Goodman was born in Boston in 1941. After graduating cum laude *from Radcliffe College in 1963, she worked as a reporter and researcher for* Newsweek. *In 1967, she began working at the* Boston Globe *and, since 1974, has been a full-time columnist. Her regular column, "At Large," is syndicated by the* Washington Post's Writer's Group *and appears in nearly four hundred newspapers across the country. In addition, her writing has appeared in* McCall's, Harper's Bazaar, *and* Family Circle, *and her commentaries have been broadcast on radio and television. Several collections of Goodman's columns have been published as books, including* Close to Home *(1979),* At Large *(1981),* Keeping in Touch *(1985),* Value Judgments *(1995), and* Making Sense *(1999). Her most recent book is* I Know Just What You Mean: The Power of Friendship in Women's Lives *(2000). In "The Company Man," taken from* Close to Home, *Goodman defines the* workaholic *by offering a poignant case-in-point example.*

FOR YOUR JOURNAL

While many jobs have regular hours, some, like journalism, medicine, high-level management, and Internet jobs, are less predictable and may require far more time. Think about your career goals. Do you anticipate a greater emphasis on your work life or your home life? How much time beyond the standard forty hours per week are you willing to sacrifice to advance your career? Has this issue influenced your choice of career in any way, or do you anticipate that it will? Explain.

H e worked himself to death, finally and precisely, at 3:00 A.M. 1
Sunday morning.

The obituary didn't say that, of course. It said that he died of a 2
coronary thrombosis—I think that was it—but everyone among his friends and acquaintances knew it instantly. He was a perfect Type

A, a workaholic, a classic, they said to each other and shook their heads — and thought for five or ten minutes about the way they lived.

This man who worked himself to death finally and precisely at   3
3:00 A.M. Sunday morning — on his day off — was fifty-one years old and a vice-president. He was, however, one of six vice-presidents, and one of three who might conceivably — if the president died or retired soon enough — have moved to the top spot. Phil knew that.

He worked six days a week, five of them until eight or nine at   4
night, during a time when his own company had begun the four-day week for everyone but the executives. He worked like the Important People. He had no outside "extracurricular interests," unless, of course, you think about a monthly golf game that way. To Phil, it was work. He always ate egg salad sandwiches at his desk. He was, of course, overweight, by 20 or 25 pounds. He thought it was okay, though, because he didn't smoke.

On Saturdays, Phil wore a sports jacket to the office instead of a   5
suit, because it was the weekend.

He had a lot of people working for him, maybe sixty, and most   6
of them liked him most of the time. Three of them will be seriously considered for his job. The obituary didn't mention that.

But it did list his "survivors" quite accurately. He is survived by   7
his wife, Helen, forty-eight years old, a good woman of no particular marketable skills, who worked in an office before marrying and mothering. She had, according to her daughter, given up trying to compete with his work years ago, when the children were small. A company friend said, "I know how much you will miss him." And she answered, "I already have."

"Missing him all these years," she must have given up part of   8
herself which had cared too much for the man. She would be "well taken care of."

His "dearly beloved" eldest of the "dearly beloved" children is a   9
hard-working executive in a manufacturing firm down South. In the day and a half before the funeral, he went around the neighborhood researching his father, asking the neighbors what he was like. They were embarrassed.

His second child is a girl, who is twenty-four and newly married.   10
She lives near her mother and they are close, but whenever she was alone with her father, in a car driving somewhere, they had nothing to say to each other.

The youngest is twenty, a boy, a high-school graduate who has   11
spent the last couple of years, like a lot of his friends, doing enough

odd jobs to stay in grass and food. He was the one who tried to grab at his father, and tried to mean enough to him to keep the man at home. He was his father's favorite. Over the last two years, Phil stayed up nights worrying about the boy.

The boy once said, "My father and I only board here." 12

At the funeral, the sixty-year-old company president told the forty- 13
eight-year-old widow that the fifty-one-year-old deceased had meant much to the company and would be missed and would be hard to re-place. The widow didn't look him in the eye. She was afraid he would read her bitterness and, after all, she would need him to straighten out the finances—the stock options and all that.

Phil was overweight and nervous and worked too hard. If he wasn't 14
at the office, he was worried about it. Phil was a Type A, a heart-attack natural. You could have picked him out in a minute from a lineup.

So when he finally worked himself to death, at precisely 3:00 15
A.M. Sunday morning, no one was really surprised.

By 5:00 P.M. the afternoon of the funeral, the company president 16
had begun, discreetly of course, with care and taste, to make inquiries about his replacement. One of three men. He asked around: "Who's been working the hardest?"

QUESTIONS FOR STUDY AND DISCUSSION

1. After reading Goodman's essay, how would you define a *com-pany man*? As you define the term, consider what such a man is not, as well as what he is. Is *company man* synonymous with *workaholic*? Explain.

2. In paragraph 4, Goodman says that Phil worked like "the Impor-tant People." How would you define that term in the context of the essay?

3. What is Goodman's purpose in this essay? (Glossary: *Purpose*) Explain your answer.

4. Do you think Goodman's unemotional tone is appropriate for her purpose? (Glossary: *Tone*) Why, or why not?

5. Describe Phil's relationship with each of his children. What does each relationship indicate about the impact of Phil's work habits on his family?

6. Goodman repeats the day and time that Phil worked himself to death. Why are those facts important enough to bear repetition? What about them is ironic?

VOCABULARY

Refer to your dictionary to define the following words as they are used in this selection. Then use each word in a sentence of your own.

obituary (2)
extracurricular (4)
discreetly (16)

CLASSROOM ACTIVITY USING DEFINITION

The connotation of the term *workaholic* depends on the context. For Phil's employers—and at his workplace in general—the term obviously had a positive connotation. For those who knew Phil outside the workplace, it had a negative one. Choose one of the terms below, and provide two definitions, one positive and one negative, that could apply to the term in different contexts.

go-getter
party animal
overachiever
mover and shaker

SUGGESTED WRITING ASSIGNMENTS

1. A procrastinator—a person who continually puts off responsibilities—is very different from a workaholic. Write an essay, modeled on Goodman's, using an extended example to define this interesting personality type.

2. One issue that Goodman does not raise is how a person becomes a workaholic. Write an essay in which you speculate about how someone might develop workaholism. How does a desirable trait like hard work begin to adversely affect someone? How might workaholism be avoided?

Division and Classification

A writer practices **division** by separating a class of things or ideas into categories following a clear principle or basis. In the following paragraph, journalist Robert MacNeil establishes categories of speech according to the level of formality:

> It fascinates me how differently we all speak in different circumstances. We have levels of formality, as in our clothing. There are very formal occasions, often requiring written English: the job application or the letter to the editor—the darksuit, serious-tie language, with everything pressed and the lint brushed off. There is our less formal out-in-the-world language—a more comfortable suit, but still respectable. There is language for close friends in the evenings, on weekends—bluejeans-and-sweat-shirt language, when it's good to get the tie off. There is family language, even more relaxed, full of grammatical short cuts, family slang, echoes of old jokes that have become intimate shorthand—the language of pajamas and uncombed hair. Finally, there is the language with no clothes on; the talk of couples—murmurs, sighs, grunts—language at its least self-conscious, open, vulnerable, and primitive.
>
> –Robert MacNeil

With **classification,** on the other hand, a writer groups individual objects or ideas into already established categories. Division and classification can operate separately but often accompany one another. Here, for example, is a passage about levers in which the writer first discusses generally how levers work. In the second paragraph, the writer uses division to establish three categories of levers and then uses classification to group individual levers into those categories:

> Every lever has one fixed point called the "fulcrum" and is acted upon by two forces—the "effort" (exertion of hand muscles) and the "weight" (object's resistance). Levers work according to a simple formula: the effort (how hard you push or pull) multiplied by its distance from the fulcrum (effort arm) equals the weight

multiplied by its distance from the fulcrum (weight arm). Thus two pounds of effort exerted at a distance of four feet from the fulcrum will raise eight pounds located one foot from the fulcrum.

There are three types of levers, conventionally called "first kind," "second kind," and "third kind." Levers of the first kind have the fulcrum located between the effort and the weight. Examples are a pump handle, an oar, a crowbar, a weighing balance, a pair of scissors, and a pair of pliers. Levers of the second kind have the weight in the middle and magnify the effort. Examples are the handcar crank and doors. Levers of the third kind, such as a power shovel or a baseball batter's forearm, have the effort in the middle and always magnify the distance.

The following paragraph introduces a classification of the kinds of buyers who purchase stereo systems:

> As stereo equipment gets better and prices go down, stereo systems are becoming household necessities rather than luxuries. People are buying stereos by the thousands. During my year as a stereo salesman, I witnessed this boom firsthand. I dealt with hundreds of customers, and it didn't take long for me to learn that people buy stereos for different reasons. Eventually, though, I was able to divide all stereo buyers into four basic categories: the looks buyer, the wattage buyer, the price buyer, and the quality buyer.
>
> –Gerald Cleary, student

In the remainder of his essays, Cleary explains in detail the distinguishing characteristics of each type of stereo system buyer.

In writing, division and classification are affected directly by the writer's practical purpose. That purpose — what the writer wants to explain or prove — determines the class of things or ideas being divided and classified. For instance, a writer might divide television programs according to their audiences — adults, families, or children — and then classify individual programs into each of these categories to show how much emphasis the television stations place on reaching each audience. A different purpose would require different categories. A writer concerned about the prevalence of violence in television programming would first divide television programs into those that include fights and murders and those that do not, and would then classify a large sample of programs into those categories. Other writers with different purposes might divide television programs differently — by the day and time of broadcast, for example, or by the number of women featured in prominent roles — and then classify individual programs accordingly.

Another example may help clarify how division and classification work hand in hand in writing. Suppose a sociologist wants to determine whether the socioeconomic status of the people in a particular neighborhood has any influence on their voting behavior. Having decided on her purpose, the sociologist chooses as her subject the fifteen families living on Maple Street. Her goal then becomes to group these families in a way that will be relevant to her purpose. She immediately knows that she wants to divide the neighborhood in two ways: (1) according to socioeconomic status (low-income earners, middle-income earners, and high-income earners) and (2) according to voting behavior (voters and nonvoters). However, her process of division won't be complete until she can classify individual families into her various groupings.

In confidential interviews with each family, the sociologist learns first its income and then whether any member of the household has

Subject: The fifteen families on Maple Street

Purpose: To group the families according to socioeconomic status and voting behavior to study the relationship between the two.

Subclasses:

Low Income (under $35,000)	Middle Income ($35,000–$90,000)	High Income (over $90,000)
Bowman	Reilly	Rigby
Packer	Santana	Kretz
Eells	Lane	Wagner
Weiss	Pfeffer	
Murray	Halstead	
Nadel		
Sikorski		

Basis: Family income

Subclasses:

Non-voting	Voting	Non-voting	Voting	Non-voting	Voting
Bowman		Lane	Reilly	Wagner	Rigby
Packer			Santana		Kretz
Eells			Pfeffer		
Weiss			Halstead		
Murray					
Nadel					
Sikorski					

Basis: Voting behavior

Conclusion: On Maple Street, there seems to be a relationship between socioeconomic status and voting behavior: the low-income families are nonvoters.

voted in a state or federal election during the last four years. Based on this information, she begins to classify each family according to her established categories and at the same time to divide the neighborhood into the subclasses crucial to her study. Her work leads her to construct a diagram of her divisions and classifications.

This diagram allows the sociologist to visualize her division and classification system and its essential components: subject; basis or principle of division; subclasses or categories; and conclusion. It is clear that her ultimate conclusion depends on her ability to work back and forth between the potential divisions or subclasses and the actual families to be classified.

The following guidelines can help you in using division and classification in your writing:

1. *Identify a clear purpose, and be sure that your principle of division is appropriate to that purpose.* If, for example, you wished to examine the common characteristics of four-year athletic scholarship recipients at your college or university, you might consider the following principles of division: program of study, sport, place of origin, or sex. In this case it would not be useful to divide students on the basis of their favorite type of music because that seems irrelevant to your purpose.

2. *Divide your subject into categories that are mutually exclusive.* An item can belong to only one category. For example, it would be unsatisfactory to divide students as men, women, and athletes.

3. *Make your division and classification complete.* Your categories should account for all items in a subject class. In dividing students on the basis of geographic origin, for example, it would be inappropriate to consider only the United States, for such a division would not account for foreign students. Then, for your classification to be complete, every student must be placed in one of the established categories.

4. *Be sure to state clearly the conclusion that your division and classification lead you to draw.* For example, after conducting your division and classification of athletic scholarship recipients, you might conclude that the majority of male athletes with athletic scholarships come from the western United States.

The Ways of Meeting Oppression

■ **Martin Luther King Jr.**

Martin Luther King Jr. (1929–1968) was the leading spokesman for the rights of African Americans during the 1950s and 1960s before his assassination in 1968. He established the Southern Christian Leadership Conference, organized many civil-rights demonstrations, and opposed the Vietnam War and the draft. In 1964, he was awarded the Nobel Peace Prize. In the following essay, taken from his book Strive toward Freedom *(1958), King classifies the three ways oppressed people throughout history have reacted to their oppressors. As you read, pay particular attention to how King's discussions within the categories of classification lead him to the conclusion he presents in paragraph 8.*

FOR YOUR JOURNAL

Isaac Asimov once said, "Violence is the last resort of the incompetent." What are your thoughts on the reasons for violent behavior on either a personal or a national level? Is violence ever justified? If so, under what circumstances?

Oppressed people deal with their oppression in three characteristic ways. One way is acquiescence: the oppressed resign themselves to their doom. They tacitly adjust themselves to oppression, and thereby become conditioned to it. In every movement toward freedom some of the oppressed prefer to remain oppressed. Almost 2800 years ago Moses[1] set out to lead the children of Israel from the slavery of Egypt to the freedom of the promised land. He soon discovered that slaves do not always welcome their deliverers. They become accustomed to being slaves. They would rather bear those ills

---

[1]*Moses:* a Hebrew prophet, teacher, and leader of the fourteenth to thirteenth centuries B.C.E. [Eds.]

they have, as Shakespeare[2] pointed out, than flee to others that they know not of. They prefer the "fleshpots of Egypt" to the ordeals of emancipation.

There is such a thing as the freedom of exhaustion. Some people 2 are so worn down by the yoke of oppression that they give up. A few years ago in the slum areas of Atlanta, a Negro guitarist used to sing almost daily: "Been down so long that down don't bother me."[3] This is the type of negative freedom and resignation that often engulfs the life of the oppressed.

But this is not the way out. To accept passively an unjust system is to 3 cooperate with that system; thereby the oppressed become as evil as the oppressor. Noncooperation with evil is as much a moral obligation as is cooperation with good. The oppressed must never allow the conscience of the oppressor to slumber. Religion reminds every man that he is his brother's keeper. To accept injustice or segregation passively is to say to the oppressor that his actions are morally right. It is a way of allowing his conscience to fall asleep. At this moment the oppressed fails to be his brother's keeper. So acquiescence — while often the easier way — is not the moral way. It is the way of the coward. The Negro cannot win the respect of his oppressor by acquiescing; he merely increases the oppressor's arrogance and contempt. Acquiescence is interpreted as proof of the Negro's inferiority. The Negro cannot win the respect of the white people of the South or the peoples of the world if he is willing to sell the future of his children for his personal and immediate comfort and safety.

A second way that oppressed people sometimes deal with oppres- 4 sion is to resort to physical violence and corroding hatred. Violence often brings about momentary results. Nations have frequently won their independence in battle. But in spite of temporary victories, violence never brings permanent peace. It solves no social problem; it merely creates new and more complicated ones.

Violence as a way of achieving racial justice is both impractical 5 and immoral. It is impractical because it is a descending spiral ending in destruction for all. The old law of an eye for an eye leaves everybody blind. It is immoral because it seeks to humiliate the opponent rather than win his understanding; it seeks to annihilate rather than to convert. Violence is immoral because it thrives on hatred rather than love. It destroys community and makes brother-

---

[2]*William Shakespeare* (1564–1616): English poet, actor, and dramatist. [Eds.]
[3]Lyric possibly adapted from "Stormy Blues" by the American jazz singer Billie Holiday (1915–1959) [Eds.]

hood impossible. It leaves society in monologue rather than dialogue. Violence ends by defeating itself. It creates bitterness in the survivors and brutality in the destroyers. A voice echoes through time saying to every potential Peter, "Put up your sword."[4] History is cluttered with the wreckage of nations that failed to follow this command.

If the American Negro and other victims of oppression succumb   6
to the temptation of using violence in the struggle for freedom, future generations will be the recipients of a desolate night of bitterness, and our chief legacy to them will be an endless reign of meaningless chaos. Violence is not the way.

The third way open to oppressed people in their quest for free-   7
dom is the way of nonviolent resistance. Like the synthesis in Hegelian[5] philosophy, the principle of nonviolent resistance seeks to reconcile the truths of two opposites — acquiescence and violence — while avoiding the extremes and immoralities of both. The nonviolent resister agrees with the person who acquiesces that one should not be physically aggressive toward his opponent; but he balances the equation by agreeing with the person of violence that evil must be resisted. He avoids the nonresistance of the former and the violent resistance of the latter. With nonviolent resistance, no individual or group need submit to any wrong, nor need anyone resort to violence in order to right a wrong.

It seems to me that this is the method that must guide the actions   8
of the Negro in the present crisis in race relations. Through nonviolent resistance the Negro will be able to rise to the noble height of opposing the unjust system while loving the perpetrators of the system. The Negro must work passionately and unrelentingly for full stature as a citizen, but he must not use inferior methods to gain it. He must never come to terms with falsehood, malice, hate, or destruction.

Nonviolent resistance makes it possible for the Negro to remain   9
in the South and struggle for his rights. The Negro's problem will not be solved by running away. He cannot listen to the glib suggestion of those who would urge him to migrate en masse to other sections of the country. By grasping his great opportunity in the South he can make a lasting contribution to the moral strength of the

---

[4]The apostle Peter had drawn his sword to defend Christ from arrest. The voice was Christ's, who surrendered himself for trial and crucifixion (John 18:11). [Eds.]
[5]*Georg Wilhelm Friedrich Hegel* (1770–1831): German philosopher. [Eds.]

nation and set a sublime example of courage for generations yet unborn.

By nonviolent resistance, the Negro can also enlist all men of good will in his struggle for equality. The problem is not a purely racial one, with Negroes set against whites. In the end, it is not a struggle between people at all, but a tension between justice and injustice. Nonviolent resistance is not aimed against oppressors but against oppression. Under its banner consciences, not racial groups, are enlisted. 10

QUESTIONS FOR STUDY AND DISCUSSION

1. What is King's purpose in writing this essay? How does classifying the three types of resistance to oppression serve this purpose? (Glossary: *Purpose*)

2. What principle of division does King use in this essay?

3. Why do you suppose King discusses acquiescence, violence, and nonviolent resistance in that order? (Glossary: *Organization*)

4. Why, according to King, do slaves not always welcome their deliverers?

5. What does King mean in paragraph 2 by the "freedom of exhaustion"?

6. King states that he favors nonviolent resistance over the other two ways of meeting oppression. What are the disadvantages that King sees in meeting oppression with acquiescence or with violence? Look closely at the words he uses to describe nonviolent resistance and those he uses to describe acquiescence and violence. How does his choice of words contribute to his argument? Show examples. (Glossary: *Connotation/Denotation*)

VOCABULARY

Refer to your dictionary to define the following words as they are used in this selection. Then use each word in a sentence of your own.

acquiescence (1)   desolate (6)
tacitly (1)   synthesis (7)
corroding (4)   sublime (9)
annihilate (5)

CLASSROOM ACTIVITY USING DIVISION AND CLASSIFICATION

Examine the following lists of hobbies, books, and buildings. Determine at least three principles that could be used to divide the items listed in each group. Finally, classify the items in each group according to one of the principles you have established.

HOBBIES
watching sports on TV
stamp collecting
scuba diving
surfing the Web
hiking
dancing
running

BOOKS
The Adventures of Huckleberry Finn
Guinness Book of World Records
The Joy of Cooking
American Heritage Dictionary
To Kill a Mockingbird
Gone with the Wind

BUILDINGS
Empire State Building
White House
The Alamo
Taj Mahal
Library of Congress
Buckingham Palace

SUGGESTED WRITING ASSIGNMENTS

1. Using King's essay as a model, write an essay about a current social or personal problem, using division and classification to discuss various possible solutions. You might discuss something personal, such as the problem of giving up smoking, or a pressing social issue, such as gun control or gay marriage. Whatever

your topic, use an appropriate principle of division to establish categories that suit the purpose of your discussion.

2. Consider any one of the following topics for an essay of classification. You may find it helpful to review the guidelines for using division and classification on page 407.

movies	country music
college courses	newspapers
sports fans	pets
teenage lifestyles	students

The Fine Art of Sighing

■ **Bernard Cooper**

Bernard Cooper was born in Hollywood, California, where he now makes his home. Recipient of the PEN/Hemingway Award, the O. Henry Prize, and a Guggenheim Award, Cooper teaches in the writing program at Antioch College in Los Angeles and the UCLA Creative Writing Program. He has published two volumes of his memoirs thus far, A Year of Rhymes *(1993) and* Truth Serum *(1996), as well as an autobiographical novel,* Maps to Anywhere *(1990). Author Amy Tan has said of his work, "Cooper injects his memoirs with pain and humor and gets to the heart of who we are and what tampers with our psyches." Cooper has also written fiction and essays, some of which have been anthologized in* The Best American Essays *(various years) as well as in* The Best American Gay Fiction of 1996. *His most recent book is* Guess Again: Short Stories *(2000). In a recent interview, Cooper gave his thoughts on reading: "A good piece of writing causes you to have a sense of identification, even if the experience . . . is remote from your own. When suddenly you feel that you've taken on a completely foreign experience and you're living it to its fullest, it's absolutely transporting. It's one of the greatest pleasures literature can offer." In "The Fine Art of Sighing," taken from* Truth Serum, *Cooper defines the human sigh, divides people according to their sighs, and imagines the cumulative expelled air from sighs being felt across the world like the weather.*

FOR YOUR JOURNAL

People are the same the world over—so goes a well-worn expression. Is there truth for you in this expression, or are people really different across the globe? If they are the same, why are we fascinated by the people we meet in our travels? If people are essentially different across the globe, why do we speak of our common humanity?

You feel a gradual welling up of pleasure, or boredom, or melancholy. Whatever the emotion, it's more abundant than you ever dreamed. You can no more contain it than your hands can cup a lake. And so you surrender and suck the air. Your esophagus opens, diaphragm expands. Poised at the crest of an exhalation, your body is about to be unburdened, second by second, cell by cell. A kettle hisses. A balloon deflates. Your shoulders fall like two ripe pears, muscles slack at last.

My mother stared out the kitchen window, ashes from her ciga-   2
rette dribbling into the sink. She'd turned her back on the rest of the house, a sentry guarding her own solitude. I'd tiptoe across the linoleum and make my lunch without making a sound. Sometimes I saw her back expand, then heard her let loose one plummeting note, a sigh so long and weary it might have been her last. Beyond our backyard, above telephone poles and apartment buildings, rose the brown horizon of the city; across it glided an occasional bird, or the blimp that advertised Goodyear tires. She might have been drifting into the distance, or lamenting her separation from it. She might have been wishing she were somewhere else, or wishing she could be happy where she was, a middle-aged housewife dreaming at her sink.

My father's sighs were more melodic. What began as a somber   3
sigh could abruptly change pitch, turn gusty and loose, and suggest by its very transformation that what begins in sorrow might end in relief. He could prolong the rounded vowel of OY, or let it ricochet like an echo, as if he were shouting in a tunnel or a cave. Where my mother sighed from ineffable sadness, my father sighed at simple things: the coldness of a drink, the softness of a pillow, or an itch that my mother, following the frantic map of his words, finally found on his back and scratched.

A friend of mine once mentioned that I was given to long and   4
ponderous sighs. Once I became aware of this habit, I heard my father's sighs in my own and knew for a moment his small satisfactions. At other times, I felt my mother's restlessness and wished I could leave my body with my breath, or be happy in the body my breath left behind.

It's a reflex and a legacy, this soulful species of breathing. Listen   5
closely: My ancestors' lungs are pumping like bellows, men towing boats along the banks of the Volga,[1] women lugging baskets of rye bread and pike. At the end of each day, they lift their weary arms in a toast; as thanks for the heat and sting of vodka, their a-h-h's condense in the cold Russian air.

---

[1] *Volga:* a river that runs through western Russia. [Eds.]

At any given moment, there must be thousands of people sighing. 6
A man in Milwaukee heaves and shivers and blesses the head of the
second wife who's not too shy to lick his toes. A judge in Munich
groans with pleasure after tasting again the silky bratwurst she ate as
a child. Every day, meaningful sighs are expelled from schoolchil-
dren, driving instructors, forensic experts, certified public accountants, and dental hygienists, just to name a few. The sighs of widows
and widowers alone must account for a significant portion of the car-
bon dioxide released into the atmosphere. Every time a girdle is removed, a foot is submerged in a tub of warm water, or a restroom is
reached on a desolate road . . . you'd think the sheer velocity of it
would create mistrals, siroccos, hurricanes; arrows should be swarm-
ing over satellite maps, weathermen talking a mile a minute, ties flap-
ping from their necks like flags.

Before I learned that Venetian[2] prisoners were led across it to 7
their execution, I imagined that the Bridge of Sighs was a feat of invisible engineering, a structure vaulting above the earth, the girders
and trusses, the stay ropes and cables, the counterweights and safety
rails connecting one human breath to the next.

QUESTIONS FOR STUDY AND DISCUSSION

1. Cooper divides the people he knows and imagines into different
   types of "sighers." Who are these people, and how does Cooper
   characterize each one or group?
2. How does Cooper define a sigh? (Glossary: *Definition*) Where in
   the essay does he offer his definition? What would be gained or
   lost if he offered the definition elsewhere in his essay? (Glossary:
   Beginnings and Endings)
3. What is the Bridge of Sighs? What point does Cooper make with
   his reference to the Bridge of Sighs? Is he using irony? (Glossary:
   Irony)
4. Cooper contrasts his mother's and father's sighs. How does he
   use the contrast he draws to reflect on his own sighing?
5. Why does Cooper go back in time to his ancestors' sighs and also
   move on to envision the sighing that goes on in distant places?
   What point is he trying to make? (Glossary: *Purpose*)

---

[2]*Venetian:* of or relating to the city of Venice, Italy. [Eds.]

6. What is Cooper's tone in this essay? (Glossary: *Tone*) How does he establish his tone?

VOCABULARY

Refer to your dictionary to define the following words as they are used in this selection. Then use each word in a sentence of your own.

melancholy (1)	ponderous (4)
esophagus (1)	bellows (5)
diaphragm (1)	forensic (6)
slack (1)	mistrals (6)
ricochet (3)	siroccos (6)
ineffable (3)	

CLASSROOM ACTIVITY USING DIVISION AND CLASSIFICATION

Divide each item in the following list into at least three different categories, and be prepared to discuss your principle of division. Also provide a few examples that might be classified into each category. For example, pets can be divided into these categories: mammals (cat, hamster, guinea pig), birds (parrot, finch, parakeet), reptiles (snake, chameleon, iguana), fish (guppy, goldfish, angelfish), and insects (ant, ladybug, cricket).

computers	colleges
fast-food restaurants	soft drinks
professional sports	checking accounts
newspapers	mall stores

SUGGESTED WRITING ASSIGNMENTS

1. As humans we sigh, but we also laugh, cry, sneeze, cough, kiss, and wink, to name a few other uniquely carried out, highly personal activities. Modeling an essay on Cooper's "The Fine Art of Sighing," divide and classify one such activity as you see it carried out by those around you. Establish a clear thesis, and develop an effective organizational pattern for your essay. Consider

what the activity that you choose to write about tells us about ourselves as humans.

2. Write an essay that divides and classifies the students at your college or university. Be sure to use principles of division that will lead to interesting insights into your school.

Friends, Good Friends—and Such Good Friends

■ **Judith Viorst**

Judith Viorst was born in Newark, New Jersey, in 1931 and attended Rutgers University. She has published several volumes of light verse and collections of prose, as well as many articles in popular magazines. Her numerous children's books include the perennial favorite Alexander and the Terrible, Horrible, No Good, Very Bad Day *(1972). Her recent books for adults include* Necessary Losses: The Loves, Illusions, Dependencies, and Impossible Expectations That All of Us Have to Give Up in Order to Grow *(1997),* Imperfect Control: Our Lifelong Struggles with Power and Surrender *(1998),* Suddenly 60: And Other Shocks of Late-Life *(2000), and* Grown-Up Marriage: What We Know, Wish We Had Known, and Still Need to Know about Being Married *(2002). The following selection appeared in her regular column in* Redbook. *In it she analyzes and classifies the various types of friends that a person can have. As you read, assess the validity of Viorst's analysis by trying to place your own friends into her categories. Determine also whether the categories themselves are mutually exclusive.*

FOR YOUR JOURNAL

Think about your friends. Do you regard them all in the same light? Would you group them in any way? On what basis would you group them?

Women are friends, I once would have said, when they totally love and support and trust each other, and bare to each other the secrets of their souls, and run—no questions asked—to help each other, and tell harsh truths to each other (no, you can't wear that dress unless you lose ten pounds first) when harsh truths must be told.

Women are friends, I once would have said, when they share the same affection for Ingmar Bergman,[1] plus train rides, cats, warm

---

[1]*Ingmar Bergman* (b. 1918): Swedish film writer and director. [Eds.]

rain, charades, Camus,[2] and hate with equal ardor Newark and Brussels sprouts and Lawrence Welk[3] and camping.

In other words, I once would have said that a friend is a friend all the way, but now I believe that's a narrow point of view. For the friendships I have and the friendships I see are conducted at many levels of intensity, serve many different functions, meet different needs, and range from those as all-the-way as the friendship of the soul sisters mentioned above to that of the most nonchalant and casual playmates. 3

Consider these varieties of friendship: 4

1. Convenience friends. These are women with whom, if our paths weren't crossing all the time, we'd have no particular reason to be friends: a next-door neighbor, a woman in our car pool, the mother of one of our children's closest friends, or maybe some mommy with whom we serve juice and cookies each week at the Glenwood Co-op Nursery. 5

Convenience friends are convenient indeed. They'll lend us their cups and silverware for a party. They'll drive our kids to soccer when we're sick. They'll take us to pick up our car when we need a lift to the garage. They'll even take our cats when we go on vacation. As we will for them. 6

But we don't, with convenience friends, ever come too close or tell too much; we maintain our public face and emotional distance. "Which means," says Elaine, "that I'll talk about being overweight but not about being depressed. Which means I'll admit being mad but not blind with rage. Which means that I might say that we're pinched this month but never that I'm worried sick over money." 7

But which doesn't mean that there isn't sufficient value to be found in these friendships of mutual aid, in convenience friends. 8

2. Special-interest friends. These friendships aren't intimate, and they needn't involve kids or silverware or cats. Their value lies in some interest jointly shared. And so we may have an office friend or a yoga friend or a tennis friend or a friend from the Women's Democratic Club. 9

"I've got one woman friend," says Joyce, "who likes, as I do, to take psychology courses. Which makes it nice for me—and nice for her. It's fun to go with someone you know and it's fun to discuss 10

---

[2]*Albert Camus* (1913–1960): French novelist, essayist, and playwright. [Eds.]
[3]*Lawrence Welk* (1903–1992): American bandleader and accordion player whose television show ran for almost thirty years. [Eds.]

what you've learned, driving back from the classes." And for the most part, she says, that's all they discuss.

"I'd say that what we're doing is *doing* together, not being to- 11 gether," Suzanne says of her Tuesday-doubles friends. "It's mainly a tennis relationship, but we play together well. And I guess we all need to have a couple of playmates."

I agree.   12

My playmate is a shopping friend, a woman of marvelous taste, a 13 woman who knows exactly *where* to buy *what*, and furthermore is a woman who always knows beyond a doubt what one ought to be buying. I don't have the time to keep up with what's new in eyeshadow, hemlines, and shoes and whether the smock look is in or finished already. But since (oh, shame!) I care a lot about eyeshadow, hemlines, and shoes, and since I don't *want* to wear smocks if the smock look is finished, I'm very glad to have a shopping friend.

3. Historical friends. We all have a friend who knew us when . . . 14 maybe way back in Miss Meltzer's second grade, when our family lived in that three-room flat in Brooklyn, when our dad was out of work for seven months, when our brother Allie got in that fight where they had to call the police, when our sister married the endodontist from Yonkers, and when, the morning after we lost our virginity, she was the first, the only, friend we told.

The years have gone by and we've gone separate ways and we've 15 little in common now, but we're still an intimate part of each other's past. And so whenever we go to Detroit we always go to visit this friend of our girlhood. Who knows how we looked before our teeth were straightened. Who knows how we talked before our voice got un-Brooklyned. Who knows what we ate before we learned about artichokes. And who, by her presence, puts us in touch with an earlier part of ourself, a part of ourself it's important never to lose.

"What this friend means to me and what I mean to her," says 16 Grace, "is having a sister without sibling rivalry. We know the texture of each other's lives. She remembers my grandmother's cabbage soup. I remember the way her uncle played the piano. There's simply no other friend who remembers those things."

4. Crossroads friends. Like historical friends, our crossroads 17 friends are important for *what was* — for the friendship we shared at a crucial, now past, time of life. A time, perhaps, when we roomed in college together; or worked as eager young singles in the Big City together; or went together, as my friend Elizabeth and I did, through pregnancy, birth, and that scary first year of new motherhood.

Crossroads friends forge powerful links, links strong enough to 18
endure with not much more contact than once-a-year letters at
Christmas. And out of respect for those crossroad years, for those
dramas and dreams we once shared, we will always be friends.

5. Cross-generational friends. Historical friends and crossroads 19
friends seem to maintain a special kind of intimacy — dormant but
always ready to be revived — and though we may rarely meet, whenever
we do connect, it's personal and intense. Another kind of intimacy exists
in the friendships that form across generations in what one woman calls
her daughter–mother and her mother–daughter relationships.

Evelyn's friend is her mother's age — "but I share so much more 20
than I ever could with my mother" — a woman she talks to of music,
of books and of life. "What I get from her is the benefit of her experience. What she gets — and enjoys — from me is a youthful perspective. It's a pleasure for both of us."

I have in my own life a precious friend, a woman of 65 who has 21
lived very hard, who is wise, who listens well; who has been where I am
and can help me understand it; and who represents not only an ultimate
ideal mother to me but also the person I'd like to be when I grow up.

In our daughter role we tend to do more than our share of self- 22
revelation; in our mother role we tend to receive what's revealed. It's
another kind of pleasure — playing wise mother to a questing
younger person. It's another very lovely kind of friendship.

6. Part-of-a-couple friends. Some of the women we call our friends 23
we never see alone — we see them as part of a couple at couples' parties.
And though we share interests in many things and respect each other's
views, we aren't moved to deepen the relationship. Whatever the reason, a lack of time or — and this is more likely — a lack of chemistry,
our friendship remains in the context of a group. But the fact that our
feeling on seeing each other is always, "I'm *so* glad she's here" and the
fact that we spend half the evening talking together says that this too,
in its own way, counts as a friendship.

(Other part-of-a-couple friends are the friends that came with the 24
marriage, and some of these are friends we could live without. But
sometimes, alas, she married our husband's best friend; and sometimes, alas, she *is* our husband's best friend. And so we find ourself
dealing with her, somewhat against our will, in a spirit of what I'll
call *reluctant* friendship.)

7. Men who are friends. I wanted to write just of women friends, 25
but the women I've talked to won't let me — they say I must mention
man–woman friendships too. For these friendships can be just as

close and as dear as those that we form with women. Listen to Lucy's description of one such friendship:

"We've found we have things to talk about that are different 26 from what he talks about with my husband and different from what I talk about with his wife. So sometimes we call on the phone or meet for lunch. There are similar intellectual interests — we always pass on to each other the books that we love — but there's also something tender and caring too."

In a couple of crises, Lucy says, "he offered himself for talking 27 and for helping. And when someone died in his family he wanted me there. The sexual, flirty part of our friendship is very small, but *some* — just enough to make it fun and different." She thinks — and I agree — that the sexual part, though small, is always *some*, is always there when a man and a woman are friends.

It's only in the past few years that I've made friends with men, in the 28 sense of a friendship that's *mine*, not just part of two couples. And achieving with them the ease and the trust I've found with women friends has value indeed. Under the dryer at home last week, putting on mascara and rouge, I comfortably sat and talked with a fellow named Peter. Peter, I finally decided, could handle the shock of me minus mascara under the dryer. Because we care for each other. Because we're friends.

8. There are medium friends, and pretty good friends, and very 29 good friends indeed, and these friendships are defined by their level of intimacy. And what we'll reveal at each of these levels of intimacy is calibrated with care. We might tell a medium friend, for example, that yesterday we had a fight with our husband. And we might tell a pretty good friend that this fight with our husband made us so mad that we slept on the couch. And we might tell a very good friend that the reason we got so mad in that fight that we slept on the couch had something to do with that girl that works in his office. But it's only to our very best friends that we're willing to tell all, to tell what's going on with that girl in his office.

The best of friends, I still believe, totally love and support and 30 trust each other, and bare to each other the secrets of their souls, and run — no questions asked — to help each other, and tell harsh truths to each other when they must be told.

But we needn't agree about everything (only 12-year-old girl 31 friends agree about *everything*) to tolerate each other's point of view. To accept without judgment. To give and to take without ever keeping score. And to *be* there, as I am for them and as they are for me, to comfort our sorrows, to celebrate our joys.

QUESTIONS FOR STUDY AND DISCUSSION

1. In her opening paragraph, Viorst explains how she once would have defined *friendship*. Why does she now think differently?
2. What is Viorst's purpose in this essay? (Glossary: *Purpose*) Why is division and classification an appropriate strategy for her to use?
3. Into what categories does Viorst divide her friends?
4. What principles of division does Viorst use to establish her categories of friends? Where does she state these principles?
5. Discuss the ways in which Viorst makes her categories distinct and memorable.
6. What is Viorst's tone in this essay? (Glossary: *Tone*) In what ways is this tone appropriate for both her audience and her subject matter? Explain.

VOCABULARY

Refer to your dictionary to define the following words as they are used in this selection. Then use each word in a sentence of your own.

ardor (2)   forge (18)
nonchalant (3)   dormant (19)
sibling (16)   perspective (20)

CLASSROOM ACTIVITY USING DIVISION AND CLASSIFICATION

The drawing on page 426 is a basic exercise in classification. By determining the features that the figures have in common, establish the general class to which they all belong. Next, establish subclasses by determining the distinctive features that distinguish one subclass from another. Finally, place each figure in an appropriate subclass within your classification system. You may wish to compare your classification system with those developed by other members of your class and to discuss any differences that exist.

SUGGESTED WRITING ASSIGNMENTS

1. Review the categories of friends that Viorst establishes in her essay. Do Viorst's categories apply to your friends? What new categories would you create? Write an essay in which you explain the types of friends in your life.

2. Music can be classified into many different types, such as jazz, country, pop, rock, hard rock, alternative, classical, big band, hip-hop, and so on. Each of these large classifications has a lot of variety within it. Write an essay in which you identify your favorite type of music, then identify at least three subclassifications of the music. Explain the characteristics of each of your categories, using at least two artists to illustrate each.

The Plot against People

■ **Russell Baker**

Russell Baker has had a long and distinguished career as a news-paper reporter and columnist. He was born in Virginia and at-tended Johns Hopkins University. In 1947, he got his first newspaper job with the Baltimore Sun, *then moved to the* New York Times *in 1954, where he wrote the "Observer" column from 1962 to 1998. His columns have been collected in numer-ous books over the years. In 1979, he was awarded the Pulitzer Prize, journalism's highest award, as well as the George Polk award for commentary. Baker's memoir* Growing Up *also re-ceived a Pulitzer in 1983. His autobiographical follow-up,* The Good Times, *appeared in 1989. Baker published an anthology entitled* Russell Baker's Book of American Humor *in 1993 and hosts the series* ExxonMobil Masterpiece Theater *on PBS. An-other essay by Baker appears on pages 195–98.*

FOR YOUR JOURNAL

How do you usually react when your car won't start or your computer won't work? How do you deal with your frustration in such situations?

Inanimate objects are classified scientifically into three major cate- 1
gories—those that break down, those that get lost, and those that don't work.

The goal of all inanimate objects is to resist man and ultimately 2
to defeat him, and the three major classifications are based on the method each object uses to achieve its purpose. As a general rule, any object capable of breaking down at the moment when it is most needed will do so. The automobile is typical of the category.

With the cunning peculiar to its breed, the automobile never 3
breaks down while entering a filling station which has a large staff of idle mechanics. It waits until it reaches a downtown intersection in the middle of the rush hour, or until it is fully loaded with family and luggage on the Ohio Turnpike. Thus it creates maximum

inconvenience, frustration, and irritability, thereby reducing its owner's lifespan.

Washing machines, garbage disposals, lawn mowers, furnaces, TV sets, tape recorders, slide projectors—all are in league with the automobile to take their turn at breaking down whenever life threatens to flow smoothly for their enemies. 4

Many inanimate objects, of course, find it extremely difficult to break down. Pliers, for example, and gloves and keys are almost totally incapable of breaking down. Therefore, they have had to evolve a different technique for resisting man. 5

They get lost. Science has still not solved the mystery of how they do it, and no man has ever caught one of them in the act. The most plausible theory is that they have developed a secret method of locomotion which they are able to conceal from human eyes. 6

It is not uncommon for a pair of pliers to climb all the way from the cellar to the attic in its single-minded determination to raise its owner's blood pressure. Keys have been known to burrow three feet under mattresses. Women's purses, despite their great weight, frequently travel through six or seven rooms to find hiding space under a couch. 7

Scientists have been struck by the fact that things that break down virtually never get lost, while things that get lost hardly ever break down. A furnace, for example, will invariably break down at the depth of the first winter cold wave, but it will never get lost. A woman's purse hardly ever breaks down; it almost invariably chooses to get lost. 8

Some persons believe this constitutes evidence that inanimate objects are not entirely hostile to man. After all, they point out, a furnace could infuriate a man even more thoroughly by getting lost than by breaking down, just as a glove could upset him far more by breaking down than by getting lost. 9

Not everyone agrees, however, that this indicates a conciliatory attitude. Many say it merely proves that furnaces, gloves, and pliers are incredibly stupid. 10

The third class of objects—those that don't work—is the most curious of all. These include such objects as barometers, car clocks . . . flashlights, and toy-train locomotives. It is inaccurate, of course, to say that they *never* work. They work once, usually for the first few hours after being brought home, and then quit. Thereafter, they never work again. 11

In fact, it is widely assumed that they are built for the purpose of not working. Some people have reached advanced ages without ever 12 seeing some of these objects—barometers, for example—in working order.

Science is utterly baffled by the entire category. There are many 13 theories about it. The most interesting holds that the things that don't work have attained the highest state possible for an inanimate object, the state to which things that break down and things that get lost can still only aspire.

They have truly defeated man by conditioning him never to ex- 14 pect anything of them. When his [car clock won't keep time] or his flashlight fails to illuminate, it does not raise his blood pressure. Objects that don't work have given man the only peace he receives from inanimate society.

QUESTIONS FOR STUDY AND DISCUSSION

1. Into what three broad categories does Baker classify inanimate objects? How do you suppose he arrived at these particular categories? In what other ways might inanimate objects be classified?

2. How does Baker organize his essay? Why do you think he waits until the conclusion to discuss objects "that don't work"? (Glossary: *Organization*)

3. How does paragraph 5 act as a transition? How does Baker use this transition to strengthen his classification? (Glossary: *Transition*)

4. Throughout his essay, Baker personifies inanimate objects. What is the effect of his doing so? Identify several specific examples of personification. (Glossary: *Figure of Speech*) Explain the meaning of Baker's title. Why does he use the word *plot*?

5. How does Baker use exemplification in paragraphs 5 and 7? Besides these paragraphs, where else does Baker offer examples? For what purposes does he use them? (Glossary: *Example*)

6. How does Baker make it clear at the beginning of the essay that his approach to the subject is humorous? How does he succeed in being more than simply silly? Point to several passages to illustrate your answer.

VOCABULARY

Refer to your dictionary to define the following words as they are used in this selection. Then use each word in a sentence of your own.

cunning (3)   conciliatory (10)
league (4)   baffled (13)
plausible (6)

CLASSROOM ACTIVITY USING DIVISION AND CLASSIFICATION

Visit a local supermarket, and select one of the many department or product areas (frozen foods, dairy products, cereals, soft drinks, meats, produce) for an exercise in classification. First, establish the general class of products in the area you have selected by determining the features that the products have in common. Next, establish subclasses by determining the features that distinguish one subclass from another. Finally, place the products from your selected area in appropriate subclasses within your classification system.

SUGGESTED WRITING ASSIGNMENTS

1. Using Baker's essay as a model, create a system of classification for one of the following topics. Then write an essay like Baker's classifying objects within that system.

   cars

   friends

   recreational activities

   sports

   Web sites

   students

   music

   pet peeves

2. Most of us have had frustrating experiences with mechanical objects that seem to have perverse minds of their own. Write a narrative recounting one such experience—with a vending machine, a television set, an automobile, a computer, a pay telephone, or any other such object. Be sure to establish a clear context for your essay. (Glossary: *Narration*)

chapter 18

Comparison and Contrast

A **comparison** points out the ways that two or more people, places, or things are alike. A **contrast** points out how they differ. The subjects of a comparison or contrast should be in the same class or general category; if they have nothing in common, there is no good reason for setting them side by side.

The function of any comparison or contrast is to clarify and explain. The writer's purpose may be simply to inform or to make readers aware of similarities or differences that are interesting and significant in themselves. Or the writer may explain something unfamiliar by comparing it with something very familiar, perhaps explaining the game of squash by comparing it with tennis. Finally, the writer can point out the superiority of one thing by contrasting it with another—for example, showing that one product is the best by contrasting it with all its competitors.

As a writer, you have two main options for organizing a comparison or contrast: the subject-by-subject pattern or the point-by-point pattern. For a short essay comparing and contrasting the Atlanta Braves and the Seattle Mariners, you would probably follow the *subject-by-subject* pattern of organization. With this pattern, you first discuss the points you wish to make about one team, and then go on to discuss the corresponding points for the other team. An outline of the body of your essay might look like this:

I. Atlanta Braves
   A. Pitching
   B. Fielding
   C. Hitting
II. Seattle Mariners
   A. Pitching
   B. Fielding
   C. Hitting

The subject-by-subject pattern presents a unified discussion of each team by placing the emphasis on the teams and not on the three points of comparison. Since these points are relatively few, readers should easily remember what was said about the Braves' pitching when you later discuss the Mariners' pitching and should be able to make the appropriate connections between them.

For a somewhat longer essay comparing and contrasting solar energy and wind energy, however, you should consider the *point-by-point* pattern of organization. With this pattern, your essay is organized according to the various points of comparison. Discussion alternates between solar and wind energy for each point of comparison. An outline of the body of your essay might look like this:

I. Installation Expenses	IV. Convenience
A. Solar	A. Solar
B. Wind	B. Wind
II. Efficiency	V. Maintenance
A. Solar	A. Solar
B. Wind	B. Wind
III. Operating Costs	VI. Safety
A. Solar	A. Solar
B. Wind	B. Wind

The point-by-point pattern allows the writer to make immediate comparisons between solar and wind energy, thus enabling readers to consider each of the similarities and differences separately.

Each organizational pattern has its advantages. In general, the subject-by-subject pattern is useful in short essays where there are few points to be considered, whereas the point-by-point pattern is preferable in long essays where there are numerous points under consideration.

A good essay of comparison and contrast tells readers something significant that they do not already know. That is, it must do more than merely point out the obvious. As a rule, therefore, writers tend to draw contrasts between things that are usually perceived as being similar or comparisons between things usually perceived as different. In fact, comparison and contrast often go together. For example, an essay about Minneapolis and St. Paul might begin by showing how much they are alike but end with a series of contrasts revealing how much they differ. A consumer magazine might report the contrasting claims made by six car manufacturers and then go on to demonstrate that the cars all actually do much the same thing in the same way.

The following essay about hunting and photography, entitled "Guns and Cameras," explores the increasing popularity of photographic safaris. After first pointing out the obvious differences between hunting with a gun and hunting with a camera, the writer focuses on the similarities between the two activities that make many hunters "willing to trade their guns for cameras." Notice how she successfully uses the subject-by-subject organizational plan in the body of her essay to explore three key similarities between hunters and photographers.

The hunter has a deep interest in the apparatus he uses to kill his prey. He carries various types of guns, different kinds of ammunition, and special sights and telescopes to increase his chances of success. He knows the mechanics of his guns and understands how and why they work. This fascination with the hardware of his sport is practical — it helps him achieve his goal — but it frequently becomes an end, almost a hobby in itself.

Not until the very end of the long process of stalking an animal does a game hunter use his gun. First he enters into the animal's world. He studies his prey, its habitat, its daily habits, its watering holes and feeding areas, its migration patterns, its enemies and allies, its diet and food chain. Eventually the hunter himself becomes animal-like, instinctively sensing the habits and moves of his prey. Of course, this instinct gives the hunter a better chance of killing the animal; he knows where and when he will get the best shot. But it gives him more than that. Hunting is not just pulling the trigger and killing the prey. Much of it is a multifaceted and ritualistic identification with nature.

After the kill, the hunter can do a number of things with his trophy. He can sell the meat or eat it himself. He can hang the animal's head on the wall or lay its hide on the floor or even sell these objects. But any of these uses is a luxury, and its cost is high. An animal has been destroyed; a life has been eliminated.

Like the hunter, the photographer has a great interest in the tools he uses. He carries various types of cameras, lenses, and film to help him get the picture he wants. He understands the way cameras work, the uses of telephoto and micro lenses, and often the technical procedures of printing and developing. Of course, the time and interest a photographer invests in these mechanical aspects of his art allow him to capture and produce the image he wants. But as with the hunter, these mechanics can and often do become fascinating in themselves.

The wildlife photographer also needs to stalk his "prey" with knowledge and skill in order to get an accurate "shot." Like the hunter, he has to understand the animal's patterns, characteristics, and habitat; he must become animal-like in order to succeed. And like the hunter's, his pursuit is much more prolonged and complicated than the shot itself. The stalking processes are almost identical and give many of the same satisfactions.

The successful photographer also has something tangible to show for his efforts. A still picture of an animal can be displayed in a home, a gallery, a shop; it can be printed in a publication, as a postcard, or as a poster. In fact, a single photograph can be used in all these ways at once; it can be reproduced countless times. And despite all these ways of using his "trophies," the photographer continues to preserve his prey.

–Barbara Bowman, student

Analogy is a special form of comparison. When a subject is unobservable, complex, or abstract—when it is so generally unfamiliar that readers may have trouble understanding it—**analogy** can be most effective. By pointing out certain similarities between a difficult subject and a more familiar or concrete subject, writers can help their readers achieve a firmer grasp of the difficult subject. Unlike a true comparison, though, which analyzes items that belong to the same class—breeds of dogs or types of engines—analogy pairs things from different classes, things that have nothing in common except through the imagination of the writer. In addition, whereas comparison seeks to illuminate specific features of both subjects, the primary purpose of analogy is to clarify the one subject that is complex or unfamiliar. For example, an exploration of the similarities (and differences) between short stories and novels—two forms of fiction—would constitute a logical comparison; short stories and novels belong to the same class (fiction), and your purpose is to reveal something about both. If, however, your purpose is to explain the craft of fiction writing, you might note its similarities to the craft of carpentry. Then you would be drawing an analogy because the two subjects clearly belong to different classes. Carpentry is the more concrete subject and the one more people will have direct experience with. If you use your imagination, you will easily see many ways the tangible work of the carpenter can be used to help readers understand the more abstract work of the novelist. Depending on its purpose, an analogy can be made in several paragraphs to clarify a particular aspect of the larger topic being discussed, as in the example below, or it can provide the organizational strategy for an entire essay.

It has long struck me that the familiar metaphor of "climbing the ladder" for describing the ascent to success or fulfillment in any field is inappropriate and misleading. There are no ladders that lead to success, although there may be some escalators for those lucky enough to follow in a family's fortunes.

A ladder proceeds vertically, rung by rung, with each rung evenly spaced, and with the whole apparatus leaning against a relatively flat and even surface. A child can climb a ladder as easily as an adult, and perhaps with a surer footing.

Making the ascent in one's vocation or profession is far less like ladder climbing than mountain climbing, and here the analogy is a very real one. Going up a mountain requires a variety of skills, and includes a diversity of dangers, that are in no way involved in mounting a ladder.

Young people starting out should be told this, both to dampen their expectations and to allay their disappointments. A mountain is rough and precipitous, with uncertain footing and a predictable number of falls and scrapes, and sometimes one has to take the long way around to reach the shortest distance.

–Sydney J. Harris

Two Ways of Seeing a River

■ **Mark Twain**

Samuel L. Clemens (1835–1910), who wrote under the pen name of Mark Twain, was born in Florida, Missouri, and raised in Hannibal, Missouri. He wrote the novels Tom Sawyer *(1876),* The Prince and the Pauper *(1882),* Huckleberry Finn *(1884), and* A Connecticut Yankee in King Arthur's Court *(1889), as well as many other works of fiction and nonfiction. One of America's most popular writers, Twain is generally regarded as the most important practitioner of the realistic school of writing, a style that emphasizes observable details. The following passage is taken from* Life on the Mississippi *(1883), Twain's study of the great river and his account of his early experiences learning to be a river steamboat pilot. As you read the passage, notice how Twain makes use of figurative language in describing two quite different ways of seeing the Mississippi River.*

FOR YOUR JOURNAL

As we age and gain experience, our interpretation of the same memory—or how we view the same scene—can change. For example, the way we view our own appearance changes all the time, and photos from our childhood or teenage years may surprise us in the decades that follow. Perhaps something we found amusing in our younger days may make us feel uncomfortable or embarrassed now, or the house we grew up in later seems smaller or less appealing. Write about a memory that has changed for you over the years. How does your interpretation of it now contrast with how you experienced it at the time?

N̲ow when I had mastered the language of this water and had come   1
to know every trifling feature that bordered the great river as familiarly as I knew the letters of the alphabet, I had made a valuable acquisition. But I had lost something, too. I had lost something which could never be restored to me while I lived. All the grace, the beauty, the poetry, had gone out of the majestic river! I still kept in mind a certain wonderful sunset which I witnessed when steamboating was new to

me. A broad expanse of the river was turned to blood; in the middle distance the red hue brightened into gold, through which a solitary log came floating, black and conspicuous; in one place a long, slanting mark lay sparkling upon the water; in another the surface was broken by boiling, tumbling rings that were as many-tinted as an opal; where the ruddy flush was faintest was a smooth spot that was covered with graceful circles and radiating lines, ever so delicately traced; the shore on our left was densely wooded, and the somber shadow that fell from this forest was broken in one place by a long, ruffled trail that shone like silver; and high above the forest wall a clean-stemmed dead tree waved a single leafy bough that glowed like a flame in the unobstructed splendor that was flowing from the sun. There were graceful curves, reflected images, woody heights, soft distances, and over the whole scene, far and near, the dissolving lights drifted steadily, enriching it every passing moment with new marvels of coloring.

I stood like one bewitched. I drank it in, in a speechless rapture.   2
The world was new to me and I had never seen anything like this at home. But as I have said, a day came when I began to cease from noting the glories and the charms which the moon and the sun and the twilight wrought upon the river's face; another day came when I ceased altogether to note them. Then, if that sunset scene had been repeated, I should have looked upon it without rapture and should have commented upon it inwardly after this fashion: "This sun means that we are going to have wind tomorrow; that floating log means that the river is rising, small thanks to it; that slanting mark on the water refers to a bluff reef which is going to kill somebody's steamboat one of these nights, if it keeps on stretching out like that; those tumbling 'boils' show a dissolving bar and a changing channel there; the lines and circles in the slick water over yonder are a warning that that troublesome place is shoaling up dangerously; that silver streak in the shadow of the forest is the 'break' from a new snag and he has located himself in the very best place he could have found to fish for steamboats; that tall dead tree, with a single living branch, is not going to last long, and then how is a body ever going to get through this blind place at night without the friendly old landmark?"

No, the romance and beauty were all gone from the river. All the   3
value any feature of it had for me now was the amount of usefulness it could furnish toward compassing the safe piloting of a steamboat. Since those days, I have pitied doctors from my heart. What does the lovely flush in a beauty's cheek mean to a doctor but a "break" that ripples above some deadly disease? Are not all her visible charms

sown thick with what are to him the signs and symbols of hidden decay? Does he ever see her beauty at all, or doesn't he simply view her professionally and comment upon her unwholesome condition all to himself? And doesn't he sometimes wonder whether he has gained most or lost most by learning his trade?

QUESTIONS FOR STUDY AND DISCUSSION

1. What method of organization does Twain use in this selection? (Glossary: *Organization*) What alternative methods might he have used? What would have been gained or lost?

2. Explain the analogy that Twain uses in paragraph 3. What is his purpose in using this analogy? (Glossary: *Analogy*)

3. Explain this sentence of Twain's: "All the grace, the beauty, the poetry, had gone out of the majestic river!" (1). What is "the poetry"? Why was it lost for him?

4. Twain uses a number of similes and metaphors in this selection. Identify three of each, and explain what Twain is comparing in each case. What do these figures of speech add to Twain's writing? (Glossary: *Figure of Speech*)

5. Now that he has learned the trade of steamboating, does Twain feel he has "gained most or lost most" (3)? What has he gained, and what has he lost?

VOCABULARY

Refer to your dictionary to define the following words as they are used in this selection. Then use each word in a sentence of your own.

acquisition (1)   rapture (2)
hue (1)   romance (3)
opal (1)

CLASSROOM ACTIVITY USING COMPARISON AND CONTRAST

Compare two places that have the same purpose. For example, compare your college cafeteria with your dining room at home, or the classroom you are in now with another one on campus. Draw up a list of descriptive adjectives for each, and discuss them with your classmates. What do you like about each place? What do you dislike?

What do you learn from comparing them? How important are your surroundings to you?

SUGGESTED WRITING ASSIGNMENTS

1. Twain's essay contrasts the perception of one person before and after acquiring a particular body of knowledge. Of course, different people usually do perceive the same scene or event differently, even if they are experiencing it simultaneously. To use an example from Twain's writing, a poet and a doctor might perceive a rosy-cheeked young woman in entirely different ways. Write a comparison and contrast essay in which you show how two people with different experience might perceive the same subject. It can be a case of profound difference, such as a musician and an electrician at the same pyrotechnic rock music concert, or more subtle, such as a novelist and a screenwriter seeing the same lovers' quarrel in a restaurant. Add a short postscript in which you explain your choice of subject-by-subject comparison or point-by-point comparison in your essay.

2. Learning how to drive a car may not be as involved as learning how to pilot a steamboat on the Mississippi River, but it still has a tremendous impact on how we function and on how we perceive our surroundings. Write an essay about a short trip you took as a passenger and as a driver. Compare and contrast your perceptions and actions. What is most important to you as a passenger? What is most important to you as a driver? How do your perceptions shift between the two roles? What changes in what you notice around you and in the way you notice it?

Loose Ends

■ Rita Dove

Pulitzer Prize–winning poet Rita Dove was born in Akron, Ohio, in 1952 and received her bachelor's degree from Miami University of Ohio in 1973. After two semesters as a Fulbright scholar at Universitat Tubingen in Germany, Dove enrolled in the University of Iowa Writers' Workshop, where she earned her master's in 1977. She has published seven poetry collections, including The Yellow House on the Corner *(1980),* Museum *(1983),* Thomas and Beulah *(1986),* Mother Love *(1995), and* On the Bus with Rosa Parks *(1999); a book of short stories,* Fifth Sunday *(1985); a novel,* Through the Ivory Gate *(1992); and a collection of essays,* The Poet's World *(1995). Dove served as poet laureate of the United States from 1993 to 1995. From 1981 to 1989, she taught at Arizona State University; currently, she is Commonwealth Professor of English at the University of Virginia. "Loose Ends" was first published in* The Poet's World. *Starting with a simple anecdote about her daughter's behavior, Dove prepares readers for what she has to say about Americans, reality, and television. Notice how she uses comparison to highlight what she sees as our culture's seeming preference for television over reality.*

FOR YOUR JOURNAL

What are your thoughts about the new "reality" television programs? What is so "real" about them? How do these shows differ from regular television programming?

For years the following scene would play daily at our house: Home from school, my daughter would heave her backpack off her shoulder and let it thud to the hall floor, then dump her jacket on top of the pile. My husband would tell her to pick it up—as he did every day—and hang it in the closet. Begrudgingly with a snort and a hrrumph, she would comply. The ritual interrogation began: 1

"Hi, Aviva. How was school?"

"Fine." 2

3

"What did you do today?" [4]

"Nothing." [5]

And so it went, every day. We cajoled, we pleaded, we threatened [6]
with rationed ice cream sandwiches and new healthy vegetable
casseroles, we attempted subterfuges such as: "What was Ms. Boyers
wearing today?" or: "Any new pets in science class?" but her answer
remained the same: I dunno.

Asked, however, about that week's episodes of "MathNet," her [7]
favorite series on Public Television's "Square One," or asked for a
quick gloss of a segment of "Lois and Clark" that we happened to
miss, and she'd spew out the details of a complicated story, complete
with character development, gestures, every twist and back-flip of the
plot.

Is TV greater than reality? Are we to take as damning evidence [8]
the soap opera stars attacked in public by viewers who obstinately
believe in the on-screen villainy of Erica or Jeannie's evil twin? Is an
estrangement from real life the catalyst behind the escalating violence
in our schools, where children imitate the gun-'em-down pyrotechnics of cop-and-robber shows?

Such a conclusion is too easy. Yes, the influence of public media [9]
on our perceptions is enormous, but the relationship of projected reality—i.e., TV—to imagined reality—i.e., an existential moment—
is much more complex. It is not that we confuse TV with reality, but
that we prefer it to reality—the manageable struggle resolved in
twenty-six minutes, the witty repartee within the family circle instead
of the grunts and silence common to most real families; the sharp-
ened conflict and defined despair instead of vague anxiety and invisible enemies. "Life, my friends, is boring. We must not say so," wrote
John Berryman,[1] and many years and Dream Songs"[2] later he leapt
from a bridge in Minneapolis. But there is a devastating corollary to
that statement: Life, friends, is ragged. Loose ends are the rule.

What happens when my daughter tells the television's story [10]
better than her own is simply this: the TV offers an easier tale to tell.
The salient points are there for the plucking—indeed, they're the
only points presented—and all she has to do is to recall them. Instant
Nostalgia! Life, on the other hand, slithers about and runs down
blind alleys and sometimes just fizzles at the climax. "The world is

---

[1]*John Berryman* (1914–1972): American poet. [Eds.]

[2]*"Dream Songs"*: two of Berryman's books of poetry that together create a sequence
of 385 "dream songs." [Eds.]

ugly, / And the people are sad," sings the country bumpkin in Wallace Stevens's[3] "Gubinnal." Who isn't tempted to ignore the inexorable fact of our insignificance on a dying planet? We all yearn for our private patch of blue.

QUESTIONS FOR STUDY AND DISCUSSION

1. What is Dove's thesis in this essay? (Glossary: *Thesis*)

2. In the first seven paragraphs, Dove contrasts her daughter's inability to tell what went on at school with her ability to relate all the details of what happened on an episode of *Lois and Clark*. How effectively do these paragraphs function as a beginning for the essay? What conclusions, if any, does Dove arrive at for the situation she describes?

3. Dove uses a number of strong action verbs in her essay to show readers her characters' actions. For example, in her second sentence she uses the descriptive, emotion-laden verbs *heave* and *dump* instead of the less-descriptive verbs *throw* and *drop*. (Glossary: *Diction*) Identify other strong verbs that Dove uses, and explain what they add to her essay.

4. Paragraph 8 consists of three rhetorical questions. (Glossary: *Rhetorical Question*) How do these questions function in the context of the essay?

5. In paragraph 9 Dove contrasts television with reality. How does Dove organize this comparison? What differences does she see between the two? Do you agree with her analysis? Explain.

6. Identify the transitional devices Dove uses to link one paragraph to the next. (Glossary: *Transition*) Which ones work best?

VOCABULARY

Refer to your dictionary to define the following words as they are used in this selection. Then use each word in a sentence of your own.

ritual (1)   subterfuges (6)
interrogation (1)   gloss (7)
cajoled (6)   segment (7)

---

[3]*Wallace Stevens* (1879–1955): American poet. [Eds.]

estrangement (8)   corollary (9)
pyrotechnics (8)   salient (10)
existential (9)   inexorable (10)
repartee (9)

CLASSROOM ACTIVITY USING COMPARISON AND CONTRAST

Carefully read and analyze the following paragraph taken from Suzanne Britt's "That Lean and Hungry Look," an essay that first appeared in *Newsweek* and later became the basis for her book *Skinny People Are Dull and Crunchy Like Carrots* (1982). Then answer the questions that follow.

> Some people say the business about the jolly fat person is a myth, that all of us chubbies are neurotic, sick, sad people. I disagree. Fat people may not be chortling all day long, but they're a hell of a lot *nicer* than the wizened and shriveled. Thin people turn surly, mean, and hard at a young age because they never learn the value of a hot-fudge sundae for easing tension. Thin people don't like gooey soft things because they themselves are neither gooey nor soft. They are crunchy and dull, like carrots. They go straight to the heart of the matter while fat people let things stay all blurry and hazy and vague, the way things actually are. Thin people want to face the truth. Fat people know there is no truth. One of my thin friends is always staring at complex, unsolvable problems and saying, "The key thing is . . . ." Fat people never say that. They know there isn't any such thing as the key thing about anything.

What is the point of Britt's paragraph? How does she use comparison and contrast to make this point? How has Britt organized her paragraph?

SUGGESTED WRITING ASSIGNMENTS

1. Do you agree with Dove's view that "It is not that we confuse TV with reality, but that we prefer it to reality" (9)? If we accept this view, what does it say about our culture and us as a people? Write an essay in which you explore this question. You may find it helpful to consider one or more of the following questions before you start writing. What are your favorite television programs? Are you intrigued by any of the new so-called reality

shows? What do you like about these programs? Do you prefer what you see on television to what is going on in your own life?

2. Dove tells us that "Life, friends, is ragged. Loose ends are the rule" (9). Unlike television, "life . . . slithers about and runs down blind alleys and sometimes just fizzles at the climax" (10). Do you agree with Dove's assessment? Write an essay in which you use examples from your own experiences or observations to support your position.

A Battle of Cultures

■ **K. Connie Kang**

K. Connie Kang was born in Korea in 1942 but grew up in Japan and the United States. After graduating from the School of Journalism at the University of Missouri, Kang went on to earn a master of science degree from the Medill School of Journalism at Northwestern University. During more than three decades in journalism, this award-winning newspaperwoman has worked as a reporter, editor, foreign correspondent, columnist, and editorial writer for the San Francisco Examiner, *the* San Francisco Chronicle, *and* United Press International. *Currently, she is a reporter for the* Los Angeles Times. *Kang's career began in June 1964, when there were only a handful of Asians in the metropolitan newsrooms in the United States. Always mindful of her Asian heritage, she wrote about Asians and the issues affecting their communities long before they were considered newsworthy. In 1995, she published* Home Was the Land of Morning Calm: A Saga of a Korean American Family. *The following essay, which first appeared in* Asian Week *in May 1990, reminds us that we need both "cultural insight" and understanding if we are to "make democracy work" in a multicultural society. Notice how Kang uses comparison and contrast when presenting aspects of Korean and African American cultures to demonstrate her point.*

FOR YOUR JOURNAL

People of different ethnic, racial, and cultural backgrounds sometimes find it difficult to achieve a common ground of understanding. What suggestions do you have for what we can do, either personally or through our institutions, to increase understanding? Rather than composing an answer, make a list of several suggestions that you would like to contribute to a classroom discussion.

A volatile inner-city drama is taking place in New York where   1
blacks have been boycotting Korean groceries for four months.

The recent attack on three Vietnamese men by a group of blacks 2
who mistook them for Koreans has brought this long-simmering tension between two minority groups to the world's attention. Korean
newspapers from San Francisco to Seoul have been running front-
page stories. Non-Asian commentators around the country, whose
knowledge of Korea may not be much more than images from the
Korean War and the ridiculous television series "M.A.S.H.,"[1] are
making all sorts of comments.

As I see it, the problem in the Flatbush area of Brooklyn started 3
with cultural misunderstanding and was compounded by a lack of
bilingual and bicultural community leaders to intervene quickly.

Frictions between Korean store owners in New York and blacks 4
had been building for years. Korean merchants have been complain-
ing about thefts. On the other hand, their black customers have been
accusing immigrant store owners of making money in their neighborhoods without putting anything back into the community. They have
also complained about store owners being brusque. Over the past
eight years, there have been sporadic boycotts but none has lasted as
long as the current one, which stemmed from an accusation by a
black customer in January that she had been attacked by a store employee. In defense, the store owner has said the employee caught the
woman stealing.

The attack on the Vietnamese on May 13 wasn't the first time 5
one group of Asians has been mistaken for another in America. But
the publicity surrounding the case has made this unfortunate situation a case study in inter-ethnic tension.

What's missing in this inner-city drama is cultural insight. 6

What struck me more than anything was a recent remark by a 7
black resident: "The Koreans are a very, very rude people. They don't
understand you have to smile."

I wondered whether her reaction would have been the same, had 8
she known that Koreans don't smile at Koreans either without a reason.
To a Korean, a smile is not a facial expression he can turn on and off
mechanically. Koreans have a word for it — "mu-ttuk-ttuk-hada"
(stiff). In other words, the Korean demeanor is "myu-po-jung" — lack
of expression.

It would be an easy thing for blacks who are naturally friendly 9
and gregarious to misunderstand Korean ways.

---

[1] "M.A.S.H.": a popular television series, set in Korea, that ran from 1972 to 1983.
The initials stand for "Mobile Army Surgical Hospital." [Eds.]

As a Korean American I've experienced this many times. When- 10
ever I'm in Korea, which is often, I'm chided for smiling too much.
"Why do you smile so easily? You act like a Westerner," people tell me.
My inclination is to retort: "Why do you always have to look like
you've got indigestion?" But I restrain myself because I know better.

In our culture, a smile is reserved for people we know and for a 11
proper occasion. Herein lies a big problem when newcomers from Korea
begin doing business in America's poor inner-city neighborhoods.

Culturally and socially, many newcomers from Korea, like other 12
Asian immigrants, are ill-equipped to run businesses in America's
inner cities. But because they are denied entry into mainstream job
markets, they pool resources and open mom-and-pop operations in
the only places where they can afford it. They work 14 and 15 hours
a day, seven days a week, dreaming of the day when their children
will graduate from prestigious schools and make their sacrifices
worthwhile.

From the other side, inner-city African Americans must wonder 13
how these new immigrants find the money to run their own businesses, when they themselves can't even get a small loan from a bank.
Their hope of getting out of the poverty cycle is grim, yet they see
newcomers living in better neighborhoods and driving new cars.

"They ask me, 'Where do you people get the money to buy a 14
business?'" Bong-jae Jang, owner of one of the grocery stores being
boycotted, told me. "How can I explain to my neighbors in my poor
English the concept of our family system, the idea of 'kye' (uniquely
Korean private money-lending system), our way of life?"

I think a little learning is in order on both sides. Korean immi- 15
grants, like other newcomers, need orientation before they leave their
country as well as when they arrive in the United States. It's also important for Korean immigrants, like other Asians who live in the
United States, to realize that they are indebted to blacks for the social
gains won by their civil rights struggle. They face less discrimination
today because blacks have paved the way. Instead of looking down
on their culture, it would be constructive to learn their history, literature, music and values and see our African American brothers and
sisters in their full humanity.

I think it is also important to remind ourselves that while the 16
Confucian culture[2] has taught us how to be good parents, sons, and

---

[2]*Confucian culture:* the traditions based on the ideas of Confucius (551–479 B.C.E.),
China's most famous and influential teacher, philosopher, and political theorist. [Eds.]

daughters and how to behave with people we know, it has not prepared us for living in a democracy. The Confucian ethos lacks the value of social conscience, which makes democracy work.

It isn't enough that we think of educating our children and send 17
them to the best schools. We need to think of other peoples' children, too. Most of all, we need to be more tolerant of other peoples' cultures. We need to celebrate our similarities as well as our differences.

Jang, the grocer, told me this experience has been painful but he 18
has learned an important lesson. "We Koreans must learn to participate in this society," he said. "When this is over, I'm going to reach out. I want to give part-time work to black youths."

He also told me that he has been keeping a journal. "I'm not a 19
writer but I've been keeping a journal," he said. "I want to write about this experience someday. It may help someone."

By reaching out, we can make a difference. The Korean grocer's 20
lesson is a reminder to us all that making democracy work in a multi-cultural society is difficult but we have no choice but to strive for it.

QUESTIONS FOR STUDY AND DISCUSSION

1. What is the "battle of cultures" named in the title? (Glossary: *Title*) How are the contrasts between the cultures helping to cause the "battle," according to Kang? What specific differences does she identify in her comparison and contrast analysis of the situation?

2. What is Kang's thesis? (Glossary: *Thesis*) How does her use of comparison and contrast help her argue her thesis?

3. Why are the Korean grocery stores being boycotted by African American customers? (Glossary: *Cause and Effect*)

4. Why are most Asian immigrants ill-equipped to run businesses in the inner cities of the United States, according to Kang? Why are they indebted to African Americans?

5. How does Kang's point of view contribute to the effectiveness of the essay? (Glossary: *Point of View*)

6. What is it about their culture that makes it difficult for Koreans to adapt to life in a multicultural society?

VOCABULARY

Refer to your dictionary to define the following words as they are used in this selection. Then use each word in a sentence of your own.

volatile (1)

boycotting (1)

bilingual (3)

intervene (3)

brusque (4)

sporadic (4)

gregarious (9)

inclination (10)

ethos (16)

CLASSROOM ACTIVITY USING COMPARISON AND CONTRAST

Review the discussion of analogy in the introduction to this chapter, and then create an analogy to explain your relationship with one of your parents or with a relative.

SUGGESTED WRITING ASSIGNMENTS

1. Choose an ethnic group other than your own that lives in or near your home community. Using Kang's essay as a model, compare and/or contrast its culture with your own. What could you do to understand the other culture better? How would you describe relations between the two groups?

2. Choose a country that you have studied, visited, or at least read about. Compare who you are now with who you think you would be if you had been born and raised in that country. How do you think you would be different? Why?

Grant and Lee: A Study in Contrasts

■ Bruce Catton

Bruce Catton (1899–1978) was born in Petoskey, Michigan, and attended Oberlin College. Early in his career, Catton *worked as a reporter for various newspapers, among them the* Cleveland Plain Dealer. Having an interest in history, Catton *became a leading authority on the Civil War and published a number of books on this subject.* These books include Mr. *Lincoln's* Army *(1951),* Glory Road *(1952),* A Stillness at Appomattox *(1953),* The Hallowed Ground *(1956),* The Coming Fury *(1961),* Never Call Retreat *(1966), and* Gettysburg: The Final Fury *(1974).* Catton was awarded both the Pulitzer Prize and the National Book Award in 1954.

The following selection was included in The American Story: The Age of Exploration to the Age of the Atom *(1956), a collection of historical essays edited by Earl Schenk Miers. In it Catton considers "two great Americans, Grant and Lee—very different, yet under everything very much alike." As you read, pay particular attention to the way Catton has organized his essay of comparison and contrast and how this organization helps readers follow Catton's thinking.*

FOR YOUR JOURNAL

Do a brief freewrite about the Civil War generals Ulysses S. Grant and Robert E. Lee. What do you know about each man and his respective role in the war? What images do you have, and what stories have you heard about each one?

W hen Ulysses S. Grant[1] and Robert E. Lee[2] met in the parlor of a modest house at Appomattox Court House, Virginia, on April 9, 1865, to work out the terms for the surrender of Lee's Army of Northern Virginia, a great chapter in American life came to a close, and a great new chapter began. 1

These men were bringing the Civil War to its virtual finish. To be sure, other armies had yet to surrender, and for a few days the fugitive Confederate government[3] would struggle desperately and vainly, trying to find some way to go on living now that its chief support was gone. But in effect it was all over when Grant and Lee signed the papers. And the little room where they wrote out the terms was the scene of one of the poignant, dramatic contrasts in American history. 2

They were two strong men, these oddly different generals, and they represented the strengths of two conflicting currents that, through them, had come into final collision. 3

Back of Robert E. Lee was the notion that the old aristocratic concept might somehow survive and be dominant in American life. 4

Lee was tidewater Virginia, and in his background were family, culture, and tradition . . . the age of chivalry transplanted to a New World which was making its own legends and its own myths. He embodied a way of life that had come down through the age of knighthood and the English country squire. America was a land that was beginning all over again, dedicated to nothing much more complicated than the rather hazy belief that all men had equal rights and should have an equal chance in the world. In such a land Lee stood for the feeling that it was somehow of advantage to human society to have a pronounced inequality in the social structure. There should be a leisure class, backed by ownership of land; in turn, society itself should be keyed to the land as the chief source of wealth and influence. It would bring forth (according to this ideal) a class of men with a strong sense of obligation to the community; men who lived not to gain advantage for themselves, but to meet the solemn obligations 5

---

[1]*Ulysses S. Grant* (1822–1885): commander of the Union armies during the late years (1864–65) of the American Civil War, and eighteenth president of the United States (1869–77). [Eds.]

[2]*Robert E. Lee* (1807–1870): Confederate general, commander of the Army of Northern Virginia, the most successful of the Southern armies during the American Civil War (1861–65). [Eds.]

[3]*Confederate government:* also called the Confederacy, the American Civil War government of 11 Southern states that seceded from the Union. [Eds.]

which had been laid on them by the very fact that they were privileged. From them the country would get its leadership; to them it could look for the higher values — of thought, of conduct, of personal deportment — to give it strength and virtue.

Lee embodied the noblest elements of this aristocratic ideal. 6 Through him, the landed nobility justified itself. For four years, the Southern states had fought a desperate war to uphold the ideals for which Lee stood. In the end, it almost seemed as if the Confederacy fought for Lee; as if he himself was the Confederacy . . . the best thing that the way of life for which the Confederacy stood could ever have to offer. He had passed into legend before Appomattox.[4] Thousands of tired, underfed, poorly clothed Confederate soldiers, long since past the simple enthusiasm of the early days of the struggle, somehow considered Lee the symbol of everything for which they had been willing to die. But they could not quite put this feeling into words. If the Lost Cause, sanctified by so much heroism and so many deaths, had a living justification, its justification was General Lee.

Grant, the son of a tanner on the Western frontier, was everything Lee was not. He had come up the hard way and embodied nothing in particular except the eternal toughness and sinewy fiber of the men who grew up beyond the mountains. He was one of a body of men who owed reverence and obeisance to no one, who were self-reliant to a fault, who cared hardly anything for the past but who had a sharp eye for the future.

These frontier men were the precise opposite of the tidewater 8 aristocrats. Back of them, in the great surge that had taken people over the Alleghenies and into the opening Western country, there was a deep, implicit dissatisfaction with a past that had settled into grooves. They stood for democracy, not from any reasoned conclusion about the proper ordering of human society, but simply because they had grown up in the middle of democracy and knew how it worked. Their society might have privileges, but they would be privileges each man had won for himself. Forms and patterns meant nothing. No man was born to anything, except perhaps to a chance to show how far he could rise. Life was competition.

Yet along with this feeling had come a deep sense of belonging to 9 a national community. The Westerner who developed a farm, opened

---

[4]*Appomattox:* a town in Virginia, site of the courthouse where the Confederate forces surrendered on April 9, 1865. [Eds.]

a shop, or set up in business as a trader, could hope to prosper only as his own community prospered—and his community ran from the Atlantic to the Pacific and from Canada down to Mexico. If the land was settled, with towns and highways and accessible markets, he could better himself. He saw his fate in terms of the nation's own destiny. As its horizons expanded, so did his. He had, in other words, an acute dollars-and-cents stake in the continued growth and development of his country.

And that, perhaps, is where the contrast between Grant and Lee 10 becomes most striking. The Virginia aristocrat, inevitably, saw himself in relation to his own region. He lived in a static society which could endure almost anything except change. Instinctively, his first loyalty would go to the locality in which that society existed. He would fight to the limit of endurance to defend it, because in defending it he was defending everything that gave his own life its deepest meaning.

The Westerner, on the other hand, would fight with an equal 11 tenacity for the broader concept of society. He fought so because everything he lived by was tied to growth, expansion, and a constantly widening horizon. What he lived by would survive or fall with the nation itself. He could not possibly stand by unmoved in the face of an attempt to destroy the Union.[5] He would combat it with everything he had, because he could only see it as an effort to cut the ground out from under his feet.

So Grant and Lee were in complete contrast, representing two 12 diametrically opposed elements in American life. Grant was the modern man emerging; beyond him, ready to come on the stage, was the great age of steel and machinery, of crowded cities and a restless burgeoning vitality. Lee might have ridden down from the old age of chivalry, lance in hand, silken banner fluttering over his head. Each man was the perfect champion of his cause, drawing both his strengths and his weaknesses from the people he led.

Yet it was not all contrast, after all. Different as they were—in 13 background, in personality, in underlying aspiration—these two great soldiers had much in common. Under everything else, they were marvelous fighters. Furthermore, their fighting qualities were really very much alike.

Each man had, to begin with, the great virtue of utter tenacity 14 and fidelity. Grant fought his way down the Mississippi Valley in

---

[5] *Union:* the federal government of the United States. [Eds.]

spite of acute personal discouragement and profound military handicaps. Lee hung on in the trenches at Petersburg after hope itself had died. In each man there was an indomitable quality . . . the born fighter's refusal to give up as long as he can still remain on his feet and lift his two fists.

Daring and resourcefulness they had, too; the ability to think 15 faster and move faster than the enemy. These were the qualities which gave Lee the dazzling campaigns of Second Manassas and Chancellorsville and won Vicksburg[6] for Grant.

Lastly, and perhaps greatest of all, there was the ability, at the 16 end, to turn quickly from war to peace once the fighting was over. Out of the way these two men behaved at Appomattox came the possibility of a peace of reconciliation. It was a possibility not wholly realized, in the years to come, but which did, in the end, help the two sections to become one nation again . . . after a war whose bitterness might have seemed to make such a reunion wholly impossible. No part of either man's life became him more than the part he played in their brief meeting in the McLean house[7] at Appomattox. Their behavior there put all succeeding generations of Americans in their debt. Two great Americans, Grant and Lee—very different, yet under everything very much alike. Their encounter at Appomattox was one of the great moments of American history.

QUESTIONS FOR STUDY AND DISCUSSION

1. In paragraphs 10–12 Catton discusses what he considers to be the most striking contrast between Grant and Lee. What is that difference?

2. List the similarities that Catton sees between Grant and Lee. What similarity does Catton believe is most important? Why?

3. What would have been lost had Catton compared Grant and Lee before contrasting them? Would anything have been gained?

4. How does Catton organize the body of his essay—paragraphs 3 through 16? You may find it helpful in answering this question

---

[6]*Second Manassas, Chancellorsville, Vicksburg:* significant battles during the American Civil War. [Eds.]
[7]*McLean house:* the specific building of the Appomattox Court House in which Lee formally surrendered to Grant. [Eds.]

to summarize the point of comparison in each paragraph and label it as being concerned with Lee, Grant, or both.

5. What attitudes and ideas does Catton describe to support the view that tidewater Virginia was a throwback to the "age of chivalry" (5)?

6. Catton claims that Grant was "the modern man emerging" (12). How does he support that statement? Do you agree?

7. Catton has constructed clear transitions between paragraphs. Identify the transitional devices he uses. How do they help you read the essay? (Glossary: *Transition*)

VOCABULARY

Refer to your dictionary to define the following words as they are used in this selection. Then use each word in a sentence of your own.

poignant (2)	obeisance (7)
chivalry (5)	tidewater (8)
sanctified (6)	tenacity (11)
sinewy (7)	aspiration (13)

CLASSROOM ACTIVITY USING COMPARISON AND CONTRAST

In preparation for writing an essay of comparison and contrast on two world leaders (or popular singers, actors, or sports figures), write out answers to the following questions:

Who could I compare and contrast?

What is my purpose?

Are the similarities or differences more interesting?

What specific points should I discuss?

What organizational pattern will best suit my purpose: subject-by-subject or point-by-point?

SUGGESTED WRITING ASSIGNMENTS

1. Using your answers to the classroom activity above as your starting point, write an essay in which you compare and contrast any two world leaders (or popular singers, actors, or sports figures).

2. Select one of the following topics, and write an essay of comparison and contrast:

two cities
two friends
two ways to heat a home
two restaurants
two sections of the town you live in
two mountains
two books by the same author
two cars
two teachers
two brands of pizza

Cause and Effect

Every time you try to answer a question that asks *why*, you engage in the process of *causal analysis*—you attempt to determine a *cause* or series of causes for a particular *effect*. When you try to answer a question that asks *what if*, you attempt to determine what *effect* will result from a particular *cause*. You will have frequent opportunity to use **cause-and-effect** analysis in the writing that you will do in college. For example, in history you might be asked to determine the causes for the 1991 breakup of the former Soviet Union; in political science you might be asked to determine the critical issues in the 2000 presidential election; in sociology you might be asked to analyze the effects that the AIDS epidemic has had on sexual-behavior patterns among Americans; and in economics you might be asked to predict what will happen to our country if we enact large tax cuts.

Fascinated by the effects that private real estate development was having on his neighborhood, a student writer decided to find out what was happening in the older sections of cities across the country.

In the first paragraph, Kevin Cunningham describes three possible effects (or fates) of a city's aging. In his second paragraph, he singles out one effect, redevelopment, and discusses in detail the impact it has had on Hoboken.

> *Effect: decay*
>
> *Effect: urban re- newal*
>
> One of three fates awaits the aging neighborhood. Decay may continue until the neighborhood becomes a slum. It may face urban renewal, with old buildings being razed and ugly new apartment houses taking their place. Or it may undergo redevelopment, in which government encourages the upgrading of existing housing stock by offering low-interest loans or outright grants; thus, the original character of the neighborhood may be retained or restored, allowing the city to keep part of its identity.
>
> *Effect: redevel- opment*
>
> *Effects of redevel- opment*
>
> An example of redevelopment at its best is Hoboken, New Jersey. In the early 1970s Hoboken

was a dying city, with rundown housing and many abandoned buildings. However, low-interest loans enabled some younger residents to refurbish their homes, and soon the area began to show signs of renewed vigor. Even outsiders moved in and rebuilt some of the abandoned houses. Today, whole blocks have been restored, and neighborhood life is active again. The city does well, too, because property values are higher and so are property taxes.

–Kevin Cunningham, student

Determining causes and effects is usually thought-provoking and quite complex. One reason for this is that there are two types of causes: *immediate causes,* which are readily apparent because they are closest to the effect, and *ultimate causes,* which, being somewhat removed, are not as apparent and may perhaps even be hidden. Furthermore, ultimate causes may bring about effects which themselves become immediate causes, thus creating a *causal chain.* Consider the following causal chain: Sally, a computer salesperson, prepared extensively for a meeting with an important client (ultimate cause), impressed the client (immediate cause), and made a very large sale (effect). The chain did not stop there: the large sale caused her to be promoted by her employer (effect). For a detailed example of a causal chain, read Barry Commoner's analysis of the near disaster at the Three Mile Island nuclear facility (pp. 107–08).

A second reason why causal analysis can be so complex is that an effect may have any number of possible or actual causes, and a cause may have any number of possible or actual effects. An upset stomach may be caused by eating spoiled food, but it may also be caused by overeating, flu, allergy, nervousness, pregnancy, or any combination of factors. Similarly, the high cost of electricity may have multiple effects: higher profits for utility companies, fewer sales of electrical appliances, higher prices for other products, and the development of alternative sources of energy.

Sound reasoning and logic, while present in all good writing, are central to any causal analysis. Writers of believable causal analysis examine their material objectively and develop their essays carefully. They examine methodically all causes and effects and evaluate them. They are convinced by their own examination of the material but are not afraid to admit other possible causes and effects. Above all, they do not let their own prejudices interfere with the logic of their analyses and presentations.

Because people are accustomed to thinking of causes with their effects, they sometimes commit an error in logic known as the "after this, therefore because of this" fallacy (in Latin, *post hoc, ergo propter hoc*). This **logical fallacy** leads people to believe that because one event occurred after another event, the first event somehow caused the second; that is, they sometimes make causal connections that are not proven. For example, if students began to perform better after a free breakfast program was instituted at their school, one could not assume that the improvement was caused by the breakfast program. There could, of course, be any number of other causes for this effect, and a responsible writer would analyze and consider them all before suggesting the cause.

Why We Crave Horror Movies

■ **Stephen King**

Stephen King's name is synonymous with horror stories. A 1970 graduate of the University of Maine, King worked as a janitor in a knitting mill, a laundry worker, and a high school English teacher before he struck it big with his writing. Many consider King to be the most successful writer of modern horror fiction today. To date, he has written dozens of novels, collections of short stories and novellas, and screenplays, among other works. His books have sold well over 250 million copies worldwide, and many of his novels have been made into popular motion pictures, including Stand by Me, Misery, The Green Mile, *and* Dreamcatcher. *His books, starting with* Carrie *in 1974, include* Salem's Lot *(1975),* The Shining *(1977),* The Dead Zone *(1979),* Christine *(1983),* Pet Sematary *(1983),* The Dark Half *(1989),* The Girl Who Loved Tom Gordon *(1999),* From a Buick 8 *(2002), and* Everything's Eventual: Five Dark Tales *(2002), his first collection of short stories in nine years. Other works of his include* Danse Macabre *(1980), a nonfiction look at horror in the media, and* On Writing: A Memoir of the Craft *(2000). Each year King and his wife, novelist Tabitha King, donate at least 10 percent of their pretaxable income to charitable organizations, many of them local. The widespread popularity of horror books and films attests to the fact that many people share King's fascination with the macabre. In the following selection, originally published in* Playboy *in 1982, a variation on "The Horror Movie as Junk Food" chapter in* Danse Macabre, *King analyzes the reasons we flock to good horror movies.*

FOR YOUR JOURNAL

What movies have you seen recently? Do you prefer watching any particular kind of movie—comedy, drama, science fiction, or horror, for example—more than others? How do you explain your preference?

I think that we're all mentally ill; those of us outside the asylums only hide it a little better—and maybe not all that much better, after all.

We've all known people who talk to themselves, people who sometimes squinch their faces into horrible grimaces when they believe no one is watching, people who have some hysterical fear—of snakes, the dark, the tight place, the long drop . . . and, of course, those final worms and grubs that are waiting so patiently underground.

When we pay our four or five bucks and seat ourselves at tenth-row center in a theater showing a horror movie, we are daring the nightmare.

Why? Some of the reasons are simple and obvious. To show that we can, that we are not afraid, that we can ride this roller coaster. Which is not to say that a really good horror movie may not surprise a scream out of us at some point, the way we may scream when a roller coaster twists through a complete 360 or plows through a lake at the bottom of the drop. And horror movies, like roller coasters, have always been the special province of the young; by the time one turns 40 or 50, one's appetite for double twists or 360-degree loops may be considerably depleted.

We also go to re-establish our feelings of essential normality; the horror movie is innately conservative, even reactionary. Freda Jackson as the horrible melting woman in *Die, Monster, Die!* confirms for us that no matter how far we may be removed from the beauty of a Robert Redford or a Diana Ross, we are still light-years from true ugliness.

And we go to have fun.

Ah, but this is where the ground starts to slope away, isn't it? Because this is a very peculiar sort of fun, indeed. The fun comes from seeing others menaced—sometimes killed. One critic has suggested that if pro football has become the voyeur's version of combat, then the horror film has become the modern version of the public lynching.

It is true that the mythic, "fairy-tale" horror film intends to take away the shades of gray. . . . It urges us to put away our more civilized and adult penchant for analysis and to become children again, seeing things in pure blacks and whites. It may be that horror movies provide psychic relief on this level because this invitation to lapse into simplicity, irrationality and even outright madness is extended so rarely. We are told we may allow our emotions a free rein . . . or no rein at all.

If we are all insane, then sanity becomes a matter of degree. If your insanity leads you to carve up women like Jack the Ripper or the Cleveland Torso Murderer,[1] we clap you away in the funny farm (but neither

2

3

4

5

6

7

8

---

[1] *Jack the Ripper, Cleveland Torso Murderer:* serial murderers who were active in the 1880s and the 1930s, respectively. [Eds.]

of those two amateur-night surgeons was ever caught, heh-heh-heh); if, on the other hand, your insanity leads you only to talk to yourself when you're under stress or to pick your nose on your morning bus, then you are left alone to go about your business . . . though it is doubtful that you will ever be invited to the best parties.

The potential lyncher is in almost all of us (excluding saints, past 9 and present; but then, most saints have been crazy in their own ways), and every now and then, he has to be let loose to scream and roll around in the grass. Our emotions and our fears form their own body, and we recognize that it demands its own exercise to maintain proper muscle tone. Certain of these emotional muscles are accepted—even exalted—in civilized society; they are, of course, the emotions that tend to maintain the status quo of civilization itself. Love, friendship, loyalty, kindness—these are all the emotions that we applaud, emotions that have been immortalized in the couplets of Hallmark cards and in the verses (I don't dare call it poetry) of Leonard Nimoy.[2]

When we exhibit these emotions, society showers us with posi- 10 tive reinforcement; we learn this even before we get out of diapers. When, as children, we hug our rotten little puke of a sister and give her a kiss, all the aunts and uncles smile and twit and cry, "Isn't he the sweetest little thing?" Such coveted treats as chocolate-covered graham crackers often follow. But if we deliberately slam the rotten little puke of a sister's fingers in the door, sanctions follow—angry remonstrance from parents, aunts, and uncles; instead of a chocolate-covered graham cracker, a spanking.

But anticivilization emotions don't go away, and they demand 11 periodic exercise. We have such "sick" jokes as, "What's the difference between a truckload of bowling balls and a truckload of dead babies? (You can't unload a truckload of bowling balls with a pitchfork. . . . a joke, by the way, that I heard originally from a ten-year-old). Such a joke may surprise a laugh or a grin out of us even as we recoil, a possibility that confirms the thesis: if we share a brotherhood of man, then we also share an insanity of man. None of which is intended as a defense of either the sick joke or insanity but merely as an explanation of why the best horror films, like the best fairy tales, manage to be reactionary, anarchistic, and revolutionary all at the same time.

---

[2]*Leonard Nimoy* (b. 1931): television and film actor. [Eds.]

The mythic horror movie, like the sick joke, has a dirty job to do. 12
It deliberately appeals to all that is worst in us. It is morbidity un-
chained, our most base instincts let free, our nastiest fantasies realized . . . and it all happens, fittingly enough, in the dark. For those
reasons, good liberals often shy away from horror films. For myself, I
like to see the most aggressive of them—*Dawn of the Dead,* for instance—as lifting a trap door in the civilized forebrain and throwing
a basket of raw meat to the hungry alligators swimming around in
that subterranean river beneath.

Why bother? Because it keeps them from getting out, man. It 13
keeps them down there and me up here. It was Lennon and McCart-
ney who said that all you need is love, and I would agree with that.

As long as you keep the gators fed. 14

QUESTIONS FOR STUDY AND DISCUSSION

1. What, according to King, causes people to crave horror movies?
   What other reasons can you add to King's list?

2. Identify the analogy King uses in paragraph 3, and explain how
   it works. (Glossary: *Analogy*)

3. What does King mean when he says, "The horror movie is innately conservative, even reactionary" (4)?

4. What emotions does society applaud? Why? Which ones does
   King label "anticivilization" emotions (11)?

5. In what ways is a horror movie like a sick joke? What is the
   "dirty job" or effect that the two have in common (12)?

6. King starts his essay with the attention-grabbing sentence, "I
   think that we're all mentally ill." How does he develop this idea
   of insanity in his essay? What does King mean when he says,
   "The potential lyncher is in almost all of us" (9)? How does
   King's last line relate to the theme of mental illness?

7. What is King's tone in this essay? (Glossary: *Tone*) Point to particular words or sentences that lead you to this conclusion.

VOCABULARY

Refer to your dictionary to define the following words as they are
used in this selection. Then use each word in a sentence of your own.

grimaces (1)	puke (10)
hysterical (1)	sanctions (10)
voyeur's (6)	remonstrance (10)
penchant (7)	recoil (11)
rein (7)	anarchistic (11)
exalted (9)	morbidity (12)
status quo (9)	subterranean (12)

CLASSROOM ACTIVITY USING CAUSE AND EFFECT

William V. Haney has developed the following test to determine your ability to analyze accurately evidence that is presented to you. After completing Haney's test, discuss your answers with other members of your class.

THE UNCRITICAL INFERENCE TEST

DIRECTIONS

1. You will read a brief story. Assume that all of the information presented in the story is definitely accurate and true. Read the story carefully. You may refer back to the story whenever you wish.

2. You will then read statements about the story. Answer them in numerical order. *Do not go back* to fill in answers or to change answers. This will only distort your test score.

3. After you read each statement carefully, determine whether the statement is:
   a. "T"—meaning: On the basis of the information presented in the story the statement is *definitely true.*
   b. "F"—meaning: On the basis of the information presented in the story the statement is *definitely false.*
   c. "?"—The statement *may* be true (or false) but on the basis of the information presented in the story you cannot be definitely certain. (If any part of the statement is doubtful, mark the statement "?".)

4. Indicate your answer by circling either "T" or "F" or "?" opposite the statement.

THE STORY

Babe Smith has been killed. Police have rounded up six suspects, all of whom are known gangsters. All of them are known to have been near the scene of the killing at the approximate time that it occurred. All had substantial motives for wanting Smith killed. However, one of these suspected gangsters, Slinky Sam, has positively been cleared of guilt.

STATEMENTS ABOUT THE STORY

1. Slinky Sam is known to have been near the scene of the killing of Babe Smith.   T   F   ?

2. All six of the rounded-up gangsters were known to have been near the scene of the murder.   T   F   ?

3. Only Slinky Sam has been cleared of guilt.   T   F   ?

4. All six of the rounded-up suspects were near the scene of Smith's killing at the approximate time that it took place.   T   F   ?

5. The police do not know who killed Smith.   T   F   ?

6. All six suspects are known to have been near the scene of the foul deed.   T   F   ?

7. Smith's murderer did not confess of his own free will.   T   F   ?

8. Slinky Sam was not cleared of guilt.   T   F   ?

9. It is known that the six suspects were in the vicinity of the cold-blooded assassination.   T   F   ?

SUGGESTED WRITING ASSIGNMENTS

1. Write an essay in which you analyze, in light of King's remarks about the causes of our cravings for horror movies, a horror movie you've seen. In what ways did the movie satisfy your "anti-civilization" emotions? How did you feel before going to the theater? How did you feel when leaving?

2. Write an essay in which you analyze the most significant reasons or causes for your going to college. You may wish to discuss such matters as your high school experiences, people and events that influenced your decision, and your goals in college as well as in later life.

Sometimes Honesty Is the Worst Policy

■ **Judy Mandell**

Judy Mandell, who makes her home in North Garden, Virginia, has published three books for writers who want inside information about how the publishing business works. She followed her first book, Fiction Writers' Guidelines *(1988), with two collections of articles on the relationship of authors to editors:* Magazine Editors Talk to Writers *(1995) and* Book Editors Talk to Writers *(1995). In her more recently published collections, she interviews a wide variety of publishing professionals and uses a question-and-answer format to convey the information quickly and clearly. In the following "My Turn" column, published in the October 21, 2002, issue of* Newsweek, *Mandell turns from the publishing world and explains why she does not want people to know her age. After a recent lunch with a New York book editor, however, she tells us she has cause to feel somewhat better about her age.*

FOR YOUR JOURNAL

What part does age play in your perceptions of the people with whom you live, attend classes, work, and play? Do you think about a person's age before all other characteristics? Or is age something you are aware of but don't think much about? Do you make judgments about people based on how old you think they are?

For as long as I've known her, an elderly relative of mine has lied about how old she is. She lives in a retirement community in the South. She looks great for her age — but I can't tell you what it is. I'm sworn to secrecy. Her friends think she's three years younger. "What's a few years among friends?" I asked her. "No one wants to be with an old lady," she answered.

She takes lying about her age to the extreme. Several years ago, when she was the only survivor of an automobile accident, she had the presence of mind to fabricate her age to the emergency medical technicians as they wheeled her into the ambulance. She was nearly arrested by U.S. Immigration officers because she crossed off and changed her birth date on her passport. For her, tampering with official documents is a way of life; she recently made me promise not to put her true age in her obituary.

I, on the other hand, had never lied about my age. I was proud, in fact, even when I turned 50. Why should I lie? I was told I looked good, and I felt great. My kids were grown, my marriage was fine, and I had a great job. I loved it when people said, "Your kids are *that* old? I can't believe it!" I thought that people who wouldn't reveal their age suffered from low self-esteem. That is, until my boss, the new, thirtysomething school headmaster, found out how old I was.

I taught part time and did fund-raising for a small private school. I was the second oldest person on the faculty. I never imagined that it could matter until the morning I met with the headmaster in his office. We chatted about the school, the students and me. "How old are you?" he asked. When I answered 50, he seemed to stop breathing. He definitely stopped talking. There was a long, strange silence.

"Why are you asking?" I said.

"Never mind," he answered.

I should have lied.

I was angry that my boss had asked that question, but I didn't want to rock the boat, so I let it pass.

Several weeks later the headmaster informed me that the school was having financial difficulties. They "just couldn't afford me," he said. I was let go.

Sure, there were age-discrimination laws 10 years ago, but I had no proof that age was the reason I was fired. I just took it on the chin, telling myself this guy was a jerk, I'd have more time for my writing and, anyhow, I must look pretty good if he was so shocked that I was 50.

My friend PJ, a book editor, never cared about who knew her age—until recently. "I don't look my age, but that doesn't matter anymore," she told me. "When younger people know I'm in my mid-50s, they treat me differently. They realize I'm their parents' age.

Another friend, a mother of three, lies about her age or avoids the subject. When her husband left her for a younger woman, she had a tummy tuck and a face-lift. She's dating, but it's hard to find a man interested in a 45-year-old woman. She says she'll tell her age if she finds someone she wants to settle down with. In the meantime, she's keeping it a secret.

After I lost my job, I decided to keep quiet, too. I even requested 13 that my date of birth be dropped from the Library of Congress data on the copyright page of my books.

Then last month I accepted an invitation to have lunch with a 14 New York book editor. We had had several phone conversations but never met in person. I knew she was under 30, but of course I had never told her how old I am.

I worried, even obsessed, about how she would react when she 15 saw me. But when we finally met, I detected no disappointment. In fact, we had fun, chatting and laughing like a couple of teenagers. After a while, I told her my age and asked her how she viewed women over 50.

Her answer surprised me. She confided that women over 50 16 made her nervous because she was afraid that they would perceive her as young. And to her, being young meant being naïve and prone to errors. She viewed older women as worldly, seasoned, deserving of respect. Although I envied her age, she seemed to envy mine.

Since that lunch, I've felt a lot better about my age. Sure, there 17 are things about getting older that aren't terrific, like memory lapses and sagging skin, but in many ways, being mature is an advantage.

Not everyone agrees, so I still avoid the subject. But the next time 18 I'm nervous or self-conscious about telling a younger person my age, I'll try to remember that she may be questioning how she will measure up to me.

QUESTIONS FOR STUDY AND DISCUSSION

1. Why does Mandell's elderly relative always lie about her age?
2. List the events that cause Mandell to change her views about telling people her age?
3. What does Mandell specifically learn when she has lunch with the young New York editor? Does it change her mind about telling people her age? Explain.
4. How does Mandell use narration as evidence to support her point of view? (Glossary: *Narration*)
5. What part does dialogue play in Mandell's essay? Is the dialogue believable? (Glossary: *Dialogue*)
6. Mandell claims that she lost her job because she told the truth about her age. She also says, however, that she didn't really care about the job. So what is her real concern? Is she in a dilemma

over telling the truth, or is she worried about growing older? Explain.

7. What is Mandell's tone in this essay? (Glossary: *Tone*) In paragraph 10, she says she told herself that the guy who fired her was a "jerk." Does the use of that word break the tone of her essay, or is it in keeping with the tone she's established?

VOCABULARY

Refer to your dictionary to define the following words as they are used in this selection. Then use each word in a sentence of your own.

fabricate (2)   confided (16)

tampering (2)   prone (16)

tummy tuck (12)   seasoned (16)

obsessed (15)

CLASSROOM ACTIVITY USING CAUSE AND EFFECT

Determining causes and effects can be quite difficult and requires thought. However, establishing a causal chain of events often brings clarity and understanding to complex issues. Consider the following example involving pollution and environmental stewardship:

ultimate cause   industrial smokestack emissions

immediate cause   smoke and acid rain damage

effect   clear air legislation

effect   improved air quality and forest growth

Develop a causal chain for each of the following cause-and-effect pairs:

terrorism/fear

giving a speech/anxiety

party/excitement

vacation/relaxation

Then mix two of the pairs. For example, develop a causal chain for vacation/anxiety. Be prepared to discuss your answers with the class.

SUGGESTED WRITING ASSIGNMENTS

1. No matter what age a person is, it seems, certain stereotypical views come into play. For example, young children are regarded as not well behaved, adolescents are seen as rebuffing adult guidance, young adults are regarded as being given to excessive behavior, adults are seen as workaholics, and older people are thought to be stubborn and set in their ways. Write an essay that examines the causes or effects of any age-related stereotypes on our behavior. In what ways do we conform to the stereotype? In what ways do we react against it? What effects do such stereotypes have on society in general?

2. Borrow Judy Mandell's title, "Sometimes Honesty Is the Worst Policy," and write a cause-and-effect essay of your own in which you explore a decision or a series of decisions that would have resulted more favorably for you if you had lied instead of telling the truth.

Surfing's Up and Grades Are Down

■ **Rene Sanchez**

Rene Sanchez, a reporter for the Washington Post, *was born in New Orleans in 1965. Shortly after graduating from Loyola University of the South in New Orleans, he went to work as a reporter for the* Washington Post. *Sanchez has covered lifestyle issues, D.C. schools and politics, as well as the controversial former mayor, Marion Barry. Sanchez is now assigned to the Los Angeles Bureau of the* Post, *where he is a general reporter for the western states. A former education editor, Sanchez now makes his home in Santa Monica, California. In "Surfing's Up and Grades Are Down," first published in the* Post *in 1996, Sanchez examines the possible causes and effects of some college students' addiction to surfing the Web and playing computer games.*

FOR YOUR JOURNAL

How many hours a day do you spend on average using a computer for recreation? How do you feel about time spent playing games or surfing the Web? Does it relax you? Does the amount of time you spend worry you? Would you consider yourself or any of your friends addicted to computer games or Web surfing?

A new campus support group called "Caught in the Web" is being 1 formed at the University of Maryland to counsel students spending too much time on computers.

At the Massachusetts Institute of Technology, students unable to 2 break their addiction to playing computer games on campus terminals have new help. At their request, the university will deny them access whenever they try to sign on.

Faculty studying the freshman dropout rate at Alfred University 3 in New York have just found that nearly half the students who quit last semester had been logging marathon, late-night time on the Internet.

Nationwide, as colleges charge into the digital age with high-tech 4
libraries, wired dormitories, and computerized course work, faculty
and campus counselors are discovering a troubling side effect: A
growing number of students are letting computers overwhelm their
lives.

It is hardly a crisis on any campus—yet. Some college officials 5
say it is merely a fad, and not nearly as harmful as other bad habits
students often fall prey to on campuses—such as binge drinking of
alcohol. But concern over the issue is spreading.

Some universities now are imposing limits on the time students 6
spend each day, or each week, on campus computers. Other colleges
are debating whether to monitor the time students spend on computer games and chat rooms, then program a warning to appear on
their screens when it gets excessive.

Some college counselors are creating workshops on the subject 7
and planning to include them in freshman orientation programs.
Others already are urging students not to plunge into on-line relationships with strangers.

"More and more students are losing themselves in this, says 8
Judith Klavans, the director of Columbia University's Center for Research on Information Access. "It's very accessible on campuses, and
students have time on their hands. We're seeing some of them really
drift off into this world at the expense of practically everything else."

Campus officials say that communicating on the Internet or 9
roaming the huge universe of information on the World Wide Web
holds an especially powerful lure for many college students because it
takes them into a vast new realm of learning and research, usually at
no cost. But for students having trouble establishing social ties at
large universities, or who are on their own, unsupervised, and facing
adult pressures for the first time, it also poses an array of new risks.

At the University of California's Berkeley campus, counselors say 10
they are dealing with a small but increasing number of student cases
linked to excessive computer use. Some students, they say, are putting
too much emphasis on electronic relationships, are neglecting course
work, and, in a few instances, are even being swindled out of money
by e-mail strangers they have come to trust.

"There can be a real sense of isolation on a large campus, and for 11
young students or new students, this seems like a safe, easy way to
form relationships," says Jeff Prince, the associate director of coun-
seling at UC-Berkeley. "But some go overboard. It becomes their only

way to connect to the world. One of the things we're really working on now is helping students balance how many social needs they try to have fulfilled by computers."

Linda Tipton, a counselor at the University of Maryland, which 12 limits students to forty hours a week on campus terminals, says she began noticing some of the same problems arise last year in individual and group therapy sessions.

Some of them, she says, spoke of spending more than six hours a 13 day on-line and considered a computerized forum the only setting in which they could express themselves or relate well to others. A few students told her of dropping or flunking courses partly because they were so preoccupied with the Internet. Others confessed to trying to get multiple computer accounts with the university to circumvent its forty-hour-a-week rule.

"Obviously, this is a wonderful tool, and for many students it's 14 perfectly fine," says Tipton, who is trying to form a campus support group and develop a workshop on Internet addiction. "But for others it's becoming a tremendous escape from the pressures of college life. Students can become whomever they want, for as long as they want, and many other things in their lives, like classes, start to suffer."

Nathaniel Cordova, a graduate student at Maryland, says his 15 problems are not that severe—but he is nevertheless heeding Tipton's advice and trying to cut back on the time he spends on computers. And he says he routinely talks to other students on campus also trying to break habits like his.

"I don't think I'm an addict," Cordova says. "But I admit, some- 16 times I'll be in my office at eight o'clock at night, and then the next thing I know it's three A.M., and I realize I forgot to eat. It's so easy to get drawn in, and not just in research, but talking to people. You tell yourself, 'Okay, just one more link-up.' But you keep going."

Other college officials, however, say the concern seems exaggerated. 17

Some say they see few signs of trouble, and others say student in- 18 terest in computer games or the Web is often intense at first, then fades. One of the venerable rites of college, they contend, is for students to find distractions from their academic burdens. They say this one is much safer than many others causing campus problems.

"There will always be something like this on college campuses," 19 says Richard Wiggins, who manages information systems and teaches computer courses at Michigan State University. "In my day, in the 1970s, it was pinball. We played that all the time to get rid of stress. Usually things like this are not that harmful."

"For some people, it's just a great new way to waste time," says 20
Jeff Boulier, a senior at George Washington University who spends
several hours a day on the Internet. "And college students have always
been quite dedicated to wasting time."

At MIT, Patrick McCormick, an undergraduate who helps admin- 21
ister computer game systems for the university, says he sees both sides
of the trend. A few students in his residence hall dropped classes, or saw
their grades sink, after they lapsed into intensive computer use. "But
others stay up all night with this stuff and still get 4.0s," he says. "It's
very easy to get sucked in, but it isn't always bad."

Still, McCormick notes one problem he spots consistently: Class- 22
mates who trust virtually everyone they meet, or everything they
read, on-line. "Some people think if it's on a computer screen, it must
be true, and they get burned," he says. "You hear them talking about
flying their dream lover up, and of course they never show."

This spring, Alfred University in upstate New York decided to 23
examine what the students who dropped out last semester had in
common. What prompted the inquiry was that twice as many students as usual—seventy-five, mostly freshmen—did not return for
classes there this spring.

Every student at Alfred receives a campus computer account, 24
which is free. So Connie Beckman, the director of Alfred's computer
center, decided to check the account records of all the students who
had dropped out. She found that half of them had been logging as
much as six hours a day on computer games or the Web, usually late
at night. "It was the only thing that correlated among so many of
them," Beckman says.

University officials say they doubt that is the only, or even the 25
primary, reason many of those students quit. But the discovery has
led to several new policies.

Next fall, for the first time, freshmen at Alfred will be told about 26
the dangers of heavy computer use as soon as they arrive on campus.
Residence halls, all of which have computer rooms, also will each
have a full-time, professional counselor to keep a close eye on late-
night computer addicts. Other campuses are studying similar moves.

"We've dealt with alcohol and drugs; we've dealt with TV and 27
video games. Now this looks like the latest pitfall for college students," Beckman says. "They're doing this all night instead of doing
their homework, or eating, or sleeping. When they're up until five
A.M. playing around on the Web, they're not going to make their
eight A.M. classes."

QUESTIONS FOR STUDY AND DISCUSSION

1. What is the possible cause-and-effect relationship between students spending too much time on computers and poor academic performance? What evidence does Sanchez provide to support the relationship? (Glossary: *Evidence*) Does he prove that the relationship exists? Explain.

2. Does Sanchez himself believe that computer addiction causes poor academic performance in college students, or is he merely reporting what others say? Point out places in the essay where you think he reveals his own opinion. (Glossary: *Attitude*)

3. Is computer addiction a problem at your school? What evidence do you have that it exists? If you think it exists, do you also think it affects students' grades?

4. Explain the function of Sanchez's first three paragraphs. (Glossary: *Beginnings and Endings*) How does he further develop those first three paragraphs in the rest of his essay? (Glossary: *Organization*)

5. What evidence does Sanchez provide that argues against the theory that too much computer use causes poor grades? How convincing is that evidence? Explain.

VOCABULARY

Refer to your dictionary to define the following words as they are used in this selection. Then use each word in a sentence of your own.

counsel (1)   heeding (15)
prey (5)   venerable (18)
monitor (6)   burned (22)
array (9)   correlated (24)
forum (13)   pitfall (27)
circumvent (13)

CLASSROOM ACTIVITY USING CAUSE AND EFFECT

In preparation for writing a cause-and-effect essay, list two effects on society and two effects on personal behavior for one of the following items: television, cell phones, e-mail, microwave ovens, DVD technology, the Internet, or an item of your choice. For example, a car could be said to have the following effects:

SOCIETY

Development of an infrastructure based on asphalt roads
Expansion of the size and influence of the petroleum and insurance industries

PERSONAL BEHAVIOR

Convenient transportation
Freedom and independence

SUGGESTED WRITING ASSIGNMENTS

1. Write an essay on the effects of computers on society. Computers have an enormous impact on society as a whole as well as on the way we live our daily lives. For example, telecommuting, in which an employee works at home and communicates with coworkers via phone, modem, and fax, could eliminate the need for much of the work force to live near cities. What other effects do you see? Which do you think are most important for society? Which are the most important to you personally? Be sure to explain your reasoning.

2. There is often more than one cause for an event. List at least six causes for one of the following:

an upset victory in a game or competition
an injury you suffered
a change in your major
a quarrel with a friend

Examine your list, and identify the causes that seem most probable. Which of these are immediate causes, and which are ultimate causes? Using this material, write a short cause-and-effect essay on one of the topics.

Where Have All the Parents Gone?

■ **Barbara Dafoe Whitehead**

Barbara Dafoe Whitehead grew up in Appleton, Minnesota, and received her bachelor's degree from the University of Wisconsin and her master's and doctorate in American social history from the University of Chicago. She researches and writes on issues of family and child well-being for many periodicals, among them the Atlantic Monthly, Boston Globe, American Enterprise, Commonweal, Woodrow Wilson Quarterly, Los Angeles Times, *and* Washington Post. *She also speaks about these issues to a wide range of audiences and is cochair, with David Popenoe, of the National Marriage Project. In a widely read and debated article in the April 1993 issue of the* Atlantic Monthly, *she wrote, "If we fail to come to terms with the relationship between family structure and declining child well-being, then it will be increasingly difficult to improve children's life prospects, no matter how many new programs the federal government funds. Nor will we be able to make progress in bettering school performance or reducing crime or improving the quality of the nation's future work force—all domestic problems closely connected to family breakup. Worse, we may contribute to the problem by pursuing policies that actually increase family instability and breakup." Whitehead has also written* The Divorce Culture: Rethinking Our Commitments to Marriage and Family *(1997) and* Why There Are No Good Men Left: The Romantic Plight of the New Single Woman *(2002). In the following article, which first appeared in* New Perspectives *Quarterly, Whitehead examines the reasons why parents are no longer at the center of American society and what that suggests about the future.*

FOR YOUR JOURNAL

What was your family like as you grew up? Were your parents married, divorced, or remarried? Were you raised by a single parent or by someone other than your birth parents? If any of your friends grew up in a different family situation, do you think you were better or worse off, or is it really impossible to compare your situation with theirs? How important is it for children to grow up in a supportive family structure?

"Invest in kids," George Bush[1] mused during his 1988 presidential campaign, "I like it." Apparently so do others. A growing number of corporate CEOs and educators, elected officials and child-welfare advocates have embraced the same language. "Invest in kids" is the bumper-sticker for an important new cause, aptly tagged the *kids as capital* argument. It runs as follows:

America's human capital comes in two forms: The active work force and the prospective work force. The bulk of tomorrow's workers are today's children, of course. So children make up much of the stockpile of America's potential human capital.

If we look at them as tomorrow's workers, we begin to appreciate our stake in today's children. They will determine when we can retire, how well we can live in retirement, how generous our health insurance will be, how strong our social safety net, how orderly our society. What's more, today's children will determine how successfully we compete in the global economy. They will be going head-to-head against Japanese, Korean, and West German children.

Unfortunately, American children aren't prepared to run the race, let alone win it. Many are illiterate, undernourished, impaired, unskilled, poor. Consider the children who started first grade in 1986: 14 percent were illegitimate; 15 percent were physically or emotionally handicapped; 15 percent spoke another language other than English; 28 percent were poor; and fully 40 percent could be expected to live in a single-parent home before they reached eighteen. Given falling birth rates, this future work force is small—all the more reason to worry about its poor quality. So "invest in kids" is not the cry of the soft-hearted altruist but the call of the hardheaded realist.

Kids as capital has caught on because it responds to a broad set of national concerns. Whether one is worried about the rise of the underclass, the decline of the family, our standing in the global economy, the nation's level of educational performance, or intergenerational conflict, kids as capital seems to offer an answer.

---

[1]*George Herbert Walker Bush* (b. 1924): forty-first president of the United States (1989–93). [Eds.]

Further, *kids as capital* offers the rationale for a new coalition for child welfare programs. The argument reaches beyond the community of traditional children's advocates and draws business into the child-saving fold. American corporations clearly have a stake in tomorrow's work force as they don't have in today's children. *Kids as capital* gives the toughminded, fifty-five-year-old CEO a reason to "care" about the eight-year-old, Hispanic school girl. 6

Nevertheless, the argument left unchallenged could easily become yet another "feel-good" formula that doesn't work. Worse, it could end up betraying those it seeks to save—the nation's children. 7

First, *kids as capital* departs from a classic American vision of the future. Most often, our history has been popularly viewed as progressive, with each generation breaking with and improving on the past. As an immigrant nation, we have always measured our progress through the progress of our children; they have been the bearers of the dream. 8

Kids as capital turns this optimistic view on its head. It conjures up a picture of a dark and disorderly future. Essentially, kids as capital is dystopic—closer to the spirit of *Blade Runner* and *Black Rain*[2] than *Wizard of Oz* or *It's a Wonderful Life*.[3] Children, in this view, do not bear the dream. They carry the seeds of our destruction. In short, *kids as capital* plays on our fears, rather than our hopes. It holds out the vision of a troubled future in order to secure a safer and more orderly present. 9

There is something troubling, too, in such an instrumental view of children. To define them narrowly as tomorrow's workers is to strip them of their full status as humans, as children: Kids can't be kids; they can only be embryonic workers. And treating *kids as capital* makes it easier to measure them solely through IQ tests, class standing, SAT scores, drop-out ratios, physical fitness tests. This leaves no place in the society for the slow starter, the handicapped, the quirky, and the nonconforming. 10

Yet kids-as-capital has an even more serious flaw. It evades the central fact of life for American children: They have parents. 11

As we all know, virtually every child in America grows up in a family with one or more parents. Parents house children. Parents feed children. Parents clothe children. Parents nurture and protect children. 12

---

[2]*Blade Runner, Black Rain:* bleak futuristic films of director Ridley Scott. [Eds.]
[3]*Wizard of Oz, It's a Wonderful Life:* optimistic films from 1939 and 1946, respectively. [Eds.]

Parents instruct children in everything from using a fork to driving a car. To be sure, there have been vast changes in family life, and, increasingly, parents must depend on teachers, doctors, day-care workers, and technology to help care for and educate their children. Even so, these changes haven't altered one fundamental fact: In American society, parents still bear the primary responsibility for the material and spiritual welfare of children. As our teachers and counselors and politicians keep reminding us, everything begins at home. So, if today's children are in trouble, it's because today's parents are in trouble.

As recently as a dozen years ago, it was the central argument of an ambitious report by the Carnegie Council on Children. The Council put it plainly: "The best way to help children tomorrow is to support parents today." Yet, that view has been lost. The *kids as capital* argument suppresses the connection between parents and children. It imagines that we can improve the standing of children without improving the standing of the parents. In the new rhetoric, it is hard even to find the word "parent." Increasingly, kids are portrayed as standing alone out there somewhere, cosmically parent-free.

13

As a result, *kids as capital* ignores rather than addresses one of the most important changes in American life: The decline in the power and standing of the nation's parents.

14

Only a generation ago, parents stood at the center of society. First of all, there were so many of them—fully half the nation's households in 1960 were parent households with one or more children under eighteen. Moreover, parents looked alike—Dad worked and Mom stayed at home. And parents marched through the stages of childbearing and child rearing in virtual lockstep: Most couples who married in the 1940s and 1950s finished having their 3.2 children by the time they were in their late twenties.

15

Their demographic dominance meant two things: First, it made for broad common ground in child rearing. Parents could do a great deal to support each other in raising the new generation. They could, and did, create a culture hospitable to children. Secondly, it made for political clout. When so many adults were parents and so many parents were part of an expanding consumer economy, private and public interests converged. The concerns of parents—housing, health, education—easily found their way into the national agenda. Locally, too, parents were dominant. In some postwar[4] suburbs like Levittown, New York, three-quarters of all residents were either parents or children under ten.

16

---

[4]*Postwar:* the stable, prosperous years following World War II. [Eds.]

Not surprisingly, there was little dissent when it came to building a new junior high or establishing a summer recreation program or installing a new playground. What's more, parents and kids drove the consumer economy. Every time they bought a pair of sneakers or a new bike, they were acting in the nation's best interest.

Behind this, of course, lurked a powerful pronatal ideology. Parenthood was the definitive credential of adulthood. More than being married, more than getting a job, it was having a child that baptized you as an adult in postwar America. In survey after survey, postwar parents rated children above marriage itself as the greatest reward of private life. For a generation forced to make personal sacrifices during the Depression[5] and the war,[6] having children and pursuing a private life represented a new kind of freedom.

17

By the 1970s, parents no longer enjoyed so central a place in the society. To baby boom children, postwar family life seemed suffocating and narrow. Women, in particular, wanted room to breathe. The rights movements of the sixties and seventies overturned the pronatal ideology, replacing it with an ideology of choice. Adults were free to choose among many options: Single, married, or divorced; career-primary or career-secondary; parent, stepparent, or child-free.

18

Thus, parenthood lost its singular status. It no longer served as the definitive credential of maturity and adult achievement. In fact, as careers and personal fulfillment beckoned, parenthood seemed just the opposite: a serious limitation on personal growth and success. As Gloria Steinem[7] put it, "I either gave birth to someone else or I gave birth to myself."

19

As the pronatal ideology vanished, so did the close connection between private families and the public interest. Raising children was no longer viewed as a valuable contribution to the society, an activity that boosted the economy, built citizen participation, and increased the nation's confidence in the future. Instead, it became one option among many. No longer a moral imperative, child rearing was just another "lifestyle choice."

20

Viewed this way, raising children looked like an economic disaster. Starting out, parents had to shell out $3,000 for basic prenatal

21

---

[5]*The Depression:* the longest and most severe economic slump in North America and Europe, which began in 1929 and lasted until about 1939. [Eds.]
[6]*The war:* World War II. [Eds.]
[7]*Gloria Steinem* (b. 1934): American feminist, political activist, writer, and cofounder of *Ms. Magazine.* [Eds.]

care and maternity costs; $3,000–$5,000 per child for day care; and $2,500 for the basic baby basket of goods and services. Crib-to-college costs for middle-class Americans could run as high as $135,000 per child. And, increasingly, the period of economic dependency for children stretched well beyond age eighteen. College tuitions and start-up subsidies for the new college graduate became part of the economic burden of parenthood. In an ad campaign, Manufacturers Hanover Trust gave prospective parents fair warning: "If you want a bundle of joy, you'll need a bundle of money."

Hard-pressed younger Americans responded to these new realities in several ways. Some simply chose not to have children. Others decided to have one or two, but only after they had a good job and solid prospects. Gradually, the number of parent households in the nation declined from one-half to one-third, and America faced a birth dearth.   22

For those who chose the parent option, there was only one way to face up to the new economic pressures of child rearing: Work longer and harder outside the home. For all but the extremely well-off, a second income became essential. But in struggling to pay the bills, parents seemed to be short-changing their children in another way. They weren't taking their moral responsibilities seriously enough. They weren't spending enough time with their kids. They weren't reading to the children or playing with the kids or supervising homework. And, most important, they weren't teaching good values.   23

This emerging critique marked a dramatic change in the way society viewed parents. In the postwar period, the stereotypical parent was self-sacrificing, responsible, caring, attentive—an impossible standard, to be sure, but one that lent enormous popular support and approval to adults engaged in the messy and difficult work of raising children. Cruel, abusive, self-absorbed parents might exist, but the popular culture failed to acknowledge them. It was not until parents began to lose their central place in the society that this flattering image faded. Then, quite rapidly, the dominant image of The Good Parent gave way to a new and equally powerful image—the image of The Bad Parent.   24

The shift occurred in two stages. The first-stage critique emerged in the seventies and focused on an important new figure: The working mother. Working mothers were destroying their children and the family, conservative critics charged. They weren't feeding kids wholesome meals, they weren't taking the kids to church, they weren't   25 serving as moral exemplars. Liberals sided with working mothers, but conceded that they were struggling with some new and difficult issues: Was day care as good as mother care? Was quality time good enough? Were the rewards of twelve-hour workdays great enough to make up for the loss of sleep and leisure-time? Where did the mother of a feverish child belong—at the crib or at her desk?

On the whole, the first-stage critique was a sympathetic critique. 26 In its view, parents might be affected by stress and guilt, but they weren't yet afflicted by serious pathology. After all, in the seventies, the nation's most suspect drug was laetrile,[8] not crack or ice.[9] Divorce was still viewed as a healthy alternative to an unhappy family life. But as the eighties began, a darker image of parents appeared. In the second-stage critique, . . . parents became toxic.

Day after day, throughout the eighties, Americans confronted an 27 ugly new reality. Parents were hurting and murdering their children. Day after day, the newspapers brought yet another story of a child abandoned or battered. Day after day, the local news told of a child sexually abused by a father or a stepfather or a mother's boyfriend. Week by week, the national media brought us into courtrooms where photographs of battered children were held up to the camera. The sheer volume of stories suggested an epidemic of historic proportion. In even the most staid publications, the news was sensational. The *New York Times* carried bizarre stories usually found only in tabloids: A father who tortured his children for years; a mother who left her baby in a suitcase in a building she then set on fire; parents who abandoned babies dead or alive, in toilets, dumpsters, and alleyways.

Drug use among parents was one clear cause of abuse. And, in- 28 creasingly child abuse and drug abuse were linked in the most direct way possible. Pregnant women were battering their children in the womb, delivering drugs through their umbilical cords. Nightly images of crack-addicted babies in neonatal units destroyed any lingering public sympathy for mothers of the underclass. And as the highly publicized Joel Steinberg case[10] made clear, middle-class parents, too, took drugs and killed babies. Even those parents who occasionally indulged were causing their children harm. The Partnership for a

---

[8]*Laetrile:* controversial drug marketed for the prevention of cancer. [Eds.]

[9]*Crack, ice:* slang terms for processed cocaine and methamphetamine. [Eds.]

[10]*Joel Steinberg case:* a first-degree murder case involving a criminal defense lawyer's pummeling of his six-year-old stepdaughter to death in 1987. [Eds.]

Drug-Free America ran ads asking: "With millions of parents doing drugs, is it any wonder their kids are too?"

More than drugs, it was divorce that lay at the heart of middle-class parental failure. It wasn't the crackhouse but the courthouse that was the scene of their collapse. Parents engaged in bitter custody battles. Parents kidnapped their own children. Parents used children as weapons against each other or simply walked away from their responsibilities. In an important new study on the long-term effects of divorce, Judith Wallerstein challenged the earlier notion that divorce is healthy for kids. She studied middle-class families for fifteen years after divorce and came up with some startling findings: Almost half of the children in the study entered adulthood as worried, underachieving, self-deprecating, and sometimes angry young men and women; one in four experienced a severe and enduring drop in their standard of living; three in five felt rejected by at least one parent. Her study concluded: "Divorce is almost always more devastating for children than for their parents. . . . [W]hile divorce can rescue a parent from an intolerable situation, it can fail to rescue the children." 29

As a group, today's parents have been portrayed as selfish and uncaring. Yuppie parents abandon the children to the au pair; working parents turn their kids over to the mall and the video arcade; single parents hang a key around their kids' necks and a list of emergency numbers on the refrigerator. Even in the healthiest families, parents fail to put their children first. 30

The indictment of parents is pervasive. In a survey by the Carnegie Foundation, 90 percent of a national sample of public school teachers say a lack of parental support is a problem in their classrooms. Librarians gathered at a national convention to draft a new policy to deal with the problem of parents who send unattended children to the library after school. Daycare workers complain to Ann Landers[11] that all too often parents hand over children with empty stomachs and full diapers. Everywhere, parents are flunking the most basic tests. 31

Declining demographically, hard-pressed economically, and disarrayed politically, parents have become part of the problem. For proponents of the *kids as capital* argument, the logic is clear: Why try to help parents—an increasingly marginal and unsympathetic bunch—when you can rescue their children? 32

---

[11]*Ann Landers:* the pseudonym of Eppie Lederer (1918–2002), a popular American advice columnist. [Eds.]

To blame parents for larger social changes is nothing new. In the   33
past, child-saving movements have depended on building a public
consensus that certain parents have failed. Child reformers in the Progressive Era,[12] for example, were able to expand the scope of public
sector responsibility for the welfare of children by exploiting mainstream fears about immigrant parents and their child-rearing practices. But what is new is the sense that the majority of parents — up
and down the social ladder — are failing. Even middle-class parents,
once solid, dependable caretakers of the next generation, don't seem
to be up to the job.

By leaving parents out of the picture, *kids as capital* conjures up   34
the image of our little workers struggling against the little workers of
Germany and the little workers of Japan. But this picture is obviously
false. For the little workers of Germany and Japan have parents too.
The difference is that their parents are strongly valued and supported
by the society for their contributions *as parents*. We won't be facing
up to reality until we are ready to pit our parents against their parents, and thus our family policy against theirs.

QUESTIONS FOR STUDY AND DISCUSSION

1. What is Whitehead's thesis in this essay? (Glossary: *Thesis*)
2. Briefly summarize the "kids as capital" argument that Whitehead discusses. (Glossary: *Argumentation*) Why did it become so
   popular? What does Whitehead say is wrong with the argument?
3. In paragraph 9, Whitehead says that "kids as capital" is dystopic. What does she mean?
4. Explain the function of paragraph 16 in developing Whitehead's
   argument.
5. Is "kids as capital" a cause or an effect or both? Explain.
6. Why are parents so important, in Whitehead's view? What do
   they provide?
7. What is the pronatal ideology Whitehead discusses in paragraph 18? What does she claim caused a change in that ideology?
8. What is causing parents to fail?
9. According to Whitehead, what causes divorce? What does she
   think divorce, in turn, causes?

---

[12]*Progressive Era:* the period during which the United States rose to world power
(1896–1920). [Eds.]

VOCABULARY

Refer to your dictionary to define the following words as they are used in this selection. Then use each word in a sentence of your own.

aptly (1)	cosmically (13)
altruist (4)	dissent (16)
embryonic (10)	dearth (22)
quirky (10)	pathology (26)
suppresses (13)	staid (27)

CLASSROOM ACTIVITY USING CAUSE AND EFFECT

Develop a causal chain in which you examine the ramifications of a past action of yours. Identify each part of the chain. For example, you decided you wanted to do well in a course (ultimate cause), so you got started on a research project early (immediate cause), which enabled you to write several drafts of your paper (immediate cause), which earned you an A for the project (effect), which earned you an excellent grade in the class (effect), which enabled you to take the advanced seminar you wanted (effect).

SUGGESTED WRITING ASSIGNMENTS

1. Perhaps you have a different view than Whitehead about the causes or effects of divorce in our society. Write a cause-and-effect essay on this topic, drawing on real-life experiences that you or your friends have had and on any reading or other research that you have done. Be careful to distinguish between remote and immediate causes.

2. Write an essay in which you establish the cause-and-effect relationship that exists in one of the following pairs:

winter and depression	health and happiness
poverty and crime	old age and wisdom
wealth and power	good looks and popularity

chapter 20

Argument

The word *argument* probably brings to mind a verbal disagreement of the sort that everyone has at least witnessed, if not participated in directly. Such disputes are occasionally satisfying: You can take pleasure in knowing you have converted someone to your point of view. More often, though, verbal arguments are inconclusive and frustrating when you realize that you have failed to make your position understood, or enraging when you feel that your opponent has been stubborn and unreasonable. Such dissatisfaction is inevitable because verbal arguments generally arise spontaneously and so cannot be thoughtfully planned or researched; it is difficult to come up with appropriate evidence on the spur of the moment or to find the language that will make a point hard to deny. Indeed, it is often not until later that the convincing piece of evidence or the forcefully phrased assertion finally comes to mind.

Written **arguments** share common goals with spoken ones: They attempt to convince a reader to agree with a particular point of view, to make a particular decision, or to pursue a particular course of action. Written arguments, however, involve the presentation of well-chosen evidence and the artful control of language. Writers of arguments have no one around to dispute their words directly, so they must imagine their probable audience to predict the sorts of objections that may be raised. Written arguments, therefore, must be much more carefully planned—the writer must settle in advance on a specific, sufficiently detailed thesis or proposition. There is a greater need for organization, for choosing the most effective types of evidence from all that is available, for determining the strategies of rhetoric, language, and style that will best suit the argument's subject, its purpose, and its thesis, as well as ensure its effect on the intended audience. In the end, however, such work can be far more satisfying than spontaneous oral argument.

Most people who specialize in the study of arguments identify two essential categories: persuasion and logic. *Persuasive appeals* are directed at readers' emotions, at their subconscious, even at their biases and prejudices. These appeals involve diction, slanting, figurative language, analogy, rhythmic patterns of speech, and the establishment of a tone that will encourage a positive response. It is important to understand, as well, that persuasion very often attempts to get the audience to take action. Examples of persuasive argument are found in the exaggerated claims of advertisers and the speech making of political and social activists.

Logical appeals, on the other hand, are directed primarily at the audience's intellectual faculties, understanding, and knowledge. Such appeals depend on the reasoned movement from assertion to evidence to conclusion and on an almost mathematical system of proof and counterproof. Logical argument, unlike persuasion, does not normally impel its audience to action. Logical argument is commonly found in scientific or philosophical articles, in legal decisions, and in technical proposals.

Most arguments, however, are neither purely persuasive nor purely logical. A well-written newspaper editorial, for example, will present a logical arrangement of assertions and evidence, but it will also employ striking diction and other persuasive patterns of language to reinforce its effectiveness. Thus the kinds of appeals a writer emphasizes depend on the nature of the topic, the thesis or proposition of the argument, the writer's purpose, the various kinds of support (for example, evidence, opinions, examples, facts, statistics) offered, and a thoughtful consideration of the audience. Knowing the differences between persuasive and logical appeals is essential in learning both to read and to write arguments.

True arguments make assertions about which there is a legitimate and recognized difference of opinion. It is unlikely that anyone will ever need to convince a reader that falling in love is a beautiful and intense experience, that crime rates should be reduced, or that computers are changing the world; most everyone would agree with such assertions. But not everyone would agree that women experience love more intensely than men, that reinstating the death penalty will reduce the incidence of crime, or that computers are changing the world for the worse; these assertions are arguable and admit of differing perspectives. Similarly, a leading heart specialist might argue in a popular magazine that too many doctors are advising patients to have pacemakers implanted when the devices are not necessary; the editorial writer for a small-town newspaper could write urging that a local agency supplying food to poor families be given a larger percentage of the town's budget; in a long and complex book, a foreign-policy specialist might attempt to prove that the current administration exhibits no consistent policy in its relationship with other countries and that the Department of State needs to be overhauled. No matter what its forum or its structure, an argument has as its chief purpose the detailed setting forth of a particular point of view and the rebuttal of any opposing views.

Argumentation frequently utilizes the other rhetorical strategies. In your efforts to argue convincingly, you may find it necessary to define, to compare and contrast, to analyze causes and effects, to classify, to describe, or to narrate. Nevertheless, it is the writer's attempt to convince, not explain, that is of primary importance in an argumentative essay. In this respect, it is helpful to keep in mind that there are two basic patterns of thinking and presenting our thoughts that are followed in argumentation: induction and deduction.

Inductive reasoning, the more common type of reasoning, moves from a set of specific examples to a general statement. In doing so, the writer makes an *inductive leap* from the evidence to the generalization. For example, after examining enrollment statistics, we can conclude that students do not like to take courses offered early in the morning or late in the afternoon.

Deductive reasoning, on the other hand, moves from a general statement to a specific conclusion. It works on the model of the *syllogism,* a simple three-part argument that consists of a major premise, a minor premise, and a conclusion, as in the following example:

a. All women are mortal. *(Major premise)*

b. Jeanne is a woman. *(Minor premise)*

c. Jeanne is mortal. *(Conclusion)*

Obviously, a syllogism will fail to work if either of the premises is untrue.

a. All living creatures are mammals. *(Major premise)*

b. A butterfly is a living creature. *(Minor premise)*

c. A butterfly is a mammal. *(Conclusion)*

The problem is immediately apparent. The major premise is obviously false: Many living creatures are not mammals, and a butterfly happens to be one of the nonmammals. Consequently, the conclusion is invalid.

Writing an argument is a challenging assignment but one that can be very rewarding. By nature, an argument must be carefully reasoned and thoughtfully structured to have maximum effect. Allow yourself, therefore, enough time to think about your thesis, to gather the evidence you need, and to draft, revise, edit, and proofread your essay. Fuzzy thinking, confused expression, and poor organization will be immediately evident to your reader and will diminish your chances for completing the assignment successfully. The following steps will remind you of some key features of arguments and will help you sequence your activities as you research and write.

I. DETERMINE THE THESIS OR PROPOSITION

Begin by deciding on a topic that interests you and about which there is some significant difference of opinion or about which you have a number of questions. Find out what's in the news about your topic, what people are saying about it, what authors and instructors are emphasizing as important intellectual arguments. As you pursue your research, consider what assertion or assertions you can make about the topic you choose. The more specific this thesis or proposition, the more directed your research can become and the more focused your ultimate argument will be. Don't hesitate along the way to modify or even reject an initial thesis as your continued research warrants.

A thesis can be placed anywhere in an argument, but it is probably best while learning to write arguments to place the statement of your controlling idea somewhere near the beginning of your composition. Explain the importance of the thesis, and make clear to your reader that you share a common concern or interest in this issue. You may wish to state your central assertion directly in your first or second paragraph so that your reader will have no doubt or confusion about your position. You may also wish to lead off with a particularly striking piece of evidence to capture your reader's interest.

2. TAKE ACCOUNT OF YOUR AUDIENCE

In no other type of writing is the question of audience more important than in argumentation. The tone you establish, the type of diction you choose, the kinds of evidence you select to buttress your assertions, and indeed the organizational pattern you follow can influence your audience to trust you and believe your assertions. If you judge the nature of your audience accurately, respect its knowledge of the subject, and correctly envision whether it is likely to be hostile, neutral, complacent, or receptive, you will be able to tailor the various aspects of your argument appropriately.

3. GATHER THE NECESSARY SUPPORTING EVIDENCE

For each point of your argument, be sure to provide appropriate and sufficient evidence: verifiable facts and statistics, illustrative examples and narratives, or quotations from authorities. Don't overwhelm your reader with evidence, but don't skimp either; it is important to demonstrate your command of the topic and control of the thesis by choosing carefully from all the evidence at your disposal.

4. SETTLE ON AN ORGANIZATIONAL PATTERN

Once you think you have sufficient evidence to make your assertion convincing, consider how best to organize your argument. To some extent, your organization will depend on your method of reasoning: inductive, deductive, or a combination of the two. For example, is it necessary to establish a major premise before moving on to discuss a minor premise? Should most of your evidence precede your direct statement of an assertion, or follow it? Will induction work better with the particular audience you have targeted? As you present your primary points, you may find it effective to move from least important to most important or from least familiar to most familiar. A scratch outline can help; but often a writer's most crucial revisions in an argument involve rearranging its components into a sharper, more coherent order. Very often it is difficult to tell what that order should be until the revision stage of the writing process.

5. CONSIDER REFUTATIONS TO YOUR ARGUMENT

As you proceed with your argument, you may wish to take into account well-known and significant opposing arguments. To ignore opposing views would be to suggest to your readers any one of the following: You don't know about the opposing views; you know about them and are obviously and unfairly weighting the arguments in your favor; or you know about them and have no reasonable answers for them. Grant the validity of opposing arguments or refute them, but respect your reader's intelligence by addressing the objections to your assertion. Your readers will in turn respect you for doing so.

6. AVOID FAULTY REASONING

Have someone read your argument for errors in judgment and for faulty reasoning. Sometimes others can see easily what you can't see because you are so intimately tied to your assertion. These errors are typically called **logical fallacies.** Review the following list of errors in reasoning, making sure that you have not committed any of them.

OVERSIMPLIFICATION: A drastically simple solution to what is clearly a complex problem: *We have a balance-of-trade deficit because foreigners make better products than we do.*

HASTY GENERALIZATION: In inductive reasoning, a generalization that is based on too little evidence or on evidence that is not representative: *My grandparents eat bran flakes for breakfast, just as most older folks do.*

POST HOC ERGO PROPTER HOC: "After this, therefore because of this." Confusing chance or coincidence with causation. The fact that one event comes after another does not necessarily mean that the first event caused the second: *I went to the hockey game last night. The next thing I knew I had a cold.*

BEGGING THE QUESTION: Assuming in a premise something that needs to be proven: *Parking fines work because they keep people from parking illegally.*

FALSE ANALOGY: Making a misleading analogy between logically unconnected ideas: *If we can clone mammals, we should be able to find a cure for cancer.*

EITHER/OR THINKING: Seeing only two alternatives when there may in fact be other possibilities: *Either you love your job, or you hate it.*

NON SEQUITUR: "It does not follow." An inference or conclusion that is not clearly related to the established premises or evidence: *She is very sincere. She must know what she's talking about.*

7. CONCLUDE FORCEFULLY

In the conclusion of your essay, be sure to restate your position in new language, at least briefly. Besides persuading your reader to accept your point of view, you may also want to encourage some specific course of action. Above all, your conclusion should not introduce new information that may surprise your reader; it should seem to follow naturally, almost seamlessly, from the series of points that you have carefully established in the body of the essay. Don't overstate your case, but at the same time don't qualify your conclusion with the use of too many words or phrases like *I think, in my opinion, maybe, sometimes,* and *probably.* These words can make you sound indecisive and fuzzy-headed rather than rational and sensible.

The Declaration of Independence

■ Thomas Jefferson

President, governor, statesman, lawyer, architect, philosopher, and writer, Thomas Jefferson (1743–1826) is one of the most important figures in U.S. history. He was born in Albemarle County, Virginia, in 1743 and attended the College of William and Mary. After being admitted to law practice in 1767, he began a long and illustrious career of public service to the colonies and, later, the new republic. In 1809, after two terms as president, Jefferson retired to Monticello, a home he had designed and helped build. Ten years later he founded the University of Virginia. Jefferson died at Monticello on July 4, 1826, the fiftieth anniversary of the signing of the Declaration of Independence. Jefferson drafted the Declaration in 1776. Although it was revised by Benjamin Franklin and his colleagues at the Continental Congress, the declaration retains in its sound logic and forceful, direct style the unmistakable qualities of Jefferson's prose.

FOR YOUR JOURNAL

In your mind, what is the meaning of *democracy*? Where do your ideas about democracy come from?

When in the course of human events, it becomes necessary for one people to dissolve the political bands which have connected them with another, and to assume among the Powers of the earth, the separate and equal station to which the Laws of Nature and of Nature's God entitle them, a decent respect to the opinions of mankind requires that they should declare the causes which impel them to the separation.

We hold these truths to be self-evident, that all men are created equal, that they are endowed by their Creator with certain unalienable Rights, that among these are Life, Liberty and the pursuit of Happiness. That to secure these rights, Governments are instituted among Men deriving their just powers from the consent of the governed. That whenever any Form of Government becomes destructive of these ends, it is the Right of the People to alter or to abolish it, and to institute new Government, laying its foundation on such principles and organizing its powers in such form, as to them shall seem most likely to effect their Safety and Happiness. Prudence, indeed, will dictate that Governments long established should not be changed for light and transient causes; and accordingly all experience hath shown, that mankind are more disposed to suffer, while evils are sufferable, than to right themselves by abolishing the forms to which they are accustomed. But when a long train of abuses and usurpations pursuing invariably the same Object evinces a design to reduce them under absolute Despotism, it is their right, it is their duty, to throw off such government, and to provide new Guards for their future security. Such has been the patient sufferance of these Colonies; and such is now the necessity which constrains them to alter their former Systems of Government. The history of the present King of Great Britain[1] is a history of repeated injuries and usurpations, all having in direct object the establishment of an absolute Tyranny over these States. To prove this, let Facts be submitted to a candid world.

He has refused his Assent to Laws, the most wholesome and necessary for the public good. 3

He has forbidden his Governors to pass Laws of immediate and pressing importance, unless suspended in their operation till his Assent should be obtained; and when so suspended, he has utterly neglected to attend to them. 4

He has refused to pass other Laws for the accommodation of large districts of people, unless those people would relinquish the right of Representation in the Legislature, a right inestimable to them and formidable to tyrants only. 5

He has called together legislative bodies at places unusual, uncomfortable, and distant from the depository of their Public Records, for the sole purpose of fatiguing them into compliance with his measures. 6

He has dissolved Representative Houses repeatedly, for opposing with manly firmness his invasions on the rights of the people. 7

He has refused for a long time, after such dissolutions, to cause others to be elected; whereby the Legislative Powers, incapable of 8

---

[1]*King of Great Britain:* King George III, who ruled the British empire from 1760 to 1820. [Eds.]

Annihilation, have returned to the People at large for their exercise; the State remaining in the mean time exposed to all the dangers of invasion from without, and convulsions within.

He has endeavoured to prevent the population of these States; for 9 that purpose obstructing the Laws of Naturalization of Foreigners; refusing to pass others to encourage their migration hither, and raising the conditions of new Appropriations of Lands.

He has obstructed the Administration of Justice, by refusing his 10 Assent to Laws for establishing Judiciary Powers.

He has made Judges dependent on his Will alone, for the tenure 11 of their offices, and the amount and payment of their salaries.

He has erected a multitude of New Offices, and sent hither 12 swarms of Officers to harass our People, and eat out their substance.

He has kept among us, in time of peace, Standing Armies without 13 the Consent of our Legislature.

He has affected to render the Military independent of and supe- 14 rior to the Civil Power.

He has combined with others to subject us to jurisdictions for- 15 eign to our constitution, and unacknowledged by our laws; giving his Assent to their acts of pretended Legislation:

For quartering large bodies of armed troops among us: 16

For protecting them, by a mock Trial, from Punishment for any 17 Murders which they should commit on the Inhabitants of these States:

For cutting off our Trade with all parts of the world: 18

For imposing Taxes on us without our Consent: 19

For depriving us in many cases, of the benefits of Trial by Jury: 20

For transporting us beyond Seas to be tried for pretended of- 21 fenses:

For abolishing the free System of English Laws in a Neighbouring 22 Province, establishing therein an Arbitrary government, and enlarging its boundaries so as to render it at once an example and fit instrument for introducing the same absolute rule into these Colonies:

For taking away our Charters, abolishing our most valuable 23 Laws, and altering fundamentally the Forms of our Governments:

For suspending our own Legislatures, and declaring themselves 24 invested with Power to legislate for us in all cases whatsoever.

He has abdicated Government here, by declaring us out of his 25 Protection and waging War against us.

He has plundered our seas, ravaged our Coasts, burnt our towns 26 and destroyed the Lives of our people.

He is at this time transporting large Armies of foreign Mercenaries 27 to compleat works of death, desolation and tyranny, already begun with circumstances of Cruelty & perfidy scarcely paralleled in the most barbarous ages, and totally unworthy the Head of a civilized nation.

He has constrained our fellow Citizens taken Captive on the high 28 Seas to bear Arms against their Country, to become the executioners of their friends and Brethren, or to fall themselves by their Hands.

He has excited domestic insurrections amongst us, and has en- 29 deavoured to bring on the inhabitants of our frontiers, the merciless Indian Savages, whose known rule of warfare, is an undistinguished destruction of all ages, sexes and conditions.

In every stage of these Oppressions We Have Petitioned for Re- 30 dress in the most humble terms: Our repeated petitions have been answered only by repeated injury. A Prince, whose character is thus marked by every act which may define a Tyrant, is unfit to be the ruler of a free People.

Nor have We been wanting in attention to our British brethren. 31 We have warned them from time to time of attempts by their legislature to extend an unwarrantable jurisdiction over us. We have reminded them of the circumstances of our emigration and settlement here. We have appealed to their native justice and magnanimity and we have conjured them by the ties of our common kindred to disavow these usurpations, which would inevitably interrupt our connections and correspondence. They too have been deaf to the voice of justice and of consanguinity. We must, therefore acquiesce in the necessity, which denounces our Separation, and hold them, as we hold the rest of mankind, Enemies in War, in Peace Friends.

We, therefore, the Representatives of the United States of Amer- 32 ica, in General Congress, Assembled, appealing to the Supreme Judge of the world for the rectitude of our intentions, do, in the Name, and by Authority of the good People of these Colonies, solemnly publish and declare, That these United Colonies are, and of Right ought to be Free and Independent States; that they are Absolved from all Allegiance to the British Crown, and that all political connection between them and the State of Great Britain, is and ought to be totally dissolved; and that as Free and Independent States, they have full power to levy War, conclude Peace, contract Alliances, establish Commerce, and to do all other Acts and Things which Independent States may of right do. And for the support of this Declaration, with a firm reliance on the protection of Divine Providence, we mutually pledge to each other our lives, our Fortunes and our sacred Honor.

QUESTIONS FOR STUDY AND DISCUSSION

1. In paragraph 2, Jefferson presents certain "self-evident" truths. What are these truths, and how are they related to his argument? Do you consider them self-evident?

2. The Declaration of Independence is a deductive argument; it can, therefore, be presented in the form of a syllogism. What are the major premise, the minor premise, and the conclusion of Jefferson's argument? (Glossary: *Syllogism*)

3. The list of charges against the king is given as evidence in support of Jefferson's minor premise. Does he offer any evidence in support of his major premise? (Glossary: *Evidence*)

4. How, specifically, does Jefferson refute the possible charge that the colonists had not tried to solve their problems by less drastic means?

5. Where in the Declaration does Jefferson use parallel structure? What does he achieve by using it? (Glossary: *Parallelism*)

6. While the basic structure of the Declaration reflects sound deductive reasoning, Jefferson's language, particularly when he lists the charges against the king, tends to be emotional. Identify as many examples of this emotional language as you can, and discuss possible reasons why Jefferson uses this kind of language. (Glossary: *Diction*)

7. What, according to the Declaration of Independence, is the purpose of government? In your opinion, are there other legitimate purposes that governments serve? If so, what are they?

VOCABULARY

Refer to your dictionary to define the following words as they are used in this selection. Then use each word in a sentence of your own.

prudence (2)	conjured (31)
transient (2)	acquiesce (31)
convulsions (8)	rectitude (32)
abdicated (25)	

CLASSROOM ACTIVITY USING ARGUMENT

Choose one of the following controversial subjects, and think about how you would write an argument for or against it. Write three sentences that summarize three important points, two based on logic and one based on persuasion/emotion. Then write one sentence that acknowledges the opposing point of view. For example, if you were to argue for stricter enforcement of a leash law and waste pickup ordinance for dog owners in your town, you might write:

logic	Dogs allowed to run free can be a menace to joggers and local wildlife.
logic	Dog waste poses a health risk, particularly in areas where children play.
emotion	How would you feel if you hit an unleashed dog with your car?
counterargument	Dogs need fresh air and exercise, too.

Gun control
Tobacco restrictions
Cutting taxes and cutting social programs
Paying college athletes
Assisted suicide for terminally ill people
Widespread legalization of gambling

SUGGESTED WRITING ASSIGNMENTS

1. In recent years, the issue of human rights has been much discussed. Review the arguments for and against our country's active and outspoken promotion of the human rights issue as reported in the press. Then write an argument of your own in favor of a continued strong human rights policy on the part of our nation's leaders.

2. Using one of the subjects listed below, develop a thesis, and then write an essay in which you argue in support of that thesis.

   the minimum wage
   Social Security
   capital punishment
   the erosion of individual rights
   welfare
   the separation of church and state
   First Amendment rights

I Have a Dream

■ Martin Luther King Jr.

Civil rights leader Martin Luther King Jr. (1929–1968) was the son of a Baptist minister in Atlanta, Georgia. Ordained at the age of eighteen, King went on to earn academic degrees from Morehouse College, Crozer Theological Seminary, Boston University, and Chicago Theological Seminary. He came to prominence in 1955 in Montgomery, Alabama, when he led a successful boycott against the city's segregated bus system. The first president of the Southern Christian Leadership Conference, King became the leading spokesman for the civil rights movement during the 1950s and 1960s, espousing a consistent philosophy of nonviolent resistance to racial injustice. He also championed women's rights and protested the Vietnam War. Named Time *magazine's Man of the Year in 1963, King was awarded the Nobel Peace Prize in 1964. King was assassinated in April 1968 after speaking at a rally in Memphis, Tennessee. "I Have a Dream," the keynote address for the March on Washington in 1963, has become one of the most renowned and recognized speeches of the past century. Note how King uses allusions and parallelism to give life to his argument.*

FOR YOUR JOURNAL

Most Americans have seen film clips of King delivering the "I Have a Dream" speech. What do you know of the speech? What do you know of the events and conditions under which King presented it over forty years ago now?

Five score years ago, a great American, in whose symbolic shadow we stand, signed the Emancipation Proclamation.[1] This momentous decree came as a great beacon light of hope to millions of Negro slaves who had been seared in the flames of withering injustice. It came as a joyous daybreak to end the long night of captivity.

---

[1]*Emancipation Proclamation:* a decree enacted by Abraham Lincoln in 1863 that freed the slaves in the southern states. [Eds.]

But one hundred years later, we must face the tragic fact that the 2
Negro is still not free. One hundred years later, the life of the Negro
is still sadly crippled by the manacles of segregation and the chains of
discrimination. One hundred years later, the Negro lives on a lonely
island of poverty in the midst of a vast ocean of material prosperity.
One hundred years later, the Negro is still languishing in the corners
of American society and finds himself an exile in his own land. So we
have come here today to dramatize an appalling condition.

In a sense we have come to our nation's Capitol to cash a check. 3
When the architects of our republic wrote the magnificent words of
the Constitution and the Declaration of Independence, they were
signing a promissory note to which every American was to fall heir.
This note was a promise that all men would be guaranteed the unalienable rights of life, liberty, and the pursuit of happiness.

It is obvious today that America has defaulted on this promissory 4
note insofar as her citizens of color are concerned. Instead of honoring
this sacred obligation, America has given the Negro people a bad check;
a check which has come back marked "insufficient funds." But we
refuse to believe that the bank of justice is bankrupt. We refuse to believe
that there are insufficient funds in the great vaults of opportunity of this
nation. So we have come to cash this check — a check that will give us
upon demand the riches of freedom and the security of justice. We have
also come to this hallowed spot to remind America of the fierce urgency
of *now*. This is no time to engage in the luxury of cooling off or to take
the tranquilizing drug of gradualism. *Now* is the time to make real the
promises of Democracy. *Now* is the time to rise from the dark and desolate valley of segregation to the sunlit path of racial justice. *Now* is the
time to open the doors of opportunity to all of God's children. *Now* is
the time to lift our nation from the quicksands of racial injustice to the
solid rock of brotherhood.

It would be fatal for the nation to overlook the urgency of the 5
moment and to underestimate the determination of the Negro. This
sweltering summer of the Negro's legitimate discontent will not pass
until there is an invigorating autumn of freedom and equality. 1963
is not an end, but a beginning. Those who hope that the Negro
needed to blow off steam and will now be content will have a
rude awakening if the nation returns to business as usual. There
will be neither rest nor tranquility in America until the Negro is
granted his citizenship rights. The whirlwinds of revolt will continue
to shake the foundations of our nation until the bright day of justice
emerges.

But there is something I must say to my people who stand on the   6
warm threshold which leads into the palace of justice. In the process
of gaining our rightful place we must not be guilty of wrongful deeds.
Let us not seek to satisfy our thirst for freedom by drinking from the
cup of bitterness and hatred. We must forever conduct our struggle
on the high plane of dignity and discipline. We must not allow our
creative protest to degenerate into physical violence. Again and again
we must rise to the majestic heights of meeting physical force with
soul force. The marvelous new militancy which has engulfed the
Negro community must not lead us to a distrust of all white people,
for many of our white brothers, as evidenced by their presence here
today, have come to realize that their destiny is tied up with our destiny and their freedom is inextricably bound to our freedom. We cannot walk alone.

And as we walk, we must make the pledge that we shall march   7
ahead. We cannot turn back. There are those who are asking the
devotees of civil rights, "When will you be satisfied?" We can never
be satisfied as long as the Negro is the victim of the unspeakable hor-
rors of police brutality. We can never be satisfied as long as our bodies, heavy with the fatigue of travel, cannot gain lodging in the motels
of the highways and the hotels of the cities. We cannot be satisfied as
long as the Negro's basic mobility is from a smaller ghetto to a larger
one. We can never be satisfied as long as a Negro in Mississippi cannot vote and a Negro in New York believes he has nothing for which
to vote. No, no, we are not satisfied, and we will not be satisfied until
justice rolls down like waters and righteousness like a mighty stream.

I am not unmindful that some of you have come here out of great   8
trials and tribulations. Some of you have come fresh from narrow jail
cells. Some of you have come from areas where your quest for freedom
left you battered by the storms of persecution and staggered by the winds
of police brutality. You have been the veterans of creative suffering. Continue to work with the faith that unearned suffering is redemptive.

Go back to Mississippi, go back to Alabama, go back to South   9
Carolina, go back to Georgia, go back to Louisiana, go back to the
slums and ghettoes of our northern cities, knowing that somehow
this situation can and will be changed. Let us not wallow in the valley
of despair.

I say to you today, my friends, that in spite of the difficulties and   10
frustrations of the moment I still have a dream. It is a dream deeply
rooted in the American dream.

I have a dream that one day this nation will rise up and live out 11
the true meaning of its creed: "We hold these truths to be self-
evident; that all men are created equal."[2]

I have a dream that one day on the red hills of Georgia the sons 12
of former slaves and the sons of former slaveowners will be able to sit
down together at the table of brotherhood.

I have a dream that the state of Mississippi, a desert state swelter- 13
ing with the heat of injustice and oppression, will be transformed into
an oasis of freedom and justice.

I have a dream that my four little children will one day live in a 14
nation where they will not be judged by the color of their skin but by
the content of their character.

I have a dream today. 15

I have a dream that the state of Alabama, whose governor's[3] lips 16
are presently dripping with the words of interposition and nullification, will be transformed into a situation where little black boys and
black girls will be able to join hands with little white boys and white
girls and walk together as sisters and brothers.

I have a dream today. 17

I have a dream that one day every valley shall be exalted, every 18
hill and mountain shall be made low, the rough places will be made
plain, and the crooked places will be made straight, and the glory of
the Lord shall be revealed, and all flesh shall see it together.

This is our hope. This is the faith with which I return to the 19
South. With this faith we will be able to hew out of the mountain of
despair a stone of hope. With this faith we will be able to transform
the jangling discords of our nation into a beautiful symphony of
brotherhood. With this faith we will be able to work together, to
pray together, to struggle together, to go to jail together, to stand up
for freedom together, knowing that we will be free one day.

This will be the day when all of God's children will be able to 20
sing with new meaning.

> My country, 'tis of thee
> Sweet land of liberty,
> Of thee I sing:

---

[2]From the Declaration of Independence by Thomas Jefferson. (See p. 494.) [Eds.]
[3]*Governor George Wallace* (b. 1919): a strong segregationist in 1963 who later received integrated political support after he changed his stance. [Eds.]

Land where my fathers died,
Land of the pilgrims' pride,
From every mountainside
    Let freedom ring.

And if America is to be a great nation this must become true. So 21
let freedom ring from the prodigious hilltops of New Hampshire. Let
freedom ring from the mighty mountains of New York. Let freedom
ring from the heightening Alleghenies of Pennsylvania!

Let freedom ring from the snowcapped Rockies of Colorado! 22

Let freedom ring from the curvaceous peaks of California! 23

But not only that; let freedom ring from Stone Mountain of 24
Georgia!

Let freedom ring from Lookout Mountain of Tennessee! 25

Let freedom ring from every hill and molehill of Mississippi. 26
From every mountainside, let freedom ring.

When we let freedom ring, when we let it ring from every village 27
and every hamlet, from every state and every city, we will be able to
speed up that day when all of God's children, black men and white
men, Jews and Gentiles, Protestants and Catholics, will be able to
join hands and sing in the words of the old Negro spiritual, "Free at
last! free at last! thank God almighty, we are free at last!"

QUESTIONS FOR STUDY AND DISCUSSION

1. What is King's thesis? (Glossary: *Thesis*) How has America "defaulted" on its promise?

2. What does King mean when he says that in gaining a rightful
   place in society "we must not be guilty of wrongful deeds"? Why
   is this issue so important to him?

3. King delivered his speech to two audiences: the huge audience
   that listened to him in person, and another, even larger audience.
   (Glossary: *Audience*) What is that larger audience? How does
   King's speech catch the audience's attention and deliver his
   point?

4. Examine the speech to determine how King organized his presentation. (Glossary: *Organization*) What are the main sections
   of the speech, and what is the purpose of each? How does
   the organization serve King's overall purpose? (Glossary:
   Purpose)

5. King uses parallel constructions and repetitions throughout his speech. (Glossary: *Parallelism*) Identify the phrases and words that he particularly emphasizes. Explain what these techniques add to the persuasiveness of his argument.

6. Explain King's choice for the title. (Glossary: *Title*) Why is that title particularly appropriate given the context in which the speech was delivered? What other titles might he have used?

VOCABULARY

Refer to your dictionary to define the following words as they are used in this selection. Then use each word in a sentence of your own.

manacles (2)
languishing (2)
gradualism (4)
inextricably (6)
tribulations (8)

redemptive (8)
nullification (16)
prodigious (21)
curvaceous (23)

CLASSROOM ACTIVITY USING ARGUMENT

King uses a variety of metaphors in his speech, but a singly encompassing metaphor can be useful to establish the tone and purpose of an essay. Write a brief description based on a metaphor that conveys an overall impression from the beginning. Try to avoid clichés ("My dorm is a beehive," "My life is an empty glass"), but make your metaphor readily understandable. For example, you could say, "A police siren is a lullaby in my neighborhood," or "My town is a car that has gone 15,000 miles since its last oil change." Carry the metaphor through the entire description.

SUGGESTED WRITING ASSIGNMENTS

1. King's language is powerful, and his imagery is vivid, but the effectiveness of any speech depends partially upon its delivery. If read in monotone, King's use of repetition and parallel language would sound almost redundant rather than inspiring. Keeping presentation in mind, write a short speech that argues a point of view about which you feel strongly. Using King's speech as a

model, incorporate imagery, repetition, and metaphor to communicate your point. Read your speech aloud to a friend to see how it flows and how effective your use of language is. Refine your presentation—both your text and how you deliver it—then present your speech to your class.

2. Using King's assessment of the condition of African Americans in 1963 as a foundation, research the changes that have occurred in the years following King's speech. How have laws changed? How have demographics changed? Present your information in an essay that assesses what still needs to be done to fulfill King's dream for America. Where do we still fall short of the racial equality envisioned by King? What are the prospects for the future?

As They Say, Drugs Kill

■ Laura Rowley

Laura Rowley is a columnist for Self *magazine and author of* On Target: How the World's Hottest Retailer Hit a Bull's-eye *(2003). Her freelance writing has appeared in the* New York Times, Parents, *and other publications. Rowley also spent five years at CNN in New York, reporting on air for "Your Money" and "Business Unusual" and producing live programs. Before going to work for CNN, she was an editor for the* United Nations Chronicle *and editor in chief of* Multi-Housing News, *a trade magazine for builders. She graduated from the University of Illinois at Urbana–Champaign in 1987 with a degree in journalism, and she received a master's in divinity from New York Theological Seminary in 1999. In the following essay, which first appeared in* Newsweek on Campus *in 1987, Rowley argues against substance abuse by recounting a particularly poignant experience. Although her narrative appeals primarily to the reader's emotions, she nonetheless attempts to persuade without preaching.*

FOR YOUR JOURNAL

What is your best argument against the use of drugs? If you could tell a story that argues against drugs and that would persuade young people not to use them, what would that story be? It might be a personal story, a story about friends who were unlucky in their use of drugs, or a story that you read about or saw portrayed in the movies or on television.

The fastest way to end a party is to have someone die in the middle of it. 1

At a party last fall I watched a 22-year-old die of cardiac arrest 2 after he had used drugs. It was a painful, undignified way to die. And I would like to think that anyone who shared the experience would feel his or her ambivalence about substance abuse dissolving.

This victim won't be singled out like Len Bias[1] as a bitter ex- 3 ample for "troubled youth." He was just another ordinary guy

---

[1]*Len Bias:* college basketball star who died of a drug overdose after signing a contract with the Boston Celtics. [Eds.]

celebrating with friends at a private house party, the kind where they roll in the keg first thing in the morning and get stupefied while watching the football games on cable all afternoon. The living room was littered with beer cans from last night's party—along with dirty socks and the stuffing from the secondhand couch.

And there were drugs, as at so many other college parties. The drug of choice this evening was psilocybin, hallucinogenic mushrooms. If you're cool you call them "'shrooms." 4

This wasn't a crowd huddled in the corner of a darkened room with a single red bulb, shooting needles in their arms. People played darts, made jokes, passed around a joint and listened to the Grateful Dead on the stereo. 5

Suddenly, a thin, tall, brown-haired young man began to gasp. His eyes rolled back in his head, and he hit the floor face first with a crash. Someone laughed, not appreciating the violence of his fall, thinking the afternoon's festivities had finally caught up with another guest. The laugh lasted only a second, as the brown-haired guest began to convulse and choke. The sound of the stereo and laughter evaporated. Bystanders shouted frantic suggestions: 6

"It's an epileptic fit, put something in his mouth!" 7

"Roll him over on his stomach!" 8

"Call an ambulance; God, somebody breathe into his mouth." 9

A girl kneeling next to him began to sob his name, and he seemed to moan. 10

"Wait, he's semicoherent." Four people grabbed for the telephone, to find no dial tone, and ran to use a neighbor's. One slammed the dead phone against the wall in frustration—and miraculously produced a dial tone. 11

But the body was now motionless on the kitchen floor. "He has a pulse, he has a pulse." 12

"But he's not breathing!" 13

"Well, get away—give him some f—ing air!" The three or four guests gathered around his body unbuttoned his shirt. 14

"Wait—is he OK? Should I call the damn ambulance?" 15

A chorus of frightened voices shouted, "Yes, yes!" 16

"Come on, come on, breathe again. Breathe!" 17

Over muffled sobs came a sudden grating, desperate breath that passed through bloody lips and echoed through the kitchen and living room. 18

"He's had this reaction before—when he did acid at a concert last spring. But he recovered in 15 seconds . . . ," one friend confided. 19

The rest of the guests looked uncomfortably at the floor or paced   20
purposelessly around the room. One or two whispered, "Oh, my God,"
over and over, like a prayer. A friend stood next to me, eyes fixed on the
kitchen floor. He mumbled, just audibly, "I've seen this before. My dad
died of a heart attack. He had the same look. . . ." I touched his shoulder and leaned against a wall, repeating reassurances to myself. People
don't die at parties. People don't die at parties.

Eventually, no more horrible, gnashing sounds tore their way   21
from the victim's lungs. I pushed my hands deep in my jeans pockets
wondering how much it costs to pump a stomach and how someone
could be so careless if he had had this reaction with another drug.
What would he tell his parents about the hospital bill?

Two uniformed paramedics finally arrived, lifted him onto a   22
stretcher and quickly rolled him out. His face was grayish blue, his
mouth hung open, rimmed with blood, and his eyes were rolled back
with a yellowish color on the rims.

The paramedics could be seen moving rhythmically forward and   23
back through the small windows of the ambulance, whose lights
threw a red wash over the stunned watchers on the porch. The paramedics' hands were massaging his chest when someone said, "Did
you tell them he took psilocybin? Did you tell them?"

"No, I . . ."   24

"My God, so tell them—do you want him to die?" Two people   25
ran to tell the paramedics the student had eaten mushrooms five minutes before the attack.

It seemed irreverent to talk as the ambulance pulled away. My   26
friend, who still saw his father's image, muttered, "That guy's dead."
I put my arms around him half to comfort him, half to stop him from
saying things I couldn't believe.

The next day, when I called someone who lived in the house, I   27
found that my friend was right.

My hands began to shake and my eyes filled with tears for some-   28
one I didn't know. Weeks later the pain has dulled, but I still can't
unravel the knot of emotion that has moved from my stomach to my
head. When I told one friend what happened, she shook her head and
spoke of the stupidity of filling your body with chemical substances.
People who would do drugs after seeing that didn't value their lives
too highly, she said.

But others refused to read any universal lessons from the inci-   29
dent. Many of those I spoke to about the event considered him the
victim of a freak accident, randomly struck down by drugs as a

pedestrian might be hit by a speeding taxi. They speculated that the student must have had special physical problems; what happened to him could not happen to them.

Couldn't it? Now when I hear people discussing drugs I'm   30
haunted by the image of him lying on the floor, his body straining to rid itself of substances he chose to take. Painful, undignified, unnecessary—like a wartime casualty. But in war, at least, lessons are supposed to be learned, so that old mistakes are not repeated. If this death cannot make people think and change, that will be an even greater tragedy.

QUESTIONS FOR STUDY AND DISCUSSION

1. Rowley uses an extended narrative example to develop her argument. How does she use dialogue, diction choices, and appropriate details to make her argument more compelling? (Glossary: *Narration; Dialogue; Diction;* and *Details*)

2. Rowley does not argue her point until the last sentence of the essay, but the purpose of her essay is clear. (Glossary: *Purpose*) What does she want us to believe? What does she want us to do? How does her anecdote serve as the foundation for her argument? (Glossary: *Anecdote*)

3. What does Rowley gain by sharing this powerful experience with her readers? How did Rowley's friends react when she told them her story?

4. Why do you think Rowley chose not to name the young man who died? In what ways is this young man different from Len Bias, the talented basketball player who died of a drug overdose?

5. What in Rowley's tone—her attitude toward her subject and audience—particularly contributes to the persuasiveness of the essay? (Glossary: *Tone*) Cite examples from the selection that support your conclusion.

6. How did Rowley's opening paragraph affect you? What would have been lost had she combined the first two paragraphs? (Glossary: *Beginnings and Endings*)

7. For what audience do you suppose Rowley wrote this essay? (Glossary: *Audience*) In your opinion, would most readers be convinced by what Rowley says about drugs? Are you convinced? Why, or why not?

VOCABULARY

Refer to your dictionary to define the following words as they are used in this selection. Then use each word in a sentence of your own.

ambivalence (2)

stupefied (3)

convulse (6)

semicoherent (11)

audibly (20)

gnashing (21)

irreverent (26)

unravel (28)

speculated (29)

tragedy (30)

CLASSROOM ACTIVITY USING ARGUMENT

Choose one of the following position statements for an exercise in argumentation:

1. More parking spaces should be provided on campus for students.
2. English should be declared the official language of the United States.
3. Performance standards in our schools should be raised.
4. The Food and Drug Administration takes too long to decide whether new drugs will be made available to consumers.
5. Job placement is not the responsibility of colleges and universities.

Make a list of the types of information and evidence you would need to write an argumentative essay on the topic you chose. Indicate where and how you might obtain this information.

SUGGESTED WRITING ASSIGNMENTS

1. Write an essay in which you argue against either drinking or smoking. What would drinkers and smokers claim are the benefits of their habits? What are the key arguments against these types of substance abuse? Like Rowley, use examples from your personal experience or from your reading to document your essay.
2. Write a persuasive essay in which you support or refute the following proposition: "Television advertising is in large part responsible for Americans' belief that over-the-counter drugs are cure-alls." Does such advertising, in fact, promote drug dependence or abuse?

3. What is the most effective way to bring about social change and to influence societal attitudes? Concentrating on the sorts of changes you have witnessed over the last ten years, write an essay in which you describe how best to influence public opinion.

Uncle Sam and Aunt Samantha

■ Anna Quindlen

Anna Quindlen was born in 1953. After graduating from Barnard College in 1974, she became a reporter for the New York Times *and later a columnist, winning the Pulitzer Prize for her "Public and Private" column in 1992. Quindlen left the* Times *in 1994 to concentrate on writing fiction and her new column at* Newsweek. *Quindlen's novels include* Object Lessons *(1991),* One True Thing *(1995), and* Black and Blue *(1998). Her most recent books,* How Reading Changed My Life *(1998) and* A Short Guide to a Happy Life *(2000), focus on everyday life issues. The following essay originally appeared in Quindlen's* Newsweek *column in November 2001, less than two months after the attacks on the World Trade Center and the Pentagon. At the time, the United States was preparing for a military confrontation with the Taliban regime in Afghanistan. Notice how she uses facts as evidence as she argues that women and men should both register for the draft.*

FOR YOUR JOURNAL

Equality between the sexes is the subject of many ongoing debates. What are the common ways women are treated differently than men? When do you think it's justified, and when isn't it?

O ne out of every five new recruits in the United States military is 1 female.

The Marines gave the Combat Action Ribbon for service in the 2 Persian Gulf[1] to 23 women.

Two female soldiers were killed in the bombing of the USS *Cole.*[2] 3

The Selective Service registers for the draft all male citizens be- 4 tween the ages of 18 and 25.

---

[1]*Persian Gulf War:* the 1991 conflict to expel Iraqi forces from Kuwait. [Eds.]
[2]*Bombing of USS* Cole: the October 2000 terrorist attack on a U.S. destroyer that killed 17 soldiers. [Eds.]

What's wrong with this picture?   5

As Americans read and realize that the lives of most women in   6
this country are as different from those of Afghan women as a Cu-
nard cruise is from maximum-security lockdown, there has nonetheless been little attention paid to one persistent gender inequity in U.S.
public policy. An astonishing anachronism, really: While women are
represented today in virtually all fields, including the armed forces,
only men are required to register for the military draft that would be
used in the event of a national-security crisis.

Since the nation is as close to such a crisis as it has been in more   7
than 60 years, it's a good moment to consider how the draft wound
up in this particular time warp. It's not the time warp of the Taliban,[3]
certainly, stuck in the worst part of the 13th century, forbidding
women to attend school or hold jobs or even reveal their arms, forc-
ing them into sex and marriage. Our own time warp is several decades old. The last time the draft was considered seriously was 20
years ago, when registration with the Selective Service was restored
by Jimmy Carter after the Soviet invasion of, yep, Afghanistan. The
president, as well as the Army chief of staff, asked at the time for the
registration of women as well as men.

Amid a welter of arguments—women interfere with esprit de   8
corps, women don't have the physical strength, women prisoners
could be sexually assaulted, women soldiers would distract male soldiers from their mission—Congress shot down the notion of gender-
blind registration. So did the Supreme Court, ruling that since women
were forbidden to serve in combat positions and the purpose of the
draft was to create a combat-ready force, it made sense not to register
them.

But that was then, and this is now. Women have indeed served in   9
combat positions, in the Balkans and the Middle East. More than
40,000 managed to serve in the Persian Gulf without destroying unit
cohesion or failing because of upper-body strength. Some are even
now taking out targets in Afghanistan from fighter jets, and apparently without any male soldier's falling prey to some predicted excess
of chivalry or lust.

Talk about cognitive dissonance. All these military personnel,   10
male and female alike, have come of age at a time when a significant
level of parity was taken for granted. Yet they are supposed to accept

[3]*Taliban:* the reactionary group that ruled Afghanistan from 1996 to 2001. [Eds.]

that only males will be required to defend their country in a time of national emergency. This is insulting to men. And it is insulting to women. Caroline Forell, an expert on women's legal rights and a professor at the University of Oregon School of Law, puts it bluntly: "Failing to require this of women makes us lesser citizens."

Neither the left nor the right has been particularly inclined to consider this issue judiciously. Many feminists came from the antiwar movement and have let their distaste for the military in general and the draft in particular mute their response. In 1980 NOW released a resolution that buried support for the registration of women beneath opposition to the draft, despite the fact that the draft had been redesigned to eliminate the vexing inequities of Vietnam, when the sons of the working class served and the sons of the Ivy League did not. Conservatives, meanwhile, used an equal-opportunity draft as the linchpin of opposition to the Equal Rights Amendment,[4] along with the terrifying specter of unisex bathrooms. (I have seen the urinal, and it is benign.) The legislative director of the right-wing group Concerned Women for America once defended the existing regulations by saying that most women "don't want to be included in the draft." All those young men who went to Canada during Vietnam and those who today register with fear and trembling in the face of the Trade Center devastation might be amazed to discover that lack of desire is an affirmative defense.

Parents face a series of unique new challenges in this more egalitarian world, not the least of which would be sending a daughter off to war. But parents all over this country are doing that right now, with daughters who enlisted; some have even expressed surprise that young women, in this day and age, are not required to register alongside their brothers and friends. While all involved in this debate over the years have invoked the assumed opposition of the people, even 10 years ago more than half of all Americans polled believed women should be made eligible for the draft. Besides, this is not about comfort but about fairness. My son has to register with the Selective Service this year, and if his sister does not when she turns 18, it makes a mockery not only of the standards of this household but of the standards of this nation.

[4]*Equal Rights Amendment:* a proposed amendment to the U.S. Constitution guaranteeing equal rights to men and women. [Eds.]

It is possible in Afghanistan for women to be treated like little 13
more than fecund pack animals precisely because gender fear and ignorance and hatred have been codified and permitted to hold sway.
In this country, largely because of the concerted efforts of those allied
with the women's movement over a century of struggle, much of that
bigotry has been beaten back, even buried. Yet in improbable places
the creaky old ways surface, the ways suggesting that we women
were made of finer stuff. The finer stuff was usually porcelain, deco-
rative and on the shelf, suitable for meals and show. Happily, the
finer stuff has been transmuted into the right stuff. But with rights
come responsibilities, as teachers like to tell their students. This is a
responsibility that should fall equally upon all, male and female alike.
If the empirical evidence is considered rationally, if the decision is di-
vested of outmoded stereotypes, that's the only possible conclusion to
be reached.

QUESTIONS FOR STUDY AND DISCUSSION

1. Quindlen begins her argument with a quick list of facts. How effective is this as a beginning for the issue she is writing about?
(Glossary: *Beginnings and Endings*)

2. What is Quindlen's thesis? (Glossary: *Thesis*) Where does she
state it in her essay? Would you have put it in a different place?
Explain.

3. Why do you think Quindlen recounts the history of the Selective
Service in paragraphs 7 and 8? What effect does this have on her
argument?

4. Toward the end of the essay, Quindlen makes a point about her
own family and the draft. What is Quindlen's purpose in using
her own family as an example? (Glossary: *Purpose*)

5. How would you describe Quindlen's tone? (Glossary: *Tone*) To
support your answer, identify specific words and phrases that she
uses.

6. Who is Quindlen trying to reach in this essay? (Glossary: *Audience*) What sentences in the essay lead you to that conclusion?

VOCABULARY

Refer to your dictionary to define the following words as they are
used in this selection. Then use each word in a sentence of your own.

persistent (6)	linchpin (11)
anachronism (6)	fecund (13)
time warp (7)	codified (13)
esprit de corps (8)	porcelain (13)
vexing (11)	transmuted (13)

CLASSROOM ACTIVITY USING ARGUMENT

Write a paragraph that argues that people should compliment one another more. Use only one of the following quotes to support your argument:

> "Compliments are the high point of a person's day," said self-help author Melodie Bronson. "Without compliments, anyone's life is sure to be much more difficult."

> "Compliments have been proven to lower blood pressure and increase endorphin production to the brain," said Dr. Ruth West of the Holistic Medicine Committee. "A compliment a day may lengthen your life span by as much as a year."

> "Compliments are a special way people communicate with each other," said Bill Goodbody, therapist at the Good Feeling Institute. "Ninety percent of our patients report happier relationships or marriages after they begin compliment therapy."

Explain why you chose the quote you did. How did you integrate it into your paragraph?

SUGGESTED WRITING ASSIGNMENTS

1. Think about a policy in which people are treated differently on the basis of gender, age, race, or some other feature. The policy could be one of either your local campus, local government, state government, or national government. For example, most states require that people be 21 to drink, 18 to buy cigarettes, or 16 to drive a car. Using "Uncle Sam and Aunt Samantha" as a model, write an argument in which you argue for or against the policy. Try to include the history of the policy in your argument so that your audience understands the policy.

2. Using your journal entry as a starting point, write an argument in favor or against a certain way men and women are treated differently. In your essay, be sure to address possible objections to your point of view. For example, if you argue that women should be allowed to play the same professional sports as men, you should refute any objections that your audience might have based on safety issues and the physical differences between men and women. Be sure to list clear and specific examples that support your argument.

In Praise of the F Word

■ Mary Sherry

Mary Sherry was born in Bay City, Michigan, and received her bachelor's degree from Rosary College in River Forest, Illinois. She owns her own research and publishing company specializing in information for economic and development organizations. Sherry also teaches in adult-literacy programs and has written essays on educational problems for various newspapers, including the Wall Street Journal *and* Newsday. *In the following essay, reprinted from* Newsweek, *Sherry takes a provocative stance—that the threat of flunking is a "positive teaching tool." She believes students would all be better off if they had a "healthy fear of failure," and she marshals a series of logical appeals to both clarify and support her argument.*

FOR YOUR JOURNAL

Comment on what you see as the relationship between learning and grades. Do teachers and students pay too much attention to grades at the expense of learning? Or are grades not seen as important enough?

Tens of thousands of 18-year-olds will graduate this year and be handed meaningless diplomas. These diplomas won't look any different from those awarded their luckier classmates. Their validity will be questioned only when their employers discover that these graduates are semiliterate.

Eventually a fortunate few will find their way into educational-repair shops—adult-literacy programs, such as the one where I teach basic grammar and writing. There, high-school graduates and high-school dropouts pursuing graduate-equivalency certificates will learn the skills they should have learned in school. They will also discover they have been cheated by our educational system.

As I teach, I learn a lot about our schools. Early in each session I ask my students to write about an unpleasant experience they had in school. No writers' block here! "I wish someone would have made me stop doing drugs and made me study." "I liked to party and no one seemed to care." "I was a good kid and didn't cause any trouble, so they just passed me along even though I didn't read well and couldn't write." And so on. 3

I am your basic do-gooder, and prior to teaching this class I blamed the poor academic skills our kids have today on drugs, divorce, and other impediments to concentration necessary for doing well in school. But, as I rediscover each time I walk into the classroom, before a teacher can expect students to concentrate, he has to get their attention, no matter what distractions may be at hand. There are many ways to do this, and they have much to do with teaching style. However, if style alone won't do it, there is another way to show who holds the winning hand in the classroom. That is to reveal the trump card of failure. 4

I will never forget a teacher who played that card to get the attention of one of my children. Our youngest, a world-class charmer, did little to develop his intellectual talents but always got by. Until Mrs. Stifter. 5

Our son was a high-school senior when he had her for English. "He sits in the back of the room talking to his friends," she told me. "Why don't you move him to the front row?" I urged, believing the embarrassment would get him to settle down. Mrs. Stifter looked at me steely-eyed over her glasses. "I don't move seniors," she said. "I flunk them." I was flustered. Our son's academic life flashed before my eyes. No teacher had ever threatened him with that before. I regained my composure and managed to say that I thought she was right. By the time I got home I was feeling pretty good about this. It was a radical approach for these times, but, well, why not? "She's going to flunk you," I told my son. I did not discuss it any further. Suddenly English became a priority in his life. He finished out the semester with an A. 6

I know one example doesn't make a case, but at night I see a parade of students who are angry and resentful for having been passed along until they could no longer even pretend to keep up. Of average intelligence or better, they eventually quit school, concluding they were too dumb to finish. "I should have been held back" is a comment I hear frequently. Even sadder are those students who are high-school graduates who say to me after a few weeks of class, "I don't know how I ever got a high-school diploma." 7

Passing students who have not mastered the work cheats them 8
and the employers who expect graduates to have basic skills. We
excuse this dishonest behavior by saying kids can't learn if they come
from terrible environments. No one seems to stop to think that—no
matter what environments they come from—most kids don't put
school first on their list unless they perceive something is at stake.
They'd rather be sailing.

Many students I see at night could give expert testimony on un- 9
employment, chemical dependency, abusive relationships. In spite of
these difficulties, they have decided to make education a priority.
They are motivated by the desire for a better job or the need to hang
on to the one they've got. They have a healthy fear of failure.

People of all ages can rise above their problems, but they need to 10
have a reason to do so. Young people generally don't have the maturity
to value education in the same way my adult students value it. But fear
of failure, whether economic or academic, can motivate both.

Flunking as a regular policy has just as much merit today as it 11
did two generations ago. We must review the threat of flunking and
see it as it really is—a positive teaching tool. It is an expression of
confidence by both teachers and parents that the students have the
ability to learn the material presented to them. However, making it
work again would take a dedicated, caring conspiracy between teachers and parents. It would mean facing the tough reality that passing
kids who haven't learned the material—while it might save them
grief for the short term—dooms them to long-term illiteracy. It
would mean that teachers would have to follow through on their
threats, and parents would have to stand behind them, knowing their
children's best interests are indeed at stake. This means no more
doing Scott's assignments for him because he might fail. No more
passing Jodi because she's such a nice kid.

This is a policy that worked in the past and can work today. A wise 12
teacher, with the support of his parents, gave our son the opportunity
to succeed—or fail. It's time we return this choice to all students.

QUESTIONS FOR STUDY AND DISCUSSION

1. What is Sherry's thesis? (Glossary: *Thesis*) What evidence does
   she use to support her argument?

2. Sherry uses dismissive terms to characterize objections to flunking: *cheats* and *excuses*. In your opinion, does she do enough to
   acknowledge the other side of the argument? Explain.

3. What is the "F word" discussed in the essay? Does referring to it as the "F word" increase the effectiveness of the essay? Why?

4. Who is Sherry's audience? (Glossary: *Audience*) Is it receptive to the "F word"? Explain your answer.

5. What does Sherry accomplish in paragraph 3?

6. In what way is Sherry qualified to comment on the potential benefits of flunking students? Do you think her induction is accurate?

7. Why does Sherry think flunking is a valuable tool for educators and for students?

VOCABULARY

Refer to your dictionary to define the following words as they are used in this selection. Then use each word in a sentence of your own.

validity (1)   trump (4)

semiliterate (1)   testimony (9)

impediments (4)

CLASSROOM ACTIVITY USING ARGUMENT

A first-year composition student, Marco Schmidt, is preparing to write an essay in which he will argue that music should be a required course for all public high school students. He has compiled the following pieces of evidence:

Informal interviews with four classmates. Three of the classmates stated that they would have enjoyed and benefited from taking a music course in high school, and the fourth stated that she would not have been interested in taking music.

An article from a professional journal for teachers comparing the study habits of students who were involved in music and those who were not. The author, a psychologist, found that students who play an instrument or sing regularly have better study habits than students who do not.

A brief article from a national newsmagazine praising an inner-city high school's experimental curriculum, in which music classes play a prominent part.

The personal Web site of a high school music teacher who posts information about the successes and achievements of her former students.

Discuss these pieces of evidence with your classmates. Which are most convincing? Which provide the least support for Marco's argument? Why? What other types of evidence might Marco find to support his argument?

SUGGESTED WRITING ASSIGNMENTS

1. Write an essay in which you argue against Sherry's thesis. In what ways is flunking bad for students? Are there techniques more positive than a "fear of failure" that can be used to motivate students?

2. Think of something that involves short-term pain or sacrifice, but can be beneficial in the long run. For example, exercising requires exertion, but it may help prevent health problems. Studying and writing papers when you'd rather be having fun or even sleeping may seem painful, but a college degree leads to personal growth and development. Even if the benefits are obvious, imagine a skeptical audience, and write an argument in favor of the short-term sacrifice over the long-term consequences of avoiding it.

The Right to Fail

■ **William Zinsser**

William Zinsser was born in New York City in 1922. After graduating from Princeton University, he worked for the New York Herald Tribune, first as a feature writer and later as its drama and film critic. He also taught writing at Yale University and served as the general editor of the Book-of-the-Month Club. He is currently the series editor for the Writer's Craft Series, publications of talks given by writers sponsored by the Book-of-the-Month Club and the New York Public Library. Zinsser's own published works cover many aspects of contemporary American culture, but he is best known as the author of lucid and accessible books about writing, including Writing to Learn *(1988) and* On Writing Well *(6th ed., 1998), a perennial favorite for college writing courses and for the general public. Zinsser now teaches at the New School for Social Research in New York City. In the following essay, he argues the benefits of failing or dropping out and uses numerous examples to illustrate his points. As you read, consider the degree to which these examples serve as compelling evidence for the validity of Zinsser's point of view.*

FOR YOUR JOURNAL

Think about a time when, despite your best efforts, you could be said to have failed at something. Perhaps it was a loss in sports, a poor performance on a test in school, or even a vocational or educational path that you tried but were not able to see through. How did it feel to fail? Were you able to learn from the experience? How long did it take you to put the failure behind you?

I like "dropout" as an addition to the American language because it's brief and it's clear. What I don't like is that we use it almost entirely as a dirty word.

We only apply it to people under twenty-one. Yet an adult who spends his days and nights watching mindless TV programs is more of a dropout than an eighteen-year-old who quits college, with its frequently mindless courses, to become, say, a VISTA volunteer. For the young, dropping out is often a way of dropping in.

To hold this opinion, however, is little short of treason in America. A boy or girl who leaves college is branded a failure—and the right to fail is one of the few freedoms that this country does not grant its citizens. The American dream is a dream of "getting ahead," painted in strokes of gold wherever we look. Our advertisements and TV commercials are a hymn to material success, our magazine articles a toast to people who made it to the top. Smoke the right cigarette or drive the right car—so the ads imply—and girls will be swooning into your deodorized arms or caressing your expensive lapels. Happiness goes to the man who has the sweet smell of achievement. He is our national idol, and everybody else is our national fink.

I want to put in a word for the fink, especially the teen-age fink, because if we give him time to get through his finkdom—if we release him from the pressure of attaining certain goals by a certain age—he has a good chance of becoming our national idol, a Jefferson or a Thoreau, a Buckminster Fuller[1] or an Adlai Stevenson,[2] a man with a mind of his own. We need mavericks and dissenters and dreamers far more than we need junior vice-presidents, but we paralyze them by insisting that every step be a step up to the next rung of the ladder. Yet in the fluid years of youth, the only way for boys and girls to find their proper road is often to take a hundred side trips, poking out in different directions, faltering, drawing back, and starting again.

"But what if we fail?" they ask, whispering the dreadful word across the Generation Gap to their parents, who are back home at the Establishment, nursing their "middle-class values" and cultivating their "goal-oriented society." The parents whisper back: "Don't!"

What they should say is "Don't be afraid to fail!" Failure isn't fatal. Countless people have had a bout with it and come out stronger as a result. Many have even come out famous. History is strewn with eminent dropouts, "loners" who followed their own trail, not worrying about its odd twists and turns because they had faith in their own sense of direction. To read their biographies is always exhilarating,

---

[1] *Buckminster Fuller* (1895–1983): noted engineer, inventor, author, and architect. [Eds.]
[2] *Adlai Stevenson* (1900–1965): eloquent politician and diplomat. [Eds.]

not only because they beat the system, but because their system was better than the one that they beat.

Luckily, such rebels still turn up often enough to prove that individualism, though badly threatened, is not extinct. Much has been written, for instance, about the fitful scholastic career of Thomas P. F. Hoving, New York's former Parks Commissioner and now director of the Metropolitan Museum of Art. Hoving was a dropout's dropout, entering and leaving schools as if they were motels, often at the request of the management. Still, he must have learned something during those unorthodox years, for he dropped in again at the top of his profession.

His case reminds me of another boyhood—that of Holden Caulfield in J. D. Salinger's *The Catcher in the Rye,* the most popular literary hero of the postwar period. There is nothing accidental about the grip that this dropout continues to hold on the affections of an entire American generation. Nobody else, real or invented, has made such an engaging shambles of our "goal-oriented society," so gratified our secret belief that the "phonies" are in power and the good guys up the creek. Whether Holden has also reached the top of his chosen field today is one of those speculations that delight fanciers of good fiction. I speculate that he has. Holden Caulfield, incidentally, is now thirty-six.

I'm not urging everyone to go out and fail just for the sheer therapy of it, or to quit college just to coddle some vague discontent. Obviously it's better to succeed than to flop, and in general a long education is more helpful than a short one. (Thanks to my own education, for example, I can tell George Eliot from T. S. Eliot. I can handle the pluperfect tense in French, and I know that Caesar beat the Helvetii[3] because he had enough frumentum.[4]) I only mean that failure isn't bad in itself, or success automatically good.

Fred Zinnemann, who has directed some of Hollywood's most honored movies, was asked by a reporter, when *A Man for All Seasons* won every prize,[5] about his previous film *Behold a Pale Horse,* which was a box-office disaster. "I don't feel any obligation to be successful," Zinnemann replied. "Success can be dangerous—you feel you know it all. I've learned a great deal from my failures." A

7

8

9

10

---

[3]Reference to Rome's conquest of the Helvetii tribe in 58 B.C.E. [Eds.]
[4]*Frumentum:* a dish of wheat boiled in milk and usually sweetened and spiced. [Eds.]
[5]*A Man for All Seasons:* a 1966 film that won Academy Awards for best actor, screenplay, director, and motion picture. [Eds.]

similar point was made by Richard Brooks about his ambitious money loser, *Lord Jim*. Recalling the three years of his life that went into it, talking almost with elation about the troubles that befell his unit in Cambodia, Brooks told me that he learned more about his craft from this considerable failure than from his many earlier hits.

It's a point, of course, that applies throughout the arts. Writers, 11 playwrights, painters, and composers work in the expectation of periodic defeat, but they wouldn't keep going back into the arena if they thought it was the end of the world. It isn't the end of the world. For an artist—and perhaps for anybody—it is the only way to grow.

Today's younger generation seems to know that this is true, 12 seems willing to take the risks in life that artists take in art. "Society," needless to say, still has the upper hand—it sets the goals and condemns as a failure everybody who won't play. But the dropouts and the hippies are not as afraid of failure as their parents and grandparents. This could mean, as their elders might say, that they are just plumb lazy, secure in the comforts of an affluent state. It could also mean, however, that they just don't buy the old standards of success and are rapidly writing new ones.

Recently it was announced, for instance, that more than two 13 hundred thousand Americans have inquired about service in VISTA (the domestic Peace Corps) and that, according to a Gallup survey, "more than three million American college students would serve VISTA in some capacity if given the opportunity." This is hardly the road to riches or to an executive suite. Yet I have met many of these young volunteers, and they are not pining for traditional success. On the contrary, they appear more fulfilled than the average vice-president with a swimming pool.

Who is to say, then, if there is any right path to the top, or even 14 to say what the top consists of? Obviously the colleges don't have more than a partial answer—otherwise the young would not be so disaffected with an education that they consider vapid. Obviously business does not have the answer—otherwise the young would not be so scornful of its call to be an organization man.

The fact is, nobody has the answer, and the dawning awareness 15 of this fact seems to me one of the best things happening in America today. Success and failure are again becoming individual visions, as they were when the country was younger, not rigid categories. Maybe we are learning again to cherish this right of every person to succeed on his own terms and to fail as often as necessary along the way.

QUESTIONS FOR STUDY AND DISCUSSION

1. What does Zinsser argue? Does he state his thesis outright? (Glossary: *Thesis*) If so, where? If not, how does he present it to the reader?

2. Zinsser defines young adulthood as "the fluid years of youth" (4). What does his use of the word *fluid* convey to you? How does he use this definition to strengthen his argument regarding the nature of failure?

3. Zinsser wrote "The Right to Fail" more than thirty years ago. His reasoning and his argument remain sound, but at times his diction places him in a different era. (Glossary: *Diction*) Find the words that you perceive as being dated. What would their modern equivalents be?

4. Look up *fink* in the dictionary. Why do you think Zinsser chose this word to characterize those who do not have the "sweet smell of achievement" (3)? In what way are those who are willing to risk failure—as defined by society—"finks"?

5. Zinsser argues that many people who are considered very successful have "failed" at various times in their careers. Why does Zinsser use movie directors to illustrate his point? (Glossary: *Illustration*) What makes them good examples?

6. Why does Zinsser use VISTA volunteers to represent those who are not pursuing society's definition of success? In what way might one say they are "dropping in," not dropping out?

VOCABULARY

Refer to your dictionary to define the following words as they are used in this selection. Then use each word in a sentence of your own.

dissenters (4)	coddle (9)
strewn (6)	affluent (12)
eminent (6)	vapid (14)

CLASSROOM ACTIVITY USING ARGUMENT

Deductive reasoning works on the model of the syllogism. After reviewing the material on syllogisms in the introduction to this chapter (pp. 489–90), analyze the following syllogisms. Which work well, and which do not?

1. All of my CDs have blue lettering on them.
   I saw the new Youssou N'Dour CD the other day.
   The new Youssou N'Dour CD has blue lettering on it.
2. I have never lost a tennis match.
   I played a tennis match yesterday.
   I won my tennis match yesterday.
3. Surfers all want to catch the perfect wave.
   Jenny is a surfer.
   Jenny wants to catch the perfect wave.
4. Writers enjoy reading books.
   Bill enjoys reading books.
   Bill is a writer.
5. Cotton candy is an incredibly sticky kind of candy.
   Amy ate some incredibly sticky candy.
   Amy ate cotton candy.

Write two effective syllogisms of your own.

SUGGESTED WRITING ASSIGNMENTS

1. Based on your own experience, argue for or against the following statement: "You learn more from failure than you do from success." If you agree with this statement, do you think that you need to fail in order to eventually achieve more than you would have otherwise? If you disagree, what do you think success teaches you? How do you get strong and adaptable if all you encounter for a long time is success? How do your views compare with those of Zinsser and Sherry?

2. Zinsser's article is critical of the tyranny of the American dream of "getting ahead." Write an essay in which you discuss Americans' materialistic tendencies. When did we lose our ability to tell the difference between what we need and what we want? How would our quality of life improve if we could be content with fewer possessions? What changes would you propose to reduce the conspicuous-consumption mentality of our society?

Diversity Is Essential . . .

 **Lee C. Bollinger**

Lee C. Bollinger is the president of Columbia University and a member of its Law School faculty. He has had a distinguished career in higher education. A native of Santa Rosa, California, and a graduate of the University of Oregon and Columbia Law School, Bollinger clerked for Chief Justice Warren Burger of the U.S. Supreme Court. In 1973 he joined the faculty of the University of Michigan Law School and then went on to become president of Dartmouth College and then president of the University of Michigan. Bollinger's major scholarly interest has been free speech and First Amendment rights. Among his many publications are The Tolerant Society: Freedom of Speech and Extremist Speech in America *(1986),* Images of a Free Press *(1991), and* Eternally Vigilant: Free Speech in the Modern Era *(2002). The following article appeared in the January 27, 2003, issue of* Newsweek *as part of a larger feature on affirmative action in public higher education and the Supreme Court case against it. In the argument, Bollinger explains why he's in favor of affirmative action for minorities.*

FOR YOUR JOURNAL

How representative of our society as a whole should the students, faculty, and staff of a college or university be? Does the college's admissions office have a larger responsibility to society than selecting for admission the most "qualified applicants" — those who, say, score the highest on standardized tests? Who should be selected, and why?

When I became president of the University of Michigan in 1997, affirmative action in higher education was under siege from the right. Buoyed by a successful lawsuit against the University of Texas Law School's admissions policy and by ballot initiatives such as California's Proposition 209, which outlawed race as a factor in college admissions, the opponents set their sights on affirmative-action programs at colleges across the country.

The rumor that Michigan would be the next target in this campaign turned out to be correct. I believed strongly that we had no choice but to mount the best legal defense ever for diversity in higher education and take special efforts to explain this complex issue, in simple and direct language, to the American public. There are many misperceptions about how race and ethnicity are considered in college admissions. Competitive colleges and universities are always looking for a mix of students with different experiences and backgrounds—academic, geographic, international, socioeconomic, athletic, public-service oriented, and, yes, racial and ethnic.

It is true that in sorting the initial rush of applications, large universities will give "points" for various factors in the selection process in order to ensure fairness as various officers review applicants. Opponents of Michigan's undergraduate system complain that an applicant is assigned more points for being black, Hispanic, or Native American than for having a perfect SAT score. This is true, but it trivializes the real issue: whether, in principle, race and ethnicity are appropriate considerations. The simple fact about the Michigan undergraduate policy is that it gives overwhelming weight to traditional academic factors—some 110 out of a total of 150 points. After that, there are some 40 points left for other factors, of which 20 can be allocated for race or socioeconomic status.

Race has been a defining element of the American experience. The historic *Brown v. Board of Education*[1] decision is almost 50 years old, yet metropolitan Detroit is more segregated now than it was in 1960. The majority of students who each year arrive on a campus like Michigan's graduated from virtually all-white or all-black high schools. The campus is their first experience living in an integrated environment.

This is vital. Diversity is not merely a desirable addition to a well-rounded education. It is as essential as the study of the Middle Ages, of international politics, and of Shakespeare. For our students to better understand the diverse country and world they inhabit, they must be immersed in a campus culture that allows them to study with, argue with, and become friends with students who may be

---

[1]*Brown v. Board of Education:* the unanimous 1954 Supreme Court decision abolishing segregated education. [Eds.]

different from them. It broadens the mind, and the intellect—essential goals of education.

Reasonable people can disagree about affirmative action. But it is important that we do not lose the sense of history, the compassion and the largeness of vision that defined the best of the civil-rights era, which has given rise to so much of what is good about America today.

6

QUESTIONS FOR STUDY AND DISCUSSION

1. What is Bollinger's thesis, and where is it most clearly stated? (Glossary: *Thesis*)

2. In paragraph 2, Bollinger says, "There are many misperceptions about how race and ethnicity are considered in college admissions." What does he say those misperceptions are, and how does he clarify them?

3. Does Bollinger deny critics who say that more points are awarded in the University of Michigan undergraduate admissions formula for race than for a perfect SAT score? How does he answer those critics? Do you accept his argument? Has he successfully countered their argument that such a formula is inherently unfair?

4. What arguments does Bollinger give in favor of diversity? Does he provide sufficient supporting evidence for his ideas and beliefs? (Glossary: *Evidence*) Explain.

5. In paragraph 4, Bollinger points to the history of diversity as part of the American experience. Is that an appropriate appeal for him to make? Explain.

6. What audience do you think Bollinger is writing this argument for—those convinced of his argument, those opposed to it, or those who are undecided? (Glossary: *Audience*)

VOCABULARY

Refer to your dictionary to define the following words as they are used in this selection. Then use each word in a sentence of your own.

siege (1)   socioeconomic (2)
initiatives (1)   trivializes (3)
misperceptions (2)   ethnicity (3)

allocated (3)   intellect (5)
virtually (4)

CLASSROOM ACTIVITY USING ARGUMENT

In preparation for a discussion about some critically important terms in the argument over affirmative action, research in your dictionary, in the library, and on the Internet the following terms:

affirmative action
antidiscrimination
California Proposition 209
discrimination
glass ceiling
institutional discrimination
prejudice
quota system
racism
reverse discrimination
reverse racism

SUGGESTED WRITING ASSIGNMENTS

1. Using Bollinger's argument in favor of diversity as a starting point, write an argument in which you further detail the case for diversity. Using personal experiences, library, and Internet sources as your research, extend his ideas and provide more examples of why diversity is in the best interest of colleges and universities and the country as a whole. As much as possible, you should present objective ideas and examples, not personal ones, when making your case. If you want to write on a more personal level, see the next writing suggestion.

2. In paragraph 5, Bollinger writes, "For our students to better understand the diverse country and world they inhabit, they must be immersed in a campus culture that allows them to study with, argue with, and become friends with students who may be different from them. It broadens the mind, and the intellect—essential goals of education." Taking Bollinger's statement as your thesis, write an argument in favor of diversity on our campuses using

examples from your own experiences as a student. How have you personally benefited from your contacts with people of other races and ethnic groups? How has arguing with and becoming friends with people from different backgrounds helped you further your education and outlook?

... But Not at This Cost

◼ Armstrong Williams

Armstrong Williams is one of the "most widely recognized conservative voices in America," according to the Washington Post. *A commentator, radio talk-show host, and columnist, Williams is also chief executive officer of the Graham Williams Group, an international public relations firm. As a provocative standard bearer for the ideals of the right, Williams has written for such publications as* USA Today, *the* Washington Post, *the* Los Angeles Times, *the* Washington Times, *and* Reader's Digest. *Williams also writes a nationally syndicated newspaper column that is carried by 75 newspapers across the country, and he hosts a daily nationally syndicated television show. "The Right Side with Armstrong Williams." His best-selling* Beyond Blame *(1995) is a book of advice for a misguided young man. A native of Marion, South Carolina, and a 1981 graduate of South Carolina State College, Williams currently lives in Washington, D.C. The following essay arguing against affirmative action appeared alongside the preceding selection written by Lee C. Bollinger in the January 27, 2003, issue of* Newsweek.

FOR YOUR JOURNAL

Do you think that special consideration should be given to students of color, athletes, and legacies (descendants of graduates) in the college admissions process? If so, how much weight should be given? If not, why not?

Back in 1977, when I was a senior in high school, I received scholarship offers to attend prestigious colleges. The schools wanted me in part because of my good academic record—but also because affirmative action mandates required them to encourage more black students to enroll. My father wouldn't let me take any of the enticements. His reasoning was straightforward: Scholarship money should go to the economically deprived. And since he could pay for my schooling, he would. In the end, I chose a historically black college—South Carolina State.

What I think my father meant, but was perhaps too stern to say,   2
was that one should always rely on hard work and personal achievement to carry the day—every day. Sadly, this rousing point seems lost on the admissions board at the University of Michigan, which wrongly and unapologetically discriminates on the basis of skin color. The university ranks applicants on a scale that awards points for SAT scores, high-school grades, and race. For example, a perfect SAT score is worth 12 points. Being black gets you 20 points. Is there anyone who can look at those two numbers and think they are fair?

Supporters maintain that the quota system is essential to creating   3
a diverse student body. And, indeed, there is some validity to this sort of thinking. A shared history of slavery and discrimination has ingrained racial hierarchies into our national identity, divisions that need to be erased. There is, however, a very real danger that we are merely reinforcing the idea that minorities are first and foremost victims. Because of this victim status, the logic goes, they are owed special treatment. But that isn't progress, it's inertia.

If the goal of affirmative action is to create a more equitable soci-   4
ety, it should be need-based. Instead, affirmative action is defined by its tendency to reduce people to fixed categories: At many universities, it seems, admissions officers look less at who you are than *what* you are. As a result, affirmative-action programs rarely help the least among us. Instead, they often benefit the children of middle- and upper-class black Americans who have been conditioned to feel they are owed something.

This is alarming. We have finally, after far too long, reached a   5
point where black Americans have pushed into the mainstream—and not just in entertainment and sports. From politics to corporate finance, blacks succeed. Yet many of us still feel entitled to special benefits—in school, in jobs, in government contracts.

It is time to stop. We must reach a point where we expect to rise   6
or fall on our own merits. We just can't continue to base opportunities on race while the needs of the poor fall by the wayside. As a child growing up on a farm, I was taught that personal responsibility was the lever that moved the world. That is why it pains me to see my peers rest their heads upon the warm pillow of victim status.

QUESTIONS FOR STUDY AND DISCUSSION

1. What is Williams's thesis in this essay? Where does he offer his thesis statement? (Glossary: *Thesis*)

2. Williams begins his essay with a short narrative about the time he applied for college. How else might he have begun his essay? What would be lost or gained by a different approach? (Glossary: *Beginnings and Endings*)

3. Williams cites the admissions policy of the University of Michigan, where an applicant to the university can get 12 points for a perfect SAT score and 20 points for being black. He asks, "Is there anyone who can look at those two numbers and think they are fair?" (2) What do you think? Are the two sets of numbers a sign of unfairness to you? Explain.

4. What objections to Williams's argument can you provide?

5. In paragraph 3, Williams refers to the University of Michigan admissions policy as a "quota system." Is that a fair assessment? Explain. What is a quota system? (Glossary: *Definition*)

6. Read the pro side of the affirmative action argument written by Lee C. Bollinger (530–32). How effective are the two arguments? Your own position on the affirmative action debate aside, which argument is better written in your view, and why? (Glossary: *Evaluation*)

VOCABULARY

Refer to your dictionary to define the following words as they are used in this selection. Then use each word in a sentence of your own.

prestigious (1)	inertia (3)
mandates (1)	equitable (4)
enticements (1)	mainstream (5)
validity (3)	

CLASSROOM ACTIVITY USING ARGUMENT

The lead article in the January 23, 2003, *Newsweek* cover story on affirmative action written by Howard Fineman and Tara Lipper includes the following statement: "At least in theory, the idea of making decisions on racial grounds is unpopular—especially among whites, who oppose preferences for blacks by a 73–22 percent margin in the new *Newsweek* poll. (Minorities are nearly as dubious, opposing preference for blacks by 56–38 percent). Indeed, Americans of all colors oppose admissions preferences of all kinds, whether it's for minorities, athletes, legacies, or the drumline." Discuss with your classmates possible reasons why preferences are not viewed more favorably. How important are the polls in such a national debate?

SUGGESTED WRITING ASSIGNMENTS

1. Included in the January 27, 2003, *Newsweek* was an article entitled "What's at Stake?" by Barbara Kantrowitz and Pat Wingert. The article asks a number of questions that you may find helpful in developing your own position regarding affirmative action:

   • What is affirmative action?
   • How did the University of Michigan become the test case?
   • How does the Michigan system work?
   • Does the Michigan system create quotas?
   • How can the court rule?
   • Will the decision affect private universities and colleges?
   • How would an anti-affirmative-action ruling affect other preferences for legacies and athletes?
   • Whom does affirmative action hurt, and whom does it help?
   • What is affirmative access?
   • What, then, is the most equitable way to select the best-qualified applicants?

   Using your answers to these questions, write an argument in favor of or against affirmative action in college admissions.

2. Write an essay in which you try to find some middle ground between the pro and con sides of the affirmative action argument. What is the best course of action for universities and colleges to follow in their admissions policies? What is the best course for the courts to take? What is best for the country?

Exposing Media Myths: TV Doesn't Affect You as Much as You Think

 **Joanmarie Kalter**

Joanmarie Kalter has written extensively about television news and about the press in the Third World. After graduating from Cornell University in 1972 and working as a freelance writer for a number of years, Kalter received her master's degree from the Columbia Graduate School of Journalism in 1981. She joined TV Guide *as a staff writer in 1984 but returned to freelancing in 1989. Her articles have appeared in numerous and diverse periodicals, including the* New York Times, *the* Christian Science Monitor, *the* Bulletin of Atomic Scientists, *and* Africa Report. *In the following selection, note how Kalter uses her evidence to chip away at some "false truths" about television news. The rhetorical mode of cause and effect also plays a significant role in Kalter's argument as she reveals the serious implications of the myths she exposes.*

FOR YOUR JOURNAL

Reflect on your sense of the importance of television news. Do you watch a news program regularly? Do you find it valuable? How much of what you see and hear do you remember, and for how long?

Once upon a time, there was a new invention—television. It be- 1 came so popular, so quickly, that more American homes now have a TV set (98 percent) than an indoor toilet (97 percent). Around this new invention, then, an industry rapidly grew, and around this industry, a whole mythology. It has become a virtual truism, often heard and often repeated, that TV—and TV news, in particular— has an unparalleled influence on our lives.

Over the past 20 years, however, communications scholars have been quietly examining such truisms and have discovered, sometimes to their surprise, that many are not so true at all. *TV Guide* asked more than a dozen leading researchers for their findings and found an eye-opening collection of mythbusters. Indeed, they suggest that an entire body of political strategy and debate has been built upon false premises. . . .

Myth No. 1: Two-thirds of the American people receive most of their news from TV. This little canard is at the heart of our story. It can be traced to the now-famous Roper polls, in which Americans are queried: "I'd like to ask you where you usually get most of your news about what's going on in the world today. . . ." In 1959, when the poll was first conducted, 51 percent answered "television," with a steady increase ever since. The latest results show that 66 percent say they get most of their news from TV; only about a third credit newspapers.

Trouble is, that innocent poll question is downright impossible to answer. Just consider: It asks you to sort through the issues in your mind, pinpoint what and where you learned about each, tag it, and come up with a final score. Not too many of us can do it, especially since we get our news from a variety of sources. Even pollster Burns Roper concedes, "Memories do get fuzzy."

Scholars have found, however, that when they ask a less general, more specific question—Did you read a newspaper yesterday? Did you watch a TV news show yesterday?—the results are quite different. Dr. John Robinson, professor of sociology at the University of Maryland, found that on a typical day 67 percent read a newspaper, while 52 percent see a local or national TV newscast. Dr. Robert Stevenson, professor of journalism at the University of North Carolina, analyzed detailed diaries of TV use, and further found that only 18 percent watch network news on an average day, and only 13 percent pay full attention to it. Says Robinson, "TV is part of our overall mix, but in no way is it our number one source of news."

Yet it's a myth with disturbing consequences. Indeed, it is so widespread, says Dr. Mark Levy, associate professor of journalism at the University of Maryland, that it shapes—or misshapes—our political process. In the words of Michael Deaver, White House deputy chief of staff during President Reagan's first term, "The majority of the people get their news from television, so . . . we construct events and craft photos that are designed for 30 seconds to a minute so that it can fit into that 'bite' on the evening news." And thus the myth, says Levy, "distorts the very dialogue of democracy, which cannot be responsibly conducted in 30-second bites."

Myth No. 2: TV news sets the public agenda. It was first said [7] succinctly in 1963, and has long been accepted: While the mass media may not tell us what to think, they definitely tell us what to think about. And on some issues, the impact of TV is indisputable: the Ethiopian famine, the Challenger explosion. Yet for the more routine story, new research has challenged that myth, suggesting TV's influence may be surprisingly more limited.

For one thing, TV news most often reacts to newspapers in framing [8] issues of public concern. Dr. David Weaver, professor of journalism at Indiana University, found that newspapers led TV through the 1976 campaign. Given the brevity of broadcasts, of course, that's understandable. "TV has no page 36," explains Dr. Maxwell McCombs, professor of communications at the University of Texas. "So TV journalists have to wait until an issue has already achieved substantial public interest." TV, then, does not so much set the public agenda as spotlight it.

Even among those issues spotlighted, viewers do make indepen- [9] dent judgments. It seems the old "hypodermic" notions no longer hold, says Dr. Doris Graber, political science professor at the University of Illinois. "We're not sponges for this stuff, and while TV may provide the raw material, people do select."

Indeed, even TV entertainment is less influential than once was [10] thought. According to Robinson, studies found no difference in racial attitudes among those who saw *Roots* and those who didn't. Ditto "The Day After" on nuclear war, and *Amerika* on the Soviets. As for news, Graber notes that the public took a long time to share the media's concern about Watergate,[1] and even now are lagging the media on Iran-Contragate.[2] And finally, there are many issues on which the press must belatedly catch up with the public. Which brings us to . . .

Myth No. 3: TV news changed public opinion about the war in [11] **Vietnam.**[3] Contrary to this most common of beliefs, research shows

---

[1]*Watergate:* U.S. political scandal in 1972–1974 involving illegal activities of former President Richard Nixon's administration. [Eds.]

[2]*Iran-Contragate:* U.S. political scandal in the 1980s involving the illegal sale of weapons to Nicaraguan rebels. [Eds.]

[3]*Vietnam:* a war fought in the 1960s–1970s by the United States and South Vietnam against North Vietnam to prevent all of Vietnam from being united under Communist leadership. [Eds.]

just the opposite. Lawrence Lichty, professor of radio/television/film at Northwestern University, analyzed network war coverage and found that it did not become relatively critical until 1967. By then, however, a majority of Americans already thought U.S. involvement in Vietnam was a mistake. And they thought so not because of TV coverage, but because of the number of young Americans dying.

Yet this fable about the "living-room war" is so accepted it has become "fact": that gory TV pictures of bloody battles undermined public support for the war; that, in a 1968 TV-news special, Walter Cronkite mistakenly presented the Tet offensive as a defeat for the U.S.; and that, because President Johnson so believed in the power of TV, he concluded then that his war effort was lost. 12

In fact, Lichty found few "gory" pictures. "TV presented a distant view," he says, with less than five percent of TV's war reports showing heavy combat. Nor, as we now know, was a rapt audience watching at home in their living rooms. As for Cronkite's report on the Tet offensive, the CBS anchor said on the evening news, "First and simplest, the Vietcong suffered a military defeat." And, in his now-famous TV special, Cronkite concluded, "we are mired in a stalemate," and should "negotiate." By that time, Lichty says, "public opinion had been on a downward trend for a year and a half. A majority of Americans agreed." And so Johnson's concern, it seems, was not that Cronkite would influence public opinion, but rather that he reflected it. 13

Indeed, Professor John Mueller of the University of Rochester has compared the curve of public opinion on the war in Vietnam, covered by TV, with that of the war in Korea, hardly covered. He found the two curves strikingly similar: In both cases, public support dropped as the number of American deaths rose. 14

Disturbingly, the misconception about TV's influence in Vietnam has had broad consequences, for it has framed an important debate ever since. Can a democratic society, with a free flow of dramatic TV footage, retain the public will to fight a war? Many argue no. And this has been the rationale more recently for censoring the Western press in the Falklands and Grenada.[4] Yet it is, says Lichty, a policy based on a myth. 15

Myth No. 4: TV today is the most effective medium in communicating news. Most of us think of TV fare as simple, direct, easy to understand — with the combination of words and pictures making it all the more powerful. But recent research shows that TV news, as 16

---

[4]Falklands, Grenada: military actions of the early 1980s. [Eds.]

distinct from entertainment, is often very confusing. In study after study, Robinson and Levy have found that viewers understand only about a third of network news stories.

Why is TV news so tough to understand? Dr. Dan Drew, profes-   17
sor of journalism at Indiana University, suggests that the verbal and visual often conflict. Unlike TV entertainment, in which the two are composed together, TV-news footage is gathered first, and the story it illustrates often diverges. We may see fighting across the Green Line in Beirut—for a story about peace talks. We may see "file footage" of Anglican envoy Terry Waite walking down the street— for a story on his disappearance. As viewers try to make sense of the visual, they lose the gist of the verbal. "The myth," says Levy, "is that since we are a visual medium, we must always have pictures. . . . But that's a disaster, a recipe for poor communication."

Journalists also are much more familiar with the world of public   18
affairs, says Levy, and rely on its technical jargon: from "leading economic indicators" to "the Druse militia." Their stories, say researchers, are overillustrated, with most pictures on the screen for less than 20 seconds. They assume, mistakenly, that viewers pay complete attention, and so they often do not repeat the main theme. Yet while understanding TV news takes concentration, watching TV is full of distractions. In one study, researchers mounted cameras on top of sets and recorded the amount of time viewers also read, talked, walked in and out of the room. They concluded that viewers actually watch only 55 percent of what's on.

The audience does recall the extraordinary, such as a man on the   19
moon, and better comprehends human-interest stories. But since most news is not covered night after night, tomorrow's broadcast tends to wash away today's. "People don't remember much from TV news," says Graber. "It's like the ocean washing over traces that have been very faintly formed."

Today's TV news is carefully watched by politicians, who keep a   20
sharp eye on how they're covered. But while it may provide theater for a handful, this research increasingly shows it's lost on the American public. And sadly, then, hard-working TV journalists may be missing an opportunity to inform.

Yet TV remains a medium with great potential. And studies show   21
that it does extend the awareness of the poor and ill-educated, who cannot afford additional sources. What's more, research suggests that the clarity of TV news can be improved—without compromising journalistic standards. "We have been glitzed by the glamour of TV,

all these gee-whiz gimmicks," says Robinson. "And we have lost sight of one of the oldest and most durable findings of communications research. . . . The most important element is the writer, who sits at a typewriter and tries to tell the story in a simple and organized way. That's the crucial link."

Research also shows that viewers want a broadcast they can understand. The success of *60 Minutes* proves there's an audience still hungry for sophisticated factual information. "When someone does this for news, they'll grab the ratings," says Levy. "Nobody loses!" Ironically, no corporation would launch an ad campaign without extensive testing on how best to reach its audience. But many broadcast journalists, working under intense pressure, remain unaware of the problems. "There's a lot we have to learn about how people comprehend," says William Rubens, NBC research vice-president. "But no, it hasn't been the thrust of our research." According to Robinson and Levy, this requires the attention of those in charge, a collective corporate will. With the networks under a financial squeeze, their news audiences having recently declined some 15 percent, "This may be the time for them to rethink their broadcasts," says Levy.   22

And if they do, they may just live . . . happily ever after.   23

QUESTIONS FOR STUDY AND DISCUSSION

1. Kalter begins by discussing television—and her title implies that the article is about television in general—but the focus of her article is television news. (Glossary: *Focus*) In what ways does narrowing her focus help her argue her point?

2. How does Kalter organize her argument in paragraphs 16–20? (Glossary: *Organization*) What does each paragraph accomplish? (Glossary: *Paragraph*)

3. Kalter uses the term *myth* to describe assumptions about TV news. Look up the definition of *myth* in your dictionary. How does the use of this term help Kalter influence her audience? (Glossary: *Audience*)

4. How can general survey questions lead to inaccurate data? How have the Roper polls contributed to the myths about television news?

5. According to Kalter, why is it a myth that TV news changed public opinion about the Vietnam War? (Glossary: *Cause and Effect*) What are the broad consequences of this myth?

6. In what ways does TV remain a "medium with great potential" (21)? How can TV news be changed to make it more effective? Why hasn't it been changed in the past?

VOCABULARY

Refer to your dictionary to define the following words as they are used in this selection. Then use each word in a sentence of your own.

truism (1)

canard (3)

succinctly (7)

brevity (8)

rapt (13)

rationale (15)

gist (17)

glitzed (21)

CLASSROOM ACTIVITY USING ARGUMENT

The effectiveness of a writer's argument depends in large part on the writer's awareness of audience. For example, if a writer wished to argue for the use of technology to solve environmental problems, that argument would normally have to be more convincing (that is, more factual, better reasoned) for an environmentalist than for an industrialist because environmentalists might tend to distrust technology.

Review each of the essays you have read thus far in this chapter. In your opinion, for what primary audience was each essay intended? What types of evidence did you use in determining your answer?

SUGGESTED WRITING ASSIGNMENTS

1. How much do you think television—and television news in particular—has affected you? Write an argumentative essay in which you either agree or disagree with Kalter's position, based on your personal experiences.

2. How would you change television news to make it more effective for you? Write a letter to the head of a network news show in which you argue for your proposed changes in the format of the show.

Life Is Precious, or It's Not

Barbara Kingsolver

The popular and prolific author Barbara Kingsolver was born in 1955 in eastern Kentucky. A born storyteller, Kingsolver has kept a journal since she was a child but nonetheless never dreamed she might one day become a published writer. After graduating from DePaul University in Indiana, where she majored in biology, Kingsolver lived in Greece and France, taking a variety of jobs to support herself. She returned to the States and received her master's of science degree in biology and ecology at the University of Arizona, where she also took a writing course with Francine Prose. Taking a job as a science writer, she gradually developed into a features writer for journals and newspapers. Kingsolver has published poetry, essays, and an oral history along with her novels, which include The Bean Trees *(1988),* Animal Dreams *(1990),* Pigs in Heaven *(1993), and* Prodigal Summer *(2002). In "Life Is Precious, or It's Not," taken from her collection of essays* Small Wonder *(2002), Kingsolver uses the tragedy at Columbine High School in Littleton, Colorado, as her starting point to argue for changes in our national attitude that promotes violence and killing as quick and easy solutions to our problems.*

FOR YOUR JOURNAL

Reflect on any of the following questions concerning the possible connection between violence and the media: Do you think that most people who watch television or movies can tell the difference between screen violence and the real thing? Does footage of the real thing, a documentary for example, blur the difference between a dramatic representation and reality? Does repeated viewing of violence encourage a culture of violence?

Columbine used to be one of my favorite flowers," my friend told   1
me, and we both fell silent. We'd been talking about what she might plant on the steep bank at the foot of the woods above her house, but a single word cut us suddenly adrift from our focus on the

uncomplicated life in which flowers could matter. I understood why she no longer had the heart to plant columbines. I feel that way, too, and at the same time I feel we ought to plant them everywhere, to make sure we remember. In our backyards, on the graves of the children lost, even on the graves of the children who murdered, whose parents must surely live with the deepest emotional pain it is possible to bear.

In the aftermath of the Columbine High School shootings in Colorado, the whole country experienced grief and shock and — very noticeably — the spectacle of a nation acting bewildered. Even the op-ed commentators who usually tell us just what to think were asking, instead, what we should think. How could this happen in an ordinary school, an ordinary neighborhood? Why would any student, however frustrated with meanspirited tormentors, believe that guns and bombs were the answer?

I'm inclined to think all of us who are really interested in these questions might have started asking them a long while ago. Why does any person or nation, including ours, persist in celebrating violence as an honorable expression of disapproval? In, let's say, Iraq, the Sudan, Waco[1] — anywhere we get fed up with meanspirited tormentors — why are we so quick to assume that guns and bombs are the answer?

Some accidents and tragedies and bizarre twists of fate are truly senseless, as random as lightning bolts out of the blue. But this one at Columbine High was not, and to say it was is irresponsible. "Senseless" sounds like "without cause," and it requires no action, so that after an appropriate interval of dismayed hand-wringing, we can go back to business as usual. What takes guts is to own up: This event made sense. Children model the behavior of adults, on whatever scale is available to them. Ours are growing up in a nation whose most important, influential men — from presidents to the coolest film characters — solve problems by killing people. Killing is quick and sure and altogether manly.

It is utterly predictable that some boys who are desperate for admiration and influence will reach for guns and bombs. And it's not surprising that this happened in a middle-class neighborhood; institutional violence is right at home in the suburbs. Don't let's point too hard at the gangsta rap in our brother's house until we've examined the video games, movies, and political choices we support in our own. The tragedy in Littleton grew out of a culture that is loudly and proudly rooting for the global shootout. That culture is us.

2

3

4

5

---

[1] *Waco:* a city in Texas where, in 1993, 70 members of a religious sect perished in a fire after a fifty-one-day standoff with federal agents. [Eds.]

Conventional wisdom tells us that Nazis, the U.S. Marines, the   6
Terminator, and the NYPD all kill for different reasons. But as every
parent knows, children are good at ignoring or seeing straight
through the subtleties we spin. Here's what they must surely see:
Killing is an exalted tool for punishment and control. Americans who
won't support it are ridiculed, shamed, or even threatened. The Vietnam War[2] was a morally equivocal conflict by any historical measure, and yet to this day, candidates for public office who avoided
being drafted into that war are widely held to be unfit for leadership.

Most Americans believe bloodshed is necessary for preserving   7
our way of life, even though it means risking the occasional misfire —
the civilians strafed because they happened to live too close to the terrorist, maybe, or the factory that actually made medicines but *might*
have been making weapons. We're willing to sacrifice the innocent
man condemned to death row because every crime must be paid for,
and no jury is perfect. The majority position in our country seems to
be that violence is an appropriate means to power, and that the loss
of certain innocents along the way is the sad but inevitable cost.

I'd like to ask those who favor this position if they would be will-   8
ing to go to Littleton and explain to some mothers what constitutes
an acceptable risk. Really. Because in a society that embraces violence, this is what "our way of life" has come to mean. The question
can't be *why* but only "Why yours and not mine?" We have taught
our children in a thousand ways, sometimes with flag-waving and
sometimes with a laugh track, that the bad guy deserves to die. But
we easily forget a crucial component of this formula: "Bad" is defined by the aggressor. Any of our children may someday be, in someone's mind, the bad guy.

For all of us who are clamoring for meaning, aching for the loss   9
of these precious young lives in Littleton to mean something, my
strongest instinct is to use the event to nail a permanent benchmark
into our hearts: Life is that precious, period. It is possible to establish
zero tolerance for murder as a solution to anything. Those of us who
agree to this contract can start by removing from our households and
lives every television program, video game, film, book, toy, and CD
that presents the killing of humans (however symbolic) as an entertainment option, rather than the appalling loss it really is. Then we

---

[2]*Vietnam War:* a war fought by the United States and South Vietnam against North
Vietnam to prevent all of Vietnam from being united under Communist leadership.
[Eds.]

can move on to harder choices, such as discussing the moral lessons of capital punishment. Demanding from our elected officials the subtleties and intelligence of diplomacy instead of an endless war budget. Looking into what we did (and are still doing) to the living souls of Iraq, if we can bear it. And—this is important—telling our kids we aren't necessarily proud of the parts of our history that involved bombing people in countries whose policies we didn't agree with.

Sounds extreme? Let's be honest. *Death* is extreme, and the children are paying attention. 10

QUESTIONS FOR STUDY AND DISCUSSION

1. What is Kingsolver's thesis, and where is it stated? (Glossary: *Thesis*)

2. In paragraph 4, Kingsolver argues against the widely held view that the killings at Columbine High School were senseless. Why doe she say that they made sense? (Glossary: *Cause and Effect*)

3. In your opinion, is Kingsolver writing for a particular audience? If so, who is that audience? How do you know? (Glossary: *Audience*)

4. Does Kingsolver present a logic-based argument or an opinion on violence in American culture? What kinds of evidence does she provide to substantiate her claims? Do you find that evidence convincing? (Glossary: *Evidence*)

5. How appropriate is Kingsolver's title? Is the title an example of the logical fallacy of either/or thinking? (Glossary: *Logical Fallacy*) Explain. Why doesn't she find an intermediate position acceptable? Can there be such a position?

6. In paragraph 9, Kingsolver says, "It is possible to establish zero tolerance for murder as a solution to anything." Is zero tolerance for murder a realistic position to take? Explain.

VOCABULARY

Refer to your dictionary to define the following words as they are used in this selection. Then use each word in a sentence of your own.

adrift (1)	dismayed (4)
op-ed (2)	strafed (7)
meanspirited (2)	clamoring (9)

CLASSROOM ACTIVITY USING ARGUMENT

Can killing ever be justified? If so, under what circumstances? Have six members of the class, three on each side of the question, volunteer to hold a debate. Team members should assign themselves different aspects of their position and should then do research in the library and on the Internet to develop ideas and evidence. The teams should be allowed equal time to present their assertions and whatever evidence they have to support them. Finally, the rest of the class should be prepared to discuss the effectiveness of the presentations on both sides of the question.

SUGGESTED WRITING ASSIGNMENTS

1. If your class held a debate on the question of whether killing can ever be justified, write an argument in which you take one side of the question. As you write, take Kingsolver's argument into account. Using ideas and information supplied by the debaters, add whatever research you yourself have done on the issue to your essay.

2. If you have not already done so, read Joanmarie Kalter's essay, "Exposing Media Myths: TV Doesn't Affect You as Much as You Think" (pp. 539–44). Write an essay in which you take a stand on the influence of media violence on our attitudes and behavior. Be sure that your essay offers supporting evidence where necessary and that you take into consideration opposing arguments and offer rebuttals. Finally, consider your audience and its special needs.

Crack and the Box

■ Pete Hamill

Pete Hamill was born in Brooklyn, New York, in 1935, and for more than four decades has worked at New York newspapers. After serving in the U.S. Navy in the early 1950s, he attended Mexico City College, Pratt Institute, and the School of Visual Arts before starting his career at the New York Post. *He has been a columnist for the* Post, *the* New York Daily News, *and the* Village Voice, *and his articles have appeared in* Playboy, *Esquire,* Conde Nast Traveler, *Vanity Fair, and the* New York Times Magazine. *Hamill is the author of sixteen books, including the novels* Snow in August *(1977) and* Forever *(2003), the memoir* A Drinking Life *(1955), and the nonfiction books* Why Sinatra Matters *(1998) and* Diego Rivera *(1999). In 1993 Hamill helped save the* New York Post *when he served as editor in chief. He currently holds that position at the* New York Daily News. *In the following selection, taken from his collection* Piecework: Writings on Men and Women, Fools and Heroes, Lost Cities, Vanished Friends, Small Pleasures, Large Calamities, and How the Weather Was *(1997), Hamill argues that television is part of the cause of our nation's drug problems.*

FOR YOUR JOURNAL

Hamill refers to one study indicating that Americans may average seven hours of television viewing each day. Think about your own viewing habits and the time you spend in front of your television. Do you think this statistic is correct? How do you feel about the amount of time you spend watching television? Can television be addicting?

One sad rainy morning last winter, I talked to a woman who was addicted to crack cocaine. She was twenty-two, stiletto-thin, with eyes as old as tombs. She was living in two rooms in a welfare hotel with her children, who were two, three, and five years of age. Her story was the usual tangle of human woe: early pregnancy, dropping out of school, vanished men, smack and then crack, tricks with johns in parked cars to pay for the dope. I asked her why she did drugs. She shrugged in an empty way and couldn't really answer beyond "makes me feel good." While we talked and she told her tale of squalor, the children ignored us. They were watching television.

Walking back to my office in the rain, I brooded about the woman, her zombielike children, and my own callous indifference. I'd heard so many versions of the same story that I almost never wrote them anymore; the sons of similar women, glimpsed a dozen years ago, are now in Dannemora or Soledad or Joliet,[1] in a hundred cities, their daughters are moving into the same loveless rooms. As I walked, a series of homeless men approached me for change, most of them junkies. Others sat in doorways, staring at nothing. They were additional casualties of our time of plague, demoralized reminders that although this country holds only 2 percent of the world's population, it consumes 65 percent of the world's supply of hard drugs.

Why, for God's sake? Why do so many millions of Americans of all ages, races, and classes choose to spend all or part of their lives stupefied? I've talked to hundreds of addicts over the years; some were my friends. But none could give sensible answers. They stutter about the pain of the world, about despair or boredom, the urgent need for magic or pleasure in a society empty of both. But then they just shrug. Americans have the money to buy drugs; the supply is plentiful. But almost nobody in power asks, Why? Least of all, George Bush[2] and his drug warriors.

William Bennett[3] talks vaguely about the heritage of sixties permissiveness, the collapse of Traditional Values, and all that. But he and Bush offer the traditional American excuse: It Is Somebody Else's Fault. This posture set the stage for the self-righteous invasion of Panama, the bloodiest drug arrest in world history. Bush even accused Manuel Noriega of "poisoning our children." But he never asked why so many Americans demand the poison.

And then, on that rainy morning in New York, I saw another one of those ragged men staring out at the rain from a doorway. I suddenly remembered the inert postures of the children in that welfare hotel, and I thought: television.

---

[1]*Dannemora, Soledad, Joliet:* cities known for their prisons. [Eds.]

[2]*George Herbert Walker Bush* (b. 1924): forty-first president of the United States (1989–93). [Eds.]

[3]*William Bennett:* family values advocate and former U.S. Secretary of Education. [Eds.]

Ah, no, I muttered to myself: too simple. Something as compli-   6
cated as drug addiction can't be blamed on television. Come on . . .
but I remembered all those desperate places I'd visited as a reporter,
where there were no books and a TV set was always playing and the
older kids had gone off somewhere to shoot smack, except for the kid
who was at the mortuary in a coffin. I also remembered when I was a
boy in the forties and early fifties, and drugs were a minor sideshow,
a kind of dark little rumor. And there was one major difference between that time and this: television.

We had unemployment then; illiteracy, poor living conditions,   7
racism, governmental stupidity, a gap between rich and poor. We
didn't have the all-consuming presence of television in our lives. Now
two generations of Americans have grown up with television from
their earliest moments of consciousness. Those same American generations are afflicted by the pox of drug addiction.

Only thirty-five years ago, drug addiction was not a major prob-   8
lem in this country. There were drug addicts. We had some at the end
of the nineteenth century, hooked on the cocaine in patent medicines.
During the placid fifties, Commissioner Harry Anslinger pumped up
the butt of the old Bureau of Narcotics with fantasies of reefer madness. Heroin was sold and used in most major American cities, while
the bebop generation of jazz musicians got jammed up with horse.

But until the early sixties, narcotics were still marginal to Ameri-   9
can life; they weren't the $120-billion market they make up today. If
anything, those years have an eerie innocence. In 1955 there were
31,700,000 TV sets in use in the country (the number is now past
184 million). But the majority of the audience had grown up without
the dazzling new medium. They embraced it, were diverted by it, perhaps even loved it, but they weren't formed by it. That year, the New
York police made a mere 1,234 felony drug arrests; in 1988 it was
43,901. They confiscated ninety-seven ounces of cocaine for the entire year; last year it was hundreds of pounds. During each year of the
fifties in New York, there were only about a hundred narcotics-
related deaths. But by the end of the sixties, when the first generation
of children formed by television had come to maturity (and thus to
the marketplace), the number of such deaths had risen to 1,200. The
same phenomenon was true in every major American city.

In the last Nielsen survey of American viewers, the average fam-   10
ily was watching television seven hours a day. This has never happened before in history. No people has ever been entertained for
seven hours a day. The Elizabethans didn't go to the theater seven

hours a day. The pre-TV generation did not go to the movies seven hours a day. Common sense tells us that this all-pervasive diet of instant imagery, sustained now for forty years, must have changed us in profound ways.

Television, like drugs, dominates the lives of its addicts. And 11 though some lonely Americans leave their sets on without watching them, using them as electronic companions, television usually absorbs its viewers the way drugs absorb their users. Viewers can't work or play while watching television; they can't read; they can't be out on the streets, falling in love with the wrong people, learning how to quarrel and compromise with other human beings. In short they are asocial. So are drug addicts.

One Michigan State University study in the early eighties offered 12 a group of four- and five-year olds the choice of giving up television or giving up their fathers. Fully one third said they would give up Daddy. Given the choice (between cocaine or heroin and father, mother, brother, sister, wife, husband, children, job), almost every stoned junkie would do the same.

There are other disturbing similarities. Television itself is a 13 consciousness-altering instrument. With the touch of a button, it takes you out of the "real" world in which you reside and can place you at a basketball game, the back alleys of Miami, the streets of Bucharest, or the cartoony living rooms of Sitcom Land. Each move from channel to channel alters mood, usually with music or a laugh track. On any given evening, you can laugh, be frightened, feel tension, thump with excitement. You can even tune in MacNeill/Lehrer and feel sober.

But none of these abrupt shifts in mood is earned. They are at- 14 tained as easily as popping a pill. Getting news from television, for example, is simply not the same experience as reading it in a newspaper. Reading is active. The reader must decode little symbols called words, then create ideas and make them connect; at its most basic level, reading is an act of the imagination. But the television viewer doesn't go through that process. The words are spoken to him by Dan Rather or Tom Brokaw or Peter Jennings. There isn't much decoding to do when watching television, no time to think or ponder before the next set of images and spoken words appears to displace the present one. The reader, being active, works at his or her own pace; the viewer, being passive, proceeds at a pace determined by the show. Except at the highest levels, television never demands that its audience take part in an act of imagination. Reading always does.

In short, television works on the same imaginative and intellec- 15
tual level as psychoactive drugs. If prolonged television viewing
makes the young passive (dozens of studies indicate that it does), then
moving to drugs has a certain coherence. Drugs provide an unearned
high (in contrast to the earned rush that comes from a feat accom-
plished, a human breakthrough earned by sweat or thought or love).

And because the television addict and the drug addict are alien- 16
ated from the hard and scary world, they also feel they make no difference in its complicated events. For the junkie, the world is reduced
to him and the needle, pipe, or vial; the self is absolutely isolated,
with no desire for choice. The television addict lives the same way.
Many Americans who fail to vote in presidential elections must believe they have no more control over such a choice than they do over
the casting of *L.A. Law.*

The drug plague also coincides with the unspoken assumption of 17
most television shows: Life should be easy. The most complicated
events are summarized on TV news in a minute or less. Cops confront
murder, chase the criminals, and bring them to justice (usually violently) within an hour. In commercials, you drink the right beer and you
get the girl. Easy! So why should real life be a grind? Why should any
American have to spend years mastering a skill or a craft, or work eight
hours a day at an unpleasant job, or endure the compromises and crises
of a marriage? Nobody works on television (except cops, doctors, and
lawyers). Love stories on television are about falling in love or breaking
up; the long, steady growth of a marriage—its essential dailiness—is
seldom explored, except as comedy. Life on television is almost always
simple: good guys and bad, nice girls and whores, smart guys and
dumb. And if life in the real world isn't that simple, well, hey, man,
have some dope, man, be happy, feel good.

The doper always whines about how he feels; drugs are used to 18
enhance his feelings or obliterate them, and in this the doper is very
American. No other people on earth spend so much time talking
about their feelings; hundreds of thousands go to shrinks, they buy
self-help books by the millions, they pour out intimate confessions to
virtual strangers in bars or discos. Our political campaigns are about
emotional issues now, stated in the simplicities of adolescence. Even
alleged statesmen can start a sentence, "I feel that the Sandinistas[4]

---

[4]*Sandinistas:* members of Nicaragua's Sandinista National Liberation Front (FSLN),
which overthrew President Anastasio Somoza in 1978–79 and stayed in power until
1990. [Eds.]

should . . ." when they once might have said, "I think . . ." I'm convinced that this exaltation of cheap emotions over logic and reason is one by-product of hundreds of thousands of hours of television.

Most Americans under the age of fifty have now spent their lives 19 absorbing television; that is, they've had the structures of drama pounded into them. Drama is always about conflict. So news shows, politics, and advertising are now all shaped by those structures. Nobody will pay attention to anything as complicated as the part played by Third World debt in the expanding production of cocaine; it's much easier to focus on Manuel Noriega, a character right out of *Miami Vice*, and believe that even in real life there's a Mister Big.

What is to be done? Television is certainly not going away, but 20 its addictive qualities can be controlled. It's a lot easier to "just say no" to television than to heroin or crack. As a beginning, parents must take immediate control of the sets, teaching children to watch specific television programs, not "television," to get out of the house and play with other kids. Elementary and high schools must begin teaching television as a subject, the way literature is taught, showing children how shows are made, how to distinguish between the true and the false, how to recognize cheap emotional manipulation. All Americans should spend more time reading. And thinking.

For years, the defenders of television have argued that the net- 21 works are only giving the people what they want. That might be true. But so is the Medellin cartel.[5]

QUESTIONS FOR STUDY AND DISCUSSION

1. What is Hamill's thesis? (Glossary: *Thesis*) Where is it stated?
2. What types of evidence does Hamill provide in support of his thesis? Are you convinced by that evidence? (Glossary: *Evidence*) Explain.
3. What is the question that plagues Hamill about drug addiction, the question that none who are concerned about addiction ever seem to address?
4. In paragraph 6, Hamill says he himself doubted the connection between drugs and television that had occurred to him. Why did he doubt the connection?

---

[5]*Medellin cartel:* an infamous group of Columbian cocaine traffickers, finally dissolved in the early 1990s. [Eds.]

5. Do you agree with Hamill that watching television causes people to use drugs and become addicted? (Glossary: *Cause and Effect*) Why, or why not?

6. Hamill sees similarities between television watching and using drugs. Does that necessarily make one activity the cause of the other? Is he guilty of trying to prove his argument by the fallacy of false analogy? (Glossary: *Logical Fallacy*) What reasoning and evidence does Hamill provide to go beyond similarities?

7. Why do you think Hamill begins his essay with the story of the drug addict? (Glossary: *Beginnings and Endings*)

VOCABULARY

Refer to your dictionary to define the following words as they are used in this selection. Then use each word in a sentence of your own.

squalor (1)	afflicted (7)
callous (2)	pox (7)
demoralized (2)	eerie (9)
stupefied (3)	decode (14)
inert (5)	obliterate (18)
smack (6)	exaltation (18)

CLASSROOM ACTIVITY USING ARGUMENT

Find an editorial in your local newspaper or in a national paper that presents a view of an issue that you disagree with. Bring the editorial to class and reread it, study it for a few minutes, and then write a brief letter to the editor of the newspaper arguing against its position. Your letter should be brief; short letters have a much better chance of being published than long ones.

During a subsequent class, form groups of two to three students to share your letters and comment on the effectiveness of each other's arguments. Revise your letter, if necessary, and consider sending it to the newspaper for possible publication.

SUGGESTED WRITING ASSIGNMENTS

1. Hamill's style as a journalist is instructive. His language runs the range from the slang of the drug trade (for example, *smack,*

reefer, and *horse*) to figures of speech that a poet would be proud of (for example, "She was twenty-two, stiletto-thin, with eyes as old as tombs," paragraph 1). He moves effortlessly among styles that are chatty, colloquial (representing everyday speech), and formal, while remaining accessible to the average reader. He adds to his very human touch by not being afraid to let us know how he comes upon an idea and that he questions if he may be oversimplifying a complex problem. Write an essay in which you argue that to be an effective and popular journalist today, one has to be extremely flexible with language, insightful, and human. Other journalists that you might reference or quote in your argument are Russell Baker (pp. 195–98 and 427–29), Anna Quindlen (pp. 513–16), K. Connie Kang (pp. 445–48), and Rene Sanchez (pp. 471–74).

2. Hamill writes that many people appear to be concerned about drug addiction, but few seem to care what brings it about. Write an essay in response in which you argue that something other than television causes drug addiction. To be sure, there are many causes of addiction, but attempt to focus your argument on what you consider the one or two major causes. Be sure, as well, to think about the various kinds of evidence that you can obtain through research, reading, and interviews with experts in the field and that you can use in building your argument.

Writing a Research Paper

The research paper is an important part of a college education—and for good reason. In writing a research paper, you acquire a number of indispensable skills that you can adapt to other college assignments and to situations after graduation.

The real value of writing a research paper, however, goes beyond acquiring basic skills; it is a unique hands-on learning experience. The purpose of a research paper is not to present a collection of quotations that show you can report what others have said about your topic. Rather, your goal is to analyze, evaluate, and synthesize the materials you research—and thereby learn how to do so with any topic. You learn how to view the results of research from your own perspective and to arrive at an informed opinion of a topic.

Writing a researched essay is not very different from the other writing you will be doing in your college writing course. You will find yourself drawing heavily on what you have learned from the four student papers in the first two chapters of this text. First you determine what you want to write about. Then you decide on a purpose, consider your audience, develop a thesis, collect your evidence, write a first draft, revise and edit, and prepare a final copy. What differentiates the research paper from other kinds of papers is your use of outside sources and how you acknowledge them.

In this appendix, you will learn how to locate and use print and Internet sources; how to evaluate these sources; how to develop a working bibliography; how to conduct directory and keyword searches; how to take useful notes; how to summarize, paraphrase, and quote your sources; how to integrate your notes into your paper; how to acknowledge your sources; and how to avoid plagiarism. You will also find extensive guidelines for documenting your essay in Modern Language Association (MLA) style. MLA guidelines are widely accepted by English and foreign-language scholars and teachers, and we encourage their use. Before you begin work on your research paper, your instructor will let you know which style you should follow.

Your library research will involve working with print as well as electronic sources. In both cases, however, the process is essentially the same. Your aim is to select the most appropriate sources for your research from the many that are available on your topic.

■ Using Print Sources

In most cases, you should use print sources (books, newspapers, journals, magazines, encyclopedias, pamphlets, brochures, and government publications) as your primary tools for research. Print sources, unlike many Internet sources, are often reviewed by experts in the field before they are published, are generally overseen by a reputable publishing company or organization, and are examined by editors and fact checkers for accuracy and reliability. Unless you are instructed otherwise, you should try to use print sources in your research.

To find print sources, search through your library's reference works, computer or card catalog, periodical indexes, and other databases to generate a preliminary listing of books, magazine and newspaper articles, public documents and reports, and other sources that may be helpful in exploring your topic. At this early stage, it is better to err on the side of listing too many sources. Then, later on, you will not have to relocate sources you discarded too hastily.

PREVIEW PRINT SOURCES

Although you want to be thorough in your research, you will soon realize that you do not have enough time to read every source you encounter. Rather, you must preview your sources to decide what you will read, what you will skim, and what you will simply eliminate. Here are some questions to ask as you preview your print sources.

Questions for Previewing Print Sources

1. Is the book or article directly related to your research topic?
2. Is the book or article obviously outdated (for example, a source on language-related brain research that is from the 1970s)?
3. Have you checked the table of contents and index in each book to locate material that may be important and relevant to your topic?
4. If an article appears to be what you are looking for, have you read the abstract (a summary of the main points of the article,

which appears in some journals) or the opening and concluding paragraphs?

5. Is it necessary to read the entire article quickly to be sure that it is relevant?

DEVELOP A WORKING BIBLIOGRAPHY

It is important to develop a working bibliography of the books, articles, and other materials that you think are relevant to your topic. Compiling a working bibliography lets you know at a glance which works you have consulted and the shape your research is taking. A working bibliography also guides you to other materials you may wish to consider. Naturally, you will want to record early on all the information you need for each work so that you do not have to return to the library at a later time to retrieve publication data for your final bibliography or list of works cited. Accuracy and completeness are, of course, essential at this final stage of the research.

For each work that you think might be helpful, make a separate bibliography card, using a 4 × 6 index card. As your collection of cards grows, alphabetize them by the authors' last names. By using a separate card for each book or article, you can continually edit your working bibliography, dropping sources that are not helpful for one reason or another and adding new ones. You will also use the cards to compile your final list of works cited.

For books, record the following information:

- all authors; any editors or translators
- title and subtitle
- edition (if not the first)
- publication data: city, publishing company, and year
- call number

For periodical articles, record the following information:

- all authors
- title and subtitle
- title of journal, magazine, or newspaper
- volume and issue numbers
- date and page numbers

Using the correct bibliographic form ensures that your entries are complete, reduces the chance of introducing careless errors, and saves time when you are ready to prepare your final list of works cited. You will find MLA style guidelines for the list of works cited on pages 580–86.

EVALUATE PRINT SOURCES

Before beginning to take notes, you should read your sources and evaluate them for their reliability and relevance in helping you explore your topic. Examine your sources for the writers' main ideas. Pay particular attention to abstracts or introductions, tables of contents, section headings, and indexes. Also, look for information about the authors themselves — information that will help you determine their authority and perspective on the issues. Here are some questions to ask as you evaluate your print sources.

Questions for Evaluating Print Sources

1. Is your source focused on your particular research topic?

2. Is your source too abstract, too general, or too technical for your needs?

3. Does your source build on current thinking and existing research in the field?

4. Does your source promote a particular view, or is it meant to provide balanced coverage of the topic? What biases, if any, does your source exhibit?

5. Is the author of your source an authority on the topic? Do other writers mention the author of your source in their work?

▮ Using Internet Sources

You will find that Internet sources can be informative and valuable additions to your research. The Internet is especially useful in providing recent data, stories, and reports. For example, you might find a just-published article from a university laboratory or a news story in your local newspaper's online archives. Generally, however, Internet sources should be used alongside print sources and not as a replacement for them. Whereas print sources are generally published under the guidance of a publisher or an organization, practically anyone with access to a computer and an Internet connection can put text and pictures on the Internet; there is often no governing body that checks for content or accuracy. The Internet offers a vast number of useful and carefully maintained resources, but it also contains much unreliable information. It is your responsibility to evaluate whether a given Internet source should be trusted.

Your Internet research will probably produce many more sources than you can reasonably use. By carefully previewing Web sites and other Internet sources, developing a working bibliography of potentially useful ones, and evaluating them for their reliability, you will ensure that you are making the best use of Internet sources in researching your topic. Once you have learned how to preview and evaluate your sources, you will better know what you should look for as you use successful and effective search techniques to find appropriate sources.

If you do not know how to access the Internet, or if you need more instruction on conducting Internet searches, go to your on-campus computer center for more information, or consult one of the many books written for Internet beginners. You can also access valuable information for searching the Internet at Diana Hacker's *Research and Documentation Online* <www.dianahacker.com/resdoc>.

PREVIEW INTERNET SOURCES

The key to successful Internet research is being able to identify the sites that will help you the most. Answering the following questions will help you weed out sources that hold no promise.

Questions for Previewing Internet Sources

1. Scan the Web site. Do the contents and links appear to be related to your research topic?
2. Can you identify the author of the site? Are the author's credentials available, and are they appropriate to the content of the site?
3. Has the site been updated within the last six months? Information about the most recent update is usually provided at the bottom of the home page of the Web site. It is not always necessary to use updated information, especially if your topic is not a current one and the information about it is fairly stable.

If you answer "no" to any of these questions, you should consider eliminating the source from further consideration.

DEVELOP A WORKING BIBLIOGRAPHY

Just as for print sources, you must maintain accurate records for the Internet sources you use. Here is what you need for each source:

- all authors or sponsoring agents
- title and subtitle of the document
- title of complete work (if applicable)
- document date (or date "last modified")
- date you accessed the site
- publishing data for print version (if available)
- address of the site, uniform resource locator (URL), or network path

See pages 583–86 for the latest MLA guidelines for electronic sources.

EVALUATE INTERNET SOURCES

Because the quality of sources on the Internet varies tremendously, it is important to evaluate the information you find there. Answering the following questions will help you evaluate the sites you have included in your working bibliography.

Questions for Evaluating Web Sites

1. *What type of Web site is it?*
   a. Who sponsors the site? A corporation? An individual? The URL indicates the sponsor of the site. Some common domain names are:

   .com   Business/commercial
   .edu   Educational institution
   .gov   Government
   .mil   Military
   .net   Various types of networks
   .org   Nonprofit organization

2. *Who is the authority or author?*
   a. What individual or company is responsible for the site?
   b. Can you verify if the site is official, actually sanctioned by an organization or company?
   c. What are the author's or company's qualifications for writing on this subject?

    d. Is there a way to verify the legitimacy of this individual or company? Are there links to a home page or résumé?

3. *What is the site's purpose and audience?*

    a. What appears to be the author's or sponsor's purpose or motivation?

    b. Who is the intended audience?

4. *Is the site objective?*

    a. Are advertising, opinion, and factual information clearly distinguished?

    b. What biases, if any, can you detect?

5. *How accurate is the site?*

    a. Is important information documented through links so that it can be verified or corroborated by other sources?

    b. Is the text well written and free of careless errors in spelling and grammar?

6. *Is the coverage thorough and current?*

    a. Is there any indication that the site is still under construction?

    b. For sources with print equivalents, is the Web version more or less extensive than the print version?

    c. How detailed is the site's treatment of its subject matter?

    d. Is there any indication of the currency of the information (the date of the last update or a statement regarding frequency of updates)?

You can also find sources on the Internet itself that offer useful guidelines for evaluating electronic sources. One excellent set of guidelines has been created by reference librarians at the Wolfgram Memorial Library at Widener University; see <http://www.widener .edu/?pageId=857>.

■ Internet Research: Subject Directories and Keyword Searches

Beyond knowing how to identify and evaluate the Web sites that will help you most, you will need to know the best methods for finding them. This will help you save time as you do your research. Keep in mind the questions for previewing and evaluating sources as you use subject directories and keyword searches to find information.

USING SUBJECT DIRECTORIES TO REFINE
YOUR RESEARCH TOPIC

The subject directories on the home pages of search engines make it easy to browse various subjects and topics, a big help if you are undecided about your exact research question or if you simply want to see if there is enough material to supplement your research work with print sources. Often the most efficient approach to Web research is to start with the subject directory of a search engine. Once you choose a subject area in the directory, you can maneuver through the directory to narrow down the subject and eventually arrive at a list of sites closely related to your topic.

Suppose you want to research acupuncture in America, and you are using the search engine Google, <http://www.google.com>. You would start your search with the "Google Directory" screen, pictured below. Your first task would be to choose, from the sixteen categories listed, the one most likely to contain information about acupuncture. Remember that just as you often need to browse through tables of contents and indexes of numerous books on a given subject to uncover the three or four sources that will be most useful

Google Directory.

to you, more than one general subject category in a Web directory may seem appropriate on the surface.

The most common question students have at this stage in a directory search is, How can I tell if I'm looking in the right place? If more than one subject category sounds plausible, you will have to dig more deeply into each of their subdirectories, using logic and the process of elimination to determine which one is likely to produce the best Web site listings for your topic. In most cases, it doesn't take long—usually just one or two clicks—to figure out whether you are searching in the right subject area. If you click on a subject category and none of the topics listed in its subdirectory seems to pertain even remotely to your research topic, try a different subject area. For example, to find acupuncture links, you might be tempted to click on "Science," which has a "Biology" link. If you do, you'll find that none of the biology topics listed relates to acupuncture, which is a strong sign that "Science" is the wrong subject category for your topic. The other logical possibility is "Health." Clicking on "Health" takes you to a screen that lists forty-two more subject categories, including "Alternative," a logical place to find sites on acupuncture and other

Google Directory categories for alternative health.

alternative medical practices. For "Alternative" alone, there are more than 6,500 Web sites listed, so chances are good that some of those sites address your subject.

When you click on "Alternative," you bring up a screen that lists categories related to alternative medicine (see page 567). Because you are interested in acupuncture, "Acupuncture and Chinese Medicine," which lists 859 Web sites, is the natural next step. Clicking on this link takes you to a screen where you find a number of subdirectory categories, including one for "Acupuncture." By clicking on "Acupuncture," you arrive at a screen that lists potentially valuable Web sites, including several sites that provide good overviews of acupuncture in America.

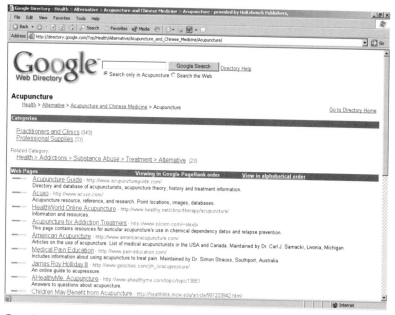

Google Directory listings for acupuncture.

USING KEYWORD SEARCHES TO FIND SPECIFIC INFORMATION

When you type in a keyword in the "Search" box on a search engine's home page, the search engine goes looking for Web sites that match your term. One problem with keyword searches is that they can produce tens of thousands of matches, making it difficult to locate sites of immediate value. For that reason, make your keywords as specific as you can, and make sure that you have the correct spelling. It is always a good idea to consult the help screens or advanced search instructions for the search engine you are using before initiating a keyword search. Once you start a search, you may want to narrow or broaden it depending on the number of hits, or matches, you get.

Refining Keyword Searches on the Web

While some variation in command terms and characters exists among electronic databases and popular Internet search engines, the following functions are almost universally accepted. If you have a particular question about refining your keyword search, seek assistance by clicking on "Help" or "Advanced Search."

- Use quotation marks or parentheses to indicate that you are searching for words in exact sequence—for example, "whooping cough"; (Supreme Court).
- Use AND or a plus sign (+) between words to narrow your search by specifying that all words need to appear in a document—for example, tobacco AND cancer; Shakespeare + sonnet.
- Use NOT or a minus sign (–) between words to narrow your search by eliminating unwanted words—for example, monopoly NOT game; cowboys – Dallas.
- Use an asterisk (*) to indicate that you will accept variations of a term—for example, "food label*."

When using a keyword search, you need to be careful about selecting the keywords that will yield the best results. If your keywords are too general, your results will be at best unwieldy and at worst not usable at all. During her initial search for her paper on monarchs, a butterfly indigenous to Central and North America, student Erin Elio typed in "monarch." To her surprise, this produced approximately 1,150,000 hits, mostly for products, services, or teams carrying the name.

After thinking about how to narrow her search, Elio decided to type in "monarch butterfly." This search yielded about 62,500 hits, still too many for her purposes. In an effort to narrow her search even more, she tried "monarch butterfly + life cycle"—a search that yielded a far more manageable 496 hits.

Search results for "monarch."

Search results for "monarch butterfly + life cycle."

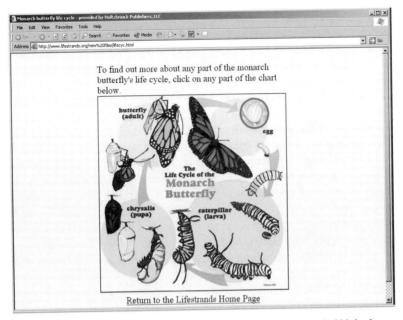

The life cycle of the monarch butterfly from the Lifestrands Web site.

Among these hits, she located a Web page entitled "Monarch butterfly life cycle" on the Lifestrands Web site, a site created by 4th and 6th grade teachers who use monarch butterflies to teach scientific inquiry to young students.

This site was the perfect starting point for Elio. Here she found information about the life cycle of monarch butterflies as well as the opportunity to learn more about any particular stage of the cycle. Equipped with a basic understanding of the monarch's life cycle, Elio continued her search to discover the relationship between the butterfly's life cycle and its heralded yearly migration.

■ Taking Notes

As you gather and sort your source materials, you'll want to record the information that you consider most pertinent to your topic. As you read, take notes. You're looking for ideas, facts, opinions, statistics, examples, and other evidence that you think will be useful as you write your paper. As you work through books and articles, look for recurring themes, and notice where writers are in agreement and where they differ. Try to remember that the effectiveness of your paper is largely determined by the quality—not necessarily the quantity—of your notes. Your purpose is not to present a collection of quotes that show you've read all the material and know what others have said about your topic. Your goal is to analyze, evaluate, and synthesize the information you collect—in other words, to enter into the discussion of the issues and thereby take ownership of your topic. You want to view the results of your research from your own perspective and arrive at an informed opinion of your topic.

Now for some practical advice on taking notes: First, be systematic in your note taking. As a rule, write one note on a card and include the author's full name, the complete title of the source, and a page number indicating the origin of the note. Use cards of uniform size, preferably 4 × 6 cards because they are large enough to accommodate even a long note on a single card and yet small enough to be easily handled and conveniently carried. Following this system will also help you when you get to the planning and writing stage because you will be able to sequence your notes according to the plan you envision for your paper. Furthermore, should you decide to alter your organizational plan, you can easily reorder your cards to reflect your revisions. You can, of course, do note taking on your computer as well, which makes it easy for you to reorder your notes. An added advantage of the computer is that the Copy and Paste features let you move notes and their citations directly into your essay.

Second, try not to take too many notes. One good way to control your note taking is to ask yourself, "How exactly does this material help prove or disprove my thesis?" Try to envision where in your paper you could use the information. If it does not seem relevant to your thesis, don't bother to take a note.

Once you decide to take a note, you must decide whether to summarize, paraphrase, or quote directly. The approach you take should be determined by the content of the passage and the way you plan to use it in your paper.

SUMMARY

When you *summarize* material from one of your sources, you capture in condensed form the essential idea of a passage, article, or entire chapter. Summaries are particularly useful when you are working with lengthy, detailed arguments or long passages of narrative or descriptive background information in which the details are not ger-mane to the overall thrust of your paper. You simply want to capture the essence of the passage because you are confident that your readers will readily understand the point being made or do not need to be convinced about its validity. Because you are distilling information, a summary is always shorter than the original; often a chapter or more can be reduced to a paragraph, or several paragraphs to a sentence or two. Remember, in writing a summary you should use your own words.

Consider the following paragraphs, in which Richard Lederer compares big words with small words in some detail:

> When you speak and write, there is no law that says you have to use big words. Short words are as good as long ones, and short, old words—like *sun* and *grass* and *home*—are best of all. A lot of small words, more than you might think, can meet your needs with a strength, grace, and charm that large words do not have.
>
> Big words can make the way dark for those who read what you write and hear what you say. Small words cast their clear light on big things—night and day, love and hate, war and peace, and life and death. Big words at times seem strange to the eye and ear and the mind and the heart. Small words are the ones we seem to have known from the time we were born, like the hearth fire that warms the home.
>
> –Richard Lederer, "The Case for Short Words," pages 303–6

A student wishing to capture the gist of Lederer's point without repeating his detailed contrast wrote the following summary.

Summary Note Card

> *Short Words*
>
> *Lederer favors short words for their clarity, familiarity, durability, and overall usefulness.*
>
> *Lederer, "The Case for Short Words," 303–6*

PARAPHRASE

When you *paraphrase* material from a source, you restate the information in your own words instead of quoting directly. Unlike a summary, which gives a brief overview of the essential information in the original, a paraphrase seeks to maintain the same level of detail as the original to aid readers in understanding or believing the information presented. A paraphrase presents the original information in approximately the same number of words, but with different wording. To put it another way, your paraphrase should closely parallel the presentation of ideas in the original, but it should not use the same words or sentence structure as the original. Even though you are using your own words in a paraphrase, it's important to remember that you are borrowing ideas and therefore must acknowledge the source of these ideas with a citation.

How would you paraphrase the following passage from "The Ways of Meeting Oppression" by Martin Luther King Jr.?

> If the American Negro and other victims of oppression succumb to the temptation of using violence in the struggle for freedom, future generations will be the recipients of a desolate night of bitterness, and our chief legacy to them will be an endless reign of meaningless chaos. Violence is not the way.
>
> –Martin Luther King Jr., "The Ways of Meeting Oppression," pages 408–11

The following note card illustrates how a student paraphrased the passage:

Paraphrase Note Card

Non-Violence

African Americans and other oppressed peoples must not resort to taking up arms against their oppressors because to do so would lead the country into an era of turmoil and confusion. Armed confrontation will not yield the desired results.

Martin Luther King Jr,
"The Ways of Meeting Oppression," 408–11

In most cases, it is best to summarize or paraphrase material—which by definition means using your own words—instead of quoting verbatim (word for word). Capturing an idea in your own words ensures that you have thought about and understood what your source is saying.

DIRECT QUOTATION

When you *quote* a source directly, you copy the words of your source exactly, putting all quoted material in quotation marks. When you make a quotation note card, check the passage carefully for accuracy, including punctuation and capitalization. Be selective about what you choose to quote; reserve direct quotation for important ideas stated memorably, for especially clear explanations by authorities, and for arguments by proponents of a particular position in their own words.

Consider, for example, the following passage from William Zinsser's "Simplicity," on page 164 in this text, emphasizing the importance—and the current rarity—of clear, concise writing:

Direct Quotation Note Card

> *Wordiness*
> *"Clutter is the disease of American writing. We are a society strangling in unnecessary words, circular constructions, pompous frills, and meaningless jargon."*
>
> *William Zinsser, "Simplicity," 164*

On occasion you'll find a long, useful passage with some memorable wording in it. Avoid the temptation to quote the whole passage; instead, try combining summary or paraphrase with direct quotation. Consider the concluding paragraph from Witold Rybczynski's essay "One Good Turn: The Importance of Machine-Made Screws":

> It is not an exaggeration to say that accurately threaded screws changed the world. Without screws, entire fields of science would have languished, navigation would have remained primitive, and naval warfare as well as routine maritime commerce in the eighteenth and nineteenth centuries would not have been possible. Without screws there would have been no machine tools, hence no industrial products and no Industrial Revolution. Think of that the next time you pick up a screwdriver to pry open a can of paint.
> –Witold Rybczynski, "One Good Turn," page 83–84

Notice how the student who took the following note was careful to put quotation marks around all the words that were borrowed directly.

Quotation and Summary Note Card

> *Impact*
>
> *Though often taken for granted, "accurately threaded screws changed the world." Screws, it appears, provided the catalyst for scientific advances as well as adventure, conquest, and trade on the seas. In the absence of screws, "there would have been no machine tools, hence no industrial products and no Industrial Revolution."*
>
> *Rybczynski, "One Good Turn," pages 83–84*

NOTES FROM INTERNET SOURCES

Working from the computer screen or from a printout, you can take notes just as you would from print sources. You will need to decide whether to summarize, paraphrase, or quote directly the information you wish to borrow. Use the same 4 × 6 index-card system that you use with print sources. The medium of the Internet, however, has an added advantage. An easy and accurate technique for capturing passages of text from the Internet is to copy the material into a separate computer file on your hard drive or diskette. In Internet Explorer, for example, you can use your mouse to highlight the portion of the text you want to save and then use the Copy and Paste commands to add it to your file of research notes. You can also use the same commands to capture the bibliographic information you will need later.

▧ Integrating Borrowed Material into Your Text

Being familiar with the material in your notes will help you decide how to integrate it into your drafts. Though it is not necessary to use all of your notes, or to use them all at once in your first draft, you do need to know which ones support your thesis, extend your ideas, offer better wording of your ideas, and reveal the opinions of noted authorities. Occasionally you will want to use notes that include ideas contrary to your own so that you can rebut them in your own argument. Once you have analyzed all of your notes, you may even alter your thesis slightly in light of the information and ideas you have found.

Whenever you want to use borrowed material, be it a summary, paraphrase, or quotation, it's best to introduce the material with a *signal phrase*—a phrase that alerts the reader that borrowed information is to follow. A signal phrase usually consists of the author's name and a verb. Well-chosen signal phrases help you integrate quotations, paraphrases, and summaries into the flow of your paper. Besides, signal phrases let your reader know who is speaking and, in the case of summaries and paraphrases, exactly where your ideas end and someone else's begin. Never confuse your reader with a quotation that appears suddenly without introduction. Unannounced quotations leave your reader wondering how the quoted material relates to the point you are trying to make. Look at the following student example. The quotation is from Rita Dove's essay "Loose Ends," which appears on pages 440–42 in this text.

UNANNOUNCED QUOTATION

> Television, it could be argued, presents life in tidy, almost predictable, 30- and 60-minute packages. As any episode of *Friends* or *West Wing* or *Law and Order* demonstrates, life on television, though exciting, is relatively easy to follow. Humor, simultaneous action, and special effects cannot overshadow the fact that each show has a beginning, a middle, and an end. "Life . . . is ragged. Loose ends are the rule" (Dove 441). For many Americans, television provides an escape from their monotonous day-to-day lives.

In the following revision, the student integrated the quotation into the text not only by means of a signal phrase, but in a number of other ways as well. By giving the name of the writer being quoted, referring to her credentials, and noting that the writer is arguing for a difference she sees between television life and real life, the student provides more context so that the reader can better understand how the quotation fits into the discussion.

INTEGRATED QUOTATION

> Television, it could be argued, presents life in tidy, almost predictable, 30- and 60-minute packages. As any episode of *Friends* or *West Wing* or *Law and Order* demonstrates, life on television, though exciting, is relatively easy to follow. Humor, simultaneous action, and special effects do not overshadow the fact that each show has a beginning, a middle, and an end. In contrast, real "life," argues Pulitzer Prize–winning poet and professor Rita Dove, "is

ragged. Loose ends rule" (441). For many Americans, television provides an escape from their monotonous day-to-day lives.

How well you integrate a quote, paraphrase, or summary into your paper depends partly on varying your signal phrases and, in particular, on choosing a verb for the signal phrase that accurately conveys the tone and intent of the writer you are citing. If a writer is arguing, use the verb *argues* (or *asserts, claims,* or *contends*); if a writer is contesting a particular position or fact, use the verb *contests* (or *denies, disputes, refutes,* or *rejects*). In using verbs that are specific to the situation in your paper, you bring your readers into the intellectual debate and avoid the monotony of such all-purpose verbs as *says* or *writes.* Following are just a few examples of how you can vary signal phrases to add precision to your paper:

Ellen Goodman asserts that . . .
To summarize Judith Viorst's observations on friends, . . .
Social activist and nutrition guru Dick Gregory demonstrates that . . .
Mary Sherry explains . . .
George Orwell rejects the widely held belief that . . .
Joanmarie Kalter exposes the myth that . . .

Other verbs that you should keep in mind when constructing signal phrases include the following:

acknowledges	declares	points out
adds	endorses	reasons
admits	grants	reports
believes	implies	responds
compares	insists	suggests
confirms		

▇ Documenting Sources

Whenever you summarize, paraphrase, or quote a person's thoughts and ideas, and whenever you use facts or statistics that are not commonly known or believed, you must properly acknowledge the source of your information. If you do not properly acknowledge ideas and information created by someone else, you are guilty of *plagiarism,* of using someone else's material but making it look as if it were your own. You must document the source of your information whenever you do the following:

- quote a source word-for-word
- refer to information and ideas from another source that you present in your own words as either a paraphrase or a summary
- cite statistics, tables, charts, or graphs

You do not need to document these types of information:

- your own observations, experiences, and ideas
- factual information available in a number of reference works (known as "common knowledge")
- proverbs, sayings, and familiar quotations

A reference to the source of your borrowed information is called a *citation.* There are many systems for making citations, and your citations must consistently follow one of these systems. As noted earlier, the documentation style recommended by the Modern Language Association is commonly used in English and the humanities and is the style used throughout this book. Another common system is the American Psychological Association (APA) style, which is generally used in the social sciences. Your instructor will probably tell you which style to use. For more information on documentation styles, consult the appropriate manual or handbook. For MLA style, consult the *MLA Handbook for Writers of Research Papers,* 6th ed. (New York: MLA, 2003) and the MLA style section on the MLA Web site <http://www.mla.org>.

There are two components of documentation: *In-text citations* are placed in the body of your paper; the *list of works cited* provides complete publication data for your in-text citations and is placed at the end of your paper. Both are necessary for complete documentation.

IN-TEXT CITATIONS

In-text citations, also known as *parenthetical citations,* give the reader citation information immediately, at the point at which it is most meaningful. Rather than having to find a footnote or an endnote, the reader sees the citation as a part of the writer's text.

Most in-text citations consist of only the author's last name and a page reference. Usually the author's name is given in an introductory or signal phrase at the beginning of the borrowed material, and the page reference is given in parentheses at the end. If the author's name is not given at the beginning, put it in parentheses along with the page reference. The parenthetical reference signals the end of the borrowed material and directs your readers to the list of works cited should they want to pursue a particular source. Treat electronic sources as you do print sources, keeping in mind that some electronic sources use paragraph numbers instead of page numbers. Consider the following examples of in-text citations, which are from student Caitlin O'Neill's paper.

IN-TEXT CITATIONS (MLA STYLE)

Citation with author's name in the signal phrase

Educators today are debating whether a flunking grade has any place in today's educational arena. In other words, is there some good that comes out of the threat of a flunking grade or even the grade of F itself? Educator Mary Sherry argues that the threat of flunking can be "a positive teaching tool" and that students with a "healthy fear of failure" (447) are motivated. On the other hand, students should not be overly afraid to fail. As one popular writer and university professor reminds us, "Failure isn't fatal. Countless people have had a bout with it and come out stronger as a result" (Zinsser 451).

Citation with author's name in parentheses

The following shows how the preceding in-text citations appeared in the list of works cited at the end of O'Neill's essay.

LIST OF WORKS CITED (MLA STYLE)

Sherry, Mary. "In Praise of the F Word." <u>Models for Writers</u>. Ed. Alfred Rosa and Paul Eschholz. 7th ed. Boston: Bedford, 2001. 445-47.

Zinsser, William. "The Right to Fail." <u>Models for Writers</u>. Ed. Alfred Rosa and Paul Eschholz. 7th ed. Boston: Bedford, 2001. 450-53.

LIST OF WORKS CITED

In this section, you will find general MLA guidelines for creating a works cited list followed by sample entries that cover the citation situations you will encounter most often. Make sure that you follow the formats as they appear on the following pages.

General Guidelines

- Begin the list on a new page following the last page of text.
- Organize the list alphabetically by author's last name. If the entry has no author name, alphabetize the first major word of the title.
- Double-space within and between entries.
- Begin each entry at the left margin. If the entry is longer than one line, indent the second and subsequent lines five spaces or one-half inch.
- Do not number entries.

Books

BOOKS BY ONE AUTHOR

List the author's last name first, followed by a comma and the first name. Underline the title. Follow with the city of publication and a shortened version of the publisher's name—for example, *Houghton* for *Houghton Mifflin,* or *Cambridge UP* for *Cambridge University Press.* End with the date of publication.

```
Pinker, Steven. The Language Instinct: How the Mind
    Creates Language. New York: Morrow, 1994.
```

BOOKS BY TWO OR THREE AUTHORS

List the first author (following order on title page) in the same way as for a single-author book; list subsequent authors, first name first, in the order in which they appear on the title page.

```
Young Bear, Severt, and R. D. Theisz. Standing in the
    Light: A Lakota Way of Seeing. Lincoln: U of
    Nebraska P, 1994.
```

BOOK BY FOUR OR MORE AUTHORS

List the first author in the same way as for a single-author book, followed by a comma and the abbreviation *et al.* ("and others").

```
Morris, Desmond, et al. Gesture Maps. London: Cape,
    1978.
```

TWO OR MORE BOOKS BY THE SAME AUTHOR

List two or more books by the same author in alphabetical order by title. List the first book by the author's name. After the first book, in place of the author's name substitute three unspaced hyphens followed by a period.

Lederer, Richard. <u>Anguished English</u>. Charleston: Wyrick, 1987.

---.<u>Crazy English</u>. New York: Pocket, 1990.

REVISED EDITION

Hassan, Ihab. <u>The Dismemberment of Orpheus: Toward a Postmodern Literature</u>. 2nd ed. Madison: U of Wisconsin P, 1982.

EDITED BOOK

Douglass, Frederick. <u>Narrative of the Life of Frederick Douglass, an American Slave, Written by Himself</u>. Ed. Benjamin Quarles. Cambridge: Belknap, 1960.

TRANSLATION

Kafka, Franz. <u>The Penal Colony: Stories and Short Pieces</u>. Trans. Willa Muir and Edwin Muir. New York: Schocken, 1984.

ANTHOLOGY

Clark, Virginia, Paul Eschholz, and Alfred Rosa, eds. <u>Language: Readings in Culture and Language</u>. 6th ed. New York: St. Martin's, 1998.

WORK IN AN ANTHOLOGY

Dao, Bei. "13 Happiness Street," <u>Contemporary Literature of Asia</u>. Ed. Arthur W. Biddle, Gloria Bien, and Vinay Dharwadker. Upper Saddle River: Prentice, 1996. 281-92.

SECTION OR CHAPTER IN A BOOK

Carver, Raymond. "Why Don't You Dance?" <u>What We Talk about When We Talk about Love</u>. New York: Knopf, 1981.

Periodicals

ARTICLE IN A JOURNAL WITH CONTINUOUS PAGINATION THROUGHOUT

Some journals paginate issues continuously, by volume; that is, the page numbers in one issue pick up where the previous issue left off. For these journals, follow the volume number by the date of publication in parentheses.

Gazzaniga, Michael S. "Right Hemisphere Language Following Brain Bisection: A Twenty-Year Perspective." American Psychologist 38 (1983): 528-49.

ARTICLE IN A JOURNAL WITH SEPARATE PAGINATION IN EACH ISSUE

Some journals paginate by issue; each issue begins with page 1. For these journals, follow the volume number with a period and the issue number. Then give the date of publication in parentheses.

Douglas, Ann. "The Failure of the New York Intellectuals." Raritan 17.4 (1998): 1-23.

ARTICLE IN A MONTHLY MAGAZINE

Keizer, Garret. "Sound and Fury: The Politics of Noise in a Loud Society." Harper's Magazine Mar. 2001: 39-48.

ARTICLE IN A WEEKLY OR BIWEEKLY MAGAZINE

Hamill, Pete. "On Lars-Erik Nelson." New York Review of Books 11 Jan. 2001: 4.

ARTICLE IN A NEWSPAPER

Wade, Nicholas. "A Prolific Genghis Khan, It Seems, Helped People the World." New York Times 11 Feb. 2003, late ed.: D3.

If an article in a newspaper or magazine appears discontinuously — that is, if it starts on one page and skips one or more pages before continuing — include only the first page followed by a plus sign.

Faison, Seth. "President Arrives in Shanghai: Focuses on Talk with Citizens." New York Times 30 June 1998, late ed.: A1+.

EDITORIAL OR LETTER TO THE EDITOR

"The Return of Fuzzy Math." Editorial. New York Times 1 Mar. 2001, late ed.: A32.

Hunter, Ted. "Historic Homer." Letter. Smithsonian Dec. 2002: 14.

Internet Sources

The following guidelines and models for citing information retrieved from the Internet have been adapted from the most recent advice of the MLA, as detailed in the *MLA Handbook for Writers of Research*

Papers, 6th ed. (2003) and from the MLA's Web site <http://www .mla.org>. When listing an electronic source in your list of works cited, include the following elements, if they are available and relevant, in the reference. All elements should be followed by a period with the exception of the date the site is accessed.

- *Author.* Write the name of the author, editor, compiler, or translator of the source with the last name first, followed by a comma and the first name. If appropriate, follow the name with an abbreviation, such as *ed.* If no author is given, begin with the title.
- *Title.* Write the title of the poem, short story, article, essay, or similar short work within a scholarly project, database, or periodical in quotation marks. If the source is a posting to a discussion list or forum, take the title from the subject line and put it in quotation marks, followed by the description *online posting.* If you are citing an entire online book, the title should be underlined.
- *Editor/translator.* Add the name of the editor, compiler, or translator of the text (if it is relevant and if not cited earlier), preceded by the appropriate abbreviation, such as *Ed.*
- *Print publication information.* Give the publication information of any print version of the source that the source provides.
- *Electronic publication information.* Give the title of the scholarly project, database, periodical, or professional or personal site (underlined) or, for a professional or personal site with no title, give a general description, such as *home page.* Follow the title with the name of the editor of the scholarly project or database (if available); a version, volume, or any other identifying number of the source (if not part of the title); the date of electronic publication, the latest update, or posting; the name of the discussion list or forum; the number range or total number of pages, paragraphs, or other sections, if they are numbered; and finally the name of the institution or organization sponsoring or associated with the Web site, if any.
- *Access information.* The final elements to add are the date you accessed the source and the electronic address, or URL, of the source (in angle brackets).

MLA style requires that you break URLs extending over more than one line only after a slash. Do *not* add spaces, hyphens, or any other punctuation to indicate the break.

SCHOLARLY PROJECT

<u>Victorian Women Writers Project</u>. Ed. Perry Willett.
June 1996. Indiana U. 27 July 2002 ⟨http://
www.indiana.edu/~letrs/vvwp/⟩.

PROFESSIONAL SITE

<u>MLA on the Web</u>. Modern Language Association. 20 Sept.
2000. 14 Feb. 2003 ⟨http://www.mla.org⟩.

PERSONAL SITE

Rosa, Alfred. <u>English 104: Language Awareness</u>. 22 Sept.
2002 ⟨http://www.uvm.edu/~arosa/1041a.htm⟩.

BOOK

Whitman, Walt. <u>Leaves of Grass</u>. 1900. <u>Bartleby.com:</u>
<u>Great Books Online</u>. 15 Dec. 2002 ⟨http://
www.bartleby.com/142⟩.

POEM

Blake, William, "London." <u>The William Blake Page</u>. Ed.
Richard Record. 10 Feb. 2003 ⟨http://
www.members.aa.net/~urizen/experience/soe.html⟩.

ARTICLE IN A JOURNAL

Cummings, William. "Interdisciplinary Social Science."
<u>Electronic Journal of Sociology</u> 5.2 (2000) 12 Jan.
2003 ⟨http://www.sociology.org/content/vol005.002/
cummings.html⟩.

ARTICLE IN A NEWSPAPER

Kessler, Glenn. "Committee Approves Reduction in Individual Tax Rates." <u>Washington Post</u> 1 Mar. 2001. 23
Jan. 2003 ⟨http://washingtonpost.com/wp-dyn/
articles/A8679-2001Mar1.html⟩

ARTICLE IN AN ONLINE REFERENCE WORK

"e. e. cummings." Encyclopedia.com 1994. <u>The Concise</u>
<u>Columbia Electronic Encyclopedia</u>. 3rd ed. 12 Sept.
2000 ⟨http://www.encyclopedia.com/articles/
03328.htm⟩.

ARTICLE FROM AN ONLINE SUBSCRIPTION SERVICE

Kappel-Smith, Diana. "Fickle Desert Blooms: Opulent One
Year, No-Shows the Next." <u>Smithsonian Magazine</u> Mar.
1995. 9pp. America Online. 18 April 2002. Keyword:
desert.

ELECTRONIC MAIL

Morrison, Ben. E-mail to the author, 11 Feb. 2003.

POSTING TO A DISCUSSION LIST

Preston, Dennis R. "Re: Basketball Terms." Online posting. 8 Nov. 1997. American Dialect Society. 10 Jan.
2003 <http://www2.et.byu.edu/~lilliek/ads/
indes.htm>.

Other Sources

TELEVISION OR RADIO PROGRAM

<u>The American Experience: Chicago 1968</u>. Writ. Chana
Gazit. Narr. W. S. Merwin. PBS. WNET, New York, 13
Nov. 1997.

MOVIE, VIDEOTAPE, RECORD, OR SLIDE PROGRAM

<u>Gladiator</u>. Dir. Ridley Scott. Perf. Russell Crowe,
Joaquin Phoenix, Connie Nielsen, Oliver Reed, Derek
Jacobi, Djimon Hounsou, and Richard Harris. Dream-
Works Pictures, 2000.

PERSONAL INTERVIEW

Eschholz, Paul. Personal interview. 6 Jan. 2003.

LECTURE

Hayford, Helen. Lecture. English 160: Literature of
Vermont. U of Vermont Department of English,
Burlington. 20 Feb. 2003.

■ A Note on Plagiarism

The importance of honesty and accuracy in doing library research
cannot be stressed enough. Any material borrowed word for word
must be placed within quotation marks and be properly cited; any

idea, explanation, or argument you have paraphrased or summarized must be documented, and it must be clear where the paraphrased material begins and ends. In short, to use someone else's ideas, whether in their original form or in an altered form, without proper acknowledgment is to be guilty of *plagiarism*. The Council of Writing Program Administrators offers the following helpful definition of plagiarism in academic settings for administrators, faculty, and students: "In an instructional setting, plagiarism occurs when a writer deliberately uses someone else's language, ideas, or other (not common-knowledge) material without acknowledging its source." Accusations of plagiarism can be substantiated even if plagiarism is accidental. A little attention and effort at the note-taking stage can go a long way toward eliminating inadvertent plagiarism. Check all direct quotations against the wording of the original, and double-check your paraphrases to be sure that you have not used the writer's wording or sentence structure. It is easy to forget to put quotation marks around material taken verbatim or to use the same sentence structure and most of the same words—substituting a synonym here and there—and treat it as a paraphrase. In working closely with the ideas and words of others, intellectual honesty demands that we distinguish between what we borrow—acknowledging it in a citation—and what is our own.

While writing your paper, be careful whenever you incorporate one of your notes into your paper. Make sure that you put quotation marks around material taken verbatim, and double-check your text against your note card—or, better yet, against the original if you have it on hand—to make sure that your quotation is accurate. When paraphrasing or summarizing, make sure you have not inadvertently borrowed key words or sentence structures from the original.

USING QUOTATION MARKS FOR LANGUAGE BORROWED DIRECTLY

When you use another person's exact words or sentences, you must enclose the borrowed language in quotation marks. Without quotation marks, you give your reader the impression that the wording is your own. Even if you cite the source, you are guilty of plagiarism if you fail to use quotation marks. The following examples demonstrate both plagiarism and a correct citation for a direct quotation.

Original Source

So Grant and Lee were in complete contrast, representing two diametrically opposed elements in American life. Grant was the modern man emerging; beyond him, ready to come on the stage, was the great age of steel and machinery, of crowded cities and a restless burgeoning vitality.

–Bruce Catton, "Grant and Lee: A Study in Contrasts," p. 453

Plagiarism

So Grant and Lee were in complete contrast, according to Civil War historian Bruce Catton, representing two diametrically opposed elements in American life. Grant was the modern man emerging; beyond him, ready to come on the stage, was the great age of steel and machinery, of crowded cities and a restless burgeoning vitality (453).

Correct Citation of Borrowed Words in Quotation Marks

"So Grant and Lee were in complete contrast," according to Civil War historian Bruce Catton, "representing two diametrically opposed elements in American life. Grant was the modern man emerging; beyond him, ready to come on the stage, was the great age of steel and machinery, of crowded cities and a restless burgeoning vitality" (453).

USING YOUR OWN WORDS AND WORD ORDER WHEN SUMMARIZING AND PARAPHRASING

When summarizing or paraphrasing a source, you must use your own language. Pay particular attention to word choice and word order, especially if you are paraphrasing. Remember, it is not enough simply to use a synonym here or there and think you have paraphrased the source; you *must* restate the original idea in your own words, using your own style and sentence structure. In the following examples, notice how plagiarism can occur when care is not taken in the wording or sentence structure of a paraphrase. Notice that in the acceptable paraphrase, the student writer uses her own language and sentence structure.

Original Source

Punctuation, one is taught, has a point: to keep up law and order. Punctuation marks are the road signs placed along the highway of our communications—to control speeds, provide directions and prevent head-on collisions. A period has the unblinking finality of a red light; the comma is a flashing yellow light that asks us only to slow down; and the semicolon is a stop sign that tells us to ease gradually to a halt, before gradually starting up again.

–Pico Iyer, "In Praise of the Humble Comma," p. 172

Unacceptably Close Wording

According to Iyer, the point of punctuation is to keep a sense of order. Like road signs, punctuation marks are placed in our written communications. We use these punctuation marks to control pace, give direction and prevent serious accidents. For example, a period can be compared to the finality of a red traffic light. The comma, on the other hand, functions like a flashing yellow light, cautioning to slow down or pause. And the semicolon acts as a stop sign, telling us to come to rest before proceeding (172).

Unacceptably Close Sentence Structure

Iyer believes that punctuation, we learn in school, has a purpose: to give meaning and structure to our writing. Marks of punctuation can be likened to traffic signs along the roads we all travel—signs that dictate speed, give directions, and prevent accidents. For example, a period, like a red traffic light, brings readers to a total stop; the comma, like a flashing yellow light, tells readers to move ahead slowly with caution; and the semicolon, like a stop sign, tells readers to come to a complete stop before moving ahead (172).

Acceptable Paraphrase

Iyer believes that punctuation is meaningful, that it provides order to our writing. People can more easily understand the meaning conveyed by marks of punctuation by thinking of them in terms of road signs that help readers navigate the streets and highways of our writing. A period, for example, has the force of a red light; it signals the reader to stop and wait. The comma, like a flashing yellow, tells readers to proceed slowly with caution. And the semicolon, like a stop sign, directs readers to come to a complete stop before moving on (172).

Finally, as you proofread your final draft, check your citations one last time. If at any time while you are taking notes or writing your paper you have a question about plagiarism, consult your instructor for clarification and guidance before proceeding.

Preventing Plagiarism

Questions to Ask about Direct Quotations
- Do quotation marks clearly indicate the language that I borrowed verbatim?
- Is the language of the quotation accurate, with no missing or misquoted words or phrases?
- Do the brackets or ellipsis marks clearly indicate any changes or omissions I have introduced?
- Does a signal phrase naming the author introduce each quotation? Does the verb in the signal phrase help establish a context for each quotation?
- Does a parenthetical page citation follow each quotation?

Questions to Ask about Summaries and Paraphrases
- Is each summary or paraphrase written in my own words and style?
- Does each summary or paraphrase accurately represent the opinion, position, or reasoning of the original writer?
- Does each summary or paraphrase start with a signal phrase so that readers know where my borrowed material begins?
- Does each summary or paraphrase conclude with a parenthetical page citation?

Questions to Ask about Facts and Statistics
- Do I use a signal phrase or some other marker to introduce each fact or statistic that is not common knowledge so that readers know where the borrowed material begins?
- Is each fact or statistic that is not common knowledge clearly documented with a parenthetical page citation?

▮ An Annotated Student Research Paper

Jake Jamieson's writing assignment was to write an argument, and he was free to choose his own topic. After considering a number of possible topics and doing some preliminary research on several of them, he turned to the material he was studying in another of his courses, which focused on the study of the English language. In that course, he had become intrigued with the English-only movement. As he said, "I chose this topic to do my paper on because it is an aspect of speech that I had previously explored, and my interest was piqued

I realized that it absolutely intrigued me, from the prospect of banning languages other than English right down to the question of funding for bilingualism."

Jamieson began by brainstorming about his topic. He made lists of ideas, facts, issues, arguments, and opposing arguments. Once he was confident that he had amassed enough information to begin writing, he made a rough outline of an organizational pattern he felt he could follow. Keeping this pattern in mind, he wrote a first draft of his essay. Then he went back and examined it carefully, assessing how it could be improved.

After he reread his first draft, he realized that his organizational pattern could be clearer and that his examples needed to be sharper and more to the point. He also struck upon the idea of asking a series of rhetorical questions in the eighth paragraph, and he took particular delight in being able to use them in this paper: "I have always enjoyed these kinds of rhetorical questions, and I was excited when I got a chance to sneak them into this paper, lampooning the air of superiority and unwillingness to accept difference that seem to fill the English-only viewpoint." Most importantly, Jamieson scoured his sources for the most appropriate and memorable quotations to include in his paper, all the while being careful to keep accurate notes on where he found them.

The final draft of Jamieson's paper illustrates that he has learned how the parts of a well-researched and well-written paper fit together and how to make the revisions that emulate some of the qualities of the model essays he has read and studied. The following is the final draft of the paper.

The English-Only Movement: Can America Proscribe
Language with a Clear Conscience?

Jake Jamieson

*Announces
melting pot
debate*

A common conception among many people in
this country is that the United States is a giant
cultural "melting pot." For these people, the
melting pot is a place where people from other
places come together and bathe in the warm
waters of assimilation. For many others, however, the melting pot analogy doesn't work. They
see the melting pot as a giant cauldron into
which immigrants are placed; here their cultures,
values, and backgrounds are boiled away in the

*Asks
question
to be an-
swered in
paper*

scalding waters of discrimination. One major
point of contention in this debate is language:
Should immigrants be pushed toward learning English or encouraged to retain their native
tongues?

Those who argue that the melting pot analogy
is valid believe that people who come to America
do so willingly and should be expected to become
a part of its culture instead of hanging on to
their past. For them, the expectation that people
who come to this country will celebrate this
country's holidays, dress as we do, embrace our
values, and most importantly speak our language
is not unreasonable. They believe that assimilation offers the only way for everyone in this
country to live together in harmony and the only
way to dissipate the tensions that inevitably

arise when cultures clash. A major problem with this argument, however, is that no one seems to be able to agree on what exactly constitutes "our way" of doing things.

Not everyone in America is of the same religious persuasion or has the same set of values, and different people affect vastly different styles of dress. There are so many sets of variables that it would be hard to defend the argument that there is only one culture in the United States. What seems to be the most widespread constant in our country is that much of the population speaks English, and a major movement is being staged in favor of making English the official language. Making English America's official language would, according to William F. Buckley, involve making it the only language in which government business can be conducted on any level, from federal dealings right down to the local level (71). Many reasons are given to support the notion that making English the official language is a good idea and that it is exactly what this country needs, especially in the face of growing multilingualism. Indeed, one Los Angeles school recently documented sixty different languages spoken in the homes of its students (National Education Association, par. 4).

Supporters of English-only contend that all government communication must be in English. Because communication is absolutely necessary for a democracy to survive, they believe that the only

Defines English as the official language

Uses in-text MLA citation format, including introductory signal phrase and parenthetical page number

Introduces English-only position

way to ensure the existence of our nation is to make sure a common language exists. Making English official would ensure that all government business, from ballots to official forms to judicial hearings, would have to be conducted in English. According to former senator and presidential candidate Bob Dole, "Promoting English as our national language is not an act of hostility but a welcoming act of inclusion." He goes on to state that while immigrants are encouraged to continue speaking their native languages, "thousands of children [are] failing to learn the language, English, that is the ticket to the 'American Dream'" (qtd. in Donegan 51).

Intro-
duces
anti-
English-
only
position

For those who do not subscribe to this way of thinking, however, this type of legislation is anything but the "welcoming act of inclusion" that it is described to be. For them, anyone attempting to regulate language is treading dangerously close to the First Amendment and must have a hidden agenda of some type. Why, it is asked, make a language official when it is already firmly entrenched and widely used in this country and, according to United States General Accounting Office statistics, 99.96 percent of all federal documents are already in English without legislation to mandate it (Underwood, par. 2)? According to author James Crawford, the answer is quite plain: discrimination. He states that "it is certainly more respectable to discriminate by language than by race." He points out that "most

people are not sensitive to language discrimination in this nation, so it is easy to argue that
you're doing someone a favor by making them speak
English" (qtd. in Donegan 51). English-only legislation has been described as bigoted, anti-
immigrant, mean-spirited, and steeped in nativism
by those who oppose it, and some go so far as to
say that this type of legislation will not foster
better communication, as is the claim, but will
instead encourage a "fear of being subsumed by a
growing 'foreignness' in our midst" (Underwood,
"At Issue" 65).

For example, when a judge in Texas ruled that
a mother was abusing her five-year-old girl by
speaking to her only in Spanish, an uproar ensued.
This ruling was accompanied by the statement that
by talking to her in a language other than English, the mother was "abusing that child and . . .
relegating her to the position of house maid."
This statement was condemned by the National Association for Bilingual Education (NABE) for "label-
ing the Spanish language as abuse." The judge,
Samuel C. Kiser, subsequently apologized to the
housekeepers of the country, adding that he held
them "in the highest esteem," but stood firm on
his ruling (qtd. in Donegan 51). One might notice
that he went out of his way to apologize to the
housekeepers he might have offended but saw no
need to apologize to the hundreds of thousands of
Spanish speakers whose language had just been be-
littled in a nationally publicized case.

Uses example to question English-only position that speaking Spanish in the home is abusive

This tendency of official-English proponents to put down other languages is one that shows up again and again, even though it is maintained that they have nothing against other languages or the people who speak them. If there is no malice toward other languages, why is the use of any language other than English tantamount to lunacy according to an almost constant barrage of literature and editorial opinions? In a recent publication of the "New Year's Resolutions" of various conservative organizations, a group called U.S. English, Inc., stated that the U.S. government was not doing its job of convincing immigrants that they "must learn English to succeed in this country." Instead, according to this publication, "in a bewildering display of irrationality, the U.S. government makes it possible to vote, file a tax return, get married, obtain a driver's license, and become a U.S. citizen in many languages" (Moore 46).

Argues against the English-only idea of multilingualism as irrational

Now, according to this mindset, not only is speaking any language other than English abusive, but it is also irrational and bewildering. What is this world coming to when people want to speak and make transactions in their native language? Why do they refuse to change and become more like us? Why can't immigrants see that speaking English is right and anything else is wrong? These and many other questions are implied by official-English proponents as they discuss the issue.

Asks rhetorical questions

Conservative attorney David Price wrote that official-English legislation is a good idea because many English-speaking Americans prefer "out of pride and convenience to speak their native language on the job" (13). Not only does this statement imply that the pride and convenience of non-English-speaking Americans is unimportant, but that their native tongues are not as important as English. The scariest prospect of all is that this opinion is quickly gaining popularity all around the country.

Points to growing popularity of English-only position

As of early 1996, six official-English bills and one amendment to the Constitution have been proposed in the House and Senate. There are twenty-two states, including Alabama, California, and Arizona, that have made English their official language, and more are debating it every day (Donegan 52). An especially disturbing fact about this debate is that official-English laws always seem to be linked to other anti-immigrant legislation, such as proposals to "limit immigration and restrict government benefits to immigrants" ("English-Only Law Faces Test" 1).

Presents status report of English-only legislation

Although official-English proponents maintain that their bid for language legislation is in the best interest of immigrants, the facts tend to show otherwise. A decision has to be made in this country about what kind of message we will send to the rest of the world. Do we plan to allow everyone in this country the freedom of

Concludes that English-only legislation is not in our best interest

speech that we profess to cherish, or will we decide to reserve it only for those who speak the
same language as we do? Will we hold firm to our
belief that everyone is deserving of life, liberty, and the pursuit of happiness in this country? Or will we show the world that we believe in
these things only when they pertain to ourselves
and people like us?

Works Cited

*Follows
MLA
citation
guidelines*

Buckley, William F. "Se Hable Ingles." National
Review 9 Oct. 1995: 70-71.

Donegan, Craig. "Debate over Bilingualism: Should
English Be the Nation's Official Language?"
CQ Researcher 19 Jan. 1996: 51-71.

"English-Only Law Faces Test." Burlington Free
Press 26 Mar. 1996: 1.

Moore, Stephen, et al. "New Year's Resolutions."
National Review 29 Jan. 1996: 46-48.

Mujica, Mauro E. "At Issue: Should English Be the
Official Language of the United States?" CQ
Researcher 19 Jan. 1996: 65.

National Education Association. "NEA Statement on
the Debate over English Only." Teacher's
College, U. of Nebraska, Lincoln. 27 Sept.
1999 <http://www.tc.unl.edu/enemeth/
biling/engonly.html>.

Price, David. "English-Only Rules: EEOC Has Gone
Too Far." USA Today 28 Mar. 1996, final ed.:
A13.

Underwood, Robert A. "At Issue: Should English Be the Official Language of the United States? CQ Researcher 19 Jan. 1996: 65.

---. "English-Only Legislation." U.S. House of Representatives, Washington, D.C., 28 Nov. 1995. 26 Sept. 1999 <http://www.house.gov/underwood/speeches/english.htm>.

Glossary of Useful Terms

Abstract See *Concrete/Abstract.*

Allusion An allusion is a passing reference to a familiar person, place, or thing, often drawn from history, the Bible, mythology, or literature. An allusion is an economical way for a writer to capture the essence of an idea, atmosphere, emotion, or historical era, as in "The scandal was his Watergate" or "He saw himself as a modern Job" or "The campaign ended not with a bang but a whimper." An allusion should be familiar to the reader; if it is not, it will add nothing to the meaning.

Analogy Analogy is a special form of comparison in which the writer explains something unfamiliar by comparing it to something familiar: "A transmission line is simply a pipeline for electricity. In the case of a water pipeline, more water will flow through the pipe as water pressure increases. The same is true of electricity in a transmission line."

Anecdote An anecdote is a short narrative about an amusing or interesting event. Writers often use anecdotes to begin essays as well as to illustrate certain points.

Argumentation Argumentation is one of the four basic types of prose. (Narration, description, and exposition are the other three.) To argue is to attempt to persuade the reader to agree with a point of view, to make a given decision, or to pursue a particular course of action. There are two basic types of argumentation: logical and persuasive. See the introduction to Chapter 20 (pp. 487–93) for a detailed discussion of argumentation.

Attitude A writer's attitude reflects his or her opinion of a subject. The writer can think very positively or very negatively about a subject or have an attitude that falls somewhere in between. See also *Tone.*

Audience   An audience is the intended readership for a piece of writing. For example, the readers of a national weekly newsmagazine come from all walks of life and have diverse interests, opinions, and educational backgrounds. In contrast, the readership for an organic chemistry journal is made up of people whose interests and education are quite similar. The essays in *Models for Writers* are intended for general readers, intelligent people who may lack specific information about the subject being discussed.

Beginnings and Endings   A beginning is the sentence, group of sentences, or section that introduces an essay. Good beginnings usually identify the thesis or controlling idea, attempt to interest readers, and establish a tone.

An ending is the sentence or group of sentences that brings an essay to a close. Good endings are purposeful and well planned. They can be a summary, a concluding example, an anecdote, or a quotation. Endings satisfy readers when they are the natural outgrowths of the essays themselves and give the readers a sense of finality or completion. Good essays do not simply stop; they conclude. See the introduction to Chapter 6 (pp. 129–35) for a detailed discussion of beginnings and endings.

Cause and Effect   Cause-and-effect analysis is a type of exposition that explains the reasons for an occurrence or the consequences of an action. See the introduction to Chapter 19 (pp. 457–59) for a detailed discussion of cause and effect. See also *Exposition*.

Classification   See *Division and Classification*.

Cliché   A cliché is an expression that has become ineffective through overuse. Expressions such as *quick as a flash, jump for joy,* and *slow as molasses* are clichés. Writers normally avoid such trite expressions and seek instead to express themselves in fresh and forceful language. See also *Diction*.

Coherence   Coherence is a quality of good writing that results when all sentences, paragraphs, and longer divisions of an essay are naturally connected. Coherent writing is achieved through (1) a logical sequence of ideas (arranged in chronological order, spatial order, order of importance, or some other appropriate order), (2) the purposeful repetition of key words and ideas, (3) a pace suitable for your topic and your reader, and (4) the use of transitional words and expressions. Coherence should not be confused with unity. (See *Unity*.) See also *Transition*.

Colloquial Expression   A colloquial expression is an expression that is characteristic of or appropriate to spoken language or to writing that seeks the effect of spoken language. Colloquial expressions are informal, as *chem, gym, come up with, be at wit's end, won't*, and *photo* illustrate. Thus, colloquial expressions are acceptable in formal writing only if they are used purposefully. See also *Diction*.

Combined Strategies   By combining rhetorical strategies, writers are able to develop their ideas in interesting ways. For example, in writing a cause-and-effect essay about a major oil spill, the writer might want to describe the damage that the spill caused, as well as explain the cleanup process step by step.

Comparison and Contrast   Comparison and contrast is a type of exposition in which the writer points out the similarities and differences between two or more subjects in the same class or category. The function of any comparison and contrast is to clarify—to reach some conclusion about the items being compared and contrasted. See the introduction to Chapter 18 (pp. 431–35) for a detailed discussion of comparison and contrast. See also *Exposition*.

Conclusions   See *Beginnings and Endings*.

Concrete/Abstract   A concrete word names a specific object, person, place, or action that can be directly perceived by the senses: *car, bread, building, book, John F. Kennedy, Chicago*, or *hiking*. An abstract word, in contrast, refers to general qualities, conditions, ideas, actions, or relationships that cannot be directly perceived by the senses: *bravery, dedication, excellence, anxiety, stress, thinking*, or *hatred*. See the introduction to Chapter 10 (pp. 237–42) for more on abstract and concrete words.

Connotation/Denotation   Both connotation and denotation refer to the meanings of words. Denotation is the dictionary meaning of a word, the literal meaning. Connotation, on the other hand, is the implied or suggested meaning of a word. For example, the denotation of *lamb* is "a young sheep." The connotations of *lamb* are numerous: *gentle, docile, weak, peaceful, blessed, sacrificial, blood, spring, frisky, pure, innocent*, and so on. See the introduction to Chapter 10 (pp. 237–42) for more on connotation and denotation.

Controlling Idea   See *Thesis*.

Coordination   Coordination is the joining of grammatical constructions of the same rank (e.g., words, phrases, clauses) to indicate that they are of equal importance. For example, *They ate hot dogs*, and *we ate hamburgers*. See the introduction to Chapter 9 (pp. 208–12) for more on coordination. See also *Subordination*.

Deduction   Deduction is the process of reasoning from stated premises to a conclusion that follows necessarily. This form of reasoning moves from the general to the specific. See the introduction to Chapter 20 (pp. 487–93) for a discussion of deductive reasoning and its relation to argumentation. See also *Syllogism*.

Definition   Definition is one of the types of exposition. Definition is a statement of the meaning of a word. A definition may be either brief or extended, part of an essay or an entire essay itself. See the introduction to Chapter 16 (pp. 388–90) for a detailed discussion of definition. See also *Exposition*.

Denotation   See *Connotation/Denotation*.

Description   Description is one of the four basic types of prose. (Narration, exposition, and argumentation are the other three.) Description tells how a person, place, or thing is perceived by the five senses. See the introduction to Chapter 14 (pp. 343–44) for a detailed discussion of description.

Details   Details are the small elements that collectively contribute to the overall impression of a person, place, thing, or idea. For example, in the sentence "The *organic, whole-grain* dog biscuits were *reddish brown, beef flavored,* and in the *shape of a bone*" the italicized words are details.

Dialogue   Dialogue is the conversation of two or more people as represented in writing. Dialogue is what people say directly to one another.

Diction   Diction refers to a writer's choice and use of words. Good diction is precise and appropriate: The words mean exactly what the writer intends, and the words are well suited to the writer's subject, intended audience, and purpose in writing. The word-conscious writer knows that there are differences among *aged, old,* and *elderly; blue, navy,* and *azure;* and *disturbed, angry,* and *irritated.* Furthermore, this writer knows in which situation to use each word. See the introduction to Chapter 10 (pp. 237–42) for a detailed discussion of diction. See also *Cliché; Colloquial Expression; Connotation/Denotation; Jargon; Slang.*

Division and Classification   Division and classification is one of the types of exposition. When dividing and classifying, the writer first establishes categories and then arranges or sorts people, places, or things into these categories according to their different characteristics, thus making them more manageable for the writer and more understandable and meaningful for the reader. See the introduction to Chapter 17 (pp. 404–7) for a detailed discussion of division and classification. See also *Exposition.*

Dominant Impression   A dominant impression is the single mood, atmosphere, or quality a writer emphasizes in a piece of descriptive writing. The dominant impression is created through the careful selection of details and is, of course, influenced by the writer's subject, audience, and purpose. See the introduction to Chapter 14 (pp. 343–44) for more on dominant impression.

Emphasis   Emphasis is the placement of important ideas and words within sentences and longer units of writing so that they have the greatest impact. In general, what comes at the end has the most impact, and at the beginning nearly as much; what comes in the middle gets the least emphasis.

Endings   See *Beginnings and Endings.*

Evaluation   An evaluation of a piece of writing is an assessment of its effectiveness or merit. In evaluating a piece of writing, one should ask the following questions: What is the writer's purpose? Is it a worthwhile purpose? Does the writer achieve the purpose? Is the writer's information sufficient and accurate? What are the strengths of the essay? What are its weaknesses? Depending on the type of writing and the purpose, more specific questions can also be asked. For example, with an argument one could ask: Does the writer follow the principles of logical thinking? Is the writer's evidence sufficient and convincing?

Evidence   Evidence is the information on which a judgment or argument is based or by which proof or probability is established. Evidence usually takes the form of statistics, facts, names, examples or illustrations, and opinions of authorities.

Example   An example illustrates a larger idea or represents something of which it is a part. An example is a basic means of developing or clarifying an idea. Furthermore, examples enable writers to show and not simply to tell readers what they mean. See the introduction to Chapter 12 (pp. 282–92) for more on example.

Exposition   Exposition is one of the four basic types of prose. (Narration, description, and argumentation are the other three.) The purpose of exposition is to clarify, explain, and inform. The methods of exposition presented in *Models for Writers* are process analysis, definition, illustration, classification, comparison and contrast, and cause and effect. For a detailed discussion of these methods of exposition, see the appropriate chapter introductions.

Facts   Facts are pieces of information presented as having objective reality, that is, having actual existence. For example, water boils at 212°F, Katherine Hepburn died in 2003, and the USSR no longer exists — these are all facts.

Fallacy   See *Logical Fallacy.*

Figure of Speech   A figure of speech is a brief, imaginative comparison that highlights the similarities between things that are basically dissimilar. Figures of speech make writing vivid, interesting, and memorable. The most common figures of speech are

> *Simile:* An explicit comparison introduced by *like* or *as.* "The fighter's hands were like stone."
> *Metaphor:* An implied comparison that makes one thing the equivalent of another. "All the world's a stage."
> *Personification:* A special kind of simile or metaphor in which human traits are assigned to an inanimate object. "The engine coughed and then stopped."

See the introduction to Chapter 11 (pp. 265–66) for a detailed discussion of figurative language.

Focus   Focus is the limitation that a writer gives his or her subject. The writer's task is to select a manageable topic given the constraints of time, space, and purpose. For example, within the general subject of sports, a writer could focus on government support of amateur athletes or narrow the focus further to government support of Olympic athletes.

General   See *Specific/General.*

Idiom   An idiom is a word or phrase that is used habitually with special meaning. The meaning of an idiom is not always readily apparent to nonnative speakers of that language. For example, *catch cold, hold a job, make up your mind,* and *give them a hand* are all idioms in English.

Illustration   Illustration is the use of examples to explain, elucidate, or corroborate. Writers rely heavily on illustration to make their ideas both clear and concrete. See the introduction to Chapter 12 (pp. 289–92) for a detailed discussion of illustration.

Induction   Induction is the process of reasoning to a conclusion about all members of a class through an examination of only a few members of the class. This form of reasoning moves from the particular to the general. See the introduction to Chapter 20 (pp. 487–93) for a discussion of inductive reasoning and its relation to argumentation.

Inductive Leap   An inductive leap is the point at which a writer of an argument, having presented sufficient evidence, moves to a generalization or conclusion. See also *Induction.*

Introductions   See *Beginnings and Endings.*

Irony   Irony is the use of words to suggest something different from their literal meaning. For example, when Jonathan Swift suggested in "A Modest Proposal" that Ireland's problems could be solved if the people of Ireland fattened their babies and sold them to the English landlords for food, he meant that almost any other solution would be preferable. A writer can use irony to establish a special relationship with the reader and to add an extra dimension or twist to the meaning. See the introduction to Chapter 10 (pp. 237–42) for more on irony.

Jargon   Jargon, or technical language, is the special vocabulary of a trade, profession, or group. Doctors, construction workers, lawyers, and teachers, for example, all have a specialized vocabulary that they use on the job. See also *Diction.*

Logical Fallacy   A logical fallacy is an error in reasoning that renders an argument invalid. See the introduction to Chapter 20 (pp. 487–93) for a discussion of the more common logical fallacies.

Metaphor   See *Figure of Speech.*

Narration   Narration is one of the four basic types of prose. (Description, exposition, and argumentation are the other three.) To narrate is to tell a story, to tell what happened. While narration is most often used in fiction, it is also important in expository writing, either by itself or in conjunction with other types of prose. See the introduction to Chapter 13 (pp. 315–18) for a detailed discussion of narration.

Opinion   An opinion is a belief or conclusion, which may or may not be substantiated by positive knowledge or proof. (If not substantiated, an opinion is a prejudice.) Even when based on evidence and sound reasoning, an opinion is personal and can be changed and is therefore less persuasive than facts and arguments.

Organization   Organization is the pattern or order that the writer imposes on his or her material. Some often-used patterns of organization include time order, space order, and order of importance. See the introduction to Chapter 5 (pp. 106–10) for a detailed discussion of organization.

Paradox   A paradox is a seemingly contradictory statement that is nonetheless true. For example, "We little know what we have until we lose it" is a paradoxical statement.

Paragraph   The paragraph, the single most important unit of thought in an essay, is a series of closely related sentences. These sentences adequately develop the central or controlling idea of the paragraph. This central or controlling idea, usually stated in a topic sentence, is necessarily related to the purpose of the whole composition. A well-written paragraph has several distinguishing characteristics: a clearly stated or implied topic sentence, adequate development, unity, coherence, and an appropriate organizational strategy. See the introduction to Chapter 7 (pp. 160–63) for a detailed discussion of paragraphs.

Parallelism   Parallel structure is the repetition of word order or grammatical form either within a single sentence or in several sentences that develop the same central idea. As a rhetorical device, parallelism can aid coherence and add emphasis. Franklin Roosevelt's statement "I see one-third of a nation ill-housed, ill-clad, and ill-nourished" illustrates effective parallelism.

Personification   See *Figure of Speech*.

Persuasion   Persuasion, or persuasive argument, is an attempt to convince readers to agree with a point of view, to make a decision, or to pursue a particular course of action. Persuasion appeals strongly to the emotions, whereas logical argument does not.

Point of View   Point of view refers to the grammatical person in an essay. For example, first-person point of view uses the pronoun *I* and is commonly found in autobiography and the personal essay; third-person point of view uses the pronouns *he, she,* or *it* and is commonly found in objective writing. See the introduction to Chapter 13 (pp. 315–18) for a discussion of point of view in narration.

Process Analysis   Process analysis is a type of exposition. Process analysis answers the question *how* and explains how something works or gives step-by-step directions for doing something. See the introduction to Chapter 15 (pp. 362–65) for a detailed discussion of process analysis. See also *Exposition.*

Purpose   Purpose is what the writer wants to accomplish in a particular piece of writing. Purposeful writing seeks to *tell* (narration), to *describe* (description), to *explain* (process analysis, definition, classification, comparison and contrast, and cause and effect), or to *convince* (argumentation).

Rhetorical Question   A rhetorical question is asked for its rhetorical effect but requires no answer from the reader. "When will nuclear proliferation end?" is such a question. Writers use rhetorical questions to introduce topics they plan to discuss or to emphasize important points. See the introduction to Chapter 6 (pp. 129–35) for another example.

Sentence   A sentence is a grammatical unit that expresses a complete thought. It consists of at least a subject (a noun) and a predicate (a verb). See the introduction to Chapter 9 (pp. 208–12) for a detailed discussion of effective sentences.

Simile   See *Figure of Speech.*

Slang   Slang is the unconventional, very informal language of particular subgroups in our culture. Slang terms, such as *bummed, sweat, dark,* and *cool,* are acceptable in formal writing only if used selectively for specific purposes.

Specific/General   General words name groups or classes of objects, qualities, or actions. Specific words, on the other hand, name individual objects, qualities, or actions within a class or group. To some extent the terms *general* and *specific* are relative. For example, *clothing* is a class of things. *Shirt,* however, is more specific than *clothing* but more general than *T-shirt.* See also *Diction.*

Strategy   A strategy is a means by which a writer achieves his or her purpose. Strategy includes the many rhetorical decisions that the writer makes about organization, paragraph structure, sentence structure, and diction. In terms of the whole essay, strategy refers to the principal rhetorical mode that a writer uses. If, for example, a writer wishes to explain how to make chocolate chip cookies, the most effective strategy would be process analysis. If it is the writer's purpose to analyze why sales of American cars have declined in recent years, the most effective strategy would be cause-and-effect analysis.

Style   Style is the individual manner in which a writer expresses his or her ideas. Style is created by the author's particular choice of words, construction of sentences, and arrangement of ideas.

Subordination   Subordination is the use of grammatical constructions to make one part of a sentence dependent on, rather than equal to, another. For example, the italicized clause in the following sentence is subordinate: They all cheered *when I finished the race.* See the introduction to Chapter 9 (pp. 208–12) for more on subordination. See also *Coordination.*

Supporting Evidence   See *Evidence.*

Syllogism   A syllogism is an argument that utilizes deductive reasoning and consists of a major premise, a minor premise, and a conclusion. For example,

All trees that lose leaves are deciduous. (major premise)
Maple trees lose their leaves. (minor premise)
Therefore, maple trees are deciduous. (conclusion)

See also *Deduction.*

Symbol   A symbol is a person, place, or thing that represents something beyond itself. For example, the bald eagle is a symbol of the United States, and the maple leaf, a symbol of Canada.

Syntax   Syntax refers to the way in which words are arranged to form phrases, clauses, and sentences, as well as to the grammatical relationship among the words themselves.

Technical Language   See *Jargon.*

Thesis   A thesis, also known as the controlling idea, is the main idea of an essay. A thesis may sometimes be implied rather than stated directly in a thesis statement. See the introduction to Chapter 3 (pp. 67–69) for a detailed discussion of thesis.

Title A title is a word or phrase set off at the beginning of an essay to identify the subject, to state the main idea of the essay, or to attract the reader's attention. A title may be explicit or suggestive. A subtitle, when used, explains or restricts the meaning of the main title.

Tone Tone is the manner in which a writer relates to an audience, the "tone of voice" used to address readers. Tone may be friendly, serious, distant, angry, cheerful, bitter, cynical, enthusiastic, morbid, resentful, warm, playful, and so forth. A particular tone results from a writer's diction, sentence structure, purpose, and attitude toward the subject. See the introduction to Chapter 10 (pp. 237–42) for several examples that display different tones.

Topic Sentence The topic sentence states the central idea of a paragraph and thus limits the content of the paragraph. Although the topic sentence normally appears at the beginning of the paragraph, it may appear at any other point, particularly if the writer is trying to create a special effect. Not all paragraphs contain topic sentences. See also *Paragraph*.

Transition A transition is a word or phrase that links sentences, paragraphs, and larger units of a composition to achieve coherence. Transitions include parallelism, pronoun references, conjunctions, and the repetition of key ideas, as well as the many conventional transitional expressions such as *moreover, on the other hand, in addition, in contrast,* and *therefore*. See the introduction to Chapter 8 (pp. 184–87) for a detailed discussion of transitions. See also *Coherence*.

Unity Unity is that quality of oneness in an essay that results when all the words, sentences, and paragraphs contribute to the thesis. The elements of a unified essay do not distract the reader. Instead, they all harmoniously support a single idea or purpose. See the introduction to Chapter 4 (pp. 86–88) for a detailed discussion of unity.

Verb Verbs can be classified as either strong verbs *(scream, pierce, gush, ravage,* and *amble)* or weak verbs *(be, has, get,* and *do)*. Writers prefer to use strong verbs to make their writing more specific, more descriptive, and more action filled.

Voice Verbs can be classified as being in either the active or the passive voice. In the active voice, the doer of the action is the

Lars Eighner. "On Dumpster Diving." From *Travels with Lizbeth* by Lars Eighner. Copyright © 1993 by Lars Eighner. Reprinted by permission of St. Martin's Press, LLC.

Thomas L. Friedman. "My Favorite Teacher." From *The New York Times*, January 9, 2001, Section A, p. 19. Copyright © 2001 by The New York Times Company. Reprinted by permission.

Martin Gansberg. "38 Who Saw Murder Didn't Call Police." From *The New York Times*, March 17, 1964. Copyright © 1964 by The New York Times Company. Reprinted by permission.

Henry Louis Gates, Jr. "What's in a Name?" Originally published in *Dissent*. Foundation for the Study of Independent Social Ideas. Reprinted by permission.

Natalie Goldberg. "Be Specific." From *Writing Down the Bones* by Natalie Goldberg. © 1986 by Natalie Goldberg. Reprinted by arrangement with Shambhala Publications, Inc., Boston. www.shambhala.com.

Ellen Goodman. "The Company Man." From *Close to Home* by Ellen Goodman. © 1979 by The Washington Post Company. Reprinted with the permission of Simon & Schuster Adult Publishing Group.

GOOGLE screen shots. www.google.com. Reprinted by permission.

Dick Gregory. "Shame." From *Nigger: An Autobiography* by Dick Gregory. Copyright © 1964 by Dick Gregory Enterprises, Inc. Used by permission of Dutton, a division of Penguin Group (USA), Inc.

Pete Hamill. "Band of Brothers: Faces of Honor." From *The New York Daily News*, September 23, 2001. Reprinted with permission by the New York Daily News, IP. "Crack and the Box." From *Piecework* by Pete Hamill. Copyright © 1996 by Deidre Enterprises, Inc. Reprinted by permission of Little, Brown and Company, Inc.

Gilbert Highet. "Subway Station." From *Talents and Geniuses* by Gilbert Highet. Copyright © 1957 by Gilbert Highet. Reprinted with the permission of Curtis Brown, Ltd.

Roger Hoffmann. "The Dare." From the column "About Men" in *The New York Times*, January 1, 1996. Originally titled "There's Always a Dare." Copyright © 1986 Robert Hoffman. Reprinted by permission.

Manny Howard. "A Tricky Stick." From *The New York Times*, December 30, 2001, Section 6, p. 61. Copyright © 2001 Manny Howard. Reprinted by permission.

Langston Hughes. "Salvation." From *The Big Sea* by Langston Hughes. Copyright © 1940 by Langston Hughes. Copyright renewed 1968 by Arna Bontemps and George Houston Bass. Reprinted by permission of Hill and Wang, a division of Farrar, Straus and Giroux, LLC.

Barbara Huttmann. "A Crime of Compassion." Originally published in *Newsweek*, August 8, 1983. Copyright © 1983 by Barbara Huttmann. Reprinted with the permission of the author.

Caroline Hwang. "The Good Daughter." From *Newsweek*, September 21, 1998, p. 16. Copyright © 1998, Newsweek, Inc. All rights reserved. Reprinted by permission.

Pico Iyer. "In Praise of the Humble Comma." From *Tropical Classical: Essays from Several Directions* by Pico Iyer. Copyright © 1997 by Pico Iyer. Used by permission of Alfred A. Knopf, a division of Random House, Inc.

K. Connie Kang. "A Battle of Cultures." First published in *Asian Week*, May 25, 1990. Copyright © K. Connie Kang. Reprinted by permission of the author.

Michael T. Kaufman. "Of My Friend Hector and My Achilles Heel." From *The New York Times*, November 11, 1992. Copyright © 1992 by The New York Times Company. Reprinted with permission.

Garrison Keillor. "How to Write a Personal Letter." From *We Are Still Married* by Garrison Keillor. Published by Viking Penguin in 1989. Originally written for *Power of the Printed Word* series by the International Paper Company.

Helen Keller. "The Most Important Day." Originally published as "Three Days to See" in the January 1993 issue of the *Atlantic Monthly*. Copyright © 1932 by The Helen Keller Foundation. Reprinted with permission.

Martin Luther King, Jr. "The Ways of Meeting Oppression" from *Stride Toward Freedom* by Martin Luther King. Copyright © 1958 Dr. Martin Luther King Jr. Copyright © 1986 by Coretta Scott King. "I Have a Dream." Copyright © 1963 Dr. Martin Luther King Jr. Copyright renewed 1991 Coretta Scott King. Reprinted by arrangement with the Estate of Martin Luther King Jr., c/o Writers House as agent for the proprietor, New York, NY.

Stephen King. "Why We Crave Horror Movies." Originally appeared in *Playboy* (1982). © Stephen King. All rights reserved. Reprinted with Permission.

Barbara Kingsolver. "Life Is Precious, or It's Not." From *Small Wonder: Essays* by Barbara Kingsolver. Copyright © 2002 by Barbara Kingsolver. Reprinted by permission of HarperCollins, Inc.

Nedra Newkirk Lamar. "Does a Finger Fing?" This article first appeared in *The Christian Science Monitor* on February 20, 1970, and is reproduced with permission. Copyright © 1970 The Christian Science Monitor (www.csmonitor.com). All rights reserved.

Richard Lederer. "The Case for Short Words." From *The Miracle of Language* by Richard Lederer. Copyright © 1991 by Richard Lederer. Reprinted with the permission of Pocket Books, a Division of Simon & Schuster, Inc.

Lifestrands, Inc. Screen shot: www.lifestrands.org. Reprinted with permission.

William Lutz. "Doubt about Doublespeak." From *State Government News*, July 1993. Copyright © 1993 William Lutz. All rights reserved. Used by permission of the author.

Judy Mandell. "Sometimes Honesty Is the Worst Policy." From *Newsweek*, October 21, 2002, p. 16. Copyright © 2002 Newsweek, Inc. Reprinted by permission. All rights reserved.

David McCullough. "I Love Washington." From *American Heritage*, April/May 1986 issue. Published by Forbes, Inc. Reprinted by permission of American Heritage.

Cherokee Paul McDonald. "A View from the Bridge." From the *Sun Sentinel*, February 12, 1989. Copyright © 1989. Reprinted by permission of Knight Ridder/Tribune Information Services.

Gloria Naylor. "The Meaning of a Word." From *What's in a Name*. Copyright © 1986 by Gloria Naylor. Reprinted by permission of Sterling Lord Literistic, Inc.

George Orwell. "A Hanging." From *Shooting an Elephant and Other Essays* by George Orwell. Copyright © 1950 by Sonia Brownell Orwell and renewed 1978 by Sonia Pitt-Rivers, reprinted by permission of Harcourt, Inc. (U.S.). Copyright ©

George Orwell 1931 by permission of Bill Hamilton as the Literary Executor of the Estate of the Late Sonia Brownell Orwell and Secker & Warburg Ltd.

Anna Quindlen. "Uncle Sam and Aunt Samantha." First appeared in *Newsweek*, November 2001. Copyright © 2001 by Anna Quindlen. Reprinted by permission of International Creative Management, Inc.

Robert Ramirez. "The Barrio." Originally titled "The Woolen Sarape" from *Pain and Promise: The Chicano Today*, edited by Edward Simmens. Published by New American Library in 1972. Reprinted by permission of the author.

Janisse Ray. "Built by Fire." From *Ecology of a Cracker Childhood* by Janisse Ray. Copyright © 1999 by Janisse Ray. Reprinted with permission from Mildweed Editions.

David Raymond. "On Being 17, Bright, and Unable to Read." From *The New York Times*, April 25, 1976. Copyright © 1976 by The New York Times Company. Reprinted by permission.

Mike Rose. Excerpt from "I Just Wanna Be Average." From *Lives on the Boundary* by Mike Rose. © 1989 by Mike Rose. Reprinted by permission of The Free Press, an imprint of Simon & Schuster.

Carl T. Rowan. "Unforgettable Miss Bessie." Copyright © 1985 by The Reader's Digest Association, Inc. Reprinted with permission from the March 1985 *Reader's Digest*.

Laura Rowley. "As They Say, Drugs Kill." First published in the February 1987 issue of *Newsweek on Campus*. Reprinted by permission of the author.

Ruth Russell. "The Wounds That Can't Be Stitched Up." From *Newsweek*, December 20, 1999, p. 11. Copyright © 1999 Newsweek, Inc. Reprinted by permission. All rights reserved.

Witold Rybczynski. "One Good Turn: How Machine-Made Screws Brought the World Together." Originally published in *The New York Times Magazine*, Special Edition, April 18, 1999, p. 133. © 1999 by Witold Rybczynski. Reprinted by permission of the author.

Rene Sanchez. "Surfing's Up and Grades are Down." Originally titled, "Hooked Online, and Sinking: Cybersurfing Crowds Out College Work." From *The Washington Post*, May 22, 1996, p. A1. © 1966, *The Washington Post*. Reprinted with permission.

Mary Sherry. "In Praise of the F Word." First published in *Newsweek*, May 6, 1991. Copyright © 1991 by Mary Sherry. Reprinted by permission of the author.

Gary Soto. "The Jacket." From *The Effects of Knut Hamsun on a Fresno Boy: Recollections and Short Essays* by Gary Soto. Copyright © 1983, 2000 by Gary Soto. Reprinted by permission of Persea Books, Inc. (New York).

James Tuite. "The Sounds of the City." From *The New York Times*, January 1, 1966. Copyright © 1966 by The New York Times Company. Reprinted with permission.

Judith Viorst. "Friends, Such Good Friends—and Such Good Friends." Copyright © 1977 by Judith Viorst. Originally appeared in *Redbook*. Reprinted by permission of Lescher & Lescher, Ltd.

Sarah Vowell. "Pop-A-Shot." From *The Partly Cloudy Patriot* by Sarah Vowell. © 2002 by Sarah Vowell. Reprinted by permission of Simon & Schuster Adult Publishing Group.

INDEX

Research and Writing Online

Whether you want to investigate the ideas behind a thought-provoking essay or conduct in-depth research for a paper, the Web resources for *Models for Writers* can help you find what you need — and then use it once you find it.

The Bedford Researcher for Developing Research Skills

bedfordresearcher.com

Formerly known as *The English Research Room, The Bedford Researcher* Web site provides interactive tools for working with both print and digital sources. You can create a virtual workspace with the Research Log, where you can log in and work through every stage in the research process, from keeping notes, to building a bibliography, to evaluating sources and more. You can also consult research manuals and tutorials, a gallery of student research projects, and downloadable research activities and checklists.

Diana Hacker's Research and Documentation Online for Incorporating Sources

dianahacker.com/resdoc

Incorporating sources correctly in a paper is often a challenge, and the Web has made it even more complex. This online version of the popular booklet *Research and Documentation in the Electronic Age*, by Diana Hacker, provides clear advice for the humanities, social sciences, history, and the sciences on:

- which Web and library sources are relevant to your topic (with links to Web sources)
- how to integrate outside material into your paper
- how to cite sources correctly, using the appropriate documentation style
- whether the final format of your paper should be MLA, APA, *Chicago*, or CBE style